# The "Who Is Johnny Dollar?" Matter

A CHARACTER PROFILE
AND PROGRAM SYNOPSIS
OF "AMERICA'S FABULOUS INSURANCE INVESTIGATOR,
THE MAN WITH THE ACTION PACKED EXPENSE ACCOUNT"

# "YOURS TRULY, JOHNNY DOLLAR"

BY JOHN C. ABBOTT

THE "WHO IS JOHNNY DOLLAR?" MATTER
A CHARACTER PROFILE AND PROGRAM SYNOPSIS
OF "AMERICA'S FABULOUS INSURANCE INVESTIGATOR,
THE MAN WITH THE ACTION PACKED EXPENSE ACCOUNT"
"YOURS TRULY, JOHNNY DOLLAR"
VOLUME TWO
© 2010 JOHN C. ABBOTT

All rights reserved.

No part of this book may be reproduced in any form or by any means,
electronic, mechanical, digital, photocopying or recording, except for the inclusion
in a review, without permission in writing from the publisher.

Published in the USA by:

BEARMANOR MEDIA
PO BOX 71426
ALBANY, GA 31708
www.BearManorMedia.com

ISBN-10: 1-59393-090-9
ISBN-13: 978-1-59393-090-5

BOOK DESIGN AND LAYOUT BY VALERIE THOMPSON.

# Table of Contents

VOLUME TWO

*Dedicated to:*

*All those wonderful actors, actresses, writers, directors, producers, technical staff and sponsors, who made radio a wonderful place for almost 40 years.*

*Special thanks also go out to J. David Goldin and Bill Brooks, for their support, and encouragement and most of all, for answering my many questions. Thanks guys.*

*Support for this project was also provided by: Jeanette Berard of the Thousand Oaks Library, Anthony L'Abatte at Eastman House, and Janet Lorenz at the National Film Information Service.*

# Section 4: Bob Bailey

To millions of Americans, there is only one Johnny Dollar. After a lapse of almost a year and a month, producer/director Jack Johnstone brought the character of Johnny Dollar back to CBS with the voice of Bob Bailey. From the first broadcast, listeners could tell that something was different. Not only was the format of the program different, with one 15-minute episode each weekday, but Bob Bailey was able to infuse energy into the character. Bob Bailey was a real person infusing his personality into the program.

Bob had come to Johnny Dollar after a long and successful run as George Valentine in *Let George Do It*. Bob had a long history of radio acting, and also played in several movies with Laurel and Hardy.

Bob played Johnny Dollar until 1960, when CBS moved the program to New York. Bob continued to write for television, but eventually he dropped out of sight, lost to the world and even to his family for over ten years.

The following are the Bob Bailey Johnny Dollar programs.

**SHOW:** THE MACORMACK MATTER
**COMPANY:** ALLIED CASUALTY AND INSURANCE COMPANY
**AGENT:** ED BARTH
**PART 1** **SHOW DATE:** **10/3/1955**

**SYNOPSIS:** Father Taggert call Johnny from Sing Sing. Michael Kearns wants Johnny to talk to Johnny, as he is dying.

Allied did not authorize the investigation but you will probably pay it. Johnny goes to Sing Sing Prison and visits Michael Kearns in the infirmary. Johnny had put Mike in prison, and now he is very sick and has to be awakened. Mike is glad to see Johnny and tells him that he was the best insurance cop. Prison is a lousy place to die and Mike was thinking about his life. He had a wife once and has to do something for her. Mike asks Johnny if he would pick up some clean easy money for him. He tells Johnny that he roomed with Joe Panning, who has been paroled. He put in his time, but he had something waiting for him outside, money. Joe yelled "Macormack" in his sleep, and a guy named Macormack was robbed a couple years back for $100,000 and Joe was in on it. There must be a reward out for it. Look into it and get the reward and send half to my old lady.

Mike dies and Johnny heads to New York City and goes to the police to look at the Macormack files. The case is open and unsolved so Johnny calls Frank Porter of Allied and asks for information on the Macormack robbery. Johnny learns that there is a $7500 reward on the case.

Johnny gets a mug shot for Joe Panning and his address from the parole officer. Johnny goes to see Joe, and tells him about Mike. Johnny asks if he can buy Joe a drink and they talk. Johnny starts to think that another man was involved in the Macormack case. Johnny wants to go to Long Island and see a friend and asks Joe to go along. When Johnny mentions Julian Macormack, Joe gets suspicious and goes back to his room. Johnny goes back to the hotel the next morning and Joe has gone.

Tomorrow, there is living proof that a pretty girl can be just as dangerous as, well, a pretty girl.

**PART 2** **SHOW DATE:** **10/4/1955**

Frank Porter calls with the information on the Macormack case and Johnny tells Frank about the tip on Joe. Frank tells Johnny not to bother Julian Macormack, as it could be dangerous.

Johnny rents a car and drives to the Macormack mansion where Julian is packing for a trip to Europe. Johnny tells Macormack who he is and about the lead on the jewelry. Johnny tells him that he may have a clue. Macormack tells Johnny that they had just returned from their honeymoon and the safe was opened, not cracked. Only he knows the combination. The police and insurance company were called and Frank Porter worked very hard to collect. Macormack did not get much, as he had violated the policy and collected only $20,000 on the jewelry, which was an heirloom. Johnny tells Macormack of the tip on Joe Panning and thinks that Mrs. Macormack will be glad to see the jewelry again. Johnny leaves and thinks that Macormack is scared of him. Johnny has lunch at Walgreens and then goes to the Allied office and meets Frank Porter. Frank shows Johnny pictures of the jewelry and hopes he has better luck. Frank gives Jules Martin as the police contact. Frank tells Johnny that someone just picked the safe and got clean away. The hardest part is that none of the goods has surfaced. Maybe the guy still has it and we can only wait. Just let me know when you find something. Johnny goes to the parole office and Panning has not called in. Johnny goes back to the police and pulls Panning's file. A police clerk tells Johnny that he had already given Johnny the address. Did you forget? Johnny rushes to the Allen Hotel and runs into a woman wearing a sable coat who tries to run past Johnny with a gun in her hand. Johnny reaches for the gun and she hits him. Johnny follows her to the street and loses her. The desk clerk saw no one, but tells Johnny that Joe is out. Johnny borrows a passkey and opens Joe's room, which was already unlocked. Joe's clothes were there and the room has been searched and trashed. Johnny gets a drink and thinks. Mike's tip was really good.

Tomorrow, a slight case of mayhem when the right guy turns up in the wrong place.

**PART 3**        **SHOW DATE:**    **10/5/1955**

Lt. Jules Martin returns Johnny's call and Johnny tells him that he wants to talk about the Macormack job.

Johnny buys drinks for Lt. Martin after looking at the room. A pickup is ordered for Panning and Johnny relates how he got involved and how the case is working out. Johnny describes the woman and her gun, but she could be anyone. Lt. Martin recalls that Macormack was kind of strange. He will call Johnny when Panning is picked up. After two days there is no news on Panning. Johnny checks the files on Panning again and finds the name of an ex-wife, Iris Carter. Vital Statistics gives a general description that could match the woman who hit him. Johnny goes to the last address and asks the manager for Iris. She tells Johnny that she knew both Iris and Joe but does not know where she is, but she used to work in a bookstore nearby. Johnny gets a description of Iris and goes looking for the bookstore where the owner tells Johnny that Iris had worked there and did not know where to find her. At the Showboat restaurant the manager remembers Iris' boyfriend and his work address at a nearby club. Johnny goes to the club and talks to the trumpet player Jack Lang. Johnny asks about Iris and her ex-husband. Jack tells Johnny that she and Joe were all washed up and she might have gone back to Ohio; she was sick of losers. Jack shows Johnny a picture, and it is the girl who Johnny saw outside of Panning's apartment. Johnny checks with Lt. Martin and nothing has turned up. Lt. Martin tells Johnny that Julian Macormack had complained about Johnny. Lt. Martin gets a call and Joe Panning has been found, in the harbor. He had been shot and his feet burnt.

Tomorrow, a phase of this case that should be called the talking corpse. Believe me, this one said plenty.

### PART 4        SHOW DATE:        10/6/1955

Frank Porter calls and Johnny tells him that Panning has been found. Johnny asks Frank to help him find Joe's wife, and Frank wants to come over and get the facts.

Johnny hires a secretary to record the events for Allied, the police and himself and gives a copy to Frank Porter. Johnny is sure that he will find the goods, as he cannot see a small-time crook pulling a big-time jewel robbery. Frank tells Johnny that he feels he is not helping a bit, so be careful if you keep on this case. Johnny goes to see Lt. Martin and reads the medical report on Panning. The Medical Examiner says that Joe had been dead 48 hours and shot twice with a .25 at close range. Johnny feels that Iris seems to be the key to opening the case, and that maybe Joe was ambushed. Lt. Martin tells him that the burns on Joe's feet indicate he was not ambushed and was dead when the feet were burned. Johnny thinks that the burns were a cover up and maybe the searched room was to throw me off. Edmond Thompson comes in and tells Lt. Martin that he had seen a guy dumped in the water. It was against the will of god and the laws of nature. Edmond was on a vacant lot and saw a long black car with a lot of chrome pull up to the water and a man dumped the body into the water. Then Edmond prayed. The car was a coupe and the man had the devil's face.

Johnny goes to his hotel where Jack Lang has called with a tip. Johnny goes to the Al-Mar Theater in the Bronx. Johnny asks for Iris Carter and a gruff doorman gives him a hard time until a girl named Gloria Ward tells Johnny that she knows Iris. Johnny tells Gloria that Joe is dead and she tells Johnny that Iris is married to a nice guy. She lives in Long Island and her name is Iris Macormack. Johnny almost has it figured but is shot in the alley behind the theater as he is leaving. Johnny is hit and the long black coupe with all the chrome got away.

Tomorrow, the end of the trail for a .38 slug.

### PART 5        SHOW DATE:        10/7/1955

Johnny calls Ed Barth and tells him he has been shot but is ok. He reviews the case and tells Ed that Mrs. Macormack is Mrs. Panning. Johnny get the go ahead to continue, as it is better that Johnny is shot than Frank Porter.

Johnny buys a bottle of scotch for medicinal purposes and then goes back to the alley and gets the .38 slugs out of a telephone pole. Johnny goes to Long Island and checks the garage and finds a 1955 Cadillac and a Jaguar there. At the house Mrs. Macormack opens the door and does not want Johnny to come in, but he does. Johnny tells her that Joe is dead, and she cries. Johnny tells her that she had helped Joe rob the safe, and she tells Johnny that Joe made her do it. She went to see him because he had wanted money, but Joe was not there. She has not seen Joe, and she loves her husband. Joe came around after the honeymoon and threatened to tell the husband about her past and she opened the safe for him. Julian comes into the room with a gun and tells Johnny that Iris is innocent as far as he is concerned. The jewels are hers to do with as she chooses. Julian offers Johnny money for him to go away. Johnny tells him that he has already tried to kill him once and hits him, as the safety on the .38 is on. Johnny takes the gun and there is cosmoline in the barrel. It had never been fired.

Johnny cabs to Queens and Frank Porter's apartment. Johnny waits in the lobby for Frank to come home but the manager does not like people loitering in his exclusive building. Johnny gives him a little bribe and gets into the luxury apartment. Frank show up thirty minutes later and is not surprised that Johnny is there. Johnny tells him what he has learned and compliments Frank on his apartment, as they cost money. Johnny tells him that Julian offered Johnny money, so he had experience doing it. It was Frank that had called the parole office and had killed Joe. Frank tells Johnny that when he was brought in to the Macormack case Frank recognized Iris and confused the clues. He tipped the cops and framed Joe. Frank offers to buy Johnny but he refuses. Frank collapses, and tells Johnny that he had hit him twice at the theater. Frank dies.

Johnny locates Joe's wife in Iowa, and she accepts half the reward.

Remarks: Gee Whiz!

Exp. Acct: $265.91

## NOTES:
- JOHNNY IS COMPLIMENTED FOR TIPPING HIS HAT IN PART 3
- JOHNNY IS SHOT FOR THE 5TH TIME IN PART 4—THE FIRST TIME FOR BOB BAILEY.
- COSMOLINE IS A FAIRLY THIN, SOFT, GREASE-LIKE MATERIAL USED TO PROTECT MACHINED MATERIALS.
- JOHN DAWSON IS E. JACK NEUMAN.
- JOHNNY NEVER MENTIONS THAT HE EARNED HIMSELF HALF OF THE $7,500.
- ROY ROWAN IS THE ANNOUNCER

Producer: Jack Johnstone    Writers: John Dawson
Cast: Mary Jane Croft, Virginia Gregg, Marvin Miller, Forrest Lewis, Frank Gerstle, Herb Butterfield, Herb Ellis, Tony Barrett, Ken Christy, Jack Kruschen, Junius Matthews

◆ ❖ ◆

SHOW: THE MOLLY K MATTER
COMPANY: MARINE AND MARITIME CASUALTY, LTD.
AGENT: DAVE BORGER
PART 1    SHOW DATE: 10/10/1955

SYNOPSIS: Dave Borger calls and he is in mourning for Molly K; she is insured for $500,000 and sank 20 miles off of the Golden Gate Bridge. Fly out and take a look and don't get killed.

Johnny goes to San Francisco, California and lands at mid-morning. The Molly K had disappeared just 36 hours earlier. Johnny gets a room and meets with the Harbor Master, Tim O'Roark, who is presiding at an inquiry. The presidings are informal and disclose that the Molly K left at 10:12 for Yokohama with a grain cargo, and Edgar Brawly is the captain. At 10:38 the pilot was dropped and the fog was medium-to-dense. At 12:49 the Coast Guard got the first distress signal. Lt. Cmdr. Barton Fields takes the stand and relates that five minutes after the first SOS, there was a second SOS. Several boats were launched and two crewmen are missing. Johnny studies the teletype messages and listens to the other testimony. The seeds of suspicion are small, but grow. Capt. Brawly takes the stand and relates that the pilot was dropped and then they hit a submerged derelict. His story is the same as the other stories; everything was normal after they dropped the pilot. All the normal precautions were taken because of the fog. Capt. Brawly felt the ship hit the derelict, surveyed the damage and got everyone top side and gave the abandon ship order. Johnny asks if he can ask a few questions and asks why there was no mention of the first sailing a week earlier when a cargo fire caused them to go back to port? An insurance claim was filed and then later cancelled. Brawly retorts that he had to get under way to keep from losing money. He does not know what started the fire. Bill Mack discovered the fire, and Mack is missing. Johnny asks how did he see the derelict in the fog as the Coast Guard found nothing when there was no fog. Mr. Hawkins says it felt like a blast. Hawkins objects and does not want to get involved in anything. Johnny thinks that an explosion caused the ship to sink and Johnny will find out who did it. Murder is involved.

After the hearing Johnny walks the Embarcadero and thinks about how the men in the hearing room were scared.

Tomorrow, a strange girl, and a strange threat, and a promise that is stranger than both.

## PART 2          SHOW DATE:    10/11/1955

A girl calls Johnny and tells him that he does not know her, but he will soon. Molly K was her mother.

Johnny eats after covering all the usual sources and then cabs to pier 29, with Alcatraz in the background. Just short of the Brawly Shipping office where a light is burning, Johnny gets that old feeling he has had before in the Orinoko jungle, in the Casbah of Algiers, London's Soho, and in Suez, that there was someone watching him. Johnny opens the office door and a man stops him with a gun. The man tells Johnny to turn around and Johnny obliges and then the man slugs him. He knows it is Johnny, and he is as tough as they say. The door opens and a girl comes out. She tells Dean to leave and invites Johnny in. The office is plush and cozy and they talk, sparring type talk. After two scotches she tells Johnny that she is Ellen Brawly, Capt. Brawly's daughter. Dean Sutton is an exporter she knows, but he is not normally so jealous. It was his cargo on the Molly K. She is a free agent and has no obligations to Dean. She mentions the hearing and Johnny tells her that there are some things that do not add up. There is a big mortgage on the Molly K and her father could have made out well from the insurance. Johnny tells Ellen that Lu Tang, Shanghai Lu, holds the mortgage and that Lu owns a nightclub in Chinatown. Johnny knows Lu Tang, and she is quite a girl. Ellen tells Johnny that her father had no part in sinking the Molly K. Ellen hopes they would be friends and kisses him. That's pretty friendly, but the papers say you are engaged to Dean Sutton. Johnny leaves and the fog is thicker. On the way out Johnny is stopped by Mr. Hawkins. He tells Johnny that he was scared, and there is something strange going on. There are some things that have not been brought out yet. Hawkins tells Johnny that the Chinese steward Benny Wong did not drown. Bennie is shot at, but the bullet may have been meant for Johnny!

Tomorrow, a dead man can tell a tale. It all depends on how he died.

**PART 3**      **SHOW DATE:**      **10/12/1955**

Lu Tang calls Johnny and tells him that it has been a long time. Johnny tells her that he has to get rid of a drunk and will meet her later. She will do anything for Johnny. He wants her to find Benny Wong. Oh, It is too bad Johnny is here for the Molly K.

Johnny gets Hawkins drunk and asks him if Mack had a girl. Someone shot at you to keep you quiet. Hawkins tells Johnny that the crew thinks the ship was sunk on purpose. The first fire was discovered by Bill Mack, and Brawly hit him and told him not to spread rumors. On the second trip, Mack slipped into the hold and had not come back out when the explosion went off in the forward hold. Hawkins does not remember seeing Benny either. Capt. Brawly had hired Benny himself. Mack was dead before the ship sank, as someone had cut his throat. Hawkins sees Brawly come in and Brawly complains about Hawkin's company. Johnny tells Brawly that there is a lot against him. So do not go spending the insurance money yet. Brawly tells Johnny that he even has tried to turn his daughter and Dean Sutton against him. Johnny tells him that he is in this up to his neck, and Brawly slugs him. Johnny hits Brawly and leaves him on the floor and Johnny notices that Brawly is carrying a gun. Johnny goes to see Lu Tang, who is wise shrewd and alert. She is a mysterious woman, and the most beautiful woman Johnny has ever known. Johnny remembers last year in Paris and Lu Tang wants to marry Johnny right now. Johnny tells her that he has been mad for her for years. Lu tells Johnny that she did not sink the Molly K, nor has she found Benny yet. She had a stake in the boat, and it was a sound business deal that was insured. The wheat cargo belonging to Dean Sutton was a good investment. A young man comes in and Lu talks to him. She asks if Johnny would send her to jail if she was involved, and of course he would. She tells Johnny that she is not part of the deal. If it was sunk, Johnny thinks an explosion did it. Lu tells Johnny that Benny Wong was a demolition sergeant in the war and an expert on explosives.

Tomorrow a double-cross and a double play, and a lovely girl forces the jealous sea to give up it's dead.

**PART 4**  **SHOW DATE:**  **10/13/1955**

Dan McKay of the harbor police calls, and Johnny is told that he under arrest for assault and battery, etc. Capt. Brawly has signed a complaint, but Johnny has witnesses. Dan is serious and wants Johnny to come down and talk about it.

Johnny cabs to the Harbor Police and talks to Dan McKay, an old friend who tells Johnny that the charges were probably filed to slow him down. Dan thinks Johnny has a strong and circumstantial case, but there are a lot of unsolved crimes in the bay. Dan tells Johnny that the human element is a good thing to work on. Brawly is a tough man but not a crook. Even under pressure he will act according to type and a knife is not his nature. Johnny thinks Brawly was strapped for cash and hauled the cargo on contingency. He got scared off and withdrew his claim. On the second trip, Benny probably killed Mack when he was caught snooping around. The phone rings and Dan gets a call for Johnny, and Lu Tang tells Johnny what he needed to know. Johnny asks Dan to come and talk to the man that blew up the Molly K. They cab to the Fa Song Fish Company where Benny is hold up armed, scared and dangerous. At the warehouse they go to a back room and open the back door. They burst in and Dean Sutton is there. They find Benny dead in a corner, shot three times. Dean says he did not shoot Benny, but that he got a phone call to meet someone about the Molly K. there, a man. Johnny discovers that Benny has been dead for hours and was shot with a .45, and Johnny remembers that Brawly was carrying a .45. Johnny goes to his hotel room to wait. There is a knock at the door and it is Ellen. She asks if her father had been there. She tells Johnny that she is scared and lonely. Her father was furious last night and left. The phone rings and Dan tells Johnny that Brawly was picked up and denies everything but his gun has been fired and the bullets match the bullets in Benny. Johnny does not tell Ellen about her father because Johnny is suspicious and uncomfortable. It is Ellen's perfume; he had smelled it in the room where Benny was murdered.

Tomorrow, a deadly rendezvous in the fog shrouded waterfront, and an explosion that rocked the city; the payoff!

**PART 5**  **SHOW DATE:**  **10/14/1955**

Lu calls and tells Johnny that the grain prices in Tokyo fell three weeks ago and are holding steady. So that is what caused the Mary K to sink. Lu tells Johnny to come over later and tell her anything, especially about a certain night in Paris.

Johnny calls Hartford and New York and then cabs to Dan's office where Brawly will not talk. Johnny tells Dan that Brawly is innocent. Johnny tells Dan that Brawly has the money in the bank to pay the mortgage on his ship. The cargo was insured by another company for top-market value, and the market broke four days before the ship sank. The shipper now gets full price for the cargo. Brawly was in the middle trying to protect his daughter. Dan issues a bulletin to pick up Dan Sutton. Dan tells Johnny to call if he finds him before we do. Johnny leaves and walks through the fog. At pier 29 Johnny sees a small boat that does not belong there. Johnny goes on board and hears nothing. Johnny opens the hatch and freezes as the boat shifts to expose a booby trap.

Johnny goes to the Brawly office and knocks. The door opens and Ellen is there. She tells Johnny that she has tried to find Dean and is trying to find a way to help her father. She tells Johnny that Dean owns a boat, and Johnny tells her that it is tied up near here. Johnny tells her that Dean had hired Benny Wong to get the insurance money, and that her father is in the clear. Ellen cries and Johnny holds her. Johnny breathes in and smells the perfume. The puzzle is solved but he feels the gun in his side. She tells Johnny that she is a dead shot, ask Benny Wong. Johnny realizes it had to be Ellen, that it was her idea as Dean was too weak. She tells Johnny that he is too honest and Johnny figures that Ellen is clever enough to get rid of Dean too. Johnny hears Dean walk in and Johnny edges back to the door. They tell Johnny that they are going to build a fire for Johnny. Dean walks between them and Johnny drags Dean outside. The railing breaks loose and they end up in the water while Ellen is firing blindly. Johnny drags Dean under the water and finally breaks free, but Dean did not come up for two days. Johnny gets out of the water but Ellen is gone and Dan McKay runs up and tells Johnny that he saw a girl running to the cruiser. Johnny yells to Ellen to stop but she gets on and the bomb goes off. It was not meant for Johnny, it was rigged by Dean to get her in a double-cross.

The company will have to pay off on this one. The sea has taken Capt. Brawly's boat, his wife and his daughter.

Exp. Acct:     $547.60

**NOTES:**
• **ROY ROWAN IS THE ANNOUNCER**

| | | | |
|---|---|---|---|
| **Producer:** | Jack Johnstone | **Writers:** | Les Crutchfield |
| **Cast:** | Virginia Gregg, Peter Leeds, Barney Phillips, Victor Perrin, James McCallion, Hy Averback | | |

◆   ❖   ◆

| | |
|---|---|
| **SHOW:** | THE CHESAPEAKE FRAUD MATTER |
| **COMPANY:** | UNIVERSAL ADJUSTMENT BUREAU |
| **AGENT:** | PAT KELLEHER |
| **PART 1** | **SHOW DATE:**     **10/17/1955** |

**SYNOPSIS:** Pat Kelleher calls Johnny from Baltimore. Pat tells Johnny that John Reardon died in 1950 and the policy was paid off. Reardon was seen two days ago.

Johnny goes to Baltimore, Maryland and arrives at Friendship International Airport where Pat is waiting. Johnny tells Pat that he has investigated a lot of alive-but-dead cases. Pat tells Johnny that when the Chairman of the Board sees someone who is supposed to be dead, we investigate. Johnny learns that the policy on Reardon was issued in 1944 with the wife as beneficiary. Reardon was lost in a boating accident, but only Reardon was not found. Atlantic States Ltd. held the policy on Reardon, and the courts declared him dead after three years and paid Mrs. Elizabeth Reardon $20,000. She is a nice person, but does not need the money, which is why she waited a month to file the claim.

Johnny visits Mr. Paul Coombs, the Chairman of the Board, who is glad Johnny is working on the case. He tells Johnny that Reardon was a close friend of his and was a fine man; you will know how to handle him. Coombs saw Reardon at the Brown Palace Hotel in Denver. Coombs tried to talk to him, but he said his name was John Bowers and had lived in Toledo, gone to Ohio University and was a mining engineer. Coombs just let the conversation drop, but everything about John Bowers pointed to Reardon. Coombs is hesitant when Johnny says he is going to visit Mrs. Reardon. Johnny is worried that maybe John was not as fine as you thought.

Johnny has dinner with Pat and is troubled over the case. Johnny is going to start with Mrs. Reardon and does not know how he will handle the case. Pat notices Mrs. Reardon at the bar and Johnny goes to introduce himself. Johnny tells her that he knew John and asks how he is. He is apologetic to learn he had been dead that long. Johnny was sure he met the Reardons in Denver three years ago. Mrs. Reardon invites Johnny out for a drink, and tells him not to mention her husband's name again.

Tomorrow a little talk to a widow who may not be a widow at all, and a strong feeling that a smile can sometimes be more dangerous than a gun.

## PART 2          SHOW DATE:          10/18/1955

Pat calls and asks about the Mrs. Reardon. Johnny found out she is upset and invited me for cocktails.

Johnny calls George Handley, a PI and asks him to get information on Reardon. Johnny calls Mrs. Reardon and is expected at 7:00 PM. She is sorry for yelling at him last night. She was shocked at this death and it disturbs her, but it is good to know he is dead. Johnny tells her that he is an investigator and almost tells why he is there. They had been married for four years, and he had given her all she needed. She was nineteen and not really grown up. She loved him, but Johnny is not convinced. She is not sure he loved her. They started not getting along and she started drinking. Hugh Brian comes in and is introduced to Johnny. You must have never met Mrs. Reardon or you would not have started drinking with her. Brian is the Reardon attorney and tells Johnny he is just leaving. You never knew John Reardon and just picked her up. Good-bye Mr. Dollar.

Johnny spends several days investigating the boating accident and meets with Lt. Jack Halverson. Jack tells Johnny that the report told all the facts. The people who took the boat out did not know what they were doing. If the body were in the bay we would have found it.

Johnny goes to visit Mrs. Reardon and Brian is there. Johnny tells Brian that is in working on a case about her husband being alive. Brian is told of the meeting with Coombs and Johnny is going to investigate. Brian says that his being alive would be wonderful for her and apologizes for thinking Johnny is a playboy after her. Brian agrees to get vital statistics on John Reardon.

Johnny gets a call from Elizabeth who tells him to drop the case, and then hangs up.

Tomorrow at trip to Denver and a look at a man whose gun makes it pretty emphatic he does not want to be looked at.

**PART 3**          **SHOW DATE:**     **10/19/1955**

Hugh Brian calls and he has the information on Reardon. Johnny wants the information and will meet him in an hour.

Johnny gets a telegram from Denver and there is little evidence that Bowers is really Reardon. Johnny wires back and tells George that Johnny will be there. Johnny sees Brian and has the necessary documents for Johnny. Johnny explains the fraud aspects of the case to Brian. Johnny gets a picture, physical data, marriage license, fingerprints, etc.

Johnny leaves for Denver, Colorado. Johnny rents a car and meets with George Handley. George has little to say about Bowers—he has an office but only goes there occasionally. He gets money from a New York bank, and has a nice bank account. He does not go with anyone and has a lot of friends. He came to Denver in 1951 from Toledo. Bowers does not seem to be hiding from anyone. George looks at the picture and it matches Bowers. George continues working on background details. Johnny visits Bowers and he tells Bowers he is making an investigation from Baltimore. Johnny reminds him of the meeting with Coombs and Bowers does not remember. Johnny shows him the picture and he does resemble the man in the picture. Johnny asks him about going to Ohio State, but Bowers says he could have told him anything; he went to Carnegie Tech. Bowers has lived in a lot of places and was married once in 1942. Bowers starts to get uncomfortable. Johnny asks for a set of fingerprints and they go to George's office and take Bower's prints. George notes that the prints do not match. Bowers is not Reardon. Johnny tells George to stay on the case.

Tomorrow another man comes to Denver. He doesn't check in to a hotel or carry luggage, at least not much luggage—just a .38 Colt.

**PART 4**          **SHOW DATE:**     **10/20/1955**

Western union calls with a wire from Baltimore about the information sent. Come home, your expenses are too high come home. Johnny wires that fingerprints do not lie but people do.

Johnny is trying to prove that John Reardon is still alive but the evidence points otherwise; but Johnny is not convinced.

Johnny meets with George while he is watching Bower's house, but nothing will change. Johnny thinks the situation over and his stubbornness—Frank Bowers was too cooperative. Frank calls and asks how he made out with the fingerprints; he was curious. Johnny offers to meet him for a drink. Johnny figures him for being over confidant. Bowers comes in, followed by George. Johnny asks Bowers what he should do? Johnny tells him he is too nice about too many things. Johnny says Bowers matches the book on him, but Johnny does not believe him. Johnny calls him a liar and Bowers wants to hit Johnny, but leaves to make a phone call for a date. Frank comes back and he does not have a date for the night.

Franks rushes out. George tells Johnny that Frank had called Baltimore. Johnny follows Frank out and they encourage each other to go to Baltimore. They walk to Frank's car and Johnny is slugged and Frank drives off. Johnny goes to his room and waits for a call.

Next morning George calls and tells Johnny that Frank had gone home. Johnny wires Frank's fingerprints to Washington. George reports in that Franks is nervous. Johnny goes to Frank's house to meet George. There is a man in Frank's house and they prepare to go in. The man leaves and there are shots and George is hit. Johnny can only lie there, as he does not have a gun.

Tomorrow proof that an insurance case is one thing; the murder of a pal is something else. Tomorrow, the windup.

### PART 5        SHOW DATE:    10/21/1955

The operator calls and Pat on one the phone. Bowers was killed, as was George. Johnny wants to find out who killed George.

Johnny talks with the police. Lt. O'Neal talks to Johnny about the case and George's involvement. Johnny describes a big man with a topcoat who shot George and Bowers. Johnny had excited Bowers and he had called Baltimore. The police tell Johnny to be careful next time. Someone must have seen something. Three different people give the police information on the case. Bowers had let the man in and argued with him. A neighbor tells Johnny that the man was taller than Bower's and had a tweed coat; she would recognize him anywhere. O'Neal turns up a cabbie who had picked up a fare at the airport. Johnny calls Pat in Baltimore and tells him that a man named Orrin Williams was the man who killed Bowers. O'Neal gives Johnny a wire from Washington. The prints Johnny had prove Bowers was John Reardon. The prints Johnny had came from Brian. O'Neal says Bowers was trying to call Brian in Baltimore.

Johnny flies back to Baltimore and goes to Brian's residence. Ellen opens the door and Johnny wants to tell Ellen and Hugh something. Ellen tells Johnny that she had married Hugh Brian this morning. Hugh comes down and Johnny tells him things were not ok. Johnny tells him the police will be there to see him. She tells Ellen to listen. Hugh tells Johnny he will only tells this once, and it will be different in court. Hugh tells them that he had gone to Denver to see John, who had been living there. John had been picked up by a fishing boat and was taken to Charleston. John had called Hugh and they arranged for John to disappear. It was John's idea. He was in debt and wanted out; it was his chance to get away from the things he hated. John told Hugh he could have Elizabeth for a price, $25,000 a year, which Hugh could afford. And then along came Johnny Dollar. Johnny tells them that John is dead—shot to death by Hugh Brian. Hugh tells them that Frank/John had called and told Hugh he was going to tell Johnny everything, so he went out and shot him. It took Elizabeth five years to decide to marry Hugh and one day for John to decide to come back.

Exp. Acct:    $1,124.98

NOTES:

- THIS PROGRAM IS AN ADAPTATION OF "THE WALTER PATTERSON MATTER" DONE BY JOHN LUND.
- FRIENDSHIP IS NOW BALTIMORE/WASHINGTON INTERNATIONAL THURGOOD MARSHALL AIRPORT
- ROY ROWAN IS THE ANNOUNCER

**Producer:** Jack Johnstone      **Writers:** John Dawson
**Cast:** Jeanne Bates, D. J. Thompson, Hy Averback, Will Wright, John Dehner, Tony Barrett, Paul Dubov, Forrest Lewis

◆   ❖   ◆

**SHOW:** THE ALVIN SUMMERS MATTER
**COMPANY:** NORTHEAST FIDELITY AND BONDING
**AGENT:** FRED WILKINS
**PART 1      SHOW DATE:** 10/24/1955

SYNOPSIS: Fred Wilkins calls Johnny with a case. Alvin Summers had embezzled $75,000 and Fred just got a call from Santa Tomas, Mexico from a man who has information about Summers.

Johnny flies to Santa Tomas and gets a room in the better hotel in town. Benito the desk clerk grabs his bag and becomes the bellboy. He tells Johnny that his cousin has a fishing boat, and he will show Johnny the sights for a small fee. In the room Benito turns on the overhead fan and looks out the balcony. You can see the ocean, if you stand up the rail and look around the building. Johnny asks if anyone has been asking for him just as the balcony door slams shut because of the fan and surprises Johnny. Benito thinks Johnny is jumpy. Benito tells Johnny that he has never heard the name Summers. It is hard to think in the heat, but a $5 bill helps Benito's memory. Benito tells Johnny that he has seen the man and Johnny tells him he might have a few more bills for him. As Johnny is resting and there is a knock at the door, and E.K. Carson wants to see Johnny. As soon as he saw Johnny, he knew he was an American and wants to get Johnny into a cribbage game. Carson is the regional salesman for the Hold-Tight Zipper Company. Carson really wants to talk, as he is really lonely. "We can talk and play a game of cribbage," he tells Johnny. Johnny goes to the cantina and meets a girl there. Gloria talks to Johnny about the guitar player and notes there is no one listening to him. She picked a great spot for a vacation, at least it was until now. Johnny notes an American watching him and then the man leaves. Gloria is going to her hotel and Johnny will meet her there on the terrace in half an hour. Johnny thinks she wants more than his manly charms. In his room Johnny finds the man from the bar, but with a gun. He searches Johnny, takes his gun and wants to know who Johnny is. Johnny tries to talk to him but the man hits him. He knows why Johnny is here. He will hate is here, and hits Johnny again. "Leave now or leave never," he tells Johnny.

Tomorrow, a threesome on a moon lit beach. A girl, me and a man with a knife.

**PART 2**      **SHOW DATE:**    **10/25/1955**

Gloria calls and Johnny tells her about the man in the bar. Gloria wants to nurse Johnny on the terrace.

Johnny gets a doctor to sew him up and then goes to meet Gloria. At the Playa del Mar Hotel, Johnny meets Gloria on the terrace. He tells her what happened in the room, and that he will find out what it is about. Gloria tells Johnny that the place is less boring now. Gloria suspects Johnny is not in town on vacation as he is not the Santa Tomas type. She tells Johnny that he came here to find or meet someone. Maybe she was looking for Johnny or vice versa. The flamenco singer is singing so they walk start to go down to the beach. Johnny sees Benito and he tells Johnny that a friend of his worked for the man in the picture as a houseboy and told him where the house is in the jungle. Benito will take him there at midnight. Benito tells Johnny that he should not have come to the Playa del Mar; he will spend all of Benito's money. Johnny runs into Carson on the way back to meet Gloria, on the path to the beach where her scarf looks bigger than her bathing suit. Johnny gets some swimming trunks and they head for the water. They sit under the cliff and talk. Johnny spots two men walking on the beach, and one is the man from the bar, and he has a friend with a machete. Johnny and Gloria hide behind the rocks until the men leave. Gloria is afraid Johnny is in some sort of trouble. She is afraid for Johnny and kisses him. It is almost midnight, so Johnny goes to his room. The balcony door is open and someone is out there. It is Benito, dead from a cut throat.

Tomorrow, there are some people you do not want to meet in a dark alley. But sometimes it cannot be helped.

**PART 3**      **SHOW DATE:**    **10/26/1955**

Lt. Gomez calls and Johnny tells him he had been making funeral arrangements. Benito was found in your room. Let's discuss the matter further.

Johnny pays for the funeral and burial of Benito and goes to visit Lt. Gomez. Johnny tells Lt. Gomez that it was obvious that Benito died of knife wounds, but Johnny tells him what happened. But Lt. Gomez wants to know what is behind the killing, but Johnny has an alibi and had no reason to kill Benito. Johnny gives Lt. Gomez his card and tells why he is in Santa Tomas. Johnny tells Lt. Gomez that Benito was going to take Johnny to the Summers house that night. Johnny tells Lt. Gomez about Carson and the man in his room. Johnny is told that the man is Señor Krause, but Lt. Gomez does not know much about him. Sgt. Romero comes in and verifies Johnny's alibi with Gloria and tells Johnny that Carson has been arrested for disturbing the peace. Johnny and Lt. Gomez talk to Carson, who tells them he was just having some fun, had grabbed the serape of one of the dancers and chased her and broke a guitar. He was just trying to have some fun. Carson is told he will have to pay a fine and damages, and Johnny is sure he will expense it. Lt. Gomez tells Johnny that before the Playa del Mar was built, the town used to be a haven for undesirables from the states. Johnny tells Lt. Gomez that Gloria says she is on vacation, and Lt. Gomez tells Johnny that she has been in town for several months. Lt. Gomez warns Johnny to be careful and not to take the law in his own hands. Gloria meets Johnny outside the police office and tells Johnny she heard about Benito. Johnny sees someone following them across the street. It is Krause. Johnny goes down an alley and tells Gloria to go to her hotel. Johnny waits for Krause and slugs him. Johnny beats him and wants to know why he is following Johnny. Krause thinks Johnny is in Mexico to take him back to the states. Johnny is sure that Krause is wanted and tells Krause that he is not a cop, and puts his lights out. Johnny goes to his room and hears someone there, so he goes in through the balcony to find Gloria going through his bags.

Tomorrow, how to fall into a trap in one easy lesson.

**PART 4**       **SHOW DATE:**     **10/27/1955**

Johnny finds Gloria in his room and tells her she was acting. She can explain, but Johnny does not want to be number two on the list of people killed in his room.

Johnny adds the expenses for entertaining Gloria Harris after he caught her searching the room. She is probably tied up with the Summers matter. She tells Johnny she is stranded because she has no passport. She has been drifting for a year and came to Santa Tomas because other fugitives were here. She was just trying to find out why Johnny is here. Gloria tells Johnny that if he can help her get a passport, she can help him. She knows that Johnny is here about Alvin Summers because she read the report in his brief case, and she has met Alvin Summers. Johnny must know someone who has an extra passport for a price. She tells Johnny that she will take him to see Alvin. She met him a couple months ago and had dinner there. Gloria tells Johnny that she only lied about one thing, why she was here. Everything else she meant. Gloria leaves and Johnny thinks about the case and then decides to go to meet her. The phone rings and Fred is tells Johnny that Alvin called again this morning and wants to know if someone is coming down. There is a knock at the door and it is Lt. Gomez, who is angry that Mr. Kraus had been beaten. Do not take the law into your hands. Johnny tells Lt. Gomez that he has to do things on his own because Lt. Gomez only has two men. Lt. Gomez is afraid he will have to attend Johnny's funeral too.

Johnny and Gloria walk down the beach and go past the path to Summers house and work their way back to the path, in case someone is watching. Johnny hears someone tailing them. Gloria walks on and Johnny circles toward the sound. Johnny trips and the man disappears. They approach the house and Johnny opens the door, but there is no one there. It looks like he has not been there for several days and there are signs of two people being in the house. Maybe he is dead. Johnny tells Gloria to talk as he goes back outside to catch whoever there was out there. Suddenly there is a gun in his back and a voice tells him to drop his gun and do not turn around. Any move might be your last.

Tomorrow, how to find out what you have been looking for the hard way.

**PART 5**       **SHOW DATE:**     **10/28/1955**

Johnny tells the voice his name. The voice tells Johnny not to move or it will be his last.

Johnny figures his life is worth 2 cents now. The man wants to talk to him. The man tells Johnny to be in his room in one hour and then disappears. Gloria comes out and the man is gone. Johnny tells Gloria that he did not find anything. She is worried about her passport and tells Johnny that her imagination is working overtime as she thinks someone is watching her. Johnny is sure that the voice is the man who called. In the lobby of his hotel is Carson. He is checking out, as half the world is waiting to get zipped up! Carson wants Johnny to keep the events of the previous night quiet, and Johnny assures him that his secret is safe. Carson tells Johnny that he will look him up in the states. When Johnny gets to his room, the phone is ringing, but no one is there. The voice is in his room and he tells Johnny that he has searched the room. The voice is Alvin Summers. He had made the calls and is ready to give up. Johnny turns on the fan as Summers starts to talk and the balcony door slams shut so Johnny turns the fan off. Alvin tells Johnny that his deal went real sour and he spent his time hiding instead of having a good time. Every shadow is someone following him. So he called the bonding company to send an investigator. Johnny tells Alvin to come home and bring the money, which Alvin tells Johnny amounts to $60,000 and is in a safe deposit box in Mexico City because he had to be careful. Alvin tells Johnny that he had come to search his room and saw Benito come in, but he did not kill him. Alvin had kept under cover so they would not find him, the man who arranged for him to come here and the woman who helped him. Gloria comes in with a gun and wants the safe deposit key. She had found out that Summers was going to turn himself in but he disappeared and she used Johnny to find him. Gloria invites Johnny to come with her, but he wants no part of it. There are shots from the balcony and Gloria is dead. Carson comes in and tells Summers that he had crossed him. He tells Johnny that he had to kill Benito. Johnny turns on the fan as Carson talks; he needs some air. When the door slams Carson wheels, Johnny knocks the lamp over and shoots Carson. Johnny tells Summers to call the police and Johnny tells Carson he finally got Johnny into a game and he lost. Johnny takes Alvin back with him to the states. He wonders if Gloria meant what she said, not that it matters.

Exp. Acct:     $923.00

**NOTES:**
- ROY ROWAN IS THE ANNOUNCER

**Producer:**     Jack Johnstone       **Writers:**    Robert Ryf
**Cast:**         **Virginia Gregg, Marvin Miller, Don Diamond, Tony Barrett, Parley Baer**

| **SHOW:** | **THE VALENTINE MATTER** |
|---|---|
| **COMPANY:** | **NEW BRITAIN INSURANCE COMPANY** |
| **AGENT:** | **ROY VICKERS** |
| **PART 1** | **SHOW DATE:** **10/31/1955** |

**SYNOPSIS:** Roy Vickers calls and tells Johnny that a bellhop has robbed a safe in a New Orleans hotel. A diamond necklace is the property of a client. Look into it for us.

Johnny goes to New Orleans, Louisiana where the police have wrapped up the case with all the goods recovered. Johnny reports the results and looks for something to do. Johnny finds a bar and runs into a rugged old man. Johnny recognizes the man as a prohibition era figurehead. Johnny sits down and introduces himself to Mr. Valentine and buys him a drink. Valentine pegs Johnny for a cop but Johnny tells him he is an insurance investigator, but was a cop once. Valentine has been in New Orleans for three months and no one has recognized him. Valentine tells Johnny about his days violating the Volstead Act and that he wants to live a nice quiet life, and is flattered that Johnny recognized him. Johnny agrees that he will not tell the police or anyone that Valentine had the dinner Johnny would buy for him at Jimmy Moran's. After dinner they listen to some jazz and drink sazaracks. Johnny prepares to leave and is given a message from Inspector Debaca of the police, who wants Johnny to come to his office to talk to him. Insp. Debaca asks Johnny about Dan Valentine and his evening with him. Johnny is told that the police have been watching Valentine and they want to know if Johnny had any business with him. Valentine has no visitors and lives alone, and you are his first visitor. The phone rings and Insp. Debaca is told that Dan Valentine has been shot. A newspaper boy found him and a neighbor carried him in. They go to the scene and Johnny tells Dan that the police had called him in. Dan tells Johnny that he shot himself cleaning his gun and asks Johnny to phone a private hospital for him. Dan is operated on and Johnny waits for him to wake up. Insp. Debaca tells Johnny that he is sticking around to make sure Dan is OK because Dan is quite a man. Dan wakes up and thanks Johnny for his help. Dan insists that he shot himself, but Johnny encourages him to go to the police. Dan tells Johnny that he will handle things himself. Johnny cabs to the airport, is delayed for five hours until his plane is fixed. Johnny gets a call from Roy Vickers in Hartford. Johnny tells Roy about the incident with Dan. Roy tells Johnny that New Britain carries a $50,000 policy on Dan, so look into it. OK, Roy!

Tomorrow all the king's men, that could be the New Orleans police force, try to keep one man alive. And they almost do it.

**PART 2          SHOW DATE:          11/1/1955**

Insp. Debaca calls and Johnny tells him that he has been assigned to look into the Valentine matter. Johnny is told that Dan has said nothing, and only Dan can keep himself alive.

Johnny requests a copy of the insurance policy and beneficiary information. Johnny meets with Insp. Debaca and tells him the insurance company wants a separate report. They want to make sure the policy is not being broken. Johnny thinks that, unofficially, the company wants Dan to stay alive. Insp. Debaca tells Johnny that that Valentine has lived quietly, but now you meet him and he is shot. "Are you a bad news boy?" Johnny is asked. Johnny tells Insp. Debaca he is wrong and Insp. Debaca gives Johnny a very thick folder on Dan Valentine, his long sorted history, prison on tax evasion and a wife and daughter. Insp. Debaca brings in a witness to the shooting, Willy Blakley. Willy was driving a milk truck and saw Valentine walking. A black car approached with two men and Valentine stopped and looked at the car and smiled a sad smile. Willy would not recognize the men again. When Valentine stopped Willy heard two noises, "Whack! Whack!" and Valentine fell down. Willy was scared and left. Insp. Debaca thinks the noises were from a silenced gun. Johnny visits Dan but he can have no visitors, as he is weak. A woman comes in to see Dan and Johnny follows her. She gets into a cab and Johnny follows her in a cab. He goes to her room and introduces himself to Mrs. Anne Valentine. Johnny tells her who he is, and she tells Johnny that she has not been called by that name in many years; in the hotel she is Anne Ward. Johnny tells her that he wants to keep Dan alive, just like she does. She tells Johnny that she has not seen or contacted Dan in thirteen years, and his daughter knows nothing of her father. Her daughter thinks that she is on vacation. Dan wanted her not to contact him, as he was ashamed of what his reputation would do to her. Johnny is sure that there is something to worry about. Johnny eats and gets a package from Hartford, checks with Insp. Debaca and goes to the hospital where Johnny gets the run around. Johnny learns that Dan has disappeared from the hospital. A nurse tells Johnny to find Mr. Valentine if you want to keep him alive. Johnny is worried about Dan taking care of the matter himself, even if it kills him.

Tomorrow, what happens to a 30 year old grudge when somebody explains it with bullets.

### PART 3          SHOW DATE:          11/2/1955

Ann Ward calls and asks Johnny if he has heard from Dan. She is worried he will die. Johnny tells her that he has not told the police she is in town. Ann wants Johnny to come over and talk.

Johnny meets with Mrs. Valentine and she is very worried about Dan. She does not know where Dan is and thinks he might have wanted to see somebody. Johnny asks why Dan came to New Orleans to live. She tells Johnny that he did not want to interfere with their lives. She has no answers to any of Johnny's other questions. Ann tells Johnny that a man named Conrad Webster lives in the area; he had done legal work for Dan in the old days. Johnny remembers that he had seen the name on Dan's insurance policy. Dan might have gone to him for help. Johnny will try to find Webster and maybe Dan. Johnny locates Webster in a crummy duplex on Gentile Street and wants to talk. Johnny has a bonded gift for him. After a long pull at the bottle, Johnny tells Webster that he is looking for a man, Dan Valentine, a friend of his. Webster tells Johnny he is not a friend of Dan's, as he does not look like an ex-prisoner. Dan is not there and he does not know where to contact him. Johnny is told that his concern is a pressing irritation to Webster. Johnny tells Webster that he is a friend, but Webster tells him that all of Dan's friends are gone. Dan should have never lived in that age; he was an explorer. Webster has not the strength to be anyone's friend and he bids Johnny goodnight. Johnny goes to his hotel and the next morning the papers are full of the story, including the news of Dan's wife and daughter. Johnny calls Anne and apologizes for the events. She is going call the daughter and tell her. Johnny suggests she change hotels and names. Johnny calls Insp. Debaca, and Dan is still missing and the two men are still unidentified. Johnny goes to the Roosevelt Hotel to see Mrs. Ward and Insp. Debaca is there. Johnny is told that Dan had come in, gone to her room and then left with Mrs. Valentine. That evening Insp. Debaca and Johnny go to a small hotel where they find Mr. and Mrs. Valentine, dead.

Tomorrow, proof that the murder of Dan Valentine and his wife are not the only murders to be solved.

**PART 4**     **SHOW DATE:**     **11/3/1955**

Roy Vickers calls and asks Johnny about Valentine. Johnny tells Roy he could not find him, let alone keep him alive. Roy has just talked with the daughter. Johnny is told to do what he can, as Roy needs a full report.

Johnny and Insp. Debaca eat dinner and discuss the case. Two men with dark suits was the description of the men who killed the Valentines. The job was a professional one and Valentine knew them. Valentine saw his wife was in town and Ann just got in the way. Johnny thinks it has something to do with his family. If Dan were expecting trouble from his enemies, he would have carried a gun. Insp. Debaca tells Johnny that Dan had spent most of his time painting and listening to music. Insp. Debaca tells Johnny to have Webster visit him as he is missing. Johnny learns that the bullets were from an Italian pistol, a Rombero of 37.5 caliber, so far untraced. Johnny goes to the Valentine house and meets the cook, Mrs. Iochino. She tells Johnny that it has been a hard day, what with the police and Miss Ward. Teresa comes in and wants to talk to Johnny, and Johnny finds Teresa to be a beautiful girl. Teresa wants to know about her father but Johnny cannot tell her much. Johnny tells her that Dan had thought about her by the things he did. When she was young, Dan had set up a trust for her, which has paid for her education. Now that he is dead, she gets the trust. She tells Johnny that she hardly knew her father but is very upset about her mother's death and cries. Johnny comforts her and they talk. They talk about Dan's paintings that look like Italian landscapes. Johnny is told that Teresa's mother came from Italy. Teresa tells Johnny that she wants to see Johnny again. Johnny leaves and goes back the next day to talk to Mrs. Iochino. Johnny helps with the funeral arrangements and goes back to work with Insp. Debaca. The police have found Webster by Lake Pontchartrain; shot to death by the same gun that killed

Valentine. Johnny goes to see Teresa who is frantic. She tells Johnny that she has been hounded by the press and by a Hollywood agent. Johnny realizes that she has grown to love her father. They walk outside and shots were fired. Terry is shot and dies as Johnny reaches for his gun, but no one is there.

Tomorrow a sober lesson on how long, how far and how deadly one man's hate can be.

## PART 5          SHOW DATE:      11/4/1955

Insp. Debaca calls and Johnny tells him what happened. Johnny checks his gun and goes looking for the killers.

After Teresa is shot, Johnny staggers down the driveway and sees a car pulling away. Johnny shoots twice at the car and is shot at twice. The car crashes and Johnny runs to it and pulls a wounded man from the car, but there is also a dead man in the car. The man's name is Cisto, and he wants a doctor. Johnny threatens to kill him if he does not talk. Insp. Debaca arrives and he takes Johnny's gun. Johnny tells Insp. Debaca that he should have killed him; he wanted to kill him. Johnny waits while the body of Teresa is taken away. Johnny and Insp. Debaca discuss the events and Cisto has told the police nothing. Insp. Debaca had found papers that identify the men as Cisto and Darvy Chianti from New York. Johnny and Insp. Debaca cannot figure things out and then they learn that Cisto has died. Johnny goes to the Valentine house and Mrs. Iochino is there. She knows nothing of the Chianti brothers. Dan had given her a thousand dollars and he was a nice man who had been forgiven. Johnny looks at the paintings and goes back to see Insp. Debaca who tells Johnny that the New York police have reported that the Chianti brothers came to America at age 18, were naturalized citizens with no records. The father was due to be processed soon, but he has disappeared. Johnny tries to sleep when Insp. Debaca calls and tells Johnny that Mr. Chianti has come to get his sons at the morgue. Insp. Debaca and Johnny talk to the man. He knows the boys had killed the others, but will not say much other than he is still alive. Johnny appears before a coroner's jury and is cleared of all charges. Johnny visits Pietro Chianti and tells him that Ann Valentine was his daughter and that Johnny has a copy of the marriage license from New York. Pietro tells him that Teresa and the others had to die because they were all bad. He had ordered it. He was the father. Only bad can come from a bad mad. Dan had taken his daughter from his village in Italy many years ago and Webster had helped. He lived to find Valentine and kill everyone involved. It was a vendetta. He was a bad man who did bad things. Johnny leaves New Orleans and has had enough of the town.

Remarks: Whenever I close my eyes, I can see a lovely girl standing at the bottom of a long curving stairway, smiling because I am in the room. That's all.

Exp. Acct:     $1,290.38

## NOTES:
• **REMAKE OF THE SAN ANTONIO MATTER OF 4/28/1953**

- THE VOLSTEAD ACT, PASSED IN 1919, ENFORCED PROHIBITION UNDER THE 18TH AMENDMENT TO THE CONSTITUTION
- THE SAZARACK IS THE QUINTESSENTIAL NEW ORLEANS COCKTAIL OF FRENCH BRANDY MIXED WITH HIS SECRET BLEND OF BITTERS, A DROP OF WATER AND A BIT OF SUGAR.
- JIMMY MORAN'S IS A FAMOUS NEW ORLEANS RESTAURANT.
- ROY ROWAN IS THE ANNOUNCER

**Producer:** Jack Johnstone     **Writers:** John Dawson
**Cast:**    Lillian Buyeff, Betty Lou Gerson, Barney Phillips, Will Wright, Forrest Lewis, Marvin Miller, Jay Novello, Jack Moyles

◆ ❖ ◆

**SHOW:**     THE LORKO DIAMONDS MATTER
**COMPANY:**     TRANSWORLD FIDELITY COMPANY
**AGENT:**     BEN TYLER
**PART 1**     **SHOW DATE:**     11/7/1955

**SYNOPSIS:** Ben Tyler calls and asks Johnny to go to Algiers. Lorko Diamonds has just lost courier with a briefcase full of diamonds in Algiers, and the briefcase is missing.

Johnny goes to Algiers, Algeria in North Africa. The easy trip was ended when Johnny lands and talks to Inspector Marcus of the Algerian police, who trusts special investigators and is sure Johnny will catch the criminals in a matter of hours. But Johnny feels a "cold wind" from the Inspector. Johnny follows Insp. Marcus to his office where a man from the local diamond firm is waiting to give Johnny the details. Johnny is sure nothing escapes the Inspector, except the diamonds. Insp. Marcus tells Johnny that the officials in Paris say that Pierre "goofed." Jan Zeindorf was very excitable about the diamonds, as Africa is for barbarians. Johnny is told that the courier had worked for Lorko for 15 years and that he never had heart failure before. Paul Gruber, the courier, was unexpectedly taken ill on the plane and died in the police clinic, and the autopsy is this afternoon. The briefcase was given to the customs property man, Andre Jourdine who was busy and did not have time to place the briefcase in the vault immediately. A few minutes later Insp. Marcus heard shots. Insp. Marcus discovered that Jourdine had been shot and the diamonds were gone. Insp. Marcus found out what was in the briefcase two hours later, $100,000 worth of diamonds in various settings. They were being sent to Countess Maria de Tolia, a beautiful sleek chic woman. She may be the only one who knew the diamonds were coming. Johnny is told that Jourdine will recover, and Zeindorf is still very nervous.

Johnny talks to the plane crew and the airport staff. Johnny thinks that maybe Jourdine might be the man. Johnny goes to the hospital and visits Jourdine and tells him who he is. Jourdine tells Johnny that he was working in the files, turned around to see a tall thin man with a gun. He ordered him to turn around and then the man hit him and took the briefcase. He fumbled for his gun and fired a shot. He did not know what was in the briefcase. Johnny examines the wound and tells Jourdine that he is lucky to be alive. Jourdine knows the Countess and she is so . . . The pet theory is limping now and Jourdine is not the suspect. Insp. Marcus meets Johnny in the hospital and asks, with a smile, how Johnny is doing. Not good is the answer. Insp. Marcus tells Johnny that the autopsy is in and the courier died of poison. The courier was poisoned on the plane by someone who knew what he was carrying — the Countess de Tolia.

Tomorrow, a lovely woman lies beautifully and a sinister whisper drifts out of the Kasbah.

### PART 2            SHOW DATE:      11/8/1955

The Countess de Tolia calls Johnny, and she is at her residence. "Did you think I would just run over to see you?" she asks. Johnny tells her that he wants to talk to her about the diamonds. I'll be there at 8:00.

At dinner Johnny is met by Insp. Marcus, who would love to have a glass of his favorite brandy. Insp. Marcus is still working on the man who sat next to the courier. Insp. Marcus is amazed that Johnny has not solved the case yet. He suggests Johnny change his plans to question the Countess, but Johnny thinks she is in this up to her neck. Johnny thinks she has everyone hypnotized by her charm, and that an accomplice could have helped her kill the courier. When Johnny asks if Insp. Marcus is the man, he tells Johnny that he wonders what he would do if the countess asked him to kill someone. The American consulate calls with some information and then Johnny goes to see the Countess who opens the door and is surprised that he came. Johnny tells her that we either play "cat-and-mouse" or do you turn yourself in now? As Johnny explains why he thinks she is involved, she asks for a cigarette and tells Johnny she expected him to be annoying but not insulting. You are under the idea I had something to do with the theft. Johnny has more than one reason; she is the only one who knew of the diamonds. She tells Johnny that dozens of her friends knew the diamonds were coming, but Johnny shows a letter telling exactly when they were coming and instructions not to tell anyone. She tells Johnny that she had told a girl she had met at a party, and Insp. Marcus was there. Johnny tells her that her title is inherited and she has moved around since the end of the war. She is well known and gets a long on her title and her looks, but is flat broke. Yet she orders diamonds on approval. So how were you going to pay for them? She throws an ashtray at Johnny and tells him to leave, and then she cries. Johnny holds her and kisses her, and tells her it was a sudden impulse. But he still thinks she is guilty. Suddenly Johnny tells her to douse the cigarette and open the windows as he heads for the kitchen to find all of the gas jets open. Johnny breaks the windows and turns off the gas. In a closet Johnny finds the body of Zeindorf, who seems to be a little bit dead.

Tomorrow, a desperate fight in an Algiers alley, a killer is named, and a lovely lady confesses her shame.

**PART 3          SHOW DATE:          11/9/1955**

The Countess' phone rings and then goes dead. The Countess tells Johnny that she knows nothing about Zeindorf. The Countess gives Zeindorf some smelling salts to wake him up. She tells Johnny that Zeindorf know some things and he will tell Johnny.

Johnny buys smelling salts for Zeindorf and scotch for himself. Zeindorf wakes up and tells Johnny that he was there because no one has found the diamonds, so he came himself. He was hiding and waiting for everyone to go to sleep but he does not know who turned on the gas. The Countess tells Johnny that her maid is not here, that she left when Johnny got there. She hired the woman through and agency, and she lives in the Casbah. Zeindorf gets ready to leave and Johnny tells him that the diamond people normally investigate their clients so why did you send diamonds to someone who is broke. The Countess tells Johnny that she was not really the client. Someone else would actually pay for the diamonds, up to $20,000. The man is Charles Barrett. He has been in Algiers for about three months and lives on a yacht. Zeindorf has a letter from Barrett promising to pay for the diamonds up to $20,000 in exchange for considerations; they are an engagement present. The Countess is sorry Johnny kissed her, as Barrett is an overbearing spoiled little boy. She tells Johnny that she has few other options. Johnny tells her she is not the first woman to marry for money. "Who said anything about marriage?" she asks. So far both suspects are off the hook. As Johnny takes a car to the yacht of Charles Barrett he notices an English car following him. The car matches speeds with him and Johnny tells the driver to block the road so he can talk to the driver. "Let's hope we have seen the same movies" muses Johnny. Johnny runs back to the car and a big beefy man comes out fighting. Johnny knocks him out and searches him as Insp. Marcus drives up. Insp. Marcus tells Johnny the man is Charles Barrett. Insp. Marcus was following him and, by the way, Insp. Marcus enjoyed the fisticuffs, but Johnny's footwork was just so-so. Insp. Marcus tells Johnny that a man named Bobo sat next to the courier, and they shared a bottle of wine. Bobo is well known in the Casbah and can be hired. Insp. Marcus has not tried to pick him up, as police in the Casbah makes people disappear. Also, Insp. Marcus tells Johnny that Jourdine has disappeared. Insp. Marcus tells Johnny that he has bugged the countess' apartment and their conversation was most interesting. Johnny calls Insp. Marcus a rat. But not to worry, Insp. Marcus tells him, he is the soul of discretion, and a Frenchman! Johnny notes that the Casbah had been mentioned twice that night. He has questions, and the trail leads to the Casbah.

Tomorrow, a bungling fool, a tightening net and a violent death in a crooked alley in the Casbah.

**PART 4          SHOW DATE:          11/10/1955**

Abdul calls Johnny and tells Johnny that he has a little business and Johnny is looking for him. Abdul runs an employment agency and he hired the countess's maid. Johnny will pay Abdul $10 for the address.

Johnny pays $15 to Abdal for the address of a girl named Chatta, who Johnny thinks was the one who turned on the gas. In his hotel room, Johnny puts a gun in his pocket when there is a knock at the door. It is Charlie Barrett who apologizes for the fight. Johnny wants to know what he wants. Charlie tells Johnny that he is in the meat business; he cans the squeal. Charlie wants to talk man-to-man. He has a claim on the countess and has bought things for her. They had a fight last week when he told her she had to stop "ginny flipping" around with other men, and that made her mad. The fight was before the diamonds were shipped here, and he cannot forget about her. Johnny tells Charles he was in the apartment for business. Charles tells Johnny that he is someone in the States, but Johnny slugs him and calls room service to drag him out to the hall. Johnny goes to the Casbah and walks through the streets, and people stop talking as he passes by. Johnny goes to the address Abdul gave him, which is a coffeehouse. Johnny goes in and asks for Chatta and is told to sit down. Johnny sits and drinks coffee and waits. Finally a man with a Peter Lorre voice sits with him. The man knows how to find Chatta, as she his wife, and he is Bobo, the man that killed the courier. He tells Johnny that he only gave him some wine but maybe it was a bad vintage. Bobo wants to talk of diamonds. It is possible Chatta turned on the gas but Bobo wants to talk of diamonds. Bobo tells Johnny that the company would like to get the diamonds back and Bobo asks about making a deal. Bobo can lead him to their location and he has at least 30 men in the room to protect him if Johnny tries anything. Johnny tells Bobo he does not make deals with killers. A voice warns of the police and Bobo disappears. Insp. Marcus comes in to find an empty coffeehouse. Johnny tells Insp. Marcus that he had had a gun on Bobo and that Insp. Marcus has goofed. There are shots outside and they run out and search the area. Johnny finds Bobo in an alley, shot three times in the back. Bobo tells Johnny that a 12-foot tall dragon shot him to protect his honor. Bobo admits that he attacked Jourdine, and dies. Insp. Marcus comes up and they look at the short stocky body of Bobo. Johnny tells Insp. Marcus that he knows the whole story, the whole filthy rotten story.

Tomorrow, the odds are set, the last chip is down, and it is the last spin of the wheel, and death is the croupier.

## PART 5          SHOW DATE:      11/11/1955

The Countess calls and tells Johnny that she is being followed. She is in a coffeehouse on the waterfront. Johnny tells her that everything was set up, now she has to stay there.

Johnny cabs to the waterfront to go to the Countess. Insp. Marcus had set a trap, but she left before he got there. The street is dark and Johnny enters the Marrakech coffeehouse. She tells Johnny that she was visiting a friend, Charlie. Johnny tells her of the conversation with Charlie; and she tells Johnny that she knew he would come around. Johnny tells her the facts just seem to point to her. Johnny asks about Charlie, and she is not sure that she will marry him. Charlie had given her his car, and someone had followed her. As they leave, shots ring out and Johnny runs for a curb to draw their fire. Johnny fires back and a man runs away and into a car. Johnny gets in Charlie's car and they follow the other car. Johnny follows the car and finally has to stop when the other car misses a turn, rolls down a hill and explodes. Johnny sees the driver of the car before it explodes. Johnny tells the Countess that now that she knows that she is safe, that the other driver, Jourdine, will not talk as he was the only one left. Oh, Maria did not know about Bobo, he is dead too. The plan was to make sure that the courier died, so that the briefcase would go to Jourdine. But Bobo was a tough cookie. He attacked Jourdine, and tried to kill him but Andre got to his gun. Andre got the idea for a double-cross and went after Bobo in the Casbah and killed him. Now Insp. Marcus is at her apartment waiting for Andre to appear. Why did both Andre and Bobo try to kill her unless she was in on it? She tries the charm routine, but it fails. Johnny tells her she is rotten and leaves the Countess to walk back to town. Johnny goes to the Customs Property office with Insp. Marcus who opens the safe that contains the briefcase with the diamonds. So beautiful. Johnny knew that Andre was lying because he described his assailant as tall and thin, but Bobo was short and stocky, so Andre had lied. The diamonds were in the vault where Andre had access to them. Insp. Marcus will probably not do anything to the Countess; as she would cry and the court would blame him.

Social Item. To be circulated widely. The Countess Maria de Tolia was married yesterday to C. K Barrett, a big tycoon in the meat business. The happy couple will make their home in Chicago. All companies in that area who may be asked to underwrite insurance on the life of C.K Barrett—DON'T!

Exp. Acct:     $1,214.60

NOTES:
- THE CASBAH IS THE OLD SECTION OF MOST NORTH AFRICAN TOWNS
- ROY ROWAN IS THE ANNOUNCER
- MUSICAL SUPERVISION IS BY AMERIGO MARINO

Producer:   Jack Johnstone        Writers:   Les Crutchfield
Cast:       Lillian Buyeff, Jack Moyles, Victor Perrin, C. K. Barrett, Lawrence Dobkin, Forrest Lewis, Jay Novello

◆  ❖  ◆

SHOW:       THE BRODERICK MATTER
COMPANY:    EASTERN TRUST INSURANCE COMPANY
AGENT:      ROBERT STEEL
PART 1      SHOW DATE:      11/14/1955

SYNOPSIS: Mr. Steel calls. The Universal Adjustment Bureau suggested that he call Johnny. They need help paying the beneficiary of a policy, as she has disappeared.

Johnny takes a bus to the Hartford, Connecticut office of Robert Steel. The policyholder was John Smith, he was malnourished and had two policies for $1,500 and the beneficiary was Lorraine Broderick. John Smith made his payments on time every month but he was broke and sold newspapers for a living. Lorraine was eleven at the time and just stopped by to talk to him one day. Smith asked an agent to help him do something for a nice little girl. It has hard for him to make the payments, so lets hope that Lorraine deserves the insurance.

Johnny goes to the last know address of Lorraine and learns that the parents were killed in 1948 and Lorraine moved out. Johnny goes to a high school in the area and speaks to Sister Mary Regina. Johnny tells her he is looking for Lorraine Broderick, who possibly went to school there. She looks in the file and she did attend the school and there is an address for a guardian uncle. Sister Mary remembers Lorraine, who had the face of an angel. Johnny tells her about the insurance policies and the Sister gets an annual and shows Johnny a picture of Lorraine. Johnny goes to the address of the uncle, but he had died, and Lorraine had moved. Johnny learns that Lorraine had worked for a dentist after that. Johnny calls Mr. Steel and asks for help tracking the agencies that hire for dentists. Johnny also tries to locate Lorraine through former students. Johnny gets the name of Dr. David Pollard who had hired Lorraine. Johnny talks to Dr. Pollard and he asks Johnny how she is. Lorraine had not worked there for several years and he does not have an address for her. She quit suddenly and never came back. Dr. Pollard goes with Johnny for a drink and tells Johnny that she was a sweet girl, but there was something about her and she had plans of her own. Many men were used by her and knew it. She was out to take people for what she could get. She is rotten, plain rotten.

Tomorrow, the expense goes way up. Yeah, it takes money to prove how wrong one man can be.

### PART 2          SHOW DATE:     11/15/1955

Carl Walden calls Johnny. Lorraine used to live in his apartment building. She moved out with no forwarding address. Carl does not think she wants to be found.

Johnny gets photographs of Lorraine from the high school photographer. Carl Walden tells Johnny that she had pulled out in the middle of the night and probably went to New York. She had walked out on some doctor who probably had it real bad for her. There was another guy too, a big man with gray hair, a homburg and a Cadillac, but he never came around again after she moved out.

Johnny places ads in the New York papers and checks with Cadillac dealers in the area. After five days Johnny gets a call from Lorraine in New York. She wants to know what Johnny wants. The line is suddenly switched and a Mr. Dameron is on the phone. He tells Johnny that he knows Lorraine. Johnny goes to New York City and meets Mr. William Dameron. Dameron is the president of the Union Brokerage Company. Dameron knew Lorraine and asks for Johnny's credentials. Johnny tells Dameron about the policies and his efforts to find Lorraine. Dameron does not know where she is. She came to New York with him and they were going to be married even though he only knew her a week. He was taking her to a party and stopped for gas. Lorraine got out of the car and disappeared. She was staying with Dameron's sister and left her clothes there. Dameron thinks that Lorraine was frightened of life. He thought he could offer her the security she longed for, but she was too immature. Dameron tells Johnny that he waited for her to return but she never came back. She just got out and left for her own reasons. Dameron gives Johnny the location of the gas station and Johnny tells him that the others had told him the truth, so why would she leave on Christmas Eve with no clothes or plans. "How much did she take?" Johnny asks. Dameron tells Johnny she took $6,500 from his wallet and notes that "there is no fool like an old fool, is here?"

Tomorrow, when the trail really gets hot and goes right down on a police blotter.

### PART 3        SHOW DATE:        11/16/1955

Bob Steel calls, and Johnny tells him he has not found Lorraine. "Do you want to go on?" asks Johnny. Steel says yes. Johnny thinks John Smith left money to a nice little girl; and he is trying to find a woman who is not so nice anymore.

Johnny goes to the gas station and talks to the man who was on duty. Edward Quinlen remembers her. She just got out and walked down the street. He felt sorry for the guy. Johnny talks to Dameron's sister who verifies his story.

Johnny requests a missing persons investigation and learns that she had been booked under an alias on drunk and disorderly charges. Johnny goes to the address on the record but Lorraine had moved. The landlady tells Johnny Lorraine was always having parties and had lots of men around.

Johnny rechecks the court record for those arrested with her. One of the men tells Johnny that he saw her at an apartment building in Manhattan. Johnny checks with the manager of the apartment building and learns that there was a Lorraine Bradley there four months ago and the picture matches. She had written a bad check and the police are looking for her. The police records for Lorraine Bradley show five warrants in New York, Chicago, and San Francisco. Three days ago she had passed a bad check in Santa Barbara. Johnny calls Mr. steel and gets permission to travel to the coast.

Johnny travels to Santa Barbara, California and talks to the operator of a hotel who is chagrined about being taken. Mr. Harrington tells Johnny that she was the best at getting what she wanted. She was there for four days and had the best of everything and paid for the $813 bill with a bad check. Johnny asks why she would check in alone, and Mr. Harrington tells Johnny that she had become friends with others in the hotel. She came in a cab and called for the manager and pretended she knew him. She said she had just been divorced and was coming from Lake Tahoe. Mr. Harrington checked the address and there was a Robert Bradley in Beverly Hills, but Mr. Harrington learned that Mr. Bradley was in Europe with his wife and family. The bill showed no phone calls and the check was a blank one.

Johnny meets with Sgt. Martin, who tells Johnny that the same woman has passed bad checks all over the area. Johnny interviews the others who had taken the bad checks, and the story is the same. Johnny calls Mr. Steel and he tells Johnny that Lorraine has just hit in Malibu Beach.

Tomorrow, a long look at what seven years can do to a woman's life.

**PART 4**      **SHOW DATE:**    **11/17/1955**

King from the Malibu Sheriff calls Johnny and he tells Johnny that he wants Lorraine, and Johnny tells King that they both want Lorraine. King is expecting some action, come on over.

Johnny travels to Malibu Beach and meets with deputy King who tells Johnny that Lorraine was in the local inn using the name Bradley. She hung out with Joe Tappan, who had driven her down town that morning. Tappan lives in the artist colony. A call comes in and Tappan is home, so Deputy King and Johnny drive out to see Joe Tappan. Johnny and deputy King stun Joe with the news that Lorraine is a phony. The picture matches and he tells Johnny that he thought he knew her when he met her at the Seaside Inn four days ago, but there must be some explanation. He dropped her bags at the Beverly Glen hotel and then took her to a bar to meet her lawyer. She was dressed in a black dress and a mink stole. The story she gave was that a baby had died and drove her away from her husband, and Joe believed her. Joe tells Johnny to try believing in people for a change.

Johnny drives to Hollywood and the luggage is still in the hotel. The lobby is watched and Johnny and deputy King go to the Topper Club, but the bartender has not seen the woman there today. The luggage is not claimed that day and so Johnny goes to see Joe Tappan again and tells him that Joe did not hear what Johnny told him. Johnny tells Joe the whole story, and that there was no baby. Johnny tells Joe that he has to find her to stop her and Joe is involved. "Where is she?" Johnny demands. Joe tells Johnny that she is at the Wentmore Hotel under the name Evelyn Brady. She had called Joe an hour ago and told Joe she loved him. What kind of crazy world is this?

Johnny goes to room 1302 in the Wentmore Hotel. Johnny finds the door open and knocks. He goes in and finds a woman on the ledge ready to jump.

Tomorrow, the end of the trail for me, and for Lorraine Broderick.

**PART 5**      **SHOW DATE:**    **11/18/1955**

The desk clerk calls and Johnny tells him to call the police. Lorraine tells Johnny it will do no good, as she is going to jump.

Lorraine tells Johnny to back off; she is going to jump. Johnny tries to calm her and offers her his coat. She asks Johnny how he knows her name. Johnny tells her of the high school picture and she wants to see his face and tells Johnny that he is not from Hartford, and she never knew him. The room clerk comes up and Lorraine screams, and Johnny tells him to call the police. She tells Johnny that she wants the police and a big crowd for when she jumps. She sees a crowd gathering. Johnny tells her that if she dies it will make him afraid to die. She is not afraid to jump, she tells Johnny. Johnny tells her that she was afraid to love any of the men she had been involved with. Johnny tells her he wants to help her. She asks Johnny why everyone died and left her alone. Johnny tells her that Mr. Dameron still loves her, but she does not love him. She says she is no good and never has been. She tells Johnny to tell Dameron she meant to send the money back. Someone runs in and she screams to get out and close the door. She finally knows what she wants to do, and that is to jump. She tells Johnny that she should have died with her parents. Johnny tells her that old John Smith had faith in her, and it meant a lot to him. She remembers buying a paper from him and talking to him that one day. Johnny tells her he had bought the policies for her. Johnny shows her the check and his identification papers. Lorraine cries over that poor old man.

It was Johnny's first and hopefully last experience with a suicide. Johnny returns the check, as Lorraine is not a responsible person, but the psychiatrist says she will be ok in time. Mr. Dameron is called and comes to Los Angeles; Joe Tappan has hired an attorney and the Insurance Company wants restitution rather than prosecution.

Exp. Acct:  $1,132.14

**NOTES:**
- REMAKE OF THE THELMA IBSEN MATTER—1/09/1953 WITH PARTS OF THE EMILY BRADDOCK MATTER
- "THE CRONIN MATTER" IS ANNOUNCED FOR NEXT WEEK, BUT MOST CATALOGS HAVE IT AIRED THREE WEEKS LATER
- ROY ROWAN IS THE ANNOUNCER
- MUSICAL SUPERVISION IS BY AMERIGO MARINO

Producer:  Jack Johnstone          Writers:  John Dawson
Cast:      Eleanor Audley, Barbara Eiler, Virginia Gregg, Carlton Young,
           Harry Bartell, Herbert Ellis, John Dehner, Marvin Miller,
           Tony Barrett, Frank Gerstle, Chester Stratton,
           Lawrence Dobkin

◆  ❖  ◆

SHOW:      THE AMY BRADSHAW MATTER
COMPANY:   NORTHWEST INDEMNITY ALLIANCE
AGENT:     GEORGE ATKINS
PART 1     SHOW DATE:     11/21/1955
SYNOPSIS: George Atkins calls Johnny about going to New York City. Someone is trying to kill the Actress Amy Bradshaw.

Johnny goes to New York City and visits the Criterion Theater where he meets David Coleman, the director. Johnny is told that the play has been running for 22 weeks, but last night Amy got a note that made her upset, and her performance is suffering. Johnny tells David that these notes are usually harmless, and maybe someone is using the note as a cover. Johnny talks to Amy after the show and he is impressed with her but she thinks Johnny is wasting his time. Johnny suggests talking over a drink but she has a date. Mike Pomeroy, her agent, comes in and leaves when he sees Johnny and the offer of the drink is taken up by Amy. She asks Johnny to leave by a different door to avoid a man who was waiting for her, Porter Caine.

Johnny and Amy talk over drinks. She tells Johnny that she has been acting for a long time and she usually gets what she wants. Johnny tells Amy that he thinks that the letter is more than a crank. She tells Johnny that last night she went for a walk and was pushed out into traffic. It was probably just a fluke, but she wonders if someone might hate her. Johnny asks of it could have come from a friend and Amy tells him her few a friends are good ones. Amy tells Johnny that the beneficiary of her policy is William York, her husband from whom she is separated.

Johnny takes Amy home and sees a man waiting in a car. Johnny watches the car and sees Mike Pomeroy go into the building. Johnny sees another man watching too.

Tomorrow, the Criterion Theater and a third act curtain that wasn't in the script.

## PART 2          SHOW DATE:     11/22/1955

Al Cintella, NYPD calls and Johnny tells him about the threat to kill Amy.

Johnny cabs to see Det. Lt. Cintella about the actress. Johnny shows Lt. Cintella the note and tells him about the push into traffic. Lt. Cintella smells a publicity stunt and thinks Johnny is stage-struck. Johnny tells Lt. Cintella that the suspects are the director, the producer, her agent, and a man named Porter Caine and her husband, who is the beneficiary.

Johnny goes to see Porter Caine at noon and he is still eating breakfast. Over coffee and Chopin, Porter tells Johnny that Amy is his career. She is a hobby and he collects things, one-of-a-kind things. He shows Johnny a signet ring supposedly owned by the Medici's and the only one in existence. He is going to add Amy to his collection, in time, and he has time.

Johnny cabs to the theater that evening and hears Mike Pomeroy tell Amy about his plans for Sheila, so don't make her look bad. When Mike leaves Johnny goes to see Amy. She thinks that her making mistakes over the note is silly. Mike meets Johnny when he leaves and Johnny tells him about the note. Mike thinks that the note is nothing and Johnny should mind his own business.

After the program Johnny talks to Caine who is going to talk to Amy later. Johnny tells him that he has a date with Amy and Caine leaves. Johnny goes in after everyone has left and Amy screams. Amy tells Johnny that a sandbag had almost hit her. Johnny investigates the catwalk and goes back to Amy. She is scared that someone really is trying to kill her.

Tomorrow, a man steps onto the stage from out of the past and into a role he does not want to play.

## PART 3          SHOW DATE:     11/23/1955

Lt. Cintella calls and Johnny tells him what happened that night. Lt. Cintella tells Johnny that maybe his hunch is right. He tells Johnny that the husband is living in Greenwich Village.

Johnny cabs to the address of Bill York, Amy's husband. The address is a rooming house. Bill tells Johnny that Amy always wanted to apologize for him. He is an artist, what more could he ask for. Johnny says he has not read any of Bills books, and Bill tells him that no one else has either. He is living the unfettered life of an artist and lives comfortably in hock. He has written a manuscript, which Mr. Pomeroy has in hock. Bill has not seen Amy in months.

Johnny goes to see Emory Taylor, the producer, who is out. His wife Dora is sweet and comfortable behind the bar in the apartment. Dora tells Johnny that she would like to kill Amy because Emory was working too hard for her. She tells Johnny that Coleman was in love with Amy, and she does not want Emory to fall either. Caine is not the type to be hurt by Amy.

Johnny meets Pomeroy in a bar and he tells Johnny to mind his own business. Johnny tells him about meeting with York and he tells Johnny that he paid Bill to stay away from Amy. He has a play lined up and wants his money. Bill could work in television but Bill thinks he is too good for that. The new play will star Sheila Mitchell.

After the show Johnny takes Amy home and again he spots the man on the street. Johnny gets behind the man and discovers that it is Bill York.

Tomorrow, I find I have even more of a reason for keeping Amy alive than I had realized.

**PART 4**      **SHOW DATE:**     **11/24/1955**

Lt. Cintella calls and Johnny tells him to come to his hotel room. He has Bill York there and he has plenty to tell them.

Johnny "invites" Bill York to his hotel room. Lt. Cintella arrives and Bill asks them why he would kill Amy. They tell Bill about the insurance money and the debt to Pomeroy. Bill tells them that he had opportunity but not motive. Amy always got what she wanted and Bill had always been a failure. Bill admits he would watch her once in a while, but that is all. Bill goes down stairs with an officer and Johnny tells Lt. Cintella what he has been up to. Lt. Cintella chastises Johnny for breaking the rules and he still believes that Johnny is smitten with Amy.

Johnny thinks about what Lt. Cintella says and goes to Amy's apartment to see if he is right. She tells Johnny that she has noticed the police guard, and she is glad Johnny is there. There is a phone call and Amy tells Porter Caine that something is out of the question. Amy tells Johnny that she is glad he is there and kisses him. She is sorry and apologizes for putting him into her life. The clock is ticking but it still is affecting her life by her getting older. Johnny decides not to see Amy after the case is closed.

Johnny visits Porter Caine and he tells Johnny that he had hoped he would meet Johnny again. Porter tells Johnny that when he gets Amy his collection will be complete. He tells Johnny that he has always gotten anything he wanted, except for a lollypop he wanted when he was nine. He could not get that, so he smashed it.

Tomorrow, well it's the wind up, and a pretty rough one.

**PART 5          SHOW DATE:     11/25/1955**

Amy calls and is frantic. She is in her dressing room. She tells Johnny that she knows who is trying to killer. Please hurry.

Johnny cabs to the theater and sees a figure in the distance. In the dark theater Johnny hears shots and runs to Amy's room where he finds Mike Pomeroy dead. Amy tells Johnny that someone outside the room had shot Mike, so Johnny runs out to search and calls Lt. Cintella. In Amy's dressing room, she tells Johnny that Mike had called and wanted her to meet him in her dressing room. They were talking and a hand appeared in the door. Mike saw it and ran to protect her and was shot. He fell against the door causing the gun to fall in the dressing room. The hand had a large signet ring on it, Porter Caines's signet ring.

Lt. Cintella arrives and Amy relates her story to him and an order to pick up Porter Caine is issued. At police headquarters, Caine is unaware that Pomeroy is dead. He admits he had called Amy and asked her to meet him. He saw her leave and followed her to the theater, but did not go in. Johnny tells him that his motive was to kill her if he could not have her.

Johnny takes Amy home and she is very quiet. The phone rings and Lt. Cintella calls. Suddenly Johnny feels old, tired, and sick. Johnny tells her that the gun had no fingerprints on it. Johnny tells Amy that she killed him and faked the attempts on her life. She tells Johnny that she loved Mike but he was drifting away from her. She felt dead so the she faked the attempts. After all, she is a very good actress. As Amy goes out into the hall to meet the police, she asks Johnny not to forget her. Amy does not look back, and Johnny is glad.

Remarks: Amy repeated her confession to Lt. Cintella; her case is coming up soon. Sweet case. Well, tomorrow is another day, so they tell me.

Exp. Acct:     $185.20

**NOTES:**
- THIS PROGRAM IS NOTED FOR THE SPECIAL "GIANT ANIMAL" OFFER.
- ROY ROWAN IS THE ANNOUNCER
- MUSICAL SUPERVISION IS BY AMERIGO MARINO

**Producer:**  Jack Johnstone          **Writers:**   Robert Ryf
**Cast:**          Virginia Gregg, Florence Wolcott, Don Diamond, Larry Thor, Vic Perrin, Carlton Young

◆   ❖   ◆

**SHOW:**         THE HENDERSON MATTER
**COMPANY:**     PARAMOUNT INSURANCE ADJUSTERS
**AGENT:**        TIM CONNORS
**PART 1**        **SHOW DATE:     11/28/1955**

**SYNOPSIS:** Tim Connors calls and tells Johnny that he is a father. Come to the office and get a cigar . . . and bring a suitcase. In Culver Montana Mr. Henderson is dead. It was either murder or suicide or an accident or all three.

Johnny buys a map and tries to find Culver, Montana and then goes to Tim Connors office (the cigars cost $2.00 a box—don't smoke it). The Henderson heirs think that the insurance company is trying to cheat them for looking into the death. The claim is for $25,000. George Henderson, a rancher, fell from a hotel window and there was no inquest. Connors has phoned the sheriff and he will help. Tim called the widow and she hung up on him.

Johnny goes to Great Falls and trains to Culver, a dingy town. Johnny gets a room in the only hotel and meets Efe Holton, the sheriff who brings a bottle to help warm things up. They have a drink and Efe tells Johnny that he is visiting unofficially; and Johnny will have to go it alone in town. Culver is a small, tight community and there are people who do not care about the details that bother the insurance companies or the people who dig up people. Efe tells Johnny that the funeral is at three. Efe likes Johnny; he is all right because he does not ask questions until he has one to ask.

Johnny goes to the cemetery for the funeral with Efe, who points out Pauline Henderson to Johnny, who is amazed that she is only 26 and George was 52. Johnny tells Efe he will ask for a Coroner's Inquest just from seeing her.

Tomorrow, I find out how hard it is to believe what I see, and I see plenty.

## PART 2        SHOW DATE:    11/29/1955

Efe calls Johnny about his filing for the inquest. The coroner left it up to Efe, and the Mayor will probably have to ok it. You have stirred up trouble and it will find you.

Johnny sits and waits until Mayor Newton visits Johnny about the inquest request. He tells Johnny that George's death was a blow to the community but Johnny replies that only half a dozen people were at the funeral. The mayor tells Johnny that an inquest would only prove George fell out of a window. Their police force is small and it would cost a lot of money. Johnny tells the mayor that he wants proof it was an accident; he wants an inquest.

Johnny meets with Efe for coffee and is told that the inquest is on for tomorrow. Johnny notes that Efe will not have time to do anything, and Johnny suspects someone is trying to stop the inquest. At the inquest the next day, the doctor testifies that George died of a broken neck. The maid testifies that she saw Mr. Henderson the morning of the accident and that Mrs. Henderson was in the lobby, but she does not know if she went up. Everyone else had the same vague story. Mrs. Henderson last saw George on Thursday when she went to see him around noon at the hotel. She was at the dentist when she heard the news. She went to talk to George about their divorce, which they had decided on a month ago. Mrs. Henderson does not think he was upset over the discussion, and she thinks he had a drink while they were talking. Johnny notes the New York clothes, the Paris perfume and the Tiffany jewelry and a Riviera look on Mrs. Henderson. The verdict comes in fifteen minutes, accidental death. Mayor Newton gloats over the results and Johnny tells him he will send a report saying that the inquest was a sham and that now people will be more relaxed and get careless.

Tomorrow, people do get careless all over Culver, Montana.

**PART 3**     **SHOW DATE:**     **11/30/1955**

Efe calls and Johnny tells him that he is ready to go to work, so help me move around the city. Efe says the case is closed officially but he will help, as it needs investigating.

Johnny wires Tim Connors and tells him he is not satisfied with the inquest and is staying. The operator wishes him luck. Johnny mails the report to Connors and then Mr. Porter, the manager, comes to his room to tell Johnny that he must give up his room as they are "filled up." It is a sort of convention. Johnny smells a rat and forces him to back down. "Go back to 'no one' and tell 'them' I am staying put, and call the police if you want" Johnny tells him. Johnny tells Efe about the manager and Efe calls it stupid. Johnny tells Efe that the company is out $50,000 now. Efe tells Johnny that Mrs. Henderson is a local girl, Pauline Underwood. She went to school in the east and spent time in Europe. Everyone knew that they were not getting along. George raised Pauline since she was fourteen and he was good to her and her father worked for George. Efe tells Johnny that she has no reason to kill him; as she was getting a generous settlement. Efe does not think it was suicide. Johnny asks who owns the hotel and Efe tells him it is Noah Baxter. Johnny asks Efe to look into all of Pauline's friends. Johnny wonders why Mrs. Henderson has not hired a lawyer to sue for the money, and Efe wonders too.

Tim wires Johnny to go see Mr. Thurber, an insurance agent in Great Falls. Johnny drives to Great Falls and Thurber tells Johnny that he had been out hunting and heard of the death yesterday. Two days before he left, Henderson wanted to change the beneficiary on his policy to Matilda Knickerbocker. It was just a name to put in. Then Henderson called back to say that he had changed his mind. He called on the same day he died, just after noon. Thurber knew both of the Hendersons and tells Johnny he wished he were married to Mrs. Henderson. George was just the opposite of Pauline. Thurber thinks she married George for his money and would have killed for it.

Tomorrow the whole affair becomes a town issue, and I become the town goat.

Bob Bailey closes this program with the following: "Incidentally, let me take a moment to say thanks for the many kind letters you have sent. We appreciate them more than you know and I only wish it were possible to answer them all personally. Again, thank you."

**PART 4**     **SHOW DATE:**     **12/1/1955**

Mrs. Henderson calls and Johnny tells her he wants to come out this afternoon. She tells Johnny that she will meet him at the Big Horn Lodge at 4:00.

Johnny buys galoshes because of the 14" of new snow. Johnny tells Efe that he might have to leave, as the company wants him to come home. Johnny borrows Efe's car for the drive to the lodge. Efe tells Johnny that he has looked for some friends of Pauline's, but has found nothing yet. "Don't let her rang dangle you" Efe tells Johnny.

As Johnny passes the cemetery he sees a car and an old woman is standing at the Henderson grave. Johnny stops and introduces himself to Mattie

Knickerbocker, the schoolteacher in the town. She tells Johnny that George was a wonderful man to her, and she will miss him, and Johnny tells her that he knew George too. Mattie comments on George's laugh and Johnny agrees. She tells Johnny that she did not come to the funeral because she did not think she could bear it. She notes the birds in the snow and how wonderful they are. She tells Johnny that she knows who Johnny is, and asks if it was curiosity that made him stop. Johnny thinks that Mattie was the first person to talk to him frankly.

Johnny meets Pauline and orders Pernod for Pauline and Bourbon for himself. Johnny tells her about meeting Thurber and Mattie, and the call to ignore the change. Johnny asks if something happened in the room. She tells Johnny that they had agreed on the divorce and that she would have a generous settlement. They met one day and had a bitter argument and George's response was to cancel her out of the insurance. They had met to apologize for the argument. Johnny tells her that it is unusual for a man to leave an ex-wife as a beneficiary. She also tells Johnny that she preferred to talk to him at the lodge rather than at her home.

That evening Johnny rereads the inquest testimony and goes to see Efe the next morning. In the personal effects there is no mention of a bottle, and no one brought him any, yet he had a drink before breakfast. Mrs. Henderson said that he had a drink before and while she was there. Johnny thinks that she put that in to make everyone believe George was tipsy. So, where did he get the drink? "That is a pretty good question, son" Efe tell Johnny.

Tomorrow the wind up. Yeah, the whole case blows sky high.

## PART 5          SHOW DATE:      12/2/1955

Johnny gets a call from Hartford and Tim asks Johnny about his wire asking to deny liability to Mrs. Henderson. Johnny has proof that Henderson did not have a drink. Tim is on his way out.

Efe promises Johnny a reinvestigation of the facts. Tim meets Johnny and tells him they should move in now, and that Henderson had not been drinking. Johnny tells Tim that Mrs. Henderson was ready for the inquiry, and she was ready for me, but she was not ready for you and that is why she hung up. Johnny has three things to go on; instinct, experience and statistics. Mrs. Henderson married an older man and would have everything in her favor. Johnny pushes to have charges filed and Tim says they need more evidence. Efe and Johnny go over the notes and Mrs. Henderson tells Johnny and Efe that she might have been mistaken. Efe tells Johnny that they need to find who helped her pull this off, and Mrs. Henderson background is searched. Johnny and Efe drive out the Henderson ranch where a servant tells them that Mrs. Henderson would take trips in the Cadillac, and Mr. Henderson would argue with her about meeting that man. She had watched Pauline grow up and was surprised when they married, as she was different. She fit in but was different. Efe's deputies uncover three men who knew Mrs. Henderson; one of which is Noah Baxter. Efe and Johnny drive to the Baxter ranch and speak with him. He denies seeing Mrs. Henderson on the sly as they were both good friends. Baxter was on the ranch when George died and was last in town three weeks ago. Johnny asks if they can talk to the help, and Baxter admits that she would come occasionally to talk. Baxter tells them that she did not kill George, because she loved him. Baxter then tells them he lied, that there was something between them. She would come to cry on his shoulder, because George wanted to divorce her and marry Mattie Knickerbocker. Baxter wanted Pauline but she wanted to be married to George. Baxter went to see George to tell him to go back to Pauline. He tells Johnny that his help would lie for him. He drove into town and went to George's room, just after Pauline left. George was mad and swung at him once and Baxter shoved him and he went out the window. He had killed him.

We still had to pay double indemnity. Mattie, Pauline and Noah will pay another way, with the hurt that comes to nice people.

Exp. Acct:     $802.50

## NOTES:

- REMAKE OF THE UNDERWOOD MATTER—2/27/1953
- THOSE IRRITATING STUFFED ANIMALS AGAIN!
- ROY ROWAN IS THE ANNOUNCER
- MUSICAL SUPERVISION IS BY AMERIGO MARINO

**Producer:**  Jack Johnstone          **Writers:**  John Dawson
**Cast:**      Lillian Buyeff, Irene Tedrow, D. J. Thompson, Herb Ellis, Marvin Miller, Forrest Lewis, Bob Bruce, Russ Thorson

◆  ❖  ◆

**SHOW:**       THE CRONIN MATTER
**COMPANY:**    SURETY MUTUAL AND TRUST COMPANY
**AGENT:**      JOE PARKER
**PART 1**      **SHOW DATE:**     12/5/1955

**SYNOPSIS:** Joe Parker calls Johnny about a gorgeous doll named Dolly McClain who married Barnaby Cronin. He gave her the "Circle of Fire" necklace worth $500,000. Dolly is coming out of seclusion, giving a party and is going to wear the necklace. We have a problem.

Johnny goes to the New York City apartment of Dolly McLain to discuss the necklace. She tells Johnny that she has been hibernating since Barnaby died. Johnny also meets Sylvia Blake, a friend of Dolly's. She asks Johnny if he is the Johnny Dollar, and that she would not want to be in his shoes for a million dollars, for a half a million, maybe. Sylvia is a writer who wrote about Dolly's necklace once. Dolly invites Johnny to the party and Johnny tells her that Joe Parker is really worried about the necklace. She tells Johnny that she wants no detectives at the party. Barnaby gave her the necklace at a party a long time ago, and she wore the necklace then and was perfectly safe. He was running two railroads and a bank at the time. Dolly relents because she likes Johnny and wants him at the party where hundreds are invited to her home in the Adirondacks.

Sylvia tells Dolly that she has a visitor and pours a drink for Johnny. The guest is named Shorty Webber who Johnny recognizes from Broadway, and Shorty has an invitation. Sylvia tells Johnny that he is a freeloader where as Johnny is working his way. Johnny accuses Sylvia of once writing a story about the necklace and its attempted theft and Sylvia tells Johnny that someone will steal the necklace. Johnny tells her that maybe it will be Sylvia Blake as she has written stories about all the famous jewel thefts for the past fifty years. She tells Johnny that the jewels are like her, beautiful and brittle.

Johnny looks for Dolly and finds Shorty Webber searching the mail of her desk. Johnny takes Shorty's .38 snub-nose, "it belongs to a friend" he tells Johnny. Shorty tells Johnny that Dolly is an old friend, and that he wanted to marry her once. Shorty tells Johnny that Dolly does not know he has served time for jewel theft, but he is looking out for Dolly; and he knows how word gets around. Dolly comes in and Johnny tells her that he and Shorty have a mutual friend, a prison warden. Dolly is sure that Shorty was doing a benefit for the prisoners. Shorty leaves and so does Johnny, but not before Dolly tells Johnny that she has had a premonition. She is old and feels that something awful will happen to her.

Tomorrow, a man who is afraid of his shadow, a girl who is afraid of nothing, and a stranger who strikes in the dark.

**PART 2**     **SHOW DATE:**     **12/6/1955**

Jason Prell calls Johnny and wants to talk to him immediately. Prell manages Dolly's trust accounts and he wants to talk before the train leaves. He tells Johnny not to get the necklace, to leave it where it is. Prell tells Johnny that he is worried about Mrs. Cronin's sanity.

Johnny cabs to the newspaper office to look at the morgue files on Dolly, who was a dancer and social butterfly in the 20's. Barnaby Cronin married her and the necklace is mentioned. Barnaby dies and then Dolly went into seclusion.

Johnny cabs to the railway station to find the train and meets Jason Prell, who is an old friend and has managed Dolly's business affairs. Prell knows how Dolly has gone downhill and this party is a bad idea. Prell wants Johnny to point out to Dolly how dangerous this party idea is. Prell is sure that she has burned herself out. She believes in people and lives in a dream world. Most of her friends were trying to use her, and he and Barnaby tried to protect her. Prell is sure that the necklace will be stolen. Prell tells Johnny that the capitol in the trusts is adequate but the necklace is her own property. Her belief in the past keeps her alive. Prell wants Johnny to call the bank and tell them not to deliver the necklace, but Johnny tells him he has it on him. "Heaven help us all" replies Prell. The train pulls out but only six people are there; Johnny, Dolly, Sylvia, Prell, Shorty and a newcomer, Laura Dean who knows who Johnny is, he is there to protect the necklace. She tells Johnny that Mrs. Cronin had sent an invitation to her aunt, who had died, so Dolly said to come. Laura dodges the question of who her aunt was. She only tells Johnny that Dolly and her aunt were the Siamese Twins. Johnny then makes the connection to Fritzy Morel. Johnny did not know her, but Laura says that she loved to party. Johnny knows that Laura is a liar, because Fritzy Morel had died with no relatives.

Prell rushes in and tells Johnny that Dolly is ill and he rushes to her stateroom. Dolly tells Johnny that it is just nerves and she is ok now and has some tablets to take. Dolly asks about the necklace and shows Johnny a letter that she wants him to sign and keep. Johnny reads it and the letter gives the necklace to Sylvia Blake. "Do not tell her, as it will be years before she gets it," she tells Johnny. Dolly is sure that her old friends went on ahead and will meet her at the house.

Johnny goes to his stateroom and catches a glint of light and is hit on the head and the leather case with the necklace is gone.

Tomorrow, an old love and an old hate and violence breaks out at midnight.

## PART 3      SHOW DATE:      12/7/1955

Dr. Bigby calls Johnny and wants him to come to the Cronin place. Dr. Bigby tells Johnny that he is very busy and cannot come out. If Johnny is a friend of Dolly's, take her back to New York City now, before it is too late.

Johnny cabs to Wells Falls, New York, the local town and looks for the doctor, but cannot find him. Johnny finds the pharmacist, but he cannot fill the prescription for Dolly. Johnny goes back to the house and gives the cab to Prell, so he can go to Tupper Lake to get the prescription filled. Johnny looks for Miss. Atherton the housekeeper and she notes a storm is brewing. She knew Barnaby, and he was just another man. But Dolly was always worshipping someone. Dolly was born and raised in the village and Miss Atherton worked with her. Dolly got Barnaby to spend a fortune to build the summerhouse. Dolly has been generous by keeping her on when the house is closed. She tells Johnny that Bigby is the coroner, and had lost his medical license ten years ago and is a drunk. Ask Bigby about his statements, he would know. She tells Johnny that Dolly has come home to die and knows it. Barnaby came back to die here too, on a stormy night like tonight. He was alone when he died and Bigby could not get here because of the storm.

Johnny notes that the house seemed out of sorts with the events, all dressed up with nowhere to go. Prell brings back the medicine and dinner is served. Shorty teaches Laura some dance steps and Johnny watches the rain. Sylvia notes the thunderstorm makes for a perfect setting. Sylvia asks Johnny about the cut on his head and he tells her it was a sudden stoop on the train. Sylvia suggests that someone got the necklace, but Johnny says nothing. Sylvia hopes that someone got the necklace, and Johnny tells her she will be sorry for saying that someday. She suggests that they smooch for excitement and Johnny obliges.

Shorty asks why everyone is gathered together, and Johnny tells him it was Dolly's suggestion. Shorty tells Johnny that he has been in love with Dolly for 35 years and would die for her. Dolly had arranged for Johnny to show everyone the necklace and they are all mesmerized by it. Prell's face goes white and Johnny tells Prell that he had taken the necklace from the case and Prell bolts. Johnny goes after him and the electricity goes out.

Tomorrow, a white lie, a bullet from the darkness and death comes in from the rain.

**PART 4     SHOW DATE:     12/8/1955**

The phone rings but the call to the sheriff is cut off. Johnny believes that the wires were cut. A shot comes in through the window and Johnny goes out to get Prell.

Johnny is shot at as he and Shorty go outside where Prell is shooting blindly. Shorty stays with Johnny because he cares for Dolly. Johnny spots Prell and circles around to his location. Johnny notes that Prell knows Johnny had him pegged. Johnny tells Prell to drop his gun and something happens and there is a shot and Prell is dead. Johnny tells Shorty that Dolly is going to be hurt by what is happening. Johnny changes clothes, retrieves the necklace and checks in with Dolly. Dolly is glad that Laura Dean is there; she is such a nice girl. Dolly thought she heard shots, but Johnny tells her it was thunder. She tells Johnny that she had good friends and good times and Barnaby, who she worshipped. He never did a wrong thing in his life. And Jason Prell has been such a good friend. She tells Johnny that she grew up in Wells Falls. Barnaby died here and she has come back. Dolly asks to see the necklace and he puts it on her and then she goes to sleep. "Good night dancing darling," Johnny tells her.

The next morning Johnny fixes some coffee and ponders the situation. He wonders how he will tell Dolly that Barnaby was as a big a crook as Prell was. Laura comes into the kitchen and talks to Johnny. She mentions the shooting and Johnny ignores it. Johnny tells her that she is lying about being the niece of Fritzy Morel's niece. Johnny tells her that she did not have a niece. Laura tells Johnny that Fritzy lived in the same rooming house and when the invitation came she just decided to go. Miss Atherton comes in with a grim and strange look. She announces that Mrs. Cronin is dead.

Tomorrow, the questions and answers for the living and the dead. The final payoff and fate itself pays the last trump.

**PART 5     SHOW DATE:     12/9/1955**

Dr. Bigby calls and Johnny tells him to come out, as they need a coroner. Johnny is calling from the forestry station and tells Dr. Bigby that Prell and Mrs. Cronin are dead. Mrs. Cronin was murdered.

Johnny gets a ride back from the forestry station and waits for Dr. Bigby. Maybe Dolly was better off now, he wonders. Sylvia comes in and has a cup of coffee. Johnny tells her that Jason Prell is dead, and so is Dolly. Johnny gives Sylvia the necklace and tells her of the will. Johnny tells her that it is a fake, worth $300 to $400 dollars. It has been in the vault and was broken up long ago, and Prell probably was in on it. He had complete control of her trusts and was stealing her blind. Barnaby had disposed of the necklace and did not tell her. He was pretty shady after he teamed up with Prell. Miss Atherton announces Dr. Bigby, and she tells Johnny not to believe him, as he is a chronic drunk. Johnny tells Sylvia that Dolly thought she was giving Sylvia the real necklace. She is glad it is a copy and will always remember that she thought it was real, like her world.

Dr. Bigby was another man under Dolly's spell and tells Johnny that everybody loved her. Johnny thinks that Jason Prell killed her because Prell got a prescription filled and the contents of the bottle are different. Bigby thinks he knows what the pills are. Dr. Bigby tells Johnny that he had been drinking when Barnaby died. He called it a heart attack, but Barnaby was poisoned. He knew he was wrong and turned to the bottle. Barnaby would come up to Dolly her every couple weeks and everyone knew it. Miss Atherton comes in and Johnny asks her why she did it. She tells Johnny that she killed Barnaby when he told her that he was breaking off their affair. She just changed the pills in the bottle; it was so easy. She asks Johnny to call the sheriff.

Dr. Bigby tells Johnny that he had substituted the poison with sugar pills after Barnaby died and Miss Atherton had given them to Dolly. So Mrs. Cronin died of natural causes.

Remarks: The insurance angle here seems a little muddy, premiums were paid for years on an item that didn't exist and yet no claim was filed and none will be. So, well, I leave it to the legal eagles. Me, I am beat and tired and a little sad. I have come out of this with a kind of nostalgia for a time and place I never even knew. And I am halfway in love with a girl back in that time and place, a girl I have never seen. Oh, sure I know it is a dream world and a dream girl and none of it exists. But it's too bad. I wish it did because she must have been a honey, a real sweet heart, a dancing darling.

Exp. Acct:    $263.30

## NOTES:

- ROY ROWAN IS THE ANNOUNCER
- MUSICAL SUPERVISION IS BY AMERIGO MARINO

**Producer:**   Jack Johnstone          **Writers:**   Les Crutchfield
**Cast:**            Virginia Gregg, Shirley Mitchell, Vivi Janiss, Barbara Fuller, Benny Rubin, John Dehner, Parley Baer

◆  ❖  ◆

**SHOW:**           THE LANSING FRAUD MATTER
**COMPANY:**     UNIVERSAL ADJUSTMENT BUREAU
**AGENT:**          JIM CARTER
**PART 1**          **SHOW DATE:**    12/12/1955

**SYNOPSIS:** Jim Carter calls from the Universal Adjustment Bureau; he is going to Phoenix where James Lansing was insured for $50,000 and died two days ago, he starved to death. Johnny will meet Jim at the airport.

Johnny flies to Tucson, Arizona with Jim Carter. Jim tells Johnny that he has advised the state insurance commission that they are holding up payment. They will be there before the letters arrive and have room to investigate, but they need to work fast, as the commission will start asking questions fast. James Lansing's sister Arlene Kennedy has asked about the payment and she was told it would be a day or two, but she could be rough. She has some money and influence in the area and is upset. James Lansing died on the street with no identification. The police did a post mortem and the county was going to bury him, but Jim had the coroner hold the body. Jim thought it might not be Lasing at all. The post mortem showed chronic heart condition, lung history and debility. He took a physical before the policy was issued and was ok when it was issued. So how did he get in that condition in two years? They will go to see Dr. Mayhood, the examining physician first. "Hey, cute stewardess" Jim remarks to Johnny. Johnny and Jim get back to business and they study the files.

In Tucson, Johnny checks into the Pioneer Hotel and goes to see Sgt. Younger who filed the DOA report. Sgt. Younger tells Johnny that the man was found dead on the street. There was no identification so the coroner performed an autopsy. They had a print match based on a traffic arrest. The sister identified the body. He had been dead an hour before he was found. Sgt. Younger tells Johnny that death was natural causes and they will have to pay off. Johnny tells Sgt. Younger that he has to be sure they insured the right man.

Johnny calls Jim who has the history on Dr. Mayhood. Johnny visits the office and talks with Dr. Mayhood. Johnny tells him that in 1953 he examined a man we need information on, but Dr. Mayhood does not remember him. He thinks he signed the exam form and the notes look like his. Johnny tells him that the forms pronounced him sound, but he died two days ago. Dr. Mayhood thinks he could have developed a heart condition since the exam. Johnny tells him that Lansing died of malnutrition. It could not have been overlooked and the coroner says he had been sick for several years. Dr. Mayhood cannot explain any of the problems, but tells Johnny that the nurse will find the exam forms for him tomorrow. Johnny wants them first thing and is riding him hard!

Tomorrow, $50,000 is a good price for a killing. Most anybody will listen for that kind of money.

**PART 2        SHOW DATE:        12/13/1955**

Dr. Mayhood calls about the report forms he sent. Johnny tells him that the forms do not straighten things out. You have to come to the morgue with me to identify Lansing.

Johnny tells Jim about going to take Dr. Mayhood to the morgue. Jim tells Johnny that the doctor is ok financially. Too bad that Lansing died on the street. Johnny tells Jim that they do not have to be careful. Call the state people and tell them we do not think this is legitimate and see who yells.

Johnny takes Dr. Mayhood to the morgue to see the body and he tells Johnny that he only examines whoever the insurance agent sends over. Dr. Mayhood tells Johnny to call his attorney for any further questions. He does not remember seeing Lansing and cannot determine if the body was the man he examined. Johnny has the doctor's staff examine the body as well, with no results.

Johnny tells Jim that the Dr. is too angry over this, so Johnny is going to Lansing's address. The apartment manager is willing to look at Lansing's body at the morgue and she recognizes him. She has seen him drunk many times. He would get up at 10 and buy some groceries and booze and drink all day. He was fried by noon for years. He tried to sell real estate and always had the money to pay his rent. Johnny wonders how he had money to buy booze and insurance. Johnny spends time gathering information on Lansing and determines that he had been drinking heavily for 18 months.

Jim tells Johnny that Lansing had lived in Los Angeles and was fired for drinking on the job. And, Mrs. Kennedy is upset at the investigation. Johnny is told that Hillary Franks sold the policy and has been in business for 17 years. Johnny is sure that only Arlene Kennedy would benefit and would need expert help to get the papers signed and the physicals taken. If Franks did something wrong, he will be looking for us. Jim checks the cylinders of a .38 and tells Johnny to carry it.

Tomorrow, there is a bit of excitement when a pair of thieves starts a falling out. Matter of fact, a lot of excitement.

### PART 3          SHOW DATE:      12/14/1955

Mrs. Kennedy returns Johnny's call and he tells her that he is investigating James Lansing's death. She tells Johnny to call her lawyer. Johnny tells her he wants to talk to her, and she hangs up.

Johnny rents a car and drives to Mrs. Kennedy's house. Mrs. Kennedy does not want to talk to Johnny and tells him to leave. Now! She tells Johnny that Jim drank himself to death; now pay me. It is cut and dry. Johnny tells her it is not and tells her of the results of the autopsy. They will have to discredit one or the other and will not pay until the matter is cleared up. She wants to know what Johnny wants. She finally tells Johnny that she was on good terms with Jim and he left her his insurance. Jim had spent his trust money long ago. Her attorney's have told her to sue. Johnny tells her that Jim died on the street, and that is what caused us to investigate. She tells Johnny that Jim came to her the day after he took the exam, and he was fine. Johnny tells her they think someone else took the exam. Sue us if you want but we will meet you in court.

Johnny and Jim have lunch and discuss Mrs. Kennedy. Jim tells Johnny that the commission wants us to act discretely and promptly. Jim also tells Johnny that her husband, a lawyer, died five years ago and left her some insurance. She has some income from an oil company and could use the money. Johnny has started on Franks, who Mrs. Kennedy has probably called.

Johnny reads Hillary Franks' file and the phone rings. It is Franks. He tells Johnny that Mrs. Kennedy has called and Johnny goes to his office where Johnny and Franks discuss the matter. Franks was surprised to hear from them, and Johnny tells him that he feels Mrs. Kennedy is involved in a fraud. Johnny tells Franks about Lansing and Franks tells him that we has interested in a house at one time and Lansing was the agent. He managed to sell Lansing the policy some time later. Lansing had a small income and did not remain in the real estate business. He was just a client and looked fine to him and does not recall if he drank. Johnny tells Frank that Lansing was an alcoholic. Franks also had never met Mrs. Kennedy. Johnny tells Franks he will leave, and Franks should think about what they talked about, and Johnny will want some better answers. Johnny notes that Franks was a bad, unprepared and awkward liar and Johnny is going to get him. But Franks did not know what to do about it.

Tomorrow, a bad liar turns into a pretty good gunman.

## PART 4          SHOW DATE:     12/15/1955

Jim Carter calls about Franks, who Johnny thinks is doing everything wrong. Mrs. Kennedy is fighting back and her lawyers have filed suit and the body has been cremated. Johnny is going back to see Franks.

Johnny composes a letter to the insurance commission and gives copies of the examinations and statements. Johnny drives back to Franks' office and asks if he wants to make a statement. Franks tells Johnny that he only sold a policy and does not know Mrs. Kennedy. Johnny tells him that he arranged for someone else to take the physical. Franks tells Johnny that he only knows Dr. Mayhood slightly and sent Lansing to him just like any other policy. Franks resents Johnny's insinuations and Johnny tells him that Franks is relying on his reputation. When Johnny tells Franks he is going to swear out a warrant for him and Mrs. Kennedy, Franks hits him with a paperweight and runs from the office.

Jim comes in and Johnny tells him what happened. Johnny wants a statement from Franks and tells Jim that he will not run far, as Franks does not know how to run.

Johnny goes to see Mrs. Kennedy and tells her about Hillary telling everything to him. Johnny tells her that Hillary helped her. He will not run far, and he will realize his life is ruined and he will blame you and probably wants to kill you, so do we talk? She tells Johnny that she had nothing to do with Jim taking out the insurance and that Johnny cannot prove any of the things he is saying.

Jim and Johnny watch Franks' office and the Kennedy home. Jim has called in the police and a warrant has been issued. Jim thinks maybe Franks went to Mexico, but Johnny thinks he will think things out and call him. The next day Johnny goes to Franks' office and talks to the receptionist Maria. She has worked for Franks for 12 years and does not believe any of the things they are saying. Johnny tells her where he is staying and tells her to have Franks call Johnny if he calls her.

At 11:00 PM Franks calls and wants to explain things so he can pass it on to the home office. Johnny tells him that the insurance company does not want to prosecute. Franks tells Johnny to meet him at the San Javier Mission, and come alone — he has a gun.

Tomorrow, $50,000 worth of murder.

## PART 5          SHOW DATE:     12/16/1955

Jim calls Johnny and he tells Jim about going to meet Franks. If Johnny gets a statement, he will try to have the charges dropped.

Johnny cabs to the Mission to meet Franks. The cabby is leery of dropping

Johnny off when he sees a man by the bell tower. Johnny meets Franks who has a .38 and is wearing the same clothes. Johnny tells Franks that Jim Carter will help have the charges dropped if they get a statement from him. They are on his side if he will help them. Franks tells Johnny that he met Arlene Kennedy after his wife died, and he became interested in her. They dated and he asked her to marry him, but she laughed at him and told him he was boring. She only wanted money from life and laughed at him. She knew they could have lived comfortably but she wanted travel and clothes and would not marry him unless they could live the way she wanted. She wanted $50,000 in cash. When her brother came to Tucson, he only had a year to live and so she paid for his apartment and booze and made Franks buy a nice fat policy on him. It was an investment because he was going to die. Franks paid a man $100 to take the physical for Lansing and then waited for Lansing to die. It was too late then, but he wanted out but couldn't. She thought he was weak. After the policy was issued she talked less about marriage. She made it clear she was innocent and Franks had done everything. Johnny takes Franks to town where he signs a statement. The police are called and the charges dropped and the insurance company agrees to waive prosecution. Franks says he will close his office and move away.

Franks leaves and Mrs. Kennedy withdraws her claims. Johnny stops by to see Mrs. Kennedy to get the papers signed and there are shots. Johnny breaks down the door and finds Mrs. Kennedy shot. There are bloodstains leading to the back and Johnny trails Franks to a ledge where he shoots at Johnny. Johnny shoots twice and Franks is hit. He tells Johnny that he came back to see her and she laughed at him. She was going to run away with someone else and had just used him. Mrs. Kennedy is dead when the police arrive and Franks dies on the way to the hospital.

Exp. Acct:     $1,121.13

### Notes:
- Remake of the Chicago Fraud Matter—2/6/1953
- In part 4 Howard McNear slips on Mayhood's name and calls him Mayherb.
- Roy Rowan is the announcer
- Musical supervision is by Amerigo Marino
- Next week's program is previewed as a quick trip to New York and its theaters and lights and actors, some very bad actors. This sounds like The Amy Bradshaw Matter, which was aired three weeks previous.

**Producer:** Jack Johnstone          **Writers:** John Dawson
**Cast:**          Mary Jane Croft, Vivi Janiss, Jean Tatum, Hy Averback, Barney Phillips, Russell Thorson, Howard McNear

SHOW: **THE NICK SHURN MATTER**
COMPANY: **TRI-MUTUAL INSURANCE, LTD.**
AGENT: **DON WILKINS**
PART 1 SHOW DATE: **12/19/1955**

SYNOPSIS: Don Wilkins calls and tells Johnny that Mel Priker, he got himself killed last night. Johnny tells Don that Priker "was born to be murdered." Don tells Johnny that Tri-Mutual has a $100,000 policy on him and Nick Shurn is the beneficiary and is being held by the police. There is one witness, but she has disappeared. Maybe some of Nick Shurn's boys have found her. Go check it out.

Johnny goes to New York City and meets with Lt. Ed Rafferty, who is complaining about shoplifters and his son's desire for a motorbike. Lt. Rafferty tells Johnny that Nick killed Priker, but they will not be able to prove it. Lt. Rafferty thinks that Mel and Nick were partners in the nightclub and Priker was killed there when they were arguing about money. Shots were heard around midnight and the cleaning crew found him at 3:00 AM shot with his own gun. Shurn was found at another club with Benny Stark. He had been at a shooting range earlier so the paraffin test was positive. Miss Kathleen O'Dare, the hatcheck girl was seen leaving at the time of the shots, but denies it. Later the cab driver changed his story too. Lt. Rafferty does not think that Nick got to her. She just went home, packed, took her daughter and disappeared. Johnny thanks Lt. Rafferty and tells him to call Ralph Sterner about the motorbike!

Johnny walks out and finds Nick Shurn and Benny out front. Nick reminds Johnny that he was cleared of the charges in their last meeting. Nick invites Johnny for a ride and but Johnny declines, so Nick tells Benny to go for a walk. Johnny talks to Nick and tells him that he is on the Priker case. Nick offers to let Johnny go to Vegas for a month with $10,000 if he just says the word. Johnny tells Nick that even if he does not make an insurance claim, Johnny will investigate. Nick tells Johnny that he did not kill Priker. Johnny is worried for Kathleen with Nick around and tells Nick he going to tag him.

Johnny goes to the rooming house of Kathleen and searches her rooms and finds nothing. On the way out Johnny makes a contribution to Santa and is met by Benny; who tells Johnny that some friends want to talk to him. Johnny fakes Benny out with the "two cops on the steps" routine and slugs him. Santa gets the contents of Benny's wallet, $500.

Tomorrow, an old lady with a broken arm, a shivering girl and bullets in the snow.

PART 2 SHOW DATE: **12/20/1955**

Mrs. Gottler calls Johnny about Kathleen, and he tells her that he wants to help Kathleen. That's want the other man said, the one that broke her good right arm.

Johnny cabs to the rooming house and meets Mrs. Gottler who is holding a gun. Johnny convinces her to put the gun down, and Johnny offers to help wrap her packages as they talk. One is a muffler for a nephew over in Brooklyn. They have those terrible winters over there. Johnny says it will be warmer this year because they won the pennant. Mrs. Gottler tells Johnny that Benny broke her arm to find out where Kathy is. Johnny asks where she is and Mrs. Gottler tells Johnny that she left in the middle of the might. She was everyone's favorite, so good luck to finding her. Johnny tells her that she helped Kathleen pack, so where did she go? You had a sample of what the others will do. Kathleen would not tell her where she was going to protect Mrs. Gottler. Mrs. Gottler gives Johnny a picture of Kathleen and he notices a photographer's name on the picture, Branberry, Michigan. Johnny kisses Mrs. Gottler and she mumbles "Mr. Dollar! . . . MR. DOLLAR!"

Johnny travels to Branberry, Michigan, a lumber village where there is a foot of new snow on the ground. The town is very quiet about giving out information. Johnny talks to the operator who asks him questions and tells Johnny that Kathleen lives in New York. Everyone was keeping quiet about Kathy. Johnny talks to the deputy, Dan Martin, who wants to know who Johnny is. Johnny tells Dan that Kathleen is a witness to a murder. Dan tells Johnny that he has been in love with Kathleen since grade school and would die for her. Johnny tells Dan that they are not helping by hiding her. He knows the men who are after her and they don't play games. Dan tells her that he does not know what Kathleen is afraid of.

Johnny drives to mill #4 to see Mike O'Dare and comments on the beauty of the village at dusk. Mike knows who Johnny is, and the answer is "no." Johnny cannot hurt her if he cannot find her. They hear a car drive up to the mill, and Benny Stark gets out. Benny shoots at Johnny and then drives away. They have found her.

Tomorrow, a lonely vigil in the snow, a killer prowls the night and a lovely lady vanishes.

## PART 3          SHOW DATE:     12/21/1955

Dan Martin calls and Johnny tells him that Benny is in town. He shot at Johnny and headed towards town. Dan tells Johnny to block the turn off and he will have 20 men with deer rifles blocking the roads within a half hour.

Mike and Johnny block the road turn off with a bottle of applejack, "the best thing to happen to an apple." Mike asks Johnny about what Kathleen is running from as she was scared and came home for help. Johnny tells Mike that he is not sure if she is mixed up in the murder, but he must talk to her. Mike tells Johnny that they will help protect her and fight to stop Johnny from taking her back. A car drives up, and it is a local man, Ted Perkins and Mike waves him through. Mike tells Johnny that people mind their business there. After two hours Johnny only sees three cars and a truck full of Christmas trees, but no Benny. As the temperature drops and the wind comes up, Mike tells Johnny that a blizzard is in the offing, maybe tomorrow. Mike tells Johnny that Kathy never hurt anyone, and now people are looking for her to kill her; it does not make sense. Johnny notes another time when men were looking for a child to kill him. A car approaches with relief from Dan. Johnny is told that Benny had been seen and broke through a shoot out. Johnny tells Mike that Benny would never run; he would do his job to kill Kathy.

Mike and Johnny go to town and Johnny looks through the parked cars for Benny's car. Johnny finds a car alongside a building, Benny's car. Johnny approaches but the car is empty. Mike takes Johnny to Dan Martin's house, where Kathy is. Dan tells Johnny that Benny has taken a different car. Johnny asks Mike to wake up Kathleen, and Dan tells Johnny to be easy on her. She had left town because she and Dan had argued. She went to New York and married some guy who left her. She belongs here. Mike comes down and tells Johnny and Dan that she had disappeared.

Tomorrow, a little girl who believes in Santa Claus, a big girl who believes in very little, and both of them facing death.

**PART 4**       **SHOW DATE:**      **12/22/1955**

Mike calls Johnny and he tells Mike that no one has seen Kathleen or Benny. Mike tells Johnny that Dan has found nothing either. We must find her; maybe Benny got her. Johnny tells Mike to pray.

Johnny buys gas for the truck and picks up Mike. Johnny tells Mike that Benny has not found Kathy because she took your car, her clothes and a rifle. Kathy knew about the roadblock and how to get around them. She is in the area, so where would she go to hide out? Mike thinks of Pine Lake Road, it dead-ends at the lake and there are cabins beyond the end of the trail. Johnny gets a lantern and batteries and they drive to Pine Lake. There are car tracks in the road and Johnny spots Mike's car in the trees. The car is empty and cold and there are footprints heading up the trail. Johnny tells Mike to go for help as Johnny follows the trail. Johnny sends Mike away so he would not know about the other car hidden in the snow, the one stolen by Benny Stark. Johnny goes up the trail following the footsteps. After almost two hours the trail disappears and the cold starts to take over and Johnny becomes disoriented. Johnny's light hits Benny beside a tree and there are shots. Johnny shoots back and stumbles on without a light. Johnny becomes lost and hears music in the woods. Johnny recognizes it as the cold and fatigue leading to a permanent sleep. Johnny moves toward the music, which becomes louder. Johnny calls out and sees a blaze of light and a girl with golden hair and a rifle.

Johnny warms up and moves away from the stove only when his shirt starts to smoke. Kathy tells Johnny that she and her daughter are ok, and have plenty of supplies. Johnny tells her that he just guessed where she was. Johnny tells Kathleen about Mrs. Gottler, and about Benny Stark, who is dead in the snow.

Tomorrow, the show down. Victory, and then disaster when a visitor to the little town of Branberry turns out to be death.

PART 5                SHOW DATE:        12/23/1955

Johnny Dollar is my name, j-o-h-n-n-y d-o-l-l-a-r. "That's not right. You forgot to capitalize" Jill tells Johnny. My name is J-i-l-l-O'-D-a-r-e. Is my mother pretty? Why don't you marry her so I can have a daddy?

Johnny gets a million-dollar feeling being with Kathleen and Jill. It is 4 AM and the storm is worse, so Jill is sent to bed. Kathleen tells Johnny that Jill is great little girl and the only thing Kathleen did right. She knows why Johnny came; he wants her to come back. She tells Johnny that she heard nothing and did not see or hear anything. Johnny tells her that Nick will send someone else. She tells Johnny that she is not wide eyed about Nick; she had a legitimate job and Nick is crazy about Jill. Johnny tells her she is letting the people in town down. The city has made a coward of her. Johnny tells her that she is scared, and that will make you do things you do not want to do. You have to fight the fear, do it for Jill; teach her courage. Kathleen finally tells Johnny that Nick and Mel were arguing. Mel yelled out and there were shots. She ran to the office and Nick was there with a gun. He told me to get out and keep quiet if I wanted to live. Kathleen agrees to make a statement and Johnny tells her he will stand by her. Kathleen and Jill sleep in Johnny's arms—that was the million-dollar feeling.

Mike and the rescue party arrive the next day and they go to town for the Christmas Eve program. Mike and Jill go in early and Kathy and Johnny arrive late and sit in the back. After 10 minutes another man comes in, Nick Shurn. Nick checks Johnny for a gun, and Johnny is not armed. Nick tells them to ease outside, or he will kill Kathy. Outside Mike gives Johnny a bag and tells Johnny "don't uncork it until you are ready for some serious business." Jill runs outside and wants to see Uncle Nick. Dan comes outside and Nick is forced to pick up Jill as Johnny takes Nick's gun. Johnny and Kathleen walk and he tells her that Jill saved Nick's life. Mike had slipped him a gun in the paper bag, and he had Nick covered. Johnny tells Kathleen that she showed a lot of courage, and she mentions another man who had courage 2,000 years ago.

Remarks: "Merry Christmas! Merry Christmas to all of you from all of us on the program. And God bless you."

Exp. Acct:      $486.20

NOTES:
• THIS IS HE FIRST BOB BAILEY JOHNNY DOLLAR CHRISTMAS PROGRAM
• ROY ROWAN IS THE ANNOUNCER
• MUSICAL SUPERVISION IS BY AMERIGO MARINO

Producer:   Jack Johnstone          Writers:   Les Crutchfield
Cast:          Virginia Gregg, Peggy Webber, Don Diamond, Ben Wright,
                Jack Kruschen, Barney Phillips, Sam Edwards, Ken Christy

| SHOW: | THE FORBES MATTER |
| --- | --- |
| COMPANY: | CONTINENTAL ADJUSTMENT BUREAU |
| AGENT: | MR. TURNER |
| PART 1 | SHOW DATE: 12/26/1955 |

**SYNOPSIS:** Pauline Morris calls for Mr. Turner. How would you like to handle a case for us while you are on vacation in New York City? There is practically no commission but Johnny will do it for Pauline, if she will go to dinner with him.

Johnny meets Pauline for dinner and gets the details on the case. Century Styles has filed a claim through their insurance company, Eastern Delaware. The auditors have found a deficit of $4,285; and your contact is Mr. Robert Elliott.

Johnny travels to New York City, gets a room at the New Westin hotel, calls Mr. Elliott and then goes to the Century Styles office. Mr. Elliott is colorfully dressed and Johnny admires the, um, merchandise, real and inanimate. The auditors have left a report of their findings. Elliott is the creator of "Patsy's Things," a thankless task, and the loss is devastating. The company operates on a shoestring and the loss is stopping a major show. A "ruthless brigand pussyfooted off with the money," Elliott tells Johnny. The auditors simply found the shortage.

Johnny goes to his hotel and reads the report, which points to an inside job. Johnny meets with the auditor and learns that the loss is legitimate. Johnny is told that Sheldon Forbes, who is still on the payroll at Century, handled the books containing the theft. Johnny goes to the District Attorney to explain the case and then goes to talk to Forbes. Johnny meets with Forbes, who is just an average type person, in his jail cell. Johnny tells Forbes who he is and why he is talking to him. Johnny shows Forbes the books and but he says nothing. Forbes admits stealing the money but cannot give the money back as he does not have it and wants to go to jail.

What makes a man steal? Everybody's tried to answer that question at one time or another. Tomorrow I'll take a crack at it.

**PART 2        SHOW DATE:        12/27/1955**

Robert Elliott calls and tells Johnny that he is terrible. He is at the District Attorney's office and they want him to sign a complaint. Elliott is worried about the claim, and Johnny tells him that the check is on the way now. Johnny is not finished, as he has to recover the money.

Johnny gets a rental car and drives to the police where Johnny is told that Forbes is being held in the central jail. Johnny drives to the office of Edward Gumby, Attorney. Gumby is the court appointed attorney for Forbes and Johnny explains who he is. Johnny wants to recover the money rather than prosecute. Gumby has not talked to Forbes yet, although he knows that Forbes was married and widowed after the war. Gumby tells Johnny that the money is probably in an old sock as that is the way these cases go. Later the police tell Johnny that there is no evidence of the money in Forbes' apartment or car.

Johnny visits Forbes in jail, but Forbes does not want to talk to anyone. Johnny tells Forbes that he has to recover the money and wants to help him. Forbes thinks that 3-12 years in jail is worth the money he took. Forbes will tell Johnny nothing about what he did with the money. Johnny tells him he will track down what happened with the money.

Johnny checks Forbes' files and meets Gumby in the jail. Gumby tells Johnny that there is not much to say. Forbes wants to plead guilty and take his medicine, but he is not a criminal. The court would listen to a mercy plea, but Forbes wants to plead guilty. Gumby calls Forbes a calendar job; born between two wars interspersed with a depression in the middle.

Tomorrow, a sudden twist in the case that throws all the usual theories right out the window. The unexpected.

**PART 3          SHOW DATE:     12/28/1955**

Ed Gumby calls Johnny and tells him that the hearing is set for this afternoon, but it will just be a formality. Sentencing will be at the end of the week. Gumby will try to get Forbes to return the money and Johnny is going to find out where the money went.

Johnny eats lunch with Mr. Haven of Century Styles' Accounting department. Johnny tells Haven that Forbes will probably go to prison. Haven has no idea why Forbes took the money. Everyone in the office is upset and Forbes did not go with any of the girls in the office. Havens remembers a change in Forbes' nature in the last six weeks; he was more anxious. Johnny goes to the Century office and talks to the staff about Forbes. Johnny goes to Forbes' apartment and talks to Mrs. Anastasia Kanopka, the manager. Johnny asks about Forbes, but she is hesitant to say anything other than Forbes had no visitors and did not cause trouble. He has no girlfriends and worked very hard. He is a poor fellow who just thinks and paints and listens to music. She gives Johnny the keys and Johnny searches the dismal apartment, but there is nothing worth $4,285 in the apartment. Johnny looks at Forbes' 1946 Ford and finds nothing.

Johnny eats at a local diner and learns that the local people knew him.

Johnny goes to the jail and meets Gumby there. The hearing was held and Forbes would say nothing; sentencing is Friday. Gumby tells Johnny that Forbes will be released on bail at 8:00 that night. Johnny follows Forbes when he leaves and follows him to the Empress Theater. Johnny then follows Forbes to his apartment and goes in 15 minutes later. Johnny smells gas and breaks down the door, breaks a window and drags Forbes out.

Tomorrow, a switch in the case that starts a real chase and a race against time.

**PART 4          SHOW DATE:     12/29/1955**

The police operator calls and tells Johnny that the ambulance is on the way.

Johnny calls an ambulance and the interns try to revive Forbes, who is barely alive, but a shot brings him around and he is taken to Belleview hospital. The police question Johnny and then he goes to the station house to sign a statement. Johnny then goes to the Empress Theater and talks to Frank the doorman about Forbes' visit earlier. The doorman remembers Forbes; he comes there to see Betsy Walker. He comes asking to see her, but she never sees him. She has gone home, and the doorman will not give Johnny an address or phone number, so Johnny asks him to call Betsy for him. Johnny goes to Betsy Walker's apartment and meets her and tells her why he is there. She knows Forbes' name but not him. She met him once and he is quite impossible. She tells Johnny that Forbes' had given her a number of presents, expensive presents. Forbes would also send her orchids at the theater. She got a card asking her to go to dinner, then the orchids and then the gifts. She gave some of the gifts away. When she did met him, he was unsophisticated and un-poised. Johnny tells her that Forbes had stolen the money to buy the gifts and tried to kill himself. Apparently you meant something to him.

Tomorrow, proof the $4,285 worth of unrequited love can spell three years of prison. But sometimes there is an angle, in this case a rather startling one.

**PART 5**       **SHOW DATE:**       **12/30/1955**

Betsy calls Johnny and she will see him in an hour to inventory the gifts. She tells Johnny that she does not mind giving the gifts back.

Johnny travels around New York recapping the value of the gifts bought by Sheldon Forbes for Betsy Walker that total $2780; all bought with stolen money. Johnny also tracks down a series of restaurants where $835 was spent on meals never eaten. $670 was also spent on flowers sent to Betsy. Total amount spent equals total amount stolen. Johnny visits Forbes in the hospital and tells him about Betsy Walker and the gifts. Neither Johnny nor Betsy think that the ordeal is funny. Johnny has taken the gifts back and Johnny asks Forbes to sign an inventory report. Forbes signs the document; and tells Johnny that all it means to him is dollars and cents. Forbes tells Johnny that Betsy was a model during a showing at office and he saw her there in a black dress, and had never seen anyone like her. He tracked down her name and thought that the money would give him a way to meet her. He was going to give the money back. There was no other alternative, as he had nothing else to give. She makes more in an hour than he made in a week. Johnny is convinced that Forbes was guilty of love at first sight.

Johnny wires the insurance company that the recovered goods comes to about $2,500 and then meets Betsy in the lobby of his hotel. Over a drink Johnny tells her that Forbes will be sentenced on Monday. Betsy is upset about the whole thing and asks Johnny what would happen if she paid the other $2,000? Johnny tells her it would be up to the court. "He did all these things for me" she tells Johnny. She tells Johnny that she is not much of an actress or singer, but he is the first man she has ever known who would go out on a limb for a girl, and she was that girl. "That poor stupid wonderful dumbbell does not belong in jail" she tells Johnny. Johnny kisses her and thanks her for renewing his faith in mankind.

Remarks: She got Forbes to change his plea. She paid back the additional money. He comes to trial next week. He might get a suspended sentence.

Exp. Acct:    $363.51

NOTES:

- REMAKE OF THE LESTER JAMES MATTER—3/31/1953
- THE WALDORF, THE STORK CLUB AND "THE 21" ARE MENTIONED—ALL ARE VERY EXPENSIVE NEW YORK RESTAURANTS OF THE TIME.
- ROY ROWAN IS THE ANNOUNCER
- MUSICAL SUPERVISION IS BY AMERIGO MARINO
- NEXT WEEK'S PROGRAM IS A TRIP SOUTH OF THE BORDER WITH ROMANCE AND TROUBLE. THIS COULD BE "THE FLIGHT SIX MATTER," WHICH IS AIRED IN FOUR WEEKS.

**Producer:**    Jack Johnstone          **Writers:**    John Dawson
**Cast:**          Lillian Buyeff, Sandra Gould, Jack Edwards, Herb Ellis, James McCallion, Parley Baer, John Stevenson, Howard McNear, Bob Bruce, Junius Matthews

◆　❖　◆

**SHOW:**         THE CAYLIN MATTER
**COMPANY:**    TRINITY MUTUAL INSURANCE COMPANY, LTD.
**AGENT:**        WALT ALBRIGHT
**PART 1**        **SHOW DATE:**    1/2/1956

SYNOPSIS: Walt Albright calls and tells Johnny that he has asthma, again. Whenever Walt gets suspicious, he gets asthma. Eddie Caylin died yesterday under mysterious circumstances, with a $4000 policy issued just 6 weeks ago at the wife's request. The beneficiary is the widow.

Johnny goes to Los Angeles, California and is met at the airport by Presley Welsh, the local agent. Johnny is daring and expenses a cup of coffee for Welsh. Welsh tells Johnny that he knew better than to write the policy and that Caylin had laughed at the retirement benefits; but Mrs. Caylin was very serious. Welsh only saw Caylin twice and no claim has been filed yet. Johnny gets a room at the Beverly Wilshire Hotel and then goes to the police. Johnny meets Det. Sgt. Renosa and is told that the case facts do not add up. A call was received at 4:20 AM for a car that appeared to have burned from an accident, but the upholstery seemed to have been soaked with gasoline. The body was burned but there were some personal effects that were used to identify Eddie Caylin. The police found a locked door and signs of a fight at his home, but the wife was away at a friends cabin, alone. Johnny is told that Eddie Caylin was a "promoter," a small time agent, bookie and gambler. He was in a poker game with Topo Leenly and supposedly won $60,000. The police had Leenly in for questioning, but he told them he had never heard of Caylin. Sgt. Renosa thinks this case is hokey and murder, but quien sabe, who knows. Johnny gets the address for Mrs. Caylin and has a hunch about the door lock. Johnny goes to the apartment of Mrs. Caylin and a man exits the apartment and comes out. It is Mr. Welsh. He tells Johnny that he got a wire from Hartford and the claim has been filed for double indemnity and Mrs. Caylin wants immediate payment. Johnny tells him that the policy probably will not be paid at all.

Tomorrow, a lovely girl lies cries and crosses her heart and hopes to die, and a killer fires from the dark.

### PART 2    SHOW DATE:    1/3/1956

Johnny meets Mrs. Caylin and tells her why he is there. She tells Johnny that she has a right to file a claim. Johnny asks her how many keys are there to the front door? The number will hang someone.

Johnny tells Mrs. Caylin that he does not have a name yet, but she will be smart to answer his questions but she asks Johnny to leave when he tries to question her. She changes her mind and tells him to stay. She tells Johnny that Eddie hung out at the Eloinaise and the Brass Monkey bars. She goes to change and tells Johnny to pour himself a drink. Johnny braces himself for a lovely woman. Twenty minutes later she comes back in dressed for "a special evening in." Johnny makes her a scotch and soda and asks her how Eddie died. She tells Johnny that Eddie had a lot of friends and no enemies. A good friend was Pete Steimer, who has also disappeared. The others drift in and out based on Eddie's finances. He also had a lot of women, mostly dancers and strippers. She tells Johnny that she did not kill him and does not know if she loves him. She could have killed him at times and loved him at others. She went to Arrowhead after a fight, and heard of the accident on the radio. She identified a wallet, a watch and a ring but not the body. She feels that Eddie is not dead. She thinks that Eddie won some money from that Topo Leenly character. She would never know, as Eddie never spent money at home, but only where it would show. She tells Johnny that she had to dress herself up so that she could feel anything and gave the wrong impression. Johnny apologizes for coming in with the wrong impression. She tells Johnny that her name is Lilah. Johnny sees a man outside and hears a sound in the next terrace. Johnny goes out and is attacked and a shot is fired. Johnny kicks the man and tells Lilah to call Sgt. Renosa. The man is big and stocky and the name in the wallet is Topo Leenly.

Tomorrow, we meet a Latin doll from Santa Monica, an erudite bartender and a terpsichorean ecdysiast and they are all in the cast.

### PART 3    SHOW DATE:    1/4/1956

Sgt. Renosa calls Johnny and tells him that Topo is not scared and says that Johnny jumped him. He claims he was calling on a girlfriend that gave him the wrong address. Johnny tells Sgt. Renosa that Topo is scared and maybe he will lead us to Eddie Caylin. Sgt. Renosa tells Johnny that Eddie is downtown on a slab. "Wanna Bet?"

Johnny is following a hunch about the locked door. Johnny cabs to the Café Eloinaise, a seedy bar on Santa Monica Blvd. The hostess has a beautifully rounded, um, Latin accent. She is Pepita, and Johnny buys her a drink. Johnny asks about meeting her after work, but she cannot, as she lives with her mother. Johnny gives her $10 for information on Eddie. She tells Johnny that she last saw him on Thursday, before he was killed. Eddie told her he loved her, bought a drink and borrowed the money to pay for it. He was in the bar for an hour with Pete, but no one has seen him either. Eddie did not seem worried or scared. Every girl was Eddies' girl, but only one girl in each bar. Pepita tells Johnny that at the Brass Money there are some strippers, and Eddie has a big thing with one of them. Her name is Marty Midnight. She is off at 1:00 AM, but Johnny does not want to bother her mother. "My mother lives in Havana, Cuba," exclaims Pepita. Johnny cabs to the Brass Monkey Inn, which is a very lively place. Johnny talks to the bartender about the seven-girl chorus line called the Pleiades. The bartender tells Johnny that he reads a lot and has a system. He reads the dictionary and has read it twice and is back up to "J." Johnny gives him a twenty for a drink and asks for information on Marty Midnight. The bartender tells Johnny that she has not been around since Eddie died. The bartender tells Johnny that Marty moved after she took up with Eddie, and Pete has not been around either. Another guy who worked for Topo Leenly, Mike Kelso disappeared that night too. Topo comes in all the time. Say, are you the guy that broke his arm? Have a drink! Johnny is told that Topo met Eddie at the bar and the bartender told Eddie to stay out of the card game. Johnny recounts how it could have happened but there are too many loose ends. Someone yells "police" and the bartender thinks the place is being raided. The raid turns out to be Sgt. Renosa who is looking for Marty Midnight. He tells Johnny that a man was found dead in her apartment. It was Eddie Caylin.

Tomorrow, a stakeout, a manhunt, and a tired intern breaking his heart to keep life in a broken body.

### PART 4  SHOW DATE: 1/5/1956

Johnny answers the phone and Lilah is calling Sgt. Renosa. Johnny tells her that he is at Marty Midnight's. Eddie is dead now in Marty's apartment.

Johnny and Sgt. Renosa go to the apartment of Marty Midnight and watch Eddie Caylin's body loaded into the ambulance. Sgt. Renosa wants to know why Johnny knew Caylin was alive. Johnny tells him about his hunch about the locked door. If it had a night latch or spring lock it would be obvious. The evidence of the fight meant that someone would have to get out fast, and who else but Eddie would stop to lock the door, out of habit. Johnny thinks that Eddie won the money and went home, so Topo sent Mike Kelso to get the money back, and Kelso ended up getting killed. Eddie put the body in the car and burned it with Pete Steiner's help. The jewelry was a plant. Eddie, Pete and Marty were going to leave the country, but now Marty and Pete are gone. Topo is out of jail now, so it could be him. The doorbell rings and a woman named Jeanette Dubois comes in. She had called the police about the shooting. She did not give her name because she was afraid of being implicated but a friend said she must go to the police. She tells Johnny that she heard shots, the door opened and a girl came out, a girl with long black hair. She wore a white raincoat, wiped something and threw it in the door and ran down the street. Miss Dubois then went home and called the police. Johnny tells Sgt. Renosa he is surprised about Marty, and then shot ring out. A man had been surprised and shot at the police and ran into the woods around Griffith Park. The police surround the area and Johnny and Sgt. Renosa go in to search. Shots are fired and the man is hit. It turns out to be Pete Steimer. Johnny goes to the hospital to wait for Steimer to wake up. Pete wakes up and asks for Eddie. "He should be here," Pete tells him. "Eddie always runs out and leaves someone else to face the music" Pete says and dies.

Tomorrow, a quarry run to earth, a strange alibi, and a shocking twist at the windup.

## PART 5          SHOW DATE:     1/6/1956

Sgt. Renosa calls at the hospital and Johnny tells him Pete is dead. Sgt. Renosa has Marty Midnight with a ticket to San Diego in her coat pocket.

Johnny cabs to police headquarters to help interrogate Marty. During the questioning, Marty says nothing except to ask for a lawyer. Sgt. Renosa tells her he will call her folks and she starts to talk. She tells Sgt. Renosa that she did not know that Eddie was married at first, but he said that he was getting a divorce. Eddie killed Kelso in self-defense and they were going to go to Mexico. She was going to go back to her folks and did not know that Eddie is dead. She thought they were after Pete at her apartment. Johnny and Sgt. Renosa talk outside and agree this case is strange. Sgt. Renosa is sure it is Marty. Johnny goes to see Lilah to tell her what has happened. Lilah is waiting for Johnny and fixes him some coffee. Johnny tells her that Marty was arrested, and Lilah feels sorry for her. She had four years of Eddie lying, and wonders why she went through it. Sgt. Renosa calls and tells Johnny that the paraffin test was negative and that Marty was not wearing a raincoat when she was picked up. Johnny tells him to come to Lilah's place. Lilah has black hair and Johnny goes to the closet and finds her damp white raincoat with smudges on it. Johnny tells Lilah to give him the facts. She tells Johnny that she wondered if Edie was alive, so she went to Marty's apartment and forced her way in. She fought with Eddie and he pulled a gun on him, it was self-defense.

Remarks: So the question still stands. Why do they do it? Why do girls go blind when the Eddie Caylins walk in? You might ask a stripteaser down in San Diego. But do not look for her under the name Marty Midnight. She is Jean Luanne Jagline now, a quiet kid. Lives at home with her folks.

Exp. Acct:     $596.85

## NOTES:

*   **TERPSICHOREAN: OF OR RELATING TO DANCING**
*   **ECDYSIAST: STRIPTEASER**
*   **THE PLEIADES, OR "SEVEN SISTERS" IS AN OPEN CLUSTER OF STARS IN THE CONSTELLATION "TAURUS THE BULL," TYPICALLY VISIBLE IN THE WINTER IN NORTH AMERICA.**
*   **ROY ROWAN IS THE ANNOUNCER**

- **MUSICAL SUPERVISION IS BY AMERIGO MARINO**

**Producer:** Jack Johnstone      **Writers:** Les Crutchfield
**Cast:** Virginia Gregg, Lucille Meredith, Alma Lawton, Gloria Blondell, Howard McNear, Harry Bartell, Peter Leeds, Byron Kane

◆   ❖   ◆

**SHOW:** THE TODD MATTER
**COMPANY:** FOUR STATE INSURANCE COMPANY
**AGENT:**
**PART 1**      **SHOW DATE:** 1/9/1956

**SYNOPSIS:** Orrin Vance calls and tells Johnny that he had sent Orrin to Ossining, but he will do Johnny a favor. He has information about the Todd case which cost your company $75,000.

Johnny calls Don Freed to discuss the Todd Burglary and requests information on the stolen goods. Johnny goes to the International Adjustment Bureau to look at the case involving Vance.

Orrin Vance comes to Johnny's apartment and asks not to be treated like a con. He tells Johnny that even his wife will not let him in the house unless he gets a job. Vance needs a stake and offers Johnny information on the robbery, specifically the serial number of a mink coat from Zellerbachs. Johnny calls Four State who tells him that the numbers match and that there is a $5,000 reward. Vance wants a check for $2,500 and will leave for Indiana in a couple hours. Johnny gives Orrin the check and gets the name of Gloria Tierney in New York City. Johnny goes to the airport to see Vance off and flies to New York City. Johnny checks in at the New Westin hotel and then with the police, where Gloria has no record.

Johnny goes to the apartment of Gloria Tierney, but she is not in so he checks with the manager, Mrs. Stromberg and leaves his name. Johnny watches the building for three hours and sees no one. Gloria calls Johnny at midnight. She tells Johnny that she will be leaving town in the morning and tells Johnny to come over now. Johnny gets there in less than 15 minutes but the apartment is dark and locked. The manager tells Johnny that Gloria was waiting in the hallway and that Gloria looked worried and she had been wearing her mink coat. Johnny goes outside and there is no one there. Johnny then sees a woman weaving as she crosses the street. Johnny runs up to her and the girl is Gloria, and she has been beaten. A 1955 Cadillac pulls up and Gloria is shot three times and falls into Johnny's arms and Mrs. Stromberg goes inside to call the police.

Tomorrow, the same old business of murder, but with a brand-new twist.

**PART 2**      **SHOW DATE:** 1/10/1956

Sgt. Dan Mapes calls about Johnny's statement. He wants Johnny to come to Headquarters.

Johnny wires Don Freed about the events and asks him to hire counsel for him, and then he goes to see Sgt. Mapes. Johnny tells Sgt. Mapes why he was at the apartment and what happened. Johnny tells Sgt. Mapes about the mink coat, which the police have as stolen property. Gloria is still in critical condition. Sgt. Mapes tells Johnny that Gloria had nothing else from the robbery, only the coat. Johnny tells Sgt. Mapes that he cannot tell him about the tip he got about the coat. Sgt. Mapes threatens to hold him, but Johnny tells him that an attorney is on the way over to see that he is treated nice. Johnny and Sgt. Mapes go to the apartment house and talk to Mrs. Stromberg. She tells them that Gloria had moved in a year ago and was a quiet girl. She did not work but always paid her rent on time with a check. Gloria has a family in California. She had a few boyfriends but Mrs. Stromberg had never seen the car. Sgt. Mapes gets rough with Mrs. Stromberg and then she remembers seeing the car there before, and the driver was Bill "something" who is tall and dark and well dressed. He was in his mid-thirties and came several times a week. Bill seemed to have money and clothes and gave Gloria the mink coat and other small gifts but no jewelry. She really did not talk about a lot of things; she was just a nice innocent girl. Sgt. Mapes calls the office and learns Gloria is dying.

Tomorrow, I take some lessons from a good policeman on how to find out what has to be found out.

**PART 3          SHOW DATE:     1/11/1956**

Dr. King calls and there has been no change in Gloria's condition. He tells Johnny and Sgt. Mapes to come over to the hospital.

Johnny and Sgt. Mapes arrive at the hospital and Dr. King tells them that they can have only two minutes. A priest is in the room and Gloria is barely conscious. Sgt. Mapes asks Gloria her name and condition and she only says that Bill shot her. Gloria relapses and then dies without telling anything.

Johnny and Sgt. Mapes have a drink and discuss the case. They agree that Gloria was not the type of girl to have a stolen mink coat. Sgt. Mapes comments, that "Boy this whiskey is really bad. Two more doubles please bartender!" Sgt. Mapes tells Johnny that he is really glad to have Johnny working on the case. Johnny tells Sgt. Mapes that he really could have gone for Gloria.

At the apartment Sgt. Mapes finds letters from the family in California and a picture from Bill. The lab reports that the bullets came from a .45 Colt. Mrs. Stromberg comes in and identifies the man in the picture as Bill. The phone rings and Sgt. Mapes asks Mrs. Stromberg if Gloria had ever mentioned being married. Sgt. Mapes tells Johnny that Gloria was married and divorced from William Powers who had no record. Johnny and Sgt. Mapes drive to see Powers and tell him about Gloria. Powers is upset and tells them that he saw her last week. Powers does not know anything about a mink coat. Powers is not the man in the picture but he has a 1955 Cadillac Coupe de Ville.

Tomorrow, well you find one killer and you find them all, and then you have to start all over again.

**PART 4        SHOW DATE:    1/12/1956**

Johnny gets a call from Don Freed, who is worried about his expenses. Johnny tells Don that Gloria had the coat but Johnny knows nothing else. Johnny gets kind of upset and Don tells Johnny that he is a real man-eater today!

Bill Powers goes to the morgue and then they all have coffee. Powers tells Johnny and Sgt. Mapes that he does not believe Gloria was wearing a stolen coat. Powers had been seeing Gloria regularly, and knew about Bill Chambers. Sgt. Mapes shows him the picture and Powers identifies it as Bill Chambers. Powers tells Johnny that he was going out with Gloria and had asked her to marry him. Powers tells them that he and Gloria broke up for all the stupid reasons and were going to be remarried. She did not want to marry Chambers. She told Powers two days ago she would remarry him. He had bought a Cadillac just like Bill's to influence her.

A check finds 24 names like Bill Chambers, but none matched the description. Later two pieces of jewelry from the robbery show up in a pawn shop and the description of the seller matches that of Chambers, but the addresses were phony. A call comes in to Sgt. Mapes and the Cadillac has been sold in the Bronx. The used car lot manager gives a description and prints are taken from the car and a check gives seven aliases and a record of car thefts for one William Charles. The check continues, and more jewelry shows up. Johnny wires Four State with an update, and then a call comes in about Bill Charles from a woman. Johnny cabs to Schraft's Restaurant to meet the caller. She asks Johnny about the reward and Johnny tells her she will only get half of the reward. She tells Johnny that she also wants legal protection and Johnny tells her he will work on it. The woman tells Johnny that she is Melva Charles, the wife of Bill Charles and that she will meet Johnny again in two hours. Johnny follows her out of the restaurant and Sgt. Mapes picks him up and they follow her. Johnny outlines the discussion and Schraft's Restaurant tells Johnny that he had been followed. Sgt. Mapes tells Johnny that Melva had been born to a wealthy family, but has been in trouble all her life. They stop at an apartment building and go into the door. There are shots and Johnny is hit.

Tomorrow, well there are times when $75,000 worth of stealing isn't worth a plugged nickel.

**PART 5        SHOW DATE:    1/13/1956**

Johnny is barely able to answer the phone in his room at the hospital. Sgt. Mapes tells Johnny that he had been shot twice, but is luckier than Gloria.

Johnny bribes and orderly to buy him breakfast and Sgt. Mapes comes in to visit. Johnny tells him that the last thing he remembers is being shot. Johnny is told that Melva got it; Charles shoved a butcher knife in her back for trying to sell him out. A man in the hallway was shot three times and a woman on the street was injured. Charles opened fire and Sgt. Mapes shot back. Charles is upstairs in critical condition. Sgt. Mapes gives Johnny a book of poetry to read.

The story is in the paper the next day and Charles' gun is the one that killed Gloria, but no jewelry was found. Sgt. Mapes brings a wheelchair and Johnny goes up to see Charles. Charles tells Johnny and Sgt. Mapes that he did not mean to kill Gloria. He had been doing ok with burglary jobs and had met Gloria through a mutual friend and wanted to marry her but she wanted to marry someone else, so he got mad and shot her. Charles will not tell Johnny about the goods from the Todd robbery and dies without saying anything.

Johnny recovers after three more days and visits Sgt. Mapes. They both wonder about the Todd jewelry. Johnny visits Mrs. Stromberg and she gives Sgt. Mapes a shot of bourbon. Johnny asks her about the night Gloria was killed, and how she said, "you'd have her call me." Johnny tells her "You sent her out so Charles could take care of her and were waiting for me in the hall because you knew I was an insurance investigator." Charles would not tell Johnny who introduced him, but Johnny tells Mrs. Stromberg that it was she and that she is keeping the goods. Johnny tells her that Melva would tell him for $2,500, but did not know where the jewels are. When Johnny tells her to go with him to see Sgt. Mapes, she tries to buy Johnny, but he wants her behind bars. The house is searched and the goods are found behind a cement block in the basement. The recovery was 90% but lives were lost in the process.

Exp. Acct:     $1,095.00

**NOTES:**
- REMAKE OF THE ROCHESTER THEFT MATTER—5/12/1953
- THIS STORY IS INTERESTING. IT INCORPORATES PARTS OF TWO OTHER STORIES BY E. JACK NEUMAN; "THE BALTIMORE MATTER" AND "THE ROCHESTER THEFT MATTER." THE BASIC STORY IS FROM THE ROCHESTER MATTER, BUT THE ENDING COMES FROM THE BALTIMORE MATTER.
- JOHNNY IS SHOT FOR THE 6TH TIME.
- ROY ROWAN IS THE ANNOUNCER
- MUSICAL SUPERVISION IS BY AMERIGO MARINO

Producer:   Jack Johnstone          Writers:   John Dawson
Cast:       Vivi Janiss, Barbara Fuller, Shirley Mitchell, Lawrence
            Dobkin, Frank Gerstle, Marvin Miller

◆   ❖   ◆

SHOW:       THE RICARDO AMERIGO MATTER
COMPANY:    PHILADELPHIA MUTUAL LIABILITY & CASUALTY COMPANY
AGENT:      HARRY BRANSON
PART 1      SHOW DATE:     1/16/1956

SYNOPSIS: Harry Branson calls from Philadelphia and asks Johnny what he knows about violins. An Amati, insured for $30,000 has been stolen.

Johnny trains to Philadelphia, Pennsylvania, checks in at the Belleview Stratford and cabs to see Harry "old sober sides" Branson. Harry tells Johnny that two policies had been issued, one for the violin and one for the owner. Ricardo Amerigo was a world famous virtuoso, but he has disappeared and the violin is gone. The Port Morris police think he might have drown in an accident. Ricardo was going to the shore, crashed through a guardrail and disappeared in a tidal creek. Johnny cabs to the office of Peter Corbin, the booking agent and "benuficiary" of the policy. Peter tells Johnny that he brought Amerigo to this country and kept him on top while he was working, but now he is working on a bottle and is not playing. Ricardo is in debt up to his ears so Peter took out the insurance for himself and the violin, but Peter has had to pay for the last few premiums. Peter gets upset when Johnny infers that he would be the most likely suspect and throws Johnny out. Peter takes a swing at Johnny but Johnny decks him.

Johnny calls Harry, who has been called by the Port Morris police; there is evidence of murder. Johnny goes to South Vineland to see Ad Boles, an old friend, retired investigator, and general know it all. Ad knows that Johnny is on the Amerigo case. Ad had contacted Barney Peters of the Port Morris police and learned about the next of kin and knew Branson would call Johnny. Ad had shown them where the steering arm had been cut, and Ad suspects Pete Corbin, as he is the most likely person because the car had been kept in Corbin's garage. Ad thinks that Pete only let Ricardo drive when he was drunk to get the insurance. Johnny bets his commission and expense account that Corbin is not the guilty party. Ad offers to fly Johnny to Port Morris in his private plane. Johnny calls Harry to learn that Pete Corbin has disappeared.

Tomorrow, a soggy day in a soggy south Jersey swamp, and a discovery almost too good to be true.

### PART 2　　　SHOW DATE:　　1/17/1956

Sgt. Peters calls about Ad and Johnny coming over. Sgt. Peters tells Johnny that Pete Corbin is there, but he cannot hold him. He might be gunning for you.

Johnny and Ad Boles fly to Port Morris in Ad's plane, weaving through the air in the process. Ad is positive that Pete is the suspect. In Port Morris Johnny and Ad meet Sgt. Peters and they drive to the site of the accident. On the way, Johnny learns the tide was on the way out at the time of the accident. A car approaches driving too fast and Johnny spots Pete Corbin driving it, but the road is too narrow to turn around and follow. At the bridge Johnny examines the site and spots a bird's nest with a fiddle case resting on it. Johnny wades into the black muck and pulls the case out and then struggles to make it back to the bridge. In the car, Johnny has the violin and finds a piece of a shirt with Amerigo's initials fastened to the case. Ad is now sure that Corbin is the suspect as he had the best opportunity. Pete staged the accident so that a deputy would see it happen, but where is the body? Sgt. Peters agrees that the case is too easy to blame on Corbin but Ad reminds Johnny to send him the check when he finds Corbin guilty.

Johnny takes a bus back to Philadelphia with the violin. Johnny calls Harry Branson and tells him that he has the violin, and Harry comes over to get it. In Johnny's room, Harry opens the case and the violin turns out to not be the right fiddle, maybe?

Tomorrow, the results of a poker game, and believe me there are times when the cards can be really be stacked against you.

**PART 3**        **SHOW DATE:**        **1/18/1956**

Pete Corbin returns Johnny's call. Johnny asks if Pete can explain what he was doing in Port Morris yesterday. Johnny tells Pete that he is on his way over to see him.

Johnny buys new clothes and Harry agrees to take the violin to an expert for an examination. Forresto Cherneglario, or whatever it is, is the man who identified the violin for the policy. Johnny confirms that the car had been tampered with and that there is no body. Harry tells Johnny that Ad Boles called and Harry tends to agree with him. Forresto Cherniarro (I knew that was it) arrives and pronounces that the violin is the Amati. All of the details of the violin verify that the violin is the Amati, including the label. Johnny tells Forresto that a fiddle player at the hotel says it could be a fake, but Forresto sells good violins, some of his sell for $65, so he knows. Harry tells Johnny that a representative of the Wurlitzer Collection had verified it. Johnny takes the violin and leaves.

Johnny goes to see Pete Corbin and shows him the violin and tells him that it was just where he planted it. Johnny thinks that putting the shirt there was too much. Corbin denies planting the violin and tells Johnny that he was just looking for Ricardo when he was in Port Morris. Pete tells Johnny that he is also "the executive" of Ricardo's will, so why would he leave a fiddle in the swamp. When Johnny tells Pete that the car had been tampered with, he is shocked and wants to know "who done it." Pete identifies the violin and Johnny tells him that the accident was a motive for repayment of the money Ricardo owed. Johnny thinks that pinning the case on Pete is wrong, he is not smart enough to do it, and will play it that way until he proves otherwise. Pete tells Johnny that at the time of the accident he was at Willie Elliott's playing poker with Jerry Goldsmith, a composer, conductor and piano player, and Eric Snowden, a fiddle maker. Johnny gets the addresses and Pete tells Johnny that Snowden was the only man Ricardo would let touch the violin. Johnny calls the poker pals to arrange to visit them.

Tomorrow, a trio of musicians. The question, which one's story was playing a little flat?

**PART 4**        **SHOW DATE:**        **1/19/1956**

A man calls Johnny about the investigation. The caller tells him it is no gag and hangs up.

Johnny goes to all of the bars frequented by Ricardo and learns nothing. At the Hangover Club Johnny is told that Ricardo would buy a few drinks and just get plastered until a friend would drag him out. Too bad he was so far gone.

Johnny cabs to the home of William Elliott who tells Johnny that he had know Ricardo for years. When Johnny goes to see Jerry Goldsmith, he takes the Amati. Johnny tells him he is an investigator and Jerry spots the case. He admits to Johnny that he had coveted the violin and wanted it more than anything, but not enough to kill for it. Jerry tells Johnny that Ricardo only had four friends and none would have killed him. Jerry looks at the violin and it is the Amati. Jerry plays it but it does not have the sound he is used to. It looks like the Amati but is sounds wrong.

Johnny cabs to Eric Snowden's violin shop on a side street amid the downtown area. Snowden immediately recognizes the violin case. Snowden locks the front door and takes the violin up to his second floor workroom to examine it. Johnny notices that the shop is full of tools and violins and hacksaws, including one with axle grease on it. Snowden verifies that the violin is Ricardo's. Johnny tells Eric that someone else had said that the sound was not quite right. Snowden looks closely and tells Johnny that the violin must have been tampered with. Someone pounds at the door and while Snowden goes downstairs Johnny looks around the shop and accidentally knocks open a cabinet with a violin in it, an exact duplicate of the Amati.

Tomorrow, well it's a wind up, but a windup with a real twist.

**PART 5          SHOW DATE:          1/20/1956**

Harry Branson calls Johnny and wonders about where Ricardo is. What if the violin was an imitation? It may be a phony.

Johnny finds a duplicate violin by accident and switches them while Snowden is gone. Johnny takes the violin and arranges to come back later before Snowden can make any adjustments to it. When Johnny leaves the shop a flowerpot almost hits him and Snowden apologizes from the window above. Johnny calls Harry to have the police watch Snowden and goes to Jerry Goldsmith's. Johnny has Goldsmith play the violin again and the sound is back! That violin is the Amati.

Johnny cabs to Harry's office and then to Erick Snowden's office. Johnny tells Snowden that the flowerpot had come from the third floor of the building. Johnny takes him back up to the second floor workroom and shows him the violin and asks if it is the Amati. After Snowden says it is, Johnny tells him to open the cabinet and Snowden tells him to leave. Johnny tells Snowden that he had found the copy and Snowden tells him that the loss of the Amati would be too great, so when Ricardo disappeared he made a copy and switched it. A door opens and Ricardo Amerigo comes in. He tells Johnny that the car wreck and the duplicate fiddle were his idea. He wanted the fiddle to come back after he disappeared so that it could be played by someone else. The insurance was his last chance to payback Pete and his other friends. Only Eric knew of the plans. Would you buy me a drink before you call in the police?

Remarks: No insurance payment necessary on either the Amati or the man. And I guess he really was a man, more than he knew. What the courts will do about him and about Eric Snowden, well the courts will do. And I am glad I have to have no part of it. You know, it's funny. Somehow I think I have a little better appreciation of music now than, ah well.

Exp. Acct:     $182.65

**NOTES:**
- ANDREA AMATI MADE MATCHED SETS, OR CONSORTS OF INSTRUMENTS DURING THE **1560'S** AND **1570'S**
- THE TITLE CHARACTER IS A PLAY ON THE NAME OF THE MUSIC DIRECTOR, AMERIGO MARINO

- MUSICAL SUPERVISOR AND VIOLINIST, AMERIGO MARINO
- DURING THE CREDITS FOR PARTS 1-4 SAM DAWSON IS CREDITED AS THE WRITER. IN THE FINAL EPISODE, ROY ROWAN CREDITS JACK JOHNSTONE WITH WRITING THIS WEEK'S STORY
- THIS IS THE FIRST TIME BOB BAILEY MENTIONS A COMMISSION
- BOB FLUBS ELLIOTT'S NAME IN EPISODE 4, CALLING HIM ELLIERTT
- THE WURLITZER COLLECTION IS A 19TH CENTURY CHAMBER MUSIC COLLECTION AT THE UNIVERSITY OF CINCINNATI
- IN THE STORY, JERRY GOLDSMITH IS MENTIONED. THE LATE AWARD-WINNING COMPOSER JERRY GOLDSMITH WAS AN EMPLOYEE OF CBS RADIO IN THE 1950'S AND COULD HAVE KNOWN JACK JOHNSTONE, WHO HAD A HABIT OF WRITING FRIENDS AND COWORKERS INTO THE SCRIPTS. THE WILLIE ELLIOTT COULD POSSIBLY BE A REFERENCE TO WILLIAM "WILD BILL" ELLIOTT, BUT I CANNOT CONFIRM THAT.

Producer: Jack Johnstone      Writers: Sam Dawson
Cast: Harry Bartell, Larry Dobkin, Vic Perrin, Barney Phillips, Forrest Lewis, Eric Snowden, Herb Vigran, James McCallion

SHOW: THE DUKE RED MATTER
COMPANY: UNIVERSAL ADJUSTMENT BUREAU
AGENT: NILES PEARSON
PART 1      SHOW DATE:    1/23/1956

SYNOPSIS: Niles Pearson calls and tells Johnny that he is worried about $65,000 worth of horseflesh. The horse Duke Red, who won the Futurity last year, was insured had been destroyed.

Johnny goes to San Francisco and then to San Piedro, California . Johnny goes to the Abbott Stables office and asks for Mr. Abbott, and Johnny is told he is always at the ranch and Mr. Monroe, the business manager who filed the claim three days ago, is no longer with the company. Mr. Abbott has fired him. The secretary Judy calls the ranch and is told that Mr. Abbott out for the day. Johnny asks where Mr. Monroe is, but is told that he has moved out of town.

Johnny rents a 1940 Terraplane and drives to the office of Dr. James Gorrey, the local Veterinarian. The Dr. Gorrey knows that Abbott and Monroe had quarreled and tells Johnny that Duke Red was worth more than $65,000 as Dr. Gorrey takes cares of all of Abbott's stock. He tells Johnny that Duke Red had stumbled up against a tractor and cut his hamstring. A report was made and Dr. Gorrey shows Johnny the report. Johnny spots that the carcass was cremated that night and is told that Ben Abbott wanted it that way. There are also no x-rays to prove the injury. Dr. Gorrey tells Johnny that it would have been wrong to not destroy the animal and that there was no use in consulting with another vet. Only Ben Abbott was there when the accident happened. Johnny tells Dr. Gorrey that he needs more than a report to substantiate the claim. Dr. Gorrey tells

Johnny he has been in business for 30 years, but Johnny tell him that he cannot take any one's word, so Dr. Gorrey tells Johnny to leave. Johnny drives back to town and wonders why Dr. Gorrey had not taken photos. Johnny checks on Dr. Gorrey with Judy, the secretary in Abbott's office and she tells him that Dr. Gorrey is a fixture here, and is the best vet in the area. Johnny asks Judy to dinner and she accepts. She tells Johnny that she has worked for Mr. Abbott for a year and a half and that Monroe and Abbott had quarreled, and she wondered about it. Judy sees Mr. Monroe at the bar. Johnny stops him and Monroe tells him to talk to Mr. Abbott. Monroe is leaving town now, and it was not his horse. Monroe tells Johnny the let Abbott handle his own dirty business.

Tomorrow, there is proof that things are as just about as wrong in this case, and as dangerous as they can get.

## PART 2          SHOW DATE:          1/24/1956

The operator calls with a call from Mr. Pearson who got the wire to hold up the claim. Johnny tells him that the case is all-wrong and something is cockeyed.

Johnny sends Dr. Gorrey's report to a veterinary service in Cleveland and then drives to the Abbott farm. Johnny is met by the butler who tries to find Mr. Abbott. A girl and an old man enter the room arguing and ignoring Johnny. She wants to live her life and he tells her she will do as he tells her. They leave and then the girl comes back in. The girl tells Johnny that her father does not approve of her company. Johnny introduces himself, and the girl tells Johnny that she is Terri Abbott, Ben's daughter. She knows that Johnny is there about Duke Red. She tells Johnny that Red was a great horse, and would have won a lot of money. Red was the only horse worth anything and he was not injured. Ben Abbott comes in and he tells her to go to her room. She tells him it was murder, and Ben slaps her. Ben explains to Johnny that she always gets upset when an animal is destroyed. Ben tells Johnny that Dr. Gorrey had called and Johnny tells him that he needs to go to everyone. Ben does not like Johnny sneaking around and tells Johnny that he does not know what he is doing. Ben tells Johnny that Monroe filed the claim too soon and that he was going to wait until the excitement died down. Losing that animal also caused a moral problem at the ranch. Johnny tells Ben that they will pay went they are satisfied the circumstances were proper, and that they are not satisfied now. Johnny tells Ben he will get his information from whoever he needs to in order to complete his investigation. In frustration, Ben tells Johnny that the horse was coming back from a training session and was scared by something, reared back into the tractor and cut his Achilles tendon. Dr. Gooey said the horse did not have a chance, so Ben shot him. Johnny wants to talk to the trainer, Tom Warner, but Ben has fired him and he is gone; he knew better than to stay around. There was no one else around at the time. Ben tells Johnny that accidents happen, and he deals with them and the insurance company cannot tell him how to run his farm. Terri did not see the accident. Ben calls Cully, the butler, and tells him to throw Johnny out if he ever comes back.

Johnny leaves and Cully stops him and apologizes for Mr. Abbott and tells Johnny that he is not just himself. Johnny tells Cully that he thinks Ben is losing his mind and Cully agrees with him.

Tomorrow, the whole case starts to fall apart like a man full of bullet wounds, which is just about the case.

### PART 3          SHOW DATE:          1/25/1956

Johnny receives a call in the stable office from Terri, where Cully had told her to call him. Did you believe all those things I told you? I'll be right down.

Terri meets Johnny in the stable office with a disdainful pout. She tells Johnny that he is so sure of himself although he knows nothing. Johnny tells her the only thing he knows about horses is that Duke Red is dead. Terri is very evasive about the things she had said earlier and has been upset lately. She tells Johnny that Duke Red was the best horse they had ever had, and that the accident has turned everyone upside down. Johnny asks what Monroe meant about the "dirty business" and where Tom Warner is. Teri tells Johnny that Warner is in Baltimore.

Johnny drives to town and gets Tom Warner's address. Johnny sends a wire to Niles Pearson for a run down on Ben Abbott's finances and then a wire to Tom Warner. At the local bank Johnny asks about Ben Abbott's credit. The manager, Dale O'Ryan gets the file and tells Johnny that there will be nothing to find in Ben's finances as $65,000 is small change to him, and that Terri runs him a couple thousand or so a month. Johnny reviews the folder and finds nothing unusual. The only questionable item is a check to Mr. Monroe marked "bonus"; strange considering that they had argued. There is also an outstanding salary for Tom Warner. Johnny wonders why doesn't he kick?

A check at the Abbott office showed no forwarding address for Tom Warner. At dinner Johnny receives a call from Baltimore. Tom Warner's father tells Johnny that Tom is in San Piedro, California. He is not at home; he is at Mr. Abbott's farm.

Tomorrow, well sometimes a dead man can answer a lot of questions.

### PART 4          SHOW DATE:          1/26/1956

The operator calls with a call from Niles Pearson. Johnny is told that Mr. Abbott does not need money, but no one knows what happened to Tom Warner. Abbott's claim has been filed for a week but he has not threatened to sue.

Johnny suspects that the death of Duke Red did not happen as reported. Johnny drives to the Abbott Ranch and Cully meets him at the door. Johnny asks for Tom Warner, but no one knows where he is. Cully takes Johnny to the stable and lets Johnny search the room used by Tom Warner, but the room is bare. Cully tells Johnny that no one saw Warner leave. Tom had a lot of friends and the others on the farm have talked. Tom was a good horse trainer and did not have a temper. Tom could even handle Mr. Abbott. Cully tells Johnny that Mr. Abbott has had a hard time since his wife died; he seems to have troubles at time. He really counted on Duke Red, and the other horses were no match. Warner did not have a car; so maybe Miss Terri drove him out. She used to drive Tom around and Mr. Abbott disapproved of it. Johnny talks to the others on the farm, and they were grumbling and complaining. Johnny goes to the house to see Mr. Abbott but meets Terri who is ready to see Johnny tossed out on his ear. Johnny asks if she is mad at Tom Warner for leaving and not saying goodbye. She tells Johnny that the argument on the first day was over Tom. She had said the things she did to try and get even at her father, to put him in a bad light. They had argued over Tom Warner for weeks. She tells Johnny that she had seen a lot of Tom after her mother and brother were killed in a car crash. Her father blamed the accident on Tom. Terri asks Johnny "do you think he is mad? The Abbott's are an angry people." Teri tells Johnny that her father seems as though he is on the edge of something. Two years ago he bought a new car and crashed it when something minor went wrong. Tom never got angry, and he would sit with her and read while she was doing things. If he had said goodbye, she would have left with him, and he knew it.

Johnny meets constable Polk and tells him about the claim on the horse. Johnny asks for assistance in finding Tom Warner and Johnny fills out a missing person's report.

Tomorrow, well it all hinges on a decent man who knows he is loved and never says goodbye.

### PART 5      SHOW DATE:     1/27/1956

Dr. Gorrey returns Johnny's call and Dr. Gorrey does not want to talk to him. Johnny says that he has reason to not believe what Dr. Gorrey told him. Johnny tells him that the matter with Tom Warner is in the hands of the police and Dr. Gorrey relents and agrees to talk to Johnny.

Johnny buys breakfast for Constable Polk and is told that there is little Polk can do with a small police force. Constable Polk is going to talk to Mr. Abbott and then they will plan. Johnny calls Hartford and has a man check for Tom Warner in Baltimore and then goes to see Dr. Gorrey. Johnny tells Dr. Gorrey that the head office is ready to close the case and not pay the claim. Dr. Gorrey tells Johnny that Abbott did not want to file the claim and fired Monroe. Abbott blamed the accident on Warner and fired him. Abbott hated Warner because he was seeing Terri. Johnny would hate to see Dr. Gorrey get the book. Abbott will have to prove his case and he cannot. Dr. Gorrey would have to go to court too. Dr. Gorrey tells Johnny that he has been Abbott's friend for 20 years. The horse was dead when he got there and Ben had just shot him and swore Dr. Gorrey to silence. The horse was not what Abbott had hoped for and would not run, or could not run. Tom Warner had seen Abbott shoot the horse. Abbott gave Tom some money and told him to go away. Dr. Gorrey seems to think that Ben is losing his mind. Johnny asks why did Abbott pay Monroe and not Warner? Dr. Gorrey tells Johnny that Ben said he did pay Warner.

Johnny drives to the farm and Cully opens the door and asks Johnny to come back later. Constable Polk was there earlier and Mr. Abbott is awful mad. Terri comes in and even in the darkened house Johnny can see that her father has beaten Terri. Ben comes in with a cane and beats Terri and Johnny while ranting about killing another man already. Johnny calls Constable Polk and tells him what happened and searches the grounds for Ben. Johnny hears a disturbance in the stables and Ben shouts at Johnny to leave. Johnny tells him he knows about Dr. Gorrey lying and tells him to throw down the shotgun. Johnny tells him he is smashing his whole life. Ben fires and Johnny shoots back. Ben tells Johnny that Warner is buried under the floor of the stable. Warner had seen him shoot Duke and told him he was crazy. "I'm not crazy, am I Dollar?" Ben dies and the police find Warner's body buried where Ben said it was.

Exp. Acct:     $802.65

NOTES:
- REMAKE OF THE OKLAHOMA RED MATTER—6/9/1953
- JOHNNY GIVES HIS HEIGHT AS NOT QUITE 6' 1"
- THE TERRAPLANE WAS MADE BY THE HUDSON AUTOMOBILE COMPANY
- ROY ROWAN IS THE ANNOUNCER
- MUSIC SUPERVISION IS BY AMERIGO MARINO

Producer: Jack Johnstone          Writers:  John Dawson
Cast:       Barbara Fuller, Barbara Eiler, Herb Butterfield,
             John Stevenson, Parley Baer, Will Wright, Robert Bruce,
             Forrest Lewis

◆     ❖     ◆

SHOW:         THE FLIGHT SIX MATTER
COMPANY:      GUARANTEE TRANSPORT INSURANCE COMPANY
AGENT:        PETE CARDLEY
PART 1        SHOW DATE:     1/30/1956
SYNOPSIS: Pete Cardley calls Johnny about an air crash in Mexico. The plane crashed in the mountains and Pete is stuck for $75,000. Somebody meant for it to crash

Johnny flies to Mexico City, Mexico and finally finds the office of the Inspector General of Civil Air Transport. Inside is Mack Macklin, an Irishman from Chicago. Mack gives Johnny the information on the crash. There were no survivors and the plane did not catch fire. A crew is working on the crash site now. The crash probably was sabotage. Some Indians were watching the plane and the tail blew off and the plane crashed. Mack is questioning the ground crew and checking on the passengers and crew. There were three flight insurance policies issued and Johnny has the names. There was no cargo on the plane so the crash was aimed at a passenger. A man enters the office demanding information on the crash. He is Ramon Delagos and one of the passengers was Maria Delagos, his wife. Ramon is saddened that she is dead. She had just come to visit him and was returning home. Marie's brother, Don Cerano, is staying at the Hotel Reje but he and Ramon are not on speaking terms. Ramon is staying at the Monte Casino and Mack tells him that he will be notified when the bodies are brought in.

Mack tells Johnny that Ramon is an exporter from Cuba, but the brother is the beneficiary if the policy. Mack guarantees Johnny complete cooperation.

Johnny rides up to the crash site in a jeep. On the site there are Army searchers and some silent Indians. Gino Romero meets Johnny and tells him that a single explosion caused the crash and they have found many pieces of the plane. The baggage is totally destroyed and burned but the seats are not burned. The clothes smell of dynamite and small pieces of the dynamite casings have been found. Drums start beating as the bodies are taken out and Johnny notices a young blonde woman. Gino tells Johnny that she is a daredevil, one who is always looking for adventure. Her name is Marvel Terrance. Johnny recognizes that Marvel Terrance is the beneficiary of two of the insurance policies.

Tomorrow, a fighting girl; and a lucky break, and then murder evens the score.

**PART 2          SHOW DATE:      1/31/1956**

Johnny receives a radio call from Mack for Gino. Johnny tells Mack that nothing is new. Mack tells Johnny that a baggage handler named Ramirez was acting strange. He had one suitcase that he would let no one touch. Johnny tells Mack that he is about to tangle with a tiger.

Johnny senses that Marvel Terrace is a real tiger, as Gino had suggested. She was watching the bodies being removed with cool dispatch. Johnny introduces himself and she is annoyed and tells him to run along. She tells Johnny that she came up because she had friends on the plane, "so beat it buster." Johnny wonders how she will spend the $50,000 from the passengers Palmer and Roarke. She does not know about the insurance policies and it is a surprise as Ed and Jim were her friends. An aggravated man tells Johnny that he brought her up, but not to be pushed around by a morbid publicity seeker. Marvel tells the man that Johnny in an investigator and about the insurance. The man is Bill Blakely and he is very angry that Johnny wants to know why he is there. Bill tells Johnny that he was a partner of the two men who were killed on the plane and is annoyed that Johnny accuses him of killing Ed and Jim to get the business. Marvel had known them for several months, they were just friends, it was just a game. She tells Johnny that she is a wealthy orphan who just drifts around and plays the game. She is at the Hotel Monte Casino and could teach Johnny the game. She tells Johnny that she knows Ramon Delagos and Johnny asks "didn't you know his wife was on the plane." She tells Johnny that she did not know he had a wife. See me and I will straighten out your ideas. She tells Johnny that she had reservations on the plane and cancelled at the last minute. She cancelled because Bill talked her out of going.

Johnny and Gino head back to town and talk about Marvel and her game. If she is guilty Johnny will pin it on her. Gino does not think she is guilty; she is very rich. Gino tells Johnny that Blakely is making a road and they all worked and played together. They were all after Marvel and in their warehouse there is much dynamite.

Johnny gets a room at the Del Prado and meets Mack Macklin in the bar.

During drinks, dinner and more drinks, Mack tells Johnny he has been in Mexico for seven years, but would like to see Chicago again and that he was last there in 1932. He tells Johnny that he flew on the wrong side of a war once and cannot go back. Mack gets a phone call and learns that Ramirez has been killed.

Tomorrow, a bereaved relative lies, a frustrated lover comes up fighting, and a lovely lady in the case just vanishes.

**PART 3**          **SHOW DATE:**          **2/1/1956**

Don Cerano calls Johnny and Johnny recognizes him as Marie Delagos' brother. Don Cerano has some information on the crash. He knows it was the evil work of a diabolical maniac, the product of the warped mind of a scheming worthless unspeakable dog, a sneaking money hungry snake, a scurrilous unprincipled . . . Don Cerano come on up!

Johnny buys breakfast for himself and Don Cerano, a classic Spanish gentleman full of hate who speaks of the duello, the honorable way to resolve these issues. Johnny tells him that Ramon Delagos was in Mexico to pursue his business, and Don Cerano tells Johnny that Ramon's business was women with money. Maria had come to meet her husband and found out about Marvel Terrace and you bought her a ticket on the flight. Don Cerano tells Johnny that Ramon always lied to her and was only interested in her wealth. Half of the estate goes to Ramon and the other reverts to Don Cerano. Don Cerano had managed the estate before Ramon got involved. Maria was a pious woman who could not divorce Ramon. They had not seen Ramon, but Ramon knew of the flight. Who else would have been so vile as to put explosives on the plane? Do you doubt me? Don Cerano knows Marvel Terrace and he thought she was going on the plane too, but he saw her talking to an American. Johnny asks why Maria took out the insurance and left him the insurance and Don Cerano tells Johnny that it was just a whim. Johnny tells Don Cerano that he would also benefit from the crash. Don Cerano wants to kill Johnny but Johnny tells Don Cerano that he is always looking to kill people, and tells him to leave.

Johnny checks out a number of leads and finds nothing. Maria, Palmer and Roarke seem to be the center of the case for which there are four suspects, Ramon, Don Cerano, Marvel and Bill Blakely. Johnny calls Marvel and sets up a lunch date, which she does not keep. Johnny goes to her hotel and the desk clerk starts to call her room and then remembers she had checked out at 11:00. After lunch Johnny runs into Ramon Delagos and asks him about Marvel Terrance, but he knows nothing of her plans. Johnny tells Ramon that Don Cerano had blamed him, but Ramon tells him that Don Cerano is only interested in money. Maria knew about Marvel and accepted it but Don Cerano hated him because he lost control of Maria's money. Johnny calls Don Cerano, Blakely, and Ramon's hotel to learn that they have all checked out, with no forwarding addresses.

Tomorrow a rendezvous in a tropic port. And a lot of things come together, like romance, desire and death.

**PART 4**          **SHOW DATE:**      **2/2/1956**

Gino calls Johnny and he has tracked the four suspects to Acapulco. Gino has reservations on flight six for himself and Johnny.

Johnny and Gino fly to Acapulco, Mexico. Gino has called his contacts and has the hotels for the suspects. Marvel and Blakely are at the Hotel Los Flamingo; Ramon is at the Hotel Caleta and Don Cerano is at the Club de Pesca. Johnny and Gino go to the Los Flamingo, as Johnny thinks Marvel is at the heart of the case. Johnny finds Marvel on the terrace by the cliffs and she is not surprised to find him here. Johnny does not want to have a social chat and Marvel is aware that Johnny knows her type, which scares her. She tells Johnny that she wants to be buried at sunset. She has no relatives and is lonely with only a large trust fund to spend. She has no confessions to make and can only guess who caused the accident, as she didn't know. She tells Johnny that she does not remember seeing Ramon or Don Cerano at the airport and that Ramon had met Bill and they hated each other. Johnny tells her that the others have followed her to Acapulco. Marvel wants Johnny to take her to dinner and dancing, and she goes to change. Johnny calls Don Cerano and Ramon, who were not in. Johnny wants to see Bill but he knocks on Johnny's door. Johnny has a gun on him because he had seen Blakely listening outside his door. Bill knows he is under suspicion as he now owns the business and has a warehouse full of dynamite. Johnny mentions that he forgot Marvel, but Bill says it would not make sense to bomb the plane, as she had a reservation in it and only changed her mind at the last minute. Bill tells Johnny that he talked her out of the flight, but not because it was going to explode.

Johnny enjoys a pleasant evening with Marvel and takes her back to her room. Later that night Johnny hears screaming and meets Gino in the hallway. They go to Marvel's room to find the door open and Marvel's slippers by a broken guardrail on the cliffs. They go down to the beach and find Marvel, dead on the beach, alone and lonely.

Tomorrow, a desperate killer is cornered and strikes back in a deadly counter attack, final showdown!

**PART 5**          **SHOW DATE:**      **2/3/1956**

Mack Macklin calls Johnny and Johnny tells Mack that he is following the suspects. Johnny tells Mack that Marvel was going to help, but he and Gino had just pulled Marvel from the surf. It was murder.

Johnny calls Mack with the news of Marvel's death. Gino comes rushing in and tells Johnny that the police have blocked the grounds. They run out and search the brush, the only place where someone can hide. They hear someone moving and quietly move in. Johnny corners Don Cerano, who tells Johnny that he was looking for Ramon, who was not in his room. He thought that Ramon was at Marvel's room. Don Cerano tells Johnny that he went there to kill Ramon. Don Cerano is turned over to the police and then they search Bill Blakely's room where the bed has been slept in. Johnny opens Bill's suitcase and inside they find an open box of .38 cartridges. Johnny and Gino rush to the Hotel Caleta with the police. In room 34 they call for Ramon and Bill Blakely opens the door. He gives Johnny his gun and tells him that Ramon has not shown up. Marvel had told Bill that Ramon had followed her and that she was scared of him. She was a great kid. Outside they hear shots and run after Ramon. The police block the beach and Johnny and Gino go after him. Gino spots a boat and thinks Ramon is near it. They split up and Ramon surprises Johnny behind the boat. Ramon tells Johnny to push the boat into the water and they row out across the bay. Johnny splashes an oar and Ramon almost hits him. Ramon admits killing Maria to get to Marvel. Marvel told him she was suspicions and was falling in love with Johnny, which made him crazy. They hear a police launch start up. Ramon turns to look and Johnny clubs him with an oar. The police pick him up but Ramon tries to take over the police boat and is killed.

Remarks: I will never see another sunset now without thinking of her, somewhere out beyond it. I hope she does not feel alone anymore.

Exp. Acct: $608.10

## NOTES:
* ROY ROWAN IS THE ANNOUNCER
* MUSICAL SUPERVISION IS BY AMERIGO MARINO

Producer: Jack Johnstone      Writers: Les Crutchfield
Cast: Virginia Gregg, Ben Wright, Edgar Barrier, Don Diamond, Russ Thorson, Jack Moyles

◆ ❖ ◆

SHOW: THE MCCLAIN MATTER
COMPANY: TRI-STATE INSURANCE UNDERWRITERS
AGENT: DON TAYLOR
PART 1      SHOW DATE: 2/6/1956
SYNOPSIS: Don Taylor at Tri-State calls. Don asks Johnny if he wants to come to his office and meet a pretty girl? She just told me the most interesting thing I have ever heard. She told me that she was dead.

Johnny cabs to Don Taylor's office to meet a pretty, well dressed woman in her late twenties. Don wants Mrs. McClain to talk to Johnny alone, as she has a most unusual story. Johnny tells her he is an investigator for whoever will hire him. She tells Johnny that she is legally dead and that her husband collected on her $10,000 insurance policy. Her husband is Dr. David McClain, and he lives in Los Angeles. She was the receptionist when a patient came in off the street that was sick. He took her into an examining room and she had a heart attack and died. He told Mrs. McClain what had happened and they searched her to see who she was. Her name was Teresa Corbit from Jersey City. They called the address and discovered that the woman's mother had died and the frantic apartment manager was trying to locate Teresa. The manager told Dave that Teresa was the only living relative. Then Dave said we are in luck. The girl had no relative and no one would know that they would use her body. Dave called Dr. Reed from next door and she hid. Dave told Dr. Reed that the body was his wife. They tried to revive her but they knew it was too late. Dr. Reed signed a death certificate and she was buried two days later. When Johnny asks why Dr. Reed did not know her if she was the receptionist, she tells Johnny that Dr. Reed was new and that they had never met. She stayed in a hotel and then went to Palm Springs. Dave collected the insurance and she came to New York. Dave was going to close his practice and come to New York. He wrote saying he was on his way and then stopped writing. Johnny asks what she wants them to do and she tells Johnny that she has been thinking about the matter for two years and does not want to get anyone in trouble. It sounds fantastic but it is the truth. It is good to tell it to someone after all this time. She tells Johnny that the whole thing was Dave's idea. She has been working in a lab in New York under the name of Patricia Kennedy. She can prove who she is in Los Angeles and can give Johnny a list of people who can identify her in Los Angeles. She tells Johnny that Dave was badly in debt and needed money, and this seemed like a good way to get it. Teresa Corbit had nobody, and she does not know who Dave contacted. She came to Hartford because the insurance company has been robbed. "What about you?" Johnny asks, "He did everything didn't he?" She tells Johnny that she read in a Los Angeles paper that Dave is going to get married in June. Johnny tells Don to get the legal staff to get a statement ready. Johnny asks if she is aware that, if the story is true, she and her husband can be criminally charged. She says yes and cries.

Tomorrow, some well thought out lies, well, believe it or not, they come true.

### PART 2          SHOW DATE:          2/7/1956

Don Taylor calls and asks what they should do now. Johnny tells him they need more facts. She has not told them the truth.

Johnny lunches with Don Taylor, who thinks they should act. Johnny recounts the whole story and how today she says she is tired of waiting. Johnny says there are holes, too many holes. Why did the doctor just decide on the trick at the last minute? Mrs. McClain was the receptionist but she allowed the woman to see the doctor without getting a name. Doctors will always get a name and address unless they know you. Everything she has said needs to be verified. Don has checked on the policy and the facts check. The death certificate gives the cause as coronary thrombosis and all the other details seem to check. Johnny is worried about all the things she didn't say.

Johnny goes to New York City and cabs to Mrs. McClain's apartment. The manager tells Johnny that she is a good tenant and has few friends. The manager is suspicious but lets Johnny look around the apartment. Johnny then goes to the medical lab where her story also checks out. Johnny calls Don and he tells Johnny that a Mrs. Corbit had died, and that the county buried the body.

Johnny flies to Los Angeles, California and sleeps. That afternoon Johnny gets a package of information from Don and rents a car. Johnny checks the addresses provided, but only the last one checks out. A Mrs. Henderson lets Johnny in and Johnny shows her a picture that is really familiar; it is Doris McClain; she died a year or so ago very suddenly. She knew Doris for about 5 years and worked with her. She tells Johnny that she read of the death in the papers, and she wants to know what this is all about. She tells Johnny that Dave probably got over it, so why didn't you go to Dr. McClain? "I'm going to call him." Johnny tells her.

Johnny calls Don Taylor and asks for a private eye to watch Mrs. Henderson; someone might want to kill her.

Tomorrow, a bit of information about a girl who had a date to die, that's right.

## PART 3          SHOW DATE:          2/8/1956

Vic Wade calls Johnny and he knows where Theresa Corbett is.

Johnny goes to see Wade who shows him a statement they have. They got a request from the boyfriend named George Reilly, but they never learned much. Johnny goes to see Reilly who admits that the police have been following him. He tells Johnny that he met Teresa in a restaurant and last saw her on January 19th, her birthday. George had gone to the police and mentioned her mother to them. Johnny tells him that Teresa is dead, and buried in Los Angeles. Johnny goes back to see Wade and he tells Johnny that they did not know about her heart condition, and that there is no record of a phone call to New Jersey from the doctor's office. Johnny is sure that Teresa's doctor was Dr. McClain.

## PART 4          SHOW DATE:          2/9/1956

Johnny gets a call from the desk, which connects him with Dr. McClain, who thinks Johnny is crazy. Johnny wants to see him and the doctor tells Johnny that he will call the police if he comes over. Well, get busy, I am on my way.

When Johnny goes to buy gas George Riley stops him. They drive out and he tells Johnny that he was thinking about Terri. The police came to see him and they are going to exhume the body. "It will he her, won't it?" he asks Johnny. George wants to get his hands on the bird that killed her. George was going to marry Terri and she just walked out. Now you tell me that she was killed, but what about me? Why is she dead? That doctor just took her and buried her, what is his name! Johnny tells him that he will know soon enough as Johnny will find out what happened.

Johnny drives to the offices of Dr. McClain and he tells Johnny that he was intrigued by the call. Johnny asks if Pauline Henderson called him, and Johnny tells him that he had seen Mrs. Henderson because she would recognize his wife. Dr. McClain is baffled at Johnny and wants to know what he wants. Johnny tells him about the investigation of Teresa Corbit in 1954, but he does not remember it. Dr. McClain searches the files but there is no record of Teresa. Johnny tells him that Teresa had come to see him several times, but McClain tells Johnny his wife was his receptionist, but she was not very good. Johnny tells him that not having a file makes Johnny suspicion. Johnny tells Dave about Mrs. McClain coming in and making the statement and that she is very much alive and he has witnesses. The doctor has nothing to say.

Johnny prefers charges against Dr. McClain and he is arrested but refuses to talk. Johnny wires Don with the events and Don wires back to tell Johnny that he is on the way out with Mrs. McClain. Johnny learns that the coroner has exhumed the body and identified it as Teresa Corbit. Johnny visits Dr. McClain one last time and tells him that his wife will be there the next day and that he wants a statement. Johnny suggests he pleads guilty, but Dr. McClain says he will never get him into court. The next morning Dr. McClain is released on bail, which worries Johnny. Johnny drives out to an address in the Pacific Palisades and hears shots as he walks into the building. Johnny shoots at the man as he runs out and then walks to George Riley, who tells Johnny that he has shot McClain. He did it for Terri, his girl.

Tomorrow, a brand new, or rather startling statement from Mrs. McClain, without lies.

## PART 5      SHOW DATE:     2/10/1956

Don Taylor calls and Johnny tells him that Dr. McClain had been shot. He is alive but barely. Don tells Johnny that he will meet him at the hospital.

Johnny rents a tape recorder and goes to Dr. McClain's room to meet Don. Johnny tells Don that Riley is being held for assault with intent to kill. Don and Johnny go to the room and Dr. McClain asks why the recorder is there. Johnny tells him that he wants a statement. Dr. McClain tells Johnny that he will talk later, and they leave. Dr. McClain recovers within a week and a trial date is set. Johnny tells Don that there is still more to it, he is not satisfied. Riley and Teresa are the ones who are suffering. Don flies home and Johnny wraps up the details.

Johnny goes to interview Mrs. McClain again in the jail. She is expecting a three-year sentence, which is not too long. Johnny tells her they have enough to charge conspiracy. Johnny reads to her from her statement about Teresa Corbit coming into the office and having never met her before and about the call to New Jersey. Johnny tells her that the phone company has no record of a call being billed. She accuses Johnny of calling her a liar. Johnny tells her that he had found out that Teresa Corbit was a patient of Dr. McClain, but she is adamant that she did not know her. Johnny tells her that the story was too real, it could not have happened as explained. Johnny tells her that she knew Teresa's history and that Teresa Corbit had only one living relative. She was a patsy right from the beginning, wasn't she? Mrs. McClain admits that Teresa had come in with a telegram about her mother dying and was upset. She asked for something to help her sleep and Dave mentioned her case being terminal, but she was not that sick. Dave went back to the examination room and she just waited. He buzzed her and when she went in to the room, Teresa was dead. She knew what he had done when she went in because there was a hypodermic on the table. They had not talked about it, but he had it all planned out. She left town that night and Dave said he would take care of anything. He said he killed her and that she would go to the gas chamber with him if she said anything. She told the story about the phone call to get back at him. She is glad it is all over.

Remarks: Murder charges have been filed against the McClains, and they stand trial next month. George Riley received three years and a suspended sentence for assault with a deadly weapon. I was wrong about practically everything in this case. All the lies came true, but so did the facts.

Exp. Acct:     $768.60

NOTES:

*   REMAKE OF "THE MADISON MATTER" OF 4/14/1953
*   ROY ROWAN IS THE ANNOUNCER
*   MUSICAL SUPERVISION IS BY AMERIGO MARINO
*   THE CONTENT FOR EPISODE 3 WAS OBTAINED FROM THE SCRIPT ON FILE IN THE KNX COLLECTION AT THE THOUSAND OAKS LIBRARY.

Producer:   Jack Johnstone          Writers:   John Dawson
Cast:       Lucille Meredith, Betty Lou Gerson, John Stevenson, Bob
            Bruce, Victor Perrin, Tony Barrett, Herb Ellis

SHOW:       THE CUI BONO MATTER
COMPANY:    SURETY MUTUAL INSURANCE LTD.
AGENT:      DON HANCOCK
PART 1           SHOW DATE:      2/13/1956

SYNOPSIS: Don Hancock calls and asks Johnny "cui bono," who benefits. Don tells Johnny that a little doll named Luanne Parker in Greenpass, Virginia does, to the tune of $100,000 double indemnity. She admits to shooting her stepfather twice with a .38. The coroner is going to call it an unavoidable accident. Seems lil' ol' Magnolia blossom thought papa was a prowler. I think you should put yourself on the payroll.

Johnny trains to Greenpass, Virginia, three miles from the railroad station. Johnny takes Jake Deegley's cab to the hotel. Jake tells Johnny that this is a one horse town, just one of everything, including one county attorney, who was Dan Parker the deceased who had been elected five times. Johnny asks if Dan had any enemies and Jake tells him that Luanne just took him for a prowler. When Johnny asks if Luanne is well liked, Jake tells him that he and his seventeen-year-old grandson and everyone else in town are in love with Luanne. She loved her stepfather and did everything with him. Dan was well to do but not rich. Jake tells Johnny to be careful about doing his job, or he will get a lot of trouble. Johnny checks into the hotel and goes to see sheriff Jim Peterson in the local poolroom. Sheriff Peterson calls it an accident and Johnny tells him it is a routine investigation. Sheriff Peterson tells Johnny that Dan's stepdaughter killed him. Dan had been to Richmond and was walking back to town. Jake was at the Happy Holler and Dan was not expected. Dan came back early and there was no one to meet him. He took a shortcut across the terrace, and hit a chair that woke up Luanne. When she heard him fumble in the lock and come up the stairs, she fired twice and killed him. She shot him in the dark. Dan taught her to shoot and she was real good. There were some prowlers and Luanne had heard noises before. Mary Jackson the housekeeper was there and she told the same story. Luanne was real close to her father and was broke up about it. She did what she thought was right and will regret it for the rest of her life. Sheriff Peterson tells Johnny to look all he wants, but the answer will come out the same. When Johnny tells Sheriff Peterson he wants to attend the inquest, Johnny is told that it was this morning and the verdict was death by misadventure with no recommendation for prosecution. Sheriff Peterson warns Johnny to walk easy. Johnny looks over the transcript and there was nothing suspect. She was a good student and everyone in town loved her, but cui bono?

Tomorrow, beauty is as beauty does, and an idol is found to be made of flesh and blood.

### PART 2      SHOW DATE:      2/14/1956

Tom Bates, the acting country attorney calls. Johnny wants to talk about the case and will come right over.

Johnny reads the local paper about the death of Dan Parker, but it did not mention that Luanne stood to get $100,000. Johnny meets with Tom Bates and Johnny convinces Tom that he has the legal resources to make it real hot for him. Tom thinks Johnny is trying to muddy things up and get out of paying the insurance. Tom tells Johnny that there was no hint of suspicion in the inquest, but not much of anything else either. Johnny traps Tom into admitting he is in love with Luanne. Johnny insists that he has not accused Luanne of anything. Johnny only wants the total story of how Dan died. Tom tells Johnny that he had worked for Dan for three years and got along well with Dan. Dan approved of his relationship with Luanne over the, uh, others, but she is not ready to settle down. Dan had no enemies, but he was too easy sometimes. Tom is going to press some issues, like the Happy Hollow Roadhouse, run by Sammie Drake, who should be run out of town. Luanne knows Drake, but everyone knows everyone here. Luanne was a dead shot and can outshoot everyone in the county. No paraffin test was done because she admits to firing the gun. Johnny asks Tom "cui bono"? Maybe someone else will benefit. Maybe someone used her.

Johnny rents the taxi and talks to various people around town and learns that Luanne was a smart, sweet, all-American girl. Johnny goes to meet Luanne and is met by Mary Jackson. She tells Johnny that Luanne is staying with Dr. Prayley and his wife. Johnny would like to talk to Mary also. He explains why he is there and learns that Mary had raised Luanne. She shows Johnny the house and where the shooting took place. She tells Johnny that when she heard the shots she turned on the lights and Luanne ripped off his tie, but he was gone. Mary tells Johnny that she makes $95 a month, that Dan has a nice new house and bought Luanne a new car last year, but he only made $5,000 a year. With all this they were still arguing. Mary tells Johnny that Luanne and Dan had argued about Sammy, who put ideas in her head. Luanne was a restless one, and he put crazy notions of going to New York into her head. That was the only thing Dan refused her. He told her that she would have to do it over his dead body.

Tomorrow the net tightens, a rat runs for cover, then the whole thing blows wide open.

**PART 3**      **SHOW DATE:**      **2/15/1956**

Tom Bates calls and Doc Prayley said you had been threatening him. Johnny only told him he would get a court order if necessary to talk to Luanne. Tom warns Johnny, and Johnny warns Tom that he will talk to Luanne one way or another.

Johnny goes to the Happy Hollow Road House and muses over the case on the way there. In the roadhouse Johnny finds a bar and jukebox and maybe a game in the back. Sammy Drake talks to Johnny (what's the word Mack) and Johnny replies "save your money and buy booze." Sammie tells Johnny that it is rough, and Johnny tells him that it will be rougher with a new County Attorney and Sammy asks, "What's the pitch Mitch?" Johnny tells Sammy who he is and Sammy tells him to "tie me up and mail me off!" Johnny wants to know about Dan's death but Sammy tells him "you're out of luck Chuck, I don't know nothing about nothing from nothing, see what I mean?" Sammy is sure that Bates is after him because his doll has been here. Sammy tells him to come into the office and asks "what did you say your name was, buzz?" Johnny tells him "Johnny Dollar, rhymes with collar." Sammy pours a drink and tells Johnny that the food is good there. Sammy cannot see any reason to worry about Johnny and tells him that no one had anything to do with killing Dan. Dan was his fix in the town, so why would he kill him? Sammy will pitch the sheriff, but does not think he will play. Sammy tells Johnny that Tom has "the drooling goose" over Luanne and did not like her hanging around him. Sammy did not like it either; she was too spoiled and thought she could do whatever she wanted. Dan did not like it but could not do anything. Sammy did not put any ideas about New York in her mind; she came in with them. She was busting her braces to get to the action. She has the whole town fooled, except for me. She is smart and colder than a fish and Sammy is tough, but he is scared of her.

Johnny has dinner and cabs to the railroad station and talks to the stationmaster. He was on duty when Dan Parker came back. Dan came in on the #8 and spoke with him. He tells Johnny that there was some fellow with him that Dan met on the train. They talked and the man got back on the train. The man said he would be seeing Dan when the train pulled out. Dan called home but got a busy signal and had to walk home.

Tomorrow, a tense interview, a subtle attack by a shrewd and dangerous opponent and complete surrender.

**PART 4**      **SHOW DATE:**      **2/16/1956**

Tom Bates calls and Tom does not want to fight Johnny and tells him that Luanne will be available at 2:00. You will go out with me and interview her while I am there.

Johnny eats a late breakfast and waits for Tom Bates to pick him up. On the way to the Parker house, Tom tells Johnny to give up and stop trying to break the claim. Tom has blocked every move Johnny has made. Johnny tells Tom that all the company wants is the facts; so what is the real reason for your actions. Maybe you know she is guilty and are covering up for her, or maybe she is covering up for you. Cui bono applies to you. You get Dan's job, you can run Sammy Drake out of town, and if you marry Luanne, you will get the insurance!

Luanne opens the door and Johnny is introduced to her. She tells Johnny that she feels fine now and has thought about what daddy would say. She is going to try to live her life for the future. Tom tells her that Johnny is trying to trick her to cheat her out of the policy, but Luanne tells Tom to leave and they talk alone. Johnny tells her what he has learned, and that only one person has said anything against you, and she knows that it was Sammy Drake. She tells Johnny that she saw right through him and she played along with him and Sammy took her seriously. She likes people and has had a wonderful life. She tells Johnny that going to New York was her only argument with her father. Luanne tells Johnny what had happened that night. After midnight something woke her and she saw a prowler out the window. She tried to get to the phone downstairs but heard someone at the door. She got the gun and heard someone in the house, so she shot without considering. She heard him fall and she turned on the light and saw it was daddy. Johnny asks why the phone was busy when Dan called at the depot. She says that the phone is usually off the hook at night. She asks Mary if the phone was off the hook and she says it was. Johnny thanks her and leaves. One way or another she was quite a girl; either she was an innocent girl or a cold-blooded killer.

Tomorrow, one slip of fate, and then the avalanche, and a wind up that will raise the hair on the back of your neck.

**PART 5**       **SHOW DATE:**    **2/17/1956**

Sheriff Peterson calls and asks Johnny about his talk with Luanne. Johnny tells him he is going back tomorrow and is sure the company will pay when the claim is filed. This is the first report that has ended with a question mark.

Johnny gets a 20-page report notarized and the case comes down to did she know she was shooting at her father. Johnny goes to the Happy Hollow for dinner to kill an evening. Sammy meets him ("Well wrap me up an mail me south, here's that Dollar man again") and buys Johnny a scotch. Johnny tells Sammy he is going back and Luanne will probably get the money. "Bang, bang and the little lady wins a prize. She was really shooting for new shoes that night." Johnny sees Sheriff Peterson come in, just in time. Sammy tells Johnny that Sheriff Peterson is going to replace Dan Parker in protecting him. A man asks Johnny to have a drink with him and asks what line Johnny is in. He is in "ladies ready to wear." He believes in living while you can. It can happen to anyone, like a guy named Parker he met on the train. You never know. Johnny asks the man if he had talked to Dan Parker. The man tells Johnny that they talked about his daughter, and Dan wanted him to meet her. Dan expected his daughter to be there and tried to call her at the station but could not get her so he got back on the train. He shows Johnny his tie, and takes him outside. He tells Johnny that Parker was wearing one, and he liked it so Dan gave him one. His daughter had given it to him three just the week before. In the shadows the man shows Johnny his tie, which glows in the dark.

Johnny goes back to Luanne's and he returns her loaded gun, and places it on the table. Johnny tells her he was planning to leave and asks her if she likes his necktie, it is just like the one her father was wearing. Johnny bought it from the man in the bar. It was a great setup, what with him wearing a tie that glowed in the dark. The tie he gave to a stranger is going to hang you. Luanne turns off the lights and fires at Johnny three times. The sheriff comes in and tells Luanne that the gun was loaded with blanks. Johnny gets up and Luanne screams that she was tricked, and Sheriff Peterson takes her to the jail

Remarks: When you gave me this assignment Don, you asked a question, a phrase in Latin: cui bono? Who benefits? So here is your answer; nobody.

Exp. Acct:     $382.65

## Notes:

- This story is the one that is most commonly misspelled in catalogs and books. The correct spelling of the Latin phrase is "cui bono" according to a check of three different dictionary sources.
- Roy Rowan is the announcer
- Musical supervision is by Amerigo Marino

**Producer:** Jack Johnstone          **Writers:** Les Crutchfield
**Cast:**         D. J. Thompson, Mary Jane Croft, Forrest Lewis,
                  Byron Kane, Russell Thorson, Sam Edwards, Dal McKennon,
                  Howard McNear

◆     ❖     ◆

**Show:**         The Bennet Matter
**Company:**      Four State Fire Insurance Corporation
**Agent:**        Andrew Cord
**Part 1**        **Show Date:**     2/20/1956

**Synopsis:** Andrew Cord calls and asks Johnny if he wants to go to San Francisco. Andrew tells Johnny that five companies have issued $100,000 each in fire insurance for a builder named Arnold Bennet, and his last project has burned to the ground. The total coverage is $500,000 and the experts say the fire is phony.

Johnny flies to San Francisco, California with Andrew Cord and on the plane learns that Bennet is a man who is the last of his kind, a man of many jobs and not one to let things stop him from getting what he wants. He has made Time and Life several times and has done well. Andrew tells Johnny that he does not like Bennet; maybe it is because of his roughshod nature. Andrew's man in San

Francisco believes that the fire was arson, and we have to prove it. Four State and National Fire Underwriters will be the only company investigating this. Andrew tells Johnny that Bennet is in financial trouble with taxes, and the fire is an out. Bill Underwood is the arson man in San Francisco. Bill will handle the fire, Andrew the finances and Johnny will handle Bennet. Tony is a little scared of Bennet, as no one has ever beaten him.

Johnny gets a room at the Fairmont Hotel and goes to the fire site with Andy to meet Bill, who tells them that the watchman remembers seeing a man around the site, as did three witnesses, but the police have no matches in their files. The newsboy remembers seeing the man catch a bus shortly before the fire began. Bennet has been out and does not like us snooping around the site. Bill is positive that it was set, it burnt too fast and too well. Amateurs mess up a fire; a bug sticks around and brags, but this one just disappeared. Bill tells Johnny to watch his step with Bennet; he does not care about anyone. Johnny attends a line up for the three witnesses, but no one is identified.

Next day Johnny goes to Bennet's office and meets Elizabeth Bennet, the niece of Arnold Bennet. Johnny tells her he is with the insurance company and she buzzes Arnold, who is a real pain. Bennet asks Johnny in and knows why he is there. Bennet tells Johnny the fire was deliberate and that Tony Midas set the fire. Get him and you get the arsonist. Midas worked for him once and was caught stealing money and was sent to prison. He is the one you want. Bennet knows his enemies and his friends; so don't waste his time. Tony Midas has just been released from prison. Bennet thinks that the insurance people are a bunch of hacks; now get busy! Johnny notes that he is paid very well to find out what he needs to find out, but sometimes it is not enough money.

Johnny reviews the trial of Tony Midas, and eventually the witnesses agree that Tony Midas was the man they saw, and the police issue and APB. Elizabeth Bennet calls Johnny and tells him that she will help Johnny find Tony. Come to my house in an hour. Then Bennet's lawyers calls and threatens a lawsuit. On the way to Elizabeth's Johnny meets Andy Card in a police car and they rush to Bennet's house. Andy tells Johnny that someone has shot Arnold Bennet.

Tomorrow, the trail gets so rough a couple of people just fall off dead.

### PART 2      SHOW DATE:      2/21/1956

Bill Underwood calls and Johnny tells him that Bennet has been shot. Bill tells Johnny that he has proof that the fire was set.

Bennet is taken to the hospital and given a 50/50 chance. Johnny thinks that the evidence is against Midas, even though he was in prison with a professional burner. Andy tells Johnny that Tony Midas is married to Elizabeth Bennet. Johnny tells Andy about the meeting with Elizabeth, and the address where she lives is the house where Bennet was shot.

Johnny goes to meet with Mr. Engle, the attorney who represented Tony Midas. Johnny tells him about the evidence of the arson and Engle tells Johnny that Bennet poured on the heat during the trial. Tony said he was framed, but there was no way he could win. Tony has not contacted Engle, but he would like to see him if he contacts Johnny. Johnny wants to know the real issues. What about the tax problems, and the relationship with his niece? Johnny thinks Engle can tell the real story. Engle personally thinks that Bennet framed Tony to cover the tax shortages. Tony had no experience and probably was used. Engle hopes Johnny never finds Tony or Elizabeth. But Johnny finds Tony Midas, in the county hospital, just before he is taken to the morgue. Tony had died of TB in the county hospital.

Tony turns out not to be the suspect and attention focuses on Arnold Bennet. Bill Underwood comes in with news. George Foley is in town. Foley is the best wick and celluloid man in the country if you want a building burnt down. The police spotted him in the hospital lobby trying to get to Arnold Bennet and he was tracked to an address on Barengo Street. Johnny, Bill and Andy rush to the address and talk to the police. They think Foley is trying to get money from Bennet for burning the building. Johnny decides to shake up Foley and they go it to talk to him. Johnny knocks, the door opens and there is shooting. Johnny and the others are ok and they take Foley out.

Tomorrow, we have an arsonist right in the palm of their hands, with very surprising results.

**PART 3**          **SHOW DATE:**     **2/22/1956**

Andy calls Johnny and the police have been talking to Foley all night, but he will not talk. They need to link Foley to Bennet and Johnny has an idea.

Johnny and Andy meet for a drink and they discuss the case. First it was Tony, now Foley, but who shot Arnold, the niece? She has a reason and Johnny wants to deal with her and offer her legal assistance.

Johnny cabs to Marty Engle's office and tells him to lock his door. Johnny tells him that Midas is dead, and wants to know what Engle has done. Johnny wants to know if he helped Bennet frame Tony, but Engle denies it. Johnny tells him that Elizabeth probably shot Bennet and she might be out to get you. There is a knock at the door and it is Elizabeth Bennet. Johnny tells Engle to hide and shots are fired. She runs out and Johnny shoots at her car stopping it. Johnny goes to Elizabeth who wants to know if she killed Engle who she blames for killing Tony. She tells Johnny that Arnold stole money and framed Tony. She knows he hired George Foley and tried to blame it on Tony. She knew Tony was dying the last time she saw him. She shot Bennet and tried to kill Engle. They killed Tony when they sent him to prison. She waited for five years to hold him and now he is dead, but what can we do now. She tells Johnny that nobody even looked at her until Tony, and now he is dead and she wants to die. The police finally arrive and Johnny tells them there is no problem. Elizabeth is taken to the jail where she makes a statement about Foley, shooting Bennet and trying to shoot Engle.

Johnny meets Engle in the jail and Engle tells Johnny that he is not going to press charges and wants to defend Elizabeth. Andy comes in and tells Johnny that they are going to go after Foley. Andy tells Johnny that the insurance company will pay for Elizabeth's' legal fees. Johnny catches a flight home at midnight but Andy Card calls the next morning and wants Johnny back in San Francisco. Jake

Eggelston is going to defend George Foley. Johnny remembers Andy's words that he would never get Bennet and gets the first plane out.

Tomorrow, a fight against a strong man and one of the cleverest lawyers in the country. Join us in court!

## PART 4          SHOW DATE:     2/23/1956

Andy calls Johnny in his hotel and tells Johnny that they still have not connected Bennet to Foley. The defense attorney is really slick.

Johnny flies back to San Francisco and goes to the court building. The case is going well, but Foley will not talk. The court calls Johnny as a witness. The District Attorney questions him and Johnny tells him he has been an investigator for 10 years or more, was in the Marine Corp for four years and was a Detective Sergeant 2nd grade for the New York Police. He has numerous letters of reliability from 13 insurance companies and adjustment bureaus and his police record. He was hired to conduct an investigation of the Bennet building fire. They determined it was arson based on the evidence. The method used was determined to be a woolen wick soaked with paraffin in a bag of celluloid. Johnny testifies that Foley had improvised the method and has used that method in several fires. Foley also had tried to contact Arnold Bennet and there was evidence on Foley's clothes to prove he was in the building. Johnny also testifies that Elizabeth Bennet told him that her uncle had hired Foley. Eggelston questions all of Johnny's testimony and requests that his testimony be stricken. Johnny goes to the Judge and asks to see Foley in jail with his attorney. In the jail, Johnny tells Foley that he will give him a break if he cooperates. The jury will throw the book at Foley, but they want Bennet. Tell them Bennet hired you and plead for mercy and save five years on the sentence. Foley risks going with the jury and tells Johnny he would like to kill him when he is set free.

Tomorrow, a verdict in and out of a courtroom. The wind up.

## SYNOPSIS:
## PART 5          SHOW DATE:     2/24/1956

Andy calls and Johnny tells him about meeting with Foley. Andy tells Johnny that the jury is coming back in.

Johnny calls the hospital and learns that Bennet is recovering. The jury comes in and they give the verdict: guilty as charged. Foley calls for Johnny to see him, as he has some things to tell him. Johnny goes to see Foley with Andy and he wants information. Johnny tells Foley that Bennet is in the hospital and Foley is in jail. Johnny tells him that they can get Bennet, and his conviction is the lever. Foley hates Bennet getting away with things. Foley tells them that Bennet hired him and paid him $2,500 to burn the building and that he could blame Tony Midas. A friend told him to contact Bennet and he called him. Bennet wanted the building burned and offered him $1,000. They haggled and settled on $2,500. Bennet left the money at the check stand in the bus terminal. Foley went to see Bennet to shake him down for more money. Foley finally admits meeting Bennet in his car on Market Street on the night the building was torched. Johnny doubts Foley's story and continues questioning him.

Johnny returns the next day to continue questioning Foley. Foley finally admits Bennet met him and paid him after the building was on fire. All this was done on one night. Johnny feels Foley is trying to make him question his sanity. Andy brings in the medical finding and Johnny tells him he is sane. Foley finally breaks down and admits he met Bennet a month before the fire. He knew Bennet was in trouble and would need a fire. Foley made the proposition and Bennet liked the idea. Bennet paid Foley $3,500 and he did the job and Foley buried the money in a can in a vacant lot and will take Johnny there.

Foley is sentenced and Bennet is charged, but he dies in the hospital. In a way you can still say that no one ever beat Arnold Bennet. He beat himself.

Exp. Acct:     $1,140.37

## NOTES:

- **REMAKE OF THE ELLIOTT CHAMPION MATTER—12/12/1952**
- **JOHNNY DOLLAR'S HISTORY: 10 YRS PLUS AS AN INVESTIGATOR, 4 YEARS IN THE MARINES, DETECTIVE SGT. 2ND GRADE, NYPD**
- **ROY ROWAN IS THE ANNOUNCER**
- **MUSICAL SUPERVISION IS BY AMERIGO MARINO**

Producer:    Jack Johnstone          Writers:    John Dawson
Cast:           Lillian Buyeff, Stacy Harris, Chet Stratton, Will Wright, Marvin Miller, Hans Conried, Edgar Barrier, Parley Baer

◆　❖　◆

SHOW:            THE FATHOM FIVE MATTER
COMPANY:       DELTA LIABILITY
AGENT:           RALPH STEEDLER
PART 1            SHOW DATE:      2/27/1956

SYNOPSIS: Ralph Steedler calls and greets Johnny with poetry from the Bard; "Full fathom five thy father lies; Of his bones are coral made; Those are pearls that were his eyes." Ralph has $75,000 in insurance lying at the bottom of the ocean, so they say. It happened in Miami Beach, check with the DA there. The insured was William Markey and the wife was the beneficiary.

Johnny goes to Miami, Florida to check in to the death of William Markey. At the DA's office, Barney Wilson is also confused. They are presuming that he is dead, but it has not been proved. Johnny knows little about the case. The dead man is William Markey, who owned a consulting engineering firm in New York. They have been here a month and he was supposedly drowned two days ago. Barney tells Johnny that Markey came to bid on a job, and that he and brought his wife and a young fellow named Danny Haines, a friend. They rented a house and three days ago Markey and Danny went fishing and rented the cruiser Fathom Five. They were anchored off a reef and were fishing from a dinghy. Danny took Markey back to the boat so he could fix breakfast, and later noticed that the boat was on fire. Danny could not get back on the boat and it sank a few minutes later. It was foggy and there were no other boats in the area, so Haines rowed back to shore and reported the accident. A salvage company is working on getting the boat up and the currents in the area are dangerous. It would be possible to swim back, and maybe Haines was lying. Maybe the boat will be raised or the body will show up. Barney wants the body declared dead to charge Haines with murder. Johnny gets the addresses for Mrs. Markey and Haines.

Johnny wires Hartford for an investigation of Markey. Johnny cabs to talk to Danny Haines. Danny tells Johnny that he has told the police the whole story, so go see them. Johnny tells Danny that Barney Wilson's mind is made up, but his is not. Danny tells Johnny that he had worked with Markey for several years and they socialized some. Edna, um Mrs. Markey suggested that Danny come along. Markey suggested that they stay and Danny was getting a free vacation. Markey and his wife were getting along ok. Markey suggested the fishing trip and he called Danny at 5:00 AM and went out. They went out to the reef and Markey went back to fix breakfast. Danny saw the flames through the fog, and the cruiser sank. Danny tells Johnny that the gasoline hotplate may have caused the fire as it was in bad shape. Johnny asks if Markey could have committed suicide. Danny gets angry when Johnny suggests that maybe he and the wife were more than just friends.

Tomorrow, a lady weeps, a lover curses, and a strange grim relic is brought up from the sea.

## PART 2       SHOW DATE:       2/28/1956

Barney Wilson calls and understands that Johnny has talked to Danny. Johnny bets 6 to 5 that Danny did not do it. Barney tells Johnny that the boat should be raised around 8:00, so meet him at the Harbor Police at 7:30.

Johnny cabs to the house of Mrs. Markey, who is a very beautiful woman. She is shocked over the death of her husband and does not know about the papers. Johnny tells her there are no papers, as he is an investigator and needs details from her. Johnny wants to know about her husband's mental attitude, and she gets huffy. Johnny needs the questions answered for the claims board. She tells Johnny that Bill was not the type to kill himself. She offers Johnny a drink and Johnny fixes a scotch on the rocks and she tells him that they were very happy. She did not know anything of the finances and she had worked as a dancer. Her husband was all for Danny coming on the trip, and did not show any resentment. She never saw any brooding from her husband. Danny only saw her as a friend. Johnny tells her that her husband supposedly died, and the insurance company will not pay until the body is found, or Johnny finds sufficient evidence of death. The police are going to fight for an immediate court decision, but we will fight it. Johnny tells her that her husband either died from an accident, suicide or murder, but no insurance will be paid until one of the causes is proved.

Johnny leaves and notices a man watching the house. He drives off as Johnny approaches him. Johnny gets the last three numbers of the plate—642.

Johnny cabs to the harbor police and meets Barney. They take a boat out to the wreck and Johnny tells him that he has not taken a position yet, but the insurance company will block any motions. Barney tells Johnny that the police found a shoe belonging to Markey on the beach. Johnny asks Barney to check the plate number he saw. At the wreck site the boat is brought up and the hull is undamaged. Johnny and Barney both spot a solid column of water from the hull. Barney declares that the seacocks were left opened. The boat was sunk deliberately and Markey was murdered.

Tomorrow, a photograph, a silver cup, a harried widow and the dead begin to stir with life.

## PART 3       SHOW DATE:     2/29/1956

Barney calls and asks if Johnny is on an expense account. So how about buying me lunch. Barney tells Johnny that he has a lead on the car tags. They were bought by John Smith but the address was an empty lot.

Johnny buys lunch for Barney Wilson and they discuss the case and the lack of the body. Barney feels that it is an old story; two men go out and only one comes back and that spells murder. Barney feels that the Markeys took a liking to Danny who then took a liking to the wife. He made a nuisance of himself and then Markey noticed that Haines needed straightening out. He took him out to talk to him and Haines knocked him out and threw Markey overboard and sank the boat and rowed ashore. Johnny feels the insurance is the key. Johnny is sure that it is fraud and Danny is the fall guy. Johnny tells Barney that he got a long wire from New York and learns that Markey is in financial trouble and has been living too high. Johnny thinks Markey fired the boat, swam ashore and is waiting for the wife to collect the insurance. The wife is acting too tense and is afraid she will say the wrong thing. The harbormaster has told Johnny that it is 1-in-100 that the body would go out to sea. Johnny has also arranged for counsel to fight any court actions.

Johnny calls Mrs. Markey and asks for a photo of her husband. She does not think she has one but Johnny remembers seeing one on a table. Johnny sends a messenger out to pick up the photo and then goes to see "Truthful Tom," the dealer who sold the car to John Smith. Tom is a typical used car salesman. Johnny tells him it looks like a car stolen from a friend, but Tom tells Johnny that he has papers on all his cars. Johnny tells him he is an investigator, but Tom is adamant about his honesty. Tom does not remember John Smith, but remembers the car. The man paid cash, long green mazoola. Johnny shows him a picture of Markey and Tom tells Johnny that he was the man who bought the car.

Johnny goes back to Mrs. Markey and returns the photo. Johnny tells her about the purchase of the car two weeks before his supposed death. Johnny tells her that it was not a smart scheme and that she must be pretty expensive to support and that she is one step away from prison. If you file a claim we will hit you with both barrels so talk to your husband before you do anything. If you want to convince me, show me his body.

Tomorrow, a crazy kid in love, a right decision by a court and then the whole case smashed wide open.

## PART 4          SHOW DATE:     3/1/1956

A call comes in for Johnny from Barney. He tells Johnny that the police are looking for the car and that the court will meet tomorrow at ten. See you there.

Johnny phones the insurance company legal department and then rejoins Mrs. Markey, who is nervous and pacing the floor. Johnny tells her that he has some facts to back up his ideas. Johnny tells her that attempted fraud is not a scheme to get out of paying the policy. Johnny outlines that her husband is broke, that he saw a chance to pull a swindle with the policy and that they worked it out together. He bought a car and has a room somewhere and was waiting for a foggy day. You played Haines along and your husband took the boat out, sank it, swam back to his car and drove off. When she doubts that her husband, or any one could swim back to shore, Johnny tells her that his report included information that Markey is a champion swimmer. Johnny tells her that the proof will come if she files a claim. The doorbell rings and Johnny muses that she wants to end the case. Mrs. Markey returns and tells Johnny the doorbell was someone looking for an address.

Johnny leaves and determines that the visitor was someone she did not want Johnny to know about. Johnny goes to see Danny Haines, who tells Johnny that he was reading and had been there all evening. Danny tells Johnny that Mrs. Markey told him how Johnny talked to her, and she has had too much of that kind of trouble from Markey. She told him about it, and Danny almost felt like hitting Markey. Danny tells Johnny that if Markey is doing something, he is doing it alone. Mrs. Markey is a swell girl and he would die for her.

Johnny goes to the court and meets with a local attorney for the insurance company. The hearing is swift and informal, and the judge rules that requests for a ruling must be unquestionable, and the evidence indicates that William Markey is possibly still alive so the court will not declare William Markey dead. Barney tells Johnny that he hates to see Danny get away with murder. Barney gets a message and tells Johnny that the coast patrol has just pulled a body from the ocean. A quick check of the prints showed it was William Markey.

Tomorrow, a dead man tells a tale, but not the tale he was meant to tell, and thereby hangs the windup.

## PART 5          SHOW DATE:     3/2/1956

Barney calls and tells Johnny that he was over confidant, and now has to apologize to Mrs. Markey. Barney tells Johnny not to be too hasty. Barney tells Johnny that he does not know what this case is. If you want to lose you mind, come over to the morgue.

Johnny cabs to the morgue to meet Barney. Barney shows Johnny the body and they are convinced it is Markey, but Johnny notices that the body does not show any signs of decomposition. The autopsy also showed that the body was only dead since last night and that Markey was alive after the sinking. He died of drowning, but the body was wearing two shoes. Also, Markey was drowned in fresh water. Barney wants to know who killed him and they both go to see Danny Haines.

At Danny's room Johnny learns that Danny is not in and had been gone most of the day. The room is searched and nothing is found. Back in his room Johnny gets a call from Barney. The car has been found in front of an apartment building. Barney picks up Johnny and they go to the apartment building. The manager tells them that he rented an apartment two weeks ago to Mr. Jones who did not stay in the apartment for the first several nights. He went out last night and did not come back. A young friend brought the car back an hour ago and he is in the apartment now, packing Mr. Jones' clothes for a trip. Barney and Johnny go up to the apartment and knock on the door. Barney calls to Danny and he shoots. They hear breaking glass and break in to find that Danny had run down the fire escape and shoots back at them. Barney warns Danny to surrender and after being shot at, Barney shoots him. "Well, he did say he would die for her, and it came to that." Barney and Johnny drive to the Markey house, force their way in and find evidence of a struggle, water in the tub and a wet dressing gown in the closet. Johnny goes to his hotel room and finds Mrs. Markey there. She tells Johnny that she heard that the police are looking for Danny and she wants to know what is happening. Johnny tells her to go to her house and talk to Wilson. Johnny tells her it was her husband, not Haines who came last night. Johnny gave her the idea to drown her husband and Danny helped her. She tells Johnny that she will get the best lawyer money can buy, but Johnny tells her there will be no money. The policy was already void when she and Haines killed her husband last night. It ended five days ago when he sank the boat. You lost your husband, your boyfriend your insurance claim and maybe your life.

Remarks: You quoted a line of Shakespeare at the start of this case, Ralph: "Full fathom five your father lies." Well you are wrong. It turns out to be the widow who lies, and lies and lies.

Exp. Acct:      $684.95

NOTES:
- FROM THE TEMPEST, ACT I, SCENE II: "FULL FATHOM FIVE THY FATHER LIES; OF HIS BONES ARE CORAL MADE; THOSE ARE PEARLS THAT WERE HIS EYES: NOTHING OF HIM THAT DOTH FADE BUT DOTH SUFFER A SEA-CHANGE INTO SOMETHING RICH AND STRANGE."
- ROY ROWAN IS THE ANNOUNCER
- MUSICAL SUPERVISION IS BY AMERIGO MARINO

Producer:    Jack Johnstone          Writers:    Les Crutchfield

Cast:    **Mary Jane Croft, Barney Phillips, Carlton Young, Eleanor Audley, Sam Edwards, Shep Menken, John Dehner**

◆    ❖    ◆

SHOW:    THE PLANTAGENT MATTER
COMPANY:    EASTERN SEABOARD CASUALTY INSURANCE COMPANY
AGENT:
PART 1    SHOW DATE:    3/5/1956

SYNOPSIS: Mr. Costello from the Plantagent Hotel calls. Johnny tells him that he is coming to investigate the burglary at the hotel after the weather clears.

Johnny travels to Vicksburg, Virginia and then to the Plantagent Hotel. Johnny learns that the case has been solved and the goods have been recovered. Johnny arranges for return travel and goes out for a walk. In the parking lot Johnny overhears a couple arguing, and the woman pleads for help. The man tells Johnny that the woman has had too much to drink and he tries to punch Johnny, who gets the best of him. The man walks off and tells Amy that he was only trying to beat some sense into her and leaves Amy and Johnny in the parking lot. Amy starts to cry and tells Johnny she had only one drink. Johnny buys her a drink in the hotel and they talk. Johnny tries to tell a joke and she thanks him for not asking about her or her troubles and gets up to leave. Johnny helps her get a cab and tells her to call him if she needs any help. The girl gets into the cab and suddenly gasps in pain. She says she didn't think he . . . and Johnny tells the cab to rush to the hospital. The girl is taken into the emergency room and Johnny waits, and waits, and waits. Finally the doctor asks Johnny to come to his office where there are two doctors and a nurse. Johnny tells the doctor what happened and the doctor wants Johnny to complete some papers and tells Johnny that the girl is dead. Johnny is confused and asks, "Under the circumstances, what would you do?"

Tomorrow, how can you help a dead girl? Somebody had to help her, and guess who?

**PART 2    SHOW DATE:    3/6/1956**

Johnny receives a call from Jim Akens of the Vicksburg police. Jim is sending a car to pick him up. They have some questions to ask him and tells Johnny that they have not identified her yet, she is just Jane Doe.

Johnny buys a paper and reads about the mysterious girl when Jim Akens meets him in the lobby. Johnny tells him who he is and about the burglary case, and shows him his identification. Johnny tells Jim how he met the girl, and what happened. Johnny tells Jim that he does not know the girl's name or the man's name. Johnny goes downtown with Lt. Akens and gives him a statement. In the morgue, Johnny identifies the girl's body. Lt. Akens asks about the girl and tells Johnny that no one seems to know the girl. All the girl's clothes were standard, and she is probably a local girl, but no one has reported her missing. Lt. Akens tells Johnny that the girls' purse is missing and wonders why Johnny did not notice the man's car. Lt. Akens gets a phone call and Johnny seems to be drawn to the dead girl. Lt. Akens tells Johnny that the lab had called and told him that a drug called perimythol killed her. It had been in her system for an hour before it killed her. Lt. Akens thinks it was suicide, but Johnny disagrees. Johnny packs and makes arrangements to leave. Johnny gets a drink and asks the bartender about the previous night, but he does not remember anything. Johnny tells him that a lady lost her purse, but none has been turned in. The bartender tells Johnny that the police had been in talking about the girl. Johnny searches the booth where he had sat and then goes to the parking lot. Johnny asks if a purse had been turned in, and then searches the lot where the attendant finds a purse under a car. Johnny looks into the green suede purse and finds no identification, but a .32 automatic that had been recently fired.

Tomorrow, a dead girls' .38 automatic comes to life.

## PART 3          SHOW DATE:     3/7/1956

The operator calls with Johnny's call and Johnny calls the police and needs information about a gun. Johnny is told to come to the licensing division and bring the gun with him.

Johnny cabs to the city hall and gets the ownership information on the girl's gun. The serial number of the Colt .38 automatic is "JJJ-4769992 X." Johnny fills out a form and the clerk searches for the information. Johnny learns that the gun was purchased by the Piedmont Banking Service in 1950, and was licensed to Raymond W. O'Connell on Polk Street. Johnny muses over talking to Lt. Akens but rents a car and drives to the Polk street address. A woman expecting Paul meets Johnny at the door. Johnny asks for Raymond O'Connell and the woman asks him in. She is Terri O'Connell, Ray's widow; he died of pneumonia a year ago. She tells Johnny that a lot of his friends from the service come by to see him. While they talk, Johnny sees a picture of the man he had met in the parking lot. Terri tells Johnny that he is Paul Dameron. She had met Paul after trying to kill herself, and they are going to be married. Terri asks Johnny to have dinner with her and Paul, but Johnny declines.

Johnny leaves and reads the paper with the girls picture on the front page. Paul Dameron arrives and Johnny stops him on the sidewalk and asks who the girl in the parking lot was. Paul tells him the girl was Amy Durand and that she works in the same office he does. Terri is Amy's sister. Johnny tells Paul of the drink and the trip to the hospital and Paul is shocked. Johnny shows him the paper and he tells Johnny that he did not think she was that desperate, he had no idea she would do it. Paul apologizes and asks Johnny to call him later.

Johnny takes the gun to Lt. Akens, but he is away working on a homicide. Johnny is told that some guy named Belden was shot three times with a .38.

Tomorrow, information about the gun that blows the case sky high.

## PART 4          SHOW DATE:     3/8/1956

Mr. Olfield calls and Johnny tells him he needs an attorney. Johnny wants him to take a statement and give some advice.

Johnny buys coffee and waits for Samuel W. Olfield, a local Attorney. Mr. Olfield arrives and Johnny tells him who he is, about the girl and about how he came into possession of the gun with three missing shells. Johnny tells him that he did not turn in the gun because he thought he could help the girl. Mr. Olfield tells Johnny that a statement might help protect him. They go to the office and Johnny completes a statement.

Johnny goes to see Lt. Akens and asks about the Belden case. Johnny is told that they are sure Belden was shot with a .38, and that Belden was an auditor who had found a shortage in the books of a textile wholesalers and the chief accountant is missing, Miss Amy Durand. Lt. Akens thinks it is apparent that Amy killed the auditor, but Johnny does not want the case closed yet. Johnny goes to see Terri O'Connell and she tells Johnny that her sister is dead and that Paul had gone to identify the body. Johnny tells her who he is and how he met Amy and took her to the hospital. Johnny got her address from the gun in Amy's purse. Johnny tells her about the murder of Belden, and Terri recognizes the name. Johnny tells her that the police have the evidence to show that Amy stole $10,000 from the textile firm. They have evidence of suicide but Johnny wants to help Amy because she was not a thief or a suicidal type. Terri tells Johnny that Amy saved her from a suicide attempt, and was always kind and decent and good. Amy had introduced her to Paul, and had bought things for her. She must have stolen the money for her.

Tomorrow, all the evidence comes true. A helpless dead girl gets her help.

## PART 5      SHOW DATE:     3/9/1956

Paul Dameron calls and wants to talk to Johnny and thanks him for Amy and Mrs. O'Connell. He tells Johnny that the papers have connected her to Amy. Johnny tells Paul that he has the gun and cannot believe Amy would shoot a man and then take poison.

Johnny gets Sam Olfield to prepare a statement and they go to the police to turn in the gun. Lt. Akens gets the gun and the statement. After an hour, Lt. Akens tells Johnny that the gun was the murder weapon, but Johnny did not need the lawyer, as no charges will be filed. He has the killer and the motive and the reason. Mr. Olfield leaves and Lt. Akens talks to Johnny and tells him that there is a bottle of perimythol in Amy Durand's medicine cabinet. Lt. Akens tells Johnny that he was a cop once and should have known better than to withhold evidence, and Lt. Akens will not be so generous the next time Johnny comes to town. Lt. Akens gets a call and starts to leave and tells Johnny that Amy had a good motive. Paul Dameron meets them in the hallway and tells them that he and Amy were arguing and he had just discovered the shortage in the accounts, but not of killing the auditor. Paul offers Johnny a check for his kindness and Johnny refuses. Lt. Akens tells Johnny of finding a certified check in Amy's apartment from a New York bank. Johnny tells him that any reasonable bank or auditor would want restitution, so why kill the auditor with a check in her hand.

Johnny interviews people who had known the auditor, and learns he was the type who would have listened to Amy and accepted repayment. So why did she shoot him and then commit suicide?

Johnny goes to visit Dameron and tells him the case is not closed yet. Dameron tells Johnny that he did not know about the check. Johnny thinks that Amy borrowed the money to cover for someone else, you. The auditor was smart and found out who took the money. He called you over to ask you about it and about repayment and you killed him. You fixed the papers to make it look like Amy stole the money. Amy was going to repay the money because you meant something to Terri; a woman who tried to kill herself once, and might do it again if she found out the man she was going to marry was a thief. You killed the auditor and then took Amy out and poisoned her. You could have fought me in the parking lot, but you had to get back and plant the poison in Amy's apartment. Paul attacks Johnny and they fight. Johnny beats Paul and forces him to call the police.

Exp. Acct:     $702.13

NOTES:
- AT THE END OF PART TWO THERE SEEMS TO BE SOME CONFUSION OVER THE CALIBER OF THE GIRL'S GUN; FIRST IT IS A .32, THEN A .38.
- DRINKS ARE $1.00 EACH AT THE HOTEL BAR.
- WHILE THIS CASE IS DIRECTED TO THE INSURANCE COMPANY AT THE BEGINNING, THE LATER EPISODES ARE TO JOHNNY, INDICATING THAT HE IS FOOTING THE BILL ON THIS ONE.
- THIS STORY WAS DONE AS THE NEW CAMBRIDGE MATTER ON 12/19/1952
- ROY ROWAN IS THE ANNOUNCER
- MUSICAL SUPERVISION IS BY AMERIGO MARINO

Producer:     Jack Johnstone          Writers:    John Dawson
Cast:         Michael Ann Barrett, Jeanne Bates, Marvin Miller,
              Frank Gerstle, Lawrence Dobkin, Jack Kruschen, Ken Peters,
              Herb Butterfield

◆    ❖    ◆

SHOW:       THE CLINTON MATTER
COMPANY:    UNITED ADJUSTMENT BUREAU
AGENT:      AL DAVIES
PART 1      SHOW DATE:     3/12/1956
SYNOPSIS: Johnny gets a Western Union message from the United Adjustment Bureau in New York to proceed to the Northern Hotel in Clinton, Colorado ASAP. Building irregularities suspected affecting several insurance companies. Johnny replies that he is on his way.

Johnny flies to Denver and then to Grand Junction where he rents a car to Clinton and drives to Clinton, a sleepy mountain town. Johnny arrives as the school building is burning. Johnny assists in fighting the fire and then goes to his hotel where he has a message. Albert Davies calls and Johnny tells him of the fire. Al asks if Julian Osborne has contacted Johnny yet. He feels that the school building is in bad shape. Johnny tells Al that the school is was burned down.

Johnny checks the local phone directory for Julian Osborne. The desk clerk tells Johnny that Osborne had been burned to death in the fire. Johnny walks to the Sheriff's office and meets Paul Daugherty, who is friendly until Johnny mentions Osborne. Johnny is told that Julian was the school janitor and Johnny tells the sheriff that Osborne had reported something wrong with the school to the insurance company. Daugherty tells Johnny that the body is in the morgue, but Osborne has no family or friends. He was the janitor of the school, and Florrie Hawkins hired him, and it is a bad night to go calling.

Johnny visits Miss Hawkins and she is thankful that school was not in session. Florrie gets a phone call from the sheriff while Johnny is there and suddenly and she cannot help Johnny and he must go as she is tired. Johnny is sure the phone call wore her out and he tells her about the report of building problems. She tells Johnny that Julian probably imagined things. Johnny tells her that if the sheriff calls again, he is in the Northern Hotel.

Johnny calls Al Davies, updates him and is told to stay around. Johnny visits the school ruins and on the way back to the hotel sees several men beating another man in an alley and Johnny chases them off. The man tells Johnny that he is David Baines and that he architected the school. The men beating him thought he was a bad architect. Johnny takes him to his room and fixes him up and tells him why he is in town. Baines tells Johnny that he designed the building, and before the building was built Roy Vickery sent him to Europe to study. Roy is the contractor who built the school, but you are wasting your time in Clinton. This is a tight, hot, mean little burg and you will not find out anything here.

Tomorrow, there is a lot if information to be had in a town that will not talk. And there are times when the silence screams all over the place.

**PART 2**      **SHOW DATE:**      **3/13/1956**

David Baines calls Johnny and tells him that he is staying off the streets and advises Johnny to do the same. Johnny tells him that the town has filed claim and Johnny must stay to investigate. Johnny tells David that he expects help from him.

Johnny wires Dodd and Company to request copies of the insurance policies. The newspaper blames the fire on overheated boilers.

Johnny visits the fire chief and is told that Julian passed out and the boilers exploded and that is that. He did not build the building and does not know why it spread, or why the boilers were on when school was not in session. Johnny tells him he will get his information one way or another, but the chief cannot hear him. Johnny and Baines have breakfast and Johnny asks for information and David tells him that the town is the playground of Vickery, Handley and Daugherty. Vickery is a builder with a million dollars and a million angles. Fire Chief Handley is a friend of Vickery and Daugherty keeps the law for Vickery.

Baines tells Johnny that the boilers had automatic shutoff mechanisms. They used the exterior plans Baines had drawn, but made up the rest as they went along. Baines tells Johnny that a delegation of townspeople has gone out to get an explanation from Vickery. Johnny goes to see Vickery and finds the police are guarding the house, and Daugherty warns Johnny to watch his step. Johnny wants to see Vickery and Daugherty tells him no one is seeing Vickery. Johnny shouts to the angry crowd that he is an investigator and is looking in to the fire and that the Sheriff will not let him go in. Johnny asks Daugherty again, and he is let in. Johnny meets Vickery, a big man in a blue suit who complements Johnny on how he handles the sheriff. Johnny wants to know about the building and Vickery tells Johnny that the civic building committee has just met and cannot find anything wrong, and that they will rebuild with the insurance money. Johnny asks for and gets a copy of the building specifications from Vickery.

Johnny and Baines go over the specifications, and they are just what Baines had specified. Johnny wants him to make a sworn statement but Baines tells Johnny that Vickery would kill him. And they will kill Johnny if he goes too far.

Roy Vickery calls and Johnny tells him he thinks the specifications are fakes. Johnny tells him he will stay and Vickery tells him to get out of town, NOW!

Tomorrow, a lady who promises to love honor and obey a building inspector but wound up a widow.

**PART 3**          **SHOW DATE:**          **3/14/1956**

Florrie Hawkins calls and wants to talk. She asks Johnny to meet her for cocktails at the Traders Inn, outside of town. She has heard of how he is not frightened of anyone, and she is sick of how things have been done.

Johnny buys dinner and waits for Florrie, who shows up late. She tells Johnny that she does not want to be seen by any of Daugherty's friends. He had called and warned her the night before. She tells Johnny that she knew Osborne had written the insurance company, and everyone knew the building was not up to specifications. She is willing to help Johnny. Johnny is sure that if she and Baines will help, others will come forward as well. She knows that 1,400 students could have been in the school. Florrie suggests that the building inspector, Richard Hobb might help. He is a decent man and might help. Johnny tells Florrie to give him a statement and then to fly to Denver. She gives Johnny a statement at the Inn and then Johnny takes her to the airport. Johnny wires a friend in Denver and asks him to watch over Florrie. Johnny calls Baines and asks for a statement and he agrees, but he will not hide in Denver. Baines gives Johnny the statement and Johnny mails it to himself at the hotel. Johnny calls Daugherty, Handley and Vickery about the statements, but they all laugh.

Johnny goes to the home of Richard Hobb, but he is not home, and his wife wants company. Johnny notices that she is slightly drunk and that Hobb has moved out, as there is nothing of his there, "When did he leave?" Johnny asks. She tells Johnny that he left during the fire. Johnny senses that she is scared and tells her to have Hobb contact Johnny.

As Johnny is leaving Vickery drives up. "She is a lovely girl, isn't she?" Vickery tells Johnny. Johnny feels he has been ordered out of town because he was going to ask some embarrassing questions. Vickery tells Johnny that he should stop while he is ahead.

Johnny calls Al Davies and tells him that the case is a mess and that he cannot expect any help from the town. Al tells Johnny that he will send help. Johnny goes to bed and a man breaks through his door calling his name. When the man collapses, Johnny sees three bullet holes in Richard Hobb's body.

Tomorrow, the town of Clinton begins to fall apart, and it takes a lot of work to pick up the pieces.

## PART 4        SHOW DATE:        3/15/1956

Al Davis calls and help is on the way and should be there soon. Johnny tells Al of Richard Hobb's murder. Al tells Johnny to be careful until we get there.

As Johnny gets his breakfast sheriff Daugherty enters his room and asks for a cup of coffee. Daugherty tells Johnny that he almost held him for murder, but he is not getting anywhere. They want to find out all they can and asks Johnny "why do you think he came to your room?" Johnny tells him that maybe his conscious told him to come and talk about a substandard building. Daugherty tells Johnny to keep out of his way and he will keep out of Johnny's.

Two hours later Al Davies shows up with help: Toby O'Brien from Continental States Insurance, Rob Schwartz and the Mix twins from Columbia Adjustment, Todd Weaver fresh from a case for Canadian Adjusters, Lou Donniger and Thad Thomas from Chicago—all experienced investigators. Johnny briefs everyone on the case and gives out assignments. Toby and Thad will look into Hobbs. Rob and Toby will look into Vickery. Jim and Al Mix will look into Julian Osborne. Lou will take Fire Chief Handley. Al will handle the Sheriff. Everyone else just spread out. Johnny wants statements and will offer protection to anyone who wants it. Don't push anyone, but don't be pushed around. Johnny knew the eight men would be conspicuous.

Johnny gets a call from a man and is told he wants to talk. Earl Kennedy will pick Johnny up down stairs. After ten minutes a car drives up with five men and Johnny gets in. They drive out of town and Earl, construction foreman on the school, introduces the men; most of who worked on the construction project and Frank Gibson the newspaper editor. They have seen the men Johnny brought into town are all willing to make statements. Earl can prove they shortchanged the town during construction, and Frank tells Johnny that the paper is at his disposal, as long as what he prints is the truth. The men are all willing to testify. Johnny is told that Hobb had big ideas and played ball with Vickery, who was born in Clinton and has built most of the town. Johnny is told that Vickery is the only person who would have the purchase orders, but Johnny will not get them. Johnny and the men go to the newspaper office to give their statements.

Al Davies meets Johnny in his room and shows Johnny seven men outside the hotel. There is a knock at the door and Daugherty yells at Al for bringing in troublemakers. Al is told that the men outside are indignant citizens. Daugherty wants Al's men withdrawn by sundown or they will suffer the consequences. Johnny tells Daugherty that his agents are armed and will not be intimidated. Johnny also demands that Daugherty resign by sundown or he will force him out of office. Johnny shows him the statements and Daugherty tries to attack Johnny and tells him "I'll kill you, Dollar!"

Tomorrow, the end and the beginning of Clinton, Colorado. It all happens when the smoke clears.

## PART 5      SHOW DATE:     3/16/1956

Toby O'Brien calls and he has heard about the run in with Daugherty. Toby has discovered that Hobbs got paid off after his inspections to the amount of $20,000.

Johnny gets photocopies of the deposits to Hobb's account and Al tells him the town is running scared. Al is told to mail the photocopies to the home office.

Johnny drives to Hobb's house and the wife meets Johnny in a slinky black dress and a glass of bourbon. She is "broken up" but cannot cry about Richard. She does not know about any money, but she suspects he spent it on other women. They both wanted more excitement than his salary could offer and she suspects that Vickery gave him the money. She tells Johnny that she has no insurance and needs money if she is forced to leave because she talked. She wants a $2000 endowment policy and Johnny tells her he will arrange it. She tells Johnny that Richard got the money from the Clinton Gravel Company. He came back last night and told her that Vickery was going to make a patsy out of him and that he was going to see you. Johnny remembers that Vickery was outside the house when he left, and he might have killed Hobbs himself.

Johnny goes to the hotel and meets Baines, who has a bottle of bourbon in his hand. He tells Johnny about a law allowing one crime to be committed to prevent another crime. He tells Johnny that he has committed two crimes. He disappointed his honor, and he engineered a theft; he got Vickery's secretary to steal the original purchase orders from Roy Vickery's office. Johnny mails the papers to a broker in Denver and 14 hours later Johnny gets a reply that the materials used were not passable, and the insurance company will not pay. Toby calls with two witnesses to Hobb's killing and tells Johnny that Vickery did it himself. In the afternoon newspaper is a story about the investigation naming Vickery, Daugherty and Hanley.

Johnny has a visit from Deputy Eagan and several others who jump Johnny and take him outside. On the street Johnny sees several of his agents coming and calls for help. They jump the deputies and take them to his room where Eagan tells Johnny that Vickery wanted him taken to the Gravel plant.

Johnny drives to the gravel plant and sees several cars there. The exits are covered and Toby goes in with Johnny. They hear shots and run in and find Vickery shot and Handley dead. Toby spots Daugherty on the back stairs and Johnny follows him. While Toby gets the others to block the doors, Daugherty surprises Johnny and tells Johnny that he will kill him, but Toby rushes in and shoots Daugherty. Daugherty's last words are about the falling out among

thieves. Vickery survives and is charged with 28 counts of murder and conspiracy.
   Exp. Acct:    $2,385.03

NOTES:
- REMAKE OF THE STORY OF THE BIG RED SCHOOLHOUSE—4/4/50
- IN PART 4, AL DAVIES TELLS THE SHERIFF THAT HE BROUGHT EIGHT AGENTS WITH HIM FOR A TOTAL OF NINE, BUT JOHNNY ONLY LISTS SEVEN IN PART 3, WHICH WITH AL MAKES EIGHT. THERE WAS ALSO A MIX-UP IN THE AGENT COUNT IN THE STORY OF THE RED SCHOOL HOUSE.
- ROY ROWAN IS THE ANNOUNCER
- MUSIC SUPERVISION IS BY AMERIGO MARINO

**Producer:**    Jack Johnstone        **Writers:**    John Dawson
**Cast:**    Jeanette Nolan, Lucille Meredith, Carlton Young, Herb Ellis, Jack Petruzzi, Bob Bruce, Herb Butterfield, Paul Richards, Edgar Barrier, Russell Thorson, Jack Moyles, Frank Gerstle

◆  ❖  ◆

**SHOW:**    THE JOLLY ROGER FRAUD MATTER
**COMPANY:**    UNIVERSAL ADJUSTMENT BUREAU
**AGENT:**    PAT MCCRACKEN
**PART 1**    **SHOW DATE:**    3/19/1956

SYNOPSIS: Pat McCracken calls with a case, but Johnny is going out on vacation in La Jolla California. Pat tells Johnny that there is enough commission to pay for two vacations, just come down to my office. OK, (sucker).

   Johnny cabs to Pat's office and prepares to argue his way out of the case. Pat is sure Johnny will solve the case in a couple days and will put the whole vacation on the old swindle sheet, plus there is the commission. Pat tells Johnny that the Jolly Roger was insured for $460,000 and Bert Parker in San Diego has the details. He gave you the Molly K Matter, and that was quite profitable, wasn't it? The boat is a floating palace with a wooden hull, which is why she burned to the water line and sank. Pat has told Bert that Johnny is on the way and has notified the Mexican Authorities. Pat grabs Johnny's bags and tells him about the case on the way down the elevator. Pat tells Johnny that the diesel yacht Jolly Roger is owned by Paulus Zanagian, an ex rumrunner, gunrunner, ship builder and suspected spy in both wars. Johnny cannot argue with Pat, so he takes on the case.

   Johnny lands in San Diego, California and is met by Jan Penny, Bert's secretary, who is going to work on the case with Johnny. Penny tells Johnny that Bert is in the hospital, the victim of a hit-and-run. Penny tells Johnny that Bert thinks he was hit deliberately. Johnny visits Bert in the hospital and he tells Johnny that he knows he is dying and that he knows he was run down. Bert tells Johnny that he had gotten threatening calls about holding up the claims on the Jolly Roger. Bert tells Johnny to drop the case and is wracked with pain and dies three hours later.

Johnny takes Penny to Ray Kemper's Cat Club to help drown their sorrows. Penny tells Johnny that she came to California to be in pictures, but did not like the life style and then she met Bert who hired her. She loved Bert for being a nice guy. Penny is glad that Johnny is a straight guy, like Bert. Johnny has two jobs now, the Jolly Roger and finding Bert's killer. Johnny takes Penny home and stops by the police to check on the hit and run and learns nothing. At his hotel, Johnny gets a phone call and Penny is hysterical. She tells Johnny that she was followed and she just got a threatening phone call. The caller told her that she will have an accident if she helps Johnny.

Tomorrow, well it may sound corny, but where there is smoke, there is fire.

## PART 2          SHOW DATE:      3/20/1956

Penny calls and tells Johnny about a threatening phone call. She was told that there will be two fatal accidents if they work on the Jolly Roger case.

This case is going to the Universal Adjustment Bureau now because Southwestern's agent has died. Johnny goes to see Penny and she lets Johnny in and tells him that the voice on the phone was the same one that threatened Bert. She warns Johnny to be careful as Zanagian is trying to get the claim processed. She tells Johnny that Bert did not want to insure the boat, but the two year's of premiums were hard to turn down. Zanagian himself put in the claim and demanded immediate payment. Bert did not want to pay and they killed Bert, and now she is frightened. Johnny tells her to get some sleep while he sleeps on the sofa with his gun.

In the morning Johnny goes to visit the police and Lt. Joe Franklin tells Johnny that they have not really learned anything. Johnny then goes to see Zanagian, who knows about Bert. Zanagian knows everything Johnny has done and he is depending on Johnny to make prompt payment on the policy. He is looking out for Johnny and has a trusted man watching Johnny during his stay. Zanagian tells Johnny that they were testing some new equipment when the ship sank. He will not bore Johnny with the details, which he will get from the Coast Guard. Zanagian tells Johnny that he must have settlement without delay so that he can leave immediately. He needs cash and is a most generous person. Johnny tells him that a claim for $460,00 must be investigated, and the claims make the case suspicious. The offer of a bribe does not help. So, sit back and wait to see if you get the money at all. Zanagian reminds Johnny of the accidents, but Johnny tells him he does not scare easily.

Johnny goes to the Coast Guard and talks to Lt. John Smith, who believes that Zanagian sunk the boat himself. They sent down divers but could see nothing. The crew was lost except for a cabin boy that was taken to a Mexican hospital. Lt. Smith offers Johnny his car so Johnny can drive to Tijuana to question the boy. Lt. Smith tells Johnny that both Holland and Switzerland have tied up Zanagian's funds. As Johnny is leaving Zanagian arrives and would offer Johnny a ride to Tijuana but, alas, he has just learned that the cabin boy has just died. What a pity.

Tomorrow, a dead man talks, and what he has to say isn't very pleasant for it all adds up to just one good solid threat to yours truly, Johnny Dollar.

**PART 3          SHOW DATE:          3/21/1956**

The operator returns Johnny's call to Dr. Hernandez in the hospital. Johnny is told that the cabin boy just died but under mysterious circumstance. He said things that you must know.

Johnny calls the hospital in Tijuana from a pay phone and then talks to Lt. Smith. Johnny relates what the Doctor said, and asks Lt. Smith to get him a rental car delivered to the hotel. Lt. Smith is sure that Zanagian needs money to get to Europe and get the impounded funds.

Johnny gets a rental car and drives to Tijuana, always watching for a tail. Johnny sees a variety of cars and trucks on the road, but no one tailing him. Johnny arrives at the hospital and meets Dr. Hernandez. Johnny tells him about the Jolly Roger and how well Zanagian resembles a pirate. Dr. Hernandez tells Johnny that after the boy was brought in a man called and wanted to see him. They operated on the boy and the operation was successful. Dr. Hernandez set up a special nurse to watch the boy. She left the boy for a minute to tell how the doctors how well he was recovering and when she returned the boy was dead. Someone got into the room and killed him with a knitting needle. The police were told but they are at a loss. The boy told Dr. Hernandez things that he wrote down. When Dr. Hernandez searches in his desk for the notes, they are gone. The boy had told Dr. Hernandez that he had seen a strange device brought on the ship. Only the captain had handled it, and it was taken to the engine room. The device looked like an alarm clock set for 2:35. Johnny wonders why, if the captain knew about it, why he would put it on board. Dr. Hernandez tells Johnny that the captain was hit by a small mast and was unconscious. Johnny tells the doctor to let no one know he has talked to Johnny. Zanagian is after Johnny and will be after anyone who helps him.

Johnny calls the coast Guard and learns that Lt. Smith is dead from a hit-and-run accident an hour after Johnny left him. Johnny tells Dr. Hernandez to "watch your step, Doctor."

Tomorrow, some real help from two close friends. You know, close enough to kill.

**PART 4          SHOW DATE:          3/22/1956**

Sgt. Franklin calls and he tells Johnny that he thinks the Jolly Roger was sunk. Johnny tells him that both Bert and Lt. Smith were killed and Jan Penny is helping him. Sgt. Franklin tells Johnny that they are sending a man to watch Jan Penny. But what about you?

Johnny was really looking for investigating the girls in bikini bathing suits, but now he is looking into the sinking of a luxury yacht. Johnny briefs Sgt. Franklin about the boy, the time bomb, the falling mast and the impounded funds. Bert Parker did not last long after refusing to pay the claim, and Johnny has been threatened. Johnny it told that Tommy Golden will watch Jan Penny and Johnny asks about the hit-and-run of Lt. Smith. Sgt. Franklin tells Johnny that the car was a black Buick Sedan, a 54 or 55 with no plates. Sgt. Franklin is that sure Zanagian is behind this and Johnny wonders if Sgt. Franklin is working for him. Sgt. Franklin notes that Zanagian usually has helpers but they have not been able to spot them. Johnny tells Sgt. Franklin about the men in Zanagian's room, and learns that they have been tailed. When Johnny tells Sgt. Franklin that he is going to go see Jan, Sgt. Franklin tells Johnny that Jan Penny drives a black Buick.

Johnny goes to Jan's apartment and she is worried about Johnny. She had taken a cab to the office and no one bothered her there, but she feel she is being followed. Jan urges Johnny to back out of the case, but Johnny will not do it, it is his job to take risks. Jan breaks down and they have a drink and talk. Johnny wonders why he cannot relax and enjoy the situation with Jan. Johnny tells her he is going to the police and she tells Johnny to take her car, an old black Buick with a new paint job. She tells Johnny that she took a cab that morning so the would not mar the new paint job.

Johnny goes to the garage and notices the new paint job and the partially open hood. Johnny opens the hood and finds a bomb wired to the ignition.

Tomorrow, the wind up, where the obvious becomes only too obvious.

**PART 5**       **SHOW DATE:**       **3/23/1956**

Johnny calls Jan and wonders why she is surprised. Johnny tells her that he changed his mind and will be back after taking a walk. She tells him to take a drive, but she does not want to go along with him.

Johnny calls Jan and does not tell her of the bomb. Johnny goes back upstairs and hears her talking to someone on the phone. Johnny calls Sgt. Franklin and tells what he has just heard and that he is going to lay it all out to Jan. Johnny goes back upstairs and tells Jan to sit down while he tells her about the open hood and the bomb and why she did not hear an explosion. Jan plays dumb and worries about the threats. Zanagian and Artiz come in via the service entrance with a gun drawn. "How awkward to take the service entrance" Zanagian tells Johnny. Zanagian takes Johnny's gun and Johnny tries to hit Artiz. Zanagian wants to talk about why Johnny suspects Jan of complicity. Johnny tells him that apart from the threatening phone calls that only Jan received, Zanagian had someone follow Johnny. Zanagian tells Johnny that Jan and Artiz are his only staff. Johnny knows how to dodge a tail, and Artiz says that Johnny is too good. Zanagian calls Johnny an intelligent man, and only Jan could provide the information he has, and Jan did a good job on Bert and Lt. Smith. Johnny gets angry and Artiz holds him back. Zanagian tells Johnny about the millions impounded in Europe. Jan tells Johnny that Zanagian's friends are well paid for their efforts. All Johnny has to do is approve the claim and he will get more than money, like Jan for example. Work with me or I will eliminate you. Johnny asks Artiz to lower his gun and Johnny asks how Zanagian knows Johnny will not double-cross him. Johnny tells Zanagian that he has good news for him; he has just given a confession to Sgt. Franklin. Johnny slugs Artiz who fires and falls to the floor when Sgt. Franklin comes in with reinforcements. Sgt. Franklin tells Johnny that he knew that the phone call was being listened to. But Zanagian is dead, shot by Artiz. Jan pleads with Johnny to listen to her, but Johnny can only tell her to "shut up!."

The fabulous crooked empire of Paulus Zanagian is kaput, the same way it happens when every man who tries to break the rules of international law and order. You might almost call it death by his own hand, though of course little Artiz will be made to pay for it. Jan, same thing I guess. Why to they do it?

Exp. Acct:    $523.23

NOTES:
- PAT McCRACKEN MAKES THE FIRST OF MANY APPEARANCES.
- IN PART 5, JOHNNY ADDRESSES THE EXPENSE ACCOUNT TO THE "UNIVERSAL ADJUSTERS BUREAU."
- IN EPISODE 1, PAT NOTES THAT BERT PARKER HAD ASSIGNED JOHNNY THE MOLLY K CASE, BUT THE ORIGINAL PROGRAM NAMES DAVE BORGER AND A DIFFERENT INSURANCE COMPANY, MARINE AND MARITIME CASUALTY LTD.
- THIS IS THE FIRST OF MANY PROGRAMS WRITTEN BY JACK JOHNSTONE.
- THE EXPENSE TOTAL IS REALLY A SUBTOTAL, PENDING WHAT JOHNNY SPENDS ON VACATION.
- THE ANNOUNCER IS ROY ROWAN
- MUSICAL SUPERVISION IS BY AMERIGO MARINO
- RAY KEMPER IS A CBS SOUNDMAN

Producer:  Jack Johnstone          Writers:  Jack Johnstone
Cast:      Virginia Gregg, Forrest Lewis, Paul Frees, Jay Novello, Harry Bartell, Don Diamond, Victor Perrin

◆    ❖    ◆

SHOW:       THE LA MARR MATTER
COMPANY:    UNIVERSAL ADJUSTMENT BUREAU
AGENT:      PAT McCRACKEN
PART 1      SHOW DATE:    3/26/1956

SYNOPSIS: Pat McCracken calls Johnny and asks about Johnny's vacation, which is on the expense account for the Jolly Roger Matter. Johnny asks Pat about approval to work on the La Marr case.

Johnny is on vacation and enjoying the beach in La Jolla where he is staying at the El Crescenta, alone except for Vonnie La Marr, who thinks Johnny runs a filling station. Johnny has told her that his rich uncle left him some money for a vacation. She is really a wonderful girl who he met after clearing up the Jolly Roger Matter. Vonnie was waiting for her father to arrive, but he had to delay the trip at the last minute. A telegram arrived for Vonnie and her father had delayed his trip because of doctor's orders. He just had a checkup with Tri-Mutual

Insurance. She senses something is wrong and Johnny lets her call home from his cottage. She tells Johnny that Daddy is ok and she tells daddy all about Johnny. Mr. La Marr tells Vonnie that he just had indigestion, and they go back to the dining room. That was three days ago.

Vonnie starts talking about love at first sight and Johnny gets a little nervous. Vonnie senses that Johnny does not run a filling station and he tells her that he might be a social bum. She tells Johnny that she has had her share of worthless fops, all trying to get into the La Marr name. She tells Johnny she is waiting for someone like Johnny as they snuggle on the beach.

Pedro arrives and he has telegrams for Johnny and Vonnie. Vonnie's is from the family doctor; her father has died. Johnny makes reservations for her to return home, and then calls Pat McCracken who had sent his wire. Pat wants him to stop in South Bend, Indiana and look into the death of Thomas Rene La Marr, insured for $1.5 million. They think it is murder.

Tomorrow, a set of circumstances arise that are enough to keep a man from trusting even himself.

## PART 2          SHOW DATE:          3/27/1956

The operator calls with Pat McCracken's call. Johnny tells Pat that he is leaving for South Bend with Vonnie La Marr. She does not know that they think it is murder.

This starts the La Marr case expenses. Johnny tells Pat that Vonnie is on vacation in La Jolla and no claim has been filed yet. Pat tells Johnny that he knew of La Marr's death through Tri-Mutual's agent, Lawrence Comstock, who is a close friend of Mr. La Marr. Comstock had been staying at La Marr's house and had called the doctor when La Marr collapsed. Comstock called Pat and specifically asked for Johnny. Johnny tells Pat that he does not want Vonnie to know he is investigating the case.

Johnny checks with Vonnie and he tells her he is going to go home with her, to help out. She is thankful that Johnny is so wonderful. Even with Vonnie, Johnny has to suspect everyone in this case, with a million and a half on the line. On the plane Johnny tells Vonnie he will be staying in South Bend and has contacted a business friend there, and she is very inquisitive over what Johnny does for a living. Vonnie has wired home to Harrison the butler, and Edward Wilson her father's doctor. The plane lands in Chicago and they take a cab to the La Marr home in South Bend. The large household staff meets Johnny and Vonnie at the door and Vonnie tells Harrison that Johnny is to be allowed in at any time.

Johnny cabs back to Chicago to talk with Larry Comstock. Larry tells Johnny that he thinks that La Marr was murdered. He had known La Marr for years and had written all of his policies. La Marr's company had just been bought out and he was getting ready to retire and take care of Vonnie, his adopted daughter. Johnny tells Larry that he knows Vonnie. Larry tells Johnny that in all the years he has known La Marr, there are things in Vonnie's past that no one but he knew. Larry tells Johnny that Dr. Wilson examined La Marr, and he was in excellent health. Larry suspects the man who could benefit by La Marr's death, the man Vonnie is really in love with.

Tomorrow, some stuff I didn't want to hear, but I had to.

## PART 3            SHOW DATE:      3/28/1956

Vonnie calls and asks Johnny to come to the house. She asks if Johnny's business is related to her father's death. "Do you too think he was murdered?" she asks Johnny.

Johnny talks to Larry Comstock, who tells Johnny that he and Dr. Wilson were the only friends Thomas La Marr had. They enjoyed the same things and belonged to the same clubs. La Marr was in excellent health, which is why he was allowed to increase his insurance, for his adopted daughter. Larry and Dr. Wilson were at the La Marr house that Friday night and they played three-handed pinochle. That night young Walter Marsen, La Marr's personal secretary was there. They played golf Saturday and just relaxed on Sunday. They quit playing cards just before midnight and went to bed. La Marr said he might need a sleeping pill, which Larry knew were only sugar pills. Larry heard a crash, ran up to his bathroom and saw La Marr on the floor. Ed was called and he suspected some rare poison. Samples of the pills were sent to Chicago and Washington. Walter Marsen is La Marr's personal secretary and has been married to Vonnie for over a year. La Marr's will leaves all of his assets to the corporation, except for the insurance, which goes to Vonnie. The only way someone could benefit was to be married to Vonnie. Larry knows that Marsen has something on Vonnie. Walter Marsen handled all of La Marr's investments and made it clear that he wanted to take his place at the company, but La Marr would not allow it. La Marr knew some of the transactions Marsen had made were not really moral and that Marsen would use the company for personal gain if given the chance. Larry is sure that Marsen poisoned La Marr. Johnny asks "What if Vonnie had something to do with it?" and wonders why she wanted Johnny if she was already married. Why did she know where Johnny was; why did she get him under her spell? Larry tells Johnny that he is striking out because he is hurt, but do not let it affect your judgment.

Tomorrow, well it doesn't take long to find out what has to be done on this case because the turning point in the thing comes straight to me, and with a vengeance.

## PART 4            SHOW DATE:      3/29/1956

Dr. Wilson calls Johnny and tells him that Larry had asked him to call. Dr. Wilson has just left the police autopsy surgeon and Thomas La Marr definitely had been poisoned. Johnny tells Dr. Wilson that he is in the La Marr will, which is a shot in the dark. Johnny is on his way to see him.

So far the evidence seems to point to Walter Marsen, married to Vonnie without La Marr's knowledge. Johnny meets with Dr. Wilson, who has heard of Johnny through Larry Comstock. Johnny took a shot at guessing that he and Larry are beneficiaries, and would therefore have a reason to cause La Marr's death. Johnny is also aware that Vonnie is married to Marsen. Dr. Wilson tells Johnny that after the death of her mother, Vonnie got involved in gambling through her "friends" and became deeply in debt. Marsen found out and told her he would pay off her debts if she married him. He quietly used the profits of La Marr's investment to pay off her debts. She was upset over the death of her mother and was desperate. Dr. Wilson tells Johnny that he too is upset. He and Larry are beneficiaries, but only in a minor way. Johnny apologizes for his suspicions. Dr. Wilson tells Johnny that La Marr died from a poison called pyradameron, which causes the heart to burst and leaves no residue. Dr. Wilson only found evidence, a strange coloration, on La Marr's tongue. It is strange, as the last known source, a small island off of Greece, died out many years ago and the Greek government had burned all of the known plants and seeds. The poison could have been mixed with the pills, but there was no evidence of the poison on them.

Johnny follows a hunch and goes to the library closest to the La Marr home, and only finds a reference to the plant "blephara purpurus kelandus." Johnny goes to the main library in Chicago, where the librarian is an expert on rare drugs and poisons. He has read about pyradameron in a mystery, "The Case Of The Yellow Lipped Monster." The plant is extinct now for many years, and is really deadly. It is in the book "Flora Exotica Mediterranean" which turns up missing when he searches for it. He is sure that it was there yesterday, and it is never taken out without his knowledge, as there is no other book that would cover the plant.

Johnny cabs back to the La Marr home and talks to Harrison. Johnny is told that Vonnie and Marsen are out making funeral arrangements and Vonnie had indicated she would travel and settle down elsewhere. The staff will probably find employment elsewhere. Harrison tells Johnny that Marsen lives in the house. Johnny finally tells Harrison who he is, and asks to see Marsen's room. Harrison is sure that Marsen had been a clever scheming young man planning to take over the corporation, and had tried once to marry Vonnie. But he has changed. Harrison had overheard conversations between Marsen and La Marr where La Marr confronted Marsen with is activities and his prison record for embezzlement. But even then, La Marr was ready to give him a second chance and Marsen changed his ways. Johnny finds a book in Marsen's room—"Flora Exotica Mediterranean."

Tomorrow the windup, and a switch that will make your head spin.

**PART 5**       **SHOW DATE:**       **3/30/1956**
Larry Comstock calls and Johnny asks about the results of the police crime lab. Larry tells Johnny that they found evidence of the poison on La Marr's toothbrush. Johnny tells Larry to send the police; he almost has the case wrapped up.

Johnny recounts the case and how the clues seem to point to Walter Marsen, and the book he found in Marsen's room. Marsen catches Johnny in his room, and Johnny shows him his identification, and tells why he is there. Johnny comments on the book he found about the poison pyradameron. Marsen tells

Johnny he got the book in the library, but did not kill La Marr. Johnny tells Marsen about his secret marriage to Vonnie, the stock deals and killing Thomas La Marr. Walter tells Johnny that he was married to Vonnie, and that he had tried to get a place in the company by showing La Marr how clever he was, but La Marr gave him a second chance and he has changed now. Walter tells him that he and Vonnie are divorced; she mailed him the papers from Reno before she went to La Jolla. Walter had taken the book to try and figure out where the poison had come from, knowing suspicion would fall on him. They had been out and Harrison told them that Johnny was there and wanted to talk to Vonnie. Walter had come upstairs, and Vonnie had gone somewhere in the house. Marsen tells Johnny that they were only married on paper, in spite of their secrets. She has been drinking and is more deeply in debt now than before. Suddenly Walter senses that maybe Vonnie is involved. The pyradameron plant is extinct, but Marsen wonders if Dimitri, the Greek gardener might know something. Before going to the gardener's cottage, Johnny checks with Harrison, phones Larry who is out, and then calls the librarian, who tells Johnny that the book had been checked out once by LaVon La Marr. Marsen and Johnny go out to meet with Dimitri. Johnny asks Dimitri if he had ever seen a flower like the one in the book. Dimitri had seen them in the old country and he had kept some seeds that Vonnie had planted in her secret garden. Vonnie had sent Dimitri a toiletries case from California and he shows it to Johnny. Johnny notices a yellow tint on the tooth-brush and Walter remembers that La Marr had gotten one also. They walk to Vonnie's secret garden to find Vonnie digging with a shovel. She is "burying her garden of things she had grown for daddy." Johnny pulls up the pyradameron plant and Vonnie tries to attack him. Walter and Johnny subdue her as she screams and tries to buy off Johnny.

Believe me, this is one case I wish I had never seen. Oh sure, you the company are all right, you will not have to pay off a million and a half in insurance: your gain. But me, I've lost something. Faith. Faith and I'm sick over the whole thing. Expense account, I'll add it up later. Right now I'm going out and get roaring . . . get some flowers, some clean flowers and just sit and look at them.

Exp. Acct:     $0.00

**NOTES:**
- BOTH THE PLANT "LOPHERA PAPORAS CALENDIS" AND PYRADAMERON ARE FICTITIOUS.
- VIRGINIA GREGG MUST CLEAR HER VOICE IN PART 1, INDICATING THAT PERHAPS THIS WAS A LIVE BROADCAST AND COULD NOT BE RE-RECORDED.
- ROY ROWAN IS THE ANNOUNCER
- MUSICAL SUPERVISION IS BY AMERIGO MARINO

**Producer:** Jack Johnstone     **Writers:** Jack Johnstone
**Cast:** Virginia Gregg, Harry Bartell, Lawrence Dobkin, Eric Snowden, Howard McNear, John Dehner, Jean Tatum, Joseph Kearns, Paul Richards, Jack Moyles

| SHOW: | THE SALT CITY MATTER |
|---|---|
| COMPANY: | SAMUEL RUBEN & ASSOCIATES |
| AGENT: | SAMUEL RUBEN |
| PART 1 | SHOW DATE: 4/2/1956 |

SYNOPSIS: Sam Ruben calls and Johnny complains about having to hock his watch on his last job for Sam in Hong Kong. Sam needs help with Ed Julian. ED JULIAN! So long, Sam, call the police. Sam is calling Johnny because he cannot call the police.

Johnny knows the name Ed Julian, as does every policeman in the country. Johnny goes to see Sam Ruben, who would like to have Johnny on his payroll. Johnny tells him that Ed Julian is a well-known criminal. Sam has a $50,000 insurance policy on Ed Julian but nothing has happened to Ed. The policy was issued a month ago, and Sam knows Julian was a bad risk. Julian is in San Francisco, and Sam wants Johnny to go to Julian and ask him to cancel the policy. Johnny knows that there is no way that he can approach Julian; what Sam really wants is for Johnny to watch Ed until Sam can figure out how to cancel the policy. Sam tells Johnny that he has heard through the grapevine that some on Ed's old friends are gathering in San Francisco, the kind who would like to kill him. Sam tells Johnny that an agent in San Francisco had sold a policy to Edwardo Saccavetti, and she only found out later who he was and sent Sam a wire. Johnny negotiates with Sam for expenses and a $2,500 commission.

Johnny flies to San Francisco, California and gets a room at the Fairmont Hotel. Johnny cabs to the address of Ed Julian on Nob Hill, where Johnny interviews a policeman that tells Johnny that Mr. Saccavetti moved out a week ago with his wife and their clothes. Johnny is troubled when he finds a listing for Edward Julian Enterprises in the phone book. Johnny calls the number and asks for Mr. Julian, and is told that he is not there, and is never expected back. Johnny goes to the address and walks in to find a man there and asks for Julian. The man tells Johnny that he wants to find Julian too. He is Ray Gumby, Julian's lawyer. Gumby pours Johnny a drink and tells Johnny that the enterprises were not much, but they have all been sold. Johnny wants to find him to protect him, but Gumby tells Johnny that he has been left holding the sack. He hopes to get Julian served so he can be put in jail. Gumby was a fool to accept Julian as a client. Johnny suggests they work together to keep Julian safe. Gumby gives Johnny a subpoena for Ed Julian and agrees to pay Johnny $200 if he can serve it.

Tomorrow, that's when I begin to find a myth can be stranger than fiction.

## PART 2          SHOW DATE:     4/3/1956

Johnny goes to see Insp. Walsh and updates him on Julian, who is out of town. Johnny tells him that the town is full of thugs and about Gumby. Johnny goes to see Eleanor Stover, Julian's agent, who fixes Johnny a cup of black coffee while he tells her why he is there. She tells Johnny that she met Julian in a restaurant and Lorraine was with him. They had dinner and she sold him the policy, in spite of the fact that Julian made a pass at her. She also tells Johnny that she knew Lorraine from high school.

Johnny has dinner and Eleanor tells Johnny about Jim Reno, and mentions Chili Winter from Chicago, Lolovitch and Pachaki from Detroit and Turkey Johnson, all gangsters. She tells Johnny that it is too bad about Lorraine. Johnny is called by Wade who tells him that Julian is at the Skyline Apartments. Johnny goes to the apartment and runs into Swifty, who Johnny knows as a hood. Johnny asks about Julian and Luke walks up and Johnny is beaten and put in a cab and sent to a Turkish bath.

### PART 3          SHOW DATE:      4/4/1956

The Skyline Apartments calls Johnny and Johnny tells the clerk that he was slugged there last night. Tell the guys that hit me I am on the way over.

Johnny gets two stitches and then calls the world's prettiest insurance broker, Eleanor Stover. Johnny goes to see Eleanor and tells her that he had a run in with two of Ed Julian's hoods and that he is trying to issue a subpoena to get him into court. Johnny then cabs to the Skyline Apartments where Johnny calls "Swifty" and asks about his partner. Luke comes over and they ridicule Johnny, who asks them what floor Julian is on. When they try to stop Johnny, he pulls his gun and pistol-whips them. Johnny goes to the fourth floor where a woman opens the door and Johnny finds that Ed Julian is gone. She tells Johnny that he is taking a chance being there. The woman is Ed's wife, Lorraine and Johnny tells her that Eleanor Stover was a friend of hers ten years ago in school. Lorraine does not expect Ed to come back but Johnny wants to wait. She asks about Swifty and Luke, Johnny tells her that Swifty and Luke were glad to see him come up. She is upset when she sees the stitches in Johnny's head. Johnny tells her he is trying to protect Ed, but she has no idea where he is. She tells Johnny that the others came from the east, and Ed was talking with "Chilly" Winters and then they left. She did not like Chilly's looks and she tells Johnny to leave or Ed will kill her.

Johnny goes to look up the record of Chilly Winters, which is long and ugly. Johnny goes back to his room and the Skyline desk clerk is waiting for him. He tells Johnny that he needs every penny, and that he knows that Johnny is not a thug, but he knows where Julian is. Johnny gives him some money and the man tells Johnny that Ed Julian is in Salt City for a big meeting. Johnny gets a map of California and finds Salt City 300 miles away. Johnny calls on Ed Gumby, and he knows that Salt City is a company town and that Johnny should not go there. Johnny is sure that something big, just out of touch is going to happen. Johnny buys a train ticket to Salt City and finds a yellow grimly little town around a yellow grimy smelter. Johnny wants a cab to the smelter works, but the cabby will not take him there. A hobo tells Johnny that Salt city is the end of the line. He has left twice never wanting to come back. This place is a dump somebody made and forgot about. Johnny senses nothing but a feeling that "it is going to happen here."

Tomorrow, well maybe I was psychic or something, because tomorrow is when that feeling, that hunch turns into action.

## PART 4          SHOW DATE:     4/5/1956

Johnny gets a call through to San Francisco and talks to Ed Gumby, and tells him that things look terrible. Johnny should be back tonight if he is lucky. There is not much law enforcement here, but Johnny will serve Ed if he can.

Johnny checks his bag and walks to the Salt City Bar and Grill, where a girl named Connie talks to him. She does not blame Johnny for not wanting to leave soon and stops talking when Mr. Reno comes in. Johnny recognizes Reno from the Landry murder case in Baltimore in 1950. He tells Johnny that he is Jim Reno, and that he runs the restaurant. He suggests that Johnny have the stew and tells Connie to fix it. Reno tells Johnny that Ed Julian is at the smelter and Reno offers to call Johnny a cab; he owns the taxi company also. Johnny finishes his coffee and then rides out to the smelter works. Johnny spots Ed Julian and another man in a room sitting on chairs. They were not dead, but kind of in between, like Johnny before he passes out. Johnny wakes up to see a man who tells him why he is there, and that Ed Julian does not need anything. Reno tells Johnny that Ed did not want you to protect him, and you got into an argument. You pulled your gun and shot Ed and Chilly Winters, like this, and Reno shoots them. The police here only need your gun and you will be arraigned and tried right here in Salt City. You walked right into it. Johnny jumps up slugs Reno and manages to hit him with a lamp. Johnny walks back to town and goes to the Bar and Grill. Johnny finds Connie and tells her what happened, and goes over the events of the morning with her. Johnny gives her $350 to buy a car and hides in her room while she gets a car. She packs and they drive to San Francisco.

Johnny calls the police and they tell him he is wanted for murder, and Johnny tells them he can explain it if they give him time. Johnny goes to Ed Gumby's office and then to his home where Ed opens the door with two bullet holes in his neck. Ed tells Johnny that Swifty and Luke did it an hour ago and then Gumby dies and Johnny wonders why people are dying wherever he goes. It was that same old feeling.

It winds up tomorrow, the whys and wherefores, love and hate, the usual ingredients for big explosions.

## PART 5          SHOW DATE:     4/6/1956

Johnny is called by Eleanor and he tells her that he is wanted for murder and needs help. She tells Johnny that she will meet him on fisherman's wharf in her blue 1952 Ford convertible.

Johnny cabs to Fisherman's Wharf, and is tired after two days of lost sleep. Eleanor drives up and he gets into her car and she drives off. Johnny will tell her what happened and asks her to go to inspector Dan Walsh and tell him what he is going to tell her. Johnny tells her about Ed Gumby and the plan to get Ed Julian into jail to keep him out of trouble. Johnny tells of the trip to Salt City and Jim Reno's involvement and about Ed Gumby being shot. Eleanor takes

Johnny to her office where Johnny sleeps.

Johnny goes to see the desk clerk at his apartment, and tells him about the men he has seen killed, and how the clerk took a chance to come to see Johnny, but your kind does not take chances. Johnny forces the man to tell him that Mr. Julian told him to tell all of them to make it difficult for Johnny. Then he sent a letter telling him where to send Johnny and then Johnny knocks the clerk out. Johnny calls Eleanor to tell the police to pick up the desk clerk, and Swifty and Luke too.

Johnny goes to the Skyline Apartments to see Mrs. Julian. She tells Johnny that she did not expect to see him and he better leave before Ed gets there. Johnny tells her that Chilly and Ed are dead, and that she has been double-crossed. Johnny tells her that they wanted Chilly out of the way and that Jim Reno is in command. Ed had told her to get Johnny to go to Salt City. Johnny asks her to sign a statement on how Ed Julian and Jim Reno planned to get rid of Chilly Winters and how Ed took Chilly to Salt City with him. About how he knew that Ed Gumby had a subpoena, and how Johnny would end up in Salt City and be a patsy for the killing of Chilly. Only Jim Reno decided he would be better off with them dead. She tells Johnny that Ed Gumby knew all about the enterprises and they killed him. Jim Reno comes in and tells Johnny that he needs to go to back Salt City, and that she has $50,000 coming to her now. Reno knew that Johnny would be there, and he wants Johnny to go back to Salt City to talk to the police. Johnny slugs Reno and Lorraine is shot. She asks Johnny to tell her she looks like a nice girl, and then she dies.

Johnny gets a lawyer to help explain what had happened and goes back to Hartford, after a long good bye to Eleanor. Johnny tells her that he will be back when the trial starts.

Exp. Acct:     $3,262.00

NOTES:
- ROY ROWAN IS THE ANNOUNCER
- MUSICAL SUPERVISION IS BY AMERIGO MARINO
- THE CONTENT FOR EPISODE 3 WAS OBTAINED FROM THE SCRIPT ON FILE IN THE KNX COLLECTION AT THE THOUSAND OAKS LIBRARY.

**Producer:** Jack Johnstone      **Writers:** John Dawson
**Cast:** Barbara Fuller, Jean Tatum, Barbara Eiler, Lawrence Dobkin, Dick Ryan, Jack Edwards, Barney Phillips, Junius Matthews, Tony Barrett

◆ ❖ ◆

**SHOW:** THE LAIRD DOUGLAS-DOUGLAS OF HEATHERSCOTE MATTER
**COMPANY:** PHILADELPHIA LIABILITY & CASUALTY COMPANY
**AGENT:** HARRY BRANSON
**PART 1**      **SHOW DATE:** 4/9/1956

SYNOPSIS: Harry Branson calls Johnny and tells him that he has a very important case. Laird Douglas-Douglas Of Heatherscote. "Can you come and see me, there is a nice retainer, expenses and commission if anything happens. Come by plane, this is urgent" Harry tells Johnny.

Johnny flies to Philadelphia, Pennsylvania and stays at the Benjamin Franklin, a nice hotel. Johnny is debating taking a shower when Harry calls and tells Johnny to come to his office immediately; this is an emergency due to the time issue. Johnny takes his .38 Colt and goes to see Harry, who Johnny finds waiting on the sidewalk. Harry tells Johnny "we have a serious problem with Laird Douglas-Douglas Of Heatherscote. He is in my office now, with Mrs. Peter Malcolm Kelly Van Piten. She insists you to act as his bodyguard, as she is aware of your work on the Ricardo Amerigo case and she is a very big policyholder." Harry tells Johnny that the Laird has a $5,000 policy, a short life expectancy and that he is four years old. Harry is positive that the life of Laird Douglas-Douglas is in danger. Johnny is told he has an expense account equal to his retainer of $750 a week. Johnny is told his services will only be required until the Laird appears at Bala Cynwyd. Harry walks Johnny into his 13th floor office to meet Mrs. Van Piten and the Laird, who is asleep in Harry's office. They enter Harry's office to meet the Laird who is a dog that goes after Johnny's leg!

Here's our star to tell you about tomorrow's intriguing . . . well tomorrow's episode: Tomorrow, well I've handled some pretty doggy cases in my time, but never as a pooch's bodyguard. But suddenly this one starts to smell to strongly of murder.

## PART 2          SHOW DATE:     4/10/1956

Johnny is called by Ray Roland, and Johnny tells Ray that he may need his help. Let's have lunch. Have you met? "Yeah, I know" Ray tells Johnny.

Johnny buys a new pair of pants and recounts the case. At the introduction the Laird goes for Johnny's leg and tears up his pants as Harry reminds Johnny of the retainer and expense account. Mrs. Van Piten gives Johnny $150 to replace is trousers and a biscuit for the Laird. Johnny gives the biscuit to the Laird, who is now Johnny's best friend. Mrs. Van Piten wants Johnny to stay at her place. When Johnny tells her that he is not sure about the case, she ups the retainer to $1,000 a week, and "the Laird, a Scotty, excuse me a Scottish Terrier," is now Johnny's best friend.

Mrs. Van Piten tells Johnny that Bala Cynwyd is a dog show that the Laird must win, and he will unless someone interferes. Someone might try to dope him as it has been tried before, once last year and a few weeks ago. Mrs. Van Piten tells Johnny that Harrison R. Kenworthy will not get away with it, but she will not divulge any names. Johnny must watch over the Laird until he wins the show.

Johnny "talks over" the case and tells Harry he is doing this only for the money. Johnny asks about Kenworthy, who owns a Kerry Blue Terrier, Lady O'Diddies Rollamar Meen, who Johnny will just call Mimi. Ray Roland arrives and Ray tells Johnny that Bala Cynwyd is the biggest dog show in the country and that Kenworthy owns Mimi who is a champion dog. And, Mimi is the better dog. Ray tells Johnny that Kenworthy is loaded and is in love with Mrs. Van Piten, but she will not marry him until the Laird beats Mimi in the dog show, but Kenworthy would never allow that. It is deadly serious to them; it is all pride. Last year the dog was poisoned and saved at the last minute, but Mrs. Van Piten did not know it was poison. Johnny believes them and the finger points to Kenworthy, but Ray tells Johnny that he and the police do not feel the same way. Ray urges Johnny to duck out on this case. Kenworthy is not guilty because on each occasion Mrs. Van Piten had a bodyguard who was murdered. Still want the case, Johnny?

Tomorrow, well the joke is no longer a joke, especially when a killer trains his sights on me.

### PART 3          SHOW DATE:          4/11/1956

Lt. Steve Howard from the police calls and Johnny asks him about a murder at the dog show last year. Johnny ask Lt. Howard if he wants to look at the setup for an attempted murder, his.

Johnny cabs to his hotel from Harry's office and his dog of an assignment. Lt. Howard arrives in Johnny's room and Johnny shows him his handbag, which is now locked. Johnny tells Lt. Howard that it was open when he left, and there was no sign of the maid in the room. Johnny had picked up the bag and it weighed too much, almost twenty pounds. Johnny shows Lt. Howard where a window had been pried open. Lt. Howard decides to call the office.

Johnny buys a new pair of pants and calls Mrs. Van Piten to advise of a delay. "Oh, have a couple of suits made and charge them to me" she tells Johnny. Johnny cabs to the police office and learns that his suitcase had explosives in it that would have gone off if he had opened it. Johnny was suspicious of because of the previous deaths of bodyguard but Lt. Howard thinks that there is more to it. Mrs. Van Piten's whole life revolves around the dog, and it would kill her if he died. She is a remnant of a fast dying class of very rich people who control others with their money, which is power. Lt. Howard has no idea who would be trying to kill her. She only has one living relative, a nephew Warren Staley, but the police can find nothing on him.

Johnny cabs to "The Maples" in Germantown where the Van Pitens live. The butler takes Johnny to the reading room, where Mrs. Van Piten and "Douggie" await him. Mrs. Van Piten asks Johnny to please call him Douglas, as Doug is such a common name. She takes Johnny to his suite and they meet Warren Staley, the nephew on the way. Warren takes Johnny to his suite and gives him the tour, including the rooms for Douglas and Mademoiselle Poirot, the dog's governess. Johnny talks to Warren, who makes scotch and sodas for them in Johnny's room. He tells Johnny that he will be a very rich man when his aunt dies, but he wants to try and stand on his own two feet. He is the only member of the empire left and he will survive to keep control of East Moreland Oil from Harrison Kenworthy with whom there has been a battle over control for years. Kenworthy has a son, Ronald, who is a good friend of Warren's. Warren fixes himself a second drink and Johnny asks him about the rivalry and the attempts on the dog.

Kenworthy should be the primary suspect, and you should be suspect number two. Warren starts to stammer, and then complains of not being able to breath, collapses and dies.

Tomorrow, things and people finally begin to line up on the case, just well enough for it to blow sky high.

**PART 4          SHOW DATE:      4/12/1956**

Lt. Howard calls and Johnny has been ordered confined to his room because he is the only one trust worthy enough to not destroy evidence.

Johnny calls the police and they arrive almost immediately. Johnny showers and shaves while waiting for Lt. Howard and the lab boys to arrive. When they get there, Johnny explains what happened. Mrs. Van Piten rushes in hysterical with Ronald Kenworthy, who blames Johnny for the death. Ronald tells Johnny that he had been there for 45 minutes and was talking to Mrs. Van Piten, and was on his way to see Warren. Ronald takes Mrs. Van Piten out, and Johnny tells Lt. Howard that Warren was also concerned, and was going to tell him whom he suspected when he died. The police doctor tells them that the poison was penorphic acid, the same poison used on the dog and the previous bodyguards. Johnny tells Lt. Howard that he had poured a drink from a bottle, and Johnny notices that the bottles have been switched. Johnny and Lt. Howard go into the dog's rooms and then to the room of Mademoiselle Poirot, who is caught dressing and screams. Lt. Howard apologizes and tells her to get dressed and assigns a guard to her. Lt. Howard tells Johnny that he goofed and allowed someone to switch the bottles while he showered. Johnny tells Lt. Howard he goofed too, by smudging any prints on the doorknobs. Lt. Howard would peg this on Johnny, except for his reputation.

Johnny and Lt. Howard go downstairs and listen to the questioning of the household staff, which turns up nothing. Johnny has a lot of suspicions, which includes everyone, but there is no evidence.

The police search the house well into the evening and find nothing. Johnny stays with Mrs. Van Piten, who holds up rather well. She tells Johnny that Warren meant a lot to her. Johnny asks her about Warren being the sole heir of the family, and that Warren told Johnny that Kenworthy and his son would acquire the Oil Company holdings if he married Mrs. Van Piten. Johnny is sure that now there is only one person who would benefit: Ronald Kenworthy. Suddenly Ronald appears and tells Johnny that he has said enough, too much for his health.

Tomorrow, all cards are laid on the table and believe me, the deck proved to have been stacked right from the beginning. Tomorrow, the windup.

**PART 5          SHOW DATE:      4/13/1956**

Ron Kenworthy calls and Johnny tells him that he is on his way over to see him. Ron tells Johnny to call the police as Johnny had accused Ron of killing Warren before Johnny threw him out of Mrs. Van Piten's house.

Mrs. Van Piten agrees that the attempt was really on Johnny's life, and he tells her of the attempt in the hotel. She agrees that Ronald stands to inherit the entire empire. "Ronald, who pretended to love me and was Warren's best friend." Johnny has no evidence, but she tells Johnny that she will help him get the evidence and Ronald will pay; and no one will stand in her way. She tells Johnny to shoot first, as Ron is a cornered rat.

Johnny walks to the Kenworthy estate and passes the garage where he sees Andy LaForte, a clever second story man who would do anything for money. He reasons that Andy could have planted the bomb and the poison. Johnny goes to the gatekeeper's cottage and calls the police. The gatekeeper tells Johnny that Andy had been there about a year or so. Johnny talks to Lt. Howard and then goes to the Kenworthy mansion. Ronald is upset about being thrown out and tells Johnny that Warren really wanted nothing of the estate and that she hated him for it. Ron tells Johnny that he and his father have been planning to dissipate their estate to benefit others. Ron will benefit, but he will have to work at it; he will be a man.

Johnny goes back to see Mrs. Van Piten and tells her about seeing Andy LaForte. Johnny tells her that he should have gotten wise sooner. He recounts her pledge to marry Kenworthy, but the real reason was to get access to his assets. When she realized that her dog was not ready to beat the Kenworthy dog, she ordered the murder of the handlers. She learned of the disposal of the Kenworthy assets and that Warren wanted to do the same. She had also learned from Ray Roland that her dog did not have a chance so she would not let it compete. She had someone booby trap Johnny's bags to get rid of him, and she killed Warren, which got another obstacle out of the way. Mrs. Van Piten offers Johnny money and then reaches for a gun. "Wouldn't it be easier if I just gave you $100,000, or $200,000?" she asks Johnny. Andy LaForte comes in with a gun drawn and tells Johnny to get up, and Mrs. Van Piten tells him to do it now. Johnny tells Andy that she will kill him as he is shooting Johnny. Lt. Howard shoots Andy and Mrs. Van Piten tries to talk her way out of the situation, but Lt. Howard tells her to SHUT UP!

Remarks: I'm glad I am poor.

Exp. Acct:     $1,113.40

NOTES:
- A KERRY BLUE TERRIER IS ANY OF AN IRISH BREED OF MEDIUM-SIZED TERRIERS WITH A LONG SQUARISH HEAD, DEEP CHEST, AND SILKY BLUISH COAT.
- A SCOTTISH TERRIER IS ANY OF AN OLD SCOTTISH BREED OF TERRIER THAT HAS SHORT LEGS, A LARGE HEAD WITH SMALL ERECT EARS AND A POWERFUL MUZZLE, A BROAD DEEP CHEST, AND A VERY HARD COAT OF WIRY HAIR
- PENORPHIC ACID IS A FICTITIOUS SUBSTANCE.
- ROY ROWAN IS THE ANNOUNCER
- MUSICAL SUPERVISION IS BY AMERIGO MARINO

Producer:    Jack Johnstone        Writers:    Jack Johnstone
Cast:        Jeanette Nolan, Harry Bartell, Byron Kane, Jack Kruschen,
             Bill James, James McCallion, Ken Christy, Dick Ryan, Bert
             Holland, Jack Edwards, Hy Averback

◆ ❖ ◆

SHOW:        THE SHEPHERD MATTER
COMPANY:     RICHARD PORTER
             AGENT:   RICHARD PORTER
PART 1       SHOW DATE:        4/16/1956

SYNOPSIS: Johnny receives a call from Dick Porter, a broker who wants to hire
him. Porter has a client who is buying too much insurance, like he is getting
ready to die.

Johnny flies to Providence, Rhode Island and has dinner with Dick Porter.
Johnny is told that Dr. Shepherd called two days ago and asked about straight
life insurance rates and bought and additional $80,000, for a total of $100,000.
He is not married, and his mother is the beneficiary. Porter is working on the
paperwork, and he wants Johnny to look into him. He has a good practice in
the area and lives over the office. Porter is suspicious because the doctor called
him. Or he could be the one person in 100 who values insurance.

Johnny rents a car and collects information on Dr. Shepherd. Johnny
learns that he is in good financial shape and belongs to several clubs. Johnny
goes to the office and asks to see the doctor. The nurse tells Johnny that the
doctor is out, but Johnny tells her that he just saw him walk in. Johnny tells
the nurse, Miss Corrine Streeter, that he wants to see the doctor and gives
her his card. She tells Johnny that the doctor is seeing no one and has been
acting strangely. Johnny looks into the office, and sees the doctor holding a
.32 automatic with the safety off. The doctor takes Johnny's credentials, and
then apologizes to Johnny about the gun. He tells Johnny that he is very
nervous and tells the nurse to leave early and lock up. Johnny has Dr.
Shepherd set the safety and they go into the office to talk. Johnny tells him
that Mr. Porter had asked him to look into the policy, but the gun indicates
he is in trouble. The doctor tells Johnny that a homicidal maniac has threatened
his life. He would go to the police but a patient's welfare is involved. Several
months ago he treated a woman named Forbes who was mentally distraught.
He talked to her and discovered that her problem is her husband. He told
her to move out and divorce the husband, as it would be the best thing to
do. Dr. Shepherd explained the situation to the husband and he ranted and
raved and attacked him. Johnny tells him that he should have called the
police. Dr. Shepherd tells Johnny that the insurance was to care for his
mother, in case something happened to him. Johnny tells Dr. Shepherd that
he does not believe him.

Tomorrow, the Shepherd matter becomes a matter even the police cannot
handle.

**PART 2        SHOW DATE:        4/17/1956**

Dick Porter calls and Johnny tells him that Dr. Shepherd has been threatened and Johnny thinks he is a liar.

Johnny buys aspirin for Dick Porter and suggests that the policy might not be a good idea. Johnny tells Dick about the call to Dr. Shepherd who Johnny thinks is nuts or very clever, so Dick asks Johnny to stay in town for a few days. Johnny goes to Dr. Shepherd's office where Miss Streeter is upset and asks if Johnny is the reason why the doctor is carrying a gun. Johnny is buzzed into the office and asks Dr. Shepherd if he wants to change his story. He tells Johnny that he still must be careful of Mrs. Forbes' condition. Johnny tells him to prefer charges, but Shepherd must be careful. He tells Johnny that he could approach Paul Forbes and talk to him. Shepherd offers to pay Johnny to speak to Forbes but Johnny tells him he was going to anyway.

Johnny drives to the Forbes home in a very nice neighborhood. A man opens the door and hits Johnny with a gun and runs away. The butler, Upton runs out and asks where Mr. Forbes is. Johnny tells Upton that Forbes hit him. Mrs. Forbes tells Upton to call the doctor and get the first aid supplies. Johnny tells Mrs. Forbes who he is and Upton gives Johnny a drink while Mrs. Forbes apologizes for her husband's temper. Mrs. Forbes tells Johnny that he has attacked her physician and now him, he is mad, but Johnny notices a black eye on Mrs. Forbes. Upton is talking to Johnny as he regains consciousness. Upton tells Johnny that he had fainted and that Forbes did attack Dr. Shepherd and Mrs. Forbes. This is an unhappy house. Dr. Shepherd arrives and Johnny asks for an aspirin. Dr. Shepherd tells Johnny that he will prefer charges against Forbes and sends Mrs. Forbes upstairs. Dr. Shepherd tells Johnny to come to his office and calls the police.

Johnny leaves and thinks maybe he should not have left. He might have saved a life.

Tomorrow, well the big lie is as true as little green apples. Join us when I bite into one and spit out a bullet.

**PART 3        SHOW DATE:        4/18/1956**

Miss Streeter calls and she tells Johnny to come in for a head x-ray. The Doctor is out right now and is most insistent.

Johnny takes a cab to see Dick Porter and they have a drink. Porter thinks that Johnny is finished, but Johnny wonders why he was hired. The doctor explained the reasons for the insurance, but not to Johnny's satisfaction. Johnny tells about Forbes and the threats and that Johnny went to see Forbes this morning and was attacked. He was given first aid while the family apologized for Forbes' behavior. Johnny still thinks that Dr. Shepherd's story is still leaky. The family said that Forbes had threatened Shepherd, but Shepherd lies. His reason for not calling the police and his description of Forbes as a homicidal maniac that Johnny could reason with. And why would Forbes hit him? Someone must have put someone up to it. Mrs. Forbes seemed ok, but she had been hit too.

Johnny cabs to the office for the x-ray, which is done by Miss Streeter. Johnny asks Miss Streeter if she is in love with Shepherd, but she dodges the question and Johnny asks her "He is a liar isn't he?" Johnny wonders why she did not ask who the friend was that hit him. Johnny drives to the home of Clara Shepherd. Johnny introduces himself, and she tells Johnny that her son must be up to something. She has not seen or talked to him in three years and he does not think much of her as a mother. "Is it too early for a cocktail?" she asks Johnny. She tells Johnny that she has told her friends that her son is successful and cares for her, and she feels that Johnny is nice to his mother. If she did get money from Charles it would make for a tax problems. Johnny has a martini with her and leaves at 4:00. Johnny goes to Shepherd's office and officer Phil Crosby is there. Officer Crosby tells Johnny that no one knows where the doctor is, and they need to get a signature on a complaint. Miss Streeter then finds a note about an emergency on Putnam Street. Johnny tells Officer Crosby that Forbes is really angry and they drive to the area of the emergency, which turns out to be a vacant lot. Johnny spots the doctor's car and Officer Crosby calls for assistance. Johnny waits and Officer Crosby drives up and tells Johnny that a report is out on Dr. Shepherd. Two blocks away they find the body of Dr. Shepherd.

Tomorrow, a liar is still lying even though he is dead. Tune in tomorrow and I'll tell you all about it.

## PART 4      SHOW DATE:     4/19/1956

Officer Crosby calls Johnny to come downtown, to room 203 City Hall. He wants a better story about Paul Forbes.

Johnny buys a paper and reads of Dr. Shepherd's murder. It appeared that Forbes lured the doctor out and killed him. Johnny visits Officer Crosby and several other police officers and Dick Porter. Johnny tells them how he had been hired and how Forbes had hit him and how he distrusted Dr. Shepherd. Officer Crosby asks why Dr. Shepherd went out on an emergency and did not carry his bag, and did not have the .32 you saw him with. Johnny suggests that someone Dr. Shepherd knew and trusted lured him out. Officer Crosby recounts all of Forbes' activities, yet Johnny still says the doctor is lying. Johnny is told that the police are looking for Forbes and they will find him.

Johnny goes to the morgue and meets Corrine Streeter. Johnny tells her that the police think Forbes killed the doctor. She wants to know why Johnny is not out helping find Forbes. She tells Johnny that she loved Doctor Shepherd more than her whole life and Johnny feels he has just heard the first truth in two days.

Johnny thinks about the case over dinner and drives to the office of Dr. Shepherd and bribes the guard to let him in. The guard tells Johnny that the police had just left, and they found the emergency bag. Johnny searches the office and finds no records for Mrs. Forbes, but he does find a record for Mr. Forbes.

Johnny goes to the apartment of Corrine Streeter, who has just gotten home. Johnny asks her who Dr. Shepherd was going to marry, because he had made reservations on the Ile de France for June. She tells Johnny that Mrs. Forbes was the only person the doctor has seen socially in the past year. Mr. Forbes came for a year and then stopped and went to another doctor in Baltimore. Johnny asks why he was brought into the case, and he suggests the wrong man was killed that night.

Johnny goes to visit Mrs. Forbes and tells her that he had been brought in to the case by the large purchase of insurance so that he would be there and back up a self-defense plea. Johnny tells her that she and Dr. Shepherd were going to France. Her husband killed her boyfriend just like he said he would; but you have lost your doctor. She screams at Johnny to get out, and he goes to his hotel.

Johnny calls Officer Crosby and tells him what he thinks happened and how it backfired. Johnny tells him that Forbes was supposed to die. While he is talking, Johnny is told to hang up by Paul Forbes, who has a gun, and is blazing mad.

Tomorrow, I find out how hard it is to kill a lie. Sometimes you have to kill it twice.

## PART 5          SHOW DATE:          4/20/1956

The hotel operator calls and Johnny tells her he was cut off, but he wants to sleep and tells her to take a message if anyone calls. Forbes tells Johnny to stay quiet or he will shoot, and Johnny tells him he is crazy.

Forbes visits Johnny at seven in the morning. He saw Johnny at his house and followed him. Forbes wants to talk and he asks where Johnny's home is and where he practices. He asks if Johnny is licensed to practice law in Rhode Island. Johnny tells Forbes that he is an insurance investigator looking into insurance for Dr. Shepherd. Forbes tells Johnny that Dr. Shepherd called him and said a lawyer named Dollar was coming over to talk about a divorce. Johnny now knows why Dr. Shepherd called him, and Forbes tells Johnny that he did not kill Shepherd. He is sure that Johnny is in on it to get his wife away from him and starts to beat Johnny, but Johnny overpowers him. Forbes looks lifeless and Johnny pours a couple of drinks and gives Forbes one and tells him to talk. Johnny sees that the gun has not been fired and Forbes tells Johnny that he does not know where he was when Shepherd was shot. After he hit Johnny he drove to Shepherd's office to see him, and then back to his house and then just drove around. He got some sandwiches and some drinks. He called Shepherd around five or six and wanted to meet him and talk to him. Forbes did not see Shepherd because he never showed up. He drove around and heard on the radio he was wanted for murder. Forbes tells Johnny that Pauline had always had other friends, and he really needed her this year. She wanted a divorce but he would not give it to her. He needed her, and she knew he would be gone soon. He has leukemia and will be dead within a year. Johnny gives Forbes some sleeping pills and calls the clinic in Baltimore, and they confirm the leukemia.

Johnny drives to see Corrine Streeter, who is expecting him. She tells Johnny that it is an old story. She applied for a job and fell in love with the boss. She knew that the doctor was plotting to get rid of Forbes and had heard the doctor call Forbes and tell him a lawyer was coming over. She was there when he got the call and followed him. She pleaded and fought with him and the gun went off. Johnny tells her that it was self-defense, but she tells him she cannot get off. She has just killed Mrs. Forbes.

Johnny tells Porter to call someone else if he ever needs a policy investigated. Exp. Acct: $485.00

NOTES:
- REMAKE OF "THE JAMES CLAYTON MATTER" OF 12/5/1952
- THE ILE DE FRANCE WAS A LUXURY OCEAN LINER—SOON TO BE REPLACED WITH TRANSATLANTIC JET TRAVEL. THE FRENCH LINER WAS KNOWN FOR LUXURY FIRST-CLASS SERVICE.
- ROY ROWAN IS THE ANNOUNCER
- MUSICAL SUPERVISION IS BY AMERIGO MARINO

Producer:   Jack Johnstone        Writers:   John Dawson
Cast:       Jeanne Bates, Virginia Gregg, Russell Thorson, Parley Baer, Herb Ellis, Barney Phillips, Lawrence Dobkin

SHOW:        THE LONELY HEARTS MATTER
COMPANY:     NORTHWEST SURETY COMPANY
AGENT:       DAVE ELWOOD
PART 1       SHOW DATE:      4/23/1956

SYNOPSIS: Dave Elwood calls and asks if Johnny is free. Dave tells Johnny to come over and meet a nice girl. Johnny mentions lonely hearts and Dave jumps. Dave tells Johnny that if the girl is telling the truth, it may mean murder.

Johnny cabs to the office of Dave Elwood and he tells Johnny about Norma Wells, who has just flown in from Chicago. Her father died suddenly three days ago of acute enteritis and he had a $50,000 term life policy written five months ago. The beneficiary is his second wife Mabel Burke, who he married six months ago. Norma thinks that Mabel killed him. He had met her through a lonely-hearts club. Johnny talks to Norma who is very nervous. Johnny has Dave send out for some food while Norma tells Johnny that Mabel is strange, fuzzy around the edges. Not batty but strange. Mabel would never let Norma be alone with her father. Norma is sure that she is not having a father fixation, but she was not suspicious until the night he died. Norma has a trust fund and some bonds, but the policy was Mabel's idea. She started talking about insurance the week they were married. Her father was taken ill and Mabel would not allow him to call Norma, and she called her doctor, who has refused to sign a death certificate. Norma went to her father's doctor who suggested she come to the insurance company because the cause of death was questionable. Norma tells Johnny that he had met Mabel through a club of some sort. Breakfast is brought in and Johnny tells Dave that the case needs looking into. Johnny will have Norma order an autopsy, but he will not bet that Norma is telling the truth.

Johnny and Norma fly to Chicago, Illinois where Johnny learns that an autopsy has ordered, but is being held pending a court order. Johnny cabs to the Rendezvous Club and meets a lovely receptionist. Johnny asks how he can joint the club and she tells Johnny that none of the women in the club are under 45. They will take his application and put the information in the bulletin. Johnny tells her he is looking for a friend named Jonathan Wells, and she suspects that Johnny is with the police. Johnny starts looking for the files and Johnny puts her on top of her desk when she complains. Johnny then enters a room where a cigar is still burning in the ashtray. Johnny learns that the receptionist is Fanny Tetler, who has worked there for a year. Johnny asks about a file on Mabel Burke and Fanny tells Johnny that Mabel owns the club.

Tomorrow, another day, another husband, another death, and a sweet little old lady rocks and smiles.

## PART 2        SHOW DATE:    4/24/1956

Max Lancer calls from the District Attorney's office. He tells Johnny that the autopsy is still in progress. The family doctor thinks Norma is suffering from temporary hysteria and he was not serious in suggesting the insurance company. The death may have caused her to imagine things.

Johnny eats and muses over the facts. Maybe it was hysterical suspicion. Norma knocks on his hotel door and she is scared and wonders if she is crazy. She had gone to sign the authorization for the autopsy and went home. The phone rang and no one was on the line. Then she heard footsteps outside her door, but no one was there. Then the phone rang again and no one was there, so she came to see Johnny. Johnny tells her that he can do nothing until the autopsy results come in. Johnny tells Norma that Mabel owns the club. Johnny mentions the cigar and Norma tells him that Burton Creely, Mabel's nephew, smokes cigars. He moved in with them right after the wedding and he is the reason she moved out as he was always after her. She does not think he works, but just sponged off of Mabel. Her father got along with Burton, but he was different around him. Johnny tells her to stay put, and goes to see Mabel Wells.

Mrs. Wells opens the door and Johnny introduces himself. She tells Johnny that he is mistaken; Mr. Morningly is her agent. Johnny tells her he is from the main office and has some questions. She tells Johnny that she thinks death is a doorway to a much greater life. Norma used to live here, but she moved out. Mabel offers Johnny some tea and cookies and tells him that Jonathan always had tea and cookies every afternoon at 4:00. That's how she won him, with cookies and cakes. She had been so lonely when she met Jonathan. Mr. Walter Maberly Burke had died two years earlier of acute indigestion. She started the club because she was lonely and Burton suggested she start the business, that's how she met Jonathan. But Burton actually runs the club. She will have to move soon and all she has is the insurance and the worst luck with husbands. Johnny goes to his hotel and meets Max Lancer in the lobby, and he has his hat in his hands. Max tells Johnny that the autopsy showed that Jonathan Wells died of ground glass, so it is murder after all. Johnny asks Max to check on the death of Walter

Maberly Burke in St. Louis.

Tomorrow, a strange attack, a scared girl, a hunt in the dark, and thirteen knots make a noose.

**PART 3**          **SHOW DATE:**     **4/25/1956**

Johnny gets a call from Dave and tells him about the autopsy report. Dave will stop the claim, which was filed that day. Johnny asks for Mutual Records Service to check on Walter Burke's records. Dave calls her Murdering Mabel, but Johnny tells him she is just a sweet old lady who has bad luck with husbands.

Johnny buys dinner for Norma and they eat in his room. Johnny is sure that Norma is right now. The autopsy report gives Johnny a green light to move forward now. Johnny is not sure that Mabel is the one who did it. Johnny tells Norma that Max Lancer had called the room, but she did not answer, and she tells Johnny that she was there.

Johnny and Norma cab to her apartment through a busy city. At her apartment the door is open; but she remembers locking it. Johnny goes in and finds no one there, but the apartment has been searched; someone was looking for something. Norma looks through the apartment and fixes some coffee. She fixes hers with cream and sugar, which Johnny thinks looks funny. Johnny looks at the sugar, and finds ground glass in the sugar. Johnny calls Max and arranges for a policewoman to escort Norma to a hotel. Johnny cabs to the Wells residence and asks for Burton, and is told that he is not there. Johnny goes to the club and opens the unlocked front door where he finds Creely with a gun. Johnny tells him the safety is on and takes it away from him. Creely tells Johnny that he is breaking in, so Johnny tells him to call the police. Johnny tells Burton who he is, and about leaving the office the other day. Creely gives an excuse about thinking Johnny was a bill collector, and then that he was late for an appointment. He saw no necessity for talking to Johnny, as his aunt could tell him everything. When asked if he went to see Norma, Creely tells Johnny that Norma is a smug self-satisfied little phony. Johnny tells Burton about finding the ground glass, the same thing that killed Jonathan Wells. Creely is amazed that Wells was killed. Who would do it? He was such a nice guy and never quarreled with anyone. Burton tells Johnny that he only tried to be friendly with Norma and is engaged to Miss Tetler. He has a heart condition and runs the club. Creely gets excited when Johnny tells him that Mabel is a suspect. "Have you considered Norma as a suspect?" asks Creely. "Yes, I have." Johnny tells him.

Tomorrow, another murder comes to light, another link in a long chain, and an old lady weeps for the lost years.

**PART 4**          **SHOW DATE:**     **4/26/1956**

Dave Elwood calls and gives Johnny an update. Johnny is told that Walter Burke died and left Mabel $50,000. Johnny wonders if there had been husbands before Walter. Johnny is visited by Max and tells Johnny that he had been a guest of Mabel's all night and wants to see Nora now. Johnny updates him on Mabel's husbands. Nora arrives with her guard and Max tells Johnny that Gertie the guard used to beat up the men she arrested and had to be transferred.

Johnny goes to see Mabel who rattles on about Max and her husband. When Johnny tells her about the ground glass, she calls that ridiculous and tells Johnny that her husband would have known. She tells Johnny that one's death is written in the stars, and that astrology is as real as reincarnation. Johnny receives a call from Max who tells Johnny that Walter Burke died of ground glass. Johnny hangs up just as Mabel collapses in pain.

**PART 5**        **SHOW DATE:**        **4/27/1956**

Max Lancer calls Johnny and asks how Mabel is. Johnny tells Max that it was ground glass, the same as her husband. Johnny tells Max that they were only going on suspicion about the insurance. Johnny thinks someone tried to murder her.

Johnny waits at the hospital for Mabel to recover. He had tagged her as a murderer, and now she has the key. Johnny meets Burton Creely in the hallway and tells him she is weaker now. He wonders who would do such a thing. There had been no visitors to the house and she had always been a lonely person. Creely tells Johnny that the police think she killed Jonathan and then tried to kill herself Norma walks up and Creely leaves. Johnny tells her about Mabel's condition and she tells Johnny that Mabel is too mean to die. Norma thinks maybe she did it for remorse, or is insane. A nurse tells Johnny that Mabel wants to see him. Johnny and Norma go into the room, and Creely comes in a few moments later. Mabel is smiling weakly and tells Johnny that she is ready to die. She tells Burton to straighten his tie, and is happy to see Norma there. Mabel tells Johnny that she has been thinking, and that death is just a doorway. She tells Johnny that she did not kill Jonathan, and Johnny tells her he knew that. She had been puzzling over who did kill him and she has decided to tell Johnny. She chides Burton for giving her a box of chocolates that morning. She can understand why he did it. She tells Johnny to take Burton and give him a good talking to, he must not go around . . . and then she dies. Burton pulls a gun and holds Norma as a hostage as he locks Johnny in a closet. Johnny finally breaks out and calls the desk only to learn that a man had stolen an ambulance. Johnny meets Max downstairs and they follow the ambulance to signs of a crash. A man yells that a man with a gun is in the woods. Johnny goes into the woods and glimpses Burton and tells at him to give up. Johnny has his gun at his side and cannot aim it. Norma pulls away from Burton and Johnny takes a chance and shoots. Johnny runs up and discovers that Norma is ok, but Burton is dead, shot in the heart.

Remarks: A heart with a bullet hole in it, there is a real lonely heart.

Exp. Acct:        $416.40

**NOTES:**
- ROY ROWAN IS THE ANNOUNCER
- MUSIC SUPERVISION IS BY AMERIGO MARINO
- THE CONTENT FOR EPISODE 4 WAS OBTAINED FROM THE SCRIPT ON FILE IN THE KNX COLLECTION AT THE THOUSAND OAKS LIBRARY.

**Producer:**  Jack Johnstone        **Writers:**  Les Crutchfield

**Cast:**     Lucille Meredith, Mary Jane Croft, Virginia Gregg, Herb Ellis,
Howard McNear, Stacy Harris

| | |
|---|---|
| SHOW: | THE CALLICLES MATTER |
| COMPANY: | EASTERN CASUALTY AND TRUST COMPANY |
| AGENT: | DAVE BLAINE |
| PART 1 | SHOW DATE:     4/30/1956 |

SYNOPSIS: Robert Ecker calls Johnny about an appointment with Mr. Parsons.
Johnny wants to talk about David Parsons who is missing. Johnny is told that
Mr. Parsons, Sr. is home ill today. Come to the office and I will arrange to take
you out there. Johnny does not want to be any trouble, but Ecker tells Johnny
that there would be more trouble if he did not come to the office.

Johnny flies to Los Angeles, California and meets Robert Ecker at Parsons
Stocks and Bonds. Ecker asks why Johnny thinks David Parsons is missing. They
do not know where he is but he is not missing. Johnny tells Ecker that David has
not been seen for ten days, and that is missing. Ecker tells Johnny that when
talking about David with his father; do not use the word missing as Mr. Parsons,
Sr. is very adamant about some matters. Johnny tells Ecker that David Parson is
insured for $100,000, and has access to large amounts of stocks and bonds, and
that is why the insurance company is interested. Ecker tells Johnny that David
Parsons is worth over a million dollars. Johnny finds copies of the insurance
policies and tells Ecker that he has looked up the answers to the questions
Johnny had just asked him.

Johnny and Ecker drive to the home of David Parson, Sr. in a new 1956
Studebaker Golden Hawk, and Ecker avoids all talk of David Parson, Jr. In the
home, Mrs. Parsons greets Johnny and tells him he is not supposed to meet her.
The matter will be handled from "up stairs" as her father in-law feels he has
extraordinary powers in this matter. Mr. Parsons screams for Ecker and Mrs.
Parsons leaves. Ecker and Johnny go to Mr. Parsons' bedroom where Mr. Parsons
is in bed. Parsons demands Johnny's ID and yells at Ecker to call Boston and
check on Johnny. Johnny tells him that his ID is real and he can call him at this
hotel. Johnny thought Mr. Parsons could straighten things out, but it appears
Johnny will have to go to someone else. Johnny tells Parsons that he must find
out about the situation, and Parsons tells Johnny he will break him in half if he
tries. Ecker is told to leave and Johnny is told he has five minutes. Johnny tells
Parsons he has five minutes, ten minutes or a million minutes if he needs them.
Johnny has a report that Parson's son has been missing for ten days; one of
David's clients reported it. Parsons says "bah" to Johnny and gets really mad
when Johnny asks if he has had an audit. Ecker is called and told to throw
Johnny out, but Johnny tells Parsons that he has Ecker by 25 pounds. Ecker tells
Johnny he will wait downstairs. Parsons relents and tells Johnny that David had
left a week ago Tuesday and they have heard nothing, and that the police have
not been called. They are waiting to hear from David. Parsons has not looked to

see if anything is missing and tells Johnny that he will post $100,000 in cash if necessary. Parsons does not want the matter in the papers. Johnny tells him that he cannot transfer liability, and you better fix it so I can talk to Mrs. Parsons.

Johnny leaves the bedroom as Parsons is looking for something to throw. Johnny meets Mrs. Parsons at the front door and he tells her he wants her to file a missing person's report. She tells Johnny to come see her at 2:00. Ecker tells Johnny to be careful, as Johnny is Parsons' kind, his dish of meat. Johnny ignores Ecker's comment, and compares Parsons to Svengali and Rasputin, but Parson is not in the same class with them, but he should have guessed it. Ecker was trying to tell me, but I would not listen.

Tomorrow, some more facts on how the earth swallowed a man.

**PART 2**        **SHOW DATE:**        **5/1/1956**

Mrs. David Parson calls Johnny and asks if she can pick him up at his hotel. If her father-in-law knew she was meeting him, he would probably kill her.

Johnny calls Dave Blain and explains the case so far, and how Parson's Sr. tried to throw him out. Dorothy Parsons picks up Johnny and he comments on how it looks as though she is going on a picnic. She is going to drive to the ocean, and tells Johnny to stop looking glum. She suggests going to lunch to talk. She stops the car and they walk along the beach. She tells Johnny that he married David when she was 18, and has been married for 14 years. They live well and David is successful, but Johnny notices that she does not talk about missing David, and he does not believe her. Why does no one want to talk about this, he wonders. Dorothy tells Johnny that she last saw David Tuesday at breakfast; he ate and left for work. She called later and he had not come in to the office. Tuesday night she was out with friend and came in late and did not look in David's bedroom. On Wednesday Ecker called and asked to speak with David, who was not at the office. She then called David's father, who said he would handle things. He hinted that David might have gone off with someone because he had gone off several times before and said nothing when he came back. She tells Johnny that David is brilliant and impeccable and a devoted husband. Johnny asks her if she expected Johnny to make love to her and she says "yes. Why?" She thinks she is attractive and Johnny asks why she stalled him all afternoon. Johnny asks why she told him she would call the police and then changed her mind. She tells Johnny that she wants to go home. While Dorothy makes a phone call at a gas station, Johnny watches southern California roll by. Dorothy tells Johnny that she had called home and Johnny tells her he is going to the police. She tells him that there is no need, as David has come home. Suddenly there is a crash; Johnny is shaken up and Dorothy is dead.

Tomorrow, trouble comes early and stays late.

**PART 3**        **SHOW DATE:**        **5/2/1956**

Dave Blaine calls and wonders why Johnny is in the Hospital. Johnny tells of meeting with Dorothy and the accident. Parsons is back, and he will wrap it up. She was a nice person and he saw her die.

Johnny gets a sedative at the hospital, and wakes up screaming "Look Out!" Sister Amadea tells Johnny to go to sleep, but Johnny wants to talk about it. He tells her about the case and what he had learned. It was a strange afternoon; he could have fallen in love with her. He tells her he never gets used to things like this, and goes back to sleep. The next day Johnny buys a paper and reads of the accident, an unidentified woman was killed. No names, no details. Ecker visits Johnny in his hotel room and tells him that Mr. Parsons, Sr. is concerned about him, and young Parsons is upset over his wife. Johnny settles up his hotel bill, buys plane tickets and goes to the Parsons home. Parsons still has a vile temper and blames Johnny for Dorothy's accident. Johnny helps himself to Parsons whiskey, and then meets David Parsons, who is not what Johnny expected. He did not look like a broker. David tells Johnny that he rode a freighter up to Seattle; he just wanted to be alone and think and decided not to tell anyone. Johnny asks David to sign some reports and Johnny asks the name of the ship, which David says was the Loreen B, a lumber ship. Johnny checks back into his hotel, cancels his plane reservations and calls Ecker, who is not in. Johnny rents a car and drives to Ecker's apartment and waits for him. Ecker comes in, and leaves with Johnny following right behind him to the Parkway Funeral Home. After waiting a few minutes, Johnny goes in to see Ecker looking at the body of Mrs. Parsons. Johnny asks Ecker who she is, because she is not Mrs. Parsons. Ecker tells Johnny that the girl is Ellen Myers, his fiancée. She was a special girl, and he loved her and she would do anything for him. Parsons had blown up and she volunteered to mislead Johnny. The "David Parsons" is just someone the old man hired; he has 23 detectives looking for the real David. Parsons wants it kept quiet because there is a merger in the offing and he wants David clean and unsullied when the merger is complete. Johnny tells Ecker that he was wise to the fake David because he was not broken up, and because he was a bad actor. He also gave some bad answers to being on a ship. Ecker tells Johnny he will help him.

Tomorrow, we find out that Callicles was a Greek, maybe the greatest one of them all.

## PART 4          SHOW DATE:          5/3/1956

The operator calls and Johnny tells Parsons that he is still looking for his son. Johnny has two signatures that constitute witness forgery. I'll be there in 20 minutes.

Johnny hires an attorney to impound the records of the brokerage house and gives him the forged reports. Johnny drives to see Parsons and tells him that he did not believe either of the actors. "You have botched up everything. You tried to drive me off the trail" he tells Parsons. Johnny gets the name of the detectives, Universal Operators, and Mr. Underwood as the detective Parsons had hired, but they have gotten no leads. Johnny tells Parsons that he has started the process of an audit and Parsons goes ballistic. Johnny is told that the real Mrs. Parsons has been sent to Palm Springs and Johnny tells Parsons to call and let them know he is on the way.

Johnny drives to Underwood's office and gets a report on what they have done. Johnny fires Underwood, and tells Parsons. Johnny drives to the home of David Parsons and speaks to the real Mrs. Parsons. She tells Johnny that she was the last person to see David, on the 13th. He had not packed any clothes and he has no enemies, but he never discussed the office at home. They have been married 18 years and have never talked of divorce. The office thinks he is on a business trip. They entertained and traveled and enjoyed their life. He liked to read and write and fancied himself a scholar of literature. David was not a drunk and was in good health and had a quiet personality. She tells Johnny that she has been seeing some friends in Palm Springs. Johnny is getting mad and tells her to file a missing person's report, as she may have fooled around too long. The police arrive and interview everyone. The District Attorney negates Johnny's court order and starts an official audit.

Johnny visits David's physician, Dr. Warner, and tells him about David being missing. Johnny is told that David was in excellent health for a man in his position. David knew how to escape from his father, and had no mental problems. They played golf and the Parsons seemed happy. He had talked to David informally once, and he could quote the classics. One time he just stared and quoted Callicles: "But if there were a man who had sufficient force, he would shake off and break through and escape from all this. He would trample under foot all our formulas, and spells and charms, and all our laws, which are against nature. The slave would rise in rebellion and be lord over us and the light of natural justice would shine forth." He quoted it the day before he disappeared.

The answer is with the Greek who lived two thousand years ago. Tomorrow, we'll find it.

### PART 5    SHOW DATE:    5/4/1956

David Parson Sr. calls Johnny and tells him that the papers are full of David's disappearance. Johnny asks if he wants him to give the papers the other half of the story, about arranging for people to impersonate your son.

Johnny buys the newspaper and reads about the story. He calls Parsons later and tells Parson that he should have called the police earlier. The District Attorney has impounded the books, and $5000 is missing from David's personal account, it was withdrawn on the morning he disappeared. Parson tells Johnny that David means nothing to him, the only reason he wants him back is to complete the merger.

Johnny goes with Officer Jerry Ingle to interview a bank teller who has the withdrawal slip. The teller tells Johnny that Parsons came up and gave him the slip. He was a little surprised, but Parsons has withdrawn large amounts before, and Parson asked for it in $100's and $50s. The teller tells them that Parsons was not in a hurry that morning; like he did not care what direction he went in. Other angles are investigated, and Parsons is spotted all over the area. Johnny locates a bartender who remembers seeing Parson there. He did not talk to anyone, and was making a long distance call and had asked for a bunch of quarters. Parsons had asked him if he knew Callicles. Johnny tells Officer Ingle that Callicles was a poet and the bartender tells them he thought he was a bookie. Officer Ingle checks with the phone company and learns that a call had been placed to Kenneth Temple in San Francisco. Johnny calls and gets no answer at the number, and then drives to the Parson's home. Mrs. Parson does not know who Temple is. Mrs. Parsons is getting upset and the phone rings with a call for Officer Ingle. Mr. Temple is on the phone and Temple says that Parsons is with him now. Mrs. Parson talks to David, who asks if she remembers the times he had asked her to talk to him. About all the time she was too busy with other things. David tells her that this is the end of things for them, and for father too. Tell him that. Tell him the merger is all his. Anger does not worry me anymore. He is going away with Temple. He is shipping out on Temple's boat and will not be coming back. Johnny asks about Callicles. So, you found out, and he repeats the verses.

The police close their case and the insurance company will have to sit on the $100,000 bond and hope David comes back.

Remarks: "Why didn't he talk about these things to me"? Mrs. Parsons asked. I told her he did but no one ever listened. She didn't understand that either.

Exp. Acct: $1,100.59

NOTES:
- GRIGORY YEFIMOVICH RASPUTIN (1872-1916) WAS A RUSSIAN MYSTIC AND COURT FIGURE WITH A PERVASIVE INFLUENCE OVER THE IMPERIAL FAMILY.
- SVENGALI WAS A MALEFICENT HYPNOTIST IN THE NOVEL "TRILBY" (1894) BY GEORGE DU MAURIER
- ONE NIGHT IN THE HOSPITAL: $14.95 – NOT A BAD DEAL.
- THE QUOTE IS FROM PLATO'S "GORGIAS": THE SPEECH OF CALLICLES IS FROM "CONVENTION" AND "NATURE." TECHNICALLY THE REFERENCES IN THE PROGRAM SHOULD HAVE BEEN TO PLATO, NOT TO CALLICLES.
- THIS STORY IS BASED ON "THE BRISBANE FRAUD MATTER."
- VIRGINIA GREGG WAS IN BOTH VERSIONS OF THIS STORY.
- ROY ROWAN IS THE ANNOUNCER
- MUSIC SUPERVISION IS BY AMERIGO MARINO

Producer: Jack Johnstone    Writers: John Dawson
Cast:    Virginia Gregg, Harry Bartell, Lillian Buyeff, Will Wright, Jeanne Bates, Carlton Young, Lawrence Dobkin, Bert Holland, Marvin Miller, Herb Vigran

| SHOW: | THE SILVER BLUE MATTER |
| --- | --- |
| COMPANY: | MONOGUARANTEE INSURANCE COMPANY |
| AGENT: | RALPH DEAN |
| PART 1 | SHOW DATE: 5/7/1956 |

**SYNOPSIS:** Ralph Dean calls, and tells Johnny that his wife wants to kill him. She wants a mink coat but he cannot afford one. Yesterday he lost 80 minks coats in Los Angeles and she wants to know why he can pay for 80 minks and not buy her one. Johnny tells him to buy her flowers and Ralph tells him he did; and they went into the disposal.

Johnny flies to Los Angeles, California and meets Lt. Ramon Garcia at the airport. Johnny is told that there is a man dying in the hospital that Johnny needs to talk to, the night watchman who saw the thieves; they were just kids, a gang.

Johnny and Lt. Garcia rush to the hospital and wait for the night watchman to wake up. Johnny learns that the guard is Albert Chrisman, who has no family, and was beaten by the gang members. He worked in a warehouse district. The police check the area regularly, and the kids hit 15 minutes after the police went by. The kids only know minks and passed up Chinchilla coats worth much more. Chrisman's partner was on his rounds and was slugged, and no one saw anything. Chrisman wakes up and asks for water and asks who Johnny and Lt. Garcia are. He tells them the kids came with a telegram, he opened the door and one of them hit him. The kid was 18 or 19, dark skinned with a dark jacket. Chrisman says he would recognize one of them; he had a mark on his arm and then he loses consciousness. Lt. Garcia tells Johnny that in that neighborhood there are 50,000 kids in who fit that description.

Johnny talks with the owner of the furs and then goes to the warehouse and inspects it. Like the police, Johnny finds nothing. Lt. Garcia tells Johnny that he grew up in the area, and it is a backwash of society. The residents are not on their side; they always are against the police. There are gangs there and some of them are pretty rough. They probably used the lunchroom across the street to case the warehouse. Red Wellers is the owner and Johnny is told that he might be able to get something from him. Lt. Garcia tells Johnny to remember that Chrisman may die before he makes any deals.

Johnny meets with Red Wellers and he knows Johnny is working on the fur case. Red knows nothing, and tells Johnny that the only people in the diner were old men with long beards. Johnny tells him that Chrisman is dying, and gives him his hotel, just in case.

Tomorrow, fear stalks the streets, closing the mouths of a sullen and suspicious people, terrifying a lonely girl and bringing death in a dusty alley.

**PART 2**        **SHOW DATE:        5/8/1956**

Red Wellers calls Johnny and asks what will happen if he talks. Red tells

Johnny that he will need money to move if he talks, and Johnny tells him he can take care of it.

Johnny calls Lt. Garcia at the hospital, and learns that Chrisman is still unconscious. Johnny waits for Wellers to arrive, but he does not show.

Johnny cabs to the warehouse and the area is deserted. Johnny goes to the diner and there is a girl working there. Johnny asks about the boss and is told that he is not there. Johnny gets Red's address but the girl tells Johnny that Red was going out somewhere. Johnny tells her that he is working on the theft of the furs and she drops the silverware. She tells Johnny that she is Carla Monte and lives in the area and has worked there for a year. Carla tells Johnny that kids do hang out there, but she does not know any of their names, and Johnny recognizes that she is plainly scared. Johnny tells Carla why she is scared and tries to convince her to talk, but she tells Johnny that he does not have to live here, and maybe the mobs have already taken over here. Johnny tells her that only a small minority turns to crime, but she cannot tell him anything. On the way out, Carla asks Johnny if someone knew someone who could help, could he keep him or her out of it? Johnny tells her that he can be lenient, and she decides to trust him. She knows someone who might be involved, her brother Eddie.

Johnny cabs to Carla's apartment and then to a drive-in and then to a pool hall looking for Eddie. Carla tells Johnny that Eddie should not hang out there, but they have no parents and he will not listen to a sister. They spot Eddie and she introduces Johnny. Carla wants Eddie to talk to him, and Johnny tells Eddie that he wants to talk. Johnny asks if Eddie knows anything about the robbery and Eddie tells Johnny that he "don't know nothin' about nothin'" and leaves. Johnny calls Lt. Garcia and learns that Eddie was involved in the robbery. Johnny tells Carla that Red Wellers has been found dead in an alley.

Tomorrow, a lonely broken-hearted girl, a blood stained shirt, and a fight with a cornered rat.

**PART 3          SHOW DATE:     5/9/1956**

Lt. Garcia calls Johnny just as he has finished his breakfast. Lt. Garcia demands that Johnny to come to headquarters; he wants to know more about Eddie Monte.

Johnny cabs to Lt. Garcia's office and they talk about the case. Lt. Garcia apologizes for yelling at Johnny and tells him that the chief was on his back. Lt. Garcia wants to know how Eddie figures in as he has a record for petty crimes. Johnny tells him the things he learned from Carla and how he went to see Eddie. She suspected Eddie and asked Johnny to help keep Eddie out of trouble. Lt. Garcia tells Johnny that Red was killed for trying to talk about the kids using the diner for a lookout spot. Johnny feels that Carla is a nice girl, and is special, in spite of everything. Lt. Garcia tells Johnny that he knows what Johnny is talking about. He had a sister who was special, but she ended up in prison.

The police have been checking Fences with no results so Johnny cabs to the diner to see Carla. The diner is closed so Johnny walks to Carla's apartment, where the door is locked. Carla lets Johnny in and tells him that Eddie did not come home last night. Johnny asks for two drinks and makes her take one to relax. Johnny tells Carla that the police are looking for Eddie in connection with Red Weller's murder. They think Eddie is a member of the gang. Carla tells Johnny that Eddie was out all night and did not come home until morning. Just as Johnny asks to look through Eddies' room he comes home. Carla tells Eddie to give himself up, and Eddie tells Carla that she sold him out because his friends told him the police were looking for him. Johnny starts to call the police and Eddie pulls a gun. Johnny is told to back off and Carla is told to pack some clothes for him. Carla tells Eddie a police car has just pulled up. Eddie threatens to kill Carla, and then runs out the door.

Tomorrow, a police net tightens and traps a frightened rat, a boy sobs in a jail cell, and an innocent man dies in his sleep.

### PART 4            SHOW DATE:      5/10/1956

Lt. Garcia calls and Johnny tells him that the police are still there, but Eddie got away. Johnny tells him that he is looking for the furs, not Eddie. Johnny is told that the police are looking for Eddie's friends on the list.

Johnny feels like 2 cents and looks out the window. Johnny surveys the slums, which have fostered Eddie and so many others and Carla blames herself for Eddie's problems. Johnny tells her she did the best she could. Carla asks why Johnny did not use his gun to kill Eddie, and he does not know why. Johnny looks thought Eddie's room and plays a record to keep him company. Johnny finds nothing but a lot of photos of hotrods. Johnny finds a recent photo of a hotrod with Eddie beside it. Obviously it is his, but Carla does not know that he owns one. Johnny thinks Eddie might have used the truck to carry the furs, and that Eddie is the leader of the gang.

Johnny cabs to Lt. Garcia's office and learns two of Eddie's friends have been picked up, but one had an alibi. Johnny shows him the photos of the truck and the license plate. Lt. Garcia does not recognize the background and he agrees to have copies made.

Johnny and Lt. Garcia question Mario Santores, who has a record for possession of stolen goods, and he claims that he was framed and does not know anything. Johnny tells him that Eddie Monte remembers a lot about what he and Mario did and who was involved, but Mario has not heard of the robbery. Mario starts to stumble and admits he heard of the robbery. Johnny tells him that Eddie told about Mario stabbing Red Wellers and Mario tells him that Eddie lied to them. Mario agrees to tell them the truth.

Tomorrow, a cautious search, an ambush, bullets and tears, and the end is violence

### PART 5            SHOW DATE:      5/11/1956

Carla calls Johnny in Lt. Garcia's office, and he tells her that the police have picked up Mario, who has just made a statement and that Mario says that Eddie planned everything. She tells Johnny that she is coming to headquarters as she wants to be there if Eddie is brought in.

Johnny reads Mario's statement, and thinks he was telling the truth about Eddie buying the truck and organizing the robbery. Chrisman's remark about a boy with a mark on his arm matches the mark on Mario's arm. Mario also told them that Chuey Martel killed Wellers, and that no one knows where Eddie took the furs. So far Eddie is only guilty of the robbery, and Lt. Garcia is glad for Carla. Lt. Garcia gets a call and learns Chuey Martel has been picked up, and that Chrisman has died. Now Eddie is wanted for murder. Johnny rents a car and searches the area with Carla looking for the area in the photograph. In an alley, Carla spots the fence and shack in the photos. Johnny tells Carla to call the police from a nearby house and then walks to the shack in the near darkness. Johnny finds Edie's truck behind the shack with the furs, and Eddie is there with a gun. Eddie knows about Chrisman, and Johnny urges him to give up, as Carla is with him. Eddie is going to kill Johnny, and Johnny keeps talking to him about Carla, and what he is doing to her. Carla calls for Johnny just as Lt. Garcia runs up to the shack. Johnny tells Lt. Garcia that Eddie has jumped the fence and is running across the railroad yard. Lt. Garcia and Johnny chase after him as Eddie is trying to outrun a train, but he does not make it. Lt. Garcia tells Johnny "there must be better ways to die."

Remarks: Well, I guess Carla made the remarks for me . "I don't know Johnny. Those 80 fur coats, they will go back into stock now and they will be sold to women who will wear them to parties and dances and night clubs, and they will be happy in them and they will never know about Eddie or me or what happened here tonight.

Exp. Acct:     $541.25

NOTES:
* ROY ROWAN IS THE ANNOUNCER
* MUSIC SUPERVISION IS BY AMERIGO MARINO

Producer:   Jack Johnstone        Writers:   Les Crutchfield
Cast:        Lucille Meredith, Edgar Barrier, Victor Perrin, Jack Kruschen,
             Tommy Cook, Richard Crenna

◆   ❖   ◆

SHOW:        THE MATTER OF THE MEDIUM, WELL DONE
COMPANY:     UNIVERSAL ADJUSTMENT BUREAU
AGENT:       PAT MCCRACKEN
PART 1       SHOW DATE:     5/14/1956

SYNOPSIS: Pat McCracken calls and asks if Johnny has had his fortune told. Johnny tells Pat that he has; a fortuneteller, Madam Ga-Ga told him he would become an insurance investigator and it has stuck. Pat asks how Johnny would like to try your hand as a psychic investigator.

Johnny cabs to Pat's office and he does not know what type of case this will turn out to be. Pat tells Johnny that Tommy Green in New York has a young, badly spoiled (Johnny loves 'em that way) client named Carol Sharpe who is a playgirl, and has a $110,000 policy with the family as beneficiaries. She just requested Tommy to change the beneficiary to a man named Tony Ricardo and a Madam Celia something. Tommy had another client turn up dead after making a medium the beneficiary.

Johnny travels to Tommy Green's office in New York City, and Tommy outlines the case. Tommy tells Johnny that spiritualism is a recognized religion, but there are charlatans, and one had bilked his mother when he was a kid. Madam Celia Morgana-Morgana is the one in this case. Tommy has not changed the beneficiary yet, but he cannot stall too much longer. Tony sounds like a playboy, but Tommy does not know much about him.

Johnny cabs to the Bell Towers on the East River and inquires about a small apartment for a few days. Johnny is told that there is a five-room penthouse available for $1,500 a month. Johnny shows the manager his card and asks for something near Miss Sharpe. She is not in trouble and Johnny does not want her to know he is there. There is a two-room apartment on floor 10 available at $325 per week, one week in advance. Johnny calls an old buddy, Randy Singer, and Johnny wants to meet with him. Johnny orders a bottle of scotch and when Randy gets there he tells Johnny that Carol Sharpe is loaded and throws her money around at the clubs. Randy also knows Madam Celia Morgana-Morgana; he has chased her all over the island of Manhattan. She sees the past, the future and right into your pocket book and is operating in Jersey now. She operates with class. She goes into a trance and makes with the voices. She claims the trances cause great agony of body and mind and tells of her medical bills and the clients pay. At each séance she tells them just a little and has them hanging and if you come back next week she will tell you more. Randy tells Johnny that he will see if he can dig up a séance to show him what goes on. There are dozens, hundreds to choose from. Randy had handled the case Tommy Green told him about. Johnny asks Randy to run a make on Tony Ricardo.

Johnny ponders how to meet Carol Sharpe and the phone rings. Randy has setup a date with a medium for tonight. Randy can write a book on Ricardo. Make sure you meet him first; and carry a gun.

Tomorrow, well sometimes the best-laid plans can take a terrible beating when a lovely girl steps into the picture.

### PART 2    SHOW DATE:    5/15/1956

Randy calls and tells Johnny that he has nothing new on Tony Ricardo; just look out for him. Randy is working on setting up a séance, and will call Johnny.

Johnny talks with Tommy Green and wonders what will happen if Madam Celia turns out to be ok? Johnny tells Tommy that Randy had hinted that Tony was not legitimate. Tommy is sure that Celia is a fraud. Johnny tells him that he is staying at the same apartment building and asks Tommy to find out how the family in Pennsylvania is doing; to run a fake news story or something, editors love to talk.

Johnny cabs back to the apartment and runs into Carol in the elevator. Johnny acts spacey and tells her that he must be psychic. He cannot believe it. He used to have a dream as a kid about a girl named Carol, and she looks just like the girl in the dream. Johnny apologies and tells her he must have just imagined it. Carol tells Johnny that he had a veridical dream, a "truth dream," a psychic experience. Johnny tells her that he does not believe in that, but she tells him that there are thousands of cases on record. Johnny apologizes again and goes to his apartment. Johnny notices that Carol noticed which apartment he went into. Fifteen minutes later Carol calls and tells Johnny that she wants to talk to Johnny about his dream. She got his name from the desk clerk. When she tells Johnny her name is Carol, they arrange to meet for drinks later. Randy calls and tells Johnny that he has a séance set up for tonight. Meet me around seven at headquarters.

Johnny and a well-dressed Carol meet in the cocktail lounge and Johnny tells her she probably thinks he was just trying to pick her up. Johnny orders sherry and bitters for Carol and VO over ice for himself. Carol talks about the dream Johnny had and she tells him that the only way he could have known her was through a psychic experience. Johnny almost tells Carol who he is, but the waiter interrupts and saves him. Carol tells Johnny about Madam Morgana-Morgana and the messages she has received. Carol begs Johnny to go to see Madam Morgana-Morgana with her and Johnny agrees and Carol agrees to set up a meeting for tomorrow.

Johnny stops by his room before going to see Randy, and there is a note under his door; "If you value your life you will stay away from Carole Sharpe."

Tomorrow, I find out a thing or two about a killer and about a medium not so well done.

## PART 3          SHOW DATE:     5/16/1956

Tony Ricardo calls and asks if Johnny has received his note. Tony is anxious when Johnny tells him the police will be interested in it. Tony wants to see Johnny and leaves his phone number, Sunrise 3-9970.

Johnny cabs to the 18th precinct where he tells Randy about meeting Carole and the dream story and going to see Madam Morgana-Morgana tomorrow. Randy shows Johnny the file on Tony Ricardo, who has a record a mile long. Johnny tells Randy that the man he talked to was much younger than the man in the file. Randy remembers that Tony has some kids, including Anthony Jr., a Rutgers graduate. Johnny and Randy cab to the location of the séance and are met at the door by a tall dark man who takes them in to the temple, an old dining room with a table and chairs. After a flash of light and a puff of smoke, the medium, Madam Clarabelle, appears in the room wearing an old bed sheet, a turban and the faint odor of gin. Each person is asked to put something personal on a tray, and Johnny puts his watch on the tray. They all join hands to form a flux, and her assistant Hemmingway passes among them asking for $5.00. The medium asks for "Votan" to join them, and there is a knocking on the floor. A ring is picked up and she sees clothing and sewing machines. She picks up

Johnny's watch and sees tall buildings and sees Tri-Mutual and Universal Adjustment, and papers with "policy" written on them. I have many things to tell you. She picks up Randy's badge and yells "A COP!" and the séance is over. Hemmingway bolts out the door, but Randy holds on to Madam Clarabelle and she tells Randy that all the money goes to charity. Johnny asks how she knew so much about him, and she tells him that Hemmingway (that bum!) asked where you came from, and Hartford is known for insurance. The clothing maker called from a hotel, so she called the hotel back and got his address in Woodbine, New Jersey. There is nothing there but farms and clothes factories, and he was not a farmer. It was so easy. Johnny goes back to his hotel and Randy tells Johnny that Madam Morgana-Morgana will not be so easy to expose, if you can expose her.

Tomorrow, the medium, well done appears.

### PART 4      SHOW DATE:     5/17/1956

Carole calls Johnny and tells him that she has made the arrangements for the séance to night at eight. Carole agrees to have dinner with Johnny at six.

Johnny meets Tony Ricardo, whose father was a well-known gangster. Tony apologizes for the threatening note, and tells Johnny that he is concerned about the spiritualist who has her hands on Carole. Johnny tells him that he knows that Tony is going to be named as a beneficiary, but Tony tells Johnny that it was Madam Morgana's idea. When Johnny tells him that the dream story was made up, Tony is speechless. Johnny tells him that he is an investigator and is meeting with the medium to try and prove that she is a fraud. Tony is afraid that Carol will change her policy and turn up dead. Tony briefs Johnny on how Madam Morgana-Morgana conducts her meetings. Johnny calls Tommy and he tells Johnny that the family is doing fine in Mauchunk, Pennsylvania. The mother and two brothers will not have to work for a living. Dave is the bad sheep, and tears around the country in a sports car and is somewhere here in New York now. Johnny calls Randy and asks him to find David Sharpe, no description, staying somewhere here in the city. Call me when you find him. Johnny cabs to a camera shop and buys a small camera, special film and very special flash bulbs. Randy calls back and tells Johnny that they have located David Sharpe; it was just dumb luck. He is staying not too far from Johnny, and Johnny asks Randy to put a tail on him.

Johnny has dinner with Carol, but is preoccupied. They take a cab to Union City and go to the house where Madam Morgana-Morgana is. Madam Morgana-Morgana, a plain woman welcomes them by name, and takes them inside. Johnny tells the woman that he doesn't think that he is psychic, but they thought his brother Richard was. The woman has a strange feeling about Richard, as that name has been on her mind all day. Johnny meets the others in the circle and the séance begins. Johnny flicks a lighter, and is told he can smoke, but Johnny says it is just a nervous habit. Johnny notes some metal horns on the floor, through which the voices of the spirits come. Johnny flicks his lighter, and Carol tells him not to light it. Madam Morgana-Morgana writhes as if in pain and the séance begins. Carol hears a voice of her father and he talks to her, as Johnny takes pictures with his camera. The voice tells Carol to always do what he instructs her to do. A voice calls "John," and Johnny calls for "Dick," his brother. Johnny carries on a brief conversation with Dick about things only a brother would know. Amazing! But Johnny notes that he never had a brother. Johnny plays it straight and even stays around afterwards but cannot wait to develop the infrared film in the camera at the police labs.

Tomorrow, the wind up, and a bit of heartbreak for a very chastened girl.

## PART 5        SHOW DATE:      5/18/1956

Carol calls and tells Johnny that he was so quiet on the way back last night. Carol tells him she paid $100 for the session. Johnny asks her to meet him for breakfast.

Johnny calls Randy and asks about the film and the tail. Randy tells Johnny that David was in the area of the séance last night. Johnny calls Mauchunk and talks to the local newspaper editor about the family, especially Dave. At breakfast, Johnny tells Carole that he wants to see Madam Morgana-Morgana again, today. Johnny mentions that Carol has a brother, David, and she tells Johnny that he is not really a brother. Her mother took him in, but she would rather not talk about it. Her father allowed it, but David's father had been a criminal, and his father was before him. Her father left money to him, but it was never enough. When Carol asks how Johnny knows these things, he tells her who he is and why he is there. She tells Johnny that she hates him, and he tells her that he is sure that Madam Morgana-Morgana is a fraud. Johnny tells Carol to call Tony and to meet him at the 18th precinct.

Johnny and Randy look at the pictures he took, and they are revealing. Carol and Tony arrive, and Johnny shows them the pictures. Carol sees Madam Morgana-Morgana moving the trumpets with a rod. She also sees a tube coming from a trumpet where a man could whisper into it. Johnny shows the trumpet in front of him, and tells Carol that the story of the brother was made up. Randy tells Carol about the fraudulent medium that could tell Johnny much more. Johnny reminds her of what he was able to find out about her, and Johnny asks if Tony was in with her. Randy tells Johnny that David is on the move again. Johnny and the others take a cab to the house of Madam Morgana-Morgana, and Johnny notices a Studebaker Golden Hawk parked in the back with Pennsylvania tags. Carole recognizes it as David's car. Johnny rings the bell and Madam Morgana-Morgana opens the door, and Johnny invites himself in, with the others. Johnny tells her that she will never have another séance; the monkey business is over. Johnny shows her the pictures and tells her about the camera he used. She tells Johnny that she was not doing anything malicious. Carol has money, as do the others who come to her. She tells Johnny that the insurance was not her idea. Johnny asks where David is, and he comes into the room. David knows all about Johnny. Tony realizes that putting him as a beneficiary would send the police after him, allowing the others to get out of town. The lights go out, and there are shots, and a fight breaks out, only Johnny ends up beating on Randy, and Tony had grabbed David when the lights went out. Randy tells

Johnny that he had sneaked in the back door and took over when he saw what was going on.

Well, what happens to David Sharpe and Madam Morgana-Morgana is up to the courts. It's a cinch she is out of the ghost rackets for awhile, a long while. And of course Carol did make a change in her policy, to cut off David. Oh, and if you don't mind, I'll hang on to that tricky little camera and stuff, in case I run into another medium, well done.

Exp. Acct:    $892.90

NOTES:
- RANDY SINGER MAKES THE FIRST OF MANY APPEARANCES AS JOHNNY'S LONG-TIME FRIEND.
- ONE HAS TO WONDER AT THE TONGUE-IN-CHEEK USE OF THE NAME CLARABELLE, AT A TIME WHEN THE HOWDY DOODY SHOW WAS ON TELEVISION WITH A CLOWN OF THE SAME NAME.
- JACK JOHNSTONE MENTIONED IN A TAPED INTERVIEW THAT HE HAD DONE A LOT OF INVESTIGATION INTO PSYCHIC PHENOMENON FOR ANOTHER RADIO PROGRAM CALLED "SOMEONE KNOWS."
- THIS IS THE SECOND REFERENCE TO A STUDEBAKER GOLDEN HAWK, A REALLY CLASSY CLASSIC CAR THAT COST AROUND $3,000.
- ROY ROWAN IS THE ANNOUNCER
- MUSIC SUPERVISION IS BY AMERIGO MARINO

Producer:    Jack Johnstone          Writers:    Jack Johnstone
Cast:        Virginia Gregg, Lawrence Dobkin, Lurene Tuttle, Harry
             Bartell, Eleanor Audley, Joseph Kearns, Herb Vigran, Junius
             Matthews, Tony Barrett, Sam Edwards

◆    ❖    ◆

SHOW:        THE TEARS OF NIGHT MATTER
COMPANY:     UNIVERSAL ADJUSTMENT BUREAU
AGENT:
PART 1          SHOW DATE:    5/21/1956
SYNOPSIS: Hilary Fukes returns Johnny's call. Johnny tells him that he is reviewing a claim from Mrs. Wendover and asks why she let a $50,000 claim lay around for two years before making a claim.

Johnny travels to Miami, Florida, and calls Hilary Fukes the next morning. Fukes is a CPA, and is surprised that Johnny came all the way to Florida to handle the claim. Fukes tells Johnny that Mrs. Wendover had hired him to get her affairs in order, as the treasury folks were after her for back taxes. Noah Wendover died two years ago last April 14. Johnny tells Fukes that the Insurance Company did not know about the death until the claim was filed. Johnny is told that the Wendovers had taken some friends out on their boat and Wendover developed appendicitis and died before they made port. Mrs. Wendover is a little wacky, or insane. The Wendovers were crazy for each other, and spent money like crazy, and they had it to spend. Now Mrs. Wendover has met someone and she is coming out of her grief. All the papers on my desk are hers and the policy was the first thing Hillary discovered, that and $90,000 in un-cashed dividend checks. Hillary is tired of looking at the papers, and leaves to play golf. Hillary tells Johnny that Mrs. Wendover has about $950,000 in the bank, so she is not trying to cheat the company.

Johnny verifies the death certificate and starts looking through the papers on the desk. Johnny leaves and goes to his hotel. Fukes calls him, and tells Johnny that Mrs. Wendover is having a fit. Johnny cabs to the office and sees a 1956 Cadillac at the curb with a purse on the front seat, a mink stole on the seat and the keys in the ignition. The car is registered to Mrs. Wendover. Johnny goes in and learns that Fukes had some papers for her to sign and told her about Johnny, and she blew up; she is right on the edge. Johnny meets Mrs. Wendover, who could be 16 or 36, with bright black eyes. Johnny tells her he is there to verify the facts. She knows her husband is dead, she saw him die. She asks Johnny if she will get the money and Johnny presumes she will be paid. Her dad owned an insurance company once. "Would one of the men sitting at desks write 'OK' on the policy if they knew about me?" she asks. Johnny asks why an adjuster would question the claim. She tells Johnny that she is indolent and irresponsible, and a curse. Noah died, and her father died, and her brother died, no one lives around her. As Mrs. Wendover goes out to her car Fukes tells Johnny that her brother died in Korea, and her father had a heart attack. Johnny rushes out to drive her home. Johnny listens to his heart beating, and it never lets him down. It always does that when trouble is around. Mrs. Wendover asks Johnny, "Mr. Dollar, do you think he'll will die too?"

Tomorrow, right out in the broad daylight, I have a look at the tears of night.

## PART 2          SHOW DATE:     5/22/1956

Hilary Fukes calls Johnny to make sure that Mrs. Wendover is ok. Johnny tells him that she is scared and thinks she is responsible for the death of her father, brother and husband. Johnny tells him that she said someone else would die.

At Mrs. Wendover's apartment, Johnny is fixed a drink. Mrs. Wendover tells Johnny that he is probably worried about the claim and she that she had handled things badly. She wanted to talk to Johnny to tell him of the curse. She tells Johnny that her father died of a heart attack, her brother in Korea, and her husband on the boat. But she still feels that she is a curse. Johnny asks who she was talking about on the ride back, but she does not remember riding in the car; she blanks out at times, and has seen a psychiatrist for it. Johnny asks who "he" is and she tells him that he is Teddy Martin. She will marry him, when he asks her. He is like Johnny and does not believe in a curse; he makes her laugh. Johnny tells her to marry this guy, and she kisses him and thanks him for talking to her. J. Dollar—oracle. Johnny is still bothered by the curse.

Johnny goes to see Fukes and tells him that he is filing his report recommending payment of the claim, and is flying back tonight. Johnny types up his report and calls for plane reservations and waits for the airlines to call him back. A man walks into the office and tells him that Costigan wants to see him. Johnny tells him he has the wrong man, but the man points his gun at Johnny, who twists his arm and takes his gun. Johnny asks if the man is Sam Costigan from Chicago, the one they kicked out a few years ago. The man, Frank Scanland, tells Johnny that Costigan wants to see Fukes about the Wendover dame. Johnny gives him his gun, tells Frank to behave himself, and tells him to take him to Costigan.

Johnny goes out to a black Packard and is driven out to see Costigan. Johnny describes Frankie as a punk, who is too obvious. Johnny is taken to a well-lit mansion where a man named Feeley opens the door and takes Johnny into the house, which is now a casino. Frankie takes Johnny upstairs and puts the .38 into his ribs and Johnny tells him he is going to be in trouble, but Frankie is looking forward to dealing with him.

Tomorrow, there is a curse that goes with the Wendover name, goes where ever it is

### PART 3          SHOW DATE:     5/23/1956

The phone rings and Johnny picks up the phone and says "Johnny Dollar" and Frankie takes it from him and asks what he is up to. Johnny walks into the room and says "Hello Sam" to which Sam Costigan replies "Johnny, Johnny Dollar!" Frankie is surprised that Johnny is not Hilary Fukes and Sam tells Frankie to leave.

Sam sits behind his desk staring at Johnny as he relates why he is in Florida and how Frankie had brought him to the casino. Sam tells Johnny he is doing ok, but the profit is not the same as in the old days. Frankie is a punk, but the best he can find. Johnny tells Sam about the claim, and Sam shows him a necklace called "The Tears of Night." Mrs. Wendover left it with Sam last week when she was here with Teddy; she is a little screwy. She sent Sam a check for $5,000 and wants Johnny to take the diamonds back to her. Johnny tells Sam he can act, but cannot lie. Sam tells Johnny the check bounced, but Johnny tells him she cannot write a check without Fukes to countersign it. Sam tells Johnny that she had called and wanted the necklace back or she would call the cops. Sam tells Johnny to take the ice back to Mrs. Wendover and he will take the loss, and show Johnny a good time at the casino. Johnny takes the necklace, but tells Sam that he will not come back; he does not trust Sam. Johnny leaves and sees Feeley wiping his face in the casino. Johnny calls a cab and goes to see Mrs. Wendover, who is expecting Teddy when she opens the door. Johnny is looking at her throat as she tells Johnny that she must call Teddy and slams the door. Johnny notes that the dress Mrs. Wendover was completed with "The Tears of Night," the same necklace in his pocket.

Johnny opens the case to see a label for "The House of Mortuous" inside and a phone number. Johnny calls the number and arranges for a meeting. Johnny cabs to the Sandy Beach hotel to meet Hannibal Mortuous and shows him the necklace. Mortuous is taken aback and asks how Johnny came to have it. Johnny tells him about Mrs. Wendover, who Mortuous calls "a lovely body propelled by a ridiculous mind. Such Conduct!" Mortuous is sure that the necklace is real, and shows Johnny how well the diamonds are mounted, an incomparable masterpiece for $25,000. When Johnny tells him he saw another one, Mortuous tells Johnny that it must be a fake. This requires an artist, and I am that artist; "latit in angius erba"—that is Latin. All Johnny tells him that all he knows is "agricola"—a snake in the grass. Mortuous is gratified to see his work. Johnny asks if she had mentioned a curse, and Johnny tells him he is only a friend in a way, off and on, and Mortuous laughs. Mortuous notes that the fog is coming in, and it is dark, so maybe Johnny should leave the necklace in his safe, but Johnny declines the offer and leaves. Mortuous leaves him with "Omnia Mortuous vomun vocal est"—"all speak well of Mortuous." Johnny notes that the fog had come in so Johnny gets some wrapping paper and stamps from the night clerk and calls a cab. When the cab arrives Johnny mails the necklace to himself at his hotel. He does not think the two hoods following him saw him mail the package as he gets into a cab and is followed to this hotel.

Tomorrow, and the old curse comes up with an old fashioned flourish.

### PART 4          SHOW DATE:     5/24/1956

Johnny makes a call to Hilary Fukes and asks him to come to his hotel. Johnny tells Fukes that some of Costigan's boys are here and might want to use him for target practice.

Johnny gets a bottle of Scotch as Hilary Fukes arrives. Johnny asks what he knows about the necklace, but Fukes tells Johnny that he has never heard of it. Johnny relates the case so far, including Costigan and the necklace and Mortuous. Johnny asks Fukes who made the necklace she was wearing, but he knows nothing. Johnny shows him the hoods outside and Hilary tells him to call the police. Johnny knows that Mrs. Wendover needs help, which is why he is staying. Johnny takes Fuke's car keys and tells Fukes to stay in his room. Johnny drives to Elise Wendover's apartment where Toby and Feeley are waiting for him. "Got a match, Dollar?" they taunt him, but Johnny remains silent. They go though his pockets and then work him over when he tells them he does not have the necklace. Johnny remembers trying to wake up, and has a very bad dream. At 6:00 AM Johnny wakes up and goes to Mrs. Wendover's apartment, where he finds her sitting in front of a window laughing with the phone in her hand. She tells Johnny that she has met some people who told them a lot about her. Did they tell you about Teddy Davis? She cried when Noah died, and when her brother died, and when Daddy died, but I must not cry anymore. Teddy asked me to marry him, and he is not interested in my money and he is such a good painter. She mumbles about Mr. Costigan and becomes hysterical. She thinks all they live for is money. Johnny turns on the lights to find Feeley and Toby on the floor dead.

Tomorrow, the tears of night come home.

### PART 5          SHOW DATE:     5/25/1956

Teddy calls for Elise and Johnny tells Teddy who he is and that here have been two murders and that Elise is going to need him. Teddy will come right over.

The police arrive and Lt. Brady thinks Johnny is crazy and calls Hilary Fukes to back up his story. Teddy arrives with a doctor and a lawyer and Elise is taken to a private hospital. Powder tests prove that Elsie did not kill Toby and Feeley. Teddy returns and talks to Johnny and is thankful for his involvement. Lt. Brady suspects Johnny and Teddy offers his lawyer. Lt. Brady tells Teddy to scram and asks for Johnny's buzzer. Johnny tells Lt. Brady why he is in town and about the curse. Teddy interrupts and Brady tells him "I am going to pop you in the cooler if you interrupt again!" Johnny tells Lt. Brady about Costigan and the necklace, and how Mrs. Wendover was wearing the necklace. He relates the beating and finding the bodies in the room. Johnny tells Lt. Brady that he has been an investigator for 14 years. Lt. Brady tells Johnny he knows that Johnny is not involved and that Costigan was shot earlier.

Johnny goes back to his hotel room to find Mortuous there. Mortuous apologizes for the actions of Toby and Feeley. He is impressed by the ingenious way Johnny used the post office to protect the necklace. Mortuous declines a drink and he tells Johnny that they will wait for the mail. Johnny wants to know about the double-cross, but Mortuous tells him it is a triple-cross. Scanland asked him to duplicate the necklace, and was going to double-cross Costigan. Costigan found out and Scanland killed him. Scanland then killed Feeley and Toby with Mortuous' help and took them to Mrs. Wendover's apartment, such a crude touch. It would keep her from complaining about a fake necklace to the police. Scanland is also dead, but what is one more murder today? Scanland is in the hotel room. Mortuous tells Johnny that the Tears of Night are really worth $100,000. Mortuous wants to live and the necklace will help him; vene vidi veci! Mortuous is going to turn the necklace into cash and will have spent the money before the police catch him. There is a knock at the door, and Scanland comes in and shoots Mortuous and Mortuous kills Scanland, again. "De Mortuous nihil nisi bonum," "Speak well of the dead" Mortuous tells Johnny and dies. Mrs. Wendover will recover.

Remarks: I'll stand for the last two days of defense myself; I didn't have any business sticking my nose in the jewelry end of it. But if you make me pay for them, don't ever try to hire me again.

Exp. Acct:    $405.16

NOTES:
- MUSICAL SUPERVISION IS BY AMERIGO MARINO AND CARL FORTINA.
- ROY ROWAN IS THE ANNOUNCER
- THERE ARE SEVERAL LATIN PHRASES IN THIS STORY, SOME OF WHICH I CAN AM NOT SURE ABOUT. FOR INSTANCE, JOHNNY TELLS MORTUOUS THAT THE ONLY LATIN HE KNOWS IS "AGRICOLA" A SNAKE IN THE GRASS. SEVERAL LATIN DICTIONARIES I CONSULTED ROUGHLY TRANSLATE THE TERM "ANGUIS IN HERBA" AS "A SNAKE IN THE GRASS."

**Producer:**    Jack Johnstone        **Writers:**    John Dawson
**Cast:**        Virginia Gregg, Victor Perrin, Jack Kruschen, Jay Novello, William Conrad, Frank Gerstle, Marvin Miller, Will Wright

| SHOW: | THE MATTER OF REASONABLE DOUBT |
|---|---|
| COMPANY: | AMERICON NORTHERN TRUST COMPANY |
| AGENT: | BEN GUARDLEY |
| PART 1 | SHOW DATE: 5/28/1956 |

SYNOPSIS: Ben Guardley calls and tells Johnny to save his money, the money he will get from this case. He has a crazy one. The case is a trust arrangement with a cumulative endowment insurance rider for up to a half million. Mrs. Ezra Gramley is leaving the money to her granddaughter Susan. She owns the Flintrock Ranch in Nevada. Jonas Parks started the deal, and got cold feet; he thinks the old lady is crazy. Maybe Jonas is crazy.

Johnny travels to Las Vegas, Nevada and checks out Jonas Parks, who is in excellent financial shape and scrupulously honest. Johnny rents a "drive-it-yourself" hired car and drives the 23.6 miles to Flintrock to meet with Jonas Parks. Jonas is glad Johnny is there as the day has been odd, with rain clouds over the river. Jonas chides Johnny for acting interested in desert storms, and Johnny tells him he was sizing him up. Johnny has determined that Jonas is not crazy and he was checking Johnny out. Jonas tells Johnny that he started the trust arrangement, and that there is something wrong at the ranch. He has a hunch and brought Johnny out on that hunch. Mrs. Gramley is a widow who runs the ranch. Her son and his wife lived there and did most of the work. They were killed three years ago and now the ranch is going to their daughter, Susan. Walter Gramley, her nephew manages the ranch. Mrs. Gramley came to town and sprung the idea of the trust on her own. She wanted the ranch transferred to Susan within three years. Walter came in and was told what was happening, and Walter said she would never go through with it. Jonas visited the ranch, and she told him to continue working on the deal. Now, Walter will not allow anyone on the ranch. Walter thinks the she is losing her mind, and wants to keep it quiet. Jonas suggests that Johnny tell them he is an investigator with the Cattleman's Association.

Johnny drives to the ranch and stalls the car a short distance from the ranch; the old "out of gas" trick. While walking to the ranch, Johnny is caught in a rainstorm, but continues walking. A shot rings out and Johnny sees a man on a horse coming towards him. Johnny hides and then gets the drop on him and tells him to drop the rifle. The man tells Johnny that he is trespassing and the ranch is missing cattle. Johnny tells his story about being from the Cattleman's Association and asks to see Mrs. Gramley, but is told that he cannot see her. The man tells Johnny to go to his car and he will send some gasoline, and then get out and stay out, as he will not miss the next time.

Johnny walks back to the car and a station wagon approaches and Susan Gramley introduces herself and tries to pour gas into the tank, but she spots that the tank is full. She tells Johnny that he is not with the Cattleman's Association; he is there to dig up the past and what is going to happen. Susan thinks that is fine and dandy. She loved her dad, and she knew what he did when he got angry. She tells Johnny he is the type that smashes ahead to find out things, but be careful; you are smashing into a bomb.

Tomorrow, the dead past speaks in a musty morgue, or tries to, and a living lady get cozy, or tries to, really tries to.

## PART 2      SHOW DATE:      5/29/1956

Jonas Parks calls and Johnny tells him he was rained on, shot at and threatened and out-smarted by a sixteen-year-old girl and he still has not seen Mrs. Gramley. He is giving up for tonight and is warming his bones over a triple brandy. Johnny asks about the accident and Jonas tells him to go see Will Conners. He runs the paper; tell him I sent you. And be careful.

Johnny buys a bottle of brandy and takes it to his room to warm up, and muse over the case. Next morning Johnny visits Will Conners at the paper. Johnny introduces himself and Will Connors tells Johnny that Jonas told him to answer any questions. Will asks if there is a story in what Johnny is doing, and asks for a scoop if there is, it would do him good, so Johnny promises him the story. Johnny asks for anything he has on Mrs. Gramley and the ranch. Will has noticed that there is something funny going on out there as Walter acts as scared as she does. Susan is strange but not one to be scared. Walter's fancy wife is too much for him, and she is scared also. Johnny asks about the accident, and Will offers to get the morgue files. He tells Johnny it had been raining and the accident happened on the road to the ranch. There had been an argument and Hilda grabbed her car to come to town. Ed ran out in his car too, it was a habit when he got mad. Mary went with him and they came upon Hilda's car in the road and hit it and were killed, but Hilda was not in the car. Johnny reads the files and learns nothing. Susan meets Johnny in the newspaper office, and notices Johnny is reading about the accident. She tells Johnny that he is not an investigator for the Cattleman's Association because Aunt Hilda had called the Cattleman's Association and they told her they never heard of you; and Mr. Parks did not know you either, but he was lying. Susan tells Johnny that she will set up a meeting for Johnny to see her grandmother and call him at the hotel.

Back in his hotel room there is a knock on Johnny's door and Hilda Gramley is there. Johnny notices a nice cigarette case and she tells Johnny that it was a gift; she is always getting gifts. Johnny asks about her about a wedding ring and she tells Johnny that it is around somewhere. Johnny pours her a brandy and she tells Johnny that likes all sorts of gifts, money, and most of all excitement. Johnny tells her he has no money, and never gives gifts. "You have brandy, so pour us a drink, and we'll talk . . . about excitement."

Tomorrow, a worried old lady shows her mettle, a gambler shows his hand, and the game gets tense, tight, and a little bit frightening.

## PART 3      SHOW DATE:      5/30/1956

Susan calls and Johnny says hello to "Mr. Wilson." Susan tells him that her grandmother will be expecting him and suspects that Hilda is there. "Has she made her pitch yet?" Susan asks Johnny and tells him that Uncle Walter will kill her some day.

Johnny calls a taxi for Hilda, and does not expense the six brandies she had. Johnny drives to the ranch and meets Mrs. Gramley. "Susan is a brash little flibbertigibbet, and I love her" she tells Johnny. Johnny tells her about the trust arrangement and why he is there. She tells Johnny that she did not know that Jonas was there earlier. Johnny tells her that Jonas thought she was losing her mind and was working in her best interests. She calls Johnny a presumptuous whelp and wishes she were thirty years younger. The last few months have been hard, but she denies that anything is wrong. Johnny tells her that she has stopped going to town and having visitors, and backed down on the trust arrangement. She tells Johnny that she had discovered that Walter and Hilda were stealing her blind, and have cut the ground out from under her. Walter found out, and stopped the trust plans, but Hilda was behind it. Johnny tells her that Hilda must have planned the accident and Walter went along with it. Mrs. Gramley is shocked to learn that her son had been murdered.

Susan tells Johnny that grandma will be ok, but she knows now that Walter and Hilda killed her parents. Susan knows that Walter gambles, and gambles and gambles, mostly at the Lead Balloon Club. It is the only club that will take his IOU's. Deuce McCoy runs the club. Hilda spent the rest. She is what is called a luxury dame. Susan does not know any of Hilda's boyfriends, but she is a cool operator.

Johnny visits Deuce McCoy at the Lead Balloon and wants to talk about Walter Gramley, who is there at the club gambling. Johnny is told that Walter is not into Deuce now, but he does buy off his IOU's. Johnny tells Deuce that Walter may be doing time for embezzlement soon. Deuce plays stupid when Johnny asks if he knows Walter's wife. Johnny notices a cigarette case on his desk and Deuce does not know who it belongs to, but Johnny does; it belongs to Hilda.

Tomorrow, the pressure hits the top and the whole mess starts to crack.

## PART 4        SHOW DATE:        5/31/1956

Susan calls and asks why Johnny is not out there, on the old Boulder cut off. Johnny's friend had told her to meet Johnny on the road, and she called the hotel on a whim. Johnny tells her to come straight to his hotel, fast, while you are still alive.

Johnny had expected results, but not that quickly. He had told Deuce McCoy who he was and what he wanted, and was surprised that the news was out so quickly. Johnny is sure that Susan would have been killed. Susan arrives at the hotel and Johnny lets her in to his room and she tells Johnny that no one followed her, and everyone was out at the ranch. Walter did not call her, and she did not recognize the voice. Johnny tells her that the phone call was not a joke. Johnny tells Susan about the plans for the trust, and that her grandmother is still in charge. Her grandmother was scared to say anything. Susan tells Johnny that Grandma is in better spirits than in months. Johnny is not sure who is behind the phone call, but Jonas and Will Conners also knew about the trust. Johnny asks Susan if she is scared, which she is not. Johnny tells her to stay in the room, and do not let anyone in.

Johnny goes to the newspaper office and talks to Will Conners who hopes Johnny might have a scoop for him. "Are you getting close to the "deneweyment"? You know when the detective closes the case?" Will asks. Will tells Johnny that Deuce runs the casino for a syndicate, but he lets woman get in the way. Johnny asks Will to go watch over Susan in his hotel. Will warns Johnny that Deuce packs a gun all the time.

At the Lead Balloon Johnny goes to Deuce's office and walks in to find a very drunken woman named Nicki, in the office. Johnny starts to go through Deuce's desk and asks if Nicki is in it too, and she pegs Johnny for the FBI. She gets real mad when Johnny asks about Hilda. She tells Johnny that Walter was here earlier, and Deuce left after they talked and he made a phone call. Johnny tells her that Deuce is not coming back; he is in a jam.

Tomorrow, I tag the pitch too late and a runner gets home. The score one to nothing, in favor of death.

## PART 5          SHOW DATE:    6/1/1956

Mrs. Gramley calls and Johnny tells her that he had told Walter that he had to put her on the phone or Johnny would come there with the police. She tells Johnny that she told Walter to not let him talk to her. She has decided not to set up the trust. Johnny tells her that he is coming to the ranch.

Johnny buys coffee for Nicki and ponders the call from Mrs. Gramley. Maybe Jonas was right about her sanity. Nicki tells Johnny that things were all right with Deuce before Hilda got there and that she will get Hilda if it is the last thing she does. Johnny tells her about the plot on Susan by Deuce to kill her. Nicki tells Johnny that it was Hilda's idea. Johnny tells her that Deuce is probably on the run, and the police will get him.

Johnny drives to the ranch and Walter meets Johnny at the door. Johnny wants to hear Mrs. Gramley tell him to leave, and he tells Walter to get out of the way. Mrs. Gramley enters the room, and Johnny walks them to the living room, where Hilda is listening. Mrs. Gramley tells Johnny that there is no case now, so please leave. She tells Johnny that her son was killed in an accident. The phone rings and Walter gives the phone to Johnny. Will Conners tells Johnny that Deuce was caught at the airport and is in jail, and Johnny tells the others. Johnny tells them that Deuce will talk. Johnny tells Mrs. Gramley that Susan has been in his hotel room. Mrs. Gramley tells Johnny that Walter and Hilda had told her that Deuce had Susan, and Walter pulls a gun on Johnny. Hilda tries to think, and Walter tells her that she has thought for ten years and look at the mess they are in. Walter tells her that Deuce was at the airport because he was running out on them. Nicki walks in and tells them that Hilda is a real brain. Nicki is not afraid of Walter's gun and she tells Walter that the money he lost at the table was going right back to Hilda via Deuce after hours. Hilda denies it, but Walter shoots her, and gives the gun to Johnny. Johnny tells Mrs. Gramley to call the police, and Walter tells Johnny that killing her was the first big thing he has none in ten years that Hilda did not plan.

Remarks: Nicki wonders why Hilda was running around when she already had a man of her own, her husband. Of course he didn't amount to much, but not many men do. What did she expect to find in this world? Pearls in all her oysters? A turkey in her soup?

Exp. Acct: $596.45

NOTES:

- MUSICAL SUPERVISION IS BY AMERIGO MARINO AND CARL FORTINA.
- A "DENEWEYMENT," OR DENOUEMENT IS THE FINAL OUTCOME OF THE MAIN DRAMATIC COMPLICATION IN A LITERARY WORK
- ROY ROWAN IS THE ANNOUNCER

Producer: Jack Johnstone      Writers: Les Crutchfield
Cast: Susan Whitney, Richard Crenna, Jeanette Nolan, Forrest Lewis, Inge Adams, Paul Richards, Jean Tatum

SHOW: THE INDESTRUCTIBLE MIKE MATTER
COMPANY: LAKESIDE LIFE AND CASUALTY INSURANCE COMPANY
AGENT: PETER BRANSON
PART 1      SHOW DATE: 6/4/1956

SYNOPSIS: Pat McCracken calls. "Oh, no, what have you got for me this time? The last case you gave me was that phony spiritualist case which is still haunting me. And the Laird Douglas-Douglas of Heatherscote case about drove me out of my mind" Johnny tells Pat. "Well you made money on them, didn't you?" Pat asks.

Johnny cabs to see Pat McCracken and Pat starts buttering him up immediately. A friend in New York, Peter Branson the brother of Harry Branson needs a favor. But Pete is different, believe me.

Johnny goes to Peter's New York City office and Peter is Harry's twin in all ways. Peter tells Johnny that Michael Jeremiah Flynn is a bum, with a $50,000 policy. The policy is only two months old, and his office assistant had issued the policy. Flynn passed a physical somehow, and paid the premium in cash. The address is the Glad Hands Mission, down in the Bowery. Pete is worried about what happened before. Four times this same type of policy has been issued, and fraud was involved. A derelict is insured by a gangster, and then collects when the policyholder is killed. The beneficiary on this one is John Wesley Cosgrave.

Johnny reviews the folder and gets a room at a dingy hotel, and buys some old clothes. Johnny visits the Glad Hands mission/flophouse and is greeted by Daddy Bill, who invites Johnny to attend the meeting tonight. Johnny tells him that he is looking for Mike Flynn. Johnny is told that Mike is staying there, and is a big contributor who has taken the pledge—many times. Johnny concocts a story for Daddy Bill and learns about the mission residents, except for Mike. The quartet starts rehearsing and Johnny is asked to join in, as he has a wonderful voice.

Johnny takes a nap in the mission and wakes up to see a man staggering into the mission. It is Mike Flynn. Mike collapses and Johnny sees why, there are two bullet holes in his chest. Someone wants to collect on Mike.

Tomorrow, well, tomorrow there is proof that life is a very tenacious thing, even in the broken body of a Bowery bum.

### PART 2        SHOW DATE:    6/5/1956

Peter calls about Johnny's message, and Johnny tells him that Mike was shot, but should pull through, and Johnny wants to talk to Mike before going to see the beneficiary.

Johnny cabs to see Mike Flynn in a room at the mission. Mike thanks Johnny for helping him, and Johnny looks at the holes where the bullets just went through him. Mike shows Johnny a stab wound he got last week. Mike tells Johnny that he was shot down near his "private place" where he goes to drink. Mike tells Johnny that Daddy Bill wants Mike to stay there in the mission. Mike pulls out a bottle of his special mix, Sterno and alcohol, and tells Johnny that he has been drinking it for years. Mike tells Johnny that he collapsed because he had overindulged, but please don't tell Daddy Bill. Mike tells Johnny that he was walking back to the mission and a car passed and there was a stinging feeling in his side. He is sure that the men in the car were probably just arguing about something. Johnny tells Mike who he is and that he is there to save his life. Mike is so pleased that Mr. Cosgrave offered to buy him insurance. Cosgrave helps the mission because he came to the mission when he was young and Daddy Bill helped him, so he gives food, money and jobs to the brothers. Mike does not know what type of jobs, because the men never come back. Johnny tells Mike that the accidents were part of a scam to collect the insurance. Mike tells Johnny that he gets the money for the insurance in an envelope at the mission, but yesterday's envelope did not come. Mike gets up and they go downstairs and Mike tells Johnny he will take him to his private place. Downstairs Mike spots his envelope with $20 in it, and he has a package. Inside are two bottles, one for him and one for Johnny. Johnny takes Mike to his room and tells him not to let anyone in, and do not leave.

Johnny cabs to the 18th precinct and talks to Randy Singer while the lab boys look at the bottle. Johnny asks Randy to look into Cosgrave. Johnny gets a report on the liquor bottle and there are no prints, but the seal was broken and the bottle has wood alcohol in it. Johnny rushes to the mission and runs to Mike's room and breaks in to see Mike lying across the bed, moaning about the hangover he will have.

Tomorrow, the would-be beneficiary of Mike turns out to be a very interesting and dangerous man.

### PART 3        SHOW DATE:    6/6/1956

Johnny calls John Cosgrave, and he tells Johnny that he has been expecting the call. Johnny tells Cosgrave that he is interested in why he is insuring a Bowery bum.

Johnny cabs to see Randy Singer and tells him that Mike is ok, and happy. Johnny tells Randy about the stab wound and the shots and Randy calls him "Indestructible Mike"! Randy tells Johnny that Cosgrave is a well-known gangster with a subsidiary of Murder Inc. He was last picked up in 1948, but no one can prove he is involved in the rackets, and that he is listed as "retired." All the witnesses against him seem to disappear or are killed.

Johnny cabs to Cosgrave's apartment, which his expensively and tastefully appointed. Cosgrave is well-built and well-dressed. Cosgrave shows Johnny a Picasso and a Salvador Dali and tells Johnny that he must have only the best. Cosgrave tells Johnny that he was born in a poor area, and received a meager education from criminals. He visited the mission one night and was helped, so he has tried to help the inhabitants from time to time. Cosgrave slips when Johnny asks him what type of jobs he has provided and asks Johnny "What business is it . . ." Cosgrave tells Johnny that Mike had wanted to own life insurance so he bought it for him. Johnny asks "Dutchy" where his money comes from and Cosgrave slips back into his former attitude. He admits making millions in the past but those days are over, he pocketed the profits and that is why he is retired. Thanks to some unexplained rub-outs he has managed to stay clean with the law. Johnny refuses to believe that Cosgrave would pass up an opportunity to make a quick buck, at Mike Flynn's expense. Cosgrave tells Johnny not to try and pin anything on him if Mike dies. Cosgrave apologizes for not offering Johnny a drink and pours him a 25-year-old Scotch. Johnny leaves with a feeling he is being followed.

Johnny cabs to his hotel and Mike is still there. Mike did not eat the food because he had nothing to drink with the food; it was so dry. Johnny takes Mike out for lunch, and only one drink. Johnny wonders if Daddy Bill is involved with Cosgrave. After lunch Johnny and Mike walk back to the mission on the back streets where a truck swerves and hits Mike. Johnny tells a bystander to call and ambulance, but the man tells Johnny that it is too late.

Tomorrow, somebody's going to have to pay for what is happening here; yes that's a promise.

## PART 4          SHOW DATE:      6/7/1956

Randy calls Johnny at Bellevue hospital. Johnny tells Randy that Mike is still alive, but Johnny is not sure he will survive this one. The First Precinct boys are working on the truck, and Johnny asks Randy to check with them and get some history on the Glad Hands Mission.

Johnny is sure that Cosgrave is behind the accidents to Mike as he waits in the hospital. Johnny gets a phone call from Cosgrave; he tells Johnny that he knows about a lot of things that do not get into the papers. "Dutchy," Cosgrave tells Johnny that he had nothing to do with it. Johnny tells him that he was there and tells Cosgrave he might have seen the driver of the truck. Johnny waits some more and is allowed to see Mike around midnight. Mike is lying in bed smiling from ear to ear. He will be ok, and is impressed with the room, and the nurses, they are so nice. And it smells so nice here; he has not even seen a bed bug!

Johnny turns off the light and tells Mike that he will be back in the morning, but Mike needs something to help him sleep. Johnny sneaks Mike three fingers of whisky into his water glass.

Johnny cabs to his hotel room thankful that Mike is alive. Johnny gets a call the next morning from Randy and tells him that Mike is ok. Johnny learns that the truck has been found, but the driver, Lefty Skillman, was found in the East River. Randy tells Johnny that the flophouse building was built in 1901 as a piano store, then a grocery store, a clothing store, a speakeasy, and a saloon. In 1944 William Grover Larson took over the lease. Johnny spots the lie Cosgrave told about getting help there as a kid, before the mission was opened. The owner of the speakeasy was Larson also. Johnny feels that Larson was the front man for Cosgrave. He is now using the flophouse to get his thugs, who are never seen again. Johnny hears someone outside his room, opens the door and is knocked out.

Johnny wakes up to the voice of Randy and strange meaningless sounds. Johnny wakes up in the hospital and realizes what had happened, and is put to sleep. Mike calls to Johnny and he wakes up in Mike's room. Mike tells Johnny that Randy had told Mike that Johnny has to be careful; they are out to get him too.

Tomorrow, well old Mike may have been indestructible, I knew by now that I wasn't. So tomorrow the windup, it had to be while I was still alive.

## PART 5          SHOW DATE:        6/8/1956

Johnny is called by Randy, and Johnny thanks Randy for his help. Johnny tells Randy that he is going to the mission to settle things with Daddy Bill. And he has his gun.

Johnny and Mike check out of the hospital and cab to the hotel. Mike is put in a room on the fifth floor. Johnny picks up his .38 and heads to the mission, walking the last few blocks. The mission is empty when Johnny gets there and he waits in a back office. A man walks in and tells Daddy Bill he is ready, but realizes that Johnny isn't Daddy Bill. He tells Johnny that his name is Emery, and that he rode the rods in from Ohio, and boy was he in a jam there. Daddy Bill promised him that the police would not find him, and he has a job for him to get him out of the country. Emery tells Johnny that Daddy Bill left a package for Mike or Johnny that contains liquor. Johnny does not want to open the package, and Emery tells Johnny that Mike always shares his stuff with Lefty Skillman. Johnny recognizes the name; Lefty was driving the truck that hit Mike. Johnny senses the package does not gurgle. Johnny tells Emery that he is going to the Waldorf, and that Mike is recovering in room 203 at the Brakley Hotel. Johnny tells Emery to tell Daddy Bill to call him at the Waldorf. Johnny calls Randy and then cabs to the 18th precinct. Johnny asks Randy to register him at the Waldorf, and then cabs to his room at the Brakley. Johnny tells the desk clerk to tell anyone looking for Mike that he is in room 203. Johnny spills some whisky in his room and checks in on Mike with a bottle. Johnny makes him promise to stay in the room and goes back to the second floor. Johnny leaves the door unlocked and waits. The phone rings and Randy tells Johnny that the package was a bomb. Johnny hangs up and gets into the bed as he hears footsteps. There is a knock at the door and Daddy Bill is outside and comes in with Cosgrave. Daddy Bill is sure that Johnny is at the Waldorf, and just as Cosgrave tells him he will do it himself, Mike knocks on the door and calls for Johnny. Cosgrave tells Johnny to get up takes his gun and opens the door to let Mike in. The door bursts open and there are shots as Randy comes in with Mike. Mike ends up is sitting on Daddy Bill, despondent that the bottle he hit him with is broken. Daddy Bill complains about Cosgrave hanging things on others and shoots Cosgrave, killing him.

The world will be a bit better without Dutchy Gordon, alias J. Wesley Cosgrave. And of course, the courts will take care of Daddy Bill Larkin, plenty. Mike, Indestructible Mike, well he will probably out-live the rest of us. I hope I can get down to see him now and then, talk over our great adventure together.

Exp. Acct:     $1,126.50

NOTES:

- WOOD ALCOHOL, OR METHYL ALCOHOL, OR METHANOL, IS THE SIMPLEST OF ALL THE ALCOHOLS. IT WAS FORMERLY MADE BY THE DESTRUCTIVE DISTILLATION OF WOOD. WHEN TAKEN INTERNALLY, BY EITHER DRINKING THE LIQUID OR INHALING THE VAPORS, METHANOL IS EXTREMELY POISONOUS.
- IN THE 1930'S LUCKY LUCIANO, AND MEYER LANSKY SUCCESSFULLY UNIFIED THE GREAT CRIMINAL GANGS INTO A VAST NATIONAL CRIME SYNDICATE WITH A BOARD OF DIRECTORS OF ORGANIZED CRIME AND AN ENFORCEMENT ARM THAT WAS TO BECOME KNOWN AS MURDER, INCORPORATED.
- JOHNNY REFERENCES THE "GLAD HAND MISSION" IN PART 1, AND COSGRAVE CALLS IT THE "HELPING HAND RESCUE MISSION" IN PART 3
- MUSICAL SUPERVISION IS BY AMERIGO MARINO AND CARL FORTINA
- THE ANNOUNCER IS ROY ROWAN
- JOHNNY NOTES THE USE OF A .38
- THE WALDORF REFERS TO THE WALDORF-ASTORIA, ONE OF NEW YORK'S MORE EXPENSIVE HOTELS AT THE TIME

Producer:  Jack Johnstone          Writers:  Jack Johnstone
Cast:      Howard McNear, Lawrence Dobkin, Harry Bartell, Herb
           Vigran, Alan Reed, Roy Glenn

◆   ❖   ◆

SHOW:       THE LAUGHING MATTER
COMPANY:    UNION STATES CASUALTY COMPANY
AGENT:      ED RENZER
PART 1      SHOW DATE:     6/11/1956

SYNOPSIS: Ed Renser calls, and tells Johnny that his plane for Encenada leaves in two hours. Charley Burton is down there, the big Nightclub/TV star, "Good old loveable Charlie." Someone has threatened to kill him and he has $500,000 in insurance.

Johnny travels to San Diego and then to Encenada, Mexico and the plush Balboa Hotel. Johnny comments on the two towns: the tourist Encenada and the poor working class section of warehouses, packing plants and slums. Frank Maltz, the executive producer meets Johnny and tells him that he has not called the police because Charlie would object because he has had crank letters before. Frank tells Johnny that Charley found a note yesterday under the door, and Charley tore it up. It said "Only the gods are immortal, Burton. You will never leave Encenada alive." Nothing has happened since the note. Frank tells Johnny that he has to form his own conclusions on who would want to kill Charley. Johnny is told to talk to the others; Gloria Dale is the feminine lead, and gorgeous. Al Schriber is a newcomer with a real talent. Frank thinks that someone in the family wrote the note and that is why he sent for Johnny. Frank hates Charley's guts, and he wants to make sure that if Burton is killed that justice is done, and the killer caught.

Johnny goes out to meet Gloria Dale, a lovely girl. Johnny tells her why he is there and she tells Johnny that everyone has heard of the note from Charley and his ingratitude that someone should pull such a practical joke. Gloria thinks anyone who knows him might have written it. She sticks around because she has a contract, as is the situation with Frank. Al Schriber joins Gloria and his reaction is "Happy Days! So that earthworm is really insured? Maybe the advertisers are out to kill him to make a profit." Al tells Johnny that he would not try to kill Charley. As Johnny savors a drink on the terrace, he sees a man move towards the terrace and argue fiercely with a girl. The man sees Johnny and flees. The girl was a maid at the hotel. The man had been heading towards Charley Burton's room.

Tomorrow, the great man condescends and shivers a little too, and a girl's hidden hate is blacker than the sea wet rocks she vents it on.

## PART 2          SHOW DATE:          6/12/1956

Charley Burton calls Johnny, who is glad that he is out of seclusion. Charley tells Johnny that he does not need protection, but Johnny tells him that the insurance company does not agree. Are you going to talk, or do I call the insurance company and your sponsors? I'll see you in an hour.

Johnny cabs to the office of the police and asks for a run down on Valena Morales, the hotel maid. Capt. Porale tells Johnny he will call him later.

Johnny calls on Charley Burton. Johnny asks for a double scotch on the rocks and Charley calls room service, and then cancels the order when Johnny will not give his room number. Charley tells Johnny that he will not tolerate that highhanded behavior from a hireling, but Johnny tells him he is not Charley's hireling. Johnny tells him he does not like Charley, and there is nothing he can do about it. Charley tells Johnny that he likes Johnny; he is uninhibited. Johnny tells Charley that everyone seems to have the same bad opinion of him. Charley recounts all of the shortcomings of his costars and how he had taken them from the bottom. He does not take the threat seriously and tells Johnny that not one of the cast members has a reason to kill him. Charley tells Johnny that those who complain the most do not lead to murder, and Johnny agrees. Charley tells

Johnny that the note was a joke. Johnny asks about the maid and Charley remembers her, she is utterly charming. Johnny reminds him that her husband might not like Charley's attitude.

Johnny walks down to the beach and finds Gloria with a bottle, and shares a glass with her. She tells Johnny that she sent Al off to bed. She likes him, but there is no click. She is trying to forget the emptiness and the hate for Charley Burton. She tells Johnny that she was leaving the show last year and was about to be married, and Charley was furious. She got a note from Jerry saying they were through, and then he went on a hunting trip to Canada. She signed a new contract and then learned that a detective had told Jerry about a faked private life, and that Charley Burton was behind it. She could not fight Charley because Jerry was killed on the way back from the trip. She hates Charley but has no nerves, so she drinks.

Johnny is awakened in the night by a gunshot and Charley Burton banging on his door. He tells Johnny that someone has shot at him through the window of his room; someone is out to kill him.

Tomorrow a thickening web; clinging and sticky. But one of the flies pulls free by using a gun.

**PART 3**       **SHOW DATE:**    **6/13/1956**

Capt. Porale calls Johnny and Johnny tells him about the shooting. "Before you get here, see if you can find Frank Maltz" Johnny tells Capt. Porale. Captain Porale tells Johnny that he will make the "APC." "No," Johnny corrects him, "it is an 'APB.' " "What is this APB?" Capt. Porale asks.

Johnny buys coffee and tries to wake up. In Burton's room, Capt. Porale asks where Charley is, and Johnny tells him he has moved rooms and is scared. Johnny relates how Charley was asleep and how the shot broke the window and landed over his head. He ran to Johnny's room and a search was made, but Johnny saw no one. Johnny tells Capt. Porale that any of the staff could have fired the shot. Johnny tells Capt. Porale who the others are, and Johnny tells him that all of them hate Charley. Capt. Porale is still looking for Valena, but she is not at home and her husband is missing. The phone rings and Capt. Porale answers and tells Johnny that Frank has been found in a cantina in town.

Johnny cabs to the cantina and finds Frank Maltz wrapped around a bottle. Frank tells Johnny he has been there forever. It is a crossroads for two different worlds, and they are all dead. He is not really drunk, and has been in every bar in town. Johnny asks where he was at 12:40 when Burton was shot at. Frank tells Johnny that he has not been back to the hotel since he left at 10:00. Frank tells Johnny that he hangs around Burton to help someone else, Al Schriber. Frank tells Johnny that it will be his show next year if he can hang on because the sponsors are tired of Charley. Frank is married, and tells Johnny that his wife is in a sanitarium, paralyzed. That is why he has to stay on with Charley. When the hate gets too much, he goes to visit his wife.

Johnny leaves and is met on the street by Capt. Porale, who tells Johnny that the maid has come home, and they rush to the house. Capt. Porale questions her about Charley and learns that he had been bothering her. When Johnny had seen him, her husband was going to see Charley, but she has not seen him since.

Tomorrow, death tries once more, and his time doesn't miss, but death you know, is blind.

**PART 4          SHOW DATE:     6/14/1956**

Charley Burton calls, and tells Johnny that he is still alive. Johnny tells him that he may be good old loveable Charley to others, but he is a pain in the neck to Johnny. "Your sponsor may think you are worth $500,000, but my price on you is three cents." Johnny tells him.

Johnny recounts how everyone around Charley Burton hates him, and about the attempt to shoot him last night. Johnny meets Frank at breakfast and he apologizes for last light, but Johnny asks when that was. Johnny tells him about talking to the maid, and the others seem to be off the hook. Johnny tells how her husband had come out to the hotel and that the police are looking for him. Al Schriber meets them and he is going to go swimming before "old blubber tummy" gets up. Frank reminds him about the schedule for today, a slapstick desert island scene. Al describes the scene and the punch line about a cousin in congress. Johnny is told that Charley has all the good lines in this scene. Charley walks up and gives Al a hard time and Al tells Charley that if he fires him, he could have another show in no time. Frank and Charley argue over Al's talent and Charley tells him he has always looked out for the welfare of his coworkers. Johnny tells him that he does not want to see Charley killed, that would mean he loused up, but Johnny takes pride in his work. Johnny tells Charley that the husband of the maid, Nacho Morales, is looking for him. "That native girl is married?" Charley asks. Charley tells Frank and Al that he is carrying them. He decides to trade roles, he will take Al's role, and allow him to change any line, and Frank jumps at the opportunity. Frank tells Johnny that the note was written in English, but Valena and her husband only speak Spanish.

The scene is set up at the end of the bay, and Johnny goes to watch. The last scene is re-filmed, and Al drinks from a glass of fake wine and collapses and dies.

Tomorrow, a frantic game of musical chairs, with every player desperate, because the loser in this game gets the electric chair.

**PART 5          SHOW DATE:     6/15/1956**

Charley calls Capt. Porale and Johnny answers. He tells Johnny that it might have been he who was killed. Johnny knows he is there to protect Charley because someone was crazy enough to insure him.

Johnny buys a beer for Capt. Porale and waits for night. Capt. Porale tells Johnny that Al was poisoned with "much cyanide." Johnny thinks that the wrong man was killed. Capt. Porale wonders about Nacho, who has disappeared, but they will find him.

Johnny cabs to the hotel and meets Gloria, who asks about what happened to Al. They go in to the bar and she asks about Charley and Al changing roles. What irony; Charley goes for the maid and Al gets killed. Johnny reminds her that the

Morales do not speak English, and that the note was written in English. Johnny gets a call from Capt. Porale and learns that Nacho has been picked up. Johnny tells Gloria that she did not know that Al was going to drink from the bottle, not Charley.

Johnny goes to see Nacho Morales, who is a small man with gnarled hands. Johnny and Capt. Porale go in and question him. Nacho tells Capt. Porale that he had been hiding on a boat because he had seen Charley fire the shot himself. Johnny goes to Charley and tells him that Nacho has been caught. "He should be beaten, that is the only way to make that kind talk," Charley tells Johnny. Johnny tells Charley that he killed Al Scriber, and wrote the letter and fired the shot at himself, and that the argument that day was phony. Charley pulls a gun on Johnny and tells him that he will not be tagged for the killing Al. Capt. Porale comes in and tells Charley to drop his gun, but Charley tries to shoot anyway and Capt. Porale kills him. Too bad Charley could not have seen the look on his face, the comedian would have appreciated it. He would have died laughing.

Remarks: Re policy on Charles Z. Burton, deceased. Refer Clause 34, sub paragraph C; "if the insured dies while committing a felony, this policy is null and void." The superior court of Baja, California rules that Charley was killed while resisting arrest and committing and assault with a deadly weapon. So you can keep your half a million bucks.

Exp. Acct: $791.55

NOTES:
- ON SEVERAL OCCASIONS, JOHNNY IS TOLD HE SHOULD GO INTO TELEVISION, BUT HIS STANDARD REPLY IS "I'LL WAIT UNTIL IT IS PERFECTED."
- THE ANNOUNCER IS ROY ROWAN
- MUSICAL SUPERVISION IS BY AMERIGO MARINO AND CARL FORTINA

Producer: Jack Johnstone    Writers:  Les Crutchfield
Cast:    Virginia Gregg, John Dehner, Lucille Meredith, Lawrence
         Dobkin, Gil Stratton, Harry Bartell, Don Diamond

SHOW:       THE PEARLING MATTER
COMPANY:    EASTERN LIABILITY & TRUST COMPANY
AGENT:      MORTIN SCOTMAN
PART 1      SHOW DATE:    6/18/1956
SYNOPSIS: Morton Scotman calls and he wants Johnny to see him. Martin tells Johnny that David Pearling was supposedly killed in a boating accident several days ago, but he is still very much alive.

Johnny tells Mr. Scotman that he is reading about Mr. Pearling now in the newspaper, but the papers will never have all of the story. Johnny meets Mr. Scotman and tags him as a meticulous man, who turns out to be Vice President and Chairman of the Board of Eastern Liability. Johnny tells Scotman that he has handled several other cases, the last being the San Antonio case. He tells Scotman that he usually works through an adjusting agency. Scotman tells Johnny that this idea was his own, and only one other person knows about it. The board may not approve what he is going to suggest. David Pearling is still alive, and the story will be retracted. The boat did explode, but he was a not on it. Pearling is well regarded in financial circles, and the report of his death affected several commodities on the New York Exchange, companies in which he holds varying positions. A report of his death could allow people to make a lot of money with very little risk. Scotman wants Johnny to find out if the situation has been taken advantage of. Johnny thinks that this case is not in his line, but Scotman thinks it is. Eastern Liability has considerable investments in some of those commodities, and Scotman wants to know if they have been cheated or are about to be cheated. Johnny has dinner with Scotman, who provides him with financial information on the companies.

Johnny flies to Key West, Florida and goes to meet Mr. Peyton, the editor of the local paper. Johnny asks him about the story on Pearling and is told they are running a retraction today. Peyton calls for Gracie Edwards and then tells Johnny that the story was a mistake. Pearling had been here for a week or ten days of fishing and rented a boat. The boat was coming back for fueling and blew up. Pearling could not be found and was presumed lost. It turns out that Pearling was sleeping in his room when it happened, and took a train back that afternoon. Johnny asks to see the reporter. Johnny is told that she had been at the dock when the boat caught fire and that Gracie has been a reporter for several years.

Gracie, a short stocky redhead comes in and Johnny tells her who he is. Johnny gives the Eastern Liability Company as his current employer and suggests that they go to lunch. Gracie tells Johnny that she did what every cub reporter would do; she turned in a story without checking the facts. Johnny is worried about Gracie being on the docks and is told that it is more or less her beat. She likes to see the boats come back in the afternoon. Johnny suggests they go to the docks and look at the boats.

They cab to the docks and Gracie points out where the boat "The Outwatcher" blew up. She had been there an hour or so, and phoned in her story just before three. Johnny thinks it is funny that she saw the boat in trouble and immediately phoned in her story and Johnny asks where she phoned it in from, as there are no phones there. Gracie tells Johnny she took a cab into town. Johnny then asks where her sunburn is; every redhead burns in an hour when the sun it like this. Gracie does not like the questions, but Johnny tells her he has to find out from her what happened. If he has to, he will talk to the adjuster who worked the insurance claim on the boat. Johnny tells her she is a good reporter, and would have checked her facts. She tells Johnny that somebody paid her to file the story; Mr. Pearling paid her to print the story he was dead.

Tomorrow, the affairs of Wall Street follow the current trend in cheating and mayhem.

PART 2        SHOW DATE:    6/19/1956

Johnny calls Mr. Scotman and tells him about Pearling paying someone to print the story. Johnny will meet Scotman at Idyllwild airport.

Johnny flies to New York City and meets Mr. Scotman in the airport coffee shop. Johnny tells him that the reporter was paid $100 in cash to print the story, but she would deny it. If the story would affect the market, it would probably happen today and Pearling would probably take advantage of brisk trading over the report. If it does happen, Scotman would probably report it to the Stock Exchange. They cab to Wall Street and watch the action, but there was is no manipulation. The question is, why did Pearling pay the reporter? There is a reason, and Johnny wants to find out why.

Johnny buys lunch for Scotman and checks into the New Westin and rents a car. Johnny drives to the Pearling estate and is met by a young woman at the door. Mrs. Pearling tells Johnny that Mr. Pearling is not there. Johnny tells her to tell Mr. Pearling that he has just come from Key West and has spoken with a reporter there. Mr. Pearling comes to the door and tells Johnny that his wife told him to throw Johnny out. Johnny tells him he is 10 pounds lighter but 15 years younger. Johnny asks him why he paid Gracie Edwards to print the story, but he tells Johnny that there is no way to prove he paid the girl. Johnny tells him that Eastern Liability thought he was trying to fix the market. Pearling tells him only that he paid the reporter and the boatman in cash for his own reason.

Johnny realizes that a man does not tell someone to leave; he invites him in and lies to him. So Johnny drives back to the hotel and waits. Later the phone rings and Celia Pearling calls from the lobby. She apologizes and asks Johnny if he is a sensation seeker. Johnny tells her that she knows who he is because she has checked on him and knew where to find him. She asks if Johnny is going to continue with the matter, and Johnny tells her that he believes that the answers David gave were unsatisfactory. She is sure that the issue was a personal one, and does not matter. Johnny buys her a drink (bourbon and water) and she finally opens up. She tells Johnny that they have a daughter named Eugenia, and she is the reason for the story. They are capable of many things but not child rearing. Genie got sick of having too much money and no attention and left town. She left a note saying that they would never see her again. They have no idea where she has gone and miss her. They have hired the Aimwell Agency to try and find her. They thought that a story about David's death might cause her to call them, but they have not heard from her.

Tomorrow, the trap is all baited and guess who walks in.

PART 3        SHOW DATE:    6/20/1956

The operator calls Johnny with a call from Aimwell detectives. Johnny asks Mr. Aimwell about the Pearling case and he hangs up.

Johnny cabs to the offices of the Aimwell Detective Agency and meets with Niles Aimwell. Niles tells Johnny that he does not know what Johnny is talking about, so please leave. Johnny tells him that he knows they are working for the Pearlings, and shows Niles his identification and license. Johnny tells him about the newspaper story and the reporter who was paid to print the story and the effort to contact the daughter. Johnny tells Niles he has had time to talk to the Pearlings, and he might lose them as a client. Johnny might want to see the operator's report on the case. Niles has the secretary call the Pearlings and tells Johnny what they have done so far. They thought they had her located in several cities but they missed her. She is probably traveling alone, and five men have been on this case for 11 months to the day, with no luck, and Niles is one of them. Johnny apologizes for riding him so hard. Mrs. Pearling calls and Niles tells Johnny that he will cooperate with Johnny. Johnny gets the files and an offer of a bottle of cold beer. The file is complete, but Johnny gets nothing from it.

Johnny meets with Scotman and updates him on the missing daughter. Scotman is relieved that there was no manipulation, and closes the case.

Johnny goes to pack, and then realizes he does not believe anybody or anything because there is money in it. Johnny thinks in the bar and then goes to see Mr. Scotman. Johnny asks him how the case strikes him and the answer is "neat." Johnny thinks it is too neat. Scotman is sure now that Pearling was not the type of man who would try to manipulate the market. Johnny wonders why the police were not brought in. Johnny is sure that Pearling is lying when he ways he wants his daughter back at home. Scotman tell Johnny to continue with the case.

Johnny visits Aimwell to tell him that they will be seeing a lot of each other. Aimwell tells Johnny that Pearling had told him to contact Johnny. Niles comments on the picture of Pearling's daughter, about how lucky he would be to be with her. Niles does not blame Johnny for wanting to meet her. Niles shows Johnny a wire. She has been located in New Orleans.

Tomorrow, well once you get in on a joke, you do what they tell you, you go along with the gag.

### PART 4          SHOW DATE:     6/21/1956

Dave Pearling calls and wants to talk to Johnny. He tells Johnny that Aimwell has reported that Johnny is looking into his private affairs. He should be annoyed, but is not. He will be home all day.

Johnny calls Scotman and he thinks that Johnny should check it out, so Johnny drives to the Pearling home. Johnny is met by a private detective who offers Johnny a drink. He is Brad Copeland, one of Niles Aimwell's operatives and he tells Johnny that Niles is in conference with Mr. Pearling. Johnny does not believe what he has said, and Brad tells him he is the one who found the girl. Johnny tells him about the story and Brad tells Johnny he got a phone call from a man telling him where the girl was. He checked it out, and she is the girl. Niles and David come into the room and Niles and Brad leave. David tells Johnny he is the most competent man he has seen, and that he has just fired Aimwell. He wants Genie to come home and wants Johnny to persuade her to come home. Johnny tells him he was going to anyway. He had not made a move to do anything, and she was found too soon after Johnny got involved.

Johnny leaves for New Orleans, Louisiana and checks into the Roosevelt Hotel. At the desk, Johnny sees a large man smile when the desk clerk calls his name for the bellboy. The man tells Johnny that they thought he would never get there, and the rest of the boys are in room 810. The Delta Cotton Growers are going to have a good time at this convention. The man leaves and Johnny asks the desk clerk about the convention and is told that it was held last month, and that there is no room 810. Johnny made the man play out the game and neither knows the other. Johnny wants to know who the man is because of the .38 under his left arm. Johnny eats and goes to the address on Ersaline Street. A blonde opens the door and Johnny asks about Genie Pearling. The girl tells Johnny that she is Janice Floyd, a roommate. Janice leads Johnny to a room containing a coffin with a girl in it. Janice tells Johnny that the girl is Genie, and that she died of Leukemia. Johnny tells her that he is an investigator and Janice tells him that there have been others there looking for her and throws Johnny out.

Johnny gets a copy of the death certificate and the medical report, and makes a show of checking out. The blonde man is in the lobby and at the airport. Johnny eludes him and follows him back to the Ersaline address. Johnny stops the man on the street and confronts him. The man tells Johnny to go back to New York and walks away. Johnny remembers that there is money in this case, plain old money.

Tomorrow, there is still money in it. More money than it takes to save a life.

**PART 5          SHOW DATE:     6/22/1956**

Janice Floyd calls Johnny and is concerned that he does not believe that Genie is dead. She had been through an ordeal lately and if he is going to interfere she will call the police.

Johnny writes to Mr. Scotman and encloses the documents, and tells of Janice's behavior. Johnny calls Janice and tells her she is being taken. He is there to find Genie Pearling and wants to talk. She tells him to see her tonight. Johnny walks to the apartment and the blonde man slugs Johnny in a dark part of the street. A cabby finds Johnny at midnight and thinks he is drunk. The cabby takes Johnny to Janice's address and he knocks on the door. Janice lets him in and he sees that she is packing. Johnny asks if the big blonde man is part of the reason. Johnny tells her that the man had come here to talk to her and that he had slugged Johnny. Johnny tells her that he carries a gun, and she is surprised. Johnny tells her that the girl who died was not Genie Pearling, and if necessary he will have the body exhumed. She tells Johnny that she is Genie Pearling and it was Janice Floyd that died. She figures that if she switched identities, her family would not bother her anymore. That was Al Brits' idea; Al saw to it that Janice had her identity. She hates her family, and wants her own life. She is going to marry Al. Johnny tells her that she is worth $100,000; an irrevocable trust she gets when she becomes 25. It would go to her father if she were dead. She realizes that Al had been paid to make love to her and arrange the switch. Al breaks in, and she tells Al she knows about him, and tells him to leave. Johnny talks with her and she is not sure what she wants to do. Johnny gets ready to leave and is met by Al Brit, who wants to talk. He tells Johnny that Johnny really messed it up with him and Genie and he is leaving town. Johnny tells Al that he does not like her father and does he not like him and what he will do if she goes back. Al tells Johnny that her father had hired him to find her, and he had planned the switch, but did not know about the trust fund. But Al made a mistake and fell in love with her. Funny how things work out.

Johnny stops by the apartment on the way to the airport. She is not going to New York, and does not want to talk to Al. She cries over what he did, but she loves him. Johnny tells her to talk to him the next time he calls. You may not have a mother or father, but you have him. I'd take him if I were you.

Remarks: She took him. They were married in Tampa this morning

Exp. Acct:    $714.35

NOTES:

• MR. SCOTMAN TELLS JOHNNY THAT HE HAD WORKED FOR THEM ON THE SAN ANTONIO MATTER. WHEN JOHN LUND DID "THE SAN ANTONIO MATTER," HE WORKED FOR "GREAT EASTERN FIDELITY & LIFE INSURANCE COMPANY," NOT THE EASTERN LIABILITY & TRUST NOTED IN THIS CASE. WHEN BOB BAILEY DID THE STORY AS "THE VALENTINE MATTER," HE WORKED FOR NEW BRITAIN INSURANCE COMPANY. ALL VERSIONS OF THE STORY WERE WRITTEN BY E. JACK NEWMAN/ JOHN DAWSON.

• ROY ROWAN IS THE ANNOUNCER

• MUSICAL SUPERVISION IS BY AMERIGO MARINO AND CARL FORTINA

**Producer:**  Jack Johnstone        **Writers:**  John Dawson
**Cast:**       Mary Jane Croft, Forrest Lewis, Jeanette Nolan, Russell Thorson, Michael Ann Barrett, Jack Petruzzi, Barbara Fuller, Herb Ellis, Marvin Miller

◆    ❖    ◆

**SHOW:**        THE LONG SHOT MATTER
**COMPANY:**     NATIONAL UNDERWRITERS ASSOCIATION
**AGENT:**       JIM DARRELL
**PART 1**       **SHOW DATE:**    6/25/1956

**SYNOPSIS:** Jim Darrell calls and welcomes Johnny to Hollywood. Jim tells Johnny that he wrote up the Palmquist policy, $100,000 double indemnity on both the doctor and his wife. Johnny tells Jim that National Underwriters is worried about the double indemnity clause, because Johnny has an anonymous letter saying that someone is going to collect.

Johnny flies to Hollywood, California and stays at the Beverly Hilton. Johnny cabs to the offices of Darrell and Clark and meets Jim Darrell, who is shaving and watching passersby and making checkmarks on a list. He tells Johnny that he counts Bermuda shorts and his partner counts gray suits; the loser buys lunch. Johnny shows Jim the letter about the policy. Jim tells Johnny that Palmquist is an old-line family, a doctor and a hunter. The wife is an invalid, and there is a son, Eric, who lives with them and is the beneficiary of the policy. Johnny walks to the Palmquist office and is met by the receptionist, Stephie Lund. Johnny is told that the doctor is not in, and Johnny tells her he will come back at five. Johnny rents a car and drives to the Palmquist home. Johnny knocks at the door and no one answers. In the back Johnny finds a woman in a wheelchair, pouring whiskey from a bottle. She tells Johnny that it is not a medicine, and that her husband thinks it is a sign of weakness, then she drops the glass and asks Johnny to wheel her into the house. Johnny notices a boy watching them from a window. Johnny asks her some questions, but she does not answer. Suddenly she seems to awaken when Eric enters the room. Eric offers to show Johnny out, and the woman seems to go back into her lethargic state. "You are a good son Paul," she tells Eric. Johnny asks Eric how he manages to go from Eric to Paul, and he tells Johnny that she is not insane. Paul was an older brother who died three years ago and that is part of the reason she is like that.

Johnny goes to visit Lt. Barrie at homicide and shows him the note, which goes to the lab. Johnny visits Dr. Palmquist at 5:00, but he is not there as he had cancelled all of his appointments. The nurse offers Johnny an appointment for the next day. Johnny visits a drive-in theater and has dinner and a double feature and then goes to his hotel where he runs into Jim Darrell who tells Johnny that someone killed Mrs. Palmquist a couple of hours ago.

Tomorrow, variations on an old theme. You pays your money and you takes your choice, but no matter how you pick it, it comes out murder.

PART 2          SHOW DATE:          6/26/1956

Lt. Barrie calls and tells Johnny that he has been busy. Come on down and I will introduce you to the killer.

Johnny rushes to police headquarters where Lt. Barrie tells Johnny that they got a call from Palmquist around 9:00 last night. The police got there and found a Colt .38 and the doctor holding a rifle on the man. The doctor had been on a house call and when he got home he saw a man through the window holding a gun on Mrs. Palmquist. He snuck in to the house and got behind the man, who became rattled and shot Mrs. Palmquist. Dr. Palmquist then hit the man with a paperweight. Johnny is suspicious, but here is evidence that the man broke in, and the gun was his. Lt. Barrie checked on the patient, and she is a real looker, Mrs. Laura Consadine. She backs up the story completely. The killer is an ex-con with a record of small stuff who has a really wild story.

Johnny meets with the suspect, Lonnie Miller a tall erect man, who does not look like a killer, who did not look like a prowler, but more like a Victorian anti-macassar. Johnny tells Lonnie who he is, and he tells Johnny that the police did not believe him. He tells Johnny that he is nearly 60, and has done nearly everything in the book, but has never killed anyone. Johnny tells him that the police seem to have evidence pointing to him. Lonnie tells Johnny that he had just gotten out of jail, and was hitchhiking when a man in a Cadillac gave him a ride. They stopped for coffee and then left and the car had a flat. Lonnie changed the flat, and the man told him to stay in town as he might have a job for him. He told

Lonnie that his name was Carter. He called last night and told me to come to his house at 9:00 to meet a man who had a job for him. The house was in the palisades. When he got there he rang the bell and the door opened and he was hit on the head. When he came to, there was a dead woman on the floor, and Carter was holding a rifle on him. But the police called him Dr. Palmquist.

Johnny leaves Miller and talks to Lt. Barrie who tells Johnny that the doctor is resting in the hospital, and has not been told what Miller has said. Johnny thinks about the case over lunch and a few martinis, and then goes to the hospital to meet Dr. Palmquist, who apologizes for being a bad advertisement for his profession. Johnny tells him he is investigating the insurance policy, and the Palmquist tells Johnny that he should look for another climate, as California does not agree with him. On the way out of the room, Johnny meets the most beautiful woman he has ever seen. Palmquist tells her she has the wrong room, but Johnny notices the initials on her purse, "LC" for Laura Consadine. The doctor is ill, and the patient comes to visit! You cannot trust anyone these days.

Tomorrow, beauty may be skin deep, but fear goes a lot further down than that, sometime as far a death.

**PART 3**          **SHOW DATE:**     **6/27/1956**

Lt. Barrie calls and tells Johnny that Dr. Palmquist has complained. He told Lt. Barrie to keep unauthorized people away from him and to call his lawyer if they want anything. Meet me for lunch and I will try to sell you that we have the killer.

Johnny thinks there are too many angles to this case. Johnny cabs to the Barkley for lunch with Lt. Barrie but on the way out of his hotel Johnny see Eric Palmquist and Stephie Lund in a white Cadillac. When they spot Johnny, they drive off. Lt. Barrie had ordered lunch and is unimpressed that Palmquist and Lund are an item. Lt. Barrie does not like the smell of this case, but it is ex-con versus respected citizen, and Lt. Barrie is watching everyone. Johnny is told that the nurse is a nice kid; that Eric gambles some and drinks and that Laura Consadine lives in Long Beach. Also, the lab report on the note shows that it is untraceable.

Johnny is paged for a phone call; Stephie Lund needs to talk to him. She will explain about the car. She wants Johnny to come to Dr. Palmquist's office, and hurry. Johnny rushes to the office and gets a speeding ticket on the way. As the officer writes the ticket, Johnny notices that he is being followed. At the office the man drives on, and Johnny goes upstairs. In the office Stephie asks what Johnny wants and tells him that she did not call him. But Johnny notices the signals in her eyes pointing to the other room. A voice tells Johnny to come into the office, and inside Johnny finds Eric Palmquist holding a .38. Stephie is hysterical, and tells Johnny that Eric is mad. Eric laughs because no one tells him what to do, and they are both afraid. Eric likes it when others are afraid and laughs. Eric suddenly has the same empty look that Mrs. Palmquist had, and he collapses. Eric recovers in a few minutes, and Stephie tells Johnny that Eric will be all right. Stephie tells Johnny that Eric has circulatory libility, a form of extreme hypertension, enough to make him faint from fear. Eric is seeing a psychologist, and a cure will take a long time. Eric is scared of his father, the nice gentle healer, and her father-in-law. He is scared of his father and has kept the marriage secret. Johnny is glad that he was too scared to shoot; otherwise he would be the primary suspect in the killing of his mother.

Johnny leaves with Stephie still upset and drives into the garage of his hotel. On the way to his room Johnny is hit by a man—the man who was following him. "You are in the wrong town punk, take the hint." Johnny does, he passes out.

Tomorrow, a study in reactions, three of them, one by a man who should know, one by a man who does not, an another by a bullet.

## PART 4          SHOW DATE:      6/28/1956

Dr. Van Klauser returns Johnny's call. Johnny tells Dr. Klauser that he would like to see him today because he is running out of time. Johnny is told that he can come in at 11:00.

Johnny sees the hotel house medic and gets a checkup. Johnny then goes to meets Dr. Van Klauser at 11, and learns that Dr. Klauser is treating Eric Palmquist. Johnny shows Dr. Klauser his ID, and asks about circulatory libility. Johnny learns that it is a form of provoked hypertension, and very dangerous. It could cause a man to kill. Johnny calls for messages, and Lt. Barrie wants to see him. Johnny drives to see Lt. Barrie and Johnny tells him about being hit. Lt. Barrie tells Johnny that Lonnie has been identified as the buyer of the gun at a pawnshop, but Johnny is not convinced. Johnny visits with Lonnie and asks him why he lied. Johnny wants to know why he bought the gun at a Burbank pawnshop, and that he had showed a driver's license at the time. Lonnie tells Johnny that his license is in his wallet in the property files. Johnny asks him to tell the story again. Johnny checks the property folder, and there is no driver's license in it. Johnny buys an old newspaper that has photos of both Lonnie Miller and Dr. Palmquist. Johnny then drives to Long Beach and finds the taco shop where Lonnie said he and Carter stopped. Johnny talks to Irving Gonzales, who tells Johnny that no one could pronounce his real name, Prutarco. Irving tells Johnny that he is looking for something, so ask the questions, as Irving can spot a cop. Johnny shows him the pictures and he remembers reading about the case, but tells Johnny that he would only be guessing. Johnny drives to see Laura Consadine, but the drive is gated. On the way out Johnny sees a car drive away from the house. On the way back to the highway Johnny hears a shot and puts the car into the cliffs. Johnny wonders about how good a shot a man must be to put a bullet into a moving tire. Johnny remembers being warned about a man who always had time to go hunting, and who was an excellent shot; Dr. Palmquist.

Tomorrow, you want to hide something, put it in plain view. Only don't go overboard on the system if you are hiding a murder.

## PART 5          SHOW DATE:      6/29/1956

Laura Consadine calls, and Johnny tells her she that she is the best friend a doctor can have. She tells Johnny that she has to talk to him and that she will meet him the hotel bar in an hour. Johnny tells her that the martinis will be waiting.

Johnny meets Mrs. Consadine and Johnny reminds her of meeting him in Palmquist's hospital room. She tells Johnny that Victor's wife was a millstone around his neck, a woman in love with a bottle. And Eric is insane and hates his father. Eric gets a fortune by his mother's death, and yet Johnny is badgering Victor Palmquist. Johnny tells her that there is a lot of hate and there is usually a good reason for it. Johnny rents a car and drives to the pawnshop in Burbank. Johnny asks Mr. Learner about the gun sale, and he tells Johnny about the information written in the logbook. Johnny shows him the newspaper with the pictures, with Johnny's arm hiding part of the pictures. Learner moves Johnny's arm and tells him that Miller bought the gun. Johnny tells him that he had to move his arm to tell which man had bought the gun. Johnny rushes back to see Lt. Barrie, who is out. Johnny talks to Lonnie, and asks him a few questions, and then meets with Lt. Barrie. Johnny tells him that Palmquist and Miller are about the same size and color, and clothes can make a difference. If Palmquist wore work clothes to buy the gun, anyone would identify Miller as the killer. Johnny tells him that Palmquist arranged for the tire to go flat. When Miller changed the tire, Palmquist lifted the wallet, bought the gun and arranged the murder. Lt. Barrie does not buy the story because Johnny still cannot find proof.

Stephie visits Johnny in his room and tells him that Erick has been drinking and ranting about Mrs. Consadine and his father being a killer. She wants help. She tells Johnny that Eric is going to get a gun at home and then go to Mrs. Consadine's to kill her. Johnny and Stephie drive to Palmquist's house, and Johnny learns about him on the way. Stephie tells Johnny that the doctor is a tyrant who despises any form of weakness in his family. Paul was the favorite son and hunted with the doctor. Paul had a cold once, and was humiliated into going hunting by his father. Paul ended up dying of pneumonia.

At the Palmquist house, Johnny finds Eric asleep on his bed. Dr. Palmquist comes home, so Johnny gets Stephie out of the house and then goes to the garage via a window to look at the trunk of the Cadillac. Suddenly Palmquist is telling Johnny he should have asked about a key. Johnny tells him there is a tire with no puncture in the trunk, and Palmquist opens fire with a gun. Johnny manages to get off a shot as Lt. Barrie comes in through the window. Lt. Barrie tells Johnny that he did not like the look in Johnny's eye when he left, and had him tailed. Johnny is told "he is easier to tail than a trolley car."

Eric Palmquist admitted sending them the original warning note out of fear of his father. He never knew until the death of his mother that he was the beneficiary.

Remarks: About Hollywood, let's call it the easterner's revenge: "it's a nice place to visit, but I wouldn't want to live there."

Exp. Acct:　　$490.80

NOTES:

- AN ANTIMACASSAR IS A COVER USED TO PROTECT THE BACK OR ARMS OF FURNITURE

- WHEN JOHNNY VISITS THE HOTEL DOCTOR, HE MENTIONS A SECOND WOUND, BUT JOHNNY WAS ONLY HIT ONCE.
- ROY ROWAN IS THE ANNOUNCER
- MUSICAL SUPERVISION IS BY AMERIGO MARINO AND CARL FORTINA

**Producer:** Jack Johnstone      **Writers:** Tony Barrett
**Cast:** Virginia Gregg, Victor Perrin, Lillian Buyeff, Russell Thorson, James McCallion, Edgar Barrier, Don Diamond, Herb Butterfield

◆ ❖ ◆

**SHOW:** THE MIDAS TOUCH MATTER
**COMPANY:** GREATER SOUTHWEST INSURANCE AND LIABILITY COMPANY
**AGENT:** JAKE KESSLER
**PART 1**      **SHOW DATE:** 7/2/1956

**SYNOPSIS:** Pat McCracken calls and wants to know where Johnny has been. Johnny tells Pat that he has been buying fishing gear for a trip New York and the Espopus or the Beaverkill for some trout. Pat suggests Lake Mojave in Arizona. Be the guest of Greater Southwest. There is a fish out there that might be worth three million bucks. "I'll be right over" Johnny tells Pat.

Johnny cabs to the office of Pat McCracken. Johnny is told that he had better be packed, as Pat has his tickets to Las Vegas. Take a car from there to Kingman and see Jake Kessler, the local agent. The case is the Midas Touch mine. With one to three million at stake, no one is going to quibble over your expense account. "Maybe I will take a look at those Lake Mojave bass" Johnny tells Pat. Johnny grabs some American Express traveler's checks and heads for the airport.

Johnny gives a vivid description of the night sky in Las Vegas and gets a room at the Flamingo Hotel and incurs some "incidentals" at the casino. Next morning Johnny rents a car and drives to Kingman, Arizona.

Johnny drives to Jake's office, where Jake is dressed in cowboy attire. Jake has reserved a room for Johnny at Lake Mojave Resort, a nice place to stay. "Too bad you are not a fisherman." Jake tells Johnny. Johnny tells Jake he just happens to have brought a rod with him. "Good, Buster Favor will show you all the spots down there" Jake tells Johnny, and tells and tells Johnny about the Midas Touch mine, which is the area of Lake Mojave. The mine was closed in the early thirties, but "Hard Luck" Dennis has been looking at the mine. He is a prospector and promoter who makes a fair living for himself and he once had some trouble in Texas over some phony oil stock. He has been poking around looking for a strike, and got a lease on the mine. The assay reports showed ore worth $1,100 a ton. He needed some money for a pumping job, as Lake Mojave had raised the water levels and the mine was pretty deep. He went to the Haskel brothers, Ernie, Kevin and George, who were brokers out east and retired in the area. They got bored and bought the 2 Lazy 2 ranch and some cattle, and with Alex Bundy as foreman they did all right. All their insurance is with Jake, $500,000 a piece with double indemnity. Dennis needed money and went to the Haskels, who wanted no part of it. He took them to the mine and let them take samples, and then they went in for $20,000 each. Three days ago there was a cave in and all three of the Haskels were killed. So was it an accident or murder? Johnny is told that he will have to find Hard Luck Dennis. The wife of Kevin Haskel is the beneficiary of all three policies. The phone rings and Hard Luck Dennis is on the phone. He wants to see Johnny.

Tomorrow, I find that one of the fishermen who hangs around Lake Mojave is a character called death.

## PART 2          SHOW DATE:     7/3/1956

Hard Luck Dennis calls and tells Johnny to come see him, and do not bring a gun. Meet me at three o'clock at the mine.

Johnny tells Jake about the phone call and tells Jake that he will handle the matter himself, without help from the police. Jake feels that the mine was salted, but Captain Tad Harding of the police will prove it. He is at the mine now. Jake is positive that Dennis is guilty and salted the mine to get the money. "Well, if he is guilty, why would he call me?" asks Johnny. Jake agrees to not get anyone else involved. Jake and Johnny go to see Tad Harding, who confirms Jake's story, and tells Johnny that he has no evidence of the mine having been salted. He learned that the cause of the cave-in had been linked to a cable attached to a rock column that had been pulled out. Johnny tells Jake that now they need to find out who might have pulled the cable.

Johnny stalls Jake by going out to the resort to check in. On the way, Johnny finds the trail Dennis had described and follows it up to a shack. Johnny sees no sign of life at the shack. Johnny sees a sudden movement that turns out to be a turtle. Inside the shack Dennis surprises Johnny. Dennis tells Johnny that he did not kill the Haskel boys, and Johnny agrees. Dennis tells Johnny that the town is against him, because the town liked the Haskels. Dennis knows that Capt. Harding had been to the mine. Dennis tells Johnny that the Haskels were murdered, but he did not kill them. He had taken them to the mine, and while they were getting samples, he went out to investigate the sound of a car. Dennis looked outside the mine and something hit him and knocked him out. When he came to, the cave-in had happened and the Haskels were dead. Dennis hears a car coming up the road and Dennis turns to look at it. There is a shot, and Dennis is shot.

Tomorrow, the so called trackless desert yields a set of tracks that lead straight to, well if I told you, you would know, wouldn't you?

## PART 3          SHOW DATE:     7/4/1956

Jake calls Johnny and he has been at the hospital. Johnny is told that Dennis may never talk as the bullet went right through his neck. Johnny tells Jake to call him when he can talk to Dennis. "In the mean time, I'm going to try and snag me some of these Lake Mojave bass."

Johnny buys gas for the rental car, and describes the resort area. Johnny gets Buster Favor, the general factotum of the resort to direct him to the Midas Tough mine. Buster agrees to take Johnny there, and on the way Johnny relates the facts of the case so far to Buster. Johnny is told that Dennis is a funny old character and was ok when he was prospecting, and when he could not make the big strike, he tried to find a sucker. At the mine, Buster and Johnny use a flashlight to go into the mine. Buster finds a rattlesnake and uses a shovel handle to get the snake to strike and then snaps the snake like a whip. When Johnny asks if the snake could have been planted, Buster mentions the old scorpion in the monument trick used by prospectors to mark their claims. Buster finds where the pillar has been picked at, and Johnny sees gold. Buster tells him that the only gold in the mine is in the pillars. Remove them and the mine collapses. Buster finds the winch and the steel rope. Buster tells Johnny that every ranch in the area has one, but this one does not belong in a mine. Johnny takes a hard swing at a pillar in the mine, and starts a cave-in. Back at the resort Johnny is ready to go fishing, and Buster provides all the fixings. At the dock Johnny has a message to call Jake. Johnny calls Jake, who tells him that Dennis will recover and will only talk to Johnny.

Johnny drives to the hospital and sees Dennis. Dennis tells Johnny that "he" probably saw him poking around the mine, and figured Dennis recognized the winch, and tells Johnny that only Alex used the Union Standard model and that Alex was in love with Kevin Haskel's wife. Dennis tells Johnny that he will tell that to the court's if necessary and that Johnny is the only friend Dennis has.

Johnny talks to Jake to get directions to the 2 Lazy 2 ranch. Johnny suddenly changes the subject and rushes to the door; he is sure that someone was listening. Johnny is sure that it was Alex Bundy. The chief calls Jake and tells him that Dennis is dead. Somebody climbed up the fire escape and killed Dennis with a baling hook.

Tomorrow, the case is closed, and then it suddenly reopens with a bang from a 30/06 rifle.

**PART 4**      **SHOW DATE:**      **7/5/1956**

Buster calls Johnny and Johnny tells Buster that Dennis has been killed. Buster tells Johnny that he has found tire tracks at the miner's shack where Dennis was shot and more of the same tracks at the resort. Johnny is on his way.

Johnny buys gas at the sign of the flying red horse, and meets Buster at an old wagon trail where Buster shows Johnny the tracks; the right front tire is almost worn smooth. Buster also found the same tracks at the shack. The trail ends up at the lake, so Buster suggests taking a boat to intercept the driver. Buster and Johnny travel up the lake by boat and notice a dust trail alongside the lake. Buster pulls in, and suddenly Johnny hears a noise. Johnny notices holes in the boat and they hear shots; someone is shooting at them. Buster pulls around a point and sees the dust heading back to the highway. Johnny tells Buster that he knows exactly where to look for the jeep that made the tracks.

Johnny and Buster head out to the 2 Lazy 2 ranch. Buster tells Johnny that the gun that was used to shoot at them was a long barreled 30/06, probably with a scope. Buster tells Johnny that Alex Bundy had drunk too much once and mouthed off about the rich millionaires and how he would help turn the worm. That is when the talk of him and Dora started. At the ranch Buster spots the jeep and Johnny drives by it so Buster can look at the tires. At the main house Buster notices Johnny has a gun which Johnny describes as a ".38 lemon squeezer." Dora opens the door and invites Buster and Johnny in. Buster introduces Johnny and Dora knows that he is there to investigate the mine accident. Johnny tells her about the evidence in the mine and the winch that came from this ranch. Dora wonders who would benefit here at the ranch? Johnny suggests that Alex Bundy would benefit by marrying into the family; he is interested in you isn't he. Dora tells Johnny that he was interested in her, but she knew he was only interested in the ranch and knew that her husband was ill and did not have a long time. Johnny tells Dora about someone killing Dennis, and overhearing him tell Jake that he was going fishing. The man who did it was a crack shot and was driving a jeep. Dora tells Johnny that the jeep was gone that afternoon. She offers to help and gives Johnny a high-powered hunting rifle. She tells Johnny that she was on the rifle team in college. Dora is about to give a gun to Buster when Alex yells at Dora about not telling him she was going to take the jeep. Suddenly Dora turns her gun on Johnny, and tells him his gun is not loaded!

Tomorrow, well sometimes justice is done by strange and devious means.

## PART 5        SHOW DATE:        7/6/1956

The phone rings and Dora tells Johnny to answer it. Jake is one the phone and asks Johnny what he is doing there, as Dora has filed a claim. Johnny tells Jake he is looking at proof of murder right now. Why don't you come on out here, and Johnny throws the phone at Dora.

Proof of murder will save the insurance company $1.5 million. Now Alex has pointed the finger at Dora. Buster pushes Dora who manages to crease Johnny's arm. As Buster starts to take the gun, Alex comes in with a gun. Alex tells Johnny that Dora lied. She shot at Johnny by the lake, but he shot Dennis. He killed Dennis because he was going to talk, and he had to protect his neck. She was smarter than me, and kept getting me in deeper and deeper. He got drunk once and told everyone he wanted the ranch. She heard about it and told him he could have the ranch with her. She plotted to get rid of her husband, and kept him involved. He helped with the boats once when the Haskels almost drowned. She told Dennis to take them to the mine. She would have killed me the way I killed Hard Luck. Johnny tells him he is in too deep now. Alex tells them he is going to kill Dora. She grabs her rifle, but Alex kills her and runs out the door. Johnny calls Jake to get the police to set up roadblocks as Buster looks for ammunition. Johnny and Buster drive out after Alex and follow him towards Davis Dam. At the top of a hill they see a police roadblock. Johnny heads towards Lake Mojave as a windstorm blows in. At the resort, Ham Pratt tells Johnny that Alex took his boat out on the lake. Buster starts his boat and they follow Alex up the lake towards Nevada. As they ride the chop up the lake they finally start to catch up with Alex. As they pull up beside him Alex rams them with his boat.

That's really all there is to it, except that Ham had followed behind and picked up Buster and Johnny. Alex sank with his boat.

Remarks: There is no question of course but that the Haskels had been murdered so double indemnity. And Dora's little scheme to collect a cool three million, well it got her exactly what she deserved. Won't people like that ever learn?

Exp. Acct:     $978.35

NOTES:

- THIS IS THE FIRST OF SEVERAL APPEARANCES OF JAKE KESSLER AND LAKE MOJAVE RESORT.
- JACK JOHNSTONE RELATED ONCE IN A TAPED INTERVIEW, THAT HE USED TO GO FISHING WITH HIS FRIEND ROBERT TAYLOR AT LAKE MOJAVE RESORT. MY FRIEND BILL BROOKS, WHO KNEW JACK, TOLD ME THAT BUSTER AND HAM WERE THE ACTUAL OWNERS OF THE RESORT.
- JACK JOHNSTONE WAS MARRIED TO A WOMAN NAMED BUNDY, SO POSSIBLY ALEX IS A RELATIVE. ALSO JACK USED JOHN BUNDY AS A PEN NAME.
- THE ESPOPUS AND BEAVERKILL ARE WELL KNOWN TROUT RIVERS IN NEW YORK STATE.
- FROM 1886 TO 1940, SMITH AND WESSON MADE A "SAFETY HAMMERLESS" .38 REVOLVER CALLED A "LEMON SQUEEZER." IT WAS POPULAR WITH GAMBLERS AND DETECTIVES BECAUSE IT COULD BE FIRED FROM INSIDE A COAT POCKET.
- JOHNNY IS NICKED, SO I GUESS THIS COUNTS AS BEING SHOT FOR THE SEVENTH TIME.
- THIS IS THE FIRST MENTION OF AMERICAN EXPRESS TRAVELER'S CHECKS.
- THE FLYING RED HORSE IS A VEILED REFERENCE TO MOBIL GASOLINE.
- ROY ROWAN IS THE ANNOUNCER
- MUSICAL SUPERVISION IS BY AMERIGO MARINO AND CARL FORTINA

Producer:   Jack Johnstone        Writers:   Jack Johnstone
Cast:       Virginia Gregg, Johnny Jacobs, Herb Butterfield, Parley Baer, Barney Phillips, Shep Menken, Roland Winters

◆   ❖   ◆

SHOW:        THE SHADY LANE MATTER
COMPANY:     STAR MUTUAL INSURANCE COMPANY
AGENT:       PETE CARLSON
PART 1       SHOW DATE:     7/9/1956

SYNOPSIS: Pete Carlson calls complaining to Johnny about working while the family is out on Cape Cod. Pete has a letter about the Bates murder that tells him to "look close to home." The signer was anonymous. The husband was the beneficiary, and the company is on the verge of paying the policy. Johnny agrees to go to Shady Lane, Vermont, if he can find it on the map.

Johnny travels to Shady Lane Vermont, a small quiet town with one of everything, including Jed Brambler, the constable. Johnny talks to Jed and is told that the killing is a mystery. The bullet was hand poured for an old-fashioned squirrel rifle. Ellen Bates was married and was shot in the heart. It could have been an accident, maybe a hunter who shot at anything that moved, but hunters do not use old-fashioned rifles though. Ellen Bates was a fine woman, but they have nothing to go on. There are no motives and no enemies. The bullet was sent to New York, but the test results told them nothing and there are about 300 of that type of rifle in these parts. Ellen was sitting in front of her window and was shot. Johnny tells Jed that people are facts, and you can check on people. Maybe she saw something that made her dangerous to someone, or maybe someone would benefit from her death. Johnny shows Jed the letter that was mailed from Shady Lane. Jed tells Johnny not to count on the letter too much. Ben Bates is the beneficiary, but Ben does not have the capacity for murder. Johnny wants to meet Ben and Jed agrees to drive him there, but Johnny will have to pay for gas, as the town is kind of frugal with its money. Johnny wants to talk to the coroner, but that is Jed.

Johnny and Jed drive to the Bates farm. On the way they stop and talk to Martin Preeny, Ben's neighbor. Johnny is introduced to Mr. Preeny, who is building a stone fence. He tells Johnny that he plans ahead and builds right. Sarah Preeny is called out and Jed mentions the investigation of the murder. When Martin Preeny mentions that Johnny comes from Hartford, Sarah is surprised. Martin tells Johnny about the operations that left Ellen an invalid. Sarah tells Johnny that Ben hardly took care of Ellen at all, but spent time with that flibbertigibbet in town. Martin calls Sarah back and Johnny thanks Sarah for sending the letter. "How did you know?" she asks. Johnny tells her he was just guessing.

Tomorrow, of two who are not even accused, one confesses and one denies, and both very strangely.

## PART 2          SHOW DATE:     7/10/1956

Johnny gets his call from Pete Carlson in Hartford. Johnny needs to know when the policy was written and Pete tells Johnny that it was about 4 years ago. There is a policy on Ben Bates as well.

Johnny buys a newspaper and wonders about this case; there is no evidence, no witnesses, no motives or leads. Jed takes Johnny up to the site where he thinks the shooting took place and Johnny notices the poor condition of the farmland. Jed tells Johnny that he had brought in dogs to search the area but found nothing. Johnny notices a stake and Jed tells him that it is a survey stake for a new highway that did not materialize. The highway could have made the farm worth something if the road had gone through here. Jed shows Johnny where the shot must have come from and mentions that Ellen was not alone at the time. Mrs. Preeny was with her at the time but did not see anyone. Johnny asks Jed about the gossip of Ben and the waitress and Jed tells him that Ben eats most of his evening meals there, and folks think that there is some interest growing between them. Johnny thinks that he would not be the first man to kill an invalid wife for a younger woman, but Jed tells Johnny that Ben was not like that. Jed also tells Johnny that Mrs. Preeny liked Ellen, but did not like Ben for some reason. It is just her nature.

Johnny and Jed walk to the house and knock on the door. Groady comes from behind the house and tells Jed that Ben is out, and Groady does not know when he will be back. Jed introduces Johnny to Groady Hawkins, who does odd jobs. Johnny asks if he was there the day Mrs. Bates was killed and he denies being there very loudly. Jed tells Johnny that Groady gets kind of excited when blamed for things, and he is a dead shot; he never misses.

Johnny and Jed leave and return to town, where Johnny eats dinner at the Inn. Johnny asks the waitress if she is Milly Wells, and she tells Johnny that he works fast. She had hoped that she and Ben would have some time. She never thought about Ellen Bates while she was alive, and Ben never looked twice at her either. "Doesn't it mean anything if a person has been acquitted?" asks Milly. When Johnny asks of what, she replies murder, and then realizes that Johnny did not know what she was talking about. Johnny tells her she should tell him about it.

Tomorrow, a sudden twist, and a cool threat, a strange revelation, and the lies come thick and fast.

**PART 3**        **SHOW DATE:**    **7/11/1956**

Jed calls Johnny and asks for Milly and Johnny tells him that she is crying at the moment. Jed tells Johnny that she is a nice woman, but Johnny tells him that everyone in town is nice to him.

Johnny buys dinner and Milly tells him that she and Ben never saw each other before his wife died, no matter what the people say. Milly tells Johnny that even being tried for murder brands a person for life. She tells Johnny that Ben has been coming in to eat here, and he knows about the trial. After Ellen died, he said that one day he would like to see more of her. Milly tells Johnny that four years ago in Chicago, she had been working as a governess. The wife died under mysterious circumstances and she was accused of killing her to marry the husband.

Johnny stops by Jed's office and tells him that Milly has stopped crying. Jed tells Johnny that she had stopped by and told Jed about it on her first day in town. Johnny is convinced that a case exists against Ben. Jed tells Johnny that the farm is mortgaged to the hilt and that Martin Preeny had loaned Ben $7,500 for Ellen's operations. The farm is only worth $4,500, so Ben feels obligated. The insurance policy would have released the pressure and still leave some money to marry Milly. Johnny asks if Ben has a squirrel gun, and Jed tells Johnny he only has a shotgun. Johnny tells Jed that the shotgun was resting on a set of hooks designed for a different gun, a squirrel rifle. Jed seems to remember seeing a squirrel rifle there many years ago.

Johnny and Jed go back to the Bates farm and find Ben at home. Ben takes them to the kitchen and offers them some lemonade. Jed tells Ben that they are there to talk to him. Johnny thinks Ben might have killed Ellen, but Ben tells him he would never harm a hair on Ellen's head. Mrs. Preeny thinks he did it, and Ben tells them she is crazy. When Jed asks about the squirrel rifle, Ben tells them it was stolen a week before Ellen was shot and he has not seen it since. Ellen thought she knew who took it, and Ellen asked him not to report it. The only people who were there at the house were Mrs. Preeny and Groady. When Johnny asks if Groady could have killed her, Jed tells Johnny that Groady is a nice boy. Johnny asks if Jed cares if the murder victim is ever identified and Ben tells Johnny that Jed is Ellen's uncle. She was, "but it don't have no bearing."

Tomorrow, a slow net tightens and the fish turn frantic, and one of them is armed and dangerous, as deadly as a shark.

## PART 4          SHOW DATE:     7/12/1956

The phone rings at Ben's house, but no one is there when Johnny answered it. Ben thinks that it probably was Milly Wells. Johnny tells Ben that she was tried for murder and your wife has been murdered and the town is talking; add up the facts, Ben.

Johnny still feels that Ben is the key to the case, but Jed tells Johnny that he is not the type. Johnny thinks that Jed is too close to everyone. Ben tells Johnny that he would never have killed his wife, and he is not involved with Milly. Ben explains about not reporting the missing rifle after the murder and Ell's desire to not report it before the killing. She was going to talk to whoever took it, but was killed before she could. Johnny asks Ben for a suspect, and he tells Johnny that Ellen had no enemies, and he would not kill her for the money.

Johnny and Jed drive back to town and go to the shack where Groady lives in return for keeping an eye on the store. They walk back to the shack and Jed trips over a box. Groady yells at them with a gun and tells them to stop until he has a light on them. Johnny asks to look at his gun and it turns out to be a .22. Jed asks Groady what he did with the rifle he took from Ben Bates' place. Groady denies taking it, and Jed walks him back to the jail.

In the jail Jed tells Johnny that he knows Groady, and he is lying about something. Jed tells Johnny that Ellen was the most liked person in the township, and Johnny still comes back to Ben as the guilty party. Johnny asks Jed how he and Ellen got along, and the answer is "just fine." Groady calls for Jed and they walk back to talk to Groady. He tells them he did steal the gun and sold it to Martin Preeny to hang in his house. Preeny gave Groady $4.00 for it about three weeks ago. When Johnny tells Groady that he had the gun in his possession when Ellen was killed, he tells Johnny that the gun has never been fired; it has rust in the barrel.

Tomorrow, one domino tips, the whole stack tumbles, and the last man falls with a crash.

## PART 5          SHOW DATE:     7/13/1956

Johnny is called by Mrs. Preeny and she wants to talk with him. Johnny tells her to come to his room but she could never do that; the town would talk. She tells Johnny that she has done a terrible thing and must confess.

Johnny and Mrs. Preeny meet in the lunchroom and she tells Johnny that she did not do it; "That girl did not warm the teapot properly." She tells Johnny that she did not want Martin to know she was meeting with Johnny and she tells Johnny about the letter. It was terrible thing to do. The things she said about Ben were not true. She knows that Ben had nothing to do with killing Ellen. She also made up the things she said about Ben and Milly. Her husband is steady and reliable, but life on a farm is not easy for a woman, and sometimes they get silly notions. She wants a little warmth and understanding. But Ben Bates never even looked at her, and that is all she wanted.

Johnny walks to Jed's office and Groady is still asleep. Johnny asks about picking up the gun from Martin, and Jed tells Johnny he can use the car, but it will cost him $3. Johnny jests about wondering how Jed made a living before he got there, and Jed tells Johnny that it was speeding tickets, but the new highway will end all that, as it misses the town completely. Johnny tells Jed that if it had come through the town, it would have saved Ellen Bates. Johnny tells Jed about the visit from Mrs. Preeny and Jed tells Johnny it was probably because Martin did not pay attention to her.

Johnny drives to the Preeny farm and Mrs. Preeny meets Johnny on the doorstep and tells him that she is on the way out. Johnny promises that he will not talk about, well you know. Johnny goes in to see Martin, who is finishing his books, and Johnny asks him about the squirrel gun and tells him that Groady had stolen it from Ben. Johnny inspects the gun, and it was all rusty. Johnny also notices the gun hooks, which had been there for years, and Johnny knows. He knows who killed Ellen Bates. It was somebody who stood to profit more than Ben did. Somebody who loaned Ben $7,500 out of kindness, something not in your nature. But it was not kindness it was good business. Johnny asks where the rifle is that originally hung by the fireplace. Martin tells Johnny that there might not have been one, but Johnny tells him that the neighbors will remember. Martin writes down the final figures in his journal and mentions that he had a good year last year. You take risks and sometimes you lose. He knew he made a mistake as soon as he pulled the trigger, and takes Johnny out behind the barn where the rifle is buried.

Exp. Acct:    $186.60

NOTES:
- REMAKE OF THE PINEY CORNERS MATTER
- ROY ROWAN IS THE ANNOUNCER
- MUSICAL SUPERVISION IS BY AMERIGO MARINO AND CARL FORTINA

Producer:    Jack Johnstone          Writers:    Les Crutchfield
Cast:        Jeanette Nolan, Forrest Lewis, Shirley Mitchell, Will Wright, Bert Holland, John Dehner

SHOW:        THE STAR OF CAPETOWN MATTER
COMPANY:     TRI-EASTERN INDEMNITY ASSOCIATES
AGENT:       JOE McNAB
PART 1       SHOW DATE:      7/16/1956

SYNOPSIS: Joe McNab calls Johnny about the Star of Capetown, a diamond about the size of a large olive. It is insured for $150,000. So far three men have been killed over it. The diamond is in Capetown, South Africa. Interested?

Johnny cabs to Joe McNab's office, and Joe is worried about Andrew Lanings Forbes, III who is an international playboy who owns the diamond now. He treats it like a piece of costume jewelry and carts it around with him. The insurance company wants him to put it in permanent custody. Forbes is in a party-giving mood now, and they are worried. Joe wants Johnny to talk to Forbes and convince him to let them take care of the diamond. Johnny is willing to take the case, but is worried about the three men who have died over the diamond. Joe tells him not to worry; that was thirty years ago.

Johnny flies to Capetown, South Africa and cabs to the mansion of Mr. Forbes, which Forbes describes as "adequate." Forbes tells Johnny that it was unnecessary for the company to send him. Forbes offers to show Johnny the diamond, and takes it from his jacket pocket. Forbes was expecting Johnny and decided to play a joke on him. Johnny looks at the diamond that he thinks is the size of a golf ball. Forbes takes Johnny to his bedroom and puts the diamond in a wall safe. Johnny is concerned because the bedroom opens on to a terrace, so Forbes agrees to put the diamond in a bank vault the next morning. Forbes is giving a party for Agatha his sister that night. She worries about him, and is ashamed of what he is doing to the family name. Johnny is invited to the party and asks Forbes for a guest list. Forbes tells him he has no idea who is going to show up.

Johnny stops by the local police office and gets Captain Van Tyle to provide a guard for the party. Johnny goes back to the house for the party, which is well under way. Johnny meets a girl named Sheila, a friend of Forbes. She tells Johnny that she attends most of his parties. Forbes walks up and welcomes Johnny and tells him that Agatha is not enjoying the party, and Forbes points her out. Forbes tells Johnny that she hates the party, Forbes and Sheila. A new arrival named Helen is pointed out by Sheila. Johnny wonders why Sheila keeps tagging along, and she tells Johnny that not going would not seem normal, and she wanders to the bar. Johnny spots Forbes showing off the diamond as Agatha talks to him and he puts the diamond away. Forbes enjoys himself with Helen and goes onto the terrace. After a while Johnny misses Forbes and looks for him on the terrace and then the bedroom where Forbes is on the floor with a knife in this ribs and no diamond.

Tomorrow, a girl who is exciting, beautiful and deadly.

**PART 2      SHOW DATE:      7/17/1956**

Lt. Van Tyle of the police calls, and tells Johnny that the diamond is still missing. He has a suspect; the whole party.

Johnny cabs to police headquarters and talks to Lt. Van Tyle, who has nothing but questions. Johnny outlines his involvement in the case and the diamond. Johnny tells Lt. Van Tyle that he was at the party the whole time and knew no one at the party. Johnny tells him about Agatha, Sheila and Helen, who was the last person Johnny saw Forbes with. Johnny tells Lt. Van Tyle that there was no guest list. Johnny gets the mug shots of known jewel thieves and recognizes one of them, Julio Biac. Johnny thinks he was there, but is not sure.

Johnny walks out for some fresh air and looks around the waterfront. Johnny spots the silhouette of a person on the roof of a building following him. Just in time, Johnny ducks as a roof tile crashes to the pavement. Johnny runs to the roof, but sees no one.

Johnny goes to his hotel room and smells the scent of perfume. Sheila is in the room waiting for him and she wants to talk about last night. She tells Johnny that she left before it happened, she thinks. Johnny tells her she was sober enough to see Forbes and Helen leave, and to know that Johnny went to Forbes' room. She tells Johnny that she had been watching and saw Helen leave the room with a bottle of perfume. That is always the first gift from Forbes to a new girlfriend. The perfume is called "Forever." She tells Johnny that she was waiting in the garden to talk to Forbes. She saw Johnny go into the bedroom and then left. Johnny thinks that the only way for her to get off the Forbes merry go round was to kill him, but she tells Johnny she did not do it. Johnny suggests she go talk to Lt. Van Tyle, and she is on her way there as Lt. Van Tyle had called her.

Johnny goes to the ship "Southern Empress" to see Agatha Forbes. She tells Johnny that Andrew had told her about him, but she is tired and does not want to talk. She will be in New York in a month; maybe she will be calm enough to talk then. Suddenly Johnny sees someone and breaks off the conversation. Johnny sees a girl who looks like Helen and goes into the lounge looking for her but sees Julio Biac who was the bartender at the party. Julio runs down a passageway, but it dead-ends and Johnny has him trapped. Julio pulls a knife and lunges at Johnny who is able to subdue him.

Lt. Van Tyle thanks Johnny for sending Biac ashore. Johnny tells him that Biac did not have the diamond, so the ship will have another passenger, Johnny! Johnny gets a room from the purser and goes to the hotel go get his bags. In his room Johnny is slugged and recovers in time to see his ship steaming out of the harbor.

Tomorrow, I take a trip all right, a one-way trip.

**PART 3      SHOW DATE:      7/18/1956**

Lt. Van Tyle calls and Johnny tells him about being slugged to keep him from sailing. Johnny feels the diamond is on the ship. Lt. Van Tyle tells him that Biac's story agrees with Johnny's, but he swears he does not have the diamond. Johnny feels it was passed to someone on the ship, or he was chasing someone who had it. Lt. Van Tyle will arrange for a helicopter to get Johnny to the ship.

Johnny gets a ride to the ship on a military helicopter with a throbbing head, still unsure the diamond is on the ship. Johnny lands on the ship and goes to his room. Johnny goes to the stateroom of Agatha, and Helen opens the door. She leaves to go to her cabin, and Agatha agrees to talk to Johnny, as it is probably her duty as long as Johnny does not drag the Forbes name through the dirt. Johnny asks if there was a motive other than the diamond, but she had not thought of that. Johnny asks her if Sheila could have done it, but Agatha refuses to discuss her. Johnny is surprised to find Helen in the stateroom, and Agatha tells Johnny that she is her traveling companion and that she is a thoroughly nice person. Agatha tells Johnny that Helen had decided to take the ship at the last moment and Agatha had hired her. Johnny tells her that Helen is suspect number one, and Agatha is surprised. Agatha tells Johnny that she will not file a claim until she gets to New York, which will give him time to find it, and the murderer.

Johnny goes to this stateroom and finds the door open. Inside is the same smell of perfume. Johnny remembers that Sheila has the perfume, and remembers it in his hotel room earlier, and thinks of Helen. In the hallway Johnny collides with a passenger, Ben Stacey a loudmouth who tells Johnny "See ya 'round, partner" as he walks away.

Johnny locks his door and goes for a martini. Johnny is sure it was Helen in his room, but then he spots Sheila at the bar. Johnny tells Sheila she took an interesting boat. She tells Johnny that there have been other women, but Andy always came back to her, so forget she is on board. Johnny is now sure that Helen is the prime suspect.

Johnny spots Helen, Agatha and Ben on the deck, and goes to talk. Helen leaves with a headache, and Ben tells Johnny that he and Forbes were the best of friends. He was not at the party, but would have been there had he known what was going to happen. Ben tells Johnny that he can show them some really interesting places in Day-Kar (Dakar) and leaves. Johnny asks Agatha if she knew Ben, but she tells Johnny that her brother had all sorts of strange friends he did not mention to her. Johnny goes to his room, and sees that he has had a visitor, as the room is torn apart. Somebody figures that Johnny has the diamond now. Johnny has to get the diamond before Dakar, the end of the trail for him.

Tomorrow, my one good lead jumps ship, the hard way.

### PART 4          SHOW DATE:     7/19/1956

The purser calls and Johnny asks for a steward to fix his room. The purser tells Johnny that a cablegram had been sent to Julio Biac to meet him at the usual place in Dakar. The sender's name was Corner, but there is no one on board by that name. The purser is going to talk to the steward who delivered the message to the radio room.

Johnny tips the purser for the good news and now knows that Julio was not working alone. Johnny starts for the purser's office and is met by Helen. She complains to Johnny about him tearing up her room. Johnny takes her to the bar to talk and she tells Johnny that she is so confused about people watching her. She tells Johnny that she did not know Forbes long, and that the party was strange. Forbes was interested in many people, and she did not encourage him. He gave her a bottle of perfume, which Johnny tells is the usual first gift. She could not believe the news of his death nor his attitude about the diamond. She made the trip suddenly to get away from Capetown, and Agatha is really a nice person. Before she goes back to work, Johnny asks her to a dance to be held that night. Johnny walks her to Agatha's stateroom and Agatha tells Johnny that he is very suspicious. Johnny tells Agatha about the cablegram and she hopes the publicity will die down soon and wishes Andrew had met Helen sooner.

That night Helen and Johnny dance and go out on the deck to talk. Helen tells him that he seems so nice now, and he kisses her. Ben Stacey walks up laughing and Johnny gets miffed. Ben wants to set up a little shore party for Dakar tomorrow. Ben can show you some places you won't believe. Johnny agrees, and Stacey walks off. The purser finds Johnny and tells him that the steward had disappeared. Johnny hears Helen screaming and goes to her. She tells Johnny that someone grabbed at her from behind a lifeboat and then ran off. Is she lying or telling the truth? Johnny puts her in her cabin, and there is a "man overboard" call. The crew recovers the body, which turns out to be the missing steward. Johnny's one good lead is gone.

Tomorrow, I finally figure out the deal, only to find my opponent is holding all the aces.

## PART 5          SHOW DATE:      7/20/1956

Ben Stacey calls Johnny to say they will be docking in an hour. That was some excitement last night wasn't it, about the steward falling overboard? Johnny tells Ben that he thinks he got pushed.

When the ship docks, Johnny goes to meet Ben, Helen and Agatha. Ben arrives and Agatha is going to stay on board. Johnny and Helen get a good tour of Dakar from Ben. Ben directs Helen to a local shop and while Helen tries on clothes Johnny worries about her passing the diamond to someone. Ben disappears and Johnny goes to look for him only to be followed by a man with a knife. In an alley Ben pulls Johnny into a room and a man named Hassan follows Johnny inside. Ben tells Johnny that he is after Johnny for the diamond. Johnny tells Ben that Biac knifed Forbes, and it was Ben that threw the steward over board. Ben had also been searching the rooms. Ben demands the diamond and Hassan starts beating Johnny to get it. Ben tells Johnny that a friend owns the store Helen is in and if she has the diamond, she will get it from her. Ben tells Johnny that the only time Helen could have passed the diamond was last night on deck. Suddenly Johnny understands the case.

Ben leaves Johnny with Hassan and Johnny tries to talk to him. Johnny asks Hassan what Ben is giving him and tells Hassan that everyone who works for Ben ends up dead or in jail. That would never happened to you, would it? Johnny knows where the diamond is and Hassan can come with him. As Hassan starts to think, Johnny slugs him and then goes after Ben, who comes back into the room. Johnny overpowers him and gets the police to hold Hassan and Ben.

Back on the ship Johnny visits Helen and thanks her for the snow job. Johnny asks her for the perfume bottle, smashes it and finds the diamond in the base. Agatha comes in with a gun and tells Johnny that she and Andrew had used Helen. Johnny asks Agatha why, and she asks Johnny if he knew how it felt to have someone drag the family name through the dirt? The family is deeply in debt, but the will precluded the sale of the diamond. They had arranged for someone to sell the diamond and get the insurance. She had not planned on Andrew dying, and the creditors had started pressing her. Johnny tells her that she has failed to keep the name clean, and is trapped. Are you going to brand it with murder? Johnny takes her gun and she tells Johnny she has failed all the way.

Johnny turns over the diamond over to the authorities and Agatha is charged with insurance fraud. Julio Biac and Ben Stacy were indicted in the murder of Forbes.

Remarks: About Agatha, I guess she did what she did because the ends justified the means, which is one of the oldest sucker traps of them all. About Helen, well now that she is no longer a suspect, could be I'm no longer building up to a big let down with her. At least it has not come yet, and I am still waiting. And the waiting is real pleasant.

Exp. Acct:     $1,283.60

NOTES:

- BOB BAILEY GIVES A PROMO FOR THE NEXT EPISODE, WHICH DESCRIBES "THE SEA LEGS MATTER." HOWEVER, THE NEXT BROADCAST IS "THE OPEN TOWN MATTER."
- DAKAR IS THE CAPITAL OF SENEGAL
- ROY ROWAN IS THE ANNOUNCER
- MUSIC SUPERVISION IS BY AMERIGO MARINO

**Producer:**  Jack Johnstone          **Writers:**   Robert Ryf
**Cast:**      Jean Tatum, Virginia Gregg, Harry Bartell, Chester Stratton, Marvin Miller, D. J. Thompson

◆   ❖   ◆

**SHOW:**      THE OPEN TOWN MATTER
**COMPANY:**   GREAT PLAINES GUARANTY COMPANY
**AGENT:**     RALPH KEARNS
**PART 1**     **SHOW DATE:**     7/23/1956

SYNOPSIS: Ralph Kearns calls and tells Johnny he is 52 and has married a 27-year-old woman, taken out a $50,000 insurance policy on a sheriff's salary with the wife as the beneficiary. Three days ago you were shot to death and your wife filed a claim less than 24 hours later. What do you think? You have 56 minutes to catch the plane to Greensport, Missouri. And watch yourself, it is supposed to be a wide-open town.

Johnny travels to Greensport and is met by Averil P. Potter, the local Great Plaines agent. Potter tells Johnny that the wife wants her money and that she had asked for a claim form less than 13 hours after the chief was shot. Johnny calls her cold-blooded, but Potter tells him that she is anything but cold-blooded, if you know what I mean, man oh man, WOW!

Johnny cabs to the home of Edward Blake, the dead sheriff. A tipsy man meets Johnny on the walk and tells Johnny that he is a copper. Johnny tells him that he is in insurance, and the man says that is just what he had been asking the widow about, and had just been thrown out of the house. He is Joe Crailey, a reporter for the local paper. Johnny gives a "no comments" response to his questions about insurance. Johnny asks Joe about where the action is in town, and Joe tells him he is pretty fast. Don't poke around, or you could get hurt. Johnny asks how the sheriff could afford a house in a nice area on his salary, and Joe tells him that his wife is even more expensive. Johnny asks Joe if the police chief was in on the gambling, and Joe gives him a "no comment." Johnny wants to talk to him later and Joe tells him to just look for "the alcoholic from the paper."

Johnny meets Mrs. Blake, and she is happy to see Johnny and did not think they would pay so quickly. Johnny tells her he is there to investigate the killing. She tells Johnny the company is trying to get out of paying; she knows how they operate. Johnny tells her he wants more information on the details of the killing. She tells Johnny that her husband was shot to death with his own gun right here in his own house. Johnny asks for her to show him how it happened, and that there will be no payment until he is satisfied. She makes a quick pass at Johnny and then it is back to business. She relates how her husband fell and his gun was lying right beside him. It was around 2:00 AM when she heard a noise and Ed went down to investigate. His gun was on the table. She went into the hall and heard shots. She ran downstairs and found him dead. The police say a prowler forced the lock. The police figure the man used the gun on the table. She does not know who the prowler was, but Ed had some enemies. Johnny asks if a friend could have done it. Johnny notices a diamond studded watch, the nice house and the new car, all on a policeman's salary, but she knows nothing abut Ed's finances. Johnny asks if Ed was in on the rackets, and she asks Johnny if he wants a drink. Johnny tells her that 24 hours is too quick for a grief-stricken widow to file a claim, and she tells Johnny that she is not grief-stricken. She tells Johnny to see Dave Sherman the city attorney to see of she is guilty. Then, if you are nice, I might even cooperate.

Tomorrow, a smash in the teeth loosens things up, and an airtight alibi gets air-conditioned, with bullets.

## PART 2        SHOW DATE:        7/24/1956

Johnny gets a call from Dave Sherman. He has made the records available, but Johnny wants to talk to him personally. Marty Blake told me to talk to you. Dave tells Johnny that if he wants to light a fuse in this town, he will give Johnny some matches.

Johnny cabs to city hall to talk with Dave Sherman and notes that the newspaper headlines are calling for action. Johnny tells Dave that he has been to see Mrs. Blake already, and she is not grieving. Dave tells Johnny that Ed had to make money after meeting Marty; he had to. Then she married him. Dave tells Johnny that he is on the wrong foot in this case. Johnny tells about her turning on her charms, and the scanty details she provided. Dave tells Johnny that she is cold-blooded and used to be a dancer who lived by her wits. Dave tells Johnny that they were not alone; he was there with them. "Well, she has a good alibi," notes Johnny. Dave tells Johnny that he was spending the night and that he and Ed were going fishing the next morning. He heard some noises and went out into the hall right after the shots were fired, and Marty was standing in her doorway. Dave tells them that he and Blake were not really good friends but their differences were not a motive for killing him. Johnny wonders if Marty was the motive, after all Dave is around her age. Dave tells Johnny that she has a built in jukebox and only plays if you put in money. Johnny tells him that Marty must have been the reason Blake got into the rackets, and Dave asks Johnny what makes him think that there are any rackets in town, and where he got his information. Mayor Will Lyons comes in and Johnny is introduced. Johnny tells him his theory has just blown up. Johnny asks for the official theory and the mayor tells him that when they find Shorty Wells, they will have the killer. Wells had been put in jail by Blake, had sworn to get him, and is out on parole now but no one can find him. When Johnny mentions rackets to the mayor he gets flustered, but Dave tells him that Johnny knows. The Mayor tells Johnny that here are rackets, but no one knows who is in charge. But find Shorty and the case will be closed.

On the way out of city hall Marty Blake honks her car horn at Johnny and wants to talk to him. Johnny tells her that he has talked to Dave and asks why she did not tell him about Dave. She tells Johnny that he is not being nice. When Johnny mentions Shorty Wells, she tenses up. There are shots from a speeding car, and Marty tells Johnny that someone is out to kill him. "How do you know they were not after you, Mrs. Blake?" asks Johnny.

Tomorrow, an old flame and a new one, and two men get burned. One becomes an alcoholic, the other a human torch.

**PART 3**　　　**SHOW DATE:**　　**7/25/1956**

Joe calls and asks how Johnny is making out? Johnny wants to talk, but Joe tells him not tonight, he is drunk and might talk too much. Johnny tells him about the shots, and Joe tells him to beat it. Greensport is a wide-open town.

Johnny cabs to the home of Will Lyons, the mayor, to get right to the top of the story. Will and Johnny talk in the library and he tells Johnny that he had heard the shots. Will tells Johnny that the town is looking into the shooting matter, but there are no witnesses. Johnny tells him that he is not sure that he was the target, but he does not know why anyone would have wanted to kill Marty. Will tells Johnny that there is a police guard at Marty's house now, and Johnny asks him if he can trust the officer, or anyone else for that matter? Will tells Johnny that every effort to carry out raids on the mob have been unsuccessful. Dave and Will suspected that Ed was on the take, but never could find any evidence. Dave and Ed were not friendly at all, and his being there was odd, but Ed had asked him to go fishing. Everything Will thinks of comes back to Shorty Wells. Johnny is doubtful about Shorty. Will tells Johnny that Dave was really close to Marty before she married Ed. Johnny asks if Will can trust Dave Sherman, but he is not sure.

Johnny calls on Marty Blake, and she tells him to join the party—her. She comments on her bodyguard, and how he blushed and stammered when she asked him to come in for a drink, which Johnny fixes. Marty tells Johnny that he probably knows how to party, and he tells her he has a system. First, he hooks up with the rackets so he can buy his wife all sorts of things, and Marty tells him to back off. Johnny tells her that the bullets were for her, so who would want to kill her. Did Dave really see the shooting or is he just giving you an alibi. Johnny asks where Shorty Wells is and she throws Johnny out.

Johnny goes looking for Joe Crailey and finds him after three martinis. Johnny asks about Marty and Joe tells him that she hates champagne, but always orders it, and that she is a four-star tramp. She is the ex-girlfriend of Shorty Wells and Ed Blake took her away from him. As for the police, some of them are useless. Like the ones who took two days to discover Ed had been shot with his own gun. Joe loves Marty, always has. She was his girl before Shorty Wells.

Tomorrow, a man with a gun, desperate, faces a blazing inferno and gambles for his life.

## PART 4          SHOW DATE:     7/26/1956

Johnny gets a call from Joe and is told to hang on. There is a big story breaking, a fire at Marty Blake's house.

Johnny rushes to the fire at Marty Blake's house, which is fully involved in flames. Dave Sherman tells Johnny that he got there after the fire engines and that Marty is ok. The police guard was there but did not see how it started. Dave and Johnny argue about Marty and their alibi, and the past boyfriends of Marty. Dave tells Johnny that Joe started drinking when she dumped him for Shorty Wells. When Dave found out that she was going with Shorty, he went after the rackets.

Johnny finds Marty in Dave's car, and she is scared. She agrees that someone is after her, why else burn her home. She does not know who though; maybe it was Shorty, to get even. She tells Johnny that she was sleeping on the sofa and woke up with flames around her. Joe walks up and asks if Marty has confessed, and they argue back and forth. Joe tells Johnny that the house is insured against fire, and too bad the car didn't burn, or everything Marty had would be in cash. Johnny hears shots and they see a man staggering out of the basement of the house. Joe and Johnny rush up to the man who is unconscious. It is Shorty Wells.

Johnny is in the hospital with Dave, waiting for Shorty Wells to recover. Dave is sure that the case is tied up with the rackets. Dave takes a call and tells the mayor that Shorty may not recover. Shorty mumbles but says nothing. Joe comes in from filing his story on the fire. They wonder why Shorty was firing the shots. Short Wells is the only lead now, and if he dies they are beat.

Tomorrow, death strikes again, leashes out violently and mistakes its target, and a wide-open town blows sky high.

### PART 5      SHOW DATE:      7/27/1956

The phone in the hospital room rings and Marty asks how Shorty is. She wants to talk to Johnny; she is ready to talk. She is at an all-night diner across from the hospital.

Johnny tells Dave about Marty, and Joe will call Johnny if Shorty recovers. Joe reminds Dave about the mistake with the sheriff's gun and the botched raids. Johnny tells them to stay with Shorty while he goes to see Marty.

Marty asks Johnny if she is hard to take. She has an alibi, and wants Johnny to convince the insurance company with a nice report. Johnny still wants some details as to why she heard the noise, why she turned on the lights and why she filed the claim. Johnny wants to wait for Shorty to recover but she offers Johnny $10,000 to file the report.

Joe comes in and tells Johnny that the basement door was padlocked on the outside and Shorty wells was shooting to get out of the basement. Johnny asks Marty if Shorty was supposed to die there. Joe asks Johnny what he wanted and tells Johnny that the nurse had told him that Johnny had called. They rush back to the hospital and meet Dave leaving and he tells them that the mayor had called him. They all go back up to the room to find that the police guard is gone. The door is open and Johnny walks in to find the mayor holding a pillow over Shorty's face, but Shorty is dead. The mayor tells Johnny that he was moving the pillow, and Dave tells him that he had suspected the mayor of being in on the rackets. Will pulls a gun and tells them to back off. Johnny asks why he had Ed killed and Dave tells Johnny that Ed Blake was going to pull out of the rackets and tell him everything; that was the purpose of the fishing trip. Johnny figures that Marty tipped off the Mayor, and Shorty was staying at Marty's house. They fight with the mayor get his gun but the mayor throws himself out of the window. "Well, he got out of being prosecuted."

Johnny goes back to Marty at the diner. "Too bad, Johnny you will have to pay off now. Shorty is dead and the mayor is dead—no witnesses" she tells Johnny. Johnny tells her that there is one witness; her claim form, which is really a confession. It says "we found my husband's body at the foot of the stairs, that he had been shot and killed with his own gun. The claim was in the office within less than 24 hours of Ed's death. The police did not find out until two days later. Real neat confession, huh Marty?"

Remarks: Marty Blake never was able to explain how she knew about that gun. She sure tried.

Exp. Acct:     $516.20

### NOTES:

*   AT THE END OF THE PROGRAM BOB THANKS "ALL THOSE WHO ARE SO

KIND ABOUT WRITING AND TELLING US HOW MUCH YOU LIKE JOHNNY DOLLAR. IT'S A VERY GRATIFYING EXPERIENCE. IT'S ENCOURAGEMENT TO ALL OF US WHO ARE INVOLVED IN PRODUCTION OF THE PROGRAM, WELL, WE APPRECIATE YOUR LETTERS MORE THAN YOU KNOW. AS ALWAYS, I WILL TRY TO ANSWER YOU PROMPTLY, BUT SOMETIME THE MAIL DOES PILE UP. IN ANY EVENT, THANKS. THANKS VERY MUCH FOR WRITING."

- THE PROMO IS FOR THE CORRECT PROGRAM THIS WEEK.
- ROY ROWAN IS THE ANNOUNCER
- MUSICAL SUPERVISION IS BY AMERIGO MARINO

Producer:     Jack Johnstone          Writers:     Les Crutchfield
Cast:         Jean Tatum, Paul Dubov, Joseph Kearns, Stacy Harris,
              Russell Thorson

◆   ❖   ◆

SHOW:          THE SEA LEGS MATTER
COMPANY:       UNIVERSAL ADJUSTMENT BUREAU
AGENT:         PAT MCCRACKEN
PART 1         SHOW DATE:     7/30/1956

SYNOPSIS: Didn't you tell me one you were a nut for fishing? This is Pat McCracken. "You know you spiked my plans to go fishing a couple of weeks ago, so what's on your mind?" Johnny asks Pat. "Big Fish, real big fish" is the answer. Did you ever hear of Douglas Landfere, the millionaire yachtsman and playboy? "Didn't I read somewhere?" asks Johnny. "Yeap, right on the bottom of the deep blue sea, and a $400,000 claim has been filed. You interested?" asks Pat.

Johnny cabs to Pat's office where Pat has a hand-full and head-full of information. Mrs. Constance Landfere has filed two claims. One is against Douglas's life policy for $250,000, and the other is $150,000 for the loss of the yacht. Landfere was cruising along the coast of Central America in his boat, "The Sea Legs." The boat hit some rocks and sank, and he and the other crewman were lost. Two and a half years ago Landfere filed a claim for a boat lost in the same place, near the Baldero Islands near Nicaragua. Mrs. Landfere is at home on Long Island.

Johnny travels to Long Island, New York to visit Mrs. Landfere. The cab driver tells Johnny that the estate has been sold off to cover their fast living. Johnny finds a manor house with new houses being built around it. Johnny rings the bell and Mrs. Landfere greets him. Johnny tells her why he is there, and she tells Johnny that the initial shock has passed. She has problems, mostly financial and does not know how to describe what happened. She was along on the trip until the day it happened. They were cruising slowly along the coast, in The Sea Legs, a 68-foot motor-sailer. Along the coast Doug put in at San Juan del Paro, where the ship was built but sandbars prevented entry so they went on to Bluefields. Doug had some radio work done, and went out to sea to test the radio near the

Baldero Islands. That is where "The Connie O." was lost two years ago. She told Doug not to go out there, because of the treacherous currents and rocks, but Doug had to go to prove a point. He blamed the loss of the other boat on poor seamanship, and wanted to prove he could take a boat through there safely. His last words were that a rock had torn the bottom out. A search party was sent out but the bodies were never found. There was no time to put on life preservers. Johnny tells her he will have to go do an investigation, and she tells Johnny that she needs the money. Johnny asks her what her plans are, and she tells Johnny she is going to sell the property and move to Europe, alone. She starts to imply that Johnny is trying to stop the claim and will tell her that Doug is still alive. The more she talks, the more Johnny is convinced that something is wrong with this case. On the way back to town, the cabby tells Johnny that the Landferes were very close to each other, and he should know; he knows everything in Cutchalk.

Johnny goes back to New York City and arranges to fly to Managua, Nicaragua after clearing the trip with Pat McCracken and telling him that he smells a rat. Johnny asks Pat to have someone keep an eye on Mrs. Landfere. Johnny is a called later by Pat and is told that Randy Singer has been asked to keep an eye on her, but she has left town. Johnny cabs to La Guardia Field when suddenly Mrs. Landfere gets on board and sits next to Johnny.

Tomorrow, the seeds of suspicion really begin to sprout, with the help of one of the wildest characters I ever met.

## PART 2     SHOW DATE:     7/31/1956

The operator gives Johnny his call to Pat McCracken, who has not found a trace of Connie Landfere. Johnny tells Pat that he knows where she is, she was sitting right beside me on the plane.

Johnny buys dinner in Dallas for Connie and then they board a midnight plane to Nicaragua, where he learns nothing about the case. Connie cannot get over the coincidence of them going to Nicaragua at the same time, and that she knows the country. Johnny is starting to feel very leery. Johnny wonders why she cares more about the lost boat than about the lost husband. Johnny eventually gets to his hotel, and is awakened at 6:00 AM by a man knocking on the door. Oscar Patrick Vladimir Poscaro lets himself into the room. Call me Oscar, since we are working together. Oscar can get Johnny anything, for a cost. Breakfast arrives: orange juice, tomato juice, creamed chipped beef on toast, eggs Benedict, lamb chops, scrambled eggs, little sausages, toast, honey jam and coffee. If Oscar is to be of service he must keep his strength up! No one else in Central America can get Johnny the kind of help Oscar can get him. Oscar knows who Johnny is, and who has not heard of the "famous freelancing insurance instigator" with the lovely big fat expense account! Who is Oscar to not learn from such a great man? Johnny is about to haggle Oscar down to $20 per day, but Johnny finally tells Oscar he is not hired. Oscar tells Johnny that he knows all about the boat and something crooked is going on with it. Oscar tells Johnny that he should go to Porto Gardo, and Oscar has a plane ready for his own personal use. Johnny wants to contact the authorities, but Oscar tells Johnny that it would be a waste of his time. Johnny wonders what his racket is and the answer is simple; money. Oscar gives Johnny the address of a small airfield and goes through Johnny's pants looking for a small tip for bringing up breakfast.

The police tell Johnny that Oscar lives on American tourists and can be trusted implicitly, and he knows the country. Johnny talks Captain Ramirez at the coast guard, and he can tell Johnny nothing more. He suggests that Johnny get a pilot and guide for the Baldero Islands, and the can recommend one named Oscar Patrick Vladimir Poscaro!

Johnny cabs to the airfield where Oscar has a plane waiting for him. The plane usually costs $35 per day but Oscar has a special rate, only $45 a day, but it is a special rate because it includes Oscar. Oscar tells Johnny that he is disappointed in Johnny because he told Mrs. Landfere what he was doing. She came rushing out to the airfield, rented a plane and took off just a few minutes ago.

Tomorrow, the sea, the rocks, and dear old Mother Nature bring some pretty startling facts to light, and the case takes a sudden twist

**PART 3**      **SHOW DATE:**     **8/1/1956**

Johnny sends a ham radio call to Pat McCracken from the airplane because there is no phone in Porto Gardo. Johnny tells Pat that Mrs. Landfere has disappeared, and that she has rented a small plane. Johnny tells Pat to watch her place in Long Island and call me if she comes back.

Johnny is sure that the claims are fraudulent, but cannot tell why. Porto Gardo is the last place where the Seal Legs had been heard from, by a ham operator named Oscar Poscaro, who complained about cranking the generator for the call! Oscar set up a transmitter in Porto Gardo because the authorities in Bluefields required him to have a license. Oscar does not have a pilot's license either, so Johnny tells him that the does and he will fly from now on. Johnny goes to the plane to fly over the islands, and Oscar tells him that is why he is so "unvaluable," to guide Johnny to the islands, until Johnny tells him he can also look at the maps. "But Mr. Dollar, that wouldn't be fair!" complains Oscar. Johnny flies over the islands and notes that they could be dangerous at night. Oscar tells Johnny that the boat went down at 10:21 AM on a clear day like today. Johnny notes the clear channel between the islands but there are no rocks. Oscar tells Johnny that only when the tide is changing is the channel dangerous. Johnny spots a packing case and wants to follow it to see where the tides take it, but Oscar tells him it will end up on the beach in front of his house; that is how he got the lumber for his radio shack. Oscar tells Johnny that when "The Connie O." sank, he got all sorts of things, but when the Sea Legs sank there was nothing.

Johnny lands the plane and cabs to the coast guard and talks to Captain Ramirez who tells Johnny that on the day in question the tide was just after neap, it was rising. Johnny goes to the airfield and gets the plane again. Johnny flies south to San Juan del Paro, where Johnny sees a small plane at an airfield; it is the one Mrs. Landfere rented. Oscar lands the plane and Johnny sees a car cutting in front of them. Johnny tries to get the plane off the ground, but the car hits their landing gear and they crash. Johnny hears a plane starting and realizes the other plane has taken off, and that he saw the man behind the wheel of the car? Douglas Landfere.

Oscar and Johnny are ok, but the plane is totaled and Oscar tells Johnny that he also recognized Douglas Landfere as well.

Tomorrow, the dark back streets of San Juan del Paro yield some valuable information, and a threat of sudden death. And believe me, it is not an idle threat.

**PART 4**         **SHOW DATE:**      **8/2/1956**

The operator calls Johnny and connects him to Pat McCracken. Pat has a man watching the Landfere place, but she has not returned. The man had let himself in, and answered the phone. It was the operator from San Juan del Paro with a call from a man on whom she has made a claim. Johnny tells Pat that Douglas is not dead; he tried to wreck their plane.

Johnny pays a man for a ride into town and Oscar comes in handy with the Indian dialects. The town has only a small number of boats and a few buildings. Johnny and Oscar get rooms in the hotel and have a doctor look at them. American dollars go far here, unless Oscar gets a hold of them. Johnny notes that on the flight in, he noticed several shipyards, and Oscar tells him that only one is still in operation. Johnny tells Oscar about the insurance claims on "The Connie O." and that the ease of collection on the first one gave Landfere ideas. He brought the second boat down and it disappeared, but Johnny does not think that the boat sank. Johnny is sure that Constance was in the other plane. Also, she had told Johnny that she heard "The Sea Legs" go down, but Oscar had told Johnny that the radio just went dead. Johnny thinks that Landfere probably brought the boat to a shipyard and had it rebuilt. Johnny also wants to find the other man on the boat, Ramon Gonzales, and he probably is still around unless Landfere killed him.

Johnny and Oscar go to the shipyard to look around. On the way, Johnny spots a man drinking beer in a saloon and thinks he might be Gonzales. Oscar might recognize him up close, so he goes in to look at the man. Oscar makes small talk with the man, who gets angry with him and tells him to leave. Oscar runs out at knifepoint, but is sure that the man is Gonzales. Johnny and Oscar go to the shipyard and find "The Sea Legs" with new paint and fittings, a moved cabin and other changes; a good job of disguise. On the transom, Johnny can feel the old name under the new paint. Johnny wants to go back to talk to Gonzales, but Oscar is afraid. Gonzales meets them in the shipyard with his knife, and Johnny manages to slug him. Johnny wants to wake him up and talk to him, but Oscar is afraid he might have a friend. He does, Mrs. Landfere with a gun pointed right at Johnny's back!

Tomorrow, sometimes when you wind up a case things take a turn, a sudden switch that makes you wish you hadn't won.

**PART 5**      **SHOW DATE:**      **8/3/1956**

Captain Ramirez returns Johnny's call and Johnny tells him to bring a plane to San Juan del Paro, where he can make several arrests, one of them a killer.

Johnny calls Captain Ramirez and recounts what has happened before that; the plane crash caused by Douglas Landfere, finding "The Sea Legs" and Ramon Gonzales. Connie Landfere surprises Johnny as he is trying to wake up Gonzales. Connie tells Johnny that she knows Oscar, "that chiseling, money grabbing. . ." until Oscar interrupts her. Johnny tells her that the disguise was good, and Connie tells Johnny that they would have gotten away without Oscar's help. She tells Johnny that they had to file the claims to get the money. Johnny tells her about the discrepancies in the story she told Johnny, and Connie warns Johnny as Gonzales tries to attack him with the knife. Connie disappears and Oscar tells Johnny that he was looking out for him and did not see Connie leave. Johnny tells Oscar that he has proof that Douglas Landfere is not dead and the boat was not lost. The case is closed except for a few details and Oscar is one of them. Johnny tells Oscar that he could have stopped Connie because he is carrying a gun and Connie did not have one. Johnny tells Oscar that he now knows why Oscar stayed so close to him. Oscar tells Johnny that he was paid by the Landferes for some services, including his radio. That is why he knew about the wreck and could help Johnny. Oscar tells Johnny that he was only trying to help, but Johnny tells Oscar that he only told Johnny what he would find out anyway. His real job was to keep Johnny away from Connie Landfere when she came to find her husband. Oscar complains about being called a crook, but Johnny tells him that he could have avoided the plane crash and had insisted that Johnny take his seat belt off while Oscar wore his, so that Oscar could be there to collect from Landfere. Oscar let all this happen for money. Oscar tells Johnny that he has always loved money, but would not have let anyone kill Johnny. Oscar tells Johnny that Mr. Landfere was responsible for the plot, and totally controlled his wife. Oscar tells Johnny that he is telling the truth, for once in his life. Oscar was hoping that Johnny would pay more than the Landferes so that he could be on Johnny's side, the good side for once. Oscar is ready to tell Johnny where Douglas Landfere is when Landfere walks in ready to kill Oscar for talking. Oscar reaches for his gun and they end up shooting each other.

Johnny calls Captain Ramirez and lets him take charge. Extradition procedures are under way for Connie, and Douglas' body is being taken to the states. Oscar's body? Johnny leaves some money with Capt. Ramirez for a decent burial.

Remarks: I wonder what kind of a deal Oscar Patrick Vladimir Poscaro was able to make at the Pearly Gates, or where ever he was headed. And, you know something, I kind of hope it was a pretty, well I hope it wasn't too bad a deal.

Exp. Acct:      $841.95

**NOTES:**
- JOHNNY TELLS OSCAR HE HAS A PILOT'S LICENSE.
- ROY ROWAN IS THE ANNOUNCER

- MUSICAL SUPERVISION IS BY AMERIGO MARINO
- DURING PART 4, SOMEONE ELSE PLAYS PAT MCCRACKEN, AS THE VOICE IS NOT THAT OF HARRY BARTELL
- PART 5 OF THIS PROGRAM WAS PROVIDED BY BILL BROOKS

Producer:    Jack Johnstone        Writers:    Jack Johnstone
Cast:        Harry Bartell, Lawrence Dobkin, Virginia Gregg, Parley Baer, Don Diamond, Russell Thorson

◆    ❖    ◆

SHOW:        THE ALDER MATTER
SHOW DATE:    8/6/1956
COMPANY:      WORLDWIDE MUTUAL INSURANCE COMPANY
AGENT:        VIC KELLY
PART 1

SYNOPSIS: Vic Kelly calls and asks Johnny about his Spanish. You may have to be more than a linguist to unscramble this one. William Billy "Up again, down again" Alder the promoter, is up to his ears in Venezuelan oil, and is insured for $250,000, and has changed the beneficiary five times in a month. What does that mean? "It means I will be right over" Johnny tells Vic.

Johnny cabs to Vic Kelly's office, and he is worrying over the policy on Alder. Johnny knows Alder is a super salesman, who has been in a bunch of businesses. The policy is not outrageous given the oil he is pumping out of the ground. The changing of beneficiaries started a month ago. Johnny thinks that Alder is worried. Vic tells Johnny that the policy has a clause that allows us to investigate irregularities.

Johnny flies to Caracas, Venezuela and goes to visit the local police chief, Jefe Velasquez who is apologizing about the lack of air conditioning in his office. He is avoids talking about Alder so he will not give Johnny the "bum cow." There is nothing to put your finger on. They seem like a nice family, but when you stay there for a while, you know something is wrong, just like an oil well that will blow up one day.

Johnny rents a car and drives to the huge and impressive Alder home. At the front door, Johnny sees a girl being kissed by a young man, who runs off when Johnny clears his throat. The girl tells Johnny that there is nothing her father can do to stop her from seeing Paul. Johnny tells her who he is, and asks to see her father. She is Peggy Alder, and father will be home in an hour. Johnny waits on the patio with a drink.

Mr. Alder arrives and is glad to see Johnny. He has read the policy and Johnny has the right to ask questions, but he does not have to answer. Johnny asks Alder what he is to do and Alder starts to waffle and will tell Johnny nothing. He asks Johnny to stay in the house and to keep him alive. Johnny senses that Alder is afraid. Johnny is put in a guestroom, and at dinner he eats only with Mr. Alder and Peggy. Johnny is told that Mrs. Alder is in town, with some guests, for the bullfights. Alder tells Peggy that she has disobeyed him by bringing Paul Kincaid here, and Peggy blames Johnny, but her father tells her that the servants have eyes too. Alder apologizes for embarrassing Johnny and tells him that Kincaid is an oilfield foreman, who will never have the chance to move up in the company or the family. Alder and Johnny talk after dinner, but Johnny learns nothing. Suddenly there is a gunshot and a bullet misses Alder and Johnny rushes out to the jungle area where the shot came from.

Tomorrow, one man dances attendance, another dances death, and a woman calls the tune.

**PART 2        SHOW DATE:        8/7/1956**

The Caracas police operator calls and Jefe Velasquez asks Johnny how things are. Johnny tells him about the gunshot, and asks to use the ballistics lab. Velasquez tells Johnny he should be worrying about the next bullet.

Johnny tips Nacho Gomez who had helped Johnny search the jungle for the gun. Nacho is very pleased that Johnny has given him the money. He was sure that Johnny would not find anything, but he is afraid for Johnny.

Johnny drives to Caracas and wonders about what Alder is up to. Johnny meets with Jefe Velasquez, gives him the bullet and then takes him to lunch, where Johnny is introduced to the Pisco Sour; "they do not solve the case for you, but they make you happy about being worried." Jefe Velasquez asks if Johnny has met Mrs. Alder, and Johnny tells him she got home late. Also, Alder does not want Johnny to mention the shooting to any of the guests either. The drinks arrive, and Jefe Velasquez tells Johnny to relax and take a sip. Very nice! Johnny asks why Jefe Velasquez is surprised that he had not met Mrs. Alder and he tells Johnny that Mrs. Alder does not object to being seen with a good-looking man.

Johnny goes back to the lab, and learns only that the bullet came from a Lugar. Johnny drives back to the house, and notices a car in front of the house, which swerves and cuts him off. The driver gets out and asks Johnny if he knows who he is. Johnny tells him that he did not tell Alder about him, and Kincaid tells Johnny to stay away. Johnny thinks that maybe he is there to look for an empty Lugar casing. Johnny asks him how badly he wants to get into the family and Kincaid answers by trying to slug Johnny, and the fight is rough, but Johnny wins out (I better get in shape or take up accounting!). Johnny goes in via the service entrance, and Nacho takes him upstairs and fixes his face. Nacho is amazed that Johnny won. Johnny asks about the music downstairs, and Nacho tells him that "El Mantante," the matador is a guest in the house. The Alders really like the corrida, and El Mantante is giving a demonstration of the passes with the cape. You should go watch it; it is lovely. "Anybody ever ask the bull?" asks Johnny.

Johnny joins the guests, about six people clapping to the motions of El Mantante, but Alder and Peggy are showing disdain for him. Constance Alder introduces herself to Johnny and will introduce him to the others when the display is over. Johnny notices Mr. Alder glaring at his wife as she sits down. Mrs. Alder moves from the room, and Johnny goes out to the patio and notices someone searching the grounds where the shot had come from the previous night. Johnny recognizes the searcher as Constance Alder.

Tomorrow, two sides of the same old yarn, and whichever side you choose you have to call it wrong.

**PART 3          SHOW DATE:     8/8/1956**

Constance Alder calls and asks if Johnny is ok. Why ask? Well, you did leave the living room. Yes, but you left too, and I was not bored. I wanted some air on the patio. You can see everything, the harbor, and the slope beside the patio and anyone who might be on it. Mrs. Alder wants to see Johnny in his car in a half hour.

Johnny wants to hear what she has to say and goes down stairs where Mr. Alder stops him and asks about the cuts on his face. Johnny tells Alder that Kincaid feels Johnny was hired to bust up the romance. Alder's only response is to call Kincaid an idiot. Johnny tells him that he is fed up with Alder; "Am I supposed to be a mind reader?" Johnny wants to know whom he is to protect Alder from. Someone has tried once so he must have some idea, but Alder clams up and will tell Johnny nothing. Johnny tells Alder that he could call the company and have his policy cancelled. Alder tells Johnny that the guests think Johnny is a friend from the states. Johnny asks which side Alder is on; his or his killer's.

Johnny goes to his car, forgets his keys and runs back in to get them. On the way he runs into a woman who apologizes and runs off. Johnny gets his keys and notices that his wallet had been moved.

In the car Mrs. Alder tells Johnny she knows who he is, and Johnny tells her never to search a pro's room, but she tells Johnny that she did not go into his room. Johnny describes the woman he ran into, and is told that she is Doris Cole, a friend from the states. Her room is right next door to Johnny's. Johnny asks what she was looking for in the jungle, and she asks him if he thinks she tried to shoot her husband. She tells Johnny that she was looking for some trace of the shooter, like a shell. Johnny tells her that her statement was a mistake, because only an automatic ejects a shell, and she knew what type of gun was used. Mrs. Alder slaps Johnny and then apologizes. She tells Johnny that her husband told her who Johnny was.

Back at the house Johnny looks out on to the patio to see Mrs. Alder arguing with Mrs. Cole. There is a knock at the door and Mrs. Cole apologizes for being so abrupt with Johnny. Johnny senses that Mrs. Cole did not know about the social graces, and is then visited by Mrs. Alder, who did. Johnny is told that El Mantante is taking everyone to dinner tonight.

The night was a gourmet dinner, jai alai and nightclubs. El Mantante was a man who knew what had to be done and did them, and Mrs. Alder had her eyes on him all night. El Mantante asks Johnny why he is watching him and Mrs. Alder, and tells Johnny that he does not chase other men's wives. Johnny asks him what he does when he is the pursued? He tells Johnny that acquisition is her game. Johnny tells him that he thought El Mantante was after the Alder fortune, but Johnny is told that El Mantante makes $10,000 for a Sunday afternoon's work. (Where does a fellow take bullfight lessons?) Johnny watches the Alders dancing and then fakes a headache to get back to the house. Johnny searches Mrs. Cole's room and finds a passport for Dora Jansen and an unsigned letter from New York about the arrival of a ship, the Caribbean Star. Mrs. Cole apologizes for Johnny's headache and tells him that there is no aspirin in her room!

Tomorrow, motives for murder are like peanuts, once you start you can't stop. One difference though, a peanut won't kill you.

## PART 4          SHOW DATE:     8/9/1956

Alder calls Johnny and thought he had rung Mrs. Cole's room. You got the right room; we were just discussing aspirin. Johnny is not going to arrest her, and tells her she had searched his room, and asks what she was looking for?

Johnny is not apologetic for searching Mrs. Cole's room and lying, as the whole house is full of lies. Johnny buys a paper the next morning and sees that the Caribbean Star is due at noon. Johnny drives to the oil field to see Alder who blows up when he tells of the passport belonging to Mrs. Cole. "How dare you search the room of a guest in my house?" Johnny asks who Mrs. Cole is and is told that she is "an old friend" and not a well woman. Johnny is sure that Alder knows who shot at him, and Alder asks if Johnny found anything else in the room.

Johnny goes to the cable office and wires Vic Kelly to ask for information on Doris Jansen/Cole, Passport #19B67943-11. Johnny tells the clerk that he will pick up the answer at the cable office. Johnny goes to the arrival pier and hides behind a newspaper while watching the passengers. Johnny sees Doris Cole meet a man and follows them to a cheap hotel. Johnny asks the desk clerk about the man who just came in, and the desk clerk plays dumb. The clerk asks Johnny for money and Johnny pays $10 for a name, Arthur Singer. Johnny goes to the room and listens to angry voices through the door.

Johnny goes to the cable office again and wires Vic for information on Arthur Singer. The cable clerk asks Johnny why his business partner is so angry. A man came in after you left, and was worried about something in the message. She showed him the message and then he got angry. Johnny describes the man to her and asks her to send the answers to Alder's house where they can read them together.

Johnny goes to the office of the shipping lines and looks at the passenger list, which does not include Arthur Singer. Johnny goes back to his car and is attacked by a man as he gets into the car. Johnny overpowers the man and gives him to a policeman.

Jefe Velasquez tells Johnny that the man was a cheap hood, who does not know who hired him. He is lying but will not change his story. Johnny asks to "talk" to him, but Jefe Velasquez does not allow it. Johnny asks Jefe Velasquez if he will follow the man if Johnny does not prefer charges, and Jefe Velasquez agrees.

Tomorrow, a puzzle never fits itself together, you've got to snoop, pry and juggle the pieces, and sometimes people get killed that way.

**PART 5          SHOW DATE:     8/10/1956**

Johnny is called by the cable office and they have the answer to his wires. Johnny will come and get them.

At the cable office Johnny gets nothing from Vic. Johnny spots Mrs. Alder watching him on the street and buys her breakfast. She says little over breakfast, and Johnny tells her she knows why he is there. Johnny tells her that she has been the beneficiary twice, and was looking for the gun and was following him. She gets angry and leaves.

Johnny follows her to the hotel of Arthur Singer where she stays for a half an hour.

Johnny goes to see Jefe Velasquez and outlines the case and players to him. Johnny figures that Mrs. Alder, Mrs. Cole and Singer are in on something together, but not to kill Alder for the money. Alder is afraid of what they know and the shot was to warn him that they mean business. Johnny is going to do some acting, and Johnny and Jefe Velasquez lay out a plan.

At the airport Johnny buys a plane ticket and goes to Alders office with the ticket. Johnny tells him he has had all he can take and is leaving at 6:00. He is going to recommend that the company cancel the policy. Alder tells Johnny that the changing of beneficiaries was to get someone down here to protect him. He is in a jam, and needs protection until it is over. Someone wants to kill him over a business deal. Alder will not tell him who, but Johnny tells Alder that the man is in town, and he is leaving.

Johnny goes back to the house, packs and says goodbye. He then drives to the airport, checks his bags and returns to Caracas and checks into a small hotel to wait. Finally the call comes and Jefe Velasquez tells Johnny to be patient. He will call him as soon as something happens, as he is watching everyone. Jefe Velasquez calls again and will pick up Johnny. Jefe Velasquez tells Johnny that as soon as his plane left Mrs. Cole picked up Singer and drove to the Alder house, but Alder saw them coming and drove to the oil fields, followed by the others.

Johnny and Jefe Velasquez drive to the oil field where Alder, Cole and Singer are in a work shack. Johnny sees Dora pointing a Lugar at Alder and Singer pleading with her to not shoot. She tells Alder that her brother Arthur had rigged the books on Alder's last bankruptcy and had gone to jail for three years. Alder pleads that he will make it right but needs time. Dora tells Alder that she had shot at Alder and his bodyguard (Johnny) is on his way home, so now she is going to kill him. Johnny rushes in and holds her at gunpoint. In a panic she shoots Alder and runs outside but runs into a protective fence around an oil well. Johnny goes to Alder who tells him that he would have paid. Alder tells Johnny that his wife only knew about it and her running around was to punish him, as he could not afford to complain as the case could be reopened

Details: Billy Alder was taken to the Caracas hospital, underwent some excellent surgery and, relax claims department, he is going to make it. As for the shady business practice, that is out of Johnny's bailiwick; that is for the law boys.

Exp. Acct:     $833.14

NOTES:
- JEFE IS THE SPANISH WORD FOR "CHIEF"
- ROY ROWAN IS THE ANNOUNCER
- MUSICAL SUPERVISION IS BY AMERIGO MARINO

**Producer:** Jack Johnstone    **Writers:** Tony Barrett
**Cast:** Gil Stratton, Harry Bartell, Barbara Fuller, John Dehner, Virginia Gregg, Don Diamond, Vivi Janis, Tony Barrett

◆ ❖ ◆

**SHOW:** THE CRYSTAL LAKE MATTER
**SHOW DATE:** 8/13/1956
**COMPANY:** AMALGAMATED LIFE ASSOCIATES
**AGENT:** TOM WILKINS
**PART 1**

SYNOPSIS: Tom Wilkins calls Johnny about a $50,000 policy on Edward Russell. Johnny has not heard of him, but no one else has either. His wife Leona in Denver has filed a missing person's report on him. Johnny thinks maybe he just got tired and Tom tells Johnny that Russell's car turned up in a storage garage with his luggage in it.

Johnny flies to Denver, Colorado and goes to visit Mrs. Russell, who is very attractive. Johnny is expected and she tells him that she has told the police everything, and Johnny asks her to repeat it. Johnny is told that Ed left to go to Boulder on real estate business, but he never got there. Johnny notes that the car was found in Colorado Springs, in the opposite direction. Mrs. Russell tells Johnny that she has heard nothing from him in a week, and that he has no enemies. She hopes that he is in a hospital and cannot call. He had not been depressed and he was not the type. They were getting along ok. She shows Johnny a brochure for Crystal Lake, a resort in the mountains. She does not think that Ed had ever been there. She tells Johnny that no amount of insurance money would make up for Ed.

Johnny looks at the brochure and rents a car to drive to Crystal Lake, Colorado. Johnny surveys the calm peaceful surroundings and the fishing possibilities. Johnny visits Ansel Garrett, the local deputy. Johnny briefs Ansel about the case, and shows him a picture of Ed, who he remembers seeing. Ansel tells Johnny that he may be looking in the wrong place. Russell came to ask about a man named "Bill," but there are several of them in town. Ansel saw him later in the bar talking to Betty Norton, a rich heiress who travels at a pretty good clip. Ansel tells Johnny to not go off half-cocked. Don't accuse until you find a body.

Johnny drives to the house of Betty Norton. She invites Johnny for a swim before she will talk to him so Johnny swims, and swims very hard to keep from freezing. After the swim Johnny asks her about Ed Russell. She does remember him, but does not know where he is. Betty asks what Johnny is doing with his time.

Back in his hotel room Ansel calls and tells Johnny that they have found Russell; he is dead.

Tomorrow, a cabin with a lovely view of a beautiful lake. A nice comfortable quiet spot for murder.

### PART 2          SHOW DATE:     8/14/1956

Ansel calls and tells Johnny that Russell is dead. He was found in cabin on the other side of the lake.

Johnny wires Tom about the murder and goes to see Ansel. Johnny is told that a man named Bixby found the body. Ansel asks Johnny to recount the story he was told, and Johnny tells him about the business trip and the tears from Mrs. Russell. Johnny tells about talking to Betty, and getting nothing. Clarence Bixby comes in. He tells Johnny that the body was found in his cabin, and that the lock had been changed. He was going to sell the place, but no one will buy it now. They drive to the cabin, and Bixby tells him that he had advertised the cabin, and a man named Putnam came up to look at it. Johnny sees where the lock had been pried off and Bixby shows him where the body was found. Bixby offers Johnny a cigar, and Johnny watches him tie the cigar wrapper into a knot, which is how Johnny feels.

Johnny goes back to town and calls Mrs. Russell. She will be coming up to confirm the identification. Johnny asks if she has heard of Clarence Bixby, but she has not. Johnny calls the Denver police to have her checked on, but they already have and she is clean. Johnny looks up Mr. Putnam in the hotel bar and he tells Johnny of going to the cabin. He had been looking for a cabin for a long time and wanted to buy Bixby's as a surprise for his wife. Putnam had ever heard of Russell. Johnny goes to the bartender and asks for a glass of I. W. Harper and soda. Johnny tells him it must have been quite a fight, referring to his black eye. He tells Johnny that he hit his head picking up a box. Johnny tells him who he is and he tells Johnny that Russell had hit him. Russell was there with Miss Norton. She called him by his first name, and Russell got angry and asked if he had lived in Denver. They went outside and had a fight and Russell left. Russell was asking for trouble. The bartender tells Johnny that Russell left with Betty Norton. Johnny goes out to think and walks along the lake. Johnny sees some movement and runs after it, but no one is there.

Tomorrow, a girl who lied, and a padlock that didn't.

### PART 3          SHOW DATE:     8/15/1956

Betty Norton calls and she tells Johnny to come over. Johnny tells her that he wants to talk about murder.

Johnny drives out to see Betty Norton, who has the bourbon ready. Johnny wants to talk, but she wants so dance. Johnny tells about her meeting with Russell, and tells her she lied. She tells Johnny her father told her she could do whatever she wanted, as long as it stayed out of the newspapers. She tells about the fight, which was the reason for the lie. She took Russell to get some coffee, and Russell kept mumbling about someone named Bill. Hiram, the cab driver came in and told him that someone was looking for him, and they left. She never saw him again. Johnny tries to call Hiram, but he does not answer. Johnny thinks he hears something outside and opens the door, but there is nothing there. Johnny tells Betty that maybe she killed Russell because he would not play things her way, but she tells Johnny that she can always find those who will play. She tells Johnny that he won't play, and she likes that, so stay for a few minutes. Johnny stays for a few minutes.

In the morning Johnny tries to reach Hiram and then goes to see Ansel, who is talking to Bixby. Bixby asks Ansel to keep his cabin out of the papers, and Ansel agrees. Bixby offers cigars and leaves. Johnny is told that Mrs. Russell has arrived and Johnny tells Ansel about meeting with Betty. Johnny wonders if Bixby is the killer, and Ansel wonders too, but Ansel has checked on him and found nothing. Johnny wonders about Putnam, and asks Ansel to call Putnam's wife.

Johnny goes to visit Bill Jensen at the boathouse and asks him about Russell. Jensen does not remember seeing him and Johnny notices that the boats in the boat house are padlocked. Johnny notices that the locks on the boats are like the ones used at Bixby's cabin.

Johnny looks for Hiram, who is still not there. After dark Johnny, goes back to look at the boats and sees that the locks are the same as on Bixby's cabin door and one is missing from one of the boats. Suddenly Johnny is shot at. Johnny becomes trapped in the office at the boathouse.

Tomorrow, a shot in the dark that missed, and another that hit the bulls-eye.

## PART 4     SHOW DATE:    8/16/1956

Ansel Garrett calls, and Johnny tells him to come to Bill Jensen's boathouse. The killer has him trapped there.

Someone is stalking Johnny in the boathouse and has tried to break down the door. Ansel comes in and turns on the light to find Bill Jensen. He tells Ansel that he had come there because he thought there was a prowler. Bill mentions that he saw someone outside, but the person disappeared. Johnny tells Ansel about the missing lock, and shows him. Bill thinks someone stole the lock. Johnny outlines the case and mentions his padlock, and the shooting. Ansel tells Bill to come to the office, as Ansel wants to check his gun.

After an hour of questioning, Bill tells them nothing new. The phone rings and it is Mrs. Putnam. Ansel asks about the cabin and she tells him that she knows nothing about it. Johnny and Ansel question Putnam, and Ansel tells him that his wife does not know about him being there. Putnam tells him that he is in trouble, with his wife. He just wanted a place to get away from her once in a while.

Johnny and Ansel talk about the case and the lack of leads. Johnny and Ansel walk to Hiram's shed, but the car is gone. Johnny wants to buy Ansel a drink, and they walk to the hotel. Johnny mentions that the killer could be someone they do not know. Mrs. Russell spots Johnny and tells him she is going home in the morning. Johnny asks her about who Bill might be, but she says that there is no connection with anyone at the lake to her husband.

Johnny looks for Ansel who is gone. Back in his room Johnny gets a phone call from Ansel. Hiram's body has been found in a ravine.

Tomorrow, the windup, the payoff. A payoff with illegal tender, hot lead.

## PART 5          SHOW DATE:      8/17/1956

Ansel calls Johnny and tells him that when he looks for somebody, they end up dead. They just found Hiram's body in a ravine.

Johnny drives to the three-mile grade and meets Ansel who tells Johnny that the car and body are at the bottom of a ravine. It was no accident; there was a bullet hole in Hiram's head. Ansel suggests Betty Norton did it, but Johnny is still suspicious of Mrs. Russell. Johnny wonders why the body was placed in a cabin?

Johnny goes to Betty Norton's, but she has gone to Denver. Johnny calls the Denver police and asks for assistance in locating her. Johnny then goes to Hiram's rooming house and finds nothing. Johnny finds Bill the bartender in the hallway. "Don't try to pin his murder on me" he tells Johnny. When Johnny asks how he knew Hiram was murdered, Bill tells him he got the news from a deputy.

Johnny goes back to the hotel and finds Bixby at the bar. Johnny tells Bixby that he can clean up the cabin now, but Bixby is not sure he will sell it. Johnny gets the key and goes to the cabin, where he searches for an hour and finds nothing.

Johnny goes to Mrs. Russell's room to say goodbye. She is leaving in the morning and will probably sell the house. Her lawyer is going to file a claim for her. Johnny spots something in the room that resolves all the issues. Johnny asks if he can use the phone to call Ansel. Johnny asks about the new lead and fakes a positive response about a lab test. Johnny leaves and listens by the door as she makes a call. She leaves and walks along the lakeshore, with Johnny following behind. Suddenly there is a gun barrel in his back; Bixby's gun barrel. Leona Russell walks back to Johnny and tells Bixby "I wanted to talk to you Bill, to warn you." Johnny tells him about the cigar wrapper in her room, and Bixby tells her that he should never have seen her. Johnny guesses that his middle name is William. Bixby tells him it is Wilford. Johnny tells him he had lured Russell up to the lake and killed him and then killed Hiram so he could not talk. He then stole a pad lock to put suspicion on Bill Jansen. And poor little Mrs. Russell is in on it. Bixby tells her that this whole thing was her idea and he is getting out. Bixby turns to Leona and Johnny lunges at him but too late as Bixby shoots Mrs. Russell. Johnny slugs Bixby, takes his gun and checks on Mrs. Russell, who is dead.

Remarks: About Bixby, in jail awaiting trial on three counts of murder; Edward Russell, Hiram, Leona Russell. About Leona, who had engineered the whole thing for a payoff, well she got paid off all right.

Exp. Acct:    $423.00

NOTES:

- FOR THE PROMO FOR THE NEXT EPISODE, BOB BAILEY TELLS THE AUDIENCE "NEXT WEEK, BEGINNING ON FRIDAY NIGHT, BECAUSE I AM SURE YOU WILL WANT TO LISTEN TO THE REPUBLICAN CONVENTION ON MONDAY, TUESDAY, WEDNESDAY AND THURSDAY OF NEXT WEEK, A

SIMPLE STRING OF BEADS, AND EACH BEAD ON IT A MOTIVE FOR
MURDER." THE NEXT PROGRAM IS THE 6 PART KRANESBURG MATTER.
- ROY ROWAN IS THE ANNOUNCER
- MUSICAL SUPERVISION IS BY AMERIGO MARINO

| | | | |
|---|---|---|---|
| Producer: | Jack Johnstone | Writers: | Robert Ryf |
| Cast: | Dick Crenna, Charlotte Lawrence, Jean Tatum, Howard McNear, Forrest Lewis, Herb Ellis | | |

◆  ❖  ◆

| | |
|---|---|
| SHOW: | THE KRANESBURG MATTER |
| COMPANY: | TRI-STATE GUARANTY COMPANY |
| AGENT: | BOB LAUDER |
| PART 1 | SHOW DATE:   8/24/1956 |

**SYNOPSIS:** Bob Lauder calls Johnny and tells him that he has had a pearl necklace worth $20,000 stolen. Smiley Prell tells us he has the necklace and is in Kranesburg, Ohio and wants to negotiate. Melba Krane is the owner. You already have your reservations.

Johnny travels to Kranesburg, Ohio where he gets a room and waits for Smiley Prell to call. Johnny is visited in his room by Phineas Krane, the uncle of Melba Krane. He tells Johnny that he and Melba are the last two members of the Krane family, and that the necklace is the property of Melba. Phineas asks if Johnny is sure that the person who called him really was a man, could it have been a woman? Phineas tells Johnny that he has met no strangers lately, and that this is a small town. Johnny asks what Krane has on his mind; is there something phony about the robbery? He tells Johnny that he only came to reassure Johnny that he would do anything Johnny requires to get the necklace. Phineas tells Johnny that Melba is headstrong and does not use good judgment, and he wanted to let Johnny know what to expect, as she is very upset. The necklace was a gift from her fiancé, Dean Sellers. The important thing is the sentimental attachment to the necklace and beauty of it. Johnny gets a call from "you know who. Meet me in the Green Lion Bar in an hour and a half, and no cops." Phineas starts to leave and Johnny asks him to finish what he was saying, but Phineas tells him that Melba is impulsive at times and does not mean any harm.

Johnny rents a car and locates the Green Lion. Johnny goes to the bank and talks to Milton Borkley, the president. Johnny asks Borkley for a financial status of the Krane Family. Milton asks if Johnny looking for the company or the family. The company is doing quite well. The family is the social leader of the town but they are flat broke. Their estate is mortgaged to the hilt but Phineas has been walking around with a lot of money lately. Milton tells Johnny to have more than an idea before he talks to any of the Kranes. Milt has wondered how Phineas was getting his money, and thinks that maybe he borrows it from Dean Sellers. He is new in town and will be rich soon. He is so busy that he has had to postpone the wedding once. There are rumors, but we will skip them, you understand.

Johnny goes to the Green Lion Bar and has two martinis waiting for Smiley. He come in late and only has a minute. Something has come up that he has to straighten out. Smiley tells Johnny to meet him at 1412 N. Oak Street, room 6. "Meet me there at nine tonight. Someone is trying to give me the old double-cross. Meet me at nine and I will give you more than the beads."

Tomorrow, when somebody kisses the wrong somebody, and somebody gets burned up over it, and then a gun is found in the ashes, man it's murder

## PART 2      SHOW DATE:      8/27/1956

J. D. Bartlett calls back and she is the Tri-State agent in town. She yells at Johnny for not looking her up when he got into town, but going to that bar instead. Johnny tells her he was going to meet the jewel thief there. Are you sure J. D. Bartlett is a woman? "You're the first man whoever doubted it," she tells Johnny.

Johnny thinks that this case is nutty, and tells J. D. Bartlett that. Smiley tells Johnny that he has to leave, and has things to do, something personal. Smiley tells him that Johnny knows he always works alone. Johnny tells Smiley that he does not have the necklace and is trying to pull a con. Smiley describes the pearls and their platinum mounts, an exact description. Meet me tonight, and no cops.

Johnny starts to leave and watches Smiley get into a cab. Johnny sees Phineas sitting in another cab watching Smiley. Johnny gets Krane out of the cab and takes him to his car. Phineas tells Johnny that Johnny is wrong for thinking he was watching that man. Krane tells Johnny that he was waiting to talk to Johnny about Melba. He thought he might have left a wrong impression about Melba, as he was upset at the time. Johnny tells Phineas that he wants to get the necklace back one way or another. Johnny tells him that he thought this was going to be a quick recovery, but it is not turning out that way.

Johnny goes to visit Miss J. D. Bartlett, the local agent. Call me "J. D." It makes me one of the boys. Johnny tells her of the various events and she tells Johnny that she only allowed the policy to be sold. She got Jim Markley to appraise the jewels and then issued the policy. She tells Johnny that Melba had Dean Sellers hooked before his bags were unpacked. That skirt has the ethics of a boa constrictor and about as much personality as a face painted on an egg. Melba is more worried with the Krane name, but they are all broke. Phineas is a rare bird, but he would commit murder to protect the Krane name.

Tomorrow, Monday, a thief stalls for time, an old man lies desperately, and a strange girl whispers the dread word murder.

## PART 3      SHOW DATE:      8/28/1956

Melba Krane calls Johnny. He tells her that he wants to talk to her about the theft, but she tells Johnny that she has talked to the local police. Johnny invites himself to come over in 45 minutes. He usually gets what he wants, but so does she.

Johnny walks to the Krane mansion while a storm gathers. Johnny sees a man in a suit and the maid in the sunroom, busy with each other. The maid answers the door and is excited when Johnny tells her who he is. Johnny asks if he interrupted her as she goes to get Miss Krane. Johnny meets Dean Sellers in the lobby and he knows Johnny is the insurance guy. Johnny tells him he has no leads yet, and is not sure that the man who contacted him has the necklace. Dean asks Johnny what happens if the necklace is recovered. Johnny tells him that if the claim has been paid, and the owner does not want to negotiate, the necklace will be sold. Dean hopes the necklace will be recovered soon. Johnny mentions the scene in the sunroom, and Dean tells Johnny that appearances can be deceiving sometimes, and Melba is very understanding. Drop into my office if I can help.

Melba Krane comes in and tells Johnny that Dean is impulsive and headstrong. But he never means any harm by it. Johnny tells her that the same words were used to describe her. Melba fixes scotch on the rock and they talk about the robbery. "Here's to pearls, the frozen tears from the eyes of Allah," Johnny calls them. Johnny tells her that the man who told him that had just knifed someone for nine pearls. Johnny tells her that he is not a cop, just interested in protecting the interests of the insurance company, and looking for fraud. She asks about the thief, and Johnny tells her he does not know and that he might be trying to pull a fast one. Johnny asks why she postponed the wedding, and she tells him it was Dean's idea. He has not called off the engagement, and won't. Johnny asks to see the safe the necklace was in, and it is behind a picture. It is an old safe, one easily opened. The robber must have gotten in with a key, while the house was empty. Johnny tells her he will meet with Smiley Prell tonight. Melba warns him about Uncle Phineas, he makes things up from time to time; he is eccentric.

Johnny walks to his car in the gathering dusk and sees Betty getting ready to burn a package in the incinerator. Johnny offers to help, but she objects and then runs off crying as Melba calls her. In the package is a .32 revolver with one chamber recently fired.

Tomorrow, a strange disappearance, a grim cry in the night, and a quarry is run to earth in room 413.

## PART 4          SHOW DATE:     8/29/1956

Betty the maid calls Johnny and asks "Have you told anyone about it?" Johnny wants to know who used the gun and she tells Johnny she found the gun and does not know anything except that she is in trouble.

Johnny rushes to meet Smiley at 9:00 on the Oak Street address. Johnny goes to room 6 and knocks. The door is unlocked and Johnny rushes in to find Phineas Krane there. Johnny tells him to sit, and Phineas can explain why he is there, alone. He came to ask questions of the man who lived there. He came here to talk to him about personal matters. He tells Johnny that he had followed him there one day. Johnny would understand if he could explain. Phineas is not scared of the threat to talk to the police; his grandfather founded the town, you know. Phineas had seen the man under unusual circumstances, before and after the robbery. Johnny tries to link Phineas to insurance fraud, but he does not bite the bait. Johnny tells him that he will have to talk to someone, so think it over.

Johnny searches the room, finds nothing, and goes to his hotel to find a man there who asks Johnny about Smiley Prell. He is Ed Durham, Chief of Police. Johnny tells him who he is and about Smiley Prell. Chief Durham tells Johnny that Prell has been shot dead. He was found in a back alley by the park. When Chief Durham tells Johnny that Prell was shot with a .32, Johnny goes to retrieve the gun from under the mattress, but Chief Durham has already found it. Johnny tells how he got the gun and Chief Durham recognizes the gun as one belonging to Phineas Krane. Johnny asks about the Kranes, and Chief Prell verifies the story told to him by the bank, including Phineas' sudden supply of cash. Johnny asks about Dean Sellers, and Chief Prell tells him nothing new. There is a knock at the door, and Betty is there. Chief Durham goes into the bathroom, and Johnny lets Betty in. She asks Johnny for the gun. She tells Johnny she found the gun hidden in a drawer in her room at the Kranes and she was trying to get rid of it. Johnny calls Chief Durham out of the bathroom.

Tomorrow, a castle crumbles, cupid goes to jail and a lovely iceberg thaws a bit. Exp. Acct:

## PART 5          SHOW DATE:     8/30/1956

Dean Sellers calls. He wants to talk to Johnny but Johnny tells Dean that he is on the way out to jail with Betty. What, was Betty there? Dean is concerned about Betty so Johnny will meet him in the bar in 5 minutes.

Johnny buys a drink for Dean Sellers, who is now concerned about Betty the maid. Dean tells Johnny that at first he was just flirting with Betty, but has fallen in love with her. He delayed the wedding because he had too much work. He was not sure if he was going to ask her to return the pearls, but then they were stolen. Johnny tells him that the man who stole the jewels was killed, but Betty had nothing to do with it, as someone is trying to frame her. Johnny tells Dean that the evidence is against her as she was found trying to destroy the gun, but most people would go to the police. Johnny tells Dean that the safe was opened when Betty was gone, supposedly. Betty could have told Prell when she was gone. Johnny tells him that maybe she wanted a whole necklace, rather than part of the insurance. Dean tells Johnny that without the necklace, he does not have a case.

Johnny drives to the jail with the hunch that the case will turn out messy. Chief Durham tells Johnny that Betty wants to talk, but will not change her story. She also did not know Prell, and the necklace has not been found. Johnny tells Chief Durham about Dean and Betty, and he agrees that maybe she is being framed, but by who. Johnny asks if a local jeweler could make a duplicate necklace, but there is no one here in town that could do it, maybe in Cincinnati. Johnny really wants to know if anyone had gone to Cincinnati to have one made. Chief Durham tells Johnny that that maybe Jim Markley can call around and find out for us. Johnny also asks for a complete rundown on Dean Sellers.

Johnny goes to his hotel and there is a knock at the door, and Melba Krane wants to talk. Johnny offers her a cognac, and she wants a double. She wants to make something clear to Johnny about Dean trying to protect Betty. Melba knows about the scene in the sunroom, and tells Johnny that she has seen others.

His alibis should not be given credence. After another double Cognac, she accuses Johnny of being on Betty's side, but Johnny tells her he is on the side of the insurance company. She asks if Johnny has seen Uncle Phineas, and Johnny tells her to sit down, they have not even started to talk.

Tomorrow, a bomb drops, the timid run for cover, and all is not as it seems, not even murder.

## PART 6      SHOW DATE:     8/31/1956

Phineas Krane calls, and he is mad. He wants to talk to Johnny, as there have been a number of changes since last night. Johnny tells him to wait, as he is waiting for a call from the police. Phineas tells Johnny that he might tell Johnny what the police call would. You should have called last night, he might have made a deal.

Johnny calls Cincinnati, and Cleveland and then waits for information. Finally the calls come in and jackpot! Johnny dives to the Krane estate and it met on the terrace by Phineas. He wants to talk to Johnny alone, while he is permitted to, as it is too late to save things now. He tells Johnny that he was in Prell's room looking for the necklace, and knew everything was over when he heard that Prell had been killed. In the beginning he was in favor of what happened, and asks Johnny to be easy on her. There is no excuse for him and his niece, and they are looking for a soft way out. Phineas was guessing that Prell had stolen the necklace. He had seen Prell hanging around and saw him talking to his employer. Melba comes to the terrace and tells Phineas to leave. Melba asks if Johnny had been pumping Phineas. Melba tells Johnny that Dean is in the Billiards room and Johnny tells her he might have some vital information. Melba asks what would happen if she withdrew the claim? Johnny tells her that the investigation would go on because the police are involved. Johnny tells Melba that the pearls were a gift of great sentimental value from Dean, who is broker than she is, and she is angry. Johnny tells her that he has a complete run down on her. Johnny asks to search Betty's room.

Johnny plays pool with Dean and tells him that Betty is innocent, even though Johnny found the necklace in her room. Johnny tells him Kranes are not so innocent. They are broke and used your interest in Melba to get cash. Johnny tells Dean that he was playing the same game and of how he milked his last wife in Florida of $150,000, of which only the necklace was left when you got here. You broke off the wedding when you found out the Kranes were broke, and used Betty as a pigeon. You used Prell to steal your investment, and when he told you the pearls were phony you accused him of a double-cross and killed him when he tried to deal with the insurance company. Johnny tells Dean that Melba sold the necklace a month after you gave it to her, and she had a copy made, which you killed Smiley over. Dean pulls his gun and tells Johnny to drop the cue. Melba comes in and Johnny slugs him with the pool cue. Johnny tells her that Dean had the pearls stolen and killed Prell. Johnny tells her that she filed a claim on a necklace she had already sold and will be prosecuted. You two were made for each other.

Johnny is sending the necklace under separate cover to the insurance company, with his sincere condolences.

Exp. Acct:     $409.10

NOTES:

- THIS IS A REMAKE OF THE BEAUREGARD MATTER OF 1/26/1954
- AT THE END OF PART 2, A REFERENCE IS MADE TO MONDAY'S PROGRAM—BUT IS IT MONDAY AND THE REFERENCE SHOULD HAVE BEEN TO TUESDAY.
- ROY ROWAN IS THE ANNOUNCER
- MUSIC SUPERVISION IS BY AMERIGO MARINO

Producer:   Jack Johnstone          Writers:   Les Crutchfield
Cast:          Howard McNear, Forrest Lewis, Paul Richards, Mary Jane Croft, Virginia Gregg, James McCallion, Shirley Mitchell, Russ Thorson

◆   ❖   ◆

SHOW:          THE CURSE OF KAMASHEK MATTER
COMPANY:    INTER-ALLIED LIFE INSURANCE COMPANY
AGENT:         JIMMY SAYER
PART 1          SHOW DATE:      9/3/1956

SYNOPSIS: Jimmy Sayer calls and tells Johnny that now he feels depends on Johnny. Have you heard of King Tut, and the curse on those who disturb his tomb? Wait until you hear of the curse of Kamashek.

Johnny cabs to the office to talk to Jim Sayer, who wants Johnny to visit Mr. Eric Turnbull, a very important client. He asked specifically for you. You handled the Parkinson case a couple years ago, and she was his sister. Johnny will take the case for the nice fee associated with it.

Johnny trains to Stamford, Connecticut and is driven to the Turnbull mansion, where a Studebaker Golden Hawk is parked in the drive. Haskins the driver-butler tells Johnny to go in, unless . . . Johnny enters the house, which is classic Victorian mansion. An older man is shaking his fist at a young lady, who has angered him by calling him Uncle Eric. Dorothy is told to leave and Johnny is offered a drink. Turnbull asks Johnny to help him, as Johnny is a man he can trust because of the case of his sister and the fraudulent relatives Johnny was able to trap. The problem is Donald, the son of his sister. All of Donald's money is tied up in a trust that Turnbull controls until Donald turns thirty. Donald has been living with him, and is now 25. He does not work, and has majored in archeology and Egyptology instead of business and finance. Donald Cronin comes in and is introduced to Johnny. Donald tells them that he is going to Thebes to work on the tomb of Kamashek, a very important find. Turnbull is tired of Donald wasting his time and money on these wasteful expeditions. Johnny mentions a collection of Donald's artifacts from Yucatan but Turnbull is adamant about exercising his rights to control the funds and tells Donald that he has to learn to increase the fortune and protect the family name, not squander it. Donald tells him he is going, and there is nothing he can do to stop him, and he does not care if he is cut off. Donald leaves, headed for Egypt. Johnny wonders why Turnbull is so protective about Donald's money when he has money of his own, and how does the girl figure in? Turnbull tells Johnny that there is another aspect to the case. Donald has insured himself for $100,000; half to the museum and half to Dorothy Harkness, his fiancée. Dorothy has been prodding Donald, and is trying to engineer Donald's death.

Johnny is driven to the train station by Haskins, and meets Dorothy, who tells Johnny to call her because Donald is in danger from the curse of Kamashek.

Tomorrow, a little order starts to come out of the department of utter confusion and a promise of murder.

**PART 2**      **SHOW DATE:**     **9/4/1956**

Johnny calls Stamford and talks to Dorothy Harkness. She wants to talk about the trip Donald is taking. Johnny asks about the curse of Kamashek, and Dorothy tells him it means murder. Johnny catches the next train.

Johnny trains to the Stamford apartment of Dorothy Harkness. She knows who Johnny is and tells Johnny that Turnbull does strange things and that she and Mr. Turnbull do not get along too well. Donald wants to marry her, but she is not sure about it. She wonders if he wants to marry her to get away from his uncle, and she is not interested in his money. Her father is the curator of the museum, who likes Donald for the money he is bringing into the museum. She tells Johnny that Donald is doing important things with his research and she is afraid of Donald getting hurt. Turnbull wants to keep as much of Donald's money has possible. His uncle knows that the best way to get Donald to do something is to tell him he cannot do it. She tells Johnny that Donald is a bit of a child and does not think things through. She does not want Donald to go, as the curse will give his uncle an opportunity to do something to him. Dorothy tells Johnny about the curse of King Tut and the mysterious deaths of those who participated in opening the tomb. Dorothy tells her that anyone who goes on one of these expeditions opens them self up to murder. She is afraid that his uncle will kill Donald to protect the fortune. She is happy with her financial situation, and hates Johnny for bringing up the insurance she will get. She tells Johnny that on his last expedition a man caused some accidents that could have killed Donald and that Turnbull had hired the man behind Donald's back. "Remember what I have told you," she implores Johnny.

Johnny calls the Turnbull home and asks for Donald, but Turnbull sends the car for him. Turnbull tells Johnny that Donald will be leaving in a few days, and he has to let him go to protect his reputation in the eyes of his colleagues and the universities interested in his work. But Johnny will be going with him, there will be no expenses spared. Arthur has arranged for Johnny to get $5,000 in American Express traveler's checks, and if you need more, wire me. Arthur tells Johnny that on his last expedition, a man had been hired by Dorothy Harkness to cause accidents. Johnny is sure that somebody is lying, and somebody is going to try and kill Donald Cronin.

Tomorrow, suddenly the reason for a carefully planned murder becomes crystal clear, and a race against death becomes a race for my own life.

### PART 3        SHOW DATE:        9/5/1956

The operator at the Explorers Club calls, and she tells Johnny that she cannot reach Mr. Cronin. Johnny tells her to leave a message for Donald, that I will meet him at the club.

Johnny trains to New York to pick up his traveler's checks and the teller makes a remark that this transaction will close out the account. Johnny cabs to the Explorers Club and leaves a message for Donald to sit tight. On the way out of the club, Johnny is stopped by Percival Thronghurst Scatterday. He heard Johnny asking for Donald and he is glad that Johnny is going with Donald to Egypt. It should be an important expedition if history is correct about Kamashek. Percival asks if Johnny knows about the curse, and warns Johnny to not be present when the inner sarcophagus is opened. There was a warning on the walls that whoever opened and touched the tomb of the king would die. Remember those who entered King Tut's tomb. Percival tells Johnny to take care of Donald, and himself. Percival tells Johnny that Donald is at this uncle's place in Stamford.

Johnny discounts the importance of Percival and cabs to the stock brokerage of Mr. Turnbull and talks to David Wilt. Johnny overhears a conversation with Mr. Turnbull, which would bring his investment down to nothing. Johnny tells him that the conversation is now part of his investigation, and is not to be told to Turnbull. So Turnbull is not so wealthy after all.

Johnny calls Dorothy to tell her he is going to Egypt with Donald. If he calls, tell Donald to call me. Johnny cabs to the Turnbull estate and Turnbull is glad to see Johnny. He is worried because no one has heard from Donald. Johnny tells him of his investigation into the financial condition, and Turnbull is really the one who will benefit from Donald's wealth. Turnbull tries to convince Johnny that he is not really broke. The phone rings and Johnny answers; it is Percival, who tells Johnny that Donald has flown to Egypt. Turnbull puts on a dramatic appeal to protect Donald, and Johnny wishes he had been lying, as two lives would have been saved.

Tomorrow, a flight into darkness, and when day has come there is blood on the desert sands.

### PART 4        SHOW DATE:        9/6/1956

Dorothy calls and asks if Johnny had found Donald. Find him before his uncle kills him she begs Johnny. Johnny tells her that her that Donald is on his way to Egypt, and that he will take the next plane.

Johnny goes to New York City and flies to Cairo, Egypt. Johnny talks to the other passengers, except for one man who pretends to sleep when Johnny wants to talk to him. But Johnny could see the man watching him when a seatmate used a makeup mirror. When the plane lands in Paris, Johnny helps Caroline, his seatmate off the plane, arranges for a date in New York, and goes back to talk to the mysterious man, but the man grabs him in a hallway and tries to beat him. Johnny overpowers him and wants to know who hired him. The man tells Johnny that Frederick Turnblow hired him and that he man does a lot of strong-arm work for Turnblow. He paid the man to get Johnny out of the way. Johnny takes the man's passport and gets back to his plane when he is paged. Eric Turnbull is calling him long distance, and tells Johnny to come back immediately, the case is closed as Donald is dead and the curse has been fulfilled. Johnny does not believe in the curse, and wants to know about the thug he hired. Suddenly Johnny realizes that the name of the man the thug gave was Frederick Turnblow, instead of Erick Turnbull, but they sound alike. Someone else instructed the thug to say that Eric Turnbull had hired him. Johnny changes planes and calls the Egyptian authorities who tell him that the tomb had been ransacked, and only two people had touched the bones after they had been sprayed with a preservative, a native worker and Donald Cronin, who shipped the bones to his uncle. Both of the men have died mysteriously. Only the men Donald brought, Carl Fortina and Walker Harkness, who is the son of the curator, have returned to the states. Johnny looks for the thug, who has disappeared. On the flight back Johnny tries to figure the angles on the case. Is it Eric Turnbull who opposed the trip, or Dorothy Harkness who would get the insurance, and her father who would benefit from the insurance, but how does Walter Harkness figure in to it?

Back in Stamford, Haskins opens the door and tells Johnny that Turnbull is broken up about Donald and has received a package that he is inspecting. Johnny rushes inside and Turnbull is dead

Tomorrow, the windup, and a sorry example of what the lust for money can do for nice people.

## PART 5          SHOW DATE:     9/7/1956

"Dr. Sinclair returning your call, Stinky." Johnny asks Dr. Sinclair to assist on a case. Johnny thinks that two people have been poisoned, and he wants Leonard to help him prove it. It they were not poisoned, it was a curse.

Dr. Leonard Sinclair, an old school chum, is a noted toxicologist who works with the police. Johnny wants him to examine the bones to see if poison was involved. Haskins tells Johnny that he had brought the package into the library, and Turnbull was dead when Johnny got there, and Johnny wants the police called later, and Johnny wonders how Haskins figures into the case. Dr. Sinclair arrives with his portable laboratory. He looks at the body, and determines that Turnbull has been poisoned. Len tells Johnny that it probably was a rare poison, and brings in his lab equipment and some white mice. Len thinks that the poison was recent, not from the time of the pharaohs. Johnny calls the coroner and then Dorothy, who is not home. Len tells Johnny that the poison was "curaba arcinium," which can be fatal if put on the skin. Len tells Johnny that the solution must have been sprayed on the bones, and Johnny remembers that the doctors had told him that the bones had been sprayed in Egypt. Dorothy and Walter Harkness arrive, and Johnny tells him he has been looking for Walter and asks if he wants to write his confession now. Johnny tells Dorothy that Donald was in love with her and made her a beneficiary if his insurance. Walter is working for the museum, which is depending on Donald's money, and is the other beneficiary. Eric was opposed to Donald's interest in the museum, as Donald's will leaves the estate to the museum. No wonder Eric was worried and hated Dorothy. She was being used as a tool, and your father only wanted money for the museum. Johnny tells Walter that he knows what killed Donald, just like he does. Johnny tells about the spraying of the bones, and the poison in the solution. Walter tells Johnny he sprayed the bones, and washed his hands afterward as he was told to do. Walter is about to tell Johnny who prepared the solution, when Walter's father arrives. He is there to pick up the bones to take to the museum. Johnny thought he would be there, and will give them to him, if he takes them out in his bare hands. He refuses, and Johnny tells him of the poison. He admits to the poison, and pulls a gun, but Len shoots him and kills him. Dr. Harkness just confirmed the results of his tests.

The museum will benefit, from the insurance and estate, without Dr. Harkness.

Remarks: Well, it doesn't mean a thing, I know. But I kinda wonder what I would have found if I have been assigned to investigate the deaths of the people who excavated some of those other old Egyptian tombs, tombs that had a curse on them. Heh, heh, heh. Interesting thought isn't it.

Exp. Acct:     $985.00

NOTES:
- AFTER PART 4, BOB BAILEY THANKS THE AUDIENCE FOR THE LETTERS THAT ARE SENT TO THE PROGRAM. "SO MANY COME IN EVERYDAY THAT IT'S BECOME QUITE A CHORE TO ANSWER THEM, BUT YOU KNOW SOMETHING, I LOVE IT. AS A MATTER OF FACT, YOUR LETTERS ARE APPRECIATED BY ALL OF US WHO ARE INVOLVED IN THE PRODUCTION AND PRESENTATION OF THE SHOW; OUR DIRECTOR, THE WRITERS, AND THE VARIOUS MEMBERS OF OUR CAST, AND OUR EXCELLENT TECHNICAL CREW. SO PLEASE DON'T STOP."
- THE POISON "CURABA ARCINIUM" IS ANOTHER JACK JOHNSTONE INVENTION.
- THIS IS THE THIRD PROGRAM TO MENTION THE STUDEBAKER GOLDEN HAWK. IT MAKES YOU WONDER IF JACK JOHNSTONE OWNED ONE AT THE TIME OF THE WRITING.
- ROY ROWAN IS THE ANNOUNCER
- MUSICAL SUPERVISION IS BY AMERIGO MARINO

**Producer:**   Jack Johnstone          **Writers:**   Jack Johnstone
**Cast:**        Paul Dubov, Alan Reed Sr, Dick Crenna, Virginia Gregg, Ben Wright, Forrest Lewis, Eric Snowden, Barney Phillips, James McCallion, Les Tremayne

◆ ❖ ◆

| SHOW: | THE CONFIDENTIAL MATTER |
|---|---|
| COMPANY: | ETERNITY MUTUAL INSURANCE COMPANY |
| AGENT: | MORT PARKINSON |
| PART I | SHOW DATE: 9/10/1956 |

SYNOPSIS: Mort Parkinson calls, and he feels bad. Mort wants Johnny to come over to his office and talk; this is confidential. It is about Ed Morgan. I know he was a good friend of yours, but it is too bad he did not die a year sooner.

Johnny cabs to Mort's office and they talk about the late Ed Morgan. Mort tells Johnny about working with Ed in the old Johnstone building, and it's furnishings. Mort tells Johnny that he liked Ed Morgan, and thought of him as a son, and hired him, and watched him become chief adjuster for the West Coast, and then just like that, he drives his car off a cliff into the Pacific. Mort shows Johnny a list of clients requesting settlements that Ed had marked paid. They sent and investigator and found that Ed's accounts had been doctored for some time. He had embezzled close to $80,000, but Johnny cannot believe it. Ed had a reputation of living like an old bachelor. Mort wants Johnny to find out what happened, but Johnny wants out of the case. Mort tells Johnny that there are too many questions, and Johnny has to do it. Mort tells Johnny that he knew Ed, and it would be better if a friend looked into the matter, rather than a stranger. Johnny gives in and takes the case.

Johnny flies to San Francisco, California on prepaid tickets, and goes to Ed Morgan's apartment at the Drakely Arms, a swank luxury apartment. The manager is only too glad to help Johnny, but there is little he can tell Johnny about Mr. Morgan. As Johnny offers him a crisp $20 to smooth the path, the manager gets a call from the Countess who wants a bucket of suds, just plain old beer, that she mixes with creme de menthe. The manager tells Johnny that Morgan had lived there for six months and paid $1,200 a month, and was a free spender. Mr. Morgan had no visitors, and no friends in the building, except for Mrs. Barrett. The Countess calls again and her dog is thirsty too. Johnny is told that Mr. Morgan and Mrs. Barrett were inseparable and that her husband had died early this year. Mr. Morgan moved in about six weeks after she moved in. He had met her when her husband died, something to do with the estate. Johnny wants to talk to Mrs. Barrett but she is not here, she is probably upset about having two deaths with tragic coincidences; her first husband also died in some sort of accident.

Tomorrow, the trail back into a man's past is a faint and twisting one, and at times it runs through quicksand.

## PART 2          SHOW DATE:     9/11/1956

Mack Woodson calls from the claims company. He is working on the files, and $80,000 is missing. The looting was carried out very cleverly. Johnny wants to meet him in the office tomorrow.

Johnny gets a $1 martini (a heck of a belt for a buck) and thinks about the luxury apartment of Ed Morgan. Johnny asks the bartender about Ed Morgan, who was an eager supplicant for his services. The bartender thought that Ed was too unrestrained for the Drakeley; he was always running out to some late nightspot, which Johnny notes was most unusual for Ed. Johnny is told that Ed always came in with Nicky, Mrs. Barrett. They would stay for a drink and then go to the opera, or dinner. He was there on the night he died, and Mrs. Barrett was not upset.

Johnny cabs to the apartment of Lisa DuVal, Ed's secretary, who was Miss Bohemian at home and listens to progressive jazz. She tells Johnny that she lives that way as an antidote for the insurance business. She stayed because of Ed; he was wonderful to work for, until the last few months. He was always tense and under pressure. She used to see him occasionally to listen to music and talk, until the last few months. She thinks that maybe he was tense because of the money. "Or were you going to say, until she came along?" asks Johnny. Lisa admits that she had been in love with Ed since she started but he never saw her. She is sorry that Johnny has to do what he is doing. Lisa has met Mrs. Barrett, who she compares to a vampire. She had come to the office with a life insurance claim on her husband, who had just died. Ed just melted down and lay down at her feet. She came to Ed because of the double indemnity on the policy.

Johnny cabs to the office of Ed Morgan to see Mr. Woodson and learns that Ed was running hog wild. He would deposit checks from Hartford into a disbursement account, withdraw the cash as a disbursement, and have the checks come back to him; very clever, but he should have known that it would not last. The seeds of the collapse were the complaints from policyholders. Johnny is looking at a file folder on Mrs. Barrett, whose husband died in an accident, unless he was murdered.

Tomorrow, $80,000 and a beautiful girl, both missing. Then one of the two is found, and a bombshell explodes.

## PART 3        SHOW DATE:    9/12/1956

Hector Nerkly calls from the Drakely Arms. Hector can give Johnny some information if he will come over. Johnny cannot find out anything, but he will be over in 30 minutes.

Johnny cabs to the Drakley Arms and Hector tells him that Mrs. Barrett can be contacted, but he wants to know why Johnny wants to talk to her. Hector asks to keep his name out of the matter, and tells him, after another $20, that Mrs. Barrett has requested that her mail be forwarded to American Express in Panama City, Panama.

Johnny sends a number of wires and then flies to Panama where Captain Garcia, of the Federal police tells Johnny that Mrs. Barrett (oh, what a lovely lady) has been located, and has not changed her name. She is at the Hotel Premeso, a small hotel on the waterfront usually used by sailors and fishermen. Johnny rents a cab, gets a room and goes to the Hotel Premeso, which is not the flophouse he expected. Johnny goes to the room of Mrs. Barrett, who is expecting a bellboy. Johnny tells her he wants to talk about Ed Morgan. Johnny tells her the reports about her were not exaggerated. She knows who Johnny is, as Ed had talked about him. She tells Johnny that she is trying to forget the accident. Johnny asks her what time she left him. She tells Johnny that Ed had taken her to dinner, and then went to see a client. They were going to be married. She knew that Ed worked for an insurance company, and Johnny asks how he would afford to live the life style he did. Johnny offers her a cigarette, but she tells him that she does not smoke. Johnny tells her he smelled smoke when he came, and searches for someone else. Johnny finds a man in the closet who knocks him down and runs out. Johnny recovers and sees Nicky Barrett cowering along the wall, but the assailant is gone. Nicky tells Johnny that she hit him, but Johnny knows that only one person tears up his cigarette papers, Ed Morgan!

Tomorrow, a search for a dead man who intends to stay dead, and who is willing to kill to do it.

### Part 4        Show Date:        9/13/1956

Captain Garcia calls and Johnny him about being hit. Johnny tells him that Ed Morgan is here in Panama, and Capt. Garcia will have the police search for him.

Johnny wires Hartford advising them that the case has taken a new direction. Mrs. Barrett meets Johnny the next morning at breakfast. Johnny offers her breakfast, fried fish and papaya, which she declines. Johnny tells her that he knows Ed Morgan was in the room the previous night, but she tells him he is wrong. She tells Johnny that it was a "friend" who hit him. He is married and should not have been there, which Johnny tells is a snow job. She tells Johnny that she learned to tear up cigarette papers from Ed. You were wrong, so why be stubborn. Johnny asks how much of the money she got, and she gets angry. Johnny tells her that Ed was his friend and it hurt when he found out that Ed was stealing, and now he is alive and he has to take him back. She tells Johnny that she and Ed were going to be married, and that Ed had told her that Johnny was cold, hard and ruthless. Captain Garcia arrives and meets Mrs. Barrett. "Take a look, you may be arresting her for fraud soon" Johnny tells him. Captain Garcia tells Johnny that they have located Ed Morgan, so Johnny and Garcia drive to a small inlet away from town. Johnny is told that Ed is on one of the boats tied to the wharf. He has been there for about a month, living alone on the boat. Johnny goes to the boat and calls for Ed, who tells him to come onboard. Ed asks why it had to be him, and Johnny asks why he did it. Ed tells Johnny that he would not understand, and that Nicky was with him all the way. She had always lived high, and he had to steal from the company to keep up with her. They decided to get out of the country, and he needed the money to get started. When Ed tells Johnny that she had sold everything she had, Johnny tells him that she still has her apartment and everything else, he saw it. Ed pulls a gun on Johnny, who asks if he would use it. Johnny lets him go, and he escapes while Capt. Garcia runs to the boat to check on Johnny.

Tomorrow, fate plays a devil's tune, collects a payment long overdue and the music ends on a scream.

### PART 5          SHOW DATE:          9/14/1956

Captain Garcia calls and tells Johnny that they still have not found Ed Morgan. The entire police force is active alert! "Do you know where he is?" "No, Señor."

Johnny cabs to Capt. Garcia's office and so far Ed has escaped, even in a stolen police car. Capt. Garcia tells Johnny that Morgan had taken the woman away just five minutes before the police got there. Johnny tells Capt. Garcia that Ed used to be his best friend, and that he only got involved after the monies were found missing. Capt. Garcia gets a phone call and tells Johnny that Morgan has been sighted on a narrow shore road. The car fell into the water and no bodies have been found. Johnny rents a boat and diver with an old fashioned diving suit and goes to the wreck sight. Johnny notices the cliff, and the similarity to the one in California. The diver comes up and tells Johnny that the car is a mess. The woman is inside the car, but the man is not there. Johnny knows that Ed would not kill Nicky and leave her there, so Johnny climbs the cliff face and finds Ed on a ledge. Ed tells Johnny that they did not make it, and it is kind of funny, just like they did it in San Francisco, only for real. Ed knows he is dying, but it does not matter anymore. He made her come with him, and she got mad and told him the whole story. She only came down to get the rest of the money and told him that she did not love him. Ed tells Johnny that if he could go back, he would do the same thing for Nicky. He came to get Nicky because he bought her and paid for her. Ed tells Johnny that the rest of the money is in his coat, and asks Johnny to give it back to Mort. Ed asks Johnny to shake hands with him one more time, but cannot find his hand and dies.

Johnny is sending, under separate cover by American Express, $62,112.30.

Remarks: No Mort, not on this one, Ed Morgan was my friend. The report stands.

Exp. Acct:     $912.61

### NOTES:

- THIS IS A REMAKE OF THE BEN BRYSON MATTER OF 12/29/1953
- IN PART ONE, THE MANAGER REMARKS ABOUT THE TIP JOHNNY GIVES, AND JOHNNY TELLS HIM TO "THINK OF IT AS EXPENSE ACCOUNT ITEM THREE."
- HUGH BRUNDAGE IS THE ANNOUNCER
- MUSICAL SUPERVISION IS BE AMERIGO MARINO

**Producer:**  Jack Johnstone          **Writers:**   Les Crutchfield
**Cast:**          Virginia Gregg, Jack Edwards, Russell Thorson, Shirley
                      Mitchell, Stacy Harris, Bob Miller, Harry Bartell, Victor
                      Perrin, Frank Gerstle

| SHOW: | THE IMPERFECT ALIBI MATTER |
|---|---|
| COMPANY: | NORTHEAST INDEMNITY ASSOCIATES |
| AGENT: | JOE MCNAB |
| PART 1 | SHOW DATE: 9/17/1956 |

**SYNOPSIS:** Joe McNab calls and is not glad to talk to Johnny. Ever hear of Harvey Stone, the industrialist? He took over from his father. He has over $100,000 in insurance. Last night a small object hit his windshield; it was a bullet.

Johnny cabs to Joe's office and is told about the case. Joe is not sure that the bullet was meant for Stone. His father had built up the business and Harvey is running it now. He lives with his father and stepmother in Westchester County and has an apartment in town. Harvey is running around with a singer named Helen Barrett, and his family is not pleased. He has one enemy, Dutch Krieger the gangster, who is putting on an act of going legitimate. Harvey was involved in a real estate deal, and when he found out Krieger was involved, he backed out, and Dutch will not forget something like that. The father and stepmother are the beneficiaries. Go down there and keep Harvey Stone alive.

Johnny travels to the Stone estate in Westchester County, New York and meets the very young Mrs. Daphne Stone, the wife of Mr. E. J. Stone who tells Johnny that Harvey will be back soon. Do not call him a stepson in front of him, as he is very sensitive. Mr. Stone Sr. is in a wheel chair and will be here soon, he will not let anyone push him. No one seems to have any reason to believe that there is anyone after Harvey. Johnny mentions Helen Barrett and Daphne tells Johnny not to mention it to EJ. Mr. Stone wheels in and tells Johnny that precautions are not necessary. Mr. Stone takes Johnny to see his orchids in the solarium as a pretext to talk. He asks Johnny about Harvey and the bullet, but Johnny has not made up his mind yet. EJ tells Johnny that Harvey is a poor businessman who does everything wrong, except for Helen. Mr. Stone did the same thing and got Daphne from a chorus line, but Daphne disapproves. Just as EJ tells Johnny that he wants to kill Harvey sometimes, Harvey walks in. Daphne offers Harvey a drink, and he tells her "yes darling," which ruffles everyone's hackles. Daphne and EJ leave and Harvey talks to Johnny about the company and Daphne. Harvey tells Johnny that his heart is not in the business. Last night he was out driving his new sports car and heard a noise and then the windshield shattered. Harvey racked it up to some kid with a gun. Johnny asks him about Dutch Krieger and Harvey tells him that he could not associate the Stone name with a criminal. Harvey does not want to talk about Helen and tells Johnny that there may not be a wedding. Harvey offers to take Johnny to the train and while Johnny waits in the driveway he is beaten up.

Tomorrow, well look, you should never get into a card game with a professional gambler. He can deal you any card he wants, even the ace of spades, the death card.

**PART 2**          **SHOW DATE:**     **9/18/1956**

Joe McNab calls and Johnny updates him on the fight. Johnny tells Joe to take out a policy on him.

Johnny describes the workout he received and suspects Dutch Krieger was behind it. Johnny goes to see Dutch who is sitting at his desk flipping a coin. On the way Johnny spots his assailant in the club. Dutch admits to Johnny that he knows Stone, and Dutch reminds Johnny about a guy named Tonelli who cannot walk, but things change.

Johnny goes to see Helen Barrett at the club. She is worried about Harvey because of Dutch. She tells Johnny that their wedding has not been cancelled, just postponed because of family pressure. Johnny goes to his hotel, and then to the financial district where he learns that the Stone Corporation is healthy financially. Johnny goes back to his hotel and is called by Helen. Johnny has to come to Harvey's apartment; he is dead. Helen tells Johnny that Harvey had called and wanted to talk about the wedding. She went back to pack while Harvey made reservations for Mexico. She came back and found Harvey dead. Johnny calls Lt, Ristelli and updates him and then goes to see Dutch, but he tells Johnny that he was at the club all night. On the way out, Johnny spots a picture of Daphne signed "To Dutchy with all my love."

**PART 3**          **SHOW DATE:**     **9/19/1956**

Joe Ristelli from homicide calls about the Harvey Stone killing and tells Johnny that they are still holding Helen Barrett. Johnny has a hunch and is coming right over.

Johnny cabs to police headquarters to talk to Lt. Joe Ristelli. Lt. Ristelli tells Johnny that Harvey was shot in the forehead at close range with a .38 Smith & Wesson found beside the body, but there were no prints and Helen was wearing gloves. She was packing to elope with Harvey and found him dead when she came back. The coroner placed the death at 11:30 to 12:00. Johnny tells Lt. Ristelli that Harvey took over the Stone companies, and the father's wife was the same age as Harvey. Both the Father and his wife were the policy beneficiaries. Johnny tells Lt. Ristelli that he had gone to Dutch Krieger's office and saw a picture of Daphne there. Lt. Ristelli thinks that maybe there was a question of whether the marriage would take place, and maybe Harvey was going to cut Helen out. The phone rings and someone wants to see Lt. Ristelli about the killing. The man comes in and tells them he is Alvin Gentry and he claims that he killed Harvey Stone. Stone was making a play for his girl, a hatcheck girl at Barney's. His girl was Doris and Stone was urging her to go away with him, so I killed him. He used a .45 Colt and shot him in the chest. Lt. Ristelli tells Gentry to leave and get his facts straight. Johnny calls Gentry a "Confessant Sam," someone who confesses out of a sense of repressed feelings of guilt. As Johnny gets ready to go see Daphne, another call comes in from a man who slit Harvey's throat with a razor.

Johnny cabs to the Stone estate and sees EJ's wheelchair without him in it. Johnny spots EJ in the solarium walking around his flowers. When EJ spots

Johnny he hobbles back to the chair. Daphne comes in and is hesitant to talk. EJ is acting bewildered. Johnny tells her that he saw EJ walk, and she tells Johnny that he can do it for short periods. Johnny tells her that he knows that she was fighting the marriage. She tells Johnny that Helen would not be able to keep the Stone name clean. Daphne had stopped an affair with his secretary Martha Winters. Johnny tells her that EJ had taken her from a chorus lines, but Daphne tells Johnny that not all chorus girls are equal and that she has put her past behind her. Johnny asks about the picture in Dutch Krieger's office, and is told that the picture was part of the past. Daphne tells Johnny that she has lost someone very dear to her because Harvey was a friend, a real friend.

Johnny goes to Helen's apartment and talks to the tenants. A woman remembers hearing Helen telling someone to quiet down. It was a friend of hers, Alvin Gentry.

Tomorrow, up pops an eyewitness and drives the final nail into the wrong coffin.

## PART 4      SHOW DATE:     9/20/1956

Lt. Ristelli calls back, and Johnny tells him about the woman hearing about Alvin, he is a friend of Helen Barrett's. Johnny learned that Martha Winters was a friend of Harvey. Lt. Ristelli tells Johnny that she is in his office.

Johnny cabs to Police headquarters again and meets Miss Winters. She lives in the same building as Harvey, as he used to work from his apartment. The night of the murder she saw Helen walking towards Harvey's apartment at 11:30. Harvey was her friend, so she decided to tell the police. Johnny asks her about their marriage plans, and she tells Johnny that they had decided mutually to change their plans. Johnny goes over the timings of the visits to Harvey's apartment by Helen. Johnny still has a hunch that Helen is innocent. Johnny tells Lt. Ristelli that EJ did not like the way Harvey was running the company, and the attention he paid to Daphne. Johnny tells Lt. Ristelli that EJ can also get out of his chair. And Daphne wants to protect the Stone name and the picture was part of her past.

Johnny mulls over the case and still does not believe that Helen killed Harvey. Johnny visits the supper club Alvin Gentry managers, and where Helen used to sing. Johnny asks why Alvin made the confession and why he lied about knowing Helen Barrett. He tells Johnny that he knows her and went to see her to ask her to come back to the club to sing. Alvin tells Johnny that Helen was with him at the time of the killing, and will swear to it. Johnny is sure that Alvin is lying, but why?

Johnny checks up on Martha Winters and goes to her apartment. Johnny asks her about her statement and about calling off the marriage. Johnny tells her that he heard another story at the Stone office, which upsets her. Johnny tells her that Harvey called off the marriage and almost fired her. Johnny tells her that she said she saw Helen at 11:30, but where were you? She tells Johnny that she was standing at the front entrance of her apartment and Johnny tells her that she could not have seen Helen, as Helen came in the side entrance. Martha tells

Johnny that it had to be her and admits that she lied. The trap about the side door pays off.

Tomorrow, the wind up. A gambler stakes his life on his hand and loses.

## PART 5          SHOW DATE:          9/21/1956

Lt. Ristelli calls and Johnny tells him that Martha had lied. Lt. Ristelli tells Johnny that Daphne was in the city on the night of the murder.

Johnny cabs to the Stone estate to question Daphne. On the terrace, Johnny tells her that the investigation is not going well, that there are problems. Johnny tells her that she has been giving him incomplete answers. Johnny reminds her that she lied about EJ being able to get out of his wheelchair. Johnny brings up Dutch, but that is part of her past too. Johnny asks about her being in the city that night. She tells Johnny that she went in to talk to Harvey about Helen, to talk him out of marrying Helen. She was there from 9:00 to 10:00, and when she left he had decided not to elope with Helen. Daphne decided to stay in a hotel that night instead of coming home. Johnny asks if that was the whole truth and she tells him that everything she has done has been to protect the Stone name. Johnny wonders what "everything" included?

Johnny goes back to the city and meets with Helen. Johnny tells about Martha's false statement and Alvin's confession. She tells Johnny that she liked Alvin, but did not see him after meeting Harvey. She tells Johnny that Alvin was there a few minutes while she was packing and Johnny tells her Alvin swore she was with him during the murder.

Johnny talks with Lt. Ristelli and is tired of show people, they act too good. Lt. Ristelli feels Alvin is holding something back. Johnny goes back to his room and mulls over the case, and gets a weird little idea. Johnny goes to Alvin's club and waits for the club to close. Alvin tells Johnny that he is tired of being a sucker and is withdrawing his statement about being with Helen. Johnny tells him that he is not a sucker, but a smart man trying to put a noose on Helen's neck. Johnny tells him that love can turn to hate fast, and Alvin needed a good reason to do what he did, maybe losing Helen was that reason. He wanted Helen bad and killed Harvey and then made the false confession to frame Helen. Alvin tells Johnny that he had found Helen standing over the body and tried to cover for her. Johnny tells him that his confession was correct, as the police had made a mistake, Harvey was killed with a .45 and Alvin blurts out that it was a Smith and Wesson .38. Johnny tells him that only the police, and the killer know that. Alvin runs from Johnny and takes a shot at him. Johnny shoots and finds Alvin hit in the shoulder.

Lt. Ristelli arrives and takes Alvin to jail, and arranges to release Helen.

Remarks: Here I thought that Dutch Krieger was the gambler in the case. But that little game of winner take all that Gentry had been playing was just about the weirdest I have ever heard of. I thought about him up there in the death house at Sing Sing and realized that the big trouble with that kind of gamble that he was taking is that the loser's seat can get awful hot.

Exp. Acct:     $192.40

NOTES:
- ROY ROWAN IS THE ANNOUNCER
- MUSIC SUPERVISION IS BY AMERIGO MARINO

Producer: Jack Johnstone          Writers:   Robert Ryf
Cast:         Virginia Gregg, Tony Barrett, Shirley Mitchell, Will Wright,
                 Chet Stratton, Ted de Corsia, Barney Phillips, Lillian Buyeff
                 Harry Bartell

◆   ❖   ◆

SHOW:          THE MEG'S PALACE MATTER
COMPANY:     INTER-COASTAL MARITIME AND LIFE INSURANCE COMPANY
AGENT:         BYRON KANE
PART 1         SHOW DATE:          9/24/1956

SYNOPSIS: Byron Kane calls and tells Johnny that things in Cod Harbor are terrible. Meg McCarthy runs an eating place and it may be murder, mayhem or whatever. I know it is Saturday, but come on over and let's talk.

Johnny travels to Boston and meets with By Kane. Johnny is told that Meg's restaurant is insured for $15,000 and that Meg has $25,000 straight life on herself. Meg has been threatened and the restaurant has been set on fire once. By promises Johnny a day of fishing or he will double the expenses.

Johnny travels to Cod Harbor and Meg's Palace, a big disreputable place. Johnny goes to the back and hears a woman arguing with a frying pan in her hand to a man about his crew getting drunk and breaking up her place. The man runs from the kitchen with Meg throwing glassware at him. "Ain't he the darlingest man?" she tells Johnny. Johnny finally gets a chance to introduce himself, but only after yelling at her about interrupting him. Meg is ranting on about how she is going to marry Billy, the man she just threw out, who is the beneficiary of her life insurance. Johnny tells her why is there, and she tells Johnny that Captain Billy Morgan is not one of those who are threatening her. There are a dozen who would like to see her place burnt, because she gives the men the most and best food. Meg tells Johnny that she is sleeping on the bar to protect herself. Meg suspects Clem Harris, who runs the Silver Plate, who is too soft and polite and soft spoken. Then there is Ernie Turner who runs the Manor house Café next to the bait house. The third suspect is Tony Fortino, who runs the Irving's Chop Suey joint. They all are conniving because they will not sell out to her. Meg loves it when Johnny yells at her, which is often. Johnny tells her that she has no evidence, but Meg is about to take him to see the site of a fire when the phone rings with a call for Johnny. "We know why you are here, Dollar. But you won't be here long, understand. Either you go quiet, the way you came, or you go out in a long wooden box, get it?" Johnny is told.

Tomorrow, well they say that darkness can cover a multitude of sins. It can also cover a strong man armed with a deadly weapon.

**PART 2        SHOW DATE:        9/25/1956**

Johnny is called by Byron Kane, who had trouble getting in touch with him. Johnny tells By that someone has threatened him and asks him to send some things to him, quietly at night, so no one knows it got here.

Johnny orders a batch of fire extinguishers from Byron. Johnny talks to the fishermen who direct him to the shack of Mr. Beasley, the chief of police, mayor and judge, all acting positions. He tells Johnny that the town is really part of Barnsboro, but has to be self-sufficient. Johnny tells Beasley about Meg's Palace and the insurance. Beasley has been told of the threats but has not done anything to look into it. He would look into it if anything serious happened. Beasley tells Johnny that he is the chief of police because he lost his boat and took the job. Johnny asks about the competitors to Meg, and Beasley tells him to go talk to them, but they do not like strangers messing around in their affairs.

Johnny walks back to the Palace and finds a Capt. Morgan shouting at group of men who are cleaning up the Palace. Capt. Morgan tells Johnny that Meg is cleaning Johnny's room, and Johnny wants to ask him some questions. Johnny asks about Capt. Morgan being the beneficiary of the life insurance policy, and Capt. Morgan explodes and wants to fight. Meg comes in and tells Capt. Morgan to get back to work and tells Johnny to go out fishing with Capt. Morgan in the morning and talk then. Johnny walks outside for some fresh air and sees someone hunched over at the front of the building. Johnny is easing up on the person when the side door opens and someone slugs Johnny.

Tomorrow, a trip to sea on the "Lily Ann" that starts out like an ordinary fishing trip, but somewhere on board lurks a man with murder in his heart. And his next intended victim, me.

**PART 3        SHOW DATE:        9/26/1956**

Johnny receives a call from Tim Beasley, who wants to talk to him. Johnny tells him that all he got was a warning the last time they talked. Beasley tells Johnny that he was the one who picked him up and carried him inside. Johnny goes to talk to him.

So far there are no expenses on this case as Meg is providing him a room and food. Johnny meets with Beasley who has taken a change of heart, and has thought about how he had talked to Johnny. Beasley tells Johnny that the locals usually try to settle things among themselves. He had gone to talk to Johnny and heard the noise from a fight and found Johnny on the ground. Johnny tells him that he heard the door open just before he was hit, so it had to be someone on Billy's crew. Beasley tells him that no one on the crew could have done it, but Johnny tells him someone did. Johnny tells him to look into the owners of the other restaurants while he is out on the boat. He also tells Beasley to check the handwriting on the threat letters while he is gone.

Johnny sleeps for a few hours and is awakened by Meg, who brings him some coffee. Meg sees the wound on his head, and Johnny tells her what happened. Johnny tells her that someone on the crew must have done it, but she hopes he is wrong. Johnny meets the crew for breakfast. There is Charlie, who is liked by all the others; Montgomery, who is the engineer; and Ollie, the first mate. After breakfast the boat casts off and heads out to sea. Johnny watches the crew from the bow and wonders about the case and how to trap one of them. Suddenly someone picks up Johnny and throws him overboard and he is run over by the boat.

Tomorrow, the motives for arson and murder begin to take definite shape in the form of a confession.

## PART 4          SHOW DATE:     9/27/1956

Dr. Champion calls, and tells Johnny that he had ordered Meg to keep Johnny in bed. Johnny was unconscious yesterday and the Dr. Champion asks how Johnny fell overboard. Johnny tells him he was pushed!

Johnny realizes he cannot walk on his leg with a splint on it, and Meg brings him a plate of food. Johnny wants to get up, but Meg tells him to stay put, or else. Johnny is told that Capt. Morgan is out fishing now, as he has to keep up the payments on the boat. Meg tells Johnny that the crew told her he had fallen overboard. She tells Johnny that the crew had seen him standing on the bow, then heard him yell, and then saw him in the water. Charlie was telling everyone he saw it all. Johnny tells her that he was thrown overboard by someone. He is sure that whoever threw him overboard did the other things too. Johnny asks if Beasley had been there to get the notes, and Megs tells him that he has not been there. Beasley has threatened to close her for violating town ordinances, so maybe Tim Beasley and Tim Harris are working in cahoots.

Dr. Champion arrives and takes off the splint, as it was there to make sure that Johnny stayed in bed. Capt. Billy arrives and then the other crewmembers to see how Johnny was. Johnny is told that Charlie did not come, as he was in Barnsboro today picking up supplies and visiting a sister. Johnny stops Montgomery and asks about Charlie, and gets the address of his sister.

Johnny goes to see Beasley who is not there. A neighbor tells Johnny that he is in Barnsboro. Johnny rents an old truck and drives to Barnsboro. Johnny stops at the house of Charlie's sister and meets Charlie there. Charlie puts on an act about Johnny being ok, and Johnny sees that he is packing. Charlie tells Johnny he is tired of fishing. Johnny asks why he did it, and Charlie tells him that "he" made him do it and that he had killed a man once and had escaped from a reformatory. He made Charley do these things so he would not go back to jail. Charlie tells Johnny he will go back with him. Charlie is ready to tell Johnny who "he" is when Charley is shot in the heart. Johnny sees a car disappearing down the road, and wonders for whom the shot was really intended.

Tomorrow, a killer strikes again, but one of his victims rises from the grave to strike back.

## PART 5          SHOW DATE:     9/28/1956

Chief Walters from the Barnsboro police calls. Johnny tells him to get there fast to pick up a body.

Johnny calls the police and Chief Walters comes to the house. Johnny leaves with the chief and Johnny tells him about the case and the various things which have happened. Johnny tells him that he has too many suspects. The chief has just seen Capt. Morgan in Barnsboro. Johnny tells him about Beasley, his cousin and the notes.

Back in Cod Harbor Johnny sees that the Palace is on fire, and the whole town is there fighting the flames with pumps from the various boats in the harbor. Chief Walters sees immediate evidence of arson, and Capt. Morgan is directing the effort to fight the fire. Johnny notices that Meg is not there and gets Chief Walters to lift him up into the front of the building so he can get to Meg's room, where she is found unconscious with a wound on her head. Johnny is able to get her out of the building.

Johnny wakes up, and Meg is tending to a burn on his arm. They are in Clem Harris' house, and she is grateful for Johnny saving her life. She tells Johnny that someone had hit her and left her in the building to burn. Chief Walters comes in with Capt. Morgan, who is angry because he has been arrested. Johnny tells him that he is guilty of arson and murder, and that the insurance was the reason. Johnny tells him that he had compared his handwriting with some other documents, and Morgan confesses. He tells Johnny that he needed money to save his boat. Meg goes ballistic because the boat is more important than her.

Meg tells Johnny that maybe she will move somewhere to get away from the town. She is Meg McCarthy and no man will get her down! If she were only younger and prettier . . . Meg asks about the letters and Johnny tells her that he had faked it and had never seen any handwriting samples. Meg breaks down about Capt. Morgan, as she really loved him.

The insurance will have to be paid on the building, and the courts will deal with Captain Billy.

Exp. Acct:     $221.60

NOTES:
- BYRON KANE USES HIS OWN NAME FOR HIS CHARACTER.
- ROY ROWAN IS THE ANNOUNCER
- MUSIC SUPERVISION IS BY AMERIGO MARINO AND CARL FORTINA

| | | | |
|---|---|---|---|
| Producer: | Jack Johnstone | Writers: | Jack Johnstone |
| Cast: | Virginia Gregg, Jack Kruschen, Byron Kane, Forrest Lewis, Bert Holland, Stan Jones, Bob Bruce, Austin Green, Harry Bartell | | |

◆ ❖ ◆

| | |
|---|---|
| SHOW: | THE PICTURE POSTCARD MATTER |
| COMPANY: | GLOBAL CASUALTY |
| AGENT: | TOM WILKINS |
| PART 1 | SHOW DATE:     10/1/1956 |

SYNOPSIS: Tom Wilkins calls and he has a $100,000 headache, uncut diamonds that have been stolen. There is a fat fee if you can recover them.

Johnny cabs to Tom Wilkin's office and is told that the diamonds were being taken from Zurich to Amsterdam and were stolen at the airport in Zurich. The courier had a briefcase that was cut off of his wrist during a fake fight. One of the men was described as stocky with a thick neck, not much help. Tom has a special delivery letter from a man named Sebastian that offers help for a reward. The letter has instructions for a meeting, and to use caution.

Johnny flies to Zurich, Switzerland and thinks about the case on the way. Johnny gets a cab to go to the Hotel Pola and a woman gets into his cab thinking Johnny was someone else. The woman tells the driver to stop and she exits the cab after giving Johnny a big kiss. Johnny notices that the woman, Ilsa Scheaffer, had left her purse in the cab. Johnny takes the purse to the cab office and then goes to the hotel. In the lobby a man stops Johnny with a gun in Johnny's ribs. They leave by the side entrance where Johnny is told to get into a car. The man is sure that Johnny has the diamonds. The woman did not leave the cab with her purse, so Johnny must have them. Johnny tells the man that the purse was empty, but to no avail. Johnny tries to slug the man and is hurt by a passing cab, allowing the man and his car to disappear. Johnny calls Tom Wilkins and updates him on the events and the need for caution.

Johnny goes to his room and waits for a call from Sebastian. Later while Johnny reads a newspaper in the lobby a man sits down behind him. As Johnny starts to leave the man tells him to hide his face in the paper as they talk. He is Sebastian and tells Johnny he can guarantee the return of the diamonds for $25,000. The man passes a postcard to Johnny signed by F. Greuner. The postcard is from the Kleibach Inn, and is part of the solution. Sebastian will provide proof tonight. His address is on an inner page of his newspaper, which Johnny is to get when he leaves.

That night Johnny goes to the address and knocks on the door, but no one answers. Johnny goes in and waits. Johnny hears a dripping faucet, and goes to the bathroom to find Sebastian floating in the bathtub.

Tomorrow, a perfect stranger wants to get acquainted, and a beautiful girl asks me to go skiing. Trouble is, either or both of them could be trying to kill me.

## PART 2          SHOW DATE:     10/2/1956

Inspector Hoeniger of the Zurich Police calls Johnny. He has no information about Sebastian, and Johnny tells him about the diamond robbery. The inspector tells Johnny that Sebastian was probably killed by a woman.

Johnny cabs to the police and meets with Insp. Hoeniger, who asks Johnny to provide the information he has. Johnny outlines the robbery, the letter and his meeting with Ilsa, the man in the lobby, and Sebastian. Johnny thinks that Sebastian was a member of the outfit that stole the diamonds and would get more from returning the diamonds than by fencing them. Johnny shows Insp. Hoeniger the post card, and tells him that the card was part of the solution to finding the diamonds. Insp. Hoeniger tells Johnny that Sebastian was hit and drown, a technique used typically by women.

Johnny leaves for Kleibach, Switzerland and gets a room in the chateau-like Inn. Johnny talks to the manager, Otto Friedrich about the post card. Otto tells Johnny that it is not a good picture and that he does not sell them anymore. The village sells them though. Johnny asks about the name Sebastian, and F. Greuner, and Otto tells Johnny that he will ask around the village.

Johnny is visited in his room by Geoffrey Harris who is looking for a Johnny Dollar from London. He thought Johnny might be old "Bunny." Geoffrey and Johnny walk out and Johnny spots a friend at the bar. Johnny goes over and sits down with Ilsa. She thanks Johnny for turning her purse to the cab company. Johnny asks if she had meant to pass something to him in the cab, but she plays ignorant. She is at the inn to go skiing and comes her often, and invites Johnny to come skiing with her tomorrow. Johnny goes to ask Otto about Ilsa and learns that this is her first visit. Johnny returns to the bar and tells Ilsa that he will ski with her tomorrow. Ilsa tells Johnny that they will ski the north slope, which some consider too dangerous. Johnny is sure that Ilsa will "take good care" of him.

Tomorrow, well skiing is a strenuous sport, so is hunting. Put them together and it is liable to kill you.

## PART 3      SHOW DATE:    10/3/1956

Otto calls with a phone call from Insp. Hoeniger who tells Johnny that there is no line on Sebastian's killer. Insp. Hoeniger tells Johnny that another postcard was sent to Sebastian, and he is sending it to Johnny. Johnny tells him that he is going skiing with Ilsa that morning.

Johnny rents ski equipment for $3.00 and goes to meet Ilsa. Johnny and Ilsa ride to the top and work their way down the mountain. Johnny notes that it has been 4 years since he skied last. They stop on a ridge and Ilsa asks for a cigarette. Ilsa points out the Inn below and the coincidence of meeting Johnny at the Inn, and suddenly there are shots. Ilsa points to a hill and Johnny leads off towards the hill for cover. Johnny sees a cliff and they stop in time. Ilsa tells Johnny that she had forgotten about an avalanche that took out the slope. Johnny tells her that this is one coincidence too many.

Back at the Inn, Johnny and Ilsa talk by the fire. Johnny tells her that she has to tell him what is going on. She tells Johnny that she knows Sebastian, but not about his murder. Sebastian was just a friend who had asked her to share the cab with Johnny and leave her purse in it. He told her that he was in trouble and needed her help. Ilsa tells Johnny that she is telling the truth about not knowing about the diamonds. Johnny tells her about the possibility of Sebastian trying to double-cross his own people or another group trying to get to the diamonds. Ilsa tells Johnny that Sebastian told her to meet him there. Johnny describes the man in the lobby, but she does not know him. Ilsa describes a friend of Sebastian with a stocky thick neck named Breuner, but Johnny suggests it is Greuner. Johnny asks about the Englishman Harris, but she does not know him. Ilsa goes to her room and Otto asks Johnny how the skiing was. Johnny asks how he knows if a woman is lying, and Otto tells Johnny to believe what he wishes. Otto gives

Johnny a letter and tells him that Mr. Harris was out climbing the rocks this morning. Johnny opens the letter and calls Insp. Hoeniger. The card came this morning and shows a small skier's shelter on the front. Johnny tells Insp. Hoeniger that he is going to the shelter to see if it is the hiding place of the diamonds. Johnny starts up the trail to the shelter and sees someone going down the rocks towards the Inn that looks like Harris. At the shelter, Johnny finds the contents all torn up.

Tomorrow, a third part of the key turns up in the form of a corpse.

**PART 4         SHOW DATE:        10/4/1956**

Insp. Hoeniger calls Johnny from the lobby of the inn. Johnny tells him that he found the shelter all torn up. Insp. Hoeniger tells Johnny that a man matching the description of the one who attacked him brought a ticket to Kleibach, so maybe the diamonds are here after all.

Johnny has coffee with Insp. Hoeniger and discusses the case. Johnny tells Insp. Hoeniger about the conversation with Ilsa about Sebastian, and Johnny tells him that after the robbery the gang split up, and Greuner was to hide the diamonds and get back to Sebastian with their location. Now Sebastian wants to double-cross them and another gang has moved in. Sebastian moved to slowly and was killed, and Greuner does not know that Sebastian is dead. Johnny tells of the Englishman who likes to climb mountains and maybe Ilsa positioned him where Harris could shoot at them. Insp. Hoeniger will have the police watch the train station, and goes back to Zurich.

Johnny looks at the mountains from his balcony and sees the doors to Harris's room open. Johnny searches the room and finds a rifle in a closet that had been fired. Johnny finds Otto and asks where Harris is, and is told that he left for the village before dinner. Johnny leaves and runs into Ilsa who wants to know what she must do to get Johnny to trust her.

Johnny and Ilsa go to the village to look for Harris. Johnny tells her about finding the rifle in Harris' closet. Johnny notices that someone is following them and goes into an alley. Ilsa is told to walk on while Johnny waits in a doorway. Johnny listens to the man as he passes the alley and then hears Ilsa scream. Johnny runs to Ilsa and sees a man on the street. Ilsa tells Johnny that the man fell from the window, and that he is Sebastian's friend Greuner.

Tomorrow, the windup. I find out that some people will not hesitate to kill anyone who gets in their way. And that is not so good when the man in the way is me.

**PART 5         SHOW DATE:        10/5/1956**

Otto calls returning Johnny's call. Johnny tells Otto to look out for Harris and call him at the hotel in the village if he comes back. He has found Greuner, dead.

Johnny and Ilsa go to Greuner's room to look around. She tells Johnny that she heard Greuner scream when she came out of the alley. Johnny opens the room and finds nothing. Johnny hears a door being locked and breaks in and from the window sees a man running down the street; it is the man who jumped him in Zurich.

Johnny goes back to the Inn and thinks about the case. Johnny shows Ilsa the two post cards, but they mean nothing. Johnny tells her of the connection between Sebastian and Greuner. Ilsa realizes that there might be a line between the two sites. Geoffrey Harris comes in and asks how Johnny is enjoying his stay. Johnny tells him about being shot at and the killing in the village, and how Harris was in the vicinity both times. Johnny asks him about his rifle, but Harris tells Johnny he does not have one and does not like Johnny's attitude and leaves. Ilsa is gone when Johnny goes back and Otto shows Johnny a postcard meant for Sebastian, which has a picture of the village square.

Johnny goes to his room and looks at the cards. Johnny realizes that there might be someplace where all three of the buildings in the pictures could be seen. Johnny walks out and finds a small barn where he is able to see the Inn, the shelter and the village square. Johnny enters the barn and finds a leather case. Johnny hears footsteps and jumps the man who comes in, the man from Zurich. He is Anton, who is trying to get the diamonds. Johnny asks who Anton is working for and Otto comes in. Johnny realizes that Otto had shot at him and let Johnny lead him to the diamonds. Otto takes the diamonds from Anton, who is shot by Otto. Johnny slugs Otto and goes to Anton, who is wounded in the shoulder.

Remarks: Otto and Anton were turned over to police inspector Hoeniger; the diamonds are in safekeeping. About Otto, well greed is one of the seven deadly sins. It sure turned out to be the deadliest one for Otto. About Ilsa, well, ah, please consider me available for any future assignments in Switzerland.

Exp. Acct:     $1,723.00

NOTES:
- ROY ROWAN IS THE ANNOUNCER
- MUSIC SUPERVISION IS BY AMERIGO MARINO

**Producer:**  Jack Johnstone          **Writers:**  Robert Ryf
**Cast:**  Lucille Meredith, Victor Perrin, Forrest Lewis, Stan Jones, Ben Wright

◆     ❖     ◆

**SHOW:**  THE PRIMROSE MATTER
**COMPANY:**  MID STATES INDUSTRIAL INSURANCE COMPANY
**AGENT:**  BRAD TAYLOR
**PART 1**  **SHOW DATE:**     10/8/1956
**SYNOPSIS:** Brad Taylor calls and Johnny asks if he has caught another chief accountant with his hand in the till. Brad tells Johnny that this is about the Kansas City Payroll stickup. It was the Jipper Nitson gang. He was recognized in Phoenix and one of his boys was shot at a roadblock, but Jipper got away with the $100,000 payroll. Johnny agrees to go out and look for the money. Brad tells Johnny to be careful, they killed a state policeman at the roadblock.

Johnny travels to Tucson, Arizona and contacts the Lt. Cal Mervin of the State Police. Johnny is told that the police were caught off guard and four men got the drop on them. One man was shot and his body was thrown out of the car later. Nitson and two others got away, but Bledsoe was the one who was shot. One of them had a tommy gun and used it. Lt. Mervin shows Johnny a map of the area, and the terrain is very rough. The Mexican authorities have told Lt. Mervin that the car has not gone to Nogales. Johnny is sure that they did not double back and are not in Mexico, so maybe they are still in the area. Johnny wonders if a civilian could stumble on them. Johnny offers to act like a rock hound to get information. Lt. Mervin tells Johnny to go to Dave Bright's place and he will set you up. Keep in touch so I can let you know when the gang has been pickled up in Portland, or Montana.

Johnny equips himself to look like a prospector and goes to Jake's Bar and Grill to get information. Johnny buys a scotch for himself and Jake. Johnny tells Jake that he is out looking for uranium. Jake tells Johnny he knows most of the country and Johnny asks how to get back away from the highway and get lost. Jake tells him that there is only road one that might fit the bill, the Santa Rosa Summit road which dead ends at Primrose Camp. Jake tells Johnny that the police have been looking for some robbers, but he is sure that they are in Mexico. The road is in good shape and goes up to about 6000 ft. The Primrose Camp is Pop Bardell's place. He runs a gas station and a store and has some cabins. He gets hunters and campers and prospectors as customers. He has a new helper, a nephew from Tulsa, but he did not have an Oklahoma accent. He was very closed-mouth as well. Jake asks Johnny what he is looking for because he is the first city person to some out here with a shoulder-holder and a gun.

Tomorrow, a talkative man freezes, a taciturn man thaws, but a dead man can't do either. All he can do is be dead.

## PART 2    SHOW DATE:    10/9/1956

Lt. Mervin calls and Johnny tells him that he is checking in. Lt. Mervin recognizes the number as Jake's. Johnny tells him he is playing a lead and going into the Santa Rosa Mountains.

Johnny drives up to Primrose Camp and talks to Pop Bardell. Johnny asks if he can get a cabin from Pop, but Pop tells Johnny that the cabins are full. Johnny wants to prospect and is reassured that there are no cabins. Pop warns Johnny about the dangers of snakes and getting lost. Johnny tells the man that he will wait to talk to Pop, but the man says he is Pop. Johnny tells him that he is nowhere as talkative as Jake described him. A man calls from the lunchroom and Pop hurries in. Johnny walks in to see the man, but Pop tells him that he cannot go in. The man comes out and asks if there is trouble. Johnny tells him he wants some cigarettes. The man asks what brand, and Johnny replies "Chesteroids" and is given a pack and told to pay Pop. Johnny asks the man if he knows Clem Wilkie who is working on the new power plant in Tulsa, which is almost finished. Johnny drives off and notes that there is no new electric plant in Tulsa. Johnny drives to the end of the road and notes that no one had been there.

Johnny is certain that the robbers are there.

Johnny walks back to the hill above the camp and watches with binoculars as two cars come and go. Johnny sees Pop and his wife but not their daughter or the nephew. A prospector surprises Johnny and asks if he is watching someone. He recognizes Dave's clothes and knows Johnny is a city slicker. Johnny asks if the man lives there, but he tells Johnny that he has been prospecting for three weeks and has seen no one. The man is Jed Marsh. He would stop by to talk to Pop, and Johnny mentions the nephew. Jed tells him that Pop has no close relatives. Pop used to be a prospector and bought the camp to settle down. Jed asks Johnny to look at a wrecked and buried car for him.

Johnny goes to the car with Jed and opens the door to find a body inside. Johnny notes that the man had been shot and Johnny tells him that the State Police killed him. Johnny tells Jed who is his and who he is after. Johnny is sure that they are at Primrose camp.

Tomorrow, a lion's den reluctantly opens its door to let a trusting victim step inside. And the victim? Me.

### PART 3    SHOW DATE:    10/10/1956

Johnny calls Lt. Mervin from a forest station phone. Johnny tells him that he has found the stolen car in the mountains with a dead man in it. Johnny tells him not to bring the police there, as something is wrong at Primrose Camp.

Johnny convinces Lt. Mervin to hold his men off for 24 hours. Johnny drives to Primrose Camp and asks if there is a vacancy, but all the cabins are dark. Pop tells him it is better if he goes to the crossroads. Johnny tells him he cannot drive, as the headlights are broken. Johnny spots a station wagon and wants to borrow it, but Pop tells him he cannot. Pop asks Johnny what he is there looking for. Pop is very nervous about Johnny staying around there, but Johnny cannot leave. The nephew walks up and asks what the trouble is, and Pop tells him that Johnny's lights are out. The man offers to let Johnny stay in cabin number 2. He would not want Johnny to go off and tell bad stories about them, as it might cause trouble. Johnny pays for the room and Myra Bardell offers to fix him some food. She tells Johnny that the people who are renting the cabins are not eating there. She mentions her daughter and tells Johnny that she is not feeling well, and starts to cry. Johnny eats his breakfast and Myra tells Johnny that Pop cannot help himself. She tells him that they are in dangerous trouble, but will not tell him what. The place is a powder keg, please leave and do not set it off.

Johnny goes to his cabin and finds Pop there with an oil lamp. Pop tells Johnny not to listen to the Misses. She is just upset; you know how women are sometimes. Johnny asks about his daughter and Pop tells Johnny that she is in Tucson. Johnny mentions the nephew and Pop tells Johnny that he has been there for a few weeks. Johnny confronts him with the things he knows, but Pop says nothing. Johnny notes that a tire is missing from his jeep, and Pop tells him it went flat and will be fixed in the morning.

Tomorrow, a tightening noose. People held fast in the grip of fear. Then violence.

**PART 4          SHOW DATE:          10/11/1956**

Jed calls Johnny from the forest ranger phone. Johnny asks Jed to meet him on the road below Primrose Camp. Johnny tells him that there is trouble and it is tied into the robbery.

Johnny goes to meet Jed March at the Ranger Patrol phone. Suddenly the nephew is behind Johnny with a gun. The man takes Johnny's gun and slugs Johnny when he gets smart with him. Johnny tells him that Jed is coming to help him. Johnny tells him that he is not Pop's nephew and that he came east from Kansas City. He recognizes him as Spade Keller, who worked with the Carzotti mob, and is now with Jipper Nitson. Johnny tells him he has found their car and is now looking for the money. Now there is no one but he and Jipper to take the heat. Spade asks if the police know about the car, and Johnny plays dumb and insinuates that he and Jed are after the money. Spade asks Johnny what he is planning to do and then knocks Johnny unconscious.

Later that evening, when Johnny wakes up Jed is being held by Spade. Jed is searched and Spade slaps him with his gun. Johnny tells Jed that Spade is jumpy. They tell Spade that one of them will jump him if he doesn't watch it. Johnny tells Jed that the gang has already killed three others. They get up and spread out along the road to spread Spade's attention. Jed tells Spade that his is standing close to the rocks by the cliff where the snakes are. There is the sound of a rattlesnake, Spade panics and falls over the cliff. Jed shows Johnny the rattles he has in his pocket. He tells Johnny that he uses them to spook tenderfeet.

Tomorrow, a lovely girl screams in terror as a cornered rat turns and fights back. Fights the way a rat fights.

**PART 5          SHOW DATE:          10/12/1956**

Lt. Mervin calls and Johnny tells him that he has another body for him, Spade Keller, who fell over a cliff. Johnny asks Lt. Mervin to hold off until noon. Johnny tells him that Jed will meet him in a green station wagon that they are going to steal.

Jed and Johnny go back to the camp and Jed steals the car and Johnny sees Pop Bardell come running out after the car. Johnny meets him and asks if anything is wrong. Johnny tells Pop that maybe his nephew took the car. Johnny tells him that the nephew seems to have taken over the place but Pop does not seem to be the kind to let anyone tell him what to do. Johnny tells Pop who he is and that he knows the gang is there. Johnny tells Pop that Spade Keller is dead and that Jed March took the car to meet the police while Johnny tries to get Jipper. Pop tells Johnny that his daughter is in Tucson, and will not take a chance.

Myra comes out and tells Pop that Johnny is right; they have to take the chance. Johnny tells them that he might be able to get to their daughter without harming her. Pop tells Johnny that Nipper is in a tunnel with their daughter. Johnny gives Pop his wallet and gun and goes up the trail with his equipment. Johnny ignores the tunnel when he gets there and then finally goes in. Johnny is slugged in the tunnel and Jipper walks outside to check on things. Johnny whispers to Jenny and tells her not to worry. She tells Johnny that the money is in the tunnel. Johnny tells her to get him with his back turned to Johnny. Jipper comes in and tells her to leave Johnny alone. Jipper tells her that something is wrong. Jenny lures him to her and Johnny gets up and hits him with a rock and takes his gun. Jenny tells Johnny that he killed Jipper but Johnny tells her the state probably will kill him.

Remarks: The state eventually did, kill him I mean.

Exp. Acct:      $914.15

## NOTES:

- ROY ROWAN IS THE ANNOUNCER
- MUSIC SUPERVISION IS BY AMERIGO MARINO

**Producer:**    Jack Johnstone         **Writers:**    Les Crutchfield
**Cast:**        Marvin Miller, Junius Matthews, Herb Ellis, D. J. Thompson, Herb Butterfield, Tony Barrett, Barbara Eiler

◆    ❖    ◆

**SHOW:**        THE PHANTOM CHASE MATTER
**COMPANY:**    UNIVERSAL ADJUSTMENT BUREAU
**AGENT:**       PAT MCCRACKEN
**PART 1**       **SHOW DATE:**     10/15/1956

**SYNOPSIS:** Pat McCracken calls Johnny and he has $120,000 on his mind. Pat thinks that Thomas Chase, partner of a Wall Street investment firm, has the money. Pat thinks that Chase has embezzled the money, but he has jumped bail and disappeared.

Johnny cabs to Pat's office and they discuss the case. Johnny is told that Everson and Chase is a high-class operation. Mr. George Everson is the senior partner and a widower. Thomas Chase is the junior partner, and a former football player, an all-American type. Chase is married to Lola Chase, and she seems to be a really nice girl. The missing money is currency, checks and negotiable securities. Everson can give you more details on how it was pulled off. Everson is not sure that Chase is guilty, but Pat asks Johnny if an innocent man would jump bail.

Johnny goes to New York City and the office of Mr. Everson, who cannot believe that Tom did it. Johnny is told that Tom became a partner 5 years ago. The firm has always maintained a fluid relationship with their customers, and a clever man could juggle figures. Tom had been managing some of the bigger accounts lately that were interested in long term growth. Everson discovered the missing money when a client decided to liquidate his account and the shortage was found. An audit was conducted and the District Attorney was brought in. Johnny gets the files and Everson shows where the documents recorded each transaction. Everson tells Johnny that Tom would not talk after being arrested, and that Everson had arranged bail, which Tom jumped. Everson had eaten dinner with them a week earlier and Lola told him that Tom was acting moody and preoccupied lately. Everson asks Johnny to find out why Tom did it.

Johnny arranges to have dinner with Lola Chase. Johnny notes that Lola is quite a dish. Lola tells Johnny that she thought she knew Tom, but apparently she did not. He liked golf and sailing, and had an extensive jazz collection and hi-fi setup. She tells Johnny that Tom had become moody lately and stayed out late at night. They had planned a trip and he cancelled out and told her to go alone. She found out Tom had been arrested when she got back from Martha's Vineyard.

Johnny is visited by Mr. Everson in his hotel room. He shows Johnny a newspaper article about New Orleans jazz. In a picture of a jazz place is Tom Chase. Everson is sure that, based on the pose, the man is Tom Chase.

Yeah, on to New Orleans where the trail proves to be pretty cold, but warms up fast.

## PART 2          SHOW DATE:      10/16/1956

George Everson calls and tells Johnny that he may not be so sure about the picture. Johnny tells him that New Orleans would be a good place, given Tom's interest in Jazz. My plane leaves in an hour.

Johnny goes to the airport and George Everson meets him there to tell him that if the trip is unfruitful, he will pay the expenses. Johnny goes over the facts of the case with Everson before leaving. Johnny asks about another woman, but George thinks that idea is not possible. Johnny flies to New Orleans, Louisiana and heads for the Latin Quarter. Johnny locates Ace's Castle, the bar in the newspaper article and orders a scotch and soda. The Bartender tells Johnny that this is not a tourist place, but for the locals who come to listen to Pops Harker and nurse their troubles. Johnny shows him the picture and points to the man in the background. The bartender does not recognize the picture or the name Tom Chase. If he is on the street, Tom will come back. Johnny goes to talk to Pops, who was just warming up. Johnny tells him he is looking for a man named Tom Chase, but Pops doesn't know the name. Pops would know the voice, but not the picture, as he is blind. Johnny waits for several hours but nothing happens. At midnight Freddy Quintana sits down with Johnny and tells him that Johnny should be glad to see him. It is his business to help people, when money is involved, and for a few bucks he can help Johnny find Tom Chase. Freddy describes Chase and Johnny tells Freddy to bring him there. Freddie tells Johnny that Tom does not want to be found. Freddy tells Johnny that Tom is going under the name Tom James. Freddy tells Johnny that he will be back in an hour with proof. On the way out Pops tells Johnny that Freddy was a bad one, he could tell from his voice.

Freddy returns with a letter he found in a trashcan. The letter was written to Lola, and a comparison of handwriting Johnny has matches.

There is a little game of chance called dealer's choice. Fine, until the dealer gets dealt out, the hard way.

## PART 3          SHOW DATE:      10/17/1956

Freddy calls Johnny and tells him that the deal is complicated. Freddy tells

Johnny that Tom is hiding again. Freddie tells Johnny to meet him at Ace's Castle at ten o'clock with the money.

Johnny calls Pat McCracken and gets agreement for the $500 payoff to Freddy. Johnny calls Everson who is happy Johnny is making progress. As Johnny waits for the meeting time, Lola Chase comes to his hotel room. She tells Johnny that George had told her about the phone call, and she decided to come there to be with Tom, if he is there. She might be able to talk to Tom. Johnny tells her of the letter from Freddy, and she asks to see it. Lola reads the letter and wants to come with Johnny to meet Freddy. Johnny and Lola eat dinner and then go to Ace's Castle. Lola comments to Johnny on his job and he tells her that sometimes he does not like it, like now. Johnny and Lola get a table at Ace's Castle and wait. Pops tells Johnny that he should stick to the good ones when Freddy comes in. Freddy tells Johnny that he has Tom James waiting for him on the pretext Freddie is getting passage for him. Freddy gives Johnny an address and tells Johnny to meet him there at midnight. Lola asks to go with Johnny and he reluctantly agrees.

Johnny and Lola go to the rooming house and go into room 8. They walk in and the room is empty, so they wait. After 30 minutes Johnny takes Lola to her hotel and goes to Aces Castle where Lt. LaFevre of the police sits down with Johnny and asks him why he is there. Johnny tells him about Freddy and tells Lt. LaFevre who he is. Lt. LaFevre takes Johnny to the ally in the back where Freddy Quintana is dead.

Somehow I manage to parlay a scrap of burnt paper into a plane ticket for what almost turns out to be a one-way trip.

## Part 4       Show Date:     10/18/1956

Lt. LaFevre calls and tells Johnny that he needs to talk about his involvement with Freddy.

Johnny cabs to police headquarters and tells Lt. LaFevre about all the details of the case he is working on, and the events so far in New Orleans. Johnny shows Lt. LaFevre the picture from the newspaper, and tells him about meeting Freddy at Ace's Castle and the letter from the trashcan. Johnny tells Lt. LaFevre about going to meet Freddy and finding him dead. Lt. LaFevre tells Johnny that Freddy was a really bad boy, and a lot of people would like to have killed him.

Johnny goes to tell the bad news to Lola and she wishes she could call off the investigation. Johnny is called by Lt. LaFevre. He has just located Tom James' room. Johnny cabs to the rooming house and meets Lt. LaFevre there. The room is empty and there are some burnt papers in a trashcan. Johnny identifies the handwriting, and finds a piece of envelope with the letterhead of "Everson and Chase" on the corner. Lt. LaFevre finds another scrap with the number "12, 23" on it. Johnny goes to the rental agent and asks about room rented to Tom James. The man tells Johnny that the rent was paid in advance, and that a friend rented the room for Mr. James. The agent would love to have a friend like that, "boy, what a woman!" Johnny returns to Lola and tells her to go back to New York. Johnny tells Lola that it looks like Tom is not traveling alone now. Lola returns to New York, and Johnny mulls over the case and the numbers "12, 23." While Johnny reads through the paper he notices the harbor news. Maybe the numbers refer to a ship and its departure time!

It's about a trail that heats up, and a girl who doesn't exactly help to cool things off.

## PART 5     SHOW DATE:     10/19/1956

Johnny is called by Lt. LaFevre and Johnny tells him of the new lead. Johnny tells him about the numbers and the harbor news article, and Lt. LaFevre tells Johnny that he will work on it.

Johnny cabs to Lt. LaFevre's office and learns that pier 23 is a busy place, but the police are working on getting more information. Johnny relates telling Lola about the woman, and her trip back to New York. Johnny tells Lt. LaFevre that he is glad he is single, based on the type of people he has to deal with. Lt. LaFevre is called and gets information on a ship, "The Caribbean Star" that left pier 23 at midnight on the night James disappeared. It is bound for Trinidad via Havana and Haiti, and there is a passenger named James on the passenger list. Everson calls and Johnny tells him about the woman who rented the room.

Johnny flies to Port au Prince, Haiti and meets the Caribbean Star. Johnny goes to James' stateroom and he has to break in to find an empty room. The purser arrives and tells Johnny that Mr. James got off in Havana. The purser tells Johnny that James had asked where the airline offices were. Johnny calls the Havana police and asks Lt. Escobar to check the airlines and find out where James went and call him back.

Lt. Escobar calls Johnny two hours later and tells Johnny that James had purchased a ticket to Barbados. Johnny flies to Bridgetown, Barbados and sees why Tom would want to come there. The island is bigger than Johnny thought. Johnny checks all the hotels for Tom and finds nothing. While Johnny is thinking in the hotel bar, a girl who asks if he is Johnny Dollar joins him. She tells Johnny that she knows where Tom James is. Her name is Connie, and she tells Johnny that she is the one that rented the room, and wants out. She wants money to get back to the states. She tells Johnny that Tom will be at the Trade Winds Bar on the waterfront at 10:00. Johnny goes to the bar and sees Connie go in. Johnny realizes that he is being followed and chases the man into a warehouse where he is knocked out.

Next, a small fishing boat and a deserted island and a man waiting there for me. A man with a gun.

## NOTES:
- THE CAST FOR THE FIRST FIVE EPISODES IS GIVEN AT THE END OF THIS WEEK'S PROGRAMS.

Cast:     **Virginia Gregg, Michael Ann Barrett, Lawrence Dobkin, Forrest Lewis, Peter Leeds, Barney Phillips, Tony Barrett, Victor Perrin**

**PART 6          SHOW DATE:    10/22/1956**

Connie calls Johnny and tells him she waited for him at the Trade Winds. Johnny tells her about getting slugged, but she knows nothing about it. She is in the lobby, and Johnny will be right down.

Johnny is ready to chuck the case for 2 cents when Connie does not show up. The desk clerk tells Johnny that he saw her leave after making a phone call. He had seen her with a large athletic man, who Johnny muses, could be Chase. Johnny visits the local police and meets Inspector Whitset. Johnny outlines the case to him and tells him where he has been so far. Johnny gives Insp. Whitset a description of Connie and he agrees to look for her. Johnny tells of meeting Connie and the meeting at the Trade Winds, but wonders why she left the hotel after calling him.

Back at the hotel the desk clerk tells Johnny that Connie has not come back. Johnny tells him that he is going to the Trade Winds, and the clerk warns Johnny that it is in a dangerous part of town. Johnny goes to the Trade Winds and buys a rum punch. Johnny spots Connie and goes out after her and finds her in the alley. She tells Johnny that she is not Chase's girlfriend, and she was trying to work something for herself. When Johnny talked about murder, she wanted to back out. Connie tells Johnny that she met Chase in Barbados two days ago and heard that Johnny was looking for him. She wanted to set up Chase for money; she is broke and wants to get back to the states. She tells Johnny that Chase had mentioned a friend who was coming and about a conversation with a fisherman on the wharf. Johnny takes her out to the docks and they look for the man Chase had talked to. Johnny talks to the man and learns that he took a passenger to Lagos Island. It is an island with an abandoned house, and the man took food with him. Johnny feels that it is on the up-and-up, or a big trap. He will have to go to Lagos Island to find out.

Getting to the island of Lagos, easy. Getting away from it in one piece, that is another story.

**PART 7          SHOW DATE:    10/24/1956**

Lola Chase calls Johnny from her hotel in Mirasol Beach, Barbados. She had to come here, after all Tom is her husband. Johnny goes to see her.

Johnny cabs to Lola's hotel and meets her on the terrace. She tells Johnny that she has discovered that it hurts to get kicked in the face, but you get over it. Deep inside she knew it had to be another woman but she cannot be hurt anymore. Lola is there because she feels obligated to be there. Johnny tells her about the island and the girl who led him on. Johnny tells her he should be back by dark.

Johnny calls Everson who does not know that Lola is in Barbados. He will fly to Barbados and take her back with him. Johnny tells him that he might have located Chase, and is going to go pick him up.

Johnny rents a power cruiser and goes to see Insp. Whitset. Johnny tells him about the island, and Insp. Whitset shows him the island on a chart. Both Johnny and Insp. Whitset feel that this could still be a trap. Insp. Whitset tells Johnny about the island, and does not think that anyone would be there. Johnny gives

Insp. Whitset his radio call letters, "6X3" and asks him to watch the fisherman he got the information from and to radio Johnny if the man goes out to sea.

Johnny gets the boat and sets course for the island. In the cabin Johnny finds Lola, who has stowed away. She wants to be there when Johnny finds Tom. She does not want Tom or Johnny to get hurt. She has thought a lot about Johnny and maybe if things were different . . . Johnny gets a call from Insp. Whitset who tells Johnny that the fisherman left about 20 minutes after he did.

Johnny gets to the island and lands at the abandoned pier. Johnny and Lola walk towards the house through the undergrowth and are suddenly shot at. Johnny hides in a gully and works his way towards the shots. Lola is scared that Johnny has a gun and is afraid that Johnny might hurt Tom. Lola notices that the next shots come from behind them, and Johnny realizes he has bee suckered in to getting away from the boat. He rushes back to find the boat leaving with a man at the helm. Lola tells Johnny that it is Tom.

Next, a friend to the rescue, and an unfriendly phone call from a killer.

**PART 8          SHOW DATE:      10/25/1956**

Johnny Dollar, "boy genius," who lets Tom get his boat away from him. Tom is no dummy. Johnny tells Lola that they are alone on the island, and there is no way off.

Johnny tells Lola that they might be there quite awhile. She asks Johnny to stop calling Tom her husband. Johnny wonders why Tom did not finish him off in the warehouse, and did not kill him when he was shooting at him. Lola tells Johnny that in other circumstances she would not mind being there with Johnny. Johnny builds a fire and goes to the house and finds some food. After eating they go back to the fire, build it up, and wait. Johnny dozes off, and Lola wakes Johnny up when she sees a boat. Johnny realizes that it is a police boat with Insp. Whitset on it. Johnny tells him what Chase had gone, and Insp. Whitset tells Johnny he had seen a boat heading back to Barbados.

Back in Bridgetown, Insp. Whitset tells Johnny and Lola that George Everson is there waiting for them. Johnny spots the boat he had rented, and Insp. Whitset starts watching the airlines and charter boats.

Johnny goes to talk to George Everson and updates him with what has happened. Everson still feels that Lola feels strongly about Tom, so maybe she could talk to him. He would tell Tom to give himself up and give back the money and work on restitution to their investors. Johnny tells him that Tom will not give himself up; he probably is the one who killed Freddy Quintana.

Johnny cabs to Insp. Whitset's office and learns that Chase is still on the island. Insp. Whitset tells Johnny that the island is big, and Chase could be anywhere. Insp. Whitset gets a phone call and learns that a man answering Chase's description has just checked into a hotel. Johnny and Insp. Whitset go to the hotel and enter the room with a passkey. The room is empty, and the window is open. Johnny just missed him again.

Johnny goes to his hotel and finds Tom Chase in his room. Tom takes his gun and Johnny asks why he did it. He tells Johnny that he did it for a woman, but that turned sour. He came to Johnny's room because he could not shake Johnny, and is tired of running. It is the end of the line for Johnny.

Tomorrow, the pay off. But who gets paid off, and how and why? Well the answers to those questions surprise me plenty, and maybe they will you too.

## PART 9      SHOW DATE:    10/26/1956

Johnny is called by Lola and Tom tells him to hang up. Lola realizes it is Tom, and she tells Johnny that she is coming over, but Johnny tells her not to. Tom has a gun and he means business.

Johnny figures his next expense item is for burial expenses. Tom asks him why Lola is involved in this. He tells Johnny that the girl turned sour and it is too late for anything. He cannot run and cannot take it anymore, and Tom slugs Johnny. When Johnny wakes up, Lola and George are there. He tells them what happened and about Tom ranting wildly. Johnny wonders why Tom did not kill him. It is almost as if . . . oh skip it.

Johnny goes to see Insp. Whitset and tells him what has happened. Insp. Whitset gets a call for Johnny. Lola tells Johnny that Tom was just there in her cottage, and that he just drove off towards the mountains. Johnny goes to the cottage and they get into a car and drive off towards where Tom had gone. She tells Johnny that Tom had just wanted to see her one more time before . . . Johnny drives up to the car, parked next to a cliff and tells Lola to stay in the car. Johnny climbs down and finds the body. Johnny drives Lola back to her hotel and calls Insp. Whitset. Johnny thinks about the case and Lola and himself who had come a long way for nothing. Johnny visits Insp. Whitset the next day and learns the inquest verdict was suicide, and that the burial will be here in Barbados. Johnny does not have the money and the chances are not to good at finding it. In Chase's pockets the police had found a book of matches. Johnny goes to the bar where the matches came from, searches the area and finds Tom Chase's last room but the money is not there. Johnny compares the handwriting on the register, gets a few wild ideas, and calls Pat McCracken with a request for information. Pat calls back and gives Johnny the information he had asked for. Yep, Johnny had come all the way to Barbados, but the case was solved in New York.

Johnny calls Lola and George and tells them to meet him at Tom's grave. Johnny tells them that he has been a jerk for two weeks because he has been chasing a dead man. Johnny tells them that they engineered the whole deal with only two people. Johnny tells Lola that she had gone to New Orleans and rented the room for Tom James instead of going to Cape Cod. Freddy's letter matched the handwriting given to him by George, but Freddie played his part well only to be killed by Lola. Johnny tells them that they hired a man to lead Johnny on a merry chase, and all the while the real Tom Chase was dead in New York. Johnny tells Everson that he is the one that juggled the books, and killed the impostor. When Johnny tells him that the body will be exhumed, George pulls a gun on Johnny. Johnny tells him that New York knows all about the case, and George tells Lola that the partnership is now dissolved. Both Johnny and Lola lunge for

George, and Lola is shot in the arm. Johnny tells her that Tom had said nothing when he was arrested because he knew what she was up to, but he loved her too much and was willing to cover for her.

Everson and Lola are turned over to the authorities and Everson gives up the keys to a safe deposit box in New York, where the money had been all the time. He also showed Johnny the spot on Long Island where he and Lola had buried the body of Tom Chase.

Remarks: Pat, the next time you call me for an assignment like this one, I hope you get a busy signal.

Exp. Acct:     $1,723.00

**NOTES:**
- ROY ROWAN IS THE ANNOUNCER
- MUSIC SUPERVISION IS BY AMERIGO MARINO

**Producer:** Jack Johnstone          **Writers:**   Robert Ryf
**Cast:**          Michael Ann Barrett, Jack Edwards, Ben Wright, Virginia Gregg, Don Diamond, Forrest Lewis, Richard Crenna

◆   ❖   ◆

**SHOW:**          THE SILENT QUEEN MATTER
**COMPANY:**      STATE UNITY LIFE
**AGENT:**         VIC CARSON
**PART 1**          **SHOW DATE:**      10/29/1956

**SYNOPSIS:** Vic Carson calls Johnny and has a job for him. His agent in Venice. "Venice, I'd love it! Soft nights along the canal . . ." Venice, California, Johnny. Vic's agent there has reported the death of Bernard Slade in Ocean Park, which is right next door to Venice. He ran a penny arcade there. The body was found there, and this apartment was plastered with pictures of Mavis Gayle, a silent screen star. The police reported that someone had drawn a question mark over each of her pictures, and she is the beneficiary of Slade's policy.

Johnny travels to Ocean Park, California and calls Sergeant McKay, who is at the amusement park. Johnny walks to the park and notices that the penny arcade is busy. Johnny asks for a dime's worth of pennies from a blonde in the change booth and asks her about Barney Slade. Johnny tells her who he is and she tells Johnny that Barney was a real nice guy. She tells Johnny that Barney did not have any enemies. His friends were everyone here along the pier, including her. The girl tells Johnny that she has never heard of Mavis Gayle. She tells Johnny that Sgt. McKay is in Barney's apartment and Johnny goes back to the room. Johnny notes that the walls are covered with pictures of silent movie stars. Johnny goes out the back door to meet Sgt. McKay who tells Johnny that the killer might have put the question marks on the pictures, and that some pictures are missing. Johnny asks if there was any missing money, and Sgt. McKay tells Johnny that Twyla, the change girl, did not think so. Twyla told Sgt. McKay that Barney rarely let anyone into his apartment. Twyla found the body in the morning. Barney was shot twice with a .38, and the apartment was messed up. Barney typically used the back entrance, which was open when the body was found. Johnny notices the heavy bolt and chain on the door and tells Sgt. McKay that Barney did not have to let someone in unless he wanted to. Sgt. McKay tells Johnny that Barney was found in his pajamas and a robe so he probably got up to let someone in, but the place was off limits to all of his friends. Sgt. McKay is looking for a friend called "the preacher," who was seen with Barney by Sam Heckstram. Sam remembers seeing the preacher come out of Barney's room. Barney had told Sam that the preacher was a dear old friend. Mavis Gayle has been told and was upset, especially about the crayon marks. Sgt. McKay did not know that she was the beneficiary of Slade's policy and tells Johnny that Mavis told him that she had never heard of Barney Slade.

Johnny calls Mavis Gayle's home and then goes to the funeral home where his friends are, and the manager tells Johnny that Mavis Gayle is not there. The man at the funeral home knows most of the people along the pier, but does not know anyone called "the preacher." Johnny looks at the guest book, and sees no one there who was a minister. Then Mavis Gayle enters; a thin woman in a well-tailored suit. Johnny goes to talk to her and she turns towards him and collapses.

Johnny calls Sgt. McKay and tells him that Gayle has just identified Barney as a former husband, Tom Sanford, who was killed in a hunting accident twenty-seven years earlier.

Tomorrow, a stagecoach ride. I get some lumps, and a surprise witness turns up.

### PART 2          SHOW DATE:     10/30/1956

Sgt. McKay calls and Johnny tells him about Mavis Gayle being married to Tom Sanford, who was killed 27 years ago. Mavis just identified Barney Slade as Tom Sanford. Mavis is still there, and Sgt. McKay is on his way over.

Johnny buys coffee for Mavis and walks outside. A man stops Johnny and asks about Mavis being Barney's wife. Mort, the manager thought he heard her say that. He learned who Johnny is from Twyla. He is Frank Jessup, who runs the mermaid game on the pier. Frank tells Johnny that Barney never mentioned her to him, and she has never been to the arcade. Twyla has been there for 5 years, and Twyla liked Barney a lot. Barney mostly talked about fishing and pinochle, which they played several times a week. They played at Frank's place or Sam's boat. Sgt. McKay arrives and Sgt. McKay goes in to talk to Mavis, alone. Mavis comes out and they put her in her car and she leaves. Sgt. McKay tells Johnny that Mavis was a good actress, and Johnny wonders if she still is.

Johnny gets a newspaper and goes to Mavis Gayle's home. The papers tell all about the hunting accident when Tom Sanford was supposedly killed with a shotgun. Sgt. McKay drives out and tells Johnny that the doctor has ordered her to see no one. Johnny tells Sgt. McKay that she and Tom had had a pretty stormy marriage. Johnny wonders if someone hired a man to kill Tom Sanford and then recently realized that the wrong man was killed, and this time he does the job himself. Sgt. McKay drives Johnny to his hotel and Johnny wonders why Sanford put his ID on a dead man and then disappeared, and about the question marks on the pictures. Maybe Barney wondered if his wife hired someone to kill him, and used the question marks to draw attention to Gayle.

Johnny travels to see an agent named Milo Martin, one of the men on the hunting trip. Johnny finds Milo on a ranch where a western movie is being filmed. Milo has read about the killing in the paper, and tells Johnny that finding the body of Tom was a horrible experience. Milo has no idea about why anyone would kill Tom, who was a client of his, as was Miss Gayle. Milo tells Johnny that Tom was a gambler and drank too much and was jealous, and they were fighting all the time. Of the men on the hunting trip, Francis Travellian, a producer is still around, as is Jarvis Pocket. Milo is called and invites Johnny to ride the stagecoach back to the ranch house. After a rough ride in the stagecoach, Johnny goes back to his hotel room where Sgt. McKay calls Johnny and tells him that there is a witness who saw Mavis at the arcade two nights before the murder.

Tomorrow, a bowl of lentil soup, and I almost end up in a cemetery.

**PART 3      SHOW DATE:      10/31/1956**

Vic Carson calls and he tells Johnny that that things are opening up on the coast, and about Sanford and Slade being the same person. Johnny tells Vic about Mavis being at the arcade, and that he has not found out anything about the pictures. Johnny tells Vic that he is looking for "the preacher."

Johnny goes to the penny arcade and Twyla tells Johnny that she is sure that she saw Mavis Gayle there. Mavis was just standing in the front door like she was waiting for someone, while Barney was helping Frank fix a machine. Mavis just waited and then left without seeing Barney. Frank walks up and tells Twyla that they are going to the funeral home again that night. Johnny asks Twyla and Frank if they know any of the names of his suspects, but they do not know any of them, besides Sgt. McKay already asked them.

Johnny goes out to try and find George Shelton, and ends up at a bar. The bartender gets Johnny a glass of I. W. Harper and soda, and tells him that George has had it rough, and could not act in talking movies because of his voice. He was involved with an actress, Josephine Hinch, and it went sour. The bartender gives Johnny and address for George in Glendale, and tells Johnny that he misses the preacher also. For $5, Johnny learns that the preacher is Jarvis Pocket, who runs a rescue mission. Johnny also learns that George has been dead for a couple years.

Johnny goes to the mission and waits to talk to Pocket. After the residents sing a hymn, Johnny is caught in the rush and ends up with a bowl of soup. Johnny meets with Jarvis Pocket in his office and Pocket tells Johnny that he had seen Tom Sanford fighting with a man when the gun went off and the other man was killed. They all agreed it was best to let the world think that Tom was dead. Pocket tells Johnny that he knows the name of the man who tried to kill Tom.

Johnny thinks that the man who hired him knows the man's name also. Pocket tells Johnny that the man was Joe Fallon, who was Mavis Gayle's personal chauffeur.

Tomorrow, audience with the queen, and a brush with a killer.

## PART 4          SHOW DATE:          11/1/1956

Sgt. McKay calls Johnny in Barney's office. Johnny tells Sgt. McKay that he is there with Jarvis Pocket, using a key Barney had given him. Johnny tells Sgt. McKay about Joe Fallon, the chauffeur of Mavis Gayle.

Pocket paces in Barney's office until Sgt. McKay arrives. Pocket is sure that the whole wall was covered with pictures and the missing ones were from a movie he made with Mavis and George Sheldon and Tom. The others were of Mavis and Tom. Johnny notes that none of the other pictures are of Tom Sanford, who had not changed too much. The question marks were to draw attention to Mavis. Maybe Barney left Mavis the money to repay Mavis for his actions earlier. Pocket leaves and Johnny talks with Sgt. McKay about the killing on the hunting trip, and how someone caught up with Tom living as Barney Slade. Sgt. McKay gets a call from headquarters, they just got a call from Francis Travellian. Mavis Gayle is at his beach house and wants to talk to them.

Johnny and Sgt. McKay drive to the beach house and meet Mavis and Travellian in the den. Sgt. McKay asks her why she told him that she did not know Slade. She tells Sgt. McKay that she did not know it until she saw Tom in the funeral home. She tells him that she had gone to the arcade two nights before the murder. She was afraid that she would be involved deeper. She had received a call that a dear old friend was in trouble and that she should go to the park, where the friend would meet her at 8:00, but no one came. Johnny asks if Joe Fallon means anything to her, and Travellian explodes. She tells Johnny that she had fired Joe just after she and Tom were married. Johnny tells her that they have learned that it was Joe who was killed, not Tom. Travellian tells them that Fallon had been mentioned to him in a phone call about a business deal. Johnny is sure that the same man made the two phone calls.

Johnny goes to his hotel and tells Sgt. McKay that the pictures bother him. Johnny walks to the amusement area and walks on into Venice. Johnny hears a shot, and sees a man collapse on a bridge. Johnny gets to the man to find Pocket, who points to an area "over there." Johnny runs after a man and loses him in the darkness. Johnny hears footsteps and then is knocked out.

Tomorrow, a man who talked too much, and it killed him. Yeah, the payoff

## PART 5          SHOW DATE:          11/2/1956

Milo Martin calls Johnny and tells him that he has just read of Jarvis Pocket's murder and his being attacked. Milo mentions that he did get a message from someone about Joe Fallon. Johnny tells Milo that the caller will call back, as he is after blackmail.

Johnny cabs to see Sgt. McKay, who tells Johnny that Pocket was killed with two slugs from the same gun that killed Slade. Johnny reviews the case to figure out where they are. Johnny tells Sgt. McKay about the call to Martin and the probable blackmail. Pocket probably did some snooping and got himself killed.

Johnny and Sgt. McKay go to the funeral for Tom Sanford/Barney Slade. Frank stops them and remarks about the nice funeral. Frank mentions how Mavis showed no tears at all. Johnny goes back to his room and sleeps for a while. Johnny goes to Barney's room and knocks over a bottle from the table. Twyla comes in and tells Johnny that Barney had been sick and they took care of him at Frank's place. He had gotten sick playing card and Doc. Ferris was called. Johnny goes to see Dr. Ferris who tells Johnny that Barney was very sick and was delirious at times, but Frank had stayed with him all night to tend to him. Johnny cabs back to the amusement park and learns that Frank had gone home early. Johnny cabs to his apartment and is told that he just left for a walk. Johnny follows him and sees a big Cadillac slow down and toss out package. Frank gets the package and runs towards Johnny, who stops him. Frank offers Johnny half the money and tells Johnny that Barney had told him about his past while he was sick. Frank tells Johnny that he went to Barney with a plan to blackmail the others, but he had to kill him. Johnny asks who gave Frank the money and Milo walks up with a gun and thanks Johnny for holding Frank. Johnny tells Milo that Frank really does not have any proof that Milo had hired Fallon to kill Tom, but Milo tells Johnny that he could not take chances. Milo had hoped to get close to Mavis when Tom was out of the way, but she ignored him. Milo tells Frank that he will not talk and Frank runs away. Milo shoots Frank and Johnny belts Milo.

Remarks: About Frank Jessup: he got his out there on the sand dunes for the murders of Tom Sanford and Jarvis Pocket. About Milo Martin: in jail awaiting trial for murder of the above mentioned F. Jessup. About Mavis Gayle: she is going to see to it that the good work at brother Pocket's rescue mission goes on, and will donate $25,000 to the cause. You guessed it, the insurance money.

Exp. Acct:     $436.25

NOTES:
- LAST OF THE FIVE-A-WEEK EPISODES.
- AT THE END OF THIS PROGRAM, BOB BAILEY TELLS THE AUDIENCE "I THINK YOU WILL BE GLAD TO KNOW THAT BEGINNING SUNDAY, INSTEAD OF FIVE TIME A WEEK, WE WILL BE ON THE AIR ONLY ONCE A WEEK, BUT WITH A COMPLETE HALF HOUR STORY. REMEMBER, THAT'S BEGINNING THIS COMING SUNDAY. SO JOIN US, WON'T YOU?"
- GEORGE SHELTON APPEARS AS A SUSPECT WITHOUT BEING MENTIONED PREVIOUSLY.
- THE ANNOUNCER IS ROY ROWAN
- MUSIC SUPERVISION BY AMERIGO MARINO

Producer:   Jack Johnstone        Writers:   Adrian Gendot
Cast:       Paula Winslowe, Virginia Gregg, Victor Perrin, Paul Dubov,
            Frank Gerstle, John Dehner, Lawrence Dobkin, Chet Stratton

This is the start of the 30-minute series of Bob Bailey programs.

**SHOW:** THE BIG SCOOP MATTER
**SHOW DATE:** 11/11/1956
**COMPANY:** NORTHEAST INDEMNITY AFFILIATES
**AGENT:** JOE McNAB
**EXP. ACCT:** $187.40

**SYNOPSIS:** Joe McNab calls Johnny with high blood pressure. He may have to pay off on a $100,000 policy on a reporter friend of Johnny's, Art Wesley. Art is working on a story someone does not want him to report on. He has been beaten and today a car made a pass at him at high speed. But it is early today.

Johnny travels to New York City to meet with Art, and finds him in a bar. Art tells Johnny that he is working on a story and cannot have anyone protecting him. Art tells Johnny that his departed wife is the beneficiary of the policy. Art tells Johnny that the story is about a national gambling syndicate run by someone in New York. He has the man's name written in a safe deposit box just in case.

Johnny goes to see Joan Wesley, who is not cooperative at all. Johnny cabs to see Det. Lt. Ristelli, his old friend who knows about the attempts on Art's life. The phone rings and Art calls for Johnny. Art tells Johnny that he is leaving town and this might be it. Johnny cabs to Art's apartment and finds "Watika" written on a pad by the phone—a reference to Lake Watika, New York where Art has a lodge.

Johnny rents a car and drives to the lake, though a heavy rainstorm, and finds a mass of mud on the road to the lake. Johnny drives up the road to Art's place, finds Art's car and Art lying in the doorway dead. Johnny drives to the sheriff and reports it.

Johnny meets the sheriff the next morning and they go over the known facts, including a hole in the roof over the foodstuffs. The coroner has reported that Art was killed about 10:30, while it was still raining. Johnny tells the sheriff about the story Art was working on, and Johnny is told that the only place to stay in the area is the Watika Inn.

Johnny drives to the inn and talks to the desk clerk who tells him that there were only two guests last night. One of the guests, Mr. Cooper, is sitting on the porch and the other has gone. Johnny goes to talk to Cooper, who tells Johnny that he enjoyed the rain by sitting in front of his fireplace and reading a book. Johnny gets a description of the other guest for the sheriff and goes back to New York.

Johnny visits Joan Wesley, who knows about Art's death. Johnny asks if Joan had known that Art had gone to the lodge. She tells Johnny that she was at home all the previous evening. Johnny checks the garage and finds a clean car. Johnny learns from the garage attendant that the car had been washed because the wheels were full of mud from last night.

Johnny confronts Joan with the mud on her car, but she is adamant that she was not at the lodge. Johnny tells her that the switchboard operator got a call from Art yesterday, and she admits she spoke to Art, but went out to meet someone else, which is why she wanted a divorce. The man is Ted Nash.

Johnny calls the apartment of Nash who is not there and goes to see Lt. Ristelli to update him on the events of the case. Lt. Ristelli tells Johnny that he will check up on Nash and he tells Johnny that a man named Cooper was involved in some rumors of a gambling ring earlier that year. Johnny and Lt. Ristelli go to Art's apartment and find the key to the safe deposit box, but it only has a number on it. Lt. Ristelli starts a search of the banks, and Johnny goes back to Lake Watika.

At the lake Johnny finds Cooper still there by the fireplace. Johnny tells him about the story Art was working on, and that he thinks Cooper is part of the gambling ring. Lt. Ristelli calls and tells Johnny that the name in the safe deposit box was Cooper. Johnny tells the clerk to call the sheriff. The clerk tells Johnny that he had taken a drink to Cooper at 10:40 the previous night, and had talked to him for fifteen minutes, so Cooper could not have killed Art Wesley. Johnny talks to the clerk again and he remembers that Cooper had called for a drink at 10:40, and that he had gotten back to the desk at 10:55. Johnny gets a call from the sheriff, who tells him that the other man has been found, but he is not the right man.

Johnny drives to Art Wesley's place and reviews the facts, including the hole in the roof and the sugar bowl. Suddenly Johnny has the solution.

Johnny drives back to the lodge and goes to Cooper's room, where he finds a picture out of place. Behind it Johnny finds what he is looking for. Johnny finds Cooper on the porch and sits down at his table. Johnny tells him that he is the man Art Wesley was looking for. Cooper recounts his alibi about the time and Johnny tells him that Art was not killed at his lodge. Johnny tells Cooper that he killed Art in his room, called the clerk and talked to him, and then took the body to the lodge and planted it there. You remembered that the slug that killed Art hit the wall, so you fired one into the ceiling to make it look like the killing took place there. Johnny tells Cooper about the sugar in the cabin, and how it was not crusty, but dry. The hole was made after the rain had stopped, and Johnny tells Cooper that he has found the hole in the wall of his room. Cooper tells him that he has Johnny covered with a gun under the table, and Johnny tells him the same thing. Cooper tries to run, but Johnny stops him and Cooper discovers that Johnny does not have a gun. "A big time gambler bluffed right out of the game. Cooper you're slipping."

Remarks. Cooper is awaiting trial. About Art Wesley, well I guess that sugar bowl was a dead man's revenge. Come to think of it, that revenge was pretty sweet.

## NOTES:

- THIS PROGRAM IS THE BEGINNING OF THE NEW SERIES OF 30-MINUTE PROGRAMS.

- THE NEXT PROGRAM IS ANNOUNCED TO BE ABOUT NEW ORLEANS, BUT THE NEXT AIRED PROGRAM, THE MARKHAM MATTER, TAKES PLACE IN SAN FRANCISCO
- DAN CUBBERLY IS THE ANNOUNCER.
- MUSIC SUPERVISION IS BY AMERIGO MARINO

| | | | |
|---|---|---|---|
| **Producer:** | Jack Johnstone | **Writers:** | Robert Ryf |
| **Cast:** | Virginia Gregg, Russell Thorson, Barney Phillips, Stacy Harris, Larry Thor, Parley Baer, Les Tremayne | | |

◆   ❖   ◆

**SHOW:** THE MARKHAM MATTER
**SHOW DATE:** 11/18/1956
**COMPANY:** WESTERN LIFE & TRUST COMPANY
**AGENT:** ED PORTER
**EXP. ACCT:** $968.20

**SYNOPSIS:** Mr. Porter returns Johnny's call, and Johnny would like to see him. Johnny tells Porter that he is always in a rush when he thinks someone is gypping us out of $100,000.

Johnny travels to San Francisco, California and gets a room at the St. Francis Hotel. Johnny walks to Ed Porter's office where Ed is nervous. Johnny asks Ed about Floyd Markham, who is the husband of Mrs. Markham. Mrs. Markham is wealthy and the husband is an industrial engineer who depends on her for money. Johnny shows Ed two checks for $50,000, payment for two endowment policies. Johnny tells Ed that Mrs. Markham's payment history is up to date, but why she would forget about a third policy for $50,000? Johnny tells Ed that Floyd had called the company and told them that he was calling for Mrs. Markham. Ed tells Johnny that they have a strange relationship, and each spends their own money. Ed tells Johnny that when he called to deliver the first check, Mrs. Markham was ill, and the second time she had just stepped out, and the check was given to Floyd. Ed has not seen Mrs. Markham since last spring.

Johnny checks with the bank, and since June the deposit slips were initialed by Floyd Markham and no unusual withdrawals had been made. Johnny checks with a hairdresser, and a car mechanic, but Mrs. Markham has not been there for months. Johnny also learns that Floyd had called to resign Mrs. Markham from the bridge club. Johnny calls the residence three times and gets a different reason each for Mrs. Markham not being there. Johnny visits Floyd's business address and tells the receptionist, Iris Bidler, that he is Steven B. Harris with the Cleveland Pump Company. Iris tells Johnny that Mr. Markham has not been in the office for 6 months.

Johnny goes to the Markham house on Fioradella Street in Ed Porter's car. Floyd answers the door and Johnny asks for Mrs. Markham. Johnny tells Floyd that he has a check for the third policy. Floyd tells him he will take it but Johnny tells him that he has to deliver it personally. Floyd tells Johnny that Mrs. Markham is ill with severe anemia. Reluctantly Floyd goes to see Mrs. Markham and Johnny notes his rich clothes. Johnny is directed to the room where Mrs. Markham is sitting by the window with a glazed look in her eyes. She asks how Mr. Porter is and asks Johnny not to tell Porter that she is ill, as she does not want to worry her friends. She is insistent that she wants some sherry, but Floyd tells her it is against her doctor's orders. Mrs. Markham tries to tell Johnny something but is too tired. Johnny calls Ed to confirm a description of Mrs. Markham, and tells him that Floyd is slowly killing her.

Johnny picks up Ed, and on the way to the Markham house tells him that Floyd is forcing his wife to sign money over to him and about her plea for some sherry so that she could be alone with Johnny. Johnny sees Iris drive up in a Cadillac and then leave with Floyd. Johnny tells Ed to be an investigator and follow her. Johnny walks to the house and makes sure that no one is there and enters the house. In her room, Johnny sees Mrs. Markham on a couch "doped to the ears." Johnny tells her that he is going to take her out of there and she remembers Johnny and does not want her friends to know that she is ill, Floyd had told her to say exactly that. She begs Johnny not to fool her and to help her get out of there. Johnny carries her to his car and takes her to the St. Regis Emergency hospital and tells the interns what has happened.

Johnny drives back to the house and meets Ed who tells Johnny that they went straight to the Bank of America to deposit the check and then he followed them to Angelo's where they are eating dinner.

Johnny and Ed drive to Angelo's on Stoker Street where the Cadillac is still parked. When Iris and Floyd leave Johnny follows them to a bar where he and Ed wait for 2 hours. Then they follow Floyd to a dark hill where Johnny and Ed watch Floyd and Iris necking. They then follow Floyd back into town where he drops off Iris. Ed follows Floyd and Johnny goes in to talk with Iris. Johnny tells Iris who he really is, and invites himself in. He tells her that he has been investigating Floyd Markham, and that she will be in jail with him unless she has some information to give Johnny. She tells Johnny that Mrs. Markham is out of town divorcing him. They had planned to move to a country estate in England to live a quiet country life, and Floyd had told her that she could start packing tonight.

Johnny takes Iris back to the Markham house and meets Ed. Johnny rings the bell and tells Floyd that his wife is in a hospital, and that Iris is in a cab. Floyd asks Johnny why he did not come around next week and Johnny tells him that next week she could be dead. Floyd tells Johnny that is the way she should have been for 16 years—dead.

Remarks: This one will wind up in court. Mrs. Markham's charges will include attempted homicide, attempt to defraud, Attempt to . . . In the end it was his attempt to run away, and it did not work. It never works. Even if you get a way you find something new to run from.

## NOTES:

* THE INTERMISSION COMMERCIAL IS FOR JACK BENNY'S NEW SEASONAL RETURN PROGRAM.

- JOHNNY NOTES THAT HE CARRIES MRS. MARKHAM TO HIS CAR, BUT HE DOES NOT HAVE ONE, HE WAS USING ED PORTER'S CAR, AND ED IS FOLLOWING FLOYD. LATER HE TAKES IRIS TO THE MARKHAM HOUSE IN HIS CAR, BUT TELLS FLOYD THAT SHE IS IN A CAB.
- BOB BAILEY OFFERS A THANKSGIVING MESSAGE: "THANKS GIVING, NOW THERE IS A DAY THAT DESERVES CELEBRATION, AND HEARTFELT THANKS TO THE GOD WHO MADE US, FOR BEING ABLE TO LIVE IN THE MOST FREE, AND PEACEFUL AND BOUNTIFUL COUNTRY IN THE WORLD. AND YET, WHY WAIT FOR NEXT THURSDAY, OR ANY THANKSGIVING DAY? FOR AMERICAN'S, IT SEEMS TO ME THAT THANKSGIVING DAY SHOULD BE EVERY DAY. THINK ABOUT IT, WON'T YOU?"
- THE PREVIEW IS FOR NEW ORLEANS AGAIN THIS WEEK.
- ROY ROWAN IS THE ANNOUNCER
- MUSIC SUPERVISION IS BY AMERIGO MARINO

**Producer:** Jack Johnstone  **Writers:** John Dawson
**Cast:** Lois Corbett, Frank Nelson, Virginia Gregg, Bert Holland, Paula Winslowe, John Dehner

◆  ❖  ◆

**SHOW:** THE ROYAL STREET MATTER
**SHOW DATE:** 11/25/1956
**COMPANY:** PROVIDENTIAL FIRE & MARINE
**AGENT:** C. D. BINFORD
**EXP. ACCT:** $517.20

**SYNOPSIS:** Angy Orsatti calls Johnny, and Angy wants to go to Andre's for dinner while Johnny is in New Orleans. Johnny tells Angy that he is in town for an insurance claim for $16,000 that someone wants to turn down.

Johnny travels to New Orleans, Louisiana and gets a room at the Roosevelt Hotel, and calls Angie Orsatti, an old friend who really knows the French Quarter. Johnny arranges for dinner with Angy and then calls Mr. C. D. Binford, who issued the policy. Johnny meets with "CD" and learns that the fire was last Thursday night. The insured is Henry Dupas, and the $48,000 policy covers his antique shop on Royal Street and the policy was issued just three months ago. Dupas had always told CD that he did not have money for the policy, but suddenly he had money for the policy, in cash, shop improvements and a receptionist, a real good looker. An antique lamp fell over and caused the fire. Henry told the fire marshal that he was talking to a customer and the lamp fell over but Dupas has not told CD anything, and that is why he is riled. CD had stopped by and saw the damage, but Dupas did not even ask for a claim form. CD talked to the fire marshal and typed up the claim but Dupas refused to sign the claim and told CD to get out.

Johnny walks to Canal Street and goes to the Antique shop, which looks like all the others in the area. Johnny knocks and Dupas opens the door. Johnny tells

Dupas who he is and Dupas asks why "you people" are always bothering him. He tells Johnny to leave him alone. Johnny goes down the alley to the back of the store but cannot see anything.

Johnny has dinner with Angy, and Johnny asks what he knows about Dupas. Angy knows Dupas, and he has heard about the 24-25 year old blonde he is hanging with. Angy will try to find out who the blonde is for Johnny.

Johnny buys a flashlight and goes to the shop, where a small truck is parked in the back with a bunch of bananas in the back. A man comes out and yells at Johnny to stop. Dupas comes out and tells the man that "Dollar" is with the insurance company. The man tells Johnny that Dupas will have to do something to keep Johnny away, and he tells Johnny to leave.

Johnny goes back to the hotel and is called by Angy in the morning. Angy tells Johnny that everyone knows the girl, but no one has seen her since she started working for Dupas. Her name is Rose Ellen, and she used to be a dancer.

Johnny gets the address from Angy and goes to see the girl. When Johnny gets there another girl, May Garbo tells Johnny that Rose is not there and invites Johnny in. She tells Johnny that she and Rose moved in together, and complements Johnny on being so polite. May tells Johnny that Rose does not come home for days sometimes, and has not mentioned a fire. May last saw Rose last Thursday, but she never came home again.

May tells Johnny that Rose has never stayed out this long, and that Rose is going with a man she had never met. Johnny goes to CD's office and waits for him to come back. Johnny wonders if something happened that Dupas is trying to cover up. CD tells Johnny that Dupas had called and cancelled all of his policies to keep Johnny away, so now the case is over. Johnny has a Scotch with CD and Johnny tells CD that Dupas is still covered until he returns the policy, so he can still snoop around. CD tells Johnny that the customer in the shop was Andrew W. DeLong, so Johnny goes to visit him but Johnny discovers that there is no such person in the city. Johnny asks CD to check on Dupas, and they go to the bank to check up on Dupas. Johnny learns that Dupas has banked over $11,000 in the past month. Johnny goes to the hotel and gets a message from May to see her. Johnny goes to May's apartment and she tells Johnny that a man called and told May that Rose is ok, and that he would come by and pick up her clothes. The man came at 4:00, and his name is Grant, the man she was dating while dating "the old antique." All she could say was "Carl this, and Carl that." Johnny calls Angy and they rush to the antique shop. Johnny breaks down the front door and they go in to find Carl on the floor with stab wounds. Carl tells Johnny that Dupas is going to kill Rose because she found out what Dupas was smuggling in banana shipments. She has been taken to the old Spanish fortress on the Bayou Slidell only 10 minutes ago.

Angy gets his swamp buggy, and they head out to the fortress. At the fortress Angy beaches the boat and they see Rose in a doorway. Johnny and Angy go in and call for Rose, who answers and asks for Carl. Johnny tells her that Dupas tried to kill him and she comes out and tells Johnny that she was tied up on the night of the fire and that Dupas had told Carl to kill her, which is when the lamp fell over.

She tells Johnny that Dupas was smuggling small boxes of powder in the bananas. Dupas comes in and shots are fired. Johnny does not have his gun, so he uses a brick to bean Dupas.

Remarks: Well where he is going, Dupas wouldn't have any use for the insurance money anyway. Carl Grant turned state's evidence and clinched the smuggling charges against him. Because of that, Carl may get off easy. I hope so. He and Rose could make a very happy couple.

NOTES:

- THE MID-PROGRAM COMMERCIAL IS ABOUT THE NEED FOR VOLUNTEERS FOR THE GROUND OBSERVER CORPS
- THE FINAL COMMERCIAL IS A REPEAT ABOUT THE NEED FOR VOLUNTEERS FOR THE GROUND OBSERVER CORPS
- DAN CUBBERLY IS THE ANNOUNCER
- MUSIC SUPERVISION IS BY AMERIGO MARINO AND CARL FORTINA

**Producer:** Jack Johnstone      **Writers:** Charles B. Smith
**Cast:** Virginia Gregg, Forrest Lewis, Lou Merrill, Lawrence Dobkin, Frank Gerstle

◆ ❖ ◆

**SHOW:** THE BURNING CAR MATTER
**SHOW DATE:** 12/9/1956
**COMPANY:** TRI-STATE LIFE & CASUALTY INSURANCE COMPANY
**AGENT:** EARLE POORMAN
**EXP. ACCT:** $385.26

SYNOPSIS: Earle Poorman calls Johnny, but Johnny is adamant that he is going on vacation to get away from the cold weather in Hartford. Earle is insistent that Johnny comes to work on an arson case in Sarasota. Johnny tells Earle that he has had a rough year and has made reservations for Sarasota and can't do it . . . umm, where did you say your branch office was? Sarasota? Florida?

Johnny travels to Sarasota, Florida and the office of Earle Poorman. Earle tells Johnny that Mike (his wife, Gertrude) will want him to stay for dinner. Johnny notes that "poor man" is a misnomer for Earle as they drive out to his "shack" in his "jalopy," a brand new 1956 Cadillac.

The house is next to a quiet bayou, with a speedboat at the dock. The "big fat overbearing broad" Earle is married to is a cute petite blonde who gives Johnny a strange look. Mike, who is a former dancer, gets Johnny a Martin's VVO Scotch and soda, and Earle tells him that they will have to wait until Arnold Carr gets back. Carr runs the lumberyard business, and his brother Ed just shares the profits. The lumberyard in Orlando is the one that just burned, and a claim for $120,000 has been filed. Mike tells Johnny that Arnold is in Orlando straightening things out. Earle tells Johnny that he and Arnold suspect arson. There have been some other small fires in other yards, but no sign of arson has been found. Earle has never met Ed Carr, who lives in Orlando. Arnold Carr calls and tells Earle that it was arson tonight in Arcadia. The whole yard went up, and he has proof it was arson. "Do not come here, I will come to your place."

Johnny and Mike are suspicious that Arnold might be setting the fires. After a 30-minute wait and several calls to the Carr home, Arnold never shows up. Johnny, Mike and Earle drive to Carr's home and see him through the window. Johnny notes that Arnold looks enough like him to be his brother. When Carr does not answer the door, Johnny looks again and Johnny sees that Arnold is dead. Johnny breaks down the door to find Arnold Carr shot in the forehead.

Earl calls the police and Johnny looks the place over. The police arrive and Johnny tells them what had happened. The policeman finds a bullet hole in the window and he tells Johnny that he does not need his help and tells them to leave.

Johnny, Earle and Mike leave and Johnny tells Earle that he had seen the hole in the window, but the shot came from inside the house, to make is look like it came from outside. Someone was trying to keep Arnold from talking. Earle confirms that Ed Carr will inherit the business and Johnny borrows a car from Earle and drives to Arcadia.

At the scene of the fire, Johnny trips over an old man sobbing over losing a part of his life. He had helped build up that business. He and Arnie had found a fire last week, and that is why he came here tonight. Arnie had seen a white car pulling away and said, "I knew that he would be involved." The car was a big Buick and Arnie told him not to tell anyone. Johnny tells the man that Arnold is dead, and the man tells Johnny that he knows him, and that Johnny was responsible for setting the fires, and the old man shoots at Johnny. Johnny slaps the old man and takes his gun. The old man, the police officer and Johnny all see a family likeness to Carr.

Johnny goes to see Lt. Harkness in Orlando, who wants to tell Johnny that his brother is dead. Lt. Harkness suddenly sees the difference. Johnny tells him that Ed Carr is the firebug, and a killer. Lt. Harkness puts out an APB for Carr, and Johnny drives to Ed's house. Johnny learns from Mrs. Harper, a neighbor, that Ed has parties and girls visit there. Johnny learns that Ed drives a white car. Mrs. Harper tells Johnny about a blonde who keeps coming into the house and drives a white car. She dresses like some showgirl. She comes from Sarasota based on the license plate and has green eyes. Johnny realizes that the description is that of Mike Poorman. Johnny calls Earl, and he tells Johnny that Mike is out. She was talking to Betty, they did a sister act, and was gone when Earle came down for breakfast.

Johnny drives back to Ed Carr's house and enters via the backdoor. Johnny suddenly feels a gun in his back and a voice telling Johnny that he owes him $5,000, and Johnny is slugged. Johnny wakes up later that night as a woman runs up to Johnny and tells him that Tony hit him for not paying for the Arcadia job. She tells "Eddie" that she was trying to raise money to pay Tony, and wonders why he is there. She tells Johnny that he had to kill Arnold. Johnny calls her Mike and turns on the light, at which time neither is who they think the other is. Ed Carr arrives and takes Johnny's gun. The girl tells Ed that Mike had told her that Johnny was coming up there. Ed tells her that he has to get rid of her and Johnny. He is going to call Tony Ricardo and get him to the house. Then he will call the police and kill all of them just before they get there, and blame it all on Tony by using Johnny's gun. Ed shoots Betty and Lt. Harness walks in and shoots Ed. Mike Poorman comes in and tells Johnny that she had come alone and brought Lt. Harkness there. She knew that Betty and Ed were going together and had not told Earl. Johnny and Mike drive back to Sarasota.

Remarks: Betty of course has already paid for her part in the deal. And I guess it is pretty obvious what will happen to Ed Carr and Tony Ricardo. The insurance money and the Carr estate will be distributed according to Florida law. Further remarks: The apparent friction between Earle and Mike was only part of a normal married life. They are really a pretty nice pair. Oh, and I thoroughly enjoyed three days of fishing in the Gulf, thanks to Earl.

NOTES:
- THIS IS THE FIRST APPEARANCE OF EARLE AND MIKE POORMAN, WHO END UP BECOMING CLOSE FRIENDS OF JOHNNY'S.
- THE MID-PROGRAM COMMERCIAL IS FOR THE PROGRAM JUKEBOX JURY
- THE CLOSING COMMERCIAL IS FOR THE UNITED COMMUNITY CAMPAIGNS
- DAN CUBBERLY IS THE ANNOUNCER.
- MUSIC SUPERVISION IS BY AMERIGO MARINO

**Producer:** Jack Johnstone      **Writers:** Jack Johnstone
**Cast:** Virginia Gregg, Parley Baer, Victor Perrin, Bob Bruce, Harry Bartell, Vivi Janis, Tony Barrett, Junius Matthews

◆　❖　◆

**SHOW:** THE RASMUSSEN MATTER
**SHOW DATE:** 12/16/1956
**COMPANY:** UNIVERSAL ADJUSTMENT BUREAU
**AGENT:**
**EXP. ACCT:** $1,965.00

**SYNOPSIS:** Hardy returns Johnny's call to Mr. Ellis Rasmussen. Johnny instructs Hardy to tell Mr. Rasmussen that he is investigating a matter concerning a member of his own family. Hardy tells Johnny that Mr. Rasmussen will send a car at 6:00.

Johnny travels to Los Angeles, California and is stonewalled on the case after three days. At 6:00 the chauffeur, Stouffer, arrives for Johnny at his hotel and drives him to the Rasmussen home. Hardy meets Johnny at the door and takes him to see Mr. Rasmussen. Mr. Rasmussen asks Hardy for 4 fingers of sour mash and gets Johnny the same. Johnny tells Mr. Rasmussen about the blanket policies issued on his son by Imperial Rubber. Johnny tells Mr. Rasmussen he is looking for the widow. Mr. Rasmussen does not know where the widow is, as he has never met her. Johnny is told that his son married her in Elko, Nevada one night and then left for Malaya. The rubber plantation was raided, and now he does not have a son. The widow has never contacted him, and he wants to see her. He lost the best son a man ever had. Johnny stays for dinner and hears the story of Ellis Rasmussen and of his son. On the way out Hardy tells Johnny that everyone wants to meet Mrs. Rasmussen, and they hope he finds her. On the way to the car, Johnny asks Stouffer if Mr. Rasmussen approved of Fred's marriage. Stouffer tells Johnny that Mr. Rasmussen approved of Fred, and if he loved the girl, that was enough. They were real people.

Johnny wires Imperial Rubber for information and calls the San Francisco agent to learn that the widow arrived in San Francisco and has disappeared.

Johnny rents a car and makes a number of stops to get information on Laura Olsen Rasmussen. Johnny receives the folder from Imperial Rubber, and now has a picture to go on now.

Johnny visits a boarding house and meets her mother. She does not know where Laura is, and she has not been here for 5 years. Johnny receives a list of passengers from the flight and tracks down a Mr. Oberland who traveled with Laura Rasmussen. He remembers her; she was pretty chummy on the flight, and had not mentioned the death of her husband.

Johnny is called by Hardy, and Johnny is told that Mr. Rasmussen is dying and they want Johnny to see him. Johnny is afraid to tell him that so far all he knows is that his daughter-in-law is a big fat bum!

Johnny arrives at the Rasmussen house and the family doctor is there. Johnny talks with Mr. Rasmussen and updates him. Mr. Rasmussen tells Johnny to level with him and tell him what he has found. Johnny tells him that they will find her. Mr. Rasmussen tells Johnny that he wants to see her.

Johnny receives a call from officer Dailey of the police, and they have Mrs. Rasmussen in the drunk tank. Johnny goes to see officer Dailey and tells him that he has a check for Mr. Rasmussen. Johnny makes bail for her and Officer Dailey shows Johnny her file, full of petty thefts and aliases. Johnny wires the other agents working on the case and tells them to halt their activities. Johnny meets Laura and tells her he got her out of jail for a friend. Johnny buys her coffee and tries to find out about her life since she left Malaya. She tells Johnny that she did not call her father-in-law because she felt that she meant nothing to him. Johnny tells her about the check and takes her to his room to fill out the paperwork. Stouffer calls and Johnny tells him that he has found nothing, and Mr. Rasmussen is waiting for him. Johnny gives her the check and she leaves.

Johnny checks out and waits in the hotel lobby. Laura Rasmussen spots Johnny, and tells him that she read that Mr. Rasmussen is dying. She tells Johnny that she wants to meet Fred's father and Johnny berates her for waiting. She tells Johnny that she loved Fred, and had met him at a cocktail lounge. He loved her with no questions asked. She told him of her past, but that did not matter to Fred. They went to Malaya and she learned what it was like to be loved, and then he was killed. She had gone to the Rasmussen house, but was afraid to go in, given her past. She still has her memories of Fred, and cannot drink that away. Johnny starts to leave and Stouffer arrives. Johnny introduces him to Mrs. Rasmussen, and he is mighty glad to meet her. On the way out to the house, Laura seems to change. At the house, she meets Hardy, who is happy to meet her. Upstairs Johnny introduces her to Mr. Rasmussen. He calls her to his side, holds her as she cries and tells her that there is nothing that she has to tell him. She is his daughter, and that is all that needs to be said. Mr. Rasmussen calls for brandy and sour mash.

Remarks: The old man has a few weeks more. Laura is moving into the house with him, to take care of him. She will not be telling him some things about herself; she does not have to. You should have stood there and seen that big arm go around her shoulder when he said 'you are my daughter.' Yeah.

**NOTES:**

- THIS IS PROBABLY ONE OF, IF NOT THE MOST TOUCHING AND HEART WRENCHING OF ALL THE JOHNNY DOLLAR STORIES.
- THE MID-PROGRAM COMMERCIAL IS FOR CBS NEWS.
- THE FINAL COMMERCIAL IS ABOUT THE BENEFITS OF THE LETTERS ABROAD PROGRAM
- DAN CUBBERLY IS THE ANNOUNCER.
- MUSIC SUPERVISION IS BY AMERIGO MARINO

| | | | |
|---|---|---|---|
| **Producer:** | Jack Johnstone | **Writers:** | John Dawson |
| **Cast:** | Virginia Gregg, Jean Tatum, Eric Snowden, Roy Glenn, Will Wright, Frank Nelson, Jack Kruschen | | |

| | |
|---|---|
| **SHOW:** | THE MISSING MOUSE MATTER |
| **SHOW DATE:** | 12/23/1956 |
| **COMPANY:** | FLOYDS OF ENGLAND |
| **AGENT:** | GEORGE REED |
| **EXP. ACCT:** | $38.20 |

**SYNOPSIS:** George Reed calls Johnny and asks if Johnny has heard of Jodiah Gillis, the man who owns most of Rhode Island. George had written a special policy written on an object that has disappeared. George hopes that Johnny is sitting down, as the insured object is a mouse. What!?!

Johnny cabs to George Reed's office, and George is concerned about the policy, which is for "one unusually talented grayish brown mouse." Floyds will insure almost anything, and would not have issued the policy except that Gillis has all of his insurance through Floyds. The mouse belongs to a man named Glaser, who is staying with him. The mouse is insured for $5,000. Gillis called last night and asked for the best investigator to be sent out. Gillis threatened to cancel his policies unless Johnny is sent out. George tells Johnny that he can write his own ticket on this case.

Johnny travels to the Gillis estate in Providence, Rhode Island. Johnny is met at the door by a tall, beautiful girl who is expecting him. She is Marian, Mr. Gillis' daughter. Johnny is taken in to Mr. Gillis who is happy to see him. Bert Glaser is there; he is the Bert in "Bert and his Pals," a dog act. Gillis tells Johnny that the mouse has been kidnapped, and they know who did it. Bert tells Johnny that Gulliver is worth at least $50,000 because he can sing; he can carry a tune. Johnny is doubtful, but Bert tells Johnny that it is a scientific fact that mice can sing, but Gulliver is a basso, so people can hear him. Bert and Jodiah take Johnny to a playroom where a cage contains two small mice, Hectaba and Ezmirelda. They can sing also, but not as well as Gulliver. Bert tells them to sing "over the waves," and they sing. Johnny is still unconvinced. Back in the library Johnny liberally samples the eggnog and learns that Harry McQueen has taken Gulliver. McQueen used to be Bert's agent, and has been here poking around, and was there long enough to take the mouse. Some children were there for the rehearsal for Bert's program, and McQueen could have taken him. McQueen was kicked out, and that is when the mouse was discovered missing.

Johnny calls George Reed, and asks him to find McQueen's home phone number. While Johnny is on the phone, he tells George that there is a big yellow cat there with a grayish brown mouse between his front paws.

Johnny manages to get the mouse away from the cat just as Marion walks in. She tells Johnny that Rama the cat was out during rehearsal so the corpse could be Gulliver. Johnny promises not to say anything until after Christmas.

The next morning Johnny has breakfast and gets a call from Harry McQueen, and Johnny asks him about a missing mouse. McQueen tells Johnny that he has taken towels from hotels, but he has never taken a mouse. McQueen tells Johnny that he was there to see Gillis about putting some of his people on the Christmas show. McQueen vowed a long time ago never to handle children, belly dancers or animals. McQueen also tells Johnny that Bert Glaser does not have a dog act, but is a topnotch ventriloquist. Johnny goes out for a walk and thinks that Bert is running a con when he is hit by a snowball thrown by Marian. Johnny tells her that Rama probably got an ordinary mouse. Marian sees a boy on the front porch. When she calls to him he runs away.

Johnny looks through the house and finds a leg clamp. The doorbell rings, and the boy is back. He had been there to see the show and Johnny asks him in. Bobby is almost eleven and is not impressed with all this Christmas stuff, especially the presents. He and his mom get along ok without all the gifts. Bobby had followed a dog to the Gillis house and was invited in to see the show. He cannot have any pets where he is living now. Bobby tells Johnny that he had taken the mouse from the cage, and decided to give the mouse back. Johnny tells him that Bobby has to give the mouse back himself.

Johnny, Marian and Bobby cab to the Children's Hospital and Bobby gives the mouse back to Jodiah. Johnny asks Bert if Gulliver will sing, and Johnny tells him that he never sang for Bobby. Bert tells him that he did not sing because he was never asked to. Bert goes on stage with Gulliver. Bert leaves Gulliver on stage alone, and Gulliver sings Jingle Bells.

Bert tells Johnny that he would not believe that mice could really sing if Johnny knew Bert was a ventriloquist.

As for my separate and additional fee, as agreed upon before I took this matter, well there is a boy names Bobby Nees who lives on Skully Avenue over in Providence, see that he gets it.

NOTES:

- BOB BAILEY TELLS DAN CUBBERLY THAT "I JUST DO NOT WANT TO PASS UP THE OPPORTUNITY TO DO TWO THINGS. FIRST, WELL, PAM AND ERIC AND FRAN, MR. AND MRS. FROLICH, HELEN WILLS, SCOTTY, OH ALL THE REST OF YOU NICE PEOPLE WHO HAVE WRITTEN IN TO TELL US HOW MUCH YOU LIKE THE PROGRAM. THANKS. I REALLY APPRECIATE HEARING FROM YOU, AND BELIEVE ME, I WILL ANSWER YOUR LETTERS AS SOON AS I CAN. SECOND, WELL, I AM SURE THAT YOU KNOW WHAT THIS IS, AND I WANT YOU TO KNOW THAT IS COMES FROM THE HEART. MERRY CHRISTMAS TO YOU. GOD BLESS."
- THE MID-PROGRAM COMMERCIAL IS FOR THE ROBERT Q. LEWIS PROGRAM.
- DAN CUBBERLY IS THE ANNOUNCER.
- MUSIC SUPERVISION IS BY AMERIGO MARINO

Producer:   Jack Johnstone          Writers:   Charles B. Smith
Cast:       Mary Jane Croft, Howard McNear, Parley Baer, G. Stanley
            Jones, Bill James, Lawrence Dobkin, Richard Beals

◆   ❖   ◆

SHOW:           THE SQUARED CIRCLE MATTER
SHOW DATE:      12/30/1956
COMPANY:        EASTERN ALLIED CASUALTY INSURANCE COMPANY
AGENT:          PAUL KENDRICK
EXP. ACCT:      $491.20

SYNOPSIS: Paul Kendrick calls and Johnny asks if he has seen any good fights lately. Paul asks if Johnny remembers Al Coronado, and Johnny tells Paul that he lost $20 on Coronado. Paul tells Johnny to come over as Eastern may lose $50,000 on him.

Johnny cabs to Paul Kendick's office and finds him pacing the floor in his cubicle worried about murder. Paul recounts how he and Johnny had followed the career of Al Coronado, and how Al used to have the quickest reflexes around. There is something wrong now. His manager took out an annuity for $50,000 and is trying to kill him. Paul wants Johnny to go to Joplin and watch Coronado fight. Paul has a hunch and wants somebody who knows Al to watch him.

Johnny travels to Joplin, Missouri and picks up a copy of the policy. Johnny then calls Paul and tells him that Ricky Malone had taken out the policy and paid the premiums, but the beneficiary is Frankie Fortina. Paul has been looking for

Fortina, but cannot find him. Johnny naps and then goes to the arena in Mt. Elba to watch the fight. The opponent in the main fight was a rank amateur. Frankie looked normal at first, but then Johnny noticed that Al was not connecting with his punches and Al almost misses his stool at the end of the round. Al goes down for the count after a slight slap on the face and is hurried out of the arena. Johnny goes to the dressing room and Ricky Malone the manager will not let Johnny in to see Al. Johnny forces his way in and slugs Malone. Johnny talks to Al and realizes that Al is not well. Johnny tries to take him out and is slugged by Malone.

When Johnny comes to, the room is empty and Johnny goes to his hotel to call Paul. Johnny tells Paul that Al must have some sort of brain injury and that Malone is forcing him to fight. Paul has a rundown on Fortina, and he owns Al Coronado. Al has not done well lately, and the only way Frankie will make any money is to kill him off. Johnny goes to police headquarters and Sgt. Danny Ruskin tells Johnny that Malone and Al checked out this morning and flew to Monterrey, Mexico. Danny tells Johnny to look up Sgt. Romilio Garcia when he gets there, and to mention his name. Johnny flies to Mexico via El Paso and goes to the Policia, but Garcia is not there, he is at the fights. Johnny goes to the arena and has Garcia paged. Sgt. Garcia is upset at being taken away from the fights, but when Johnny mentions Danny, Sgt. Garcia changes his attitude and tells Johnny that Al Coronado is fighting tomorrow and he will lose. The opponent is "El Toro Negro" who weights 240 lbs. against Al Coronado's 181. El Toro is a killer and has thrown three men out of the ring. Johnny tells Sgt. Garcia about the last fight and who he is. Sgt. Garcia agrees to help Johnny find Al. Johnny goes to his hotel and discovers that he is right next door to Al. Johnny talks to Al and he tells Johnny that he has insurance, and will retire soon. Johnny notices a bottle of aspirin, and Al tells Johnny that he has been having headaches lately. Johnny tells Al that he has a brain injury and will get killed if he gets hit. Johnny calls Sgt. Garcia and tells him to bring a doctor to the hotel. Frankie Fortina comes in with Ricky and tells Johnny to hang up. Malone had called him in Joplin and they have checked up on Johnny. Frankie tells Johnny that he will be dead before Sgt. Garcia gets there. Frankie tells Johnny that he has never been in Mexico, as his tourist card has a different name on it. Frankie tells Malone that Johnny has to have an accident, and that he has been stalling with Al. Frankie tells Malone that he will be taken care of after he takes care of Johnny. Frankie tells Malone that he is to kill Al as well. The scene will look like a fight and all three will be killed. Malone agrees to kill Johnny and Johnny fights with him until Malone goes out the window. Johnny goes after Fortina, but Al had hit him with a clean left hook. Sgt. Garcia comes in and he wonders why Johnny thinks Al Coronado has lost his punch.

Johnny recommends that the company make some adjustment to the policy so that Al Coronado can start collecting immediately, as they never should have issued the policy.

NOTES:
- INCIDENTALS INCLUDED A SPORT SHIRT LOUD ENOUGH TO STARTLE THE ENTIRE STATE OF ARIZONA, RAZOR BLADES AND A NEW TOOTHBRUSH, AND $3 FOR FLOWERS FOR THE STEWARDESS WHO FOUND HIM A BOTTLE OF CHAMPAGNE. NOT VERY EGREGIOUS BY MY ACCOUNT.
- JOHNNY MAKES REFERENCE TO PAUL WORKING IN A CUBICLE. THAT IS KIND OF DILBERTESQUE!
- DAN CUBBERLY IS THE ANNOUNCER.
- MUSIC SUPERVISION IS BY AMERIGO MARINO

Producer:   Jack Johnstone          Writers:   Jack Johnstone
Cast:       Harry Bartell, Herb Ellis, Victor Perrin, Jack Kruschen, Les Tremayne, Lawrence Dobkin

◆   ❖   ◆

SHOW:        THE ELLEN DEAR MATTER
SHOW DATE:   1/6/1957
COMPANY:     WESTERN MARITIME & PROPERTY
AGENT:       ARTHUR ARTHUR
EXP. ACCT:   $453.95

SYNOPSIS: Pat McCracken calls about the sleek lovely Ellen Dear. She is loaded with $325,000 in jewels. Johnny is interested until he finds out that she is a boat. Pat wants Johnny to find out what is going on.

Johnny cabs to Pat's office and Pat is not smiling. Johnny is to bill Western Maritime and Property. Pat tells Johnny about Randolph Berman, who everyone thinks is a crook, but seems to handle some of the finest jewels in the world. He is involved with the Betanhouse collection out of Hungary. A man in Mexico sold the collection to Berman. The boat is a 72-foot motor cruiser and was Berman was sailing in the pacific. When Berman heard about the jewels, he bought them. He had Western Maritime insure the jewels after he had them appraised by a gemologist named Jacques Giampiere in Guadalajara. So far there is no problem, but there have been incidents in the past, but Berman got out of them. Western is worried and Johnny is to watch the jewels until they get to the states. The boat is in Mazatlan undergoing some engine work.

Johnny flies to Los Angeles, California where he is paged in the airport. Johnny goes to the PanAm desk and meets Arthur Arthur, the local Western Maritime agent, and Jacques Giampiere who had appraised the Betanhouse collection in Mexico. Giampiere has bad news. He had tried to buy pieces of the collection, and knows all of the stones. While in Mexico Giampiere watched a friend, Garcia Hernandez, work on a mount for a stone from the Betanhouse collection, the Calabar diamond. He is sure of the identity of the stone. Arthur thinks that maybe the jewels are not on the boat. Berman is now on his way to Los Angeles, but Arthur is not sure where he will dock. Johnny and Arthur drive to Berman's office and Johnny notices a vault in the wall of the office. Johnny meets Mr. Carrillo and he gives Arthur a revision to the policy to exclude the Calabar Diamond, which has been sold. Carrillo tells Johnny that the boat is due in San Pedro tonight, and Johnny arranges to go with Carrillo to meet the boat. The phone rings and Carrillo learns that the Ellen Dear has sunk in 600 feet of water.

Johnny cabs to Coast Guard headquarters and meets Capt. Barney Thorson. Capt. Thorson tells Johnny that the passengers have been rescued and brought in to the Coast Guard. They had received a call and the boat was sinking when they got there. The engine was too big and had broken loose and destroyed the boat. There was a big safe on board and the owner was crying like a baby over the loss. The only thing Berman saved was two hats, a fishing rod, some nylons and a hatbox. Johnny is told that the Berman's are staying at the Beverly Wilshire hotel.

Johnny calls the police in Mazatlan to make sure the jewels were on board when they left. Johnny then cabs back to Berman's office and the Bermans have not been there, but they are due in soon, and have asked for claim forms to be brought in. Johnny gets a wild idea about something that happened when the Andrea Doria sank; the passengers were brought in without going through customs. Johnny wonders that if he could think of it, maybe Berman could too. Johnny calls Capt. Thorson who tells Johnny that the Berman's did not go through customs. Johnny calls Arthur and tells him to get to Berman's office to make sure that Berman does not bring in the jewels; and to keep him there as long a possible. Johnny goes to the hotel and watches Berman leave, and then goes to his suite on the 9th floor. Vy Berman opens the door, and she tells Johnny to leave, as Randy does not want anyone in the apartment. Johnny tells her that Garcia Hernandez sent him and she lets Johnny in. Johnny tells her that Randy had sold Hernandez the wrong stone, and she tells Johnny that Randy gave Hernandez the diamond so he could make a legitimate change to the policy. Johnny tells her that he has to switch the diamonds when Randy gets there. Johnny tells her about the other diamonds in the hatbox and she asks if Randy read about the Andrea Doria too. Vy starts to wise up and Johnny forces his way into the apartment to search it, and threatens to call the police if she continues to scream. Vy tells Johnny the jewels are in the closet and Johnny gets them. There is a knock at the door and Berman tells Vy to open it. Johnny opens the door and tells Berman who he is and why he is there. Berman pulls a gun and threatens to kill Johnny and Vy, "that dizzy blonde." Vy runs out with a bottle and hits Berman with it as he tries to shoot her.

By way of getting off as easily as possible, Vy sang like a canary and incidentally cleared up a couple of other of his shady deals. Result, by the time his prison sentence runs out, he'll be too long dead to collect the insurance on his yacht.

NOTES:

- THE STAR OF CAPETOWN DIAMOND AND KAMANDU EMERALD ARE MENTIONED IN THE STORY. THE STAR OF CAPETOWN WAS FEATURED IN A FIVE PART SERIES THE PREVIOUS YEAR.

- The mid-program commercial is an **AFRS** spot about the economies of democratic countries.
- **$245** was spent for a couple of days of relaxation in the California sun. Now that is padding the expense account!
- The Andrea Doria was an Italian ocean liner built in Genoa and launched in 1951. On Wednesday, July 25th 1956 she collided with the MV Stockholm near Nantucket, Massachusetts and 46 passengers and 5 crewmen were killed.
- Dan Cubberly is the announcer.
- Music supervision is by Amerigo Marino

Producer:    Jack Johnstone      Writers:    Jack Johnstone
Cast:        Virginia Gregg, Lawrence Dobkin, Howard McNear, Jay Novello, Jack Edwards, Barney Phillips, Raymond Burr

SHOW:          The Desalles Matter
SHOW DATE:     1/13/1957
COMPANY:       Continental Insurance & Trust Company
AGENT:         Hillary Fukes
EXP. ACCT:      $416.00

SYNOPSIS: Hillary Fukes calls Johnny and asks how his time is? Hillary has a claim for a $100,000 straight life policy he wants investigated. He is afraid that they will be taken this time.

Johnny notes that everyone has heard of Dave Desalles, the industrialist. Johnny meets with Hillary Fukes in his office and has two drinks with Hillary who tells Johnny that he is not going to give $100,000 to anyone. Desalles drowned four days ago on the west coast. The policy is designed for people with big money who look at it for the accident double indemnity features. Desalles bought one of these policies three months ago and now he is dead. Hillary is not sure that it was an accident, and the widow has filed a claim. The inquest in San Media was inconclusive, as was the police investigation. Bert Kenyon was assigned to the case and has recommended paying the claim. Johnny is to go out and reinvestigate the accident.

Johnny flies to Los Angeles, California and meets Bert in the airport. Johnny muses over having worked with Bert before on the San Antonio case in New Orleans, and how he seems nervous now. Bert and Johnny drive to the hotel and Johnny tells Bert that Hillary does not like the report he submitted. Bert tells Johnny that the widow is worth $8 million, and that Desalles had bought the policy at the racetrack because his agent had given him a tip on a horse. Bert is insistent that the widow does not need the money and is nervous about why Johnny was sent out to help him.

Johnny gets a room in San Medio, and goes over the reports and meets with Mrs. Desalles who tells Johnny that she and her husband were on their boat having drinks with friends, and Dave had gone up for some air. A Mr. Burke came looking for Dave, was told he was on the deck. They went up to find Dave's hat floating in the water. They looked around and found Dave's body in the water. They tried artificial respiration, but to no avail.

Back in his room, Johnny is visited by Bert while reading the reports and Johnny tells Bert that the wife had help killing Desalles, as Desalles was an ex channel swimmer and could have easily made it to shore. And why did he not yell? And suppose that the bruises on his head were there before he was in the water. Johnny suggests getting and exhumation and Bert tells Johnny that Mrs. Desalles offered him the $100,000 to let the case go. Bert tells Johnny that Desalles means nothing to them, and Bert offers to split the money with Johnny. Bert pulls his gun and slugs Johnny. Johnny tries to get up but can only watch Bert leave before he faints.

Johnny slowly wakes up and thinks about Bert and how there is no way that he will collect the money. There is a knock at the door and two men are there. One is named Blair and the other is Sgt. LaFreeda. They ask Johnny why he is in town and if the has a license for his gun. Johnny tells him who he is and about the case he is working on. They ask where Bert is and Johnny tells them that he had last seen Bert last a couple hours ago. Blair asks Johnny what is new on the case? They think that Johnny is there because there is something new on the case. They tell Johnny that Bert is dead and they go to the site of Bert's killing. Blair asks a witness named Posey if he has ever seen Johnny, and he tells Blair that he has not, and then Blair and Johnny drive off. Blair tells Johnny that Posey heard shots and then saw Bert staggering in the road. Johnny tells Blair that he and Bert have not been friends for three hours.

Johnny buys coffee for Lt. George Blair who apologizes for being so hard on him in his room. Lt. Blair asks Johnny for help. He tells Johnny that his deputies are incompetent, and had messed up the crime scene by hitting Desalles head on the dock while they were recovering the body. Lt. Blair is sure that Desalles was murdered. The coroner runs a drug store and would tell you a man was dead for Scotch. Bert Kenyon's going along with the coroner's report confuses Lt. Blair. Johnny tells him that Bert had sold out and about the covered over reports which Johnny was sent out to look into.

Johnny and Lt. Blair drive to the Desalles home and tell the butler to tell Mrs. Desalles that the police are there. Sgt. LaFreeda is there and he is upset that Johnny is giving assistance in the case, so Lt. Blair sends him home. Lt. Blair gives Johnny his gun, and tells Johnny that Tom was the first one there on the night of the killing. Lt. Blair and Johnny walk into Mrs. Desalles bedroom to find her crying and beaten up. She tells them that Tom beat her and had helped her get rid of her husband. He beat her because he did not want her to talk to anyone. Tom comes back in and opens fire on Lt. Blair and Johnny, but Johnny gets him. Lt. Blair tells Johnny that he thinks that all the "knick knacks" of the Desalles home were an enticement to Tom.

Johnny calls Hillary and tells him of the events, buys flowers for Bert and has a drink with George Blair.

NOTES:
- THE PROGRAM I HAVE IS AN **AFRS** COPY AND IS VERY NOISY, AND SOME OF THE DETAIL IS HARD TO DECIPHER.
- THE MID-PROGRAM COMMERCIAL IS AN **AFRS** SPOT ABOUT THE ORIGINS OF DEMOCRACY.
- DAN CUBBERLY IS THE ANNOUNCER.
- MUSIC SUPERVISION IS BY AMERIGO MARINO

Producer:  Jack Johnstone          Writers:  John Dawson
Cast:      Virginia Gregg, Harry Bartell, John Stevenson, Will Wright, James McCallion, Ben Wright

◆   ❖   ◆

SHOW:        THE BLOOMING BLOSSOM MATTER
SHOW DATE:   1/20/1957
COMPANY:     INTER ALLIED INSURANCE COMPANY
AGENT:       PAUL BRANNON
EXP. ACCT:   $61.55

SYNOPSIS: Paul Brannon calls and tells Johnny that he has troubles. Alfred W. Winkler has disappeared with an emerald worth $100,000. Well? Sure.

Johnny cabs to Paul Brennan's office and is told that Winkler was a partner in a New York jewelry firm. They got a hold of a stone called the Green Eye of Calcutta, big enough to choke a horse. The stone is insured for $100,000 and Winkler is insured for $10,000. Winkler took the stone home to work on in preparation for a show in Chicago. His partner tried to call him on Sunday, but there was no answer. He went to the office but the stone and Winkler were not there. The police called him while he was there and they are looking for Winkler too. The apartment manager had called them after the maid found Winkler's apartment ransacked. Sgt. Randy Singer has been assigned to the case.

Johnny returns home to pack and is called by Rubert McKenworthy Blossom, who is pleased that he will be working with Johnny. Blossom follows all of Johnny's cases on the radio and the newspapers, and is Johnny's biggest fan. He is calling about Winkler and Blossom will be waiting for Johnny in New York at 875 East 73rd street.

Johnny travels to New York City and the brownstone home of Mr. Blossom who is expecting Johnny. The inside of the home is filled with Victorian furniture, old books and all sort of old junk; "you never can tell when you might need something," Johnny is told. Interspersed among the junk are priceless art works. Blossom tells Johnny that he bought them all at auction sales, he cannot resist a bargain. Blossom tells Johnny that he knows Winkler very well, and has seen him at his office. Blossom tells Johnny that he was going to go to an auction on Saturday, but did not feel well and stayed home. A friend sent him something from the auction that will solve the case for Johnny. The item is an old trunk. Blossom tells Johnny he wanted to call the police but called Johnny instead.

Johnny opens the trunk, finds a body inside, and calls Randy Singer. Randy arrives with the lab crew and interrogates Blossom to get the names of the friends who were going to the auction with him.

Johnny cabs to the apartment of Elwood Blueit, the partner of Winkler. Elwood tells Johnny that Winkler often took jewels home with him as he felt it was safer. Blueit tells Johnny that Mr. Blossom was in the office often looking at the jewelry, but he never bought any. Blossom was last there on Friday and insisted on seeing the emerald.

Johnny calls Randy and is told that nothing has turned up with Blossom's friends who went to the auction. Johnny tells Randy he is going to the Winkler house, and wants a picture of the trunk, and wants Blossom watched. Johnny goes to Winkler's apartment and the officer guarding the house tells Johnny that Randy is on the phone. Randy tells Johnny that someone has attacked Blossom and beaten him.

Johnny cabs to 18th Precinct headquarters and meets with Randy, who tells Johnny about Blossom getting beaten. Johnny gets the picture of the trunk and the names of the friends from Randy. Johnny wonders who killed Winkler and then shipped the body to Blossom. Johnny cabs to the offices of the railroad in New Jersey and talks to a Mr. McKinney about their auctions of unclaimed baggage. McKinney remembers the auction and Johnny shows him the names on the list, but none had been there. McKinney remembers selling the trunk to a man named Albert Winkler. Johnny cabs back to Randy's office and learns that the prints from Blossom's attack belong to a "Caro Berlesconi," who was in on a hijacking a couple years ago and drove the truck. He is being held, and Randy is sure that he killed Winkler and beat up Blossom. Johnny calls McKinney who gives a detailed description of the man he sold the trunk to. Johnny and Randy talk to Berlesconi, and they learn that he delivered a trunk for Winkler and gives him a description, but he never saw Blossom, and just left the trunk in the lobby. He heard about the missing stone and went back to Blossom's to look for the rock but was scared off by a prowl car. Johnny cabs back to Blossom and tells him that he can help him. Johnny reviews the facts with him, about the house full of junk and fine things, and that Johnny was told that Blossom would do anything to own the emerald. Blossom had reached the same conclusion. When Blossom learned that InterAllied was involved, it would be smart for the killer to bring Johnny in as a cover-up, wouldn't it? Johnny tells Blossom that the body was packed in old newspapers; the kind the house is full of. Johnny tells him that Winkler was a small man, but the man that bought the trunk and ordered it delivered had thick old-fashioned glasses and Blossom's build. Blossom goes to a box and gives Johnny the emerald. Blossom would have bought the stone if Winkler would have sold it at a bargain price.

Why? Just this overpowering passion to have things? Maybe, or maybe it was a reaction, a desperate attempt to some way, any way break from a lifetime of lonely, dull, drab loneliness. I dunno, and I'm sorry for, well, the funny little old character who turned killer."

NOTES:

- THE COPY OF THE PROGRAM THAT I HAVE HAS SOME SERIOUS TAPE DAMAGE AT THE END, AND MOST OF THE FINAL PART, INCLUDING THE EXPENSE ACCOUNT TOTAL, CAST AND CREW IS UNINTELLIGIBLE. THE CLOSING DETAILS WERE OBTAINED AT THE THOUSAND OAKS LIBRARY.
- THIS IS THE FIRST TIME WHERE PUBLICATION OF JOHNNY DOLLAR'S CASES IS MENTIONED.
- DAN CUBBERLY IS THE ANNOUNCER.
- MUSIC SUPERVISION IS BY AMERIGO MARINO

**Producer:** Jack Johnstone  **Writers:** Jack Johnstone
**Cast:** Howard McNear, Herb Vigran, Junius Matthews

◆ ❖ ◆

**SHOW:** THE MAD HATTER MATTER
**SHOW DATE:** 1/27/1957
**COMPANY:** FLOYDS OF ENGLAND
**AGENT:** GEORGE REED
**EXP. ACCT:** $870.40

**SYNOPSIS:** George Reed calls with a riddle and a blonde photographer's model. The model married the former owner of the Preen Hat Company, but she has disappeared. The riddle is whether Preen told the truth or not about her disappearance.

Johnny cabs to George Reed's office to find George reading a copy of Playmate magazine, where Mrs. Preen is the center attraction. George tells Johnny that Mrs. Preen had been a very successful model, but after she married Preen she retired. Johnny notices that the magazine is the current issue and assumes that the photo is an old one. George tells Johnny that Mr. Preen is twice her age and has a lot of money, and has been living near Los Angeles. Det. Steiner is handling the case, and Preen carries no life insurance on his wife, but her face is insured. She bought a policy while she was modeling and renewed it 10 days before she disappeared.

Johnny buys a copy of Playmate and goes home to pack. Johnny flies to Los Angeles, California and gets a room at the Statler. Johnny calls Det. Steiner and then drives to the Preen home. At the front door a knockout blonde nurse meets Johnny. She tells Johnny that Mr. Preen can see no one, as he is in shock and cannot be disturbed. Mr. Preen calls out and tells Johnny to come in and meet him in the orchid room. In the heat of the orchid room Preen tells Johnny that he is pollinating his plants. He has over two hundred different varieties. Preen is anxious that Johnny find his wife. Preen tells Johnny that he is not satisfied with the actions of the police, and will cooperate totally with Johnny. Preen tells Johnny that his wife disappeared 10 days ago after coming back from their home at Lake Arrowhead. Mr. Preen was in bed when she returned and later that night she was gone. A search of the house turned up nothing. She had said nothing about going out, but mentioned that she wanted to go back to Arrowhead the next day. Preen has no idea what happened to her. On the way out Johnny feels that something is wrong. Helen, the nurse, tells Johnny that the police feel that his wife's body is buried somewhere on the property. Helen hated the wife and feels that Mr. Preen was a kind man. She tells Johnny that Mrs. Preen would kill herself if anything happened to her face. Mrs. Preen has no friends, and Helen is sure that she is dead. She shows Johnny a set of plastic dental caps, and tells Johnny that Mrs. Preen would never leave the house without them. Helen had found them in the garage two days after she disappeared.

Johnny drives back to Los Angeles and suddenly realizes that he had not seen any pictures of Mrs. Preen in the house. Det. Steiner comes to Johnny's room and tells him that the case is sewed up. They have been checking up on Mrs. Preen, and she had been taking a lot of weekend trips. They figure she has a new man and disappeared with him and left her clothes at home because she was too proud to take anything from Preen. Johnny tells Steiner about the dental caps. Steiner shows him her dental records and tells Johnny that they are going to arrest Webster Preen for murder. Johnny calls Playmate Magazine and asks Mr. Howard about the picture of Bridget Randall Preen in the current issue. Howard tells Johnny that Russell Tracy, who lives in Lake Arrowhead, took the picture in the magazine. Johnny drives to Lake Arrowhead and asks the post office about Tracy's address, which turns out to be right next to the Preen house. Johnny drives to Tracy's house and meets Russell. Johnny asks about the picture in the magazine and Russell tells Johnny that all he did was take pictures of Bridget, and has no reason to kill her. When Johnny asks him why he thinks she is dead, Russell opens up and tells Johnny that Bridget loved to model, and when she found out that he was a photographer she was always visiting him. He had been in trouble with the law once and needed money. He had the picture of Bridget and sold it to the magazine without her knowledge. Other photographers called the house and Preen answered one of them. Preen wanted to get back at him and killed his wife and threw her body in an old well on his property. He moved the body before the police got there. Preen killed her because she loved Russell and was going to divorce Preen. Johnny tells Russell to bring his camera and film and they go to the gravesite. Johnny calls Los Angeles and then picks up Russell and they drive back to town. Johnny calls Helen and learns that Det. Steiner has arrested Preen, but he was released two hours later. Johnny tells her to stay there and keep out of the way; he is on his way over. Johnny drives to the Preen's house after leaving Russell with Det. Steiner. Helen offers to fix Johnny dinner as he goes up to see Mr. Preen. Johnny meets Preen in the hothouse and tells him that he has something just as beautiful as his orchids, and shows him pictures of his dead wife. Preen tells Johnny that he had to kill her as she was going to leave him, like everyone else has. He could not let her go.

Johnny notes that Preen had removed all the pictures of his wife from the house after he killed her. One photograph caused his death; the other put him away for the rest of his life.

NOTES:

- THE MID-PROGRAM COMMERCIAL IS AN **AFRS** SPOT ABOUT DEMOCRACY AND FARMERS

Producer:   Jack Johnstone          Writers:   Charles B. Smith
Cast:        Parley Baer, G. Stanley Jones, Charlotte Lawrence, Forrest Lewis, Stacy Harris

◆  ❖  ◆

SHOW:         THE KIRBY WILL MATTER
SHOW DATE:    2/3/1957
COMPANY:      TRI-STATE LIFE & CASUALTY INSURANCE COMPANY
AGENT:        DANNY NEWCUM
EXP. ACCT:    $331.25

SYNOPSIS: Buster Favor calls Johnny from Lake Mojave Resort. Do you remember Mike Kirby, the guide? Buster tells Johnny that Mike has died, and Buster thinks it was murder.

Johnny makes reservations to fly to Las Vegas and gets a handful of American Express Travelers Checks. Danny Newcum calls and wants Johnny to work on a case, but Johnny tries to turn the case down until he learns that it is at Lake Mojave Resort. Johnny flies to Las Vegas and gets there at 7 AM and comments on the cacophony of the casinos at that hour. Johnny rents a car and drives to Lake Mojave Resort and meets Buster Favor, who is sure that it was murder. Johnny is told that Mike Kirby owned a string of restaurants and retired a few years ago, and settled down here to go fishing. He often acted as a guide, but usually forgot to charge for his services. About six months ago he transferred title to all of his property to the Resort; he did not like his relatives, as they were just waiting for him to die to get his money. He also paid Buster $10,000 for rent on his cabin for as long as he lived. Last Friday a rental boat came in and reported finding Mike dead beside his boat. Buster and Ham went out and found him, and Ham saw a rattlesnake bite mark on his leg. Chief Harding was called and he agreed about the snakebite. Buster felt that something was wrong, as there are not too many rattlers in that part of country because of the heat. Buster tells Johnny that he went back to the spot and could not find anything that Mike could have hit his head on, or signs of a snake trail. Buster noticed where another boat had been beached, and how Mike looked as though he had been rolled out of a boat. Buster tells Johnny that the relatives will be there soon. Miss Martha Woodbury arrives and announces her presence as "primary heir" and expresses her desire to have the will read as soon as possible. Johnny asks her about her job, and she tells Johnny that she teaches toxicology at Armond College. Chester Kirby, the "heir to the fortune" arrives, and then Henry Kirby the black sheep of the family arrives. The only one missing is Lolita LaVerne, Martha's sister, who is a nightclub dancer. Chester is a playboy and a gambler according to Martha. Hank is a roust-about at circuses and carnivals. He is working at a rare animal show now and is in charge of the snake pit. Chief Harding calls and tells Johnny and Buster that the venom was injected into the armpit and that the fang marks were fakes. Johnny asks him to determine if the venom was injected before or after Kirby died. Buster arranges for rooms and Johnny tells them all to stay put.

Buster and Johnny go back up the lake and reminisce about the Midas Touch Matter. Buster sees a boat in the landing where Mike's boat was and then bullets start hitting their boat. Buster and Johnny return to the landing and confirm that the three heirs are still there. Buster tells Henry that the Kingman operator has not been able to reach his party. Henry tells them that he was trying to call Lita, and she is on her way.

Johnny calls Armond College, and confirms that Martha had left last night; Chester's private club verified he had been there when Mike was killed, and the carnival where Hank worked said he had been there, and Lita had not missed a show in weeks. Johnny realizes that the other boat came from Cottonwood Landing and calls them to learn that they had rented a boat to a Lucy Hancock on Friday. Lawyer Gilford arrives and the heirs assemble for the reading. Gilford tells them that the estate is valued at $10,000 that has been transferred to the resort. The rest of his estate was converted to cash years ago. There is an insurance policy for $5,000 meant to cover burial expenses. In the will, Mike Kirby has carefully spent every dollar he has ever owned. Martha wishes that Lucy, Lucy Hancock Woodberry, had been there to see them make fools of themselves. Johnny leaves and acts on a hunch. He tells Buster to change the number of Chester's room to his on the register, and then goes to wait in his room. After midnight a car arrives and Johnny hears feminine footsteps approaching. A woman enters his room and calls him darling, and tells him he was stupid to shoot at the boat and that the police will never find the needle she used as it is at the bottom of the lake. Johnny turns on the lights and Lita screams and tries to leave, but Buster stops her from leaving.

"Yeah, all four of them had wanted to see old Mike dead, but Hank, the only honest working man of the lot, didn't have the brains. Martha wouldn't have used the means that tied in with her toxicology work probably and didn't have the nerve. So Chet, who lived by his wits, and Lita, who was a real cheap no-account, well the courts will take good care of them. And I still have to chuckle over poor old Mike's will, "Being of sound mind, I have spent all my money.""

## NOTES:

- THE MID-PROGRAM COMMERCIAL IS AN **AFRS** SPOT ABOUT DEMOCRACY AND HOW IT EFFECTS THE LIVES OF EVERYONE
- DAN CUBBERLY IS THE ANNOUNCER
- MUSIC SUPERVISION IS BY AMERIGO MARINO

**Producer:** Jack Johnstone      **Writers:** Jack Johnstone
**Cast:**      Virginia Gregg, Barney Phillips, Shirley Mitchell, Stacy Harris, Carlton Young, Forrest Lewis, Frank Nelson, John Dehner

| | |
|---|---|
| **SHOW:** | **THE TEMPLETON MATTER** |
| **SHOW DATE:** | **2/10/1957** |
| **COMPANY:** | **MID EASTERN INDEMNITY CORPORATION** |
| **AGENT:** | **LUD BARLOW** |
| **EXP. ACCT:** | **$413.28** |

**SYNOPSIS:** Lud Barlow calls and tells Johnny that he is in a pinch. The Templeton House was robbed last night and they have a $100,000 loss. Johnny is going to check on the plane situation, but Lud tells him to rush to hangar 12 at the airport, he is chartering a plane for him.

Johnny cabs to hangar 12 where a twin engine Bonanza is being fueled. Lud Barlow is there and gives Johnny all the necessary paperwork. Lud tells Johnny that Templeton House is the biggest jewelry house in Boston and was burgled during the night, and that Mid Eastern has a blanket policy. Lud tells Johnny to see Lt. Roebuck as the engines start.

In Boston, Massachusetts Johnny gets a room at the Independence Hotel and goes to Templeton House. The police are there and Johnny meets Lt. Roebuck, who is watching the ambulance crew working on an injured man. The man was a special patrolman who must have walked into the robbery. When the ambulance leaves Johnny is shown where the door was jimmied to get in so that the thieves could open the vault and take the most easily moved things from the safe.

Johnny gets an inventory of the missing goods from Mr. Dorian Templeton. Johnny tells him that the insurance company will pay once the claim is filed, and that recovery is slim. Johnny tells him that whoever pulled the job opened the safe like his front door, and they have probably disappeared by now. Shooting the policeman complicated their getaway. Lt. Roebuck takes Dorian for his statement and tells Johnny that the policeman has died. The usual gang of suspects is collected, and Johnny buys dinner for Lt. Roebuck who tells him that one of the employees, the janitor named Taber, has a record, but denies being involved.

Johnny goes to visit Taber in jail and he tells Johnny that he does not know anything about the robbery. Johnny tells him that he can offer him legal assistance if he can provide information that would incriminate him. Taber tells Johnny nothing other than he will not get a fair deal from the police. Johnny tells Lt. Roebuck to turn Taber loose and then follow him.

By the next morning three witnesses to the shooting have been found, but no one saw the killers. A police audit revealed no financial problems and that Dorian Templeton was the only person who had the combination to the vault. Several days later a check for the full claim is given to Templeton. Lt. Roebuck picks up Johnny and tells him that a man was found in the harbor that was killed with the same gun that killed the police guard.

Johnny goes to the morgue to see the body, which has no labels in the clothing, and the fingerprints are sent to Washington. Lud calls and Johnny updates him and tells him that there might be a recovery, but Johnny needs time. Johnny rents a car and drives to the company that manufactured the vault. Mr. Grantland is standing in a new vault destined for South America. "Beauty. Strength." is how he describes the vault. Johnny asks him for the records on the Templeton vault and learns that Mr. Keating had set the final combination, and that Grantland has a record of the combination in his vault, and no one else other than Mr. Templeton has the combination. Johnny asks to see Keating, but that is impossible as Keating is dead. Later that day Dorian Templeton calls and asks to have lunch with Johnny. Templeton tells Johnny that the previous evening he and Mrs. Templeton had gone to a dinner dance at the country club and noticed a girl with a handbag that was sample stock and one of those stolen. That morning he got the bag back in a package. Templeton had later learned that the girl was Helen Taber.

Johnny calls Lt. Roebuck to check on the Taber tail and then goes to see Taber. The daughter lets Johnny in and he tells her that he saw her last night at the dance. When Taber comes in Johnny tells about Templeton being at the club last night and noticing the bag. Taber tells Johnny that he borrowed the handbag two days ago, and had been borrowing things for two years. He did it whenever his daughter needed something nice, and the goods were always brought back in good shape. He did it so that his daughter would have the best chances, and Johnny tells him he believes him and will not take him in. On the way out Taber tells Johnny that the man in the harbor is Billy Kiley from Philadelphia; he used to know him.

Johnny and Lt. Roebuck drive to Kiley's apartment but find nothing. On the way out the phone rings and Johnny answers and mumbles some answers to the caller, who knows that he is not Tim, but Johnny recognizes the voice. Johnny and Lt. Roebuck drive to the Grantland vault plant and are met with shots. Grantland asks Johnny what he is doing there and Johnny tells him he is looking for jewels. Johnny tells him he is alone while Lt. Roebuck circles him. Lt. Roebuck shoots Grantland and he dies before making a statement.

Johnny figures that Grantland opened the vaults with Kiley's help, and that Grantland killed him. Tim's identity was never discovered.

Remarks: Put that against the $100,000 the insurance company didn't have to pay off. Lud Barlow calls and tells Johnny that there are no jewels at the plant. Johnny tells him that there is a Grantland vault in the Harbor of New York and if Lud hurries over there . . . Lud suddenly hangs up.

NOTES:
- THIS IS ANOTHER **AFRS** PROGRAM WITH NO CREDITS
- THIS STORY IS A VARIATION ON THE EDMOND O'BRIEN PROGRAM "THE 85 MISSING MINKS" IN WHICH THE JANITOR BORROWED A MINK COAT FOR HIS DAUGHTER. JOHNNY STAYS IN BOSTON A FEW MORE DAYS OF SIGHTSEEING, UNTIL THE DAUGHTER'S EYES START SAYING MARRIAGE!
- CAST INFORMATION FROM THE **KNX** COLLECTION AT THE THOUSAND OAKS LIBRARY.

**Producer:**    Jack Johnstone        **Writers:**    John Dawson
**Cast:**        John Dehner, Peter Leeds, Vic Perrin, Jimmy McCallion, Stacy Harris, Virginia Gregg, Marvin Miller

**SHOW:**        THE GOLDEN TOUCH MATTER
**SHOW DATE:**    2/17/1957
**COMPANY:**     PROVIDENTIAL LIFE & CASUALTY
**AGENT:**       STEVE KILMER
**EXP. ACCT:**     $240.00

**SYNOPSIS:** Steve Kilmer calls Johnny from New York City. Steve has a report about the death of Mrs. Martha Mayfield Merryman "the girl with the golden touch." Steve has a $500,000 policy on Mrs. Merryman, and wants Johnny to investigate how she died. Johnny is told that Mrs. Merryman holds a controlling interest in "Consolidated Tire and Rubber Co."

Johnny trains to New York and goes to the residence of Mrs. Mrs. Merryman, only to find her alive and kicking, and the perpetrator of many a practical joke. Johnny is told that the report of her death is false, but has touched off a steep decline in the value of the company stock, which is being bought up for a song. When Mrs. Merryman hears this, she falls into a dead faint and winds up in the hospital. Her hospitalization causes the price of the Consolidated stock to drop even further. Johnny wonders if this was all the work of "the Syndicate" which has been trying to acquire the Consolidated stock? Maybe it was Mrs. Merryman's son, Edgar? Johnny discovers that Mrs. Merryman has been merrily buying up all the devalued stock to stop a takeover by "the syndicate."

Johnny reports that Mrs. Merryman now owns her company, and that she and her son are on good terms and actually worked together to pull off the stunt. And to celebrate, Mrs. Merryman and Johnny go out and paint the town red. The matter is closed, and changed names mean no problems with the Securities commission.

**NOTES:**
- MUSIC DIRECTION IS BY AMERIGO MARINO
- THE ANNOUNCER IS DAN CUBBERLY
- STORY INFORMATION OBTAINED FROM THE KNX COLLECTION IN THE THOUSAND OAKS LIBRARY

**Producer:**    Jack Johnstone        **Writers**    Jack Johnstone
**Cast:**        Virginia Gregg, Lucille Meredith, Lillian Buyeff, Forrest Lewis, Herb Butterfield, Edgar Barrier, Chester Stratton

**SHOW:**        THE MEEK MEMORIAL MATTER
**SHOW DATE:**    3/3/1957

COMPANY:     ASSURED EQUITY & TRUST COMPANY
AGENT:       MAX GREEN
EXP. ACCT:   $98.30

SYNOPSIS: Max Green calls and wonders where Johnny has been for the past twenty minutes. "I was in the shower," Johnny tells Max. "For twenty minutes?" "Ok, so, I am a shiny dollar!" Ugh! Max quotes the Gettysburg address and asks if Johnny knows about the Meeks. Mariah Meek has lost her copy and it might cost them $100,000.

Johnny cabs to Max's office where Max asks Johnny how many words are in the Gettysburg Address, the answer is 268. Two drafts only have 266, with the two words "under God" added at the time of the speech. Mrs. Meek has a copy without the two words and insured for $100,000. It was bought from Jason Penrod and has been kept under glass in the Meek Memorial. Max tells Johnny that he is going to run newspaper ads and a reward to try and recover the document. Max tells Johnny that some people would keep the document in a safe, just for pride of possession.

Johnny cabs back home and then travels to New Bedford, Massachusetts and gets a room. Johnny calls Mrs. Meek, who arranges for a car to pick Johnny up. There is a knock at the door and someone asks for "Mr. J." Johnny opens the door and the man tells Johnny he got the wrong room. Johnny watches the man and then travels to the Meek home, and is met on the stairs by Paul Meek, the grandson of Mrs. Meek. Paul and his wife Janet, who is having another drink, tell Johnny that Mrs. Meek is blind. Paul wonders how Johnny is going to find the document, and Janet is concerned about the money that the old woman is spending. Paul and Johnny go up to Mrs. Meek's room where Martha wants to speak with Johnny alone. Martha wants to know when Johnny is going to arrest the crook that took the document. She tells Johnny that only the guard was there, and he got hit on the head that night. The memorial is not open to the public. Mr. Penrod was there on the night of the theft discussing business. He is probably either in his room or in the memorial. Mrs. Meek asks Johnny for a cigarette. When Johnny asks about her son and daughter-in-law she asks if Johnny suspects then, and he tells Mrs. Meek that he suspects everyone, including her. "Well, bless you Boy!" she tells Johnny.

Johnny speaks with Pete Vesuvio the guard, who knows his history by reading the documents in the memorial. Pete offers to repeat the Gettysburg Address to Johnny, he knows it by heart and learned it from the president's own writing. Johnny then meets with Mr. Penrod in the memorial. He is taking inventory of the things Mrs. Meek cannot see. Penrod tells Johnny that he was there on the night of the theft and was the one who discovered the manuscript missing. Mrs. Meek has given out too many keys to the memorial in his opinion. Penrod tells Johnny that Mrs. Meek had asked him to come up and take inventory. Johnny asks Penrod if he had stolen the document, how would he sell it. Penrod tells Johnny that he would sell it in Europe. He also tells Johnny that Paul and Janet are going to Paris in a few days. Johnny goes to the house and Paul tells him that they are have reservations to Paris, but is not sure they are going to go. They have friends there, so it will not cost too much to live there, and they will pay for it when they get back. "Fly now, pay later," Janet calls it. Janet thinks that Mrs. Meek is using her heart condition to keep Paul there. Johnny goes to his hotel and wires Max to check into the Meek finances and then gets a phone call from a man calling about the ad in the paper about something missing from a memorial. He tells Johnny to meet him in the alley behind the Borne Whaling Museum, alone. Johnny cabs to the museum and finds a man curled up dead in the alley. It was the man who had knocked on his door. Johnny calls the police and goes back to the hotel to ask who had his room before he got there. Johnny shows the clerk a $5 bill and the clerk shows Johnny the register. Johnny recognizes the name, and files it away until he finds some proof. Johnny goes back to the Meeks house and meets with Janet, who tells him that Mrs. Meek is ill, and not expected to live and wants to see Johnny. Pete is with Mrs. Meek and she asks Pete to finish quoting the Gettysburg Address. Pete leaves and Mrs. Meek tells Johnny that she lied to him. She is broke and only has the house and the memorial. Mr. Penrod is going to purchase the memorial and is evaluating the contents. Johnny leaves and asks Pete why he lied to him about learning the address from the original document. When Pete protests, Johnny tells him that he was just testing him. Johnny tells Paul that he knows which one of them stole the document, and that one of them hired Leo Jones to help them. Leo had called Johnny because he did not like the deal he was getting but one of you killed him. Johnny asks Penrod if he was trying to blackmail Leo, because he came to the hotel room looking for him. Johnny tells Penrod that he switched copies of the address document after Mrs. Penrod started losing her sight and closed the museum. Pete had learned from the document that had been switched after the sale. Penrod pulls a gun, and Pete lunges for him to protect the family and Penrod shoots him. Pete tells them to tell Mrs. Meek he is a much better guard now.

Pete Vesuvio will live to apply for his second papers, and in time probably will open a spaghetti joint in New Bedford. Penrod will be tried for murder. As yet he has not disclosed the name of the person who purchased the stolen manuscript, but in time I'm sure he will. As for the Meeks, well Mariah passed on later that night, but as she said, there was nothing left for her but to rest.

NOTES:
- ON SEVERAL OCCASION MRS. MEEK IS CALLED MARIAH. WHEN JOHNNY FIRST MEETS HER, HE CALLS HER MARTHA. ALSO, PAUL DESCRIBES HIMSELF AS A GRANDSON, BUT LATER JOHNNY ASKS MRS. MEEK ABOUT PAUL, HER SON.
- BASED ON THE LIBRARY OF CONGRESS WEB SITE, THERE ARE SEVERAL DIFFERENT VERSIONS OF THE SPEECH, SOME OF WHICH DO NOT INCLUDE THE PHRASE "UNDER GOD" AS NOTED IN THE STORY.
- CAST INFORMATION FROM THE KNX COLLECTION AT THE THOUSAND OAKS LIBRARY.
- DAN CUBBERLY IS THE ANNOUNCER
- MUSIC SUPERVISION IS BY AMERIGO MARINO

Producer:    Jack Johnstone          Writers:    Charles B. Smith
Cast:        Lawrence Dobkin, Marvin Miller, Bert Holland, Virginia
             Gregg, Peggy Webber, Jack Moyles, Hans Conried

◆   ❖   ◆

| | |
|---|---|
| SHOW: | THE SUNTAN OIL MATTER |
| SHOW DATE: | 3/10/1957 |
| COMPANY: | SURETY MUTUAL & TRUST COMPANY |
| AGENT: | DAVE LAWLER |
| EXP. ACCT: | $474.84 |

SYNOPSIS: Dave Lawler calls and asks if Johnny owns sunglasses and some real loud sport shirts? Johnny tells him his are so loud he has to keep them in a sound proof drawer. Dave tells Johnny he is going where "the summer spends the winter," Palm Springs. Johnny tells Dave this will be expensive and Dave tells Johnny it will cost $75,000 unless he can prove the bracelet Dan Galloway gave to his child bride wasn't really stolen. Johnny tells him that, for a trip to Palm Springs at this time of year, he can prove anything.

Johnny flies to Palm Springs, California and registers at the Casa des Paz Hotel, and then goes to lunch with Det. Sgt. Lacey. Sgt. Lacey tells Johnny that he doubts that the bracelet was stolen. Dan Galloway is drilling down by the Salton Sea; he figures that that if there is oil in the Gulf of Mexico salt domes, there is oil under the Salton Sea, which is all salt deposits. Sgt. Lacey does not know how Dan can afford the jewelry, or the expensive Italian sports car she got two weeks ago. Roberta, his wife, is much younger that Dan by about 35-40 years, and there is talk about their relationship. There is talk of her and Sonny Wyman who is about her age and a playboy who always has something intriguing to interest his rich friends. This season it is Italian sports cars; Cosmo Romas they are called.

Johnny rents a car and drives to the Galloway house and sees a sports car in the driveway. The houseboy gets his name and takes him to see Mrs. Galloway. On the Lanai, she cannot tell Johnny anything about the bracelet other than it was stolen. She asks Johnny how he will recover the bracelet, and Johnny tells her that they might offer a reward. She asks Johnny how much he will get, and he tells her 10-30%. Johnny hears a door close and then the sound of a loud car leaving, but Roberta hears nothing. Johnny drives back to town to meet with Wilhoit van Hooke the jeweler, but is stopped on the street by Sonny Wyman in his sports car. Sonny tells Johnny that he must have heard him out at Roberta's and offers to sell him a Cosmo Roma. Sonny offers to help and tells Johnny that he sold van Hooke a Cosmo just like his. They are going to be in a rally next weekend. He also offers to take Johnny to see Dan Galloway. Johnny meets with van Hooke and gets a complete set of records on the bracelet. van Hooke tells Johnny that the bracelet was an exception to what he normally carries, and had ordered it on consignment. He asks Johnny to keep it quiet that Dan had come in and asked for cash and wanted him to refund the money on the bracelet, but van Hooke did not have the money as he had paid off some over due bills. Dan needed money for his test well; something had broken on the rig necessitating a costly repair job. Berta probably does not even know about the well, and Dan has competition.

Sonny drives Johnny to the well site in his Cosmo Roma and tells Johnny that there is talk about him and Berta. There is nothing serious; they just have fun together. The house is always open, so anyone could have taken the bracelet. Sonny tells Johnny that recovered stolen jewelry usually gets a reward of 20 cents on the dollar, but Johnny tells him sometimes it gets you twenty years. Sonny tells Johnny that the car business is great and he is going to work on the racecourse for this weekend. Van Hooke is quite a racing fan, and they are running a match race on Saturday. Sonny drops Johnny at the drilling site office where Johnny meets Mrs. Flora Galloway, the first and former Mrs. Galloway. She has been waiting for three hours and is upset about $18,000 in back alimony. Johnny tells her the gun in her handbag will not help. She tells him that killing would be too good for Dan, so Johnny takes the gun from her. They drive to the well in her car and find Dan Galloway in the road, run over several times by a car.

Johnny calls Sgt. Lacey and drops Flora off at the Galloway house with Roberta. Sgt. Lacey tells Johnny that whoever ran over Galloway did it several times. Sgt. Lacey thinks that Flora might have run him down, but Johnny reminds him that the tires on her car do not match the tracks. Officer Levin calls and tells them that the tire prints match those on Sonny Wyman's car, so Sgt. Lacey orders Sonny picked up. Johnny and Sgt. Lacey drive to Roberta's, and they learn that Sonny has not been there. There is a phone call for Sgt. Lacey and he is told that Wyman has been found. His car ran over a cliff and he is dead. Johnny and Sgt. Lacey go to the site of the wreck and Johnny notices that the car looks as though it had been sideswiped, but Sgt. Lacey notices that there is no paint on the fender, and Johnny tells him he is wrong; there would be no difference if the car was sideswiped by a car of the same color. Johnny finds a phone and calls several jewelers in Los Angeles. After several calls, Johnny asks a Mr. Menkin if he had shipped a bracelet to van Hooke. He tells Johnny that he had sent three bracelets, but he sent two back immediately and the last one last Thursday.

Johnny and Sgt. Lacey drive to van Hooke's ranch. On the way, Johnny tells Sgt. Lacey that the paint on the two cars matched, which is why Lacey had seen nothing. Also, van Hooke had told Johnny he used the money from Galloway to pay off his bills, but he also bought an $8,000 sports car. Van Hooke had seen Johnny drive off with Sonny, so he had to cover his tracks and must have killed Galloway. At the ranch the police surround the house. They hear a car start up and call to van Hooke to turn off the car. He speeds out through the garage doors and gets away. Johnny and Sgt. Lacey follow along the main road. Sgt. Lacey spots van Hooke trying to squeeze through two trucks, but, as Johnny notes, "he squeezed through alright. Squeezed right through the pearly gates.

Remarks: Well, justice is done in pretty strange ways is sometimes. Kinda makes you think. Maybe it pays to tread the straight and narrow, doesn't it?

NOTES:

- JOHNNY MAKES NOTE OF HIS COMMISSION ON RECOVERED JEWELRY, WHICH RANGES FROM TEN TO THIRTY PERCENT. ON THIS CASE ALONE THAT WOULD BE $7,500 TO $22,500—NOT BAD FOR SEVERAL DAYS WORK EVEN TODAY.
- DAN CUBBERLY IS THE ANNOUNCER
- MUSIC SUPERVISION IS BY AMERIGO MARINO

Producer: Jack Johnstone     Writers: Paul Franklin
Cast: Barbara Eiler, Paula Winslowe, Forrest Lewis, Frank Nelson, Sam Edwards, Austin Green, Shep Menken

SHOW: THE CLEVER CHEMIST MATTER
SHOW DATE: 3/17/1957
COMPANY: PHILADELPHIA MUTUAL LIFE & CASUALTY INSURANCE
COMPANY AGENT: HARRY BRANSON
EXP. ACCT: $84.35

SYNOPSIS: Harry Branson calls and has a case for John. It is somewhat unusual. Harry is apprehensive about one of his clients, Dr. Walter Merrill the scientist and Nobel Prize winner.

Johnny travels to Philadelphia and Harry Branson's office where Harry meets him on the sidewalk. Harry has rented a car so Johnny can drive to New Jersey where Dr. Merrill and his colleague Dr. Theodore Nash have a lab. They are working on some top secret project, probably missiles or satellites. Dr. Merrill has a $25,000 policy and has made Dr. Nash the beneficiary. Dr. Nash also bought a $10,000 policy and made Merrill his beneficiary. Harry has received a letter of protest from Dr. Merrill's daughter who feels her father has been coerced into changing his policy. The rental car arrives and Johnny drives to Malaga, New Jersey. At the Post Office, Johnny gets directions to Wampusbung where Dr. Merrill has a cottage. Johnny is told to announce himself at the gate or he will get shot at. Johnny drives to the cottage, honks his horn at the gate and Dr. Merrill opens the door. He lets Johnny in and tells Johnny that Dr. Nash is in the lab. Dr. Merrill tells Johnny that they should talk in private, but Dr. Nash comes out and wants to know what is going on. Johnny tells him he is making a routine check on the insurance policies and Dr. Nash takes Johnny into the lab and tells Merrill to finish his experiment. The molecular balance check is ready, so Dr. Merrill tells them to leave and locks the door to the lab, and Nash bolts the door. Johnny questions it, so Nash says it is force of habit and undoes the bolt. Johnny tells him that he is there about the change in the policy and Nash tells Johnny that Merrill's daughter is married to a day laborer that is waiting for him to die. Johnny leaves with the excuse that he needs to get a room, and leaves with the feeling that something is wrong. Johnny drives back to the cottage hears someone calling for help and finds the bolt to the lab locked. The door is unlocked and Dr. Nash comes out and tells Johnny that a man beat him and threw acid on him and killed Merrill with a gun.

Johnny calls Dr. Foote, who comes out and Dr. Merrill is pronounced dead. The sheriff is called and he gets the state police. Dr. Foote tells Johnny that Dr. Nash has lost the use of his left eye because of the acid. Johnny speaks with Dr. Nash who tells Johnny that he saw the man, and describes him as a young stocky man with black curly hair and working man's hands. Johnny gives Dr. Nash a drink of water and Nash tells him he tried to stop him but could not. Johnny goes back to the cottage and finds a copy of a wedding picture with a perfect match for the description of the killer, Howard Harding, Dr. Merrill's son-in-law. Johnny thinks about Nash's comments and of the conversation in the doctor's office. The police arrive and find a .38 calibur Luger that has no prints. No Prints! Johnny rushes back to Dr. Foote's office and picks up the water glass and goes to Harry's office to get the Harding's address and tells Harry to send the glass to Ray Kemper at the Bureau.

Johnny drives to the Harding residence and Mrs. Harding meets him. Johnny tells her who he is, and she tells Johnny that someone is poisoning daddy's mind. Howard is an officer of the company and is off fishing alone today. She tells Johnny that there is something wrong with Nash. Her father always worked alone and is such an alert, bright-eyed busybody in spite of his age. Johnny tells her that when he saw Dr. Merrill, he seemed to be in a daze. Howard comes home and tells Johnny that he has heard of Johnny. Howard has been fishing at a private lake near Mount Holly. Johnny tells Howard that he has been identified as Dr. Merrill's killer, but Howard tells Johnny that Nash was the killer. Johnny gets a phone call and Harry tells him that Ray Kemper must see him immediately. Johnny tells Howard to stay put and Johnny goes to see Ray Kemper at the Bureau. Ray tells Johnny that he found three sets of prints on the glass: Johnny's, Dr. Foote's and those of Theodore Machevsky, a chemist from one of our not so friendly countries who is an expert on explosives. Ray has pictures of Machevsky and one shows a picture of a boy with a patch on his left eye. Johnny rushes back to Malaga with an FBI tail. At the state police office Johnny learns that Dr. Nash is in the clear because of Johnny's testimony that he was in the locked lab. At Dr. Foote's office, Johnny gives him some instructions and then goes to talk to Dr. Nash. Johnny tells Nash that his government does not pay him too well. Dr. Merrill was doing important work and you would have been paid well by your country. Johnny tells him he gave himself away when he reached for the water and did not hesitate because he had lost his sight long ago. Nash tells Johnny that he found him locked in the lab. Johnny tells him he found the cord that was looped over the door, so that it could be locked from the inside. Nash tells him that he could not have, he destroyed it in a vat of acid and Johnny tells him he was bluffing and made a lucky guess. Machevsky tries to swallow a capsule but Johnny prevents him and closes his other eye with his knuckles and Machevsky is saved from Johnny by the police.

Remarks: Don't beef on this one Harry. The criminal, in spite of being the named beneficiary doesn't get paid.

NOTES:

- RAY KEMPER WAS A CBS SOUND MAN WHO WORKED ON A NUMBER OF PROGRAMS, INCLUDING GUNSMOKE.
- THE MID PROGRAM COMMERCIAL IS AN AFRS SPOT ABOUT DEMOCRACY AND FREE CHOICE.
- JOHNNY MENTIONS A .38 CALIBER LUGER. I SEARCHED THE WEB, AND FOUND ONE ARTICLE NOTING THAT THERE WERE SOME LUGERS MANUFACTURED IN .38 CALIBER BUT THEY ARE VERY RARE. THE MOST COMMON CALIBER FOR A LUGER IS 7.65 AND 9 MM.
- DAN CUBBERLY IS THE ANNOUNCER
- MUSIC SUPERVISION IS BY AMERIGO MARINO

Producer:   Jack Johnstone          Writers:   Jack Johnstone
Cast:       Virginia Gregg, Harry Bartell, Howard McNear, Forrest Lewis,
            Jack Kruschen, Russell Thorson, Frank Gerstle, Bob Bruce

◆   ❖   ◆

SHOW:          THE HOLLYWOOD MATTER
SHOW DATE:     3/24/1957
COMPANY:       NATIONAL MARINE INDEMNITY
AGENT:         ABE SANDSTROM
EXP. ACCT:     $618.45

SYNOPSIS: Abe Sandstrom calls Johnny and tells him to go to Los Angeles. This is urgent, $1,000,000 urgent.

Johnny goes to Abe's office and Abe asks Johnny if he knows about guarantee policies, also called good faith policies where the insurer acts as a bond for the business venture. Abe tells Johnny that Sidney Sperry, who has been in Hollywood for 25 years, has organized the "Best American" company to make a motion picture. The film has been delayed and he wants his money.

Johnny flies to Los Angeles, and goes to Beverly Hills, California and gets a room at the Beverly Wilshire Hotel. During a downpour Johnny notes that he always seems to go to Beverly Hills during the rainy season. Johnny calls Sperry who tells Johnny that he will pick him up for lunch. Johnny buys a copy of Variety and sees a note about the movie. Sperry picks up Johnny and they go to lunch. Sperry tells Johnny that a man from New York had called about the delay, and he had blamed the weather. The star of the movie is Booth Templeton, but he will not come to the studio. Templeton signed a contract but did not show up. He has made over 300 movies and even his agent cannot get in to see him.

Johnny rents a car and drives to the Templeton house. As the butler goes to get Booth, Johnny spots a woman and a much younger man at the bar. The butler returns and tells Johnny that Mr. Templeton is not there. Johnny asks to see Mrs. Templeton and the woman at the bar tells Johnny that she is Mrs. Templeton, and tells Johnny to get out. Johnny explains who he is and Mrs. Templeton gives Johnny a phone number to call. Johnny leaves and calls the number, but there is no answer. Johnny goes to Sperry's office and tells him about the man at the Templeton house and learns that the boyfriend is named Tyler, and that Templeton puts up with it. Johnny wants to call in the police, but Sperry tells Johnny to find Templeton.

Johnny calls the number, Hollywood 6-2289, and a woman answers. Johnny asks for Templeton, and the woman tells Johnny to come to 1224 Berendo. Johnny drives to the address and Judith Ford answers the door. She tells Johnny that she is an actress and a good friend, and that Templeton is out getting some food. Templeton is staying there because he has no place else to go. Templeton returns and Johnny tells him why he is there. Johnny leaves with Templeton and on the drive Templeton tells Johnny all about his many films, and that his first wife Laura died at 25. They stop for a drink and Templeton tells Johnny that he cannot go back. Johnny and Templeton arrive at his house and Sarah and Tyler are surprised to see him. Templeton tells Johnny that he is 61 and seeking peace. He agrees to go to the studio, and come back and go to bed while Sarah plays. Templeton tells Johnny that he has been looking for contented moments all his life, but he has not found many.

Remarks: The advertising notices say that "The Best American" is a smash hit and Templeton's greatest performance and a cinch for an academy award. I hope he gets it. I hope he gets something better that what he's got as an excuse for a life."

NOTES:
- THE ANNOUNCER IS DAN CUBBERLY
- MUSIC DIRECTION IS BY AMERIGO MARINO
- STORY INFORMATION OBTAINED FROM THE KNX COLLECTION IN THE THOUSAND OAKS LIBRARY

**Producer:** Jack Johnstone         **Writers**    **John Dawson**
**Cast:** Herb Ellis, Virginia Gregg, Alan Reed, Jay Novello, Carlton Young, Jean Tatum, John Dehner

◆    ❖    ◆

**SHOW:** THE MOONSHINE MURDER MATTER
**SHOW DATE:** 3/31/1957
**COMPANY:** PHILADELPHIA MUTUAL LIFE & CASUALTY INSURANCE
**AGENT:** HARRY BRANSON
**EXP. ACCT:** $299.50
**SYNOPSIS:** Harry Branson calls Johnny and asks if Johnny knows what moonshine is. Johnny tells Harry to send him a case, and is told that it may cost him $30,000.

Johnny travels to Philadelphia, Pennsylvania where Harry has a bus ticket ready for Johnny to go to Pine Grove, Pennsylvania where Harry has already made reservations for Johnny at the Sterling Hotel. While Johnny tries to remind

Harry that he makes his own travel arrangements, Harry rattles on about all of the wonderful adventures Johnny has on his assignments. Harry even tells Johnny that when he took his last vacation, he came into the office to work. Johnny invites Harry to come along so see what it is like on a case. Harry checks with his boss and surprises Johnny by getting authorization to accompany him.

Johnny rents a car and they drive to Pine Grove. Harry tells Johnny that Horace Eckert has a policy for $30,000 and the beneficiary is his daughter Elaine. Horace has had his life threatened but has not called the police because he was a bootlegger a long time ago.

Johnny and Harry have a big dinner in Reading and drive to Piney Grove where they meet Elaine, who recognizes Harry and is very glad to see him. Horace arrives and, after introductions, he tells Johnny and Harry that he has had several car problems, the last of which was loose wheel nuts. Horace has not called the police because he hates them. Horace tells them that he used to make moonshine but has stopped and has been doing good works for the commission. Horace tells Johnny that Mug Malloy killed a revenue agent and got thirty years and said that he would get even with Horace, and that Elaine has been seeing Al Hartwell. Elaine tells Horace that he really should call in the police and there are shots fired through the window. Elaine tells Johnny that the shots might have been meant for him. When Johnny notes that they might have been meant for Harry, he faints.

Johnny calls the police to try and locate Mug Mallow and tells them about the attempt on "Stoopy Eckert." Johnny is told that Mug is in Frackville, so he drives there and meets Mug's parole officer who tells Johnny that Mug is a miner now and is clean. Johnny meets Mug and he tells Johnny that he has not heard about Eckert, and admits to having killed the officer, but what is past, is past. Johnny gets a phone call from Harry who tells Johnny that Horace is mad and wants to go after Mug, but Harry is holding a gun on him. Mug tells Johnny that the revenue agent was named Barney Hartwell. Johnny rushes back to Harry and tells Horace that Mug is not after him. Johnny gets an idea after being told that Al Hartwell is a police officer. Johnny goes to Al's house where Al tells Johnny that his father was killed when he was just a boy, and that he had planned revenge for a long time. He was trying to scare Eckert into killing Malloy. He knew that his father was a cruel man and destined to die, especially for what he did to his mother. Al's mother enters the room carrying a rifle and tells Johnny that she is not crazy and shoots out the window. She tells Johnny that she did the things to Eckert. She aims the rifle and there are shots and the gun is shot from her hand. Harry rushes in and tells Johnny that he had shot the gun from outside the window. When Elaine tells Harry that here is a hole in his coat from the first shot, Harry faints.

NOTES:
- THE ANNOUNCER IS DAN CUBBERLY
- MUSIC DIRECTION IS BY AMERIGO MARINO

- PINE GROVE AND FRACKVILLE ARE BOTH IN EASTERN PENNSYLVANIA, NORTHEAST OF READING.
- STORY INFORMATION OBTAINED FROM THE KNX COLLECTION IN THE THOUSAND OAKS LIBRARY

Producer: Jack Johnstone       Writers    Jack Johnstone
Cast: Harry Bartell, Virginia Gregg, Will Wright, Herb Butterfield, Bob Bruce, Peggy Webber, Vic Perrin

◆ ❖ ◆

SHOW: THE MING TOY MURPHY MATTER
SHOW DATE: 4/14/1957
COMPANY: FLOYDS OF ENGLAND
AGENT: GEORGE REED
EXP. ACCT: $225.70

SYNOPSIS: George Reed calls and tells Johnny it is a bad morning. Jodiah Gillis has talked them into issuing another special policy. This time it is on an articulate canine, a talking dog. Oh, No!

Johnny cabs to George's office and learns that Iron Mike Murphy is the former owner of the dog. Gillis bought the dog three weeks ago and bought a $7,500 policy on the dog. Johnny wants to refuse the policy as his commission is not worth it, but Gillis wants Johnny. After finding his mouse, Gillis thinks Johnny is a miracle worker. George offers Johnny liberal expenses but Johnny has to find the dog or keep Gillis happy. If he cannot, the auditors will be all over Johnny's expense account. It is a real sucker bet, but Johnny accepts.

Johnny travels to New York City and gets a room at the Statler Hotel. Johnny calls the Gillis number and Marian answers the phone and tells Johnny to come over for the celebration. Johnny cabs to Marion's apartment on the East River, and she takes Johnny in through the kitchen because her dad wants to see Johnny alone in the den. The celebration is for her engagement to Bill Fisher, who is with the Powers Advertising Agency, and who just talked a client into a new TV show. Bill walks in and meets Johnny and then Josiah walks in and tells Johnny to get to work. Johnny calls the missing object a dog, and Gillis chews him out; she is a lady, a canine and her name is Ming Toy Murphy. She is a Chinese, er, a Pekinese. She was locked up in the den and disappeared from the apartment. The front door was left open when they got back from breakfast. Gillis tells Johnny that all dogs can speak, but she can talk! Gillis tells Johnny that Ming Toy will be on a new TV program that is called "The Big Shock." They were looking for a dog that could say "Happy Hollow Dog Food, yum, yum, yummy!" Gillis was going to take Ming Toy to the studio and claim the $50,000 reward for a dog that could repeat the slogan. Gillis bought the dog from Murphy before the ad came out because Murphy had told Gillis that the dog could talk. Marion had told Jodiah that Bill had talked the Happy Hollow people into looking for the talking dog for their show. Gillis starts the tape and Johnny hears a dog talking, sort of.

Gillis has looked for the dog and posted a reward. Gillis feels that Iron Mike stole the dog back. Mike thinks that Gillis cheated him, which he admitted to. Gillis tells Johnny that the window to the den was open, but there is nothing below but the East River. Johnny cabs to his hotel and next morning gets an appointment to see Iron Mike Murphy. Johnny goes to Marion's apartment to get Gillis and meets the janitor. He tells Johnny that they are out for breakfast. He also tells Johnny that he picks up the trash every morning at nine o'clock. He did not see anyone who did not belong there on the morning the dog disappeared, but he did see Miss Gillis' future husband carrying a present for her.

Johnny goes down stairs and meets the Gillis'. Johnny asks Marion to go to lunch with him and she suggests '21' at 12:30, and then he and Gillis cab to Iron Mike Murphy's house on Long Island. Mike tells Johnny how Gillis stole a beautiful dog from him and Gillis accuses him of stealing the dog back after the ads appeared. Gillis and Murphy square off at each other and a black eye and bloody nose result.

Johnny goes to "The 21" to meet Marion for lunch. Johnny tells Marian about going to Iron Mike's, and is about to tell Marian about meeting Morris the janitor when Bill arrives. Johnny asks Bill about being at Marian's at 9:00 and he swears he was not there. Johnny leaves and calls Bill's secretary and learns that he had lied. Johnny cabs to his hotel, makes some more calls and waits. Bill calls and asks Johnny to meet him at a bar where he accuses Johnny of calling his secretary and the agency. Bill tells him that the whole thing was for publicity and the $50,000 was safe, as dogs could not talk. He admits getting rid of the dog. He was going to take her out in the box, but ended up throwing the dog out of the window into the river when it made too much noise. After all, it was only a dog.

Johnny calls Marian and, in a park near the apartment, tells her what happened. Johnny hears an ambulance heading towards the apartment and they run there where a policeman tells them that it sounds like a little girl is stuck in a drain. It has to be a girl, as it sounds like she is talking about a dog food being "yum, yum, yummy." Johnny goes down with the power and light men, stays a minute and then leaves. Gillis arrives and Johnny takes him down to hear Ming Toy barking and talking. When they get to her Gillis he finds out that Ming Toy has had puppies. "She disappeared to have her family! And she called me Papa! Johnny, I am a grandfather!" Gillis tells Johnny.

Johnny never did tell Gillis how the dog had been helped out of the apartment. All he knew was that Marian, for reasons of her own, had called off her engagement to Bill. Ming Toy spent a week in bed recovering from her ordeal, and naturally since Gillis refused to allow her to appear on TV that night, the $50,000 went unclaimed. And, alas, the long-suffering public has yet to hear the dulcet tones of a talking dog named Ming Toy Murphy.

NOTES:
- JOHNNY CALLS THE JANITOR "MORRIS," EVEN THOUGH HE HAD NOT TOLD JOHNNY HIS NAME.
- DAN CUBBERLY IS THE ANNOUNCER

• MUSIC SUPERVISION IS BY AMERIGO MARINO

**Producer:**   Jack Johnstone          **Writers:**   Charles Smith
**Cast:**          Virginia Gregg, G. Stanley Jones, Herb Ellis, Joseph Kearns,
                  Jay Novello, Bill James, Howard McNear

◆    ❖    ◆

**SHOW:**          THE MARLEY K. MATTER
**SHOW DATE:**     4/21/1957
**COMPANY:**       INTERCOASTAL MARITIME & LIFE
**AGENT:**         BYRON KAY
**EXP. ACCT:**     $81.00

**SYNOPSIS:** Byron Kay calls Johnny from Boston. "Remember Meg McCarthy?" he asks Johnny. Byron tells Johnny that Meg may not be long for this world, but he is not sure what is wrong.

Johnny flies to Boston and goes to Byron's office to learn that Meg had been calling hourly, but the calls have stopped. Meg is living in Fortescue, New Jersey now and is running a hotel. Meg has $10,000 on her hotel and $10,000 on her life. Johnny flies to Philadelphia and rents a car. Johnny recounts his other cases with Meg McCarthy as he arrives at Meg's Palace Hotel, a real dive. On the way in Johnny is passed by three men being thrown out. Meg is yelling at them but as soon as Meg sees "her ever lovin' darling boy" she quiets down and is glad to see Johnny. Meg tells Johnny that she has no trouble, but just stopped calling Byron to scare him and get Johnny there. Meg tells Johnny that Capt. Billy towed in a boat called the "Skate." The skipper of the boat went to Port Norris while the boat is being repaired. Meg thinks that he is Blackie Harmon, a crook from Cod Harbor. Meg tells Johnny that Blackie lost a boat called the "Marley K." in a storm, and was paid $18,000. Meg is sure that the Skate is really the Marley K.

Johnny and Meg go to look at the Skate and find a new paint job and new brass on an old boat and Johnny is able to see the letters "Mar" along the bow. While they are looking, Blackie appears with a gun and his assistant Alec. Johnny and Meg are put on the boat and told that they are "going for a ride" while Alec starts the engines. Blackie tells Meg that he thinks that Meg brought Johnny in to get him and tells Johnny that the waters are full of sharks. Meg tries to get up and Blackie hits her causing Johnny to react and get hit as well. Blackie yells at Alec about the course and tells him that Johnny is going to be thrown overboard. Johnny tries to scare Alec about being involved in murder and Blackie shouts at Alec, allowing Johnny to slug Blackie, who shoots Alec and then knocks Johnny out.

Johnny wakes up tied up in the cabin. Megs tells Johnny that Alec has been thrown overboard. Johnny spots a set of duplicate controls and an engine switch. Johnny gets up and fakes being dizzy so that he can fall on the switch and kill the engine. Blackie comes in and aims his gun at Johnny, causing Meg to give him a body slam. Blackie falls to the deck and Johnny kicks him many times. Blackie is tied up and Meg drives the boat back to port.

Remarks: Meg should get a couple of grand for the return of the Marley K.

NOTES:
* THE ANNOUNCER IS DAN CUBBERLY
* MUSIC DIRECTION IS BY AMERIGO MARINO
* STORY INFORMATION OBTAINED FROM THE KNX COLLECTION IN THE THOUSAND OAKS LIBRARY

Producer:    Jack Johnstone          Writers    Jack Johnstone
Cast:        Byron Kane, Virginia Gregg, Vic Perrin, Ben Wright

◆   ❖   ◆

SHOW:         THE MELANCHOLY MEMORY MATTER
SHOW DATE:    4/28/1957
COMPANY:      PROVIDENTIAL ASSURANCE COMPANY
AGENT:        BERT MCGRAW
EXP. ACCT:    $579.12

SYNOPSIS: Bert McGraw calls and tells Johnny about Hailey's Comet. Harry Hailey the pitcher for the Spartans, whose fastball is called "Hailey's Comet," has disappeared. He is makes $60,000, but has disappeared right in the middle of spring training. Bert has a $50,000 policy on him.

Johnny cabs to Bert's office. Bert is described as a big man who played ball in the bush leagues and played with the Spartans for a year. Bert wants Johnny to find Hailey. The policy was sold 6 months ago and Mildred Womac, his sister in Omaha, was the original beneficiary, but his wife is on the policy now. Harry has been married since he started spring training but no one has seen him for a week. Harry only thinks about baseball, but Johnny reminds Bert that he did get married. Bert has a telegram from Mildred and she is sure that Harry has been murdered. She sent the wire from Tucson, where the Spartans are training.

Johnny buys a paper to read a story about Harry Hailey, and then flies to Tucson, Arizona and gets a room at the Westerner Hotel. Johnny rents a car and goes to meet Mildred Womac at her hotel. Mildred is sure that Harry's new contract is the reason why he is dead. She had hired a detective to see what her brother was doing when he stopped writing to her. He is twenty-five years old, but much younger mentally. With his new contract Mildred is sure that he is like a ripe melon for some young chippie to pick off the vine. It was the detective who told Mildred that Harry was married. "How would you feel if you woke up some morning and found out you were married to someone named Juanita Torres?" she asks Johnny. Johnny tells her that he has never met the lady, and Mildred tells him that she isn't a lady; she is a Mexican. The detective Oglethorpe told her that Juanita worked for a nightclub as a dancer, and Harry must have been really drunk to marry her. She is a gold digger, a horrible cheap tainted dancing girl! Changing her to the beneficiary was like putting a gun in her hand. Mildred is sure that she murdered Harry.

Johnny goes to visit Oglethorpe who is not in, and then to the police where he meets Lt. Snyder who offers Johnny a hard-boiled egg. Lt. Snyder has no idea what has happened to Harry. Nothing has turned up, and his car is missing. Lt. Snyder tells Johnny that Harry's wife is missing also. Johnny goes to the ballpark and talks to Crawfish Crawford, the catcher. Johnny is told that Harry roomed with Crawfish and that Harry left everything behind when he disappeared. Johnny mentions his wife, but Crawfish claims to not know about her. Johnny learns that Harry's pitching was off this year, he must have been in love.

Back at his hotel Johnny is met by Lt. Snyder who tells Johnny that Harry's car was found, abandoned south of Nogales, and dried blood was found on the front seat.

Johnny goes to his room and returns a call to Oglethorpe. Johnny him asks about Mrs. Hailey, and Oglethorpe tells him that she is from Magdalena, about fifty miles south of the border. Crawfish comes to Johnny's room and tells him that Harry had been going to a doctor in Tucson, a Dr. Wolfe. Johnny checks the phone book, and realizes why Harry disappeared. Johnny drives to Mildred's hotel, where she has been thinking about Harry. She has given up hope ever since he married that girl. Johnny reminds her that she had said she would change her mind about Juanita if there were a good reason for him to disappear, and Johnny tells her that he has a reason, and she should be ready to go with him in the morning.

Johnny and Mildred drive to Magdalena over rough roads and through loose chickens. Mildred does not care for the Mexicans because they are poor and dirty. She points to some children in a field as an example, and Johnny stops and talks to one of them. Johnny asks who taught them to play baseball with five bases, and a boy tells Johnny that a lady taught them, Señora Torres. The boy takes them to the Torres house and a servant takes them to the living room. Mildred is sure that her brother is dead because of the blood in his car. Johnny tells her to ask her brother what happened, he is standing in the doorway. Mildred is ecstatic to see Harry and wants him pack his things and go back with them to civilization. Harry tells Mildred that he wanted to get away from her for good and hates her for what she said about his wife. Harry tells Johnny that Mildred tried to get him to leave Juanita and called him names. Mildred has been bothering over him since he was a kid. Harry tells her that she needs a husband, but she tells him that a husband would only leave, like Joe did. Harry tells her that Joe left because she was always looking after him, and never even cooked a meal for Joe. Harry tells Johnny that the blood in the car was from a chicken that they hit. They had not taken his clothes, mainly because Mildred had bought them for him. He tells Mildred to go back to Omaha and stomps out of the room. Juanita comes in and tells Mildred that she really loves Harry. He is not well and has gotten bad news from a doctor in Tucson. Harry calls to her and she leaves. Johnny tells Mildred that Harry had been going to a specialist for eye diseases, and that Harry is going blind.

Some people, you just can't figure. Mildred Womac stayed on in Magdalena. Yeah, she rented a small adobe house and did what she could to help her less fortunate neighbors. Harry Hailey never played ball again, but he retained enough of his sight to show the Magdalena Spartans the difference between four bases and five.

NOTES:

- CHIPPY IS SLANG FOR A WOMAN PROSTITUTE.
- DAN CUBBERLY IS THE ANNOUNCER
- MUSIC SUPERVISION IS BY AMERIGO MARINO
- CAST AND CREW FROM RADIOGOLDINDEX.

**Producer:** Jack Johnstone        **Writers:** Charles B. Smith
**Cast:**        Virginia Gregg, Lillian Buyeff, Richard Beals, Barney Phillips, Frank Nelson, Harry Bartell, Dick Crenna, Lawrence Dobkin

**SHOW:**        THE PEERLESS FIRE MATTER
**SHOW DATE:**   5/5/1957
**COMPANY:**     FOUR-STATE MUTUAL INSURANCE COMPANY
**AGENT:**       HENRY WILLOWBY
**EXP. ACCT:**   $14.46

SYNOPSIS: "Do you smell smoke Johnny?" asks Henry Willowby. The kind of smoke that $5,000 makes when hit goes up in flames. The fire is at the Peerless Junkyard in Cranford, Connecticut. "If it is only a $5,000 loss, how can you afford me?" asks Johnny. Because Henry smells arson.

Johnny cabs to Hank's office and learns that the policy was issued four years ago to Oscar H. Lehman, the owner. The fire started at 4:00 AM and the claim was in Hanks office when he got there. Johnny calls Mr. Lehman and he wants to know if Johnny has the check. Johnny trains to Cranford and cabs to Lehman's home. Johnny comments on the new development of Cranford after the closing of the big clock company after World War II. The cabby stops at the site of the fire and tells Johnny that he hates to see the junkyard gone, as that is where he got the parts for his cab. The cabby mentions that with the junkyard gone, the whole area can be residential, like it ought to. When the cabby tells Johnny he should burn up his cab and get the insurance money, Johnny tells him to be careful whom he talks to, especially to an insurance investigator! Johnny gets out and looks at the yard with the fire chief, Dale Marley, who agrees that the residents of the area are glad to see the eyesore go up in flames. Johnny sees where the fire started, and the owner of a store next door reported that the fire started with a boom. The Chief suspects arson, and has called for the experts from New Haven. Johnny has an idea, and relates how lumberyards and furniture factories are the worst place to look for signs of arson. Johnny goes to the store next door and buys a loaf of white bread. Johnny tells the chief to chew on a piece of bread and swallow it. Johnny drops a piece into the ashes and then uses the taste of the bread to find traces of kerosene. The chief wants to arrest the owner, but Johnny tells him to hold off. Johnny cabs to Lehman's address located in a has-been area. Lehman tells Johnny that he is waiting at home for the insurance company to pay him and that he did not know about the fire until 7:00 AM. He did not want to sit around and wait, so he filed the claim. Johnny asks why he burned the yard, and Lehman tells Johnny that he did not burn the yard, and that he has a conditional license. If he is not in business every day, he loses his lease and the development company will take the land away. Johnny thinks he has already met the arsonist, and was too blind to see it.

Johnny remembers something the cab driver said about the neighbors beefing since the junkyard got its license. Back at the junkyard Chief Marley shows Johnny where a sliding door on the shed is still locked, and the window on the Howard Street side was open. Across the street are a number of houses with nice gardens surrounded by rocks. The chief has found a rock inside the remains of the shed. He thinks that someone broke the glass with a rock, climbed in, spread the kerosene, climbed out and threw in a light and left in a hurry. Johnny tells him he has a good suspect and goes across the street to talk to the neighbors. At the first house Johnny talks to Howard McNeal who yells at Johnny for trying to sell him insurance. McNeal tells Johnny not to investigate the fire, as it was a blessing. It was the only way to get rid of the junkyard. But hate it enough to set it on fire? "Oh, no not me." McNeal would never do that; he does not believe in insurance. McNeal tells Johnny to ask that Nazi Lehman. He is German isn't he? Ask him if he had insurance. Mr. McNeal mentions the widow Cummings, and Miss Gertrude Mary Anastasia Conroy the nice spinster; they would like to see it gone too. What spirit Miss Conroy has. McNeal will ask her for a date one of these days. Johnny visits Miss Conroy, an Irish woman who is cleaning her house. She wants to see Johnny's badge and is tired of answering questions. She had wanted go get rid of the junkyard for years. But now that poor Mr. Lehman has lost everything, she could cry her eyes out. And the horrible things that Hitler did to him. He escaped from Germany and put all his savings into that "lovely secondhand lot" so he could earn an honest living. Such a gentleman he is. And the way he would click his heels and bow when he came to visit on Sunday afternoons. She used to hate the lot until she met Mr. Lehman, and now she has "set her cap" for him. She will marry him before she is through. Johnny mentions Mr. McNeal and she calls him an old coot. She tells Johnny that Mr. Lehman was not in need of money, and the accident will help bring them together. She thinks that Johnny is sure that Lehman burned the shop, and he is wrong. She had told him to get the claim in real early. She is going to fix him corned beef and cabbage for dinner tonight. "What an offbeat insurance matter" Johnny muses. Johnny visits the widow Cummings and the door slowly opens to show a small woman in a wheelchair. She has been waiting and listening to what the neighbors had told Johnny. She tells Johnny that he must take Rudolph, her stepson away. He is keeping her there until she dies to get the money her husband left her. He is smart and thought the fire would burn down the house and trap her there, but the wind changed. He had told her that he would be away at work all night, but came home early. She saw him take the kerosene can across the street, put it in the shed and run away after he lit the fire. She had lied to the police, as she hoped that he would give up when he saw she was still alive. Johnny is glad she told him, and she tells Johnny that Rudolph would just find some other way.

Johnny stays an extra day to clear things up, and for Rudolph to return. Johnny finds the kerosene can in the basement, and the Chief finds the top in the ashes, with only Rudolph's fingerprints on it. Rudolph is in the city jail and Johnny is sure that Mrs. Cummings will testify against him, after all her life is at stake. And Oscar Lehman's claim will be paid in full and Johnny hopes he and Miss Conroy will live happily ever after.

NOTES:
- THE MID-PROGRAM COMMERCIAL IS AN **AFRS** SPOT ABOUT THE FLAG OF MISSOURI
- DAN CUBBERLY IS THE ANNOUNCER
- MUSIC SUPERVISION IS BY AMERIGO MARINO

Producer:     Jack Johnstone          Writers:   Jack Johnstone
Cast:         Virginia Gregg, Peggy Webber, John Stevenson, Herb Vigran, Hans Conried, Forrest Lewis, Parley Baer

◆   ❖   ◆

SHOW:          THE GLACIER GHOST MATTER
SHOW DATE:     5/12/1957
COMPANY:       TRI-WESTERN LIFE & CASUALTY COMPANY
AGENT:         WALTER BASCOMB
EXP. ACCT:     $431.60
SYNOPSIS: Johnny is called by Walter Bascomb. Walt has a $100,000 claim to pay, but can't. Walt wants Johnny to find the body.

Johnny flies to Los Angeles and gets a room at the Ambassador Hotel. The next day Johnny goes to see Walt who tells Johnny that the insured was Raymond R. Shelton, who was part of Rycoff-Shelton Plastics. The beneficiary of the police is his wife, Gloria, who lives in Westwood. Ray and his partner loved to hunt and fish and had gone to a lake up near the Palisade Glacier, California. They had gone to Lone Horse glacier and got caught in a blizzard. They made camp, but Ray fell into a crevasse. His partner came out two days later. Johnny's assignment is to find Shelton's body. Search parties have gone out, but they cannot find the body. The wife really needs the money and must wait for a year without the body. Walt also tells Johnny that he is in love with Gloria.

Johnny goes to the plant and talks to Al Rycoff, who tells Johnny the same story, and tells Johnny that he owes his position to Ray Shelton, and will get the business. Johnny goes to see the widow and she tells Johnny that her husband worked hard, but they were never close. He was thirteen years older and it was her social connections that got him his financing. Gloria tells Johnny that Al

Rycoff was in love with her, and became a member of the family, but now she is in love with Walter Bascomb. While they are talking Al comes in with a gun and tells Johnny that he will not let Johnny intimidate Gloria. He tells Johnny that he knows that he is the most likely suspect because he has the most to gain, but Johnny cannot prove that he killed Ray. Johnny calms him down and they arrange to go to the Sierras in Al's plane the next day. Al flies Johnny over the glacier and they spot a body, but Johnny cannot prove it is Ray. Al and Johnny land at Forrest Lewis' Pack Station and Forrest tells Johnny that there is no way that he can get to the body to get it out, so it must stay there. Al leaves when Johnny tells him that he has accepted an offer from Forrest to stay and fish for a couple days.

After Al leaves Johnny gets some dynamite, some 30/30 cartridges and makes an impact fuse. After testing it, Johnny arranges with Joe Gracey to fly to the glacier with the dynamite. Joe and Johnny fly over the glacier and Johnny drops a bomb onto the glacier, causing the ice ridge with the body to fall into the lake. Joe lands his plane on the lake and they retrieve the body to discover a bullet hole in its back. Joe takes off and heads back to the pack station when he spots Al Rycoff's plane, which buzzes them and shoots at his plane. Joe tells Johnny that he will head for Anchor Pass, which has very bad downdrafts if you do not know how to fly there. Joe gets his plane through, but Al crashes.

Remarks: "Justice was done in its own strange way."

NOTES:
- THE ANNOUNCER IS DAN CUBBERLY
- MUSIC DIRECTION IS BY AMERIGO MARINO
- STORY INFORMATION OBTAINED FROM THE KNX COLLECTION IN THE THOUSAND OAKS LIBRARY

**Producer:** Jack Johnstone       **Writers** Jack Johnstone
**Cast:** John Dehner, Herb Ellis, Virginia Gregg, Forrest Lewis, James McCallion, Tom Hanley, John James

**SHOW:** THE MICHAEL MEANY MIRAGE MATTER
**SHOW DATE:** 5/19/1957
**COMPANY:** FLOYDS OF ENGLAND
**AGENT:** GEORGE REED
**EXP. ACCT:** $420.10
**SYNOPSIS:** George Reed calls, and it is not a good morning, even thought the birds are singing and the bees are buzzing for Johnny. George asks Johnny if he knows anything about whales. Neither Johnny or George or the agent in Gulf Port, Mississippi does. Floyds has a floater policy on 80 pounds of ambergris, which is used in the manufacturing of perfume. The ambergris is worth $20,000 and has disappeared. The Agent is W. C. Owen. George tells Johnny that the

ambergris will be easy to find as it "smells worse than a hound dog which has caught a skunk."

Johnny flies to Gulf Port, Mississippi and calls Owen, who visits Johnny in his hotel room to tell Johnny to find the ambergris within the next 48 hours. It is packed in dry ice that will last that long, and Michael Meany, Owen's client, was promised that Johnny could find it in that time. Meany has told Owen that the ambergris is worth upwards of $60,000. Billy Fisher, who works for Meany, found it. Meany puts his boats out on share, and takes a share of everything that is caught, so the ambergris belongs to Meany. Owen tells Johnny that Meany is waiting to talk in Mississippi City. Owen takes Johnny to see Meany, a huge man and Johnny tells him he is an investigator. Johnny is told that the ambergris was stolen from the platform of the American Express office in Tuscaloosa, Alabama. It was being sent to an agent in New Orleans. The freight had not been paid, as the delivery person, Meany's nephew TJ, spotted a girl and neglected the box. Meany tells Johnny that he has forty-five hours to find the ambergris. Johnny and Owen leave and Owen tells Johnny that Meany owns most of the business along the beach. Owen takes Johnny to Billy Fisher's boarding house where Billy is in his room with Jane Higgins. Jane and Billy come out and Johnny wants to talk to him alone. Billy tells Johnny that he found the ambergris floating in the channel. He took it into the boat not realizing it would belong to Meany. Cliff Dillinger, the checker for Meany, spotted the ambergris and took it away from him. Johnny turns down dinner with Miss Harvey and goes to his hotel where he has a message from George that tells Johnny that a friend of a man in the office is an ichthyologist. He has told George that ambergris comes only from the sperm whale, and there never has been a sperm whale in the Gulf of Mexico. Well, if there never has been a sperm whale in the gulf, what is the stuff that is insured?

Johnny calls Owen, and he is shocked when he finds out what has happened. Owen is sure that Meany is not pulling a fraud as a chemist in Biloxi analyzed the ambergris, and said it was real. Owen tells Johnny that he should have checked on the chemist, and Johnny feels sorry for him, as the company might pull his franchise. Next morning Johnny walks up the street looking for a place to eat breakfast when he meets Jane. She is on a shopping spree looking for something to get married in, and the lucky man is Billy Fisher. Jane tells Johnny that her father will be angry, but there is nothing he can do, as she is over eighteen. And she is going to change his mind about Billy. Johnny asks her to join him for breakfast, but she suddenly remembers something important she has to do. Johnny enters the "All Night Diner," and orders ham and eggs over easy and coffee. The counterman is TJ, Meany's nephew and his uncle has told him about Johnny. He tells Johnny that he was waiting to put the package on the train when a girl drove up and gave him a great big come-on. TJ went across the street to talk to her and she told him that her name was Betty Lou Miller. TJ tells Johnny the he was just talking to her on the street. After breakfast Johnny meets Owen and they go to the depot where the agent remembers everything, including the name of the woman who bought the ticket. Johnny goes to see Meany and tells him he thinks he knows who has the ambergris, and Meany wants the name. Johnny tells him he will know for sure, if Meany will help him. Johnny asks Meany for the letter from the chemist who analyzed the ambergris and then leaves to see a lady. Johnny drives Owen's car to the Harvey boarding house. Johnny tells her what he knows and she tells Johnny that it was her fault. She had put Billy up to it, and had bought the train ticket. She knew that TJ would leave the package, because he has a weakness for girls. Johnny tells Miss Harvey that she timed it just like a professional as Billy was in the woods waiting for Jane to get TJ all mixed up, and then Billy grabbed the package and ran back to the woods where Jane picked him up later. The ambergris was shipped to Atlanta, where a man will sell it for Billy. Johnny tells her that he had run into Jane, and Miss Harvey tells Johnny that they will get married, even if the ambergris turns out to be something else. Meany drives up with Owen calling for Johnny and asking what he is doing. Meany wants to arrest Billy and Jane for stealing the ambergris, and Miss Harvey tells Meany that Billy took the ambergris because it belonged to him all the time. Johnny agrees, if it was ambergris. Owen has called the chemist, but he has quit his job, and no record was found of the tests. Meany tells them that it was ambergris, and Miss Harvey tells Meany he was seeing a mirage. Johnny tells Meany that the contract he had with Billy only covers fish and fish by-products, which belong to Meany. But, the ambergris does not, because a whale is not a fish, it is a mammal.

"They say that young love can work miracles, and I guess it must be true, because later that day a huge sperm whale was sighted about three miles offshore near the Cat Island channel. Proving as I have always said, you can't figure whales anymore than you can people."

NOTES:

- THE MID-PROGRAM COMMERCIAL IS AN **AFRS** SPOT ABOUT THE FLAG OF NEW MEXICO.
- AMBERGRIS IS A FATTY OR PITCH-LIKE SUBSTANCE PRODUCED BY SPERM WHALES. AMBERGRIS IS TYPICALLY FOUND FLOATING IN THE WATER, OR ON THE SEASHORE. WHEN FRESH, AMBERGRIS SMELLS STRONG AND UNPLEASANT. IT IS USED AS A FIXATIVE IN EXPENSIVE PERFUMES.
- DAN CUBBERLY IS THE ANNOUNCER
- MUSIC SUPERVISION IS BY AMERIGO MARINO

| | | | |
|---|---|---|---|
| **Producer:** | Jack Johnstone | **Writers:** | Charles B. Smith |
| **Cast:** | Virginia Gregg, Jeanette Nolan, G. Stanley Jones, Junius Matthews, Gil Stratton, Dick Crenna, John Dehner | | |

◆   ❖   ◆

| | |
|---|---|
| **SHOW:** | THE WAYWARD TRUCK MATTER |
| **SHOW DATE:** | 5/26/1957 |
| **COMPANY:** | TRI-WESTERN INDEMNITY COMPANY |

**AGENT:**      **TED ORLOFF**

**EXP. ACCT:**      **$501.05**

**SYNOPSIS:** Ted Orloff calls from Los Angeles and he wants Johnny to come out right away. The problem is a wayward truck insured for nearly $20,000. The driver disappeared, and he is insured for $10,000 and the cargo of copper tubing is insured for $9,500. Johnny will grab the next plane.

Johnny flies to Los Angeles, California and is met at the airport by Ted. Ted tells Johnny that a truck carrying copper tubing used in airplanes has disappeared. It was shipped from Marlowe Copper Products in East Los Angeles. Jacky McCallion was scheduled to deliver the tubing and made the run at night to avoid the heat of the desert. After midnight, Jackie signed out the shipment and by the next morning Belden Aircraft was screaming about the delivery. The market for copper tubing is good because it is expensive and hard to get. Lockheed and Belden have built plants in the area and subcontract to smaller companies. The tubing would be worth its weight in gold to the smaller plants. The driver is an honest man according to the employer, and they would trust him with a load of pure gold. Johnny infers that Jacky would know where to sell the tubing, and could make a lot of money for himself. Johnny meets Mr. Marlowe and Willie, the night watchman. Johnny is told that Jacky left at 12:05 and has not been seen since. When asked about how much money Jacky makes, Mr. Marlowe tells Johnny he is dead wrong if he is thinking that Jacky stole the tubing, and that Marlowe will take care of whoever has done him in as that is the only way he would give up the goods. Johnny asks Willie if there was anything unusual about Jacky when he got the truck, and is told that everything seemed normal. When Willie leaves Johnny tells Mr. Marlowe that he needs better night watchman. Johnny is told that the hijackers could get the information on the shipment from a lot of different sources. The route has been gone over by the police, and nothing had been found. Johnny gets Jacky's address and borrows a well-marked company car. At the house the front door is open and Jacky's apartment is open. Inside someone is emptying the dresser drawers. Johnny enters and asks what is going on and fights with the man. Johnny overpowers the man, who is Jacky McCallion.

Jacky tells Johnny that he is handy with his dukes for a skinny guy. Johnny tells Jacky who he is and Jacky tells Johnny that the shipment was called off. It was supposed to go out Wednesday night, on "Betsy" his truck, but a girl in the office called and told him that the order got cancelled out and Jacky was told he could start his vacation right away. Jacky was in San Diego fishing for Yellowtail. Jackie is surprised when Johnny tells him that the shipment went out and has not been heard of since. Jacky tells Johnny that he was in San Diego by 1:00 AM, ask his sister. "And if some dirty guy took my Betsy out, I'll kill him!" As Johnny and Jacky drive back to the Marlowe warehouse, Johnny is sure that Jacky is on the level, and Johnny wonders who could be enough of a double to fool the night watchman? Or could Marlowe himself have contrived to take the copper. At the plant, Mr. Marlowe is happy to see Jacky. Marlowe tells Johnny that Jacky helped Marlowe build the company. Jacky tells Johnny that he only wanted to be a truck driver, even with the big retirement Marlowe gave him he just wants to drive Betsy, and go fishing once in a while. Johnny asks to talk to Willie, and Marlowe calls him to the office. Johnny remembers that there was something unusual in the way Willie had said Jacky picked up the truck. There were no positive answers. Marlowe tells Johnny that Willie carries a time clock and Johnny asks for the record and the manifest and the shipping order for the copper tubing. Willie arrives and Johnny takes him to the watchman's booth and is told that it is Willie's "own private office." Willie tells Johnny that he had not talked to Jackie, as he had no reason to. Johnny tells Willie that he knew what time Jacky was coming and did not see him, or see him sign the manifest or drive out with the truck. Knowing Jacky, or someone, was coming, Willie had left the gate open, and was a partner to the theft as Jacky did not pick up the truck. Johnny takes out the time clock record and goes over the record of the checks. Johnny looks at the time clock record and tells Willie that he was on the far side of he plant when the truck went out. Willie admits that he had often left the gate open, like he usually does. He had left the catch on the main gate so it would look like it was set. He did that for the other drivers, but not for Jacky because he was too close to the boss. Johnny tells Willie he is in trouble and turns him over to Marlowe, but Johnny is no closer to finding the truck. Over lunch, Jacky tells Johnny that the only ones who would know when the load was going out were Willie and Red Kingsley. Johnny remembers he had borrowed Red's car, and Jacky is about to tell him about Red when Marlowe rushes in and tells Johnny that the sheriff in Victorville has picked up some of the tubing. Johnny is told to borrow Red's car and Jacky goes with him. Johnny rushes to the area, past Edwards Air Force Base as Jacky checks out all the trucks. As Johnny passes a truck the driver yells at him and Jacky recognizes the truck as Betsy. Johnny realizes that the driver had yelled "Hey Red" because of the car. The truck catches up and rams the car. Later Johnny is awakened by a man slapping him. The man tells Johnny that he had edged the other truck off the highway, and it flipped over spilling its load. The police had seen the truck ram Red's car and had chased him, but it took a big truck like "Clara-belle," his tractor-trailer, to do that. It's not the first time he has helped the police."

Yeah, they've given a lot of people a hand, those boys who drive the big interstate trucks and trailers. They're a pretty fine bunch to have on the road. Well I guess it's pretty obvious that Red Kingsley in Marlowe's shipping department was back of the hijacking operation. The two who were aboard the stolen truck turned state's evidence and sang plenty, and the courts will take care of them.

NOTES:
- THE MID-PROGRAM COMMERCIAL IS AN AFRS SPOT ABOUT THE FLAG OF NEW JERSEY.
- DAN CUBBERLY IS THE ANNOUNCER
- MUSIC SUPERVISION IS BY AMERIGO MARINO

**Producer:** Jack Johnstone      **Writers:** Jack Johnstone

Cast:      **Forrest Lewis, John Dehner, Junius Matthews, Stacy Harris, Jack Kruschen**

◆   ❖   ◆

SHOW:          THE LOSS OF MEMORY MATTER
SHOW DATE:     6/2/1957
COMPANY:       CONTINENTAL INSURANCE COMPANY
AGENT:         LES CRUTCH
EXP. ACCT:     $95.00

SYNOPSIS: Johnny is called by Les Crutch who asks Johnny if he knows about the Preece expedition that went to the city of Ur, in the valley of the Euphrates. Les has the insurance on the collection, but nothing has happed yet, but come on over.

Johnny goes to the library to read up on Babylon so that he can be ready for a trip to the Middle East. Johnny goes to Les' office and learns that the relics are located in Lakeview, Connecticut, and are owned by that crackpot, Alvin Peabody Cartwright. Johnny is shown a pillow made of mud with some hieroglyphics on it, and is told that is it a receipt for 24 fat sheep, 12 oxen, and 12 goats that dates from 2350 BC and is typical of the collection. Alvin has sold the collection to the museum, and his nephew Alfred Hocking is going to deliver it, but Alvin is worried. There is a $20,000 transit policy, but Alvin wants Johnny to act as a guard for $250 plus expenses.

Johnny rents a car and drives to Lakeview and meets Alvin, and sees a sealed box with the relics. Johnny meets Alfred and Alvin tells Johnny that he wants the cash brought back tonight! Johnny leaves for Hartford with Alfred, who tells Johnny that he would take the money because scrooge never let him have any, even though he has a safe full of money in the basement. The car crashes and Johnny wakes up with a headache, and amnesia. Al tells Johnny that Johnny is really Alfred Hocking, and they are making a delivery and will part company later. Al tells Johnny that he is Johnny Dollar. Johnny looks at this wallet, and his driver's license says he is Alfred Hocking.

A moving van stops and picks up Johnny and Al and takes them to the museum, where Al shows the director, Mr. Waring, his credentials. Al leaves the box and gets the $21,000 in cash from Mr. Waring. Al and Johnny go to a car rental office and Al rents a car. Al and Johnny drive towards Danbury and Al tells Johnny that he is taking Johnny to a hospital in New York, but Johnny realizes that something is wrong. Johnny asks for Al's gun permit, looks at the picture and into the mirror, when Al slugs Johnny. The car stops on a gravel road and Johnny calls Al by name. Johnny starts to remember what had happened and Al fights with Johnny and two shots are fired.

Johnny gets the money back to Alvin, and Alfred is arrested. Johnny gets a $500 bonus from Alvin.

"Not bad for just a couple of wallops on the head, eh?"

NOTES:

- THE ANNOUNCER IS DAN CUBBERLY
- MUSIC DIRECTION IS BY AMERIGO MARINO
- THIS IS THE FIRST APPEARANCE OF ALVIN PEABODY CARTWRIGHT
- ALVIN LIVES IN LAKEVIEW IN THIS STORY, BUT LATER STORIES PUT HIM IN LAKEWOOD.
- PARLEY BAER PLAYS ALVIN, BUT HE IS LATER PLAYED TO A "T" BY HOWARD MCNEAR
- STORY INFORMATION OBTAINED FROM THE KNX COLLECTION IN THE THOUSAND OAKS LIBRARY

Producer: Jack Johnstone        Writers    Jack Johnstone
Cast:       Les Tremayne, Parley Baer, Shep Menken, Joseph Kearns, Barney Phillips, Tom Hanley

◆  ❖  ◆

SHOW:          THE MASON-DIXON MISMATCH MATTER
SHOW DATE:     6/9/1957
COMPANY:       PROVIDENTIAL ASSURANCE COMPANY
AGENT:         BERT MCGRAW
EXP. ACCT:     $319.00

SYNOPSIS: Bert McGraw calls Johnny about Darla Mason, niece of Sylvester Mason of Mason Steel and Iron. She disappeared six weeks ago and Bert has a $25,000 policy with double indemnity on her. A body washed up on Newport Beach yesterday and her father says it is Darla. Bert was going to pay off the policy until a man named Dixon showed up and claimed the body as his daughter.

Johnny cabs to Bert's office where Bert is in the process of hanging a picture of himself pitching for the Valgusta Lions. He did not win the game for them, the umpire cheated. Bert tells Johnny that so far the authorities have not been able to identify the body. Bert gets a call from Capt. Miller of the Newport police, and he tells Bert that the body was shot with a .38. The Steel girl has been missing for six weeks and the Mason girl for three months, so Johnny is going to find the living girl.

Johnny cabs to his apartment and travels to Newport, Rhode Island and gets a room at the Ogden Hotel. Johnny rents a car and drives to the Mason estate where Darla's sister Joan meets him at the door and takes him to see her mother. Mrs. Mason tells Johnny that he is there for nothing, as her husband has released a statement to the press saying that the body was not his daughter. Mr. Mason comes in and tells Johnny to talk to him if he wants answers. He tells Johnny that as soon as his wife found out that the girl had been murdered his wife felt that it was not her daughter, as their kind of people only die in bed. He tells Johnny that his daughter was a real nice girl. He is certain that the body is his daughter, as she had no reason to leave. He had given her everything she could want. She was last seen at the Newport Yacht club. Joan saw her talking to a stranger, and she has never been seen since. Johnny tells Mr. Mason that he is going to find her, or the Dixon girl. Mr. Mason is sure that Darla did not know the other girl, as his wife had drilled it into her daughter to not mix with people who were beneath her. Johnny gets a small picture of Darla and drives to town.

Johnny calls Henry Dixon and then goes to visit them. Mr. Dixon tells Johnny that this thing has not been easy on his wife, and they are almost sure that the body is not their daughter. Lucille comes out and they sit on the porch. They only have a small insurance policy on their daughter. Henry had been a schoolteacher but had to slow down for health reasons. They have been in Newport for five months. Lucille tells Johnny that Ruth was spoiled and they moved to Newport hoping they could find some friends on her own level. She mentioned once that the Mason girl had been at the store where she worked. Ruth seems to be happy with her job as a hostess. Johnny gets a picture of her that was taken at the Newport Yacht Club where she worked.

At his hotel Johnny has a message from Capt. Miller and goes to see him. The Masons are in Capt. Millers' office, and she is happy about the good news. She has proof that Darla is alive. Mrs. Mason got a bill for Darla from Kennedy's Department Store over in Providence. The bill came today, and a fur wrap had been charged by Darla just last week.

Johnny gets the sales slip with Darla's name of it. Capt. Miller arranges to get a copy of the driver's license to compare the signature and then Johnny and Capt. Miller drive to Kennedy's. The clerk in the fur department is sure that it was Darla, even though she had not met her before. Johnny shows her the photographs after altering them slightly with paper hats. With the hair covered up the two girls look almost identical. Johnny and Capt. Miller go back to the office and compare the driver's license signature and are sure what had happened. Johnny goes to his hotel and is called by Joan, who comes up to his room for her date. She tells Johnny that everyone knows about Darla charging the fur. Johnny asks about the day at the yacht club and the need for a guest pass to get in. Joan tells Johnny that the man was Peter Hansen, their tutor.

Next morning Johnny calls the employment agency that referred Hansen to the Masons and gets a Providence address and drives to the address followed by a battered blue sedan. Three addresses later Johnny stops and Mr. Dixon gets out of the car. He tells Johnny that he just had to do something. Johnny goes to the house and finally Peter Hansen opens the door and laughs when Johnny tells him he is with an insurance company. Peter tries to close the door and Johnny pushes his way in and knocks Pete out while Darla screams about finding them. She tells Johnny that she would be happier if they thought she was dead. She left because she was bored of living the way her family wanted her to. She shows Johnny some sea birds that are free, just the way she wants to be. Johnny tells Darla that he found her because of the bill sent to her house, and she tells Johnny that it was supposed to be sent to the beach house. Mr. Dixon comes in and is disappointed and tells Darla he wished she were dead.

Like Bert McGraw told me a long time ago, someone has to handle the rough ones, for me, this was it. Henry Dixon was in no condition to drive his car, so he rode back with us, and on the way, well Darla Mason will never forget the things he said to her; neither will I. As for Ruth Dixon, who murdered her and why, well that is up to the Newport police.

NOTES:
* THE MID PROGRAM COMMERCIAL IS AND **AFRS** SPOT ABOUT A BULL THAT THREW A MAN
* DAN CUBBERLY IS THE ANNOUNCER
* MUSIC SUPERVISION IS BY AMERIGO MARINO

Producer:  Jack Johnstone          Writers:  Charles B. Smith
Cast:      Virginia Gregg, Mary Jane Croft, Jeanette Nolan, Jean Tatum,
           Frank Nelson, Will Wright, Austin Green Marvin Miller

SHOW:         THE DIXON MURDER MATTER
SHOW DATE:    6/16/1957
COMPANY:      PROVIDENTIAL ASSURANCE COMPANY
AGENT:        BERT MCGRAW
EXP. ACCT:    $968.20

SYNOPSIS: Bert McGraw greets Johnny with "The Bases are loaded, and there is nobody out, and you're pitching, Johnny boy!" as Johnny answers the phone. Bert is calling about the job Johnny did not finish, the Mason-Dixon Murder. Johnny tells Bert that it is up to the police now, but Bert tells Johnny that police want to talk to Johnny about the case and so does Bert. Ruth Dixon was insured for $1,000, but if Johnny will come up, they will foot the bill. Johnny is interested now.

Johnny cabs to Bert's office and thinks about the case in Newport Beach where two families had claimed a girl's body. Bert tells Johnny that Ruth had a $1,000 policy, and that the police have a lot to do with the company. Capt. Lewis of homicide, called and he is very unhappy with Johnny for not giving them all the information on the Mason girl. The police chewed out the company, the company chewed out Bert, and Bert is chewing out Johnny. Bert tells Johnny to go build up the good will, and keep Capt. Lewis informed. "I hope you understand. No hard feelings?" Bert asks Johnny. Johnny tells Bert "For an expense account like the one you are going to get, I could understand the theory of relativity!"

Johnny travels to Newport, Rhode Island, gets a room and calls Capt. Pete Lewis, who is not in. Johnny calls Darla Mason and asks if she can have dinner with him. Johnny buys roses for Mrs. Lucille Dixon and then drives to the Dixon home, which has the scent or oriental incense coming from a burner on the mantle. Lucille tells Johnny that Ruth will like the flowers, and she will take them to her. She thinks that those who pass on never really leave us, and that Ruth is still there. Lucille asks Johnny to come with her to visit Madam DeSau.

She has wonderful occult powers and she will help talk to Ruth when the time is right. Henry Dixon comes home and Johnny is invited to dinner. Henry tells Johnny that the mantle looks like a heathen altar, and would not blame Johnny if he were afraid to stay. Johnny asks Henry about any men Ruth might have been seeing, and he tells Johnny that she dated too much. She did have an older friend, Sam Hood who runs a craft repair shop on Viking Beach. Johnny drives to Viking Beach and finds the repair shop and an old PT boat. A fat man with thick glasses and dirty clothes on the boat tells Johnny that Sam Hood is on vacation. Johnny goes down to the boat, "The Conomore," to talk to Sam's brother, Leroy. Leroy tells Johnny that he found the name in a book, and that the name fits him and the boat. Leroy opens a plug of Brown Mule Chewing Tobacco and tells Johnny that the boat belongs to him and Sam. Sam is visiting their folks in Augusta. Johnny asks about Ruth Dixon, and Leroy tells Johnny that Sam and Ruth used to talk a lot. Leroy thinks Ruth was a two-timing woman, and that Sam left town after her death. Leroy tells Johnny that Sam owns a .38 revolver like everyone else with a boat. Leroy is sure that Sam did not kill Ruth. Johnny goes to meet Darla for dinner, but she does not show up. Later Capt. Lewis pounds on Johnny's door and tells Johnny that Darla Mason was shot tonight; by the same gun that shot Ruth Dixon.

Johnny buys coffee for Capt. Lewis, who tells Johnny that Darla had gone to the boathouse to take the cruiser to the yacht club, and someone shot and wounded her. Capt. Lewis tells Johnny that the Masons have their boat repaired by Sam Hood, but he is still in Georgia. Capt. Lewis arranges to call the Georgia police, and Johnny suggests he tell them about Darla. Johnny has a hunch, but wants to sleep on it. The next day Johnny runs into Mrs. Dixon in the lobby and she wants to talk. Last night Madam DeSau let Lucille talk to Ruth. Ruth told her that a young woman with dark hair, brown eyes, and a big red scar on the back of her left hand shot her, so all Johnny has to do is find a girl with that scar. Johnny calls Capt. Lewis, and learns that Sam is in Georgia, and that they service the Mason cruiser. Capt. Lewis asks Johnny about his hunch, but Johnny asks Capt. Lewis to call Augusta again and ask Sam Hood who named his boat. Johnny goes to the library, finds what he is looking for and goes to Capt. Lewis' office to tells him of his hunch. Sam Hood calls with the answer to Johnny's questions, and Johnny goes to see Leroy. Johnny asks how long it would take to go over to the Mason home and Leroy answers "no time at all." Leroy admits to hearing about Darla Mason being shot, and Johnny asks why he tried to kill her. Johnny tells Leroy that Darla told him that he had shot her, and Leroy tells Johnny that it was too dark. Johnny tells Leroy that Sam told the police that Leroy cannot stand to have a woman laugh at him, and when they do he tries to make them sorry for it. Johnny tells Leroy that Sam left to think about what to do with his brother, and that Johnny is going to take Leroy in. Leroy runs into the shop and comes out with a gun and shoots at Johnny. Capt. Lewis arrives and shoots Leroy. Johnny tells Capt. Lewis that Leroy wanted to be a lady-killer, but they all laughed at him. Also, the name of the boat, "Conomore" is the name of a real lady-killer, Bluebeard.

I saw Mrs. Dixon late that same afternoon. I am afraid she was a bit disillusioned. Having been so sure that the person who killed her daughter was a woman. But there was one funny thing. On the back of Leroy's left hand was a long red scar.

NOTES:

- THE MID-PROGRAM COMMERCIAL IS AN **AFRS** STORY ABOUT THE SYMBOLS IN A TOWN IN SPAIN AND AN AIR FORCE HELICOPTER USED TO REPAIR A STATUE.
- BLUEBEARD IS A FABLE ABOUT A MAN WHO MARRIES A SERIES OF WIVES AND KILLS THEM ALL.
- THANKS TO JEANETTE BERAND AT THE THOUSAND OAKS LIBRARY FOR HELPING ME FIND OUT THAT CONOMORE (WHO WAS KING OF BRETON [BRITTANY] IN THE 6TH CENTURY) WAS KNOWN AS THE BRETON BLUEBEARD.
- BROWN'S MULE WAS A CHEWING TOBACCO MADE BY R.J. REYNOLDS
- NOW THIS IS A CASE WITH A PADDED EXPENSE ACCOUNT!
- DAN CUBBERLY IS THE ANNOUNCER
- MUSIC SUPERVISION IS BY AMERIGO MARINO

| | | | |
|---|---|---|---|
| **Producer:** | Jack Johnstone | **Writers:** | Charles B. Smith |
| **Cast:** | Jean Tatum, Jeanette Nolan, Frank Nelson, Russell Thorson, Sam Edwards, Austin Green | | |

◆ ❖ ◆

| | |
|---|---|
| SHOW: | THE PARLEY BARRON MATTER |
| SHOW DATE: | 6/23/1957 |
| COMPANY: | TRI-STATE LIFE & CASUALTY COMPANY |
| AGENT: | EARLE POORMAN |
| EXP. ACCT: | $421.50 |

SYNOPSIS: Earle Poorman calls Johnny from the land of infernal sunshine. Earle may have a case for Johnny, maybe murder.

Johnny flies to Sarasota, Florida and goes to Earle's office where he gets a promise of a fishing trip before he goes home. Earle tells Johnny that a customer named Parley Barron bought a property near him on Lido Key, and he is insured for $50,000. His wife Laura is the beneficiary. Parley left on some errands and his car was found on the docks at 11 PM, but he was not out fishing. Barron got along well with everyone and has no enemies, so Earle thinks that Barron is dead. Johnny goes to Lido Key and meets Mrs. Barron, a fragile woman who is clutching her Bible. She tells Johnny that only prayer can help now. She is very religious, but her husband worked in a sinful job; he was a chemist who made explosives for the Dufresne Chemical Company, and retired in 1951. Johnny is told that Barron went fishing every day but never caught anything, and she feels that it was retribution. As Johnny is leaving, Mrs. Barron gives him a number of religious pamphlets to read. Johnny thinks that maybe he left because of the stifling atmosphere in the house.

Johnny and Earle go fishing to talk over the case and spot a hat and a body in the water. The body is unrecognizable, but Earle is sure that body is Barron as they take it to the police. Johnny goes to the dock of Will Bright and he tells Johnny that he had been in Gainesville, and that Barron only rented his boat from him. When he got back, he found the boat, but in a different spot and wondered if someone else brought it back. Johnny looks at the boat and notices a tackle box that had not been moved in months. Johnny goes to the police and talks to Sgt. Brackett who tells Johnny that the autopsy showed that the body was dead before it went into the water. A kid told them that he saw Barron leave alone, but the skiff was back that night. Johnny is not sure that the body is that of Barron. Sgt. Brackett tells Johnny that he is waiting for Barron's dentist, Dr. Dayner, to come from Tampa. Johnny asks if he is the same Jerrod Dayner who got so much publicity for the Atomic Radiation studies.

Johnny has lunch and calls Mrs. Dayner posing as Mr. Larkin from the Federal Bureau and asks if her husband followed his instructions and she mentions Dufresne. Johnny drives to the Dufresne Chemical Company and goes to the office of the president where he is invited in to the conference room, where Johnny meets Dr. Dayner, and Mac McLaughlin from the Federal Bureau, all of whom are expecting Johnny. Johnny is told that he has been followed and is a very sharp person, something they were not expecting. Johnny is told that Barley Barron is alive, and is making a valuable contribution to national security, and that his fishing trips were a cover for his work. Johnny is told that Barron is working on a nuclear project, somewhere in New Mexico and that the body was that of a derelict. Johnny is told that Dr. Dayner will identify the body with reservations, and that Johnny is to prevent an insurance claim.

For obvious reasons, this case used fictitious names and will be delayed until getting a clearance.

NOTES:
- THE ANNOUNCER IS DAN CUBBERLY
- MUSIC DIRECTION IS BY AMERIGO MARINO
- STORY INFORMATION OBTAINED FROM THE KNX COLLECTION IN THE THOUSAND OAKS LIBRARY

Producer:   Jack Johnstone          Writers   Jack Johnstone
Cast:       Lawrence Dobkin, Jeanette Nolan, Will Wright, Harry Bartell,
            Virginia Gregg, Barney Phillips, Stacy Harris

◆   ❖   ◆

SHOW:        THE FUNNY MONEY MATTER
SHOW DATE:   6/30/1957
COMPANY:     FLOYDS OF ENGLAND
AGENT:       GEORGE REED
EXP. ACCT:   $171.25

**SYNOPSIS:** George Reed calls Johnny and tells him that things are going bad. An old client, Durango Laramie Dalhart just made his $4,500 premium payment in crisp $100 bills. They are still on my desk. Every one of these bills is counterfeit. "Ah, I'll be right over" Johnny replies to George.

Johnny cabs to George Reed's office and sees the money. All of the bills look like they were made with washed out ink. Johnny notices that the serial numbers are all different and the paper is very good and the engraving is almost perfect. George tells Johnny that Durango is as honest as the day is long. He lives on a ranch in a place called Bum Spung, Oklahoma. Johnny suggests calling the Secret Service, but George wants Johnny to handle it. Durango has always paid his premiums in cash. George wants Johnny to handle this on an expenses plus special fee basis. Every year Durango comes east for a spree drops off his policy and heads back. Johnny agrees to take the case, but only to see what kind of a place deserves the name Bum Spung!

Johnny uses a ticket from George to fly to Enid, Oklahoma, eats and heads for Bum Spung. Johnny spots a sign and heads up a dirt road to an old farm house and old barn, two sad looking bovines, chickens and other old animals and a brand new Cadillac. On the other side of the house Johnny spots a young lady who (rowf!) is really pretty. She calls to Johnny and tells him to come in. She is Carol Dalhart, Durango's niece. She tells Johnny that Bum Spung means bad water. Durango liked the name and bought the place. Johnny asks to meet Durango, and suddenly Carol pulls a .45 and shoots a gopher snake twice. She tells Johnny that she looks after the place for Durango from time to time. Durango buys her a new car every year and supposedly has a barrel of money. When he dies she will get his money and can sell her filling station; Durango says a girl has to do something. Carol asks Johnny why he is there and suddenly she trips and sprains her ankle and Johnny is forced to carry her inside. Inside the ramshackle shack is a thoroughly modern house, with all the latest appliances. Johnny cares for the ankle and starts to fix some dinner while Carol naps. Durango comes in ready to kill and shoots at Johnny several times.

Durango accuses Johnny of robbing his house until Carol calls him off. Johnny is able to take Durango's gun away from him, and Durango tells Carol he was having some fun with her boyfriend. He gives Carol $500 to buy a new stove and other destroyed goods. Durango offers Johnny a jug and tells Johnny he gets tired of sitting around and has to go out to get some excitement. Durango tells Johnny that he has spunk, not like Carol's other boyfriends. While Durango starts to fix dinner, Carol and Johnny "talk" on the sofa. Carol wants to know why Johnny is there, and he manages to put her off, while Durango constantly interrupts. After dinner Johnny learns of Durango's past, and how he has made more money than he can ever spend. After retiring for the night, Johnny hears Durango go out of the house and follows him to an out building where Johnny hears the noise of what he thinks is a printing press. Suddenly Carol surprises him and Johnny tells her he is looking for what is in the building. Carol tells Johnny not to break Durango's heart; he thinks that no one, not even she, knows what is going on in there. He does not mean any harm to anyone. Durango comes out and Johnny pulls his gun on him. Johnny tells him to open the door so he can see what is going on. Durango tells Johnny that he always goes to the bank and gets brand new $100 bills but the banks did not have any the last time he was there. Johnny goes into the building to find where Durango is washing, starching and ironing his money to make it look brand new.

Well, there you have it George, a full report on the funny money that turned out to be only cleaned up a bit. And the next time, call in the Secret Service will ya. No, no, I didn't mean that. Just don't question the charges on this account for the extra week I spent out here. If you could see this pretty little Carol, oh that Carol. And if I ever get enough money so help me I think I'll retire to Bum Spung, Oklahoma.

NOTES:
- THIS IS THE FIRST APPEARANCE OF THE DALHART CLAN, DURANGO AND CAROL.
- DAN CUBBERLY IS THE ANNOUNCER

Producer:    Jack Johnstone          Writers:    Jack Johnstone
Cast:        Virginia Gregg, G. Stanley Jones, John McIntire

SHOW:          THE FELICITY FELINE MATTER
SHOW DATE:     7/7/1957
COMPANY:       CONTINENTAL ASSURANCE COMPANY
AGENT:         HENRY PARKER
EXP. ACCT:     $407.20

SYNOPSIS: Henry Parker calls Johnny from Reno, and things are terrible in Nevada. Parker turns the phone over to a man who addresses Johnny as a "sloth-eyed Pinkerton." Johnny recognizes the voice as that of cantankerous old Jodiah Gillis, and he wants Johnny to get there before a feline friend of his gets killed. The cat is has inherited $60,000 but someone is trying to make sure that he does not live long enough to spend it.

Johnny flies to Reno, Nevada and wonders about what Gillis is doing in Reno. Gillis meets Johnny at the airport with a tall, cadaverous man, who is Gillis' friend and business partner Henry Parker. Parker tells Johnny that Gillis is quite concerned about Felicity, and goes to get Johnny's bags. Johnny tells Gillis that no one has heard of Continental Assurance, and Gillis tells Johnny that it is a local company, and Parker is the president and Jodiah is the Chairman of the Board. He used to be covered by Floyds, but dropped them when they told him he could not insure an African Anteater named Archie. Archie over indulged on a house full of termites and died of acute indigestion. Gillis tells Johnny that Continental paid off on the anteater and on the policy that Felicity inherited from poor old Mrs. Hammelmeyer. She left a brother, a nephew and a niece, but Felicity was the beneficiary. Mrs. Hawkins, a trusted friend of Mrs.

Hammelmeyer is the trustee, but there have been two attempts on Felicity in two weeks. Johnny is taken to the Mapes Hotel and then goes to the Hammelmeyer residence where Oscar Emmett, the nephew of Mrs. Hammelmeyer answers the door. Johnny and Jodiah go in and Johnny is told that Emmett does not work, and spends his time in the casinos picking up change left in the slot machines. Suddenly there is a scream when Johnny steps on Felicity's tail. Mrs. Hawkins comes in and Jodiah is talked into getting Felicity calmed down for her dish of scallops. Leona is happy to see Jodiah and is pleased to meet Johnny. She tells Johnny that a week ago Wednesday the cat was let out and when it started to rain, Mrs. Hawkins opened the door to let him in. It was then that she heard a big car zoom right for Felicity. Last Thursday Felicity was poisoned. According to the vet, somebody put arsenic in Felicity's lobster. Johnny is told that Mrs. Hammelmeyer left instructions that Felicity was to have lobster once a week, steak three times and boiled chicken every Sunday. As long as she does that Leona can live there rent-free just like her kin, the Emmetts. No one knows who gets the money if Felicity dies, and Mrs. Hammelmeyer left a sealed envelope to be opened only when Felicity dies. Leona is sure that the Emmetts will get all of the money. Joyce Emmett comes in and she bets eight to five that Johnny will not find the cat killer. Joyce tells Johnny that Aunt Mildred had no business leaving the money to that cat, and everyone else feels that way too. Mr. Emmett asks what interest Johnny has, and he tells him that Gillis sent for him. Emmett tells Johnny that he is a dog man, and it costs $23 a week to keep the cat. It will take 50 years to spend that money. Felicity comes in and everyone is sure that Felicity thinks he owns them. Johnny goes back to the hotel and feels that the cat should be taken out of the house. At 3:30 AM the phone rings and Leona tells Johnny that Felicity was let out and has disappeared, and she is sure he has been killed!

Johnny and Jodiah rush to the house and Joyce and Leona meet them, but Oscar is not there. Leona tells Johnny that she first noticed Felicity was gone an hour ago. Joyce and Mr. Emmett tell Johnny that they were at a movie, so Johnny decides to cruise the nightspots looking for Oscar. Johnny visits all the casinos and finds Oscar at a roulette wheel with a large stack of chips. Oscar had been around town all night, and when he tries to leave after missing a winning spin, he pushes Jodiah down and then apologizes. Oscar tells Johnny that he did not mean to push Jodiah, but Mrs. Hawkins had been making a fool of Gillis. He has heard what is going on, and she has been giving the same line to Mr. Emmett, and she really loves him. Johnny takes Jodiah to his room and then goes to the Hammelmeyer house where Joyce and Mr. Emmett and Leona are hunting for Felicity. Joyce offers Johnny coffee and tells her that Oscar was downtown, and asks what will happen if they cannot find Felicity. Mr. Emmett calls them to the garage and Johnny sees a hatchet, blood and cat fur. Johnny takes Joyce out and Leona asks Johnny to tell Jodiah. Johnny returns to the hotel and tells Jodiah about the events of the night. Johnny then calls the local banks and gets the information he was after. Back at the Hammelmeyer house Jodiah calls Leona a miserable Jezebel and Johnny tells her it was for the way she planned to use

Jodiah to get her out of trouble in case her scheme failed. Johnny tells Leona that she killed Felicity, and that Jodiah is having copies made of all her bank deposits since she moved in with Mrs. Hammelmeyer fifteen years ago and started paying her bills, buying her food and medicine and pocketing a good share of the money for herself. Johnny tells her that she has $47,000 in the bank, and Leona asks why not, as Mildred did not pay her a salary. Leona tells Johnny that she will pay it back and that her name is in the envelope. Joyce comes in with the envelope and everyone sits down. The envelope is opened and the codicil states that the unspent monies shall go the descendants of the original heir. Since Felicity was the original heir, the money goes to his descendants. Since he was a tomcat who loved to go prowling at night, did he ever have descendants! Hundreds of them!

"Well what happened later proves that miracles can happen. For at one o'clock on Friday afternoon, we got phone call from the Pretty Kitty Beauty Shop. A large tomcat with a bad cut on the back of his neck has shown up for his usual shampoo and manicure. Maybe they do have nine lives."

## Notes:

- This is an **AFRS** program with a story about the various types of milk issued to servicemen.
- Cast Information from the **KNX** Collection at the Thousand Oaks Library.
- Dan Cubberly is the announcer

| | | | |
|---|---|---|---|
| **Producer:** | Jack Johnstone | **Writers:** | Charles B. Smith |
| **Cast:** | Jack Edwards, Howard McNear, Edgar Barrier, Chester Stratton, Virginia Gregg, Will Wright, Joan Banks, Bill James | | |

◆ ❖ ◆

| | |
|---|---|
| **Show:** | The Heatherstone Players Matter |
| **Show Date:** | 7/14/1957 |
| **Company:** | New Jersey State Mutual Life Insurance Company |
| **Agent:** | Garrett Reynolds |
| **Exp. Acct:** | $51.25 |

**Synopsis:** "Ah, how weary stale flat and unprofitable seem to me all the uses of this world" greets Johnny when Garrett Reynolds calls. "Alas I would a tale unfold whose lightest word would harrow up thy soul, freeze thy young blood, make thy two eyes like stars start from their spheres, thy knotted and combined locks to part and each particular hair to stand an end, like quills on the fretful porpentine." "Garrett, have you gone off your rocker?" asks Johnny. Come on down and see.

Johnny trains to Trenton, New Jersey and cabs to Garrett's office. Garrett tells Johnny about the Heatherstone players and Cyril Peter Saint George Heatherstone who is just as bad as he sounds, and is on his way over spouting his Shakespearean quotes. Heatherstone travels around teaching and performing, and after he gets the local money he leaves a lot of enemies and broken hearts behind. He is back in Trenton and is putting on a festival over radio station WVGR. Johnny thinks he could join the cast, but Garrett tells Johnny that everyone there hates Heatherstone, except Joanie Carter who was picked to play the lead and promised a career. Heatherstone did it to lure her away from Charlie Cubberly, also a cast member. The cast would leave but Heatherstone has them under contract until the festival is over, or he is killed. Garrett has had to change the beneficiary on the policy so many times because Heatherstone uses it as a come-on. Heatherstone walks in quoting King John, Act III scene I. Johnny is introduced and Heatherstone is told that Johnny is going to be his bodyguard until the festival is over. Three threats have been received, and the police have said nothing, which is why Johnny was called. Garrett notes that Charlie is mad with jealousy. Johnny mentions that Heatherstone has a reputation of being harsh with the cast, and Heatherstone tells Johnny he must be cruel to only to be kind. They are so ambitious, but so inadequate. Johnny considers all of Heatherstone's associates as a threat, but Heatherstone does not believe it. Johnny is told that he festival will go on, and the next rehearsal is this afternoon. Johnny is going to be there to check up on the threats, but Heatherstone is sure that they are real, but nothing can touch him. Heatherstone leaves and Garrett wants a drink. Garrett arranges to Johnny to sit with the engineers, and Johnny accuses Garrett of wanting to kill Heatherstone himself. Johnny cabs to the studio and enters the control room and meets Gordon Mitchell. Johnny gets the layout of the microphones and Gordon phases in the mike on the table where the cast is rehearing. Gordon tells Johnny that Heatherstone is the most hated man in town and a fast dealer. He convinced Gordon to invest all his savings in the festival, and it is only Beneficial Finance that is keeping him on his uppers. Gordon phases in the mike when Joan is talking, and it is clear that Heatherstone is definitely using her. Gordon slips that he had sent notes to the insurance man that someone would kill Heatherstone. Heatherstone goes into the isolation booth to show the cast how to do something when the other sound effects man, Dan Ringo enters. Heatherstone starts speaking and suddenly falters in his speech and collapses. Joan runs into the room and screams that he is dead.

Johnny runs to the isolation booth and finds Heatherstone dead. Johnny searches the stage and booth and finds nothing. Charlie is glad he is dead, and Don tells Joan that he was taking her, the way he took everyone else. Johnny tells Gordon to call the police and notes that the door to the isolation booth is open. Joan tells Johnny that she opened it, and inside it Johnny smells something and suddenly Johnny knows what killed Heatherstone. There is a faint odor of peach blossoms in the isolation booth, the odor of potassium payatin, a deadly poison. Johnny talks to the cast and tells them what killed Heatherstone, and Don wonders if Heatherstone killed himself. Johnny tells Don that he was the last one near Heatherstone, which angers Don. Johnny asks Charlie if anyone had a better reason than he did, and Gordon tells Johnny he would like to have killed Heatherstone. Johnny notes that the only one who admits to wanting to kill Heatherstone was nowhere near him, and had been with Johnny the whole time.

Johnny suggests one of the others could have slipped Heatherstone the drug but Johnny had searched the booth and found nothing. Johnny is told that Joan went in and could have removed any evidence. Joan tells Charlie that she thought she was in love with him, but now realizes she was not. The police and the doctor arrive and agree with Johnny's conclusion on the death, but no evidence is found. The police suspect everyone but Gordon, but Johnny notes that he should be the most likely suspect. Gordon asks if he can put his equipment away and starts picking up the cables. Johnny tells Gordon that the booth mike cable is thicker, and Gordon notes that it is an older cable with more wires. They go to the booth and take the faceplate off of the mike. Johnny thinks that the poison, potassium payatin, a crystal of potassium thayatin was vaporized in the booth. In the mike, Johnny spots the remains of a small heating element that was used to vaporize the poison, thanks to the extra wires in the cable. Johnny shows the police the chemical discoloration and tells the police that only one man was vocal enough to admit that he wanted to kill Heatherstone, and who had an alibi because Johnny was with him. Johnny tells Gordon he disconnected the power leads when he called the police, and Gordon tells him he is right. But it was a good try. "No flight of angels will sing him to his rest."

"So, that was it. And the company will have to pay the claim."

NOTES:
- THERE IS AN **AFRS** SPOT ABOUT THE **US** SHIP **HOPE**.
- THE OPENING QUOTES ARE FROM HAMLET, ACT I, SCENE II, AND HAMLET ACT V, SCENE V.
- THE CLOSING QUOTE IS HAMLET ACT V, SCENE II.
- DAN CUBBERLY IS THE ANNOUNCER

Producer: Jack Johnstone     Writers: Jack Johnstone
Cast: Virginia Gregg, Lawrence Dobkin, Dick Crenna, Sam Edwards, Frank Gerstle, Herb Vigran, Hans Conried

SHOW: THE YOURS TRULY MATTER
SHOW DATE: 7/21/1957
COMPANY: UNIVERSAL ADJUSTMENT BUREAU
AGENT: PAT McCRACKEN
EXP. ACCT: $528.00

SYNOPSIS: The operator calls Johnny with a call from Pat McCracken and Johnny tells him that the Kincaid case is finished. Johnny calls him to ok a case for his most important client and the one deserving the most attention, "Me"!

Johnny travels from Los Angeles to Las Vegas, Nevada and gets a room at the Flamingo Hotel. Johnny calls Buster Favor to tell him he is on his way to Lake Mojave Resort. Buster is going to have work done on his car, so he will ride back with Johnny. Johnny rents a brand new air-conditioned 1957 Cadillac. After dinner with Buster, they leave for the Lake Mojave Resort. Buster tells Johnny not to drive too fast, or the police will stop him. Johnny comments on the old roads, and Buster tell Johnny that they go up to mines in the hills. Buster sees lights approaching from behind him and they turn into a red flashing light. Johnny stops and waits for the officer to walk to the car, but the door opens and a man with a gun gets into the back seat. He tells Buster that he used a flashlight to stop them. Johnny tries to upend him by starting in reverse but it does not work. He tells Johnny that this is just a stick up. After driving down the road for a while, the man tells Johnny to pull off onto a side road and Buster whispers to him is the road to the McKinny mine. They drive up the road until they get to a wide spot and the man tells Johnny and Buster to get out. As they turn around, the man frisks them and takes their money and jewelry. When a card falls from Johnny's wallet, the man laughs at holding up a private dick. Buster tries to attack the man, but he is shot. The man drives away and Johnny runs to Buster.

Johnny gets to Buster, who is ok; the man was a lousy shot. Buster wanted to get onto the ground so he could bury some sharp rocks under the tires and work on the tire with his knife. Buster tells Johnny that the tire will go flat soon, so they start walking back to the road, picking up some rocks along the way for ammunition. As Johnny and Buster walk down the mountain they spot lights coming up the road. They hide and wait for the car. Buster notices that the car is not the Cadillac. Johnny hails the car and it stops. Buster recognizes the driver as Mack McKinney, a miner friend. Mack tells Buster that he helped the man change his tire a few minutes ago. Buster tells Mack what happened to them. Mack feels bad that he forgot to tell the man that the gate to the main road is locked. So, he cannot get back on the highway without wrecking his car. Mack remembers seeing a bulge under the man's coat, so he had an urge to get back to the mine and call the police. Johnny gives him the license number for a 1956 gray and white Chevy, license plate number CGJ-158, the car the crook is using, and tells Mack to walk up to the mine and call the police. Johnny and Buster take Mack's jeep and drive cross-country down to the main road. Buster asks how Johnny got the plate number for the crook's car, and Johnny tells him that is why he started up in reverse, to turn on the back up lights and illuminate the plates. When they get to the gate they find the Cadillac crashed into it. Johnny searches the Cadillac and the man is not there. Buster searches the jeep and finds wire cutters in the toolbox, which will allow them to cut the fence and reach the main road. As they are driving back to the Chevy, Johnny thinks he sees a car under a storm bridge. Suddenly the man has the gun in their backs again, he tells Buster that he got in the jeep while they were at the gate. At the man's car he takes the keys for the jeep. He tells Johnny that his plans are messed up now, and he cannot take a chance with them getting away so he is going to have to kill them. Johnny tells Buster that there was a car under the bridge, a police car. Johnny tells the man that there is a police officer in the back seat of his car, and Johnny throws a rock he had been carrying into the windshield. The man fires at the car until Johnny hits him. The police arrive and Johnny tells Buster he really did think he saw a car under the bridge.

Expenses include $50 to Mack McKinney for the use of his jeep, and $81.50 for repairs on Buster's car as a way of thanking him. The car rental company will bill Pat separately. Oh, the windshield on the Chevy will have to be replaced, and it was covered by one of Pat's companies. So Pat, you can just charge off this whole case to the recovery of that car.

NOTES:
• DAN CUBBERLY IS THE ANNOUNCER

Producer: Jack Johnstone          Writers: Jack Johnstone
Cast:        Virginia Gregg, Lawrence Dobkin, Barney Phillips,
               Chet Stratton, Junius Matthews

◆   ❖   ◆

SHOW:          THE CONFEDERATE COINAGE MATTER
SHOW DATE:   7/28/1957
COMPANY:     PROVIDENTIAL ASSURANCE COMPANY
AGENT:        BERT MCGRAW
EXP. ACCT:    $405.10

SYNOPSIS: Bert McGraw calls and tells Johnny that Henry Samson, a newspaper owner in the south, collects confederate currency. He has a 50-cent piece worth $20,000 and it has disappeared.

Johnny cabs to Bert's office where Bert is reading a magazine about an old friend of his, Bob Feller. Bert tells Johnny that he helped Bob out many times until Johnny reminds Bert that he never played for the Cleveland Indians. Bert chokes and tells him it was Bob Faller of the Apalachicola Alligators. Bert tells Johnny that Samson's secretary had called to tell that the coin was stolen. The coin was minted in New Orleans, and the mint only produced 4 such coins. Samson lives outside of Birmingham, Alabama at a place called Shade Mountain.

Johnny travels to Birmingham and is met my Mike Kopeck, Mr. Samson's secretary, who will take Johnny to Zora, which is named after Samson's village in the Bible. The estate is large with a number of buildings, pools, a zoo and a turkey farm. In the library Mr. Samson is standing beside a large desk accompanied by a most beautiful woman named Delilah, who is Mr. Samson's wife. Samson shows Johnny the display case from which the coin was stolen. The thief did not try to pick the lock but broke the glass. Delilah tells Johnny that Mr. Samson suspects her. There were no visitors that night, and Samson did some work and then they played casino until 10:00. The only people in the house were the Samsons, Kopeck, Mary Williams the maid and Digger the manservant. Samson tells Johnny that only four coins were made because the Confederacy did not have the bullion to make more—"dirty union blockade." The coin was a regular 1861 Union 50-cent piece. The reverse side was ground off and stamped with the shield of the confederacy. Delilah offers Johnny a drink, again, and then fixes one for herself. Kopeck is called and told to take Delilah to her room where Samson will have her dinner sent. Johnny is told that Jefferson Davis gave the coin to his great grand-pappy personally. He refused $10,000 for it in 1879 so it must be worth more now. Samson tells Johnny to earn his pay and find the coin. The gates to Zora have been locked and no one can leave until the coin is found.

Johnny goes to his room, unpacks and calls Bert. Johnny wants Bert to find out how many of those coins were made. There is a knock at the door, and Marry Williams and Digger are there. They tell Johnny that they have snuck off to see him. They are glad he is working for a company instead of the police, and Digger is scared to death. Digger tells Johnny that Mr. Samson needs a lot of help here to run the farm, and he gets them from the prison. When someone is ready to get out, they get a job working for Mr. Samson. If they do not like it, they are sent back to prison. Johnny tells them that this is 1957, and things like that do not happen anymore. Digger tells Johnny that he does not want to go back to that place. Mary tells Johnny that they want to get married, and they are afraid Samson will send Digger back if they ask him to let them get married. Digger will not tell Johnny anything unless he promises not to send him back. Mary tells Johnny that Digger knows who took that half dollar piece.

After dinner in the dining room Samson goes off to work. Kopeck asks Johnny about his progress, and Johnny tells him he has not started yet. Johnny asks Kopeck about the servants. He knows everything about them and will have their records sent to Johnny. Kopeck goes off to see Samson and Delilah calls to Johnny and asks if he likes to ride. Johnny says yes, and she tells him to meet her at the stables before breakfast. In his room Johnny gets the files on Mary and Digger and all the facts about prison are true.

Next morning, Johnny goes riding with Delilah down by the river. At the river Delilah just stares at the river and tells Johnny that she married Samson for his money, but Samson is a collector. He married her because she is named Delilah. At 11:00 Johnny calls Bert and he tells Johnny that he coin is only worth $5,000. A man named Scott had the dies and made 500 copies back in 1879. That lowered the price of the original. There are 504 in total. Johnny tells Bert he is out $20,000 unless he lets Johnny try something.

Johnny sends word to Digger and Marry. Johnny tells digger that he cannot promise he will not be sent back to prison, but Johnny will help him all he can. Mary reluctantly tells Johnny that Digger had stolen the coin. Digger broke in because Delilah threatened to tell Samson something real bad about Digger. Digger took the coin and ran down to the river to meet Mrs. Samson, but he tripped and lost the coin. They looked everywhere, but there is a good reason why they cannot find it. They take Johnny to the site and he agrees that there is a good reason.

Johnny goes back to the house and tells Kopeck he wants to see Samson. Delilah comes down and notes that Johnny's bags are packed. He tells her he knows where the coin is and how it got there. He asks her why she did it, and she tells Johnny that the reason was money to get away. Johnny tells her that he has to tell Samson and she leaves. In Samson's office Johnny tells him what he knows. Samson orders Kopeck to take Digger to the place where the coin was lost, and

Johnny and Samson meet them there. In the middle of the turkey farm, Johnny tells Samson that Digger lost the coin in the field and one of the 2,000 turkeys ate the coin. Samson tells Johnny that they will have to pay him the insurance money. Johnny tells Samson that he will buy the turkeys from Samson for $5,000, and will guarantee return of the coin in 90 days, provided he lets Mary and Digger leave the estate and be responsible for the recovery of the coin. Johnny tells Samson that he is going to give them the turkeys. Samson agrees, and Johnny gets his 2,000 turkeys.

A couple weeks after I left Birmingham, I received a letter from Mr. and Mrs. Digger telling me that they found the coin in the craw of the bird they killed for their first Sunday dinner together. Which proves once again, miracles do happen

.

NOTES:

* THE MID-PROGRAM COMMERCIAL IS AN **AFRS** SPOT ABOUT THE VALUE OF BOOKS AND A LIBRARY GIVEN TO A VILLAGE IN AFRICA.
* THE ANNOUNCER IS DAN CUBBERLY

**Producer:** Jack Johnstone      **Writers:** Charles B. Smith
**Cast:** Virginia Gregg, Eleanor Audley, Herb Ellis, Herb Vigran, Forrest Lewis, Vic Perrin

◆ ❖ ◆

SHOW: THE WAYWARD WIDOW MATTER
SHOW DATE: 8/4/1957
COMPANY: PHILADELPHIA MUTUAL LIABILITY & CASUALTY COMPANY
AGENT: HARRY BRANSON
EXP. ACCT: $365.50

SYNOPSIS: Harry Branson calls and tells Johnny that there is no case. Harry wants Johnny to take a motor trip with a most important client, Betty Charlene Winters, a very wealthy client. Harry wants Johnny to accompany Mrs. Winters to her summer residence on Lake Wawayanda in New Jersey. Johnny will be on expense account along with a fee of $1,000 for the week. Johnny runs to grab the first train.

Johnny trains to Philadelphia, Pennsylvania and Harry is waiting for him. Johnny is told that Mrs. Winters lost her husband a short time ago, and she is very wealthy. She got half a million from her husband's insurance alone. Their home is an art gallery and she is going to give her art to the museums and sell the family estate. She is taking some things to the house in Lake Wawayanda. Johnny is going to take Mrs. Winters and a statue to the summerhouse. Harry drives Johnny to Mrs. Winters' house and Harry tells Johnny that Mr. Winters died in a car accident and that his body was never recovered. Johnny is expecting a young, rich widow, but Eric the butler takes Johnny to the library to meet Mrs. Winters, all 70 years of her. Haskins, the chauffeur and handy man is there, and he starts to take the statue to the car. The statue is a "cherub" and really ugly.

Haskins takes the statue to the car where it will be placed in a special box. Mrs. Winters asks Johnny if he can drive a Pierce Arrow. Haskins is going on vacation, and she is not sure if he will come back. Mrs. Winters calls Harry a rascal for bringing a detective, especially such a young good looking one! Johnny gets a tour of the house and the art works. Johnny inspects the 1928 Pierce Arrow, and the car is immaculate. At 5:00 cocktails are served. Johnny tells Harry that the statue is junk, and this case is very strange. At midnight Johnny retires and waits for everyone to go to sleep so he can get a look at the car. Johnny leaves his room and a door opens in the hallway and Johnny is knocked unconscious.

Johnny wakes up in the morning in his pajamas and in his bed. Johnny gets up and checks out the room down the hall, but it is empty. At breakfast Mrs. Winters is concerned and they go out to check out the car. In the trunk is the box with the statute. Haskins is not there, and Johnny wants to inspect the box, but Mrs. Winters talks him out of it. She tells Johnny that Eric the butler has been with her for 30 years and is a gentleman, more so than her late husband. She tells Johnny that she married her husband for his money and to get out of the chorus line. For the last few years they stayed buttoned up in the house while her friends were traveling. The summerhouse was her idea, and it was a relief from the main house. Mrs. Winters wants to call the police, but Johnny tells her not to, he does not want to scare the attacker off. Besides, Mrs. Winters tells Johnny that the house has a very sophisticated burglar alarm system, which was on the previous evening. There was no one else in the house but the cook, who is as old as Mrs. Winters. Eric serves breakfast, and gives Johnny a strange look. Eric tells Johnny that he found him while inspecting the house and put him in his room. He thought Johnny had imbibed too much brandy, but Johnny tells him he was slugged. The burglar alarm was set, so whoever did it was inside the house. Johnny tells him it was dark, so the attacker may have been after Eric.

Mrs. Winters comes in and is ready to leave. She will be happy to leave and get the estate settled so she and Martha can live in peace at the lake. Johnny starts getting a wild idea on the drive to the lake, and Mrs. Winters talks the whole trip. Johnny buys gas at the sign of the flying red horse and calls Harry and asks him to go to the Winters home and call him back at the lake. At the lake outside of Andover, New Jersey Johnny has to drive up a steep hill overlooking the lake to get to the garage. When Johnny mentions that he hopes the brakes will hold, Mrs. Winters mentions that the lake is over 100 feet deep at the end of the driveway. Mrs. Winters goes in to answer the phone while Johnny unpacks the car. The box in the trunk is very heavy and Johnny leaves the box perched on the trunk door to go to the phone. On the phone, Harry tells Johnny that it is terrible. How did Johnny know that Eric the butler is dead? He fell down the main staircase, and Martha is beside herself. Johnny tells Harry to call the police. Mrs. Winters calls from outside and Johnny runs out to see the box rolling down the driveway and into the lake. Mrs. Winters tells Johnny that she must have bumped it. Johnny offers to get a diver to come to the lake but she declines and decides to leave the box there in the lake; it would only be another memory of the old place. Johnny tells her she is wrong; they will get it back and whatever is in it.

Johnny hires a diver and gets the two boxes. One box has the body of Haskins; the other has the body of Mr. Winters who was supposed to have been washed out to sea. Mrs. Winters tells Johnny that Haskins had helped to get rid of Charles, so she and Martha had to do something with him. Haskins was the one who had hit Johnny, and Eric stopped him. Martha killed Eric; she had to, as Eric is the one who killed Haskins. She and Martha had planned so many wonderful things together. And now, oh dear.

Remarks: Well, I would rather not say how I feel about a case like this, Harry. A whole crime wave by a couple of apparently sweet old ladies. The legal procedures, and there will be plenty of them, are up to you and the company, as well as recovery of the insurance paid on poor old Charles Winters. Hey, next time give me case what does not turn my stomach, will ya?

NOTES:
- THE MID-PROGRAM COMMERCIAL IS AN **AFRS** SPOT ABOUT THE KALEIDOSCOPE AND THE VALUE OF SIGHT.
- ANDOVER NEW JERSEY IS IN THE NORTHERN PART OF THE STATE. THERE IS A LAKE WAWAYONDA AND A PARK CLOSE TO THE NEW YORK LINE.
- THE ANNOUNCER IS JOE WALTERS

Producer:    Jack Johnstone          Writers:    Jack Johnstone
Cast:        Virginia Gregg, Harry Bartell, Eric Snowden, Frank Gerstle

◆    ❖    ◆

SHOW:         THE KILLER'S BRAND MATTER
SHOW DATE:    8/11/1957
COMPANY:      UNIVERSAL ADJUSTMENT BUREAU
AGENT:        PAT MCCRACKEN
EXP. ACCT:    $528.00

SYNOPSIS: Pat McCracken calls and tells Johnny that Cooper's Bend Nevada is having their big celebration, Frontier Week. Pat suggests that Johnny start growing a beard and get a ten-gallon hat. Cooper's Bend was just a sleepy western town, dying on its feet, until last week. A publicity man, Bill Williams is trying to wake the town up with Frontier Week, and somebody is trying to put Bill Williams to sleep, the hard way.

Johnny cabs to Pat's office where he tells Johnny that this case is worth looking at. There is a big policy on William's life and Pat is worried. Williams does freelance publicity, and someone has taken a shot at him. Johnny thinks it might have been an accident, but Pat tells Johnny that the folks in Cooper's Bend are asleep at two in the morning, so watch yourself.

Johnny flies west and rents a car to drive to Cooper's Bend, Nevada. The town could pass as a set for a western movie, complete with a horse trough in front of the hotel. A crowd gathers and tells Johnny that anyone without a ten-gallon hat goes into the water trough. Johnny is thrown in; welcome to town! Johnny looks for Bill Williams and is directed to the newspaper office where Johnny meets "Miss Cooper's Bend Frontier Week," also known as Lois. Johnny is told that Bill is with the editor, Fred Kirby, and should be back soon. Fred comes back and Johnny tells her that Fred had helped him take a swim earlier. Fred laughs and tells Johnny that Bill is out making arrangements for the rodeo later that day, and should be back soon. Lois takes Johnny to get a cup of coffee, and Fred tells her to take her time. Johnny suspects an undercurrent between them as they drink their coffee. Lois tells Johnny that today is the last day of the celebration, and she is going away, as far away as possible. Dan Biggers comes in looking for Lois. He tells her that she is going to go to the dance with him, and a frustrated Lois leaves. Dan tells Johnny that Lois and he are engaged, so stay away from her.

Bill Williams comes in, and Johnny recognizes him as the ring-leader of the dunking committee. Bill tells Johnny to get a hat to protect himself. Bill tells Johnny that he was driving through and saw the possibility of waking the town up, for the money. Bill shows Johnny his car where a bullet hole is in the windshield. Bill feels that Dan Biggers did it because he smiled at Lois and she smiled back. Bill tells Johnny that Biggers is so jealous he cannot see straight. Johnny tells him that Fred has been watching them, so maybe he is interested in Lois too? Bill tells Johnny that after the dance tonight, he is getting his money and leaving town. Johnny tells Bill that Lois mentioned leaving town too, and Bill tells Johnny that she probably does not mean it. Bill leaves and Johnny goes to buy a hat, but is caught by the swimming team again.

Johnny goes to the dance and spots Bill, who is excited about cleaning up. Johnny goes back to his hotel and has a message from Lois to see her. Johnny drives to her house on a back road. When no one answers the door, Johnny goes in and finds Lois very dead in front of the hearth.

Johnny finds Lois in front of the fireplace with a poker lying nearby. Johnny sees where she had hit her head after what looked like a struggle. Johnny hears a noise and eases outside to see a station wagon driving away with the lights off. Johnny calls the sheriff and they go over the facts. Johnny tells him about the message and how it ties into the attempt on Bill's life. The sheriff tells Johnny that Biggers had beat up another man for asking Lois for a date. Johnny tells him about Lois' comment about leaving town and they drive to Dan's ranch.

At the Biggers ranch, they are shot at by Dan. He tells them they are not going to take him in until he finds out who killed Lois. Johnny tells him that he could not know about it unless he was there, but he tells Johnny that a deputy had told him when the call came in. Johnny tells Dan that he found out about her leaving and hit her, but Dan tells him he is crazy and fires at him. Johnny and the sheriff leave and head back to town. The sheriff tells Johnny that Dan does not own a station wagon, and that there are a lot of them in the area.

Johnny ponders the facts over a drink and decides to talk to Fred. At the newspaper office, Bill and Fred are talking. Fred is sure that Dan did it, and he had heard Lois tell that to Dan in the office. Johnny asks Bill if he and Lois were planning on leaving together, and he tells Johnny that there was nothing to it; they had only joked about it in the office. Bill leaves and Johnny tells Fred that he is trying awful hard to pin this on Dan, and that he has been carrying a flame for Lois. Johnny tells of spotting a station wagon at the house, the same kind of car Fred drives. Fred finally admits that he had driven to the house to talk Lois out of leaving, but did not go inside. The sheriff is called and Fred is taken in. Next morning Johnny meets Bill and he has his money and is ready to leave when the sheriff tells him he is finished. The crowd gathers and is ready to throw the hat-less Bill into the trough, but he tells them he is sick of the whole idea and they leave. Johnny realizes that the hot poker was the key to the murder. Johnny tells Bill that he is going to throw Bill into the trough and rips off his shirt to find burns and scratches. Johnny tells Bill that Lois did that and Bill tells Johnny that he has a gun in his pocket. Bill tells Johnny that he was trying to shake Lois off, as he did not want to take someone like her to San Francisco. He told her that, and she attacked him. Bill starts to take Johnny to the alley when Johnny splashes water in his face from the trough and gets the gun from him and slugs him into the trough. Bill got dunked after all.

Remarks: "About Dan Biggers, he really was not such a bad guy except that he had a knot in his head about Lois. He sold his ranch and moved away. About Bill Williams, you better cancel out his policy, Pat. He is due to go on trial soon, and in my book, he is a pretty bad risk."

### NOTES:
- THE CAST INFORMATION IS FROM RadioGOLDINdex.
- THE MID-PROGRAM COMMERCIAL IS AN AFRS SPOT ABOUT HELPING ONE'S NEIGHBORS AROUND THE WORLD.
- THE FINAL COMMERCIAL IS AN AFRS SPOT ABOUT THE FLAG OF OKLAHOMA

| | | | |
|---|---|---|---|
| **Producer:** | Jack Johnstone | **Writers:** | Jack Johnstone |
| **Cast:** | Mary Jane Croft, Harry Bartell, Joseph Kearns, Lawrence Dobkin | | |

◆ ❖ ◆

| | |
|---|---|
| **SHOW:** | THE WINNIPESAUKEE WONDER MATTER |
| **SHOW DATE:** | 8/18/1957 |
| **COMPANY:** | INTERNATIONAL LIFE & CASUALTY COMPANY |
| **AGENT:** | CHRISTIAN ALBECK |
| **EXP. ACCT:** | $0.00 |

**SYNOPSIS:** Johnny is called from Boston by Christian Albeck who has a routine matter for Johnny concerning a $100,000 policy, and Christian will be checking the expense account on this one.

Johnny flies to Boston and goes to Christian's office, only to be told that he should have driven to Lake Winnipesaukee, near Center Harbor, New Hampshire.

Johnny is asked if he is familiar with Hardon, Carmon & Fisher, the big brokerage house, but Johnny tells Christian that he has only bought Allis Chalmers, and Sonocy Mobil. Johnny is told that Franklin Hardon is the senior partner in the firm, and that he summers in Lake Kanasatka, which is next to Lake Winnipesaukee. He went to the lake in June with his daughter Grace, and his sons Anthony and Ben. Franklin went fishing and a storm blew in and he has not been seen since and has been pronounced dead. The policy is double indemnity and the children have filed a claim. Christian is suspicious, so he wants Johnny to investigate.

Johnny drives to Center Harbor and gets a room at the Garnet Inn. Early the next morning, police chief Mike Sharp calls and arranges to meet Johnny for breakfast. Johnny meets the chief who tells him that the storm was really bad, just like the one that is brewing now. Frank knew the lake, but his boat was found on Bear Island. A search was made and Frank's hat was found. Three weeks later his fishing vest was found, and his coat was found all eaten by fish. The chief tells Johnny that he should go talk to the kids.

Johnny goes to the Harden cottage in a rainstorm and spots three sports cars out front: a Mercedes-Benz, a Jaguar and a Maserati. As Johnny reaches the door he hears gunshots. After knocking on the door, a boy comes out and holds Johnny at gunpoint. When the boy tells Johnny that he was expecting someone else, Johnny takes the gun and slugs him. The others come out and Johnny is introduced to them. Tony recognizes who Johnny is and tells him that the gunshots were target practice that they did on rainy days; it was a suggestion from their father. Tony tells Johnny that they were expecting a friend, and the gun was a gag. Grace tells Johnny that she is sure that their father is not dead, and tells Johnny that all of them are adopted children, and they want their father back very much. She tells Johnny that filing the claim was the idea of the family attorney, Mr. Webster. Johnny is told that all of the children work in the business, and their father makes them work really hard. They tell Johnny that they have agreed to sign over their inheritances if their father is ever found alive.

Johnny is convinced that the children are on the level and is ready to leave when Grace spots her father's face in a window. They all rush outside to their father, who is standing on a bucket, and falls in the mud. Johnny goes outside to find Mr. Harden and the sheriff hiding outside the house. Johnny is told that the stunt was the idea of their attorney to test the faith of the children. He thought that the kids cared more about the money than their father. There is a big party that night, and everyone is happy.

NOTES:
- THE ANNOUNCER IS BUD SEWELL
- THERE IS THE FIRST OF SEVERAL VEILED REFERENCES TO HARMON-KARDON & FISCHER STEREO EQUIPMENT.
- STORY INFORMATION OBTAINED FROM THE KNX COLLECTION IN THE THOUSAND OAKS LIBRARY

Producer:   Jack Johnstone          Writers   Jack Johnstone

Cast:        **Bob Bruce, Forrest Lewis, Virginia Gregg, Gil Stratton, Stacy Harris, Edgar Stehli**

◆     ❖     ◆

SHOW:          THE SMOKEY SLEEPER MATTER
SHOW DATE:     8/25/1957
COMPANY:       NEW JERSEY FIRE & CASUALTY INSURANCE COMPANY
AGENT:         FED LARKIN
EXP. ACCT:     $130.49

SYNOPSIS: Fred Larkin calls early in the morning and tells Johnny that things are fine in Trenton, but not fine in Vineland, New Jersey. There was a fire there and Fred suspects arson in a fire that destroyed $83,000 in mattresses and box springs.

Johnny travels to Trenton and Fred's office where he is told that the total loss in the fire was for $83,000. Ben Murray, who is the owner of the BenMur stores scattered around the Philadelphia area, filed the claim. The warehouse was in Vineland, where storage costs are lower. Murray has had a lot of inventory insurance and is a good client. They specialize in specialty sales. The inventory in the warehouse was for his next sale. Murray is famous for switching—advertising one product and selling something else in its place. He is also suspected of label switching; putting a recognized label on inferior goods. The insurance was based on the invoice of goods as provided by the manufacturer's bills. The order was made up by one manufacturer for this sale.

Johnny calls Adam Boles, a friend, and leaves a message to meet him in Vineland, New Jersey. Johnny trains to Philadelphia and meets with Ben Murray. Murray is a real wheeler-dealer, not afraid of setting up deals in front of Johnny. Murray tells Johnny that he works on volume and narrow margins, but the prices Johnny hears discussed tell him otherwise. While Ben is on one phone, Johnny answers the other phone for Ben, where a salesman is complaining about a dissatisfied customer who did not get what she bought and is threatening to go to the authorities. Ben grabs the phone and tells him to give her anything she wants. Ben is accusative of Johnny's reasons for talking to him, but Johnny tells Ben that they always investigate fires of this size. Ben calls Johnny a punk and tells him to leave.

Johnny rents a "drive your own" car and drives to Vineland, in the heart of the agricultural area of South Jersey. Johnny goes to the police in Vineland and meets Sgt. Luis Tomaso, who agrees to take Johnny to the fire scene. Sgt. Tomaso tells Johnny that they have been over the building with a fine-toothed comb, and Adam Boles has been helping them. At the scene Johnny finds a totally destroyed building. In some of the mattresses Johnny finds the best possible evidence for burning up the building. Ad Boles arrives and greetings are exchanged (Ad: You didn't send for a half-wit like Dollar did you? Johnny: Well hold on "Stinky."). Ad tells Johnny that he is too late; Ad knows who started the fire. It was Jerry Cumber, the town wino. Ad tells Johnny and Sgt. Tomaso that Jerry was wandering around and went to sleep off a bottle of wine in the warehouse with a lighted cigarette. Ad tells Johnny to pay the claim and go home, but Johnny tells him that the case is just starting.

The fire looked accidental, but Johnny has doubts. Johnny calls Fred and tells him that he can prove fraud. Johnny tells Fred to read off the information on the invoices. Johnny asks for the label information on the "Night Cloud Sleep-rest" mattresses. The invoice shows a cost of $25.50 each. Johnny tells Fred that the labels showed a retail price of $69.00 each and Johnny remembers hearing Murray give a different cost when he was in the office. The "Night Cloud Super Sleep" is listed at $26.20 each. The "Perfection Sleep" is $27.14 each. The manufacturer is the Golden Bedding Corporation in Woodbine. Johnny asks for the name of another bedding company in some other city, and Johnny gets the name of Lauder Brothers, a very disreputable firm in New York.

Johnny drives to Woodbine and finds the Golden Bedding plant. Johnny goes in and presents himself as Barney Lauder. Mr. Golden tells "Barney" that he knows his father. "Barney" is now in the business and wants to talk business. Golden tells Johnny/Barney that he has a really good business in Philadelphia, but will do business with him, and will pre-ticket the merchandise for him—he will put any price on the merchandise Barney wants. Golden can put any name on them, and they each have 196 springs—however the demonstrator model has 392 springs. The price for 10,000 units is $14.93, but Johnny tells him the price is too high. Golden agrees to bill him on the books for $29.96. That way, it looks like he paid twice as much for the units. The phone rings and Ben Murray is calling. Golden describes his customer as wearing a blue shirt and a bow tie. Oh, no! Golden now knows that Barney really is Johnny Dollar, insurance investigator. Johnny tells him that both he and Murray will be out of business soon when the Better Business Bureau and the Federal Trade Commission get hold of this case. Golden offers Johnny a $10,000 "commission," and Johnny tells him that he is going to get it. Golden calls Johnny a "dirty crook, a faker, a liar, a cheating dirty conniving chiseling . . . you ruined me!"

Yes Fred, I am afraid that your "nice client" Ben Murray based his insurance claim on a lot of values that didn't exist. On hiked up prices, hiked up to cheat you and the income tax boys. And if that is not outright fraud, I'll eat my shirt. So you can just forget about paying that claim, or any part of it. And I hope that you and the company will take whatever legal step necessary to put these guys out of business.

NOTES:
- THE MID-PROGRAM COMMERCIAL IS AN **AFRS** SPOT ABOUT THE EARTH SHRINKING BECAUSE OF FASTER TRANSPORTATION, AND HELPING ONE'S NEIGHBORS.
- THE FINAL COMMERCIAL IS AN **AFRS** SPOT ABOUT THE FLAG OF KANSAS
- THE ANNOUNCER IS BUD SEWELL

Producer:   Jack Johnstone          Writers:   Jack Johnstone

Cast:     **Russell Thorson, Jack Edwards, Will Wright, Paul Dubov,
Lawrence Dobkin, Vic Perrin**

◆　❖　◆

SHOW:          THE POOR LITTLE RICH GIRL MATTER
SHOW DATE:     9/1/1957
COMPANY:       MASTERS INSURANCE & TRUST COMPANY
AGENT:         BERT MAJOR
EXP. ACCT:     $317.75

**SYNOPSIS:** Bert Major calls about a poor little rich girl who wants to take out a $200,000 straight life policy on her husband effective in two weeks. And hush—hush, a surprise. Nice piece of change for the company and for the girl, if she is playing a game. All the arrangements have been through the girl's lawyer.

Johnny flies to Los Angeles, California with a new pair of sunglasses to meet Roger Hackey the local agent, a repressed comic. Johnny goes to the Beverly Hilton and finally gets the details of the case from Roger. The girl is Cynthia Dervin, and she is a strange one, like a chameleon. Roger met her in the office and she is a real trim and expensive person. She asked about various policies and how they paid off. She is a fixture in the society pages in Hollywood. Her husband, Peter, is a public figure ever since they got married three years ago. Cynthia told Roger that her husband had just had a physical and gave Roger the report and the name of her attorney, Crane Collins. Roger went to see him and he just asked routine questions, about expediting the procedures and the importance of secrecy. Roger could not ask any questions as Cynthia was there sitting like "a mouse waiting to be pounced on" while the papers were filled out, and signed them like they were a death warrant.

Johnny cabs to Collins' office and Collins does not understand why Johnny is there. Johnny tells him that insurance is not a surprise gift to the covered person. Collins tells Johnny that he has known Cynthia since she was born and is her guardian since the death of her parents. The husband plays an excellent game of golf, and gets on with people when he wants to. Collins does not like Peter, but tells Johnny that he only represents people and does not have an opinion on them or their wishes. Johnny gets the address for Cynthia, and tells Collins not to tell anyone he was there, or the policy will not be issued. Johnny makes a call and then cabs to Roger's office to borrow his car. Johnny drives to the Dervin home and meets Cynthia, who is all Johnny expected. As soon as Johnny starts asking questions she gets edgy. Johnny joins Cynthia by the pool and asks her the questions he needs to. Johnny learns that the issue date of the policy is Peter's birthday. When Johnny notes that Peter would be worth a lot of money, Cynthia gets a headache and leaves.

Johnny has seen both sides of her personality and her actions seem compulsory and not natural. The phone by the pool rings and Johnny listens in to hear

Cynthia crying to a man named Eric, who tells her to meet him. Johnny leaves and drives down the block to watch the house. Cynthia leaves and Johnny follows her, only to lose her within ten blocks. Back in the office, Roger has no idea about Eric's identity. Roger shows Johnny a newspaper article on Peter who is playing in a golf tournament. Johnny runs out to interview Peter, posing as a reporter. Johnny spots Peter and asks him where his wife is, only to learn that she never watches Peter play. Johnny asks Peter about his upcoming birthday, and he tells Johnny that he is going to drive in the annual western road races that day. He has won the last two years.

Johnny cabs to Crane Collins' office and he is still there. In the office are voices, which stop when Johnny enters. Johnny waits in the lobby until Collins comes out and closes the door to his office. Johnny asks about Peter being a racing enthusiast, and Collins tells him he did not think to mention it to him. Johnny tells him that no company will issue a policy on a racing driver. Johnny asks who Eric is and then barges into the office to find Cynthia gone.

Johnny eats and regrets not writing a report and going home. In the society page of the paper Johnny sees the answer to Eric's identity. Johnny cabs to the police and chats with the captain who is one duty, and then goes to rent a tuxedo. Johnny cabs to the Hilton with a special pass that gets him into a society benefit, where he runs into Collins. Johnny spots Cynthia who tells Johnny that she is glad to see him. They dance and she tells Johnny that Peter is resting up for his golf tournament. Cynthia is warm and wants to go to the terrace. On the way to the terrace Johnny spots a man following them. Cynthia tells Johnny he is charming and she tells Johnny that she wishes . . . Johnny asks Cynthia who Eric is. He tells her that she is planning an accident to kill her husband during the upcoming race and she screams. Johnny turns and ducks and then slugs Eric as Cynthia sobs on the floor.

The house dick and I got them out of there; hawk-nose to police headquarters, Cynthia to a hospital. Eric turned out to be a quack psychiatrist who preyed on unstable rich women, and who was wanted in New York and Florida. He had a perfect setup in Cynthia Dervin, until he went for murder and the big money. Mrs. Dervin? Well the doctors tell me she ought to be normal mentally in a couple of years with proper psychiatric treatment.

## NOTES:

- THE MID-PROGRAM COMMERCIAL IS AND **AFRS** SPOT ABOUT THE VALUE OF PEOPLE TALKING TO EACH OTHER ALL OVER THE WORLD
- THE FINAL COMMERCIAL IS AN **AFRS** SPOT ABOUT THE FLAG OF NORTH CAROLINA
- BUD SEWELL IS THE ANNOUNCER

**Producer:** Jack Johnstone    **Writers:** Allen Botzer
**Cast:** Virginia Gregg, Herb Ellis, Frank Nelson, Marvin Miller, Peter Leeds

| SHOW: | THE CHARMONA MATTER |
| --- | --- |
| SHOW DATE: | 9/8/1957 |
| COMPANY: | INTER-COASTAL MARITIME & LIFE INSURANCE COMPANY |
| AGENT: | BYRON KAYE |
| EXP. ACCT: | $103.80 |

SYNOPSIS: Byron Kaye calls and asks if Johnny remembers hurricane Audrey. They have paid all the claims to the people in Louisiana and the neighboring area, as they really needed it. They just got a claim the other day from Buffalo, New York, and By wants to talk to Johnny.

Johnny flies to Byron's office in Boston where he is told that Charles Francis Keeley used to be a crooked promoter, who has been trying to change his life since the FTC and the SEC cracked down on him. Keeley has enough money to live comfortably with a nice wife, home and a 62-foot cruiser, and the boat is the problem. Early in June he took his boat to Detroit for some work to be done on it. A couple of weeks later, on the way back, hurricane Audrey was working its way north. His wife was not worried that he had not come home, as he had often stopped in Cleveland in the past to see old friends. When he was not home by July 20th she got worried. Calls to friends and the Coast Guard turned up nothing. A few days later the life preservers from the boat turned up on the south shore of Lake Erie near Linsey. Keeley had a $35,000 policy on himself and a $106,000 policy on the boat.

Johnny travels to Buffalo, New York, gets a room at the Statler Hotel, and goes to the Keeley home. Johnny is pleasantly surprised at Keeley's wife Mona, who is young and attractive, and tells Johnny that he could have stayed at the house, it is so empty and she gets lonely. Mona tells Johnny that every effort has been made to find the boat and Paul the pilot, who was very nice. The phone rings and Johnny feels that something is wrong with this case. The call was from the Coast Guard, and Mona tells Johnny that Charles is all right, he has been found. Johnny is sure because of the look in her eyes, that she is lying through her teeth.

Mona tells Johnny that a farmer had picked up Charles and took care of him. Charles was out of his mind because of what had happened to him. Johnny tells Mona that she is not glad he is alive, and she agrees. They were married nine years ago, but the things he did to make his money were not quite right. But who worries about conscious when things are going right. Charlie started giving monies to religions and charities, money she could have used. He got moody and would not pay attention to her. And Paul . . . That is why she is not overjoyed that Charlie is alive.

Mona goes upstairs to change clothes for the drive to Cleveland and Johnny waits and wonders about the case as he walks through the house. In the den Johnny sees a piece of paper sticking out of a desk drawer on the desk. The paper is a bill from an exclusive New York shop, for some very expensive gowns. In the drawer are thousands of unpaid bills, many with firm but polite warnings on them. No wonder she wished he was gone, and maybe she had a hand in getting rid of Charles. Johnny hears a noise and turns to find Mona in the doorway with a pearl handled .25 Colt in her hand.

Mona tells Johnny he should not have looked in the drawer. Johnny surmises why the wreck was no accident. Maybe he did not anticipate the storm. Mona tells Johnny that Charles is in the hospital. They are going for a ride but not to the hospital. Johnny tells her to put down the gun and she tells Johnny that Charles did not sink the boat. Mona tells Johnny the Paul must have gone down with the boat. When the boat sank she hoped she could take the money and run away with Paul. Johnny shows her a gold paperweight and throws it into a mirror. Mona is distracted, and Johnny takes the gun away from her, the gun with the safety on. She tells Johnny that she could not have killed him. The phone rings and a man asks for Charlie. Johnny tells him that Charlie is in the hospital. The man tells Johnny that he was going to buy the Charmona for $98,000 when he got back from Detroit, but since the boat is lost, he wants his deposit back.

Johnny drives Mona to Cleveland and Mona says nothing on the five-hour trip. At the hospital there is a police lieutenant and a stenographer. Mona sinks to a chair and is handcuffed to it. Charles talks and makes the case crystal clear. He tells them that Paul refused to come on the trip back with him. The police were notified and have picked up Paul and found where he bought the various parts for the device. Charles knew that he and Mona were carrying on behind his back. He wanted to get back to sell the boat, but the boat exploded after leaving. He was lucky that he was sailing close to shore, as it saved his life. The Coast Guard divers have found the boat and there is a hole as big as a house in it. The storm might have taken a lot of lives, but it really saved Charles' life.

Johnny is glad there are courts to take care of situations like this. I would have hated to dirty my hands any further. Yeah, it probably does take all kinds to make a world but believe me; the world would be a lot better off without some of those kind. The claim on the yacht, sure it will have to be paid, and to a man who is honestly trying to live a decent life for a change.

NOTES:
- DAN CUBBERLY IS THE ANNOUNCER
- THIS PROGRAM INTRODUCES A THREE-ACT PROGRAM. ALL PREVIOUS PROGRAMS IN ALL THE SERIES, EXCEPT FOR THE 5-A-WEEK PROGRAMS, HAD BEEN TWO ACTS.
- THE FIRST COMMERCIAL BREAK IS AN AFRS SPOT ABOUT DR. TOM DOOLEY
- THE SECOND COMMERCIAL SPOT IS ABOUT THE FLAG OF WISCONSIN
- THE FINAL COMMERCIAL IS ABOUT FRIENDSHIP AND THE EFFORT TO PROVIDE MEDICINE FOR A SPANISH YOUTH
- CAST INFORMATION FROM THE KNX COLLECTION AT THE THOUSAND OAKS LIBRARY.

| **Producer:** | Jack Johnstone | **Writers:** | Jack Johnstone |
|---|---|---|---|

**Cast:** Les Tremayne, Mary Jane Croft, Harry Bartell, Vic Perrin, Bob Bruce

◆ ❖ ◆

| **SHOW:** | THE JPD MATTER |
|---|---|
| **SHOW DATE:** | 9/15/1957 |
| **COMPANY:** | FLOYDS OF ENGLAND |
| **AGENT:** | GEORGE REED |
| **EXP. ACCT:** | $204.80 |

**SYNOPSIS:** George Reed calls, and Johnny wonders what Floyds of England has insured this time; singing mice, wayward cats, or counterfeit money? Maybe they did a switch and insured someone again living this time? George tells Johnny that they have such a policy, but this case is something else. Floyds has a policy on a small brewery near Tamaqua, Pennsylvania. The Dortmund Brewery is insured against damage from a nearby construction project. George tells Johnny to come over and get the details.

Johnny cabs to George's office where George shows Johnny a map of the area around Tamaqua, near the Pixatawney Creek. The brewery is near the creek. Johnny tells George that he will rent a car in New York, but George tells him that he can get most of the way there by train, anything to save a dollar on the expense account. The plant is insured for $820,000. A new brewery is being built next door, and J. P. Dortmund is afraid of what might happen.

Johnny travels to New York, rents a car and drives to Tamaqua in the evening. The next day Johnny goes to the brewery, which needs a coat of paint. On top of a cliff behind the brewery, the construction project is in full swing. At the door a large raw-boned woman in a faded dress meets Johnny. She is J. P. Dortmund, and she accuses Johnny of being a lawyer for the outfit up on the hill. Johnny tells her he is there on behalf of the insurance company and she takes him into her private office, which is run down, just like her. Johnny is told that there is nothing fancy here; all they care about is the beer. Gretchen is called and told to bring Johnny a pitcher and a glass. J. P. tells Johnny that the creek is the secret to their beer; it is the finest water for beer in the country. That is why the Carlson-Kemper bunch is building up on the cliff. But all their fancy equipment cannot make a beer equal to hers. J. P. tells Johnny that she ages the materials for three full months, and they come up with a better brew. They are getting ready to blast up on the hill, and the whole thing will come down and wreck her equipment. She tells Johnny to see if he can stop them. Johnny thinks that maybe she is on to something.

Johnny drives to the construction site on the cliff and talks to James Carlson. He tells Johnny that they are not going to do any harm to the Dortmund brewery. He cannot understand how she stays in business; her methods were out of date fifty years ago. He had offered to buy the plant for half a million (well it was actually $450,000), but she would not sell. Carlson shows Johnny the permits and he tells Johnny that he has hired one of the best blasters in the country. The blast is scheduled for tonight. Johnny meets Sidney Crutchfield, who is working with a slide rule. Johnny learns that he has done the blasting on some of the biggest construction jobs in the country. Sidney tells Johnny that he will set the charges tonight at two o'clock, and no one is to be there. Sidney gives Johnny a tour of the site and shows Johnny the entire layout of the charges and how they will be set off. Johnny is sure that this man could do nothing wrong.

Johnny drives to the brewery and finds the place totally deserted. Johnny slips the lock on the door and goes into the office to find it in shambles. Someone had been taking papers from the files. Johnny hears J. P. say "I'm sorry Johnny." and then she knocks him out, takes some papers and leaves.

Johnny comes to with a bad headache wondering why J. P. hit him. On the floor Johnny finds a bill addressed to J. P. personally for 21 cases of dynamite. Johnny looks at his watch and it is 1:52 AM. Johnny now knows where the rocks will land and why he was left there to be crushed by the rocks. Johnny phones the operator and tells her to call the construction site, but she tells him that their lines were disconnected earlier that day. Johnny stumbles to his car and somehow drives to the top of the cliff. Johnny yells at Sidney to not blast and pulls his gun to stop him. Sidney realizes that something is wrong when Johnny faints.

Johnny realizes that Sidney saw the bill for dynamite that Johnny had taken with him, and good sense told him to stop the blasts. That morning Sidney finds where J. P. had set a charge, which would go off from concussion and divert the rocks onto her brewery. No one would have ever known. When the police catch her, she has the books to the brewery with her, and they showed that she was broke.

## NOTES:

- TAMAQUA, PA. IS ABOUT 30-40 MILES NW OF ALLENTOWN, PENNSYLVANIA
- THE MID-PROGRAM COMMERCIAL AS AN AFRS SPOT ABOUT A MILK PROCESSING PLANT IN THE AZORES
- THE SECOND COMMERCIAL SPOT IS ABOUT THE FLAG OF HAWAII
- THE ANNOUNCER IS DAN CUBBERLY

| | | | |
|---|---|---|---|
| **Producer:** | Jack Johnstone | **Writers:** | Jack Johnstone |
| **Cast:** | Eleanor Audley, Jeanne Bates, G. Stanley Jones, Alan Reed, Austin Green | | |

◆   ❖   ◆

| | |
|---|---|
| **SHOW:** | THE IDEAL VACATION MATTER |
| **SHOW DATE:** | 9/22/1957 |
| **COMPANY:** | UNIVERSAL ADJUSTMENT BUREAU |
| **AGENT:** | PAT MCCRACKEN |
| **EXP. ACCT:** | $115.25 |

**SYNOPSIS:** Pat McCracken calls, and Johnny thought he was on vacation. Pat was, but Ned Grant, the Broadway columnist, has forced him to cancel his vacation. Grant is heavily insured and is taking his vacation. He has made a lot of enemies in his time and one of his enemies is trying to make his vacation permanent.

Johnny cabs to Pat's office and Pat is waiting for him. Johnny is told that Ned prints some pretty blunt stuff some time. He dug up some evidence on Willie Bemis a couple years ago, and Bemis went to jail. Bemis broke out last night, and Grant probably does not know about it. The police want to protect Grant. But no one knows where he is to protect him. Johnny is to find Grant before Bemis does.

Johnny heads to New York City and talks to the manager of Grant's apartment. He has no idea where Grant went on vacation and was only told to hold his mail. Grant is unpredictable and has phone calls all the time and strange people seeing him at all hours. Grant had his phone disconnected before he left. Johnny tells the manager about Bemis' escape, and the need to find Grant before Bemis does. Johnny is referred to Doris Anthony, a close friend of Grant's. Johnny hails a cab, but sees Willie Bemis going into the service entrance. Johnny runs back to the manager's office, breaks down the door to find the manager on the floor. He tells Johnny a man had barged in after Johnny left, and that he only told the man what he told Johnny.

Johnny looks up Doris Anthony's address and cabs there. She does not know where Grant is. Doris looks familiar to Johnny and she tells Johnny that Grant helped her in his column. She thinks the ideal vacation for Ned is where ever girls are. Johnny tells her about Bemis, and she becomes anxious. She remembers Ned stopping at a travel agency last week.

Johnny stops in to see a friend at the newspaper and in the morgue Johnny finds a picture of Doris sitting at a table with Willie Bemis. Johnny rushes back to Doris' apartment, but she is gone and the manager tells Johnny that she left with a suitcase. Johnny goes to the travel agent and he tells Johnny that he had made a number of reservations for Grant. Grant always makes reservations and then never shows up. Doris calls Johnny at the travel agent and tells Johnny that she is no longer a friend of Willie's. She thinks that Ned might be at a ski lodge in Vermont. He has gone there before to get away from things. It is called Hastings Lodge, and is located about 20 miles beyond Bradberry. Johnny travels to Hastings Ski Lodge and arrives after dark to find the lodge dark. Johnny goes into the lodge and senses that someone is there with him. Johnny calls for Grant and Bemis tells Johnny that he has the wrong person; that Ned is not there yet.

Bemis takes Johnny's gun and tells Johnny that Doris had told him where Grant was, after a little talk. Johnny wishes he had stayed at home and realizes what the ideal vacation is and where Ned Grant is. A car drives up and Bemis tells Johnny to answer the door. Johnny opens he door and Doris is there. Johnny throws open the door against Bemis grabs Doris and they drive to New York in her car. Johnny calls the local sheriff to have them pick up Bemis, and arrive in New York at dawn.

Johnny rings the doorbell at the manager's office and he does not answer. Johnny tells Doris to call the police and goes to Grant's apartment. No one answers the door, so Johnny climbs out on a ledge and goes to the bedroom window to see Ned Grant asleep, with an empty bottle beside the bed. So the ideal vacation is to tell everyone you are going out of town, and then lock your self in your apartment where no one will bother you.

Johnny lets himself in and opens the door to let Doris in, along with Bemis, who has a gun. Bemis thanks Johnny for finding Grant for him. Bemis starts to shoot Johnny when the hallway if full of police who shoot Bemis' gun away from him. Ned wakes up and asks what is going on, and why Bemis is there? Johnny tells him to write it off as a bad dream.

Look, the next time you send me out to protect a guy, don't pick one who is going to sleep all the way through the deal, huh. I don't know, it kind of takes the sport out of it. And Pat, since I didn't find a man who ran away for you, on account of he never really ran away, well how about sending my fee on this one to the community chest.

NOTES:
- JOHNNY DONATES HIS FEE TO THE COMMUNITY CHEST ON THIS ONE
- DAN CUBBERLY IS THE ANNOUNCER

**Producer:** Jack Johnstone          **Writers:**   Robert Ryf
**Cast:**          Mary Jane Croft, Lawrence Dobkin, Joseph Kearns,
          Jack Edwards, Barney Phillips Byron Kane

SHOW:          THE DOUBTFUL DIARY MATTER
SHOW DATE:    9/29/1957
COMPANY:      TRI-WESTERN PROPERTY & CASUALTY INSURANCE COMPANY
AGENT:         PETER HARDY
EXP. ACCT:     $418.00

SYNOPSIS: Peter Hardy calls and tells Johnny that there is trouble with the Amenian dairy farm near Reno. Last year they lost a silo and it cost Peter $21,000. Amenian just lost a compound Silo and the cost is $56,000. Peter thinks it is arson.

Johnny travels to Reno, Nevada and meets with Peter. The Amenian dairies are just north of Reno, and the silos are specially made for him. The claim was filed the same day for the last one.

Johnny rents a car and drives to the Amenian dairy and is impressed with its size and efficiency. Aram Armenian shows Johnny the silo remains, which only has the concrete base left. Johnny is told that only Mr. Barnwell and Amenian know how the silo was built. The secret was in the ventilation. He is building a new one based on a better design. Johnny tells Amenian that it was to his benefit to lose the silo, and that the fire came at just the right time for a new and better silo. Amenian tells Johnny that he does not think the silos were burned, and if they were, Johnny will never be able to prove it.

Johnny calls Lt. Brady of the police, and he tells Johnny that he could find nothing to prove arson. Johnny remembers an old trick and buys a loaf of white bread. Johnny goes back to Amenian's ranch and drops a piece of bread in the ashes and then puts it in his mouth. Amenian is confused until Johnny tells him that it was a sure test for the presence of kerosene. Amenian tells Johnny to leave and not come back.

Johnny calls Herb Calbert at the bank and then goes to see Herb. Johnny asks Herb for information on Amenian. Herb tells Johnny that Amenian banks with Herb, and is the biggest account they have, and his financial condition is excellent. Herb tells Johnny that he is wrong when Johnny tells him that he has found evidence of arson. Herb tells Johnny that his employees love Amenian, as do his competitors. Johnny has dinner and drinks with Herb and gets a list of firms who do business with Amenian.

After visiting a casino with Herb, Johnny goes back to his hotel where the clerk tells Johnny that a man had been waiting for him, but it was not Amenian. The clerk spots the man leaving the hotel and Johnny follows. Johnny runs down the street after the man and follows him down an alley where the man attacks Johnny and beats him.

A moving van interrupts the beating and the driver carries Johnny back to the hotel. The hotel doctor patches up Johnny and notices a ring from the YMCA Johnny got for helping with a softball team. The doctor gives Johnny a shot and Johnny vaguely hears the doctor mentioning that the ring must have made a mark on the man who hit him as he goes out for the night.

The next morning Johnny goes to see Herb, who tells him that a man Johnny is curious about is in need of money and owes the bank money, and did so last year. Herb tells him that the man must be at the Amenian ranch. Johnny and Herb drive to the ranch and meet Amenian coming out the pasteurizing plant. Amenian tells Herb that he heard a car and thought it was Barnwell. Johnny is about to apologize to Amenian until he sees a bandage on his face. Amenian tells Johnny that he cut himself shaving. Johnny is about to pull the bandage off when Barnwell comes up and Johnny tells him that he knows Barnwell because of his bruised and bandaged face. Johnny rips off Barnwell's bandage and there is a mark on his face where Johnny had hit him. Johnny beats Barnwell to get him to talk about burning Armenian's silos.

Yeah, he talked all right, plenty, about a racket so old I hadn't heard of it in years. A crooked businessman who burned out his own clients to get himself more work. And in this case, a natural, because he was the only one who shared Aram's secret construction plans. And by the time I was through with him, he blabbed about some of his other clients he had taken the same way.

**NOTES:**
- THE FIRST COMMERCIAL IS AN **AFRS** SPOT ABOUT LT. FRED HARGISHIEMER, AND HIS FRIENDSHIP WITH NATIVES ON AN ISLAND.
- THE FINAL COMMERCIAL IS AN **AFS** SPOT ABOUT MERCY AND TRUTH MEETING EACH OTHER VIA HELP GIVEN TO EARTHQUAKE VICTIMS IN CHILE
- THE ANNOUNCER IS DAN CUBBERLY

| Producer: | Jack Johnstone | Writers: | Jack Johnstone |
|---|---|---|---|
| Cast: | Paul Dubov, Will Wright, John Dehner, Harry Bartell, | | |
| | Parley Baer, Forrest Lewis | | |

◆    ❖    ◆

| SHOW: | THE BUM STEER MATTER |
|---|---|
| SHOW DATE: | 10/6/1957 |
| COMPANY: | TRI-WESTERN INSURANCE COMPANY |
| AGENT: | HAL VERSKI |
| EXP. ACCT: | $0.00 |

SYNOPSIS: Jake Denim calls Johnny from Colorado. He has a cattle ranch there and a policy with Tri-Western in Denver. He has no trouble, but his brand is the "Lazy JD," and "JD" are Johnny's initials. Jake listens to the radio programs every week, and he is sure that Johnny would want to come out and get some local color for his program. Johnny hems and haws about some reports that are due and Jake tells him that he will be expecting him. Johnny feels that Jake is lying through his teeth.

Johnny calls Hal Verski in Denver and asks him to ok an expense account for him. Hal tells Johnny that Jake has about $40,000 in insurance and Johnny tells Hal about the call from Jake. Hal tells Johnny that if he finds something they will pay for it, otherwise Johnny will have a nice vacation to pay for.

Johnny clears up the paperwork in four days and flies to Denver, rents a car and drives to Jake's ranch in Craig, Colorado. Johnny eats lunch at the hotel in Craig and gets directions to the ranch. The waitress asks if Johnny is a relative, tells him it was real nice and that everyone was there and then runs off. Johnny drives to the ranch and sees a piece of black crepe on the doorframe. A woman meets Johnny at the door and asks Johnny why he did not come earlier. Jake was buried this morning, and she thinks he was murdered.

The girl was dressed in black and had been crying. The girl is Virginia, Jake's daughter. She tells Johnny that Big Mike Craven who owns the "C Lucky Star" ranch, and who wants to own all the other ranches in the area, was responsible for Jake's death. Jake died from anthrax; at least that is what they said it was. Johnny talks to Virginia and she confirms that she thinks someone is trying to infect her herd. A young man comes in and asks Johnny who he is. The man tells Virginia that the hands will take their orders from her now, and he asks her to marry him. He will give up medical school to marry her, and she needs him to help run the ranch. Johnny asks who he is, and he is Peter Trimmer, and his father owns a small ranch nearby. Pete tells Johnny that Jake died from "galloping anthrax" that he got from a steer. Pete tells Johnny that the steer has been buried on orders of the Vet and the state inspector. Johnny leaves and calls the state inspector, who tells Johnny he has never seen the steer as he was confined to bed at the time. Johnny calls the vet, who is out at the moment. In the hotel Johnny reads an article in a magazine that makes him call the vet again. The vet tells

Johnny that he was going to see Mike Craven, an old college roommate. The vet had spotted the anthrax, which was only in one Hereford steer. He tells Johnny that the steer is buried in a far corner of the "Lazy JD" property. Johnny tells him that they are going out to look at the steer.

Johnny gets two assistants to handle the shovels, some flashlights and then they all go to dig up the steer. Once the cow is uncovered the vet tells Johnny that the color is not right, that there is no sigh of anthrax in the cow. Johnny asks if a poison could have caused it, and tells the vet that strychnine often produces signs similar to tetanus or lockjaw. The vet tells Johnny that he remembers a poison from his school days, quintanigen sulfide. He tells Johnny that it still would not explain why Jake died. Johnny notices that the brand looks like it was put on over another brand. Johnny asks the vet to skin off the hide to determine what the original brand was. The vet tells Johnny that only a small amount of the poison would have killed Jake. The vet gets the hide off, and the original brand was the "C Lucky Star."

Johnny and the Vet drive back and discuss the implications. The vet is sure that Big Mike did not do it. Instead of going to the Craven ranch, Johnny drives to the "K bar K" ranch and the vet tells Johnny that Carl Trimmer is just holding on. At the ranch Pete calls out and Johnny opens the door and they go up to Pete's room. Johnny tells him that the "Lazy JD" would be a nice place to get hold of. Johnny asks Pete where he got the quintanigen sulfide, and Pete tells him he does not know what he is talking about. Johnny shows him a marker in a toxicology book, and Pete is speechless. When Johnny asks how he gave the poison to Jake, Pete pulls a gun and the vet hits Pete with a chair.

Johnny waits around for the autopsy, which shows the same poison in Jake's body. A small bottle of the rare drug was found in Pete's trunk. So Pete has not only lost an opportunity for a nice ranch, but also for living very long.

Expenses were $618.50, but Johnny requests that the money be sent to the Community Chest, so he will feel right about this case, and about himself too.

NOTES:
- THE FIRST COMMERCIAL IS AN **AFRS** SPOT ABOUT THE VALUE OF BOOKS SENT TO TANGANYIKA
- THE SECOND COMMERCIAL IS AN **AFRS** SPOT ABOUT FRIENDSHIP AND HOW THE ARMED FORCES USES FRIENDSHIP TO AID OTHERS
- THIS IS THE SECOND CASE WHERE JOHNNY REQUESTS THAT THE MONIES BE DONATED TO THE COMMUNITY
- QUINTANIGEN SULFIDE IS ANOTHER JACK JOHNSTONE ORIGINAL POISON.
- THE ANNOUNCER IS DAN CUBBERLY

**Producer:** Jack Johnstone  **Writers:** Jack Johnstone
**Cast:** Virginia Gregg, Jean Tatum, Will Wright, Jack Edwards, Howard McNear, Sam Edwards, Forrest Lewis

◆ ❖ ◆

| | |
|---|---|
| SHOW: | THE SILVER BELLE MATTER |
| SHOW DATE: | 10/13/1957 |
| COMPANY: | FLOYDS OF ENGLAND |
| AGENT: | GEORGE REED |
| EXP. ACCT: | $317.10 |

SYNOPSIS: George Reed calls Johnny with a $25,0000, possibly $50,000 problem. Mercedes Crabtree has had a policy for 30 years. Someone took a shot at her, and last night she disappeared.

Johnny cabs to George's office and George tells Johnny that this case is important. Mrs. Crabtree was one of the first American clients of Floyds, and Mr. Murdock Morton, the president of the company personally sold the policy. At the time they became good friends and still correspond regularly. Mrs. Henrietta Scott, the only friend of Mrs. Crabtree's in Silver Gulch, Montana, wrote to Mr. Morton to tell him of the problem. Mrs. Scott was supposed to have dinner with Mrs. Crabtree but she was not there. After two days she wired Mr. Morton. The beneficiary is Mrs. Crabtree's favorite charity.

Johnny travels to Butte and takes a bus to Silver Gulch, rents a car and drives to the home of Mrs. Scott, who thinks that Johnny is from the antique shop. Mrs. Scott tells Johnny that Mrs. Crabtree is still missing, and that the Sheriff is still looking for her. Most of the residents in town have no use for her because she is stopping progress. Charlie Greenpaw is trying to turn the town into a tourist attraction and Mercedes will not sell any of her land. She owns half of Main Street and the Silver Belle mine, the richest silver mine in Montana at one time. Mercedes was walking up to her mine when she was shot at. Mrs. Scott looks out the window and "well I'll be first cousin to a stink bug," she sees Charlie Greenpaw and Slim Richards, the sheriff's deputy walking towards the mine.

Johnny drives to the mine and introduces himself to them at a new "No Trespassing" sign that they take seriously. They are not going in, but are considering it seriously. They tell Johnny if he wants to go in, there is nothing stopping him. Johnny goes into the mine and walks down a tunnel only to be shot at.

Johnny throws a rock into the tunnel, gets a shot in return and feigns being shot. When a woman calls out, Johnny calls out to Mrs. Crabtree and tells her that Mr. Morton is worried about her. Johnny walks up to her and tells her that Mrs. Scott had written to Mr. Morton. She tells Johnny that she came into the mine and hurt herself, and Johnny will have to carry her out.

Johnny takes her to her cabin and Mrs. Scott comes in. Mercedes tells Henrietta to go get the doctor. Johnny asks her why she shot at him, and she tells Johnny that she thought Johnny might be one of Charlie's men. She will not sell the mine because that is where her husband and his men are buried. She told everyone that if anyone sets foot on her property, she would shoot first and ask questions later.

Johnny goes to his hotel for dinner and is stopped by Charlie Greenpaw. Johnny asks him why he did not go into the mine. Charlie tells Johnny that his wife put him up to looking in the mine for Mrs. Crabtree otherwise it might look like he was responsible for hurting her. Charlie tells Johnny that Mrs. Crabtree has taken a shine to Johnny, as that was all she could talk about when the doctor was there. Charlie tells Johnny that he will give him $1,000 if he will get Mrs. Crabtree to sell him the mine and the acreage beside Mrs. Scott. Johnny tells Charlie that he really wants the property and Charlie tells Johnny he wants to open a dude ranch. The fire bell rings, and Slim Richards runs in to tell Charlie that Mrs. Crabtree's cabin is on fire.

Johnny rushes to the cabin, and finds Mrs. Crabtree wrapped in a blanket beside the sheriff's car. She tells Johnny to tell Charlie that she will sell to him, as there is nothing left to stay for. Charlie comes up and Johnny asks him for a map of the area. In Charlie's office Johnny looks at the map and gets sick to his stomach. Johnny drives to Mrs. Scott's and knocks at the door. She lets Johnny in and he asks to see Mrs. Crabtree, but she cannot do that, as the doctor does not want her disturbed. Johnny accuses her of burning the cabin with her in it. "She trusted you, she thought you were the only person she could trust. When she found out different she decided to sell her land and get away from here" and Henrietta calls them lies. Johnny tells her that she owns most of the property along the Crabtree property, and Charlie would not buy hers without buying Crabtree's as well. And when Mrs. Crabtree would not sell, you decided to get the land the hard way. Johnny tells her that she shot at Mrs. Crabtree to set up her alibi. Johnny forces his way into the bedroom and wakes up Mrs. Crabtree. Henrietta comes in with a gun and tells Johnny to get back. Mercedes tells Johnny that Henrietta started the fire and there is a struggle and Johnny gets the rifle away from Henrietta. Henrietta yells at Johnny for ruining the whole thing.

I was ready to leave Silver Gulch the next day, but I stayed over an extra week for a little English gentleman named Murdock Morton to arrive and claim his bride. Yeah, just about everybody in Montana came to Mrs. Crabtree's, excuse me, Mrs. Morton's wedding, everybody that is except her old friend Mrs. Henrietta Scott.

## NOTES:
- THE FIRST COMMERCIAL IS AN **AFRS** SPOT ABOUT DR. TOM DOOLEY
- THE SECOND COMMERCIAL IS AN **AFRS** SPOT ABOUT BRITISH DIVERS WHO DIVE TO THE BOTTOM OF THE OCEAN AND FIND PORTUGUESE RELICS
- THERE WAS A SILVER BELLE MINE IN MONTANA, WHICH OPERATED IN THE 1880's.
- THE ANNOUNCER IS DAN CUBBERLY

**Producer:** Jack Johnstone      **Writers:** Charles B. Smith
**Cast:**      Virginia Gregg, D. J. Thompson, G. Stanley Jones, Frank Nelson, Sam Edwards, Will Wright

| **SHOW:** | THE MARY GRACE MATTER |
| **SHOW DATE:** | 10/20/1957 |
| **COMPANY:** | MID-EASTERN LIFE & CASUALTY COMPANY |
| **AGENT:** | BEN PERRIN |
| **EXP. ACCT:** | $0.00 |

**SYNOPSIS:** Randy Singer calls and tells Johnny he is not doing so fine. You better come down here on account of Mary Grace Marshall. Oh, you know her too? I just spent a weekend with her in New York and we had a ball. Johnny, your little girlfriend has been murdered. I'll grab the first plane. Yeah, you better.

Johnny makes reservations to fly to New York City and then calls Ben Perrin at Mid-Eastern to tell him that a policyholder, Mary Grace Marshall has been killed. Ben tells Johnny that he has to wait until authorization has been obtained. When Johnny tells him that she was a personal friend, Ben approves the expense account.

Johnny thinks about Mary Grace on the flight to New York, and it hurts. Johnny wanted to marry her some years ago, but she had a career, and Johnny was not really the marrying kind anyway, so they remained friends, good friends. Johnny cabs to the 18th precinct and Randy tells Johnny that all the clues point to the one person who was known to be with her when she was killed. She struggled and fell and hit her head on the fireplace. Randy offers Johnny a cigarette and lights it with a lighter. Randy tells Johnny that the coroner says that she was killed late Sunday night by someone who spent several hours with her. Johnny realizes that he was with her late Sunday night. Randy is flicking the lighter and Johnny recognizes it. Randy tells him that it was left in the apartment by whoever killed Mary Grace Marshall.

Randy reads the inscription on the lighter, and Johnny tells Randy that he must have left it there. The wife of the building superintendent saw Johnny leave, fingerprints and cigarette butts prove that Johnny was there. Randy asks Johnny what he was doing there and Johnny explodes at him, and then apologizes. Johnny tells Randy that they spent the afternoon at the Bronx zoo and had dinner and drinks in the apartment and listened to music. Johnny had picked up a bottle of scotch and had one or two light drinks, but Randy tells him the bottle was almost empty. Mrs. Walker the wife of the building super found the body. She went up to the apartment when she heard the screams. Randy tells Johnny that he ought to go see her. Randy tells Johnny that he is the prime suspect until he can help Randy prove he is wrong.

Johnny and Randy drive to the apartment and Johnny sees the signs of the struggle in the apartment. Johnny finds the bottle of Scotch in the living room and tells Randy that he left the bottle in the kitchenette. In the refrigerator Johnny finds a bottle of soda almost full. Nobody drinks that much Scotch straight unless they are a lush, or unless you need a jolt for your nerves adds Randy. Johnny and Randy talk to Mrs. Walker, a young doll with too much makeup. Johnny notices a strange spicy odor, but forgets about it. She tells Randy that her husband has been sick and stays in bed. She heard screams, and she asked him what to do about it, but he told her to go back to sleep. She tried to sleep and heard noises later, like her husband was trying to get up. At 2:00 AM she went upstairs and found the body. Johnny asks to talk to the husband, and she says sure, if he is sober enough. Johnny smells the odor again as he goes into the wife's bedroom. In the husband's bedroom Johnny smells the odor of stale booze and finds the walls plastered with pinup pictures and photos of Mary Grace. The husband tells his wife that he does not want anymore of that stuff. He tells Johnny that he heard screaming in the apartment, and then it stopped and he wrote it off as a nightmare and the wife tells him that he was dreaming about the doll upstairs instead of paying attention to her and about sneaking around to see her. The doctor comes in and reprimands everyone for disturbing the patient. He has a serious heart condition and an infection. Johnny tells Randy to come back upstairs and he can clinch the case.

Johnny shows Randy the scotch bottle and the smears where someone tried to hide the prints. In the living room Johnny shows Randy the hi-fi with the same record they were listening to Sunday night, the Dolorema by Vinghetti still in it. They had shut it off because it became too noisy with the screams during the death scene. Randy tells him that the husband was responsible for it and killed her because she would not have him. He sees you with Mary Grace, he hears the screaming and he wakes up his wife and does not let her go up. After you leave he goes up and kills her. The wife ties it all up with the screams. Johnny and Randy go back down stairs and Johnny tells him the same circumstances would work for her if she killed Mary Grace. Johnny tells Randy that the strange odor is cardamom, the drunkard's friend. You can drink all night, chew on some and no one will know. The odor was so strong in her room; maybe she is the lush. In the hallway the doctor tells them that the husband does not even drink and could not have gotten out of bed. The wife comes out and she tells them that her husband is dead. She asks if they are going to try and pin the murder on her, and Johnny tells her that she has already pinned it on herself. "You thought you left no fingerprints on the bottle" Johnny tells her and she blurs out that she used a handkerchief. She pulls a gun and admits killing the dame on the second floor and the doctor slugs her from behind. Randy is happy now, but it does not bring back Mary Grace.

I took on this case myself because of Mary Grace, and whatever she may have meant to me is none of the company's business. Oh, sure you will have to pay the claim on her policy, so let it go at that, will ya? The rest is on me; I want it that way. Understand? For old times' sake.

## NOTES:
- ANOTHER **AFRS** PROGRAM WITH THE CREDITS CUT.
- I SEARCHED THROUGH GROVES MUSICAL DICTIONARY, AND HAVE COME TO THE CONCLUSION THAT THE COMPOSER AND OPERA NOTED IN THE STORY ARE ANOTHER EXCELLENT PIECE OF JACK JOHNSTONE FICTION.

- JOHNNY WAIVES HIS EXPENSES FOR PERSONAL REASONS ON THIS CASE.
- CAST INFORMATION FROM THE KNX COLLECTION AT THE THOUSAND OAKS LIBRARY.
- THE ANNOUNCER IS DAN CUBBERLY

Producer:   Jack Johnstone          Writers:   Jack Johnstone
Cast:       Vic Perrin, Les Tremayne, Paula Winslowe, Frank Nelson,
            Byron Kane, Jean Tatum

◆   ❖   ◆

SHOW:        THE THREE SISTERS MATTER
SHOW DATE:   10/27/1957
COMPANY:     TRI-STATE LIFE & CASUALTY COMPANY
AGENT:       EARLE POORMAN
EXP. ACCT:   $351.20

SYNOPSIS: Earle Poorman calls from Green Mountain Falls, Colorado. Earle wants Johnny to join him. An important client has disappeared.

Johnny travels to Colorado Springs, Colorado where Earle meets Johnny at the airport. Earle tells Johnny that Green Mountain Falls is just east of here. Earle is staying at the Lucky-4 ranch, the last place that Misha Rolonov, the pianist was seen. He has a place up on the mountain where he and his three daughters, actually they are stepdaughters, live. They all got here ten days ago after a concert tour of Europe. Misha likes to take long walks and left on one three days ago. He stopped in at the Lucky 4 for coffee and has not been seen since. There has been snow, which covered up the any tracks he might have made. Earle knew him well, and Misha really loved the girls. At the Lucky-4 ranch Johnny meets Ray Mishney who tells Earle and Johnny that Rolonov's body has been found near a bear cave with a bullet in the back of his head.

Johnny and the others go to the cave in a jeep, and Ray tells Johnny that the bear ate off of the garbage every day and he was going to kill it, but he has not seen it for several days before Rolonov was killed so maybe someone else has killed the bear. Ray has also found a .257 Roberts cartridge near the cave. All the hunters in the area use either a 30/06, a .270 or a 30/30. The only .257 belongs to one of the girls at the Rolonov cabin, and one of the daughters is a good shot. Ray cannot believe that it was one of them. Earle and Johnny drive to the Rolonov cabin and Earle cannot think of anyone who would kill Misha. The policy has no direct beneficiary; it is based on his will, which no one knows the location of. Misha had made it clear that the will would show up at the proper time. At the cabin Johnny meets a beautiful girl dressed like a model from Charles of the Ritz. She is Olga, the oldest sister, and she is very glad to meet Johnny. Johnny tells her that they have not found out anything about their father. Johnny meets another sister, Ada who is at the piano playing a piece that her father had written on the morning her father left. She thinks it has some special meaning. Ada bristles at Olga when Olga mentions that Ada thinks she should be the pianist in the family. Johnny asks Olga where she was on the morning her father left, and Olga tells Johnny that she was in Colorado Springs shopping. Maria and Ada were doing the dishes when she left. Maria arrives and meets Johnny. Johnny is surprised as Maria is dressed in hunting clothes and carrying a high-powered rifle.

Maria gives Johnny the rifle and Olga tells Johnny that all she does is tramp around and shoot at things. Johnny notes that the rifle is a 30/06, and she tells Johnny that she has another rifle, a .22. Johnny finally tells them that their father's body has been found, shot by a high-powered rifle. Maria and Olga yell at each other while Ada is playing the piece her father wrote. Johnny tells her to play the piece again and notes that the first three notes are "A D A." She plays the rest of the piece to spell out the message "D E F A C E E D G E C A G E B E D," the canary cage. Johnny opens the canary cage and finds the Last Will and Testament and a note. The note tells Johnny that Rolonov has fingered his killer. The note reads "and my reason for deliberately omitting her from my will is not only because of the self centered life she has always led, not only because of her constant completely selfish extravagance, an extravagance which finally led her to forging my name on checks. Then when I discovered that she was sneaking out and practicing with the old rifle over the mantle." Suddenly Olga has the rifle. She tells them that the rifle has five shots in it, one for each of them, including one for her. There is no other way out. She tries to fire the rifle but it is empty. Maria attacks her and takes the gun from her. Maria and Ada tell Johnny that they had taken the bullets from the gun and suspected Olga .

Why, why, what kind of a mind can be so twisted?

NOTES:
- THE PROGRAM I HAVE MAY BE AN **AFRS** PROGRAM, AS ALL OF THE CREDITS HAVE BEEN CUT OUT.
- THE .257 ROBERTS WAS INTRODUCED IN 1934, AND WAS A VERY POPULAR AND VERSATILE CARTRIDGE.
- CAST INFORMATION FROM THE KNX COLLECTION AT THE THOUSAND OAKS LIBRARY.
- THE ANNOUNCER IS DAN CUBBERLY

**Producer:** Jack Johnstone    **Writers:** Jack Johnstone
**Cast:** Joseph Kearns, Vic Perrin, Virginia Gregg, Lucille Meredith, Lillian Buyeff, Bill James

◆ ❖ ◆

**SHOW:** THE MODEL PICTURE MATTER
**SHOW DATE:** 11/3/1957
**COMPANY:** UNIVERSAL ADJUSTMENT BUREAU
**AGENT:** PAT MCCRACKEN
**EXP. ACCT:** $103.00
**SYNOPSIS:** Pat McCracken calls Johnny about a beautiful model, Dorothy Blair.

Johnny recognizes her as the girl with the million-dollar face who is on a lot of people's minds. "Well she is no daydream to me—she is a nightmare," replies Pat. That face of hers is insured for $100,000 and someone is trying to tear it up. She got slugged last night.

Johnny cabs to Pat's office where Johnny gets the address for Dorothy Blair and heads for New York City. Johnny arrives at Dorothy's apartment just as the doctor is leaving. Dorothy tells Johnny that there will not be any permanent scars. She came home last night and a man hit her inside her apartment and then he left. She does not think it was a burglar. She is sure that it was Jerry Dunsmuir, a real creep, the real article. She modeled for him a year ago and swore that she never would again, but she did so just the other day. He wanted to take some street shots of winter clothes. After the second picture he started up on her, and she left.

Johnny goes to see Jerry Dunsmuir, but his office is closed. Johnny contacts an old friend, Lt. Al Ricco at 18th precinct. Lt. Ricco tells Johnny that he has an unsolved murder with no leads. Johnny tells Lt. Ricco about Jerry Dunsmuir, but Lt. Ricco does not know anything about him. Lt. Ricco gets a phone call and learns that Jerry Dunsmuir has been found floating in the river.

Johnny cabs to Dorothy's apartment, and Edward Chandler is there. Edward leaves and Johnny asks Dorothy about the picture shoot, then tells her about Jerry. Dorothy asks if Johnny suspects her, and he tells her no. She can prove that Jerry took pictures, and she gets the envelope with prints of the pictures taken. Dorothy tells Johnny that Jerry looked strangely at her when she told him not to bother her anymore. After leaving Johnny vaguely remembers Ed Chandlers face, but cannot remember where.

Johnny goes to Dunsmuir's studio where the secretary Susan Billings is closing up and does not want to answer anymore questions. Johnny buys her a drink and she tells Johnny that she does not know who would kill Jerry. Susan tells Johnny that Jerry had changed about women, and does not know Ed Chandler. She tells Johnny that she and Jerry were going to be married.

Johnny goes to see Lt. Ricco, who tells Johnny that Dunsmuir had a weakness for women. Johnny and Lt. Ricco go to see Dorothy and observe Dorothy coming out of her apartment with Ed Chandler. Lt. Ricco tells Johnny that the man is Ed Chatsworth and then Johnny remembers seeing his picture in the paper.

Now Johnny has two murders on his hand and a connection to the two of them. The first victim was Edith Summers, who the police believe was killed by her boyfriend Ed Chatsworth. Dorothy is now seeing Edith's boyfriend. Maybe Chatsworth was to get out of town while Dorothy handled Edith Summers. Dunsmuir found out and tried to blackmail her. She, or Chatsworth, or both of them, decided to close Dunsmuir's mouth for keeps. It is a possibility. Johnny thinks over the case in his hotel, but there is something wrong. Johnny goes back to see Dorothy at 10:00 PM and she is just coming home. She has a business meeting with Ed, and he is on his way up. Johnny tells her that Ed's real name is Chatsworth. Johnny mentions Edith Summers, but Dorothy did not know her and she tells Johnny that Jerry was not trying to blackmail her. Dorothy tells Johnny that she met Ed yesterday. He told her he was organizing a big promotion and wanted to include her in it and wants to see some outdoors pictures. Dorothy tells Johnny that the pictures were taken on the same day Edith Summers was killed. Johnny looks at the pictures sent from Dunsmuir and spots a shot in front of an apartment house, the Blackton Arms, the same place where Edith Summers lived. Dorothy spots a man in the background coming out of the building. Johnny hears a sound and asks about a service entrance and tells Dorothy to get down as he turns off the lights. Johnny throws a cigarette lighter into the kitchen and the intruder shoots. Johnny shoots and hits Ed Chatsworth. Johnny tells Dorothy that Ed was the one who killed Edith Summers. He had an alibi but spoiled it by getting into the picture that Dunsmuir took. He also was the one in her apartment the other night. Most pictures do not do people justice, but I guess this one will do him all right.

Remarks: Well, there is a little snapper to the story Pat. You know that picture Chatsworth was knocking himself out to get? He did not realize it, but his face in the background was far too blurred to make an identification.

NOTES:
- THE PROGRAM I HAVE IS ANOTHER **AFRS** COPY WITH NO CREDITS. THE CAST INFORMATION I HAVE IS FROM RadioGOLDINdex.
- THERE ARE TWO LISTINGS IN RadioGOLDINdex FOR THIS PROGRAM. THE AFRS PROGRAM I HAVE HAS VOICES THAT MATCH WITH #45827. THE OTHER ENTRY #45825 HAS TOO MANY VOICES LISTED FOR THE CHARACTERS IN THE SHOW.
- TERRY SALOMONSON LISTS ROBERT RYF AS THE WRITER OF THIS PROGRAM; RadioGOLDINdex LISTS ROBERT WRIGHT.

Producer:    Jack Johnstone          Writers:    Robert Ryf
Cast:        Virginia Gregg, Lillian Buyeff, Lawrence Dobkin, Herb Ellis, Harry Bartell

◆   ❖   ◆

SHOW:           THE ALKALI MIKE MATTER
SHOW DATE:      11/10/1957
COMPANY:        WESTERN LIFE & TRUST INSURANCE COMPANY
AGENT:          BILL KEMPER
EXP. ACCT:      $525.00
SYNOPSIS: Meg McCarthy calls her lover boy Johnny Dollar. She is in trouble in Port Hopeful. Port Hopeful, Nevada. There is insurance trouble out here. The company is Western Life and Trust; the very company that insured what is lying dead at my feet. But I did not do him in. Ah, forgive me lover boy, my skirts are clean. Don't be putting those handcuffs on me now. Oh, Johnny boy, I am in trouble now.

Johnny calls Bill Kemper at Western Life and flies to San Francisco. The next morning Bill asks Johnny if he knows about Alkali Mike Murphy, who discovered gold out in the desert, built a house and named it Port Hopeful. The original Alkali Mike was a ship captain who died, supposedly of suicide. His son, Alkali Mike Jr. has lived there for 40 years, and he has died, and how he died will affect the payout on the policy of $200,000. The beneficiaries are two nephews, a niece and an old housekeeper, all sharing equally. Johnny tells Bill that if Meg McCarthy is guilty, he will handle the case for nothing and quit the insurance business.

Johnny flies to Reno, rents a car and drives to Winnemucca and visits the police. Sgt. Otis Framley tells Johnny that they have the number one suspect, Meg McCarthy. If she did not poison Alkali Mike, he will eat his shirt. Johnny asks him how he wants his shirt cooked, because he knows Meg. Sgt. Framley tells Johnny that she has been at Port Hopeful about six months and already she is a beneficiary. In her jail cell, Meg is pitching a fit until she sees Johnny. Meg tells Johnny that she will tell Johnny all she knows, but the evidence she can give is enough to hang her.

Meg tells Johnny that she got tired of all the drunken sailors on the east coast. When she heard that Alkali Mike was looking for a housekeeper she took the job, and they got along just fine. She told him that she did not need the money. She knows the other beneficiaries and they are just hanging around waiting for Mike to die. Edgar Murphy has a job at the bank over at Lovelock. Margaret is a disgrace to her name, playing around from one man to another, looking for the man with the most money. And Danny is always gambling. They are all out at Port Hopeful trying to cheat each other out of what is left. The doctor says that Mike died of poison from something he ate, but Meg was the only one with him and the only one to touch his food. And Meg ate the same things Mike did. The doctor called the poison quintanigen sulfanate. Johnny remembers that the poison is related to the old Indian arrow poisons. Johnny wants to go to the house with her. Johnny gets a local attorney to get Meg released into Sgt. Framley's custody. Johnny, Meg and Sgt. Framley drive to Port Hopeful, which Johnny thinks should have been called Port Hopeless, as the place was a mess and poorly built. Johnny notices three new cars in the driveway when they arrive. Sgt. Framley tells Johnny that none of the family killed Mike because people out here have too much respect for their kin. At the front door, Edgar complains to Sgt. Framley about bringing Meg back. Sgt. Framley tells them who Johnny is and Margie recognizes Johnny, and is sure that everything will be all right, won't it, Johnny? Inside, Margie gives Johnny a seat and Danny comes in and complains about Meg being there and the argument starts among them. They all agree that they wanted Mike gone, and that it was Danny who talked Mike into the insurance. Johnny tells them that Meg was probably the only one who showed Mike any kindness in years and Edgar concedes that Meg probably deserves the money as much as anybody. Somebody killed their uncle, and they have all tried to make it look like Meg did it. Johnny is going to play a hunch that maybe he was not murdered after all.

Johnny tells Sgt. Framley that maybe Mike committed suicide. They all start quibbling about Meg paying attention to Mike. Edgar tells Johnny that Mike's father committed suicide by drinking an old Indian poison. Meg mumbles something about a cup and takes them to the dining room where she shows them a cup in the china closet, the one old Mike used to kill himself. Meg tells Johnny that Mike would have his whiskey every night from a different cup, but he would never touch that one, he called it the death cup and joked about it. The night before he died he talked about the cup again and said it was making a superstitious old fool out of him. Edgar gets the cup and gives it to Johnny. Meg tells them that Mike said that his father drank from it and died, so he was going to drink from it and live to show everyone he was not superstitious. Johnny finds a deposit of deep purple quintanigen sulfanate in the bottom of the cup after forty years. Meg tells Johnny that she had tried to wash it, but that did nothing. Johnny tells them that the alcohol in the whiskey would have released enough to kill Mike.

The police took a long time over this one, but they finally reached the same conclusion I had, accidental death. So the relatives will collect the insurance, and Meg, bless her heart. But I am afraid that mere money will never take the place of her friend, Alkali Mike.

NOTES:
- THIS IS PROBABLY ANOTHER AFRS PROGRAM AS THERE ARE NO CREDITS AT ALL
- WINNEMUCCA IS NORTH EAST OF RENO, AND LOVELOCK IS HALFWAY BETWEEN RENO AND WINNEMUCCA.
- CAST INFORMATION FROM THE KNX COLLECTION AT THE THOUSAND OAKS LIBRARY.
- THE ANNOUNCER IS DAN CUBBERLY

Producer: Jack Johnstone     Writers: Jack Johnstone
Cast: Harry Bartell, Virginia Gregg, Dick Kieth, Peter Leeds, Jean Tatum, Frank Gerstle

◆ ❖ ◆

SHOW: THE SHY BENEFICIARY MATTER
SHOW DATE: 11/17/1957
COMPANY: UNIVERSAL ADJUSTMENT BUREAU
AGENT: PAT MCCRACKEN
EXP. ACCT: $410.00
SYNOPSIS: Pat McCracken calls Johnny with a problem. "Did you ever have trouble getting rid of money? I have $25,000 and have been trying to get rid if it for two weeks and can't." Johnny tells Pat, "Boy, you do have a problem, I'll be right over."

Johnny cabs to Pat's office and learns that Helen Gazeworth died, and Pat cannot find the beneficiary, Elijah Summers. Pat has advertised in the New York papers and has found nothing. Also, Helen has no relatives. The landlady told the Universal Adjustment Bureau that Miss Gazeworth was an eccentric lived all alone and felt the world was against her, except for Summers, who was nice to her sometime in the past. "Pat, you don't have much to go on." Johnny tells Pat. "Correction Johnny, YOU don't have anything to go on."

Johnny travels to New York City and visits the landlady where Miss Gazeworth lived, and then a previous landlady only to learn that Helen moved from place to place. Johnny finds a first landlady who thought that Gazeworth came from San Francisco. Johnny flies to San Francisco, California and places ads in the local papers. On the first day, Johnny gets results, with blond hair and blue eyes. The woman is Janet Blake, and Johnny tells her that he has not heard from Elijah. She is a friend of Elijah's and tells Johnny about a small town called South Fork on the Yuba River in the Sierra's. He might be up there, just call it a hunch.

Johnny rents a car and drives to South Fork, California, a barely populated town. Johnny finds the local law, a deputy named Rawlins. Rawlins tells Johnny "good luck" on finding Elijah, but if you find him let me know, he is wanted for murder. Johnny tells Rawlins that Elijah is the beneficiary of an insurance policy. Rawlins tells Johnny that the killing took place last year at Jess Tyler's place. Elijah worked at the Tyler place as a hired hand. He and Jess got into an argument and Elijah shot him and took off into the hills. The widow took it hard for a year and Ben Watts pulled her out of it and married her last month. She and Ben are living on the ranch. Johnny asks where Elijah might have gone and Rawlins tells Johnny that he might have gone to Tough Luck Canyon where some hermits are panning gold. Rawlins has been up there, but a man has to be careful, as Elijah is a dead shot with a 30/30, and there are a lot of places to hide up there. Rawlins has not given up on Elijah. The longer he stays up there, the more curious he will get. One of these days Rawlins will get him.

Johnny drives to the Tyler ranch and they are expecting Johnny. Mrs. Watts has gotten over the killing, and feels sorry for Elijah, as Jess had kept him on when it did not pay to. No one knows what the argument was about. Johnny asks Ben how to get to the canyon, and Ben tells him it is dangerous. Johnny gets directions and Johnny is warned that Elijah is a good shot. Ben was winged by Elijah on the night Jess was killed.

Johnny gets some camping equipment and follows the road to the timberline and starts hiking. When Johnny starts into the canyon he stops when he hears someone following him. Johnny lunges at the stalker who turns out to be Janet Blake. She tells Johnny that her name is Janet Tyler, and Jess Tyler was her father. She wants to find Elijah and bring him back. She thinks that she can find Elijah, as he had a favorite spot up there and had brought her to it once. Shots ring out, and Johnny thinks that they have found Elijah the hard way.

Janet tells Johnny that Elijah is shooting at them with a .22. She found a .22 cartridge that came from Elijah's gun on the night her father was killed. Janet calls out to Elijah and he recognizes her voice and Janet tells him that she and Johnny, who is a friend, want to talk to him. Johnny is told to throw his gun out and come into the open. Johnny tosses out his gun, and Elijah comes out and he looks terrible. He had seen the deputy snooping around and could have gotten him. He remembers when Janet gave the .22 to him for ground squirrels. He has never used any other rifle. Johnny remembers that Jess was killed with a 30/30, and Janet tells Johnny that she saw someone pull the .22 slug from Ben's shoulder on the night her father was killed. She heard Ben tell everyone he had been hit with a 30/30. She is sure that Ben Watts killed her father and that Elijah was trying to protect Jess. Elijah remembers that there was a big fight and he ran away. Ben has been poking around too with his 30/30. A shot rings out and Elijah is hit. Johnny scoops up his automatic and circles around behind the shooter. Johnny slips but is able to draw the fire of the shooter and hits him; it is Ben Watts.

Remarks: Well I turned Ben Watts over to the local law, and I helped old Elijah fill out his claim for $25,000 insurance money Miss Gazeworth gave him. It ought to keep him real comfortable for the rest of his life. You know Pat, once in a while I get the feeling this job of mine is worthwhile after all.

NOTES:
* ANOTHER AFRS PROGRAM WITH NO CREDITS.
* JOHNNY NOTES IN THIS EPISODE THAT HE IS CARRYING AN AUTOMATIC.
* CAST INFORMATION FROM THE KNX COLLECTION AT THE THOUSAND OAKS LIBRARY.
* THE ANNOUNCER IS DAN CUBBERLY

Producer:     Jack Johnstone          Writers:    Robert Ryf
Cast:         Larry Dobkin, Virginia Gregg, Jack Kruschen, Jeanette Nolan, Russell Thorson, Howard McNear

◆   ❖   ◆

SHOW:          THE HOPE TO DIE MATTER
SHOW DATE:     11/24/1957
COMPANY:       FLOYDS OF ENGLAND
AGENT:         GEORGE REED
EXP. ACCT:     $0.00

SYNOPSIS: A very hesitant George Reed calls Johnny and Johnny is glad, because he has no assignment, and therefore no expense account to pad. "Remember you had asked me once if we had issued a policy against living?" George asks Johnny. "Oh, Don't tell me." "I am afraid so. The company is saddled with a death insurance policy." Floyds has insured someone against living.

Johnny cabs to George's office where George is pacing the floor. George tells Johnny that Harry Baxter issued the policy while George was on vacation. Usually they pay the face value when the insured dies, but on this policy they will have to pay $250,000 if the insured does not die. Floyds is proud that they will insure anything. George does not know what the policy is about and Floyds has paid Johnny some nice fees in the past. Johnny wants to turn the case down, but

George tells Johnny that he will ok the expense report without even reading it. Johnny tells George "there are some things a conniving, chiseling unprincipled rascal like myself . . . won't . . . even . . ." "Unlimited expense account, Johnny" adds George. "Ok, George, I'll take it."

Johnny is taking this case because of his friendship with George Reed, and the promise of an unlimited expense account. The insured is Mary Ellen Markham, who lives in New York. Albert Schwinner has taken out the policy, and is the beneficiary, but George does not know who he is, except that he is a doctor. You have to find out who he is, what he is and why he has bought insurance against this woman living beyond November 10th, which is only a few days from now. George wants Johnny to find some legal reason to cancel the policy. The paperwork lists Dr. Schwinner, CL in Union City New Jersey, and Johnny wonders what "CL" is? Johnny gets an address for Harry Baxter in New York City.

Johnny travels to New York City and Harry Baxter's address, which is luxury from stem-to-stern. Harry has heard of Johnny from George, and he tells Johnny that he has so many social events to keep up with. George gave him no chance to explain why he sold the policy, and George will have to calm down before Harry will tell him. Harry will tell George, but not Johnny, as to why he issued the policy. Johnny puts his foot in the door and asks Harry how Dr. Schwinner fits into this, and Harry tells Johnny that he is a close personal friend, and slams the door. Johnny calls George Reed, but he is out. Johnny tells the receptionist to tell George he wants a complete rundown on Harry Baxter. The receptionist tells Johnny she can tell him all there is to know, but Johnny wants George to do it.

Johnny cabs to Miss Markham's apartment where Johnny meets a pale, wan, tired woman who looked to be 65 or 70, in a room full of flowers. Johnny tells Miss Markham that someone has taken a policy out on her, and she tells Johnny that it was nice of Harry Baxter to do so. She is suffering from a rare incurable disease of the blood, and will not live long. Johnny asks about Dr. Schwinner, and is told that he is a great friend. Johnny asks her why he would take out a policy hoping she would not die. She tells Johnny that November 10th would be her fiftieth birthday, and Dr. Schwinner is her physician.

Johnny leaves and calls George who has just tried to call Harry Baxter to apologize for getting upset. George tells Johnny that Baxter is the majority stockholder and Chairman of the Board of the company. Johnny tells George that Harry has left for Europe. If Mary Ellen Markham dies before November 10th, Floyds pays out $250,000 to Dr. Schwinner who is the physician of Miss Markham. Johnny thinks that there is something wrong with this deal. Johnny cabs to Dr. Schwinner's office and learns that CL is for the Albert Schwinner Clinic for the Study of Rare Diseases of the Blood. The doctor is at Miss Markham's, so Johnny cabs back to her apartment, and meets the doctor. He tells Johnny that Miss Markham is better. Johnny tells Dr. Schwinner that if she lives, he loses out on $250,000. But he corrects Johnny and tells him the clinic will lose the money. Dr. Schwinner tells Johnny that when Miss Markham first became ill, she had only 5 years to live. But because of the work of the clinic, she has lived much longer. She has told them that if she lives to be 50, that would prove that the methods of the clinic are right, and they could prolong and possibly save lives. If she lives to 50, she will give the clinic $250,000, money which is much needed. She is the one who suggested the policy. Dr. Schwinner tells Johnny that Harry Baxter's own mother died of the same disease, so, he knew how necessary the money is, and that is why he chose the policy as a means to guarantee the money. Dr. Schwinner tells Johnny that it is probably his duty to try and cancel the policy. Johnny tells him that his duty is to do just exactly nothing.

Mary Ellen Markham did live to see, 50, but only by a few days. Just long enough to make the gift to the clinic. Harry Baxter and the company? Well, Harry came back from Europe and he said he found some "mistake" in the policy that required the company to payoff anyway. Eccentric? We should have more like that. Expense account total, are you kidding?

**NOTES:**

- JOHNNY MENTIONS SINGING MICE (THE MISSING MOUSE MATTER), AND OLD ALLEY CAT (THE FELICITY FELINE MATTER), AND A SICK WHALE (THE MICHAEL MEANY MIRAGE MATTER) AS WHACKO THINGS FLOYDS HAS INSURED.
- CAST INFORMATION FROM THE KNX COLLECTION AT THE THOUSAND OAKS LIBRARY.
- THE ANNOUNCER IS DAN CUBBERLY

Producer:   Jack Johnstone         Writers:   Jack Johnstone
Cast:       G. Stanley Jones, Ben Wright, Virginia Gregg, Shirley Mitchell, Marvin Miller

◆   ❖   ◆

SHOW:        THE SUNNY DREAM MATTER
SHOW DATE:   12/1/1957
COMPANY:     UNIVERSAL ADJUSTMENT BUREAU
AGENT:       PAT MCCRACKEN
EXP. ACCT:   $12.00

**SYNOPSIS:** Frank Skinner, who operates the Sunny Dream home in Buckland Center, calls Johnny. Something is wrong and they have never had anything like this before. Most of their residents are well insured, but they have been having a lot of deaths lately, too many. These have been accidental deaths and Mr. Skinner tells Johnny that he does not think that they were accidents. If something is not done to stop this . . . well, I think you better come up here.

Johnny calls Pat McCracken and tells him he will not be available for a few days, he is working on something that interests him. Pat tells Johnny that he has an assignment in Buckland Center. The Sunny Dream home for the aged? How did you know? Pat tells Johnny that the number of deaths over there have made the actuarial tables look like a big mistake. Pat had promised the insurance companies that he would send Johnny to look into things. Also, the beneficiary of all the policies has been the Sunny Dream home for the aged.

Johnny gases up his jalopy at the sign of the flying red horse, and drives to the Sunny Dream home. Frank Skinner comes over and greets Johnny in a wheelchair. Frank asks Johnny to act like he is looking over the place, like he is going to send an old relative there. There have been five deaths in the past six months and they all look like accidents. Miss Epp died in a small fire in her cottage; Mr. Pearly had food poisoning the doctor called it; Miss Sharmley fell down the main stairs to the living room; Miss Lizzy Belle fell out the window of her bedroom; and Miss Betsler fell down the stairs too. Frank tells Johnny that most can handle the stairs, and the others had their rooms on the first floor and Miss Lizzy Bell never left her room. Johnny tells him that so far there is no reason to suspect anything. All of the accidents happened late at night, when the guests would have no reason to be up and about, when there was no one to help them. Each had their own bathrooms and if they wanted anything, all they had to do was ring the buzzer. Mrs. Skinner comes in and tells Frank he is blabbing his mouth off. She tells Johnny to get out or she will throw him out, and she is strong enough to do it. Johnny asks if she is strong enough to push someone down the stairs or out of a window, and she tells him to get out.

Martha Skinner, the real manager, was a big strong woman, much younger than Mr. Skinner. She tells Johnny that she does not want anyone snooping around. She tells Johnny that she has nothing to hide, and his snooping will ruin their reputation, and that all the deaths were accidental. Johnny tells her that Frank thought they were accidents until a minute ago. She said a lot of things because the people who died were her friends. She mentions that the police had been there and found nothing. Martha mellows and asks Johnny if she could possibly do anything to these kind people. Johnny mentions the insurance and Martha tells Johnny that making them the beneficiary was their guest's idea. Johnny starts to leave for town and is told he will stay there for dinner, and can have a room. Walter comes in and complains about having another room to take care of. Johnny is introduced, and Walter recognizes the name from the radio programs he listens to all the time. "So what is your business here?" he asks. Martha tells Walter that Frank called Johnny, and Walter tells Johnny that his mother has enough trouble without him being here. He is sick of this nonsense, and taking care of these old fogies. He takes care of the place while Franks handles all the money. He mentions how Frank keeps talking about getting enough money to move away from here. Johnny tells Walter he is pretty husky, and Walter asks Johnny is he would like a demonstration of how strong he is. Johnny tells them he will stay until he is satisfied. Walter tells Johnny that he will not be there for long, if he can help it and Martha apologizes for Walter. Martha is the owner, and if anything happened the place would go to Walter and Frank. "You can't think that Walter would do anything to get the money, would you?" asks Martha.

At dinner Johnny talks to as many guests as possible, and they feel sorry for Walter, who stays to help his mother who is really devoted to them. Mr. Skinner was the one who convinced them to make out their insurance to the home. Frank wheels up and asks Johnny if his room, at the top of the stairs is ok. Johnny tells him that he found something; marks from some kind of struggle, and a piece of cloth. He is going to leave them there for the police, as they might be clues to the killer.

Johnny waits in his room to see if his hunch will pay off. He remembers Pat telling him that he had notified Frank Skinner that he was coming, so maybe that is why Skinner called him, to allay any concern Johnny might have had. Johnny hears a noise at midnight and opens his door to see Frank standing there on his own two feet. Johnny surprises him, and tells him that there is nothing there. He had a nasty racket, convincing people to sign over their insurance and then pushing them down the stairs. Franks jumps at Johnny and is thrown down the stairs.

Yeah, he'll will live to go to trial, and whatever sentence they hand him will be much too short. The Sunny Dream home, well I hope it will be the quiet peaceful place his wife wants it to be.

NOTES:

- THIS IS THE FIRST INSTANCE OF JOHNNY MENTIONING A PERSONAL AUTOMOBILE, OR USING IT ON A CASE.
- THIS PROGRAM CONTAINS ANOTHER REFERENCE TO JOHNNY'S RADIO PROGRAMS.
- CAST INFORMATION FROM THE KNX COLLECTION AT THE THOUSAND OAKS LIBRARY.
- THE ANNOUNCER IS DAN CUBBERLY

Producer: Jack Johnstone        Writers: Jack Johnstone
Cast: Junius Matthews, Larry Dobkin, Virginia Gregg, Bert Holland, Peggy Webber

◆  ❖  ◆

SHOW: THE HAPLESS HUNTER MATTER
SHOW DATE: 12/8/1957
COMPANY: TRI-MUTUAL INSURANCE COMPANY LTD.
AGENT: JERRY HOLLAND
EXP. ACCT: $13.13

SYNOPSIS: Jerry Holland calls Johnny and asks if Curtis Randall means anything. He is a big banker in Hartford, isn't he? Well, Randall and Byron Peters went deer hunting over near Kingman, New York and hired a local guide who was an alcoholic. They raised cane with Curly because they had not found any deer, and got into a big argument. Curly got drunk and shot Randall and himself. Jerry asks Johnny to investigate; it is typical on policies over $500,000. The beneficiary is Byron Peters. Johnny tells Jerry that this case looks too easy.

Johnny cabs to Jerry's office where Jerry meets him at the door. Jerry tells Johnny that Byron Peters is in the hospital; he was shot by Curly too. Jerry rebukes Johnny for going off half-cocked on this case. The local police told Jerry that Peters supplied the all the arrangements for the trip and arranged the guide. Jerry wonders if Curly had it in for Randall. Johnny gets the address for Peters and learns that Randall only had an occasional drink before dinner, but does not know about Peters. Johnny suspects Byron Peters based on a hunch.

Johnny drives to Kingman, New York and goes to the hospital where Peters is sedated after the police had questioned him. Johnny asks the chief resident doctor if the police suspect that Peters killed Randall and Curly and wounded himself, and the doctor there calls it ridiculous. The doctor tells Johnny that the extent of Peter's wounds make that impossible, as he narrowly escaped death.

Johnny looks at Peter's wounds and x-rays, and then talks with police Captain McManus. The police had talked to Peters, and Capt. McManus tells Johnny that Peters had lunged at Curly and was hit in the head. Peters called Capt. McManus from the cabin when he came to by dragging the phone to the floor. Randall was near the front door, and Curly was between Randall and Peters. Capt. McManus tells Johnny that Curly was the town drunk who worked odd jobs and used the money to buy cheap booze, but he never drank during hunting season. He was a good guide made a lot of money, and that is why Capt. McManus cannot explain him getting drunk during hunting season. Johnny and Capt. McManus go to the coroner's office and Johnny finds something suspicious. Peters had a powder burn on his forehead, and Randall had none. But Curly showed no powder burns, even though he was supposed to have shot himself upwards through the jaw with his 30/30. Johnny asks, for the sake of argument, what if Randall shot first? Or suppose Peters started the whole thing? Johnny gets directions to the cabin and drives there.

The cabin is a shack surrounded by cheap liquor bottles, but is comfortable inside. In the kitchen is a case of Prince Francis Scotch, nearly full. On the floor Johnny notices the angle of entry of the slug that hit Peters, and a heavy cord hanging from the rafter. Suppose that someone had hung a rifle up there and carefully fired it at himself? Capt. McManus and the doctor call and tell Johnny he might be right. The doctor tells Johnny that Peters has left the hospital. Peters had asked the doctor who was in to see him, and a few minutes later the doctor heard his car leaving. Capt. McManus tells Johnny to leave the cabin just as Johnny hears the door opening and Peters walks in.

Peters was not as badly injured as Johnny thought. Johnny tells Peters how he rigged the incident, but Peters sticks to his story about Curly being drunk. Johnny tells him that he made a mistake by bring up expensive scotch to the cabin, because Curly only drank cheap liquor. Johnny tells Peters that he did not plan on the accident, and came back because he remembers leaving the cord in the ceiling. Johnny tells him that the angle of the bullet was all-wrong for what supposedly happened. Johnny tells Peters that there were no power burns on Curly when there should have been, because Peters had killed both Randall and Curly. Peters pulls a .38 and Johnny tells him he will not get away with it. Peters tells Johnny that he had forced Randall to make him the beneficiary because he knew of some shady business deals and had been blackmailing Randall. Johnny tells Peters that he hopes Capt. McManus will slug him before he shoots, and Peters calls it a ruse—until Capt. McManus calls out and shots are fired. McManus yells at Johnny for not leaving.

Remarks: Why? Why don't they ever learn?

NOTES:

* CAST INFORMATION FROM THE KNX COLLECTION AT THE THOUSAND OAKS LIBRARY.
* THE ANNOUNCER IS DAN CUBBERLY

| | | | |
|---|---|---|---|
| **Producer:** | Jack Johnstone | **Writers:** | Jack Johnstone |
| **Cast:** | John Stephenson, Parley Baer, Forrest Lewis, Carleton G. Young | | |

◆  ❖  ◆

| | |
|---|---|
| **SHOW:** | THE HAPPY FAMILY MATTER |
| **SHOW DATE:** | 12/15/1957 |
| **COMPANY:** | ESTATE OF E. P. WATKINS |
| **AGENT:** | |
| **EXP. ACCT:** | $73.00 |

SYNOPSIS: Johnny is called and told to come over here right away. "Who is this, and where is here?" asks Johnny. The man is Ellis Watkins the industrialist, and here is Broad Acres in Fairfield, Connecticut. Watkins has $100,000 to give away and Johnny is going to tell him who to give it to.

Johnny cabs to the Universal Adjustment Bureau and talks to Pat McCracken, who had talked to Watkins. Johnny is told that Watkins has a $100,000 policy, and the beneficiary was his wife, but she died several months ago. Watkins wants a new beneficiary, and he wants Johnny to do it. Johnny tells Pat he wants no part of this case, but Pat tells Johnny that Watkins does not have much time to live, so Johnny relents.

Johnny drives to Broad Acres and is shown into the library, where Mr. Watkins is sitting by the fire. Watkins tells Johnny that he has from one week to one year to live. Johnny tells him he is sorry, but Watkins tells him that he is not; his wife is gone, his business is failing and his children are strangers, so there is no reason to be sorry. He has three possible beneficiaries: Sheila, a 28 year old daughter; Michael, a 26 year old son; and Elizabeth, a 24 year old daughter; and he does not want to divide up the policy among them. Watkins also tells Johnny that the policy is the only estate. He wants the money kept in the family and only to one member of the family. He intends to leave the other two out in the cold. Watkins tells Johnny that Sheila seems to thinks that she should be managing her father's affairs. Michael prefers the life of an artist. Elizabeth is stubborn and is married to James Lovett, who thinks he knows more about business than Watkins does. Johnny tells Watkins that the others are not going to like the decision Johnny makes, so Watkins is going to pay Johnny a considerable fee, but he will earn it, every penny of it.

This is a weird assignment, but Johnny feels sorry for Ellis Watkins, as he is really alone. On the way out Johnny meets Sheila, who tells Johnny that her father was not always like he is now. He feels that his children have let him down. He resents Sheila as the oldest, because she is not a man. She is more like father and could have taken over for him, but he resents her helping him. Elizabeth is in Cranford, New Jersey, and Michael lives in New York. Johnny senses that Sheila is under a great deal of stress.

Johnny goes to see Michael in Greenwich Village. Michael tells Johnny that he does not want the money. He is doing what he wants to do—paint. Sheila is trying to hold the family together, but it will not work. Father had been trying to shove the business down Michael's throat, but he wants no part of it, but that did not matter to him. Michael tells Johnny that Sheila deserves to have the money. Johnny goes to the Lovett home and talks to Elizabeth. She thinks that this is some kind of scheme. Her husband tells Johnny to give the money to Elizabeth so he can buy a controlling interest in the company and rescue it. James tells Johnny that he once worked for the company but Watkins is running the company the way he did 30 years ago, and that will not work today, so he left. James tells Johnny that Watkins tried to get Michael into the company, but all he wants to do is paint his lousy pictures. James had sent Watkins a written contract guaranteeing the financing necessary to fix the company, and asked for six months but Watkins would not even listen to him. He tore up the contract and told Jim to leave.

Johnny looks for an art dealer and learns that Mike really is a lousy painter. Johnny gets a message to visit the Watkins attorney in his hotel. Halfway into the room Johnny feels a gun in his back. A voice tells Johnny to drop the case, or he will get dropped.

Johnny asks the voice who hired him. When the man tries to slug him, Johnny anticipates what will happen and deflects the gun butt, but the man gets away. Johnny turns on the light and sees something that tells him that the truth was under his nose all the time.

Johnny calls the family members to a meeting and drives to Broad Acres. Ellis Watkins resents the theatrics, but Johnny tells him that it is necessary. Theirs is not a happy family because someone in the family does not want Johnny to finish his job. Johnny asks Mike why he quit and started painting, and Mike tells him that his father was trying to shove the business down his throat. He could not take it any longer and quit when Sheila said it was best. Sheila tells Johnny that Mike should have a live of his own. Watkins tells Sheila that she had said she begged Mike to stay. Sheila says that she was acting in the best interests of the family. Johnny asks Jim why he quit, and Jim tells him about the contract, but Watkins tells Jim that he never saw a contract. Jim had given it to Sheila, who said that her father had refused to look at it. Johnny notes Sheila's habit of shredding cellophane, and how he found some in the hotel room. Watkins asks her why, and she is not sure. Johnny tells Sheila that she was trying to punish her father, but she is not sure. She tells them that everyone had a life of their own but her, and she could not help it. Watkins is bewildered and asks if Sheila was trying to tear the family apart to punish him, and Johnny agrees. Johnny asks if she was ever allowed to have a life? Watkins tells Johnny to suspend further action, as the matter requires further thought.

Remarks: Sheila is now undergoing treatment, and outlook is favorable. Elizabeth's husband Jim is now managing the affairs of Watkins and Company, Mike is helping him, and I guess he is doing a good job. Mr. Watkins, well he is still alive and his doctor tells that now the old gentleman has found some reasons to be alive he'll probably be with us quite awhile, and make all three of his children his beneficiaries.

NOTES:
- CAST INFORMATION FROM THE KNX COLLECTION AT THE THOUSAND OAKS LIBRARY.
- THE ANNOUNCER IS DAN CUBBERLY

Producer: Jack Johnstone       Writers:   Robert Ryf
Cast:         John Dehner, Lawrence Dobkin, Peter Leeds, Virginia Gregg, Shirley Mitchell, Paul Dubov

◆   ❖   ◆

SHOW:          THE CARMEN KRINGLE MATTER
SHOW DATE:  12/22/1957
COMPANY:     UNIVERSAL ADJUSTMENT BUREAU
AGENT:         PAT MCCRACKEN
EXP. ACCT:     $0.00

SYNOPSIS: Pat McCracken calls Johnny and asks how the weather is in Palm Springs. Pat has a matter nearby and wants Johnny to work on it, as it will only take a day. Johnny tells Pat that he is spending this Christmas in Palm Springs, not freezing like he did last year. Johnny wants to decline the case, but Pat mentions the bonus list in the office, and Johnny's name might be on it. Pat tells Johnny about an old ghost town named Calico. An old prospector named Kringle is breathing his last and wants to change his beneficiary, but a nephew, Ned Kringle will sue if he does. Contact our agent in Barstow, Gene Craig. The new beneficiary is Carmen Kringle, a burro.

Johnny wires Gene Craig of his arrival plans, rents Al Sterner's plane, and flies to Calico, California located in the Mojave desert. The plane lands on a dry lakebed and Johnny waits for his contact. Johnny gets the old feeling he is not alone. Then Johnny sees a car approach and a herd of burros disperses. A man tells Johnny to walk towards him with his hands up. Johnny sees another car approaching as Johnny recognizes the marshal's badge. Jean Craig arrives and tells the marshal who Johnny is. Jean Craig tells Johnny and the marshal that Kris has had another setback, and that someone has let his burros loose. Jean and Johnny drive back to Calico, and Jean tells Johnny all about Kris who, every year, loads up his burro with gifts for the families of the miners in the area. This year will not be very joyful with Kris ill. Ned seems to be ok, but Willie D'Agostino seems to do all the talking for Ned. Jean asks if a burro can be a beneficiary, and Johnny tells him that Kris can leave his money to a boat if he wants to, but a trust will have to be set up. Johnny asks what will happen when Carmen dies, but Jean tells him that here will always be burros in Calico.

In Calico Johnny sees a page from the past. Walter Knott of Knott's Berry Farm had bought the town and restored it to its colorful past. Jean asks Johnny to spend the holiday with them, and is very disappointed when Johnny tells her that he has other plans. At Kris' place, Doc Spangler asks Jean to drive him back to town. He has not seen Kris because he will not argue with a gun. Johnny pounds on the door and a nasty Willie D'Agostino tells Johnny that there will be no changes to the policy at this late date and just family will be admitted in the hour of the old man's demise. Johnny puts his foot in the door and pushes the door open and shoves Willie aside and is hit on the head.

Johnny wakes up to Jean fussing over him. Jean asks Willie to go up to see Kris and Ned wants to go also, but Willie tells them to go away. Willie tells them that the old man always was borrowing money from Ned to give to other people, and who loaned Ned the money? Willie. Now, Willie is going to get his money back. Ned tells Johnny that he had loaned his uncle the money, as he was sure his uncle would hit a big strike some day. Willie tells them all to leave but the marshal comes in with his rifle and tells Willie to drop his gun. The marshal tells Willie to leave, as he is guilty of carrying a gun and threatening people. Willie leaves, but Ned says he will stay. Doc calls Johnny, Jean and Ned upstairs to hear Kris tell them something, but Johnny hears a shot outside and rushes out with Jean and the marshal to find Carmen dead, killed by Willie as he left town.

The marshal tells Johnny that he figured that Willie would do something like this as he takes the bells off of the dead burro and puts them on the real Carmen. The marshal stays to tend the $50,000 jackass while the others go inside.

Kris tells them that he is not going to scratch Ned's name off the policy, he just wanted to scare off D'Agostino. He was afraid that he would have to die to square off the gambling debts. Johnny is asked to take a heavy bag from a footlocker and Kris tells them that the bag is full of uranium. The last batch assayed at $900 a ton, and he has a whole mountain of it in his and Ned's name. Kris tells them that the bank will extend credit on the assay value, and asks Jean if she can spend the next two days buying presents for the folks in the area.

Johnny calls four major cities where Willie D'Agostino might be remembered and Johnny gets a long list of reasons why he is remembered. That was Johnny's present to them. Johnny rents a truck to haul the presents back to Calico so Ned could give them away.

And then there was Christmas Eve. We sat on the Kringle porch and watched the procession up to the magi mine, the flickering lights from the miner's lamps reflecting on the faces of the happy children. Old Kris was bundled up in blankets, his little eyes twinkling and chuckling to himself like he knew all of the answers to the universe . Jean was there too. Marshal Ed Noler was one of the wise men in the procession; I could recognize the sideburns. And Doc Spangler couldn't hide his height, and he wore an awful beard. Ned Kringle led the burro that carried the blessed mother. Yeah, you guessed it. The burro was Carmen Kringle.

Johnny tells Pat that the $275 in expenses are on him.

NOTES:

- BOB BAILEY WISHES EVERYONE "FROM ALL OF US TO ALL OF YOU, MAY THIS BE YOUR VERY MERRIEST CHRISTMAS EVER."
- THIS CHRISTMAS PROGRAM WAS WRITTEN BY BOB BAILEY, UNDER THE PSEUDONYM OF ROBERT BAINTER, BAINTER BEING HIS MIDDLE NAME.
- CALICO, CALIFORNIA IS NORTH EAST OF BARSTOW, ABOUT HALF WAY BETWEEN LOS ANGELES AND LAS VEGAS.
- WALTER KNOTT WAS THE FOUNDER OF KNOTT'S BERRY FARM, AND HELPED DEVELOP THE BOYSENBERRY. IN 1952 HE PURCHASED CALICO, CALIFORNIA, WHICH HAD ONCE BEEN A PROSPEROUS SILVER MINING TOWN IN THE 1880s.
- THE ANNOUNCER IS DAN CUBBERLY
- CAST INFORMATION FROM THE KNX COLLECTION AT THE THOUSAND OAKS LIBRARY

| | | | |
|---|---|---|---|
| Producer: | Jack Johnstone | Writers: | Robert Bainter |
| Cast: | Herb Vigran, Howard McNear, Jean Tatum, Junius Matthews, Lawrence Dobkin, Forrest Lewis. Jack Kruschen, Dick Crenna, Bill James | | |

| | |
|---|---|
| SHOW: | THE LATIN LOVELY MATTER |
| SHOW DATE: | 12/29/1957 |
| COMPANY: | UNIVERSAL ADJUSTMENT BUREAU |
| AGENT: | PAT MCCRACKEN |
| EXP. ACCT: | $0.00 |

SYNOPSIS: "I love you" Johnny is told on the phone. A nervous Johnny wants to get to get together, to which she agrees. The woman identifies herself as Carmela Jocales. Johnny tells her that he usually gets calls on Sunday night for an insurance problem. Carmela tells Johnny that she has an insurance problem and it will not be dull. Tell your friend Pat McCracken that I called.

Johnny tries to call Pat McCracken on Monday and finally cabs to his office. Johnny mentions Carmela Jocales and Pat snickers. Johnny asks if she is like she sounds on the phone and Pat suggests that maybe special investigator Martha Mayberry Balderdale should handle her case. Pat tells Johnny that Carmela is a dancer, but not a very good one, and Pat will put Balderdale on the case to have someone objective on the case. Surety Mutual has issued a $50,000 retirement policy on Carmela. If she dies, her beneficiary gets the money. She dances in nightclubs and usually has a new partner every month. Her partner is the beneficiary of the policy. The cost of servicing the policy is getting ridiculous. The company has tried to stall making changes but she just yells at them. Surety has turned the case over to Pat and Carmela has specifically asked for Johnny. Pat tells Johnny that Carmela heard about Johnny on the radio, and you are her dreamboat. Get her married or settle her down. Married? Yes that's it Johnny, marry her. Johnny tells Pat that there is no way, but Pat laughs and tells Johnny that the Universal Adjustment Bureau will not defend him in case of a breach of promise case.

Johnny flies to New York City and Carmela's apartment where the doorman asks for his credentials. In the lobby the doorman calls Carmela but she does not answer the phone. Johnny and the doorman walk up and he tells Johnny that Carmela had been fearful of something lately. Johnny pounds on the door and then gets the passkey, enters the apartment and finds Carmel lying on the floor, barely alive.

The doorman discovers the service entrance open and Johnny sends him for a doctor as he gives her a drink to wake her up. Johnny puts her on the sofa and she tells Johnny that a man hit her. She found him in the apartment looking for something and he hit her. He was short and dark. She tells Johnny that a man from Mexico has been threatening her, telling her "she has done it one time to many." "Oh, hold me tight, Johnny" she tells him. She tells Johnny that she only wants one little change to the policy. The doorman comes back and she tells Billy the doorman to cancel the doctor. Johnny is suspicious, as there are no marks on Carmela. Johnny leaves and goes to see Randy Singer to get a run down on Carmela. Johnny cuts down an alley and gets a gun in his back. The man takes him into a doorway and tells him that he is Frederico. He was listening at the back stairway, and Johnny will not help Carmela, as he will kill Johnny first.

Frederico will kill Johnny before he lets Johnny help Carmela and ruin his son. He will not let Johnny change the beneficiary. Johnny distracts him and takes the gun from him. The man tells Johnny that he is Frederico Gomez, and is the father of Armando Gomez, the next fly in the web of the spider. Armando is a dancer and Carmela is going to make him her next victim. Armando is a fine dancer, and she will charm him and bring him to the city to dance with her. She will bring boys to the city to dance with her, they will fall in love with her and she will name them as the beneficiary to dazzle them. She has blinded so many young boys and taken their money. She laughs and spits at them when they want her to marry them. Frederico tells Johnny that Pedro Fernandez, and the son of a friend committed suicide when she rejected him. The boys are unwise to the ways of the world and Carmela, and he will do anything to protect his son. Johnny tells him to go back to his hotel and stay there until he hears from Johnny.

Johnny goes back to Carmela and she admits that she had used the insurance money to lure the dancers to further her career, and was proud of the broken hearts and minds she left behind. Johnny tears into her and tells her about the death of the two boys. Johnny tells her that the police will be after her no matter where she goes. Johnny tells her that the insurance will be canceled unless she changes the beneficiary to someone she cannot hurt. Carmela promises to make up for the things she has done.

As Johnny finishes his report the phone rings and Pat McCracken tells Johnny to forget the expense account. Pat has just gotten a copy of the new and last rider, which cannot ever be changed ever again. And you, you sly dog, you are the beneficiary!

Yours Truly, Juanito Peso.

NOTES:
- THIS PROGRAM CONTAINS ANOTHER REFERENCE TO JOHNNY'S RADIO PROGRAMS.
- THIS AN AFRS PROGRAM WITH NO COMMERCIAL BREAKS
- CAST INFORMATION FROM THE KNX COLLECTION AT THE THOUSAND OAKS LIBRARY.
- THE ANNOUNCER IS DAN CUBBERLY

| | | | |
|---|---|---|---|
| **Producer:** | Jack Johnstone | **Writers:** | Jack Johnstone |
| **Cast:** | Lucille Meredith, Lawrence Dobkin, Jimmy McCallion, Harry Bartell | | |

◆　❖　◆

| | |
|---|---|
| SHOW: | THE INGENUOUS JEWELER MATTER |
| SHOW DATE: | 1/5/1958 |
| COMPANY: | PHILADELPHIA MUTUAL LIABILITY & CASUALTY INSURANCE |
| COMPANY | AGENT: HARRY BRANSON |
| EXP. ACCT: | $181.00 |

SYNOPSIS: Harry Branson calls Johnny and tells him that this thing has him really upset. Harry wants Johnny to come to Philadelphia. If Johnny can clear up this matter, I mean $985,000, well any criminal could have done it. But the murder, it just does not make sense. What do you think, Johnny? Johnny suggests the butler, and Harry is confused.

Johnny travels to Philadelphia, Pennsylvania and goes to Harry's office. Harry tells Johnny that the Beaufort Collection, which is insured for almost a million dollars, has been stolen from J. Harold Whipset. Johnny remembers that Whipset was tagged by customs for trying to smuggle jewels into the country several years ago. Harry had some misgivings, but Whipset is in the clear now. Miss Winkle is Whipset's secretary, Miss Perri Winkle; she was almost killed in their office last night on Walnut Street. The collection has several emerald and diamond brooches made up of small stones that could easily be remounted. Johnny and Harry start to go to the office and Harry tells Johnny that Miss Winkle was shot and Whipset was not. Johnny gets the whole story on the jewels on the cab ride, but Johnny wants more information on Whipset. Lt. Bart Stanley is in Whipset's office and he tells Johnny that they know nothing. Lt. Stanley knows about the reputation of Whipset. Johnny is told that Whipset and Miss Winkle were there late last night working on the books. A man knocked on the door and Whipset let him in, and the man demanded the Beaufort Collection. Whipset gave him the jewels, but Miss Winkle tried to run and was shot. The man tied Winkle up, tore out the phone line and locked him in his office. Johnny asks how, as the door locks from the inside? Lt. Stanley shows Johnny a rubber doorstop, which is proof that Whipset could not have rigged the deal.

Lt. Stanley shows Johnny how all the doors open out into the corridor. The man slammed the door on Whipset and used the wedge to hold the door closed. The harder Whipset pushed, the more the door was locked. A policeman heard the shots and they got there quickly. Whipset was more upset about Winkle than the jewels. They thought that she was dead at first, but she is unconscious and will probably not make it. Mr. Whipset comes in with Officer Conroy, and he is upset about Miss Winkle. Whipset tells Johnny that Miss Winkle was his secretary, and he is in love with her. Johnny tells Whipset that Miss Winkle has not regained consciousness, but she will recover, and Whipset acts glad. Johnny told the lie to gets Whipset's reaction. Whipset leaves to go home and Lt. Stanley asks Johnny about his recovery story. Johnny tells them he is going to the hospital in case she recovers. Harry talks Johnny out of going so Johnny calls the hospital and the doctor tells him that Miss Winkle has just died.

Johnny tells Bart and Harry that the girl is dead, and Johnny asks for a key to the office. Johnny tells Lt. Stanley to go to the hospital in case Whipset goes there. Johnny goes to the office and looks at the doorstop. Johnny notices a burr where a tiny hole has been pierced into the rubber. Johnny finds a piece of platinum wire in a desk. Whipset returns and tells Johnny that he did not like his attitude. He sees Johnny has found the wire that Whipset had used to pull the wedge against the door. Johnny asks if the gloves he is wearing and the gun he has are the ones he used to shoot Miss Winkle and leave no prints. Whipset tells Johnny that Miss Winkle was against him taking the stones and remounting the jewels at home and claiming the insurance. Whipset tells Johnny that that he will kill him with the gun and lock him in the office, a kind of a trademark of the killer. As Whipset tells Johnny to turn around Lt. Stanley comes in and tells him that he has a better idea. Lt. Stanley knew Johnny had an idea, so he decided to come back up. Johnny does not tell Lt. Stanley how it was done. He will let Whipset do it. He loves to talk.

Harry, I think I will have to figure out some way to pad my expense account even more than usual in cases like this. I mean where a .38 slug nearly ends up in me. After all, fun is fun, a job is a job, but some of these laddies carry thing too far. Come to think of it, I'll have to run down to New York again to appear against Whipset, so expense account total, including that and transportation back to Hartford, and all the incidentals I could possibly think of, $181, even.

NOTES:

- THIS AN **AFRS** PROGRAM WITH NO COMMERCIAL BREAKS
- CAST INFORMATION FROM THE **KNX** COLLECTION AT THE THOUSAND OAKS LIBRARY.
- THE ANNOUNCER IS DAN CUBBERLY

Producer:    Jack Johnstone          Writers:    Jack Johnstone
Cast:        Harry Bartell, Byron Kane, Vic Perrin, Joseph Kearns, Austin Green

◆    ❖    ◆

SHOW:          THE BORON 112 MATTER
SHOW DATE:     1/12/1958
COMPANY:       FLOYDS OF ENGLAND
AGENT:         GEORGE REED
EXP. ACCT:     $2,431.00

SYNOPSIS: George Reed calls and Johnny shudders because of the wild crazy and impossible policies George issues. George tells Johnny that he has a normal policy he is worried about now. The insured is Josef Hantler, and inventor, and the invention is what is insured. The invention is for making some sort of boron-based compounds, the sort of things the government is interested in. "Can you come over?" "Yeah, I think I better. I'm on my way."

Johnny cabs to George Reed's Hartford, Connecticut office and George calls Louise on the intercom. Johnny is told that the policy on Hantler's device is for $20,000. The device is for making Boron 112, and is used for high-powered fuels. Many things once used as explosives are now being used as fuels. George has never seen the device, and Johnny calls it a pig in a poke. George has had Dr. Hugo von Brauer look at the machine, and von Brauer says that Hantler is on the right track. George is worried about Hantler. George introduces Johnny to Louise Larkin, who goes gaga over Johnny. Louise tells Johnny that a couple years ago some of the kids she went around with had some pretty funny ideas. They thought they were smart by attending meetings that the FBI watched. She went to one meeting with her boyfriend Charlie White and the meeting was awful. They left in a hurry and the FBI later busted up the meeting. This morning she saw the name on a policy, and Josef Hantler was one of the men she had seen at one of those meetings. Hantler had told George that the machine was vital to the government, but George is suspicious as to which government is involved. Johnny thinks about calling the FBI, but decides to investigate first.

Johnny rents a car and drives with Louise to rural Connecticut and the Salmon Branch stream, where the lab of Josef Hantler's is located. Johnny tells Louise to just nod if she remembers the man. Hantler calls out for them to stop and Johnny tells him he is an insurance investigator and Floyds has sent him to look at the machine, but Hantler tells Johnny that no one will see it.

Johnny asks to see his government contract, but he has none. He will allow no one to see his laboratory. Hantler pulls a gun and tells them to leave, as they are trespassing. Johnny takes Louise back to the office and calls Lee Hauk of the FBI to meet him for lunch. Louise tells Johnny that Charley would go out and kill that man. Johnny leaves for lunch as Louise answers the phone, and talks to Charlie about meeting her dream man.

At lunch, Lee tells Johnny that Hantler is just a crackpot and they know he attended one meeting. Lee mentions that Louise was at one of those meetings too, and he also tells Johnny to watch out for her boyfriend, as he is the kind to take the law into his own hands. Lee tells Johnny that Hantler is harmless and usually makes crackpot inventions. Lee tells Johnny that von Brauer had a breakdown last fall. If George sold the policy to Hantler on von Brauers' ok, he is in trouble. Johnny knows that he needs to see the machine. Johnny drives to the lab and blows his horn, but gets no response. Johnny hears a thud and then the building explodes.

Johnny drags himself out of his destroyed rental car and sees Louise walking towards him with a husky football type who tells Louise that Hantler must have gone up with the building. Louise introduces him as Charley White and Johnny asks if he killed Hantler, but they say that they just got there and that they were going to give him to the FBI. Hantler walks up and tells them that it was wonderful. He introduces Johnny to Dr. Steiner from "the commission." The final test was final proof that is invention works. Dr. Steiner tells Johnny that they had watched the explosion from a hill, and that Dr. Hantler has developed a controlled power source from his compounds of great importance to the government's rocket program, but he cannot understand why it is called Boron 112. Hantler tells them it was experiment 112 with his converter. Dr. Steiner tells Charley that he is from Washington and that the government will take over the project immediately. Hantler tells Johnny that the converter went up with the building, and can now he can build a bigger one for the government. Johnny tells him that now he will have the money to build another one, but Hantler tells Johnny that he is a great man now, and is above such things and does not want the money.

There you are George, full report; payment on the policy is up to you and if you do pay, at least it's in a good cause. Also, I guess both you and I have learned a lesson about jumping to conclusions.

NOTES:
- EXPENSES INCLUDE REPLACEMENT OF THE RENTAL CAR.
- THE ANNOUNCER IS DAN CUBBERLY

| Producer: | Jack Johnstone | Writers: | Jack Johnstone |
|---|---|---|---|
| Cast: | Shirley Mitchell, G. Stanley Jones, Parley Baer, Russell Thorson, Frank Gerstle, Lou Merrill | | |

◆ ❖ ◆

| SHOW: | THE ELEVEN O'CLOCK MATTER |
|---|---|
| SHOW DATE: | 1/19/1958 |
| COMPANY: | EASTERN TRUST & INSURANCE COMPANY |
| AGENT: | |
| EXP. ACCT: | $21.40 |

SYNOPSIS: Pat McCracken calls and asks Johnny if he has heard of A, B and C? Not the alphabet, but the ad agency. The "A" stands for Alfred Appleton, 55 years old and Eastern Trust has his life insured for $100,000. It is an annuity, which pays off at 65, and Pat thinks someone doesn't want him to make it. He thinks someone is trying to kill him. He is staying at his place up on Skeleton Point.

Johnny drives to Skeleton Point, Connecticut in a rainstorm. At the Appleton home, Mrs. Gregory meets Johnny at the door. She bluntly tells Johnny that Mr. Appleton only leases the house. Mrs. Gregory is the housekeeper, and she shows Johnny to the library where Mr. Appleton and his lawyer John Hillman are meeting. Hillman tells Johnny that Mr. Appleton has received some crank letters. He did not report it to the police because he did not want any bad publicity in the middle of landing a new account. Tom Baker is the "B" and his only partner but there is some question as to whether he still is. Appleton will not accuse anyone until he has seen the books. The "C" stands for nothing. Mrs. Laura Appleton comes in and Hillman goes to get something from his room. Mrs. Appleton seems not too happy to have Johnny stay overnight. Johnny asks if she was expecting someone else. Johnny sees someone outside in the lightening and goes out to see who it was. Johnny comes in to call the police, but the phone lines are dead.

Hillman asks Johnny if he saw anyone, and Johnny tells him the rain was coming down too hard. Mrs. Gregory announces Tom Baker, who is introduced to Johnny. He is soaked because he had to walk to the house when his car stalled in a deep puddle. Hillman suggests that they all go to the beach house and have some fun. Everyone goes down on the stairway, but no one seems to have fun. The intercom buzzer rings and Mrs. Gregory is told she can go to bed. Baker asks Appleton if they can have their talk, so Johnny and Hillman go to the house. Johnny asks Hillman about accusing Baker of anything. Hillman is not sure, but Appleton thinks that there are some irregularities in the books. Hillman manages most of Appleton's affairs, so if anything is wrong it may be his fault. Hillman asks Johnny to call him at midnight to go over the books when Johnny is suddenly hit on the head as the clock is chiming 11:00. Johnny comes to while the clock is still chiming. Hillman tells Johnny that he tried to grab the attacker but he got away. Johnny and Hillman search the house and end up at an open window. Mrs. Gregory comes in and Hillman tells her about the attack. Johnny buzzes the beach house, gets no answer and goes to the stairs and hears a scream. Mrs. Appleton is standing at the top of the stairs where some of the railing is broken away. Alfred Appleton's body is at the bottom of the stairs on the beach.

Johnny looks at the body and Mrs. Gregory takes Mrs. Appleton back to the house. Johnny and Hillman go down to find Appleton's watch stopped at 11:10. Both Hillman and Johnny wonder where Tom Baker is. Johnny goes back and calls the police, and they will get someone out as soon as possible. Hillman tells Johnny that the books seem to show a shortage of up to $50,000. Johnny goes to see Mrs. Appleton and asks her what happened. She tells Johnny that after Johnny left, she and Tom sat there for a while and then Tom left. Mr. Appleton was called on the intercom and left a few minutes after eleven. She went to the top of the stairs she saw the broken rail and looked down to see his body. Johnny asks why Baker was there and he tells her that she had been trying to signal Baker all night. Also, Appleton suspected a shortage and Hillman has confirmed it. Johnny suggests that maybe Baker came up to square things with Appleton. Mrs. Appleton tells Johnny that Baker came up because she was going to ask her husband for a divorce so she could marry Baker, and they wanted everything to be in the open. They did not know that Johnny and Hillman were going to be there and that is why she tried to signal Baker. Hillman come in and tells Johnny that Baker has just come back. Hillman is told by Johnny to question Mrs. Gregory, who could have made the call to Appleton around eleven, while Johnny questions Baker. Baker tells Johnny he had taken a walk on the beach and did not know that Appleton was dead until Hillman told him. Johnny calls the police again and they will have someone there as soon as possible. Johnny notes that the policeman on the phone is not the same one he talked to earlier, and is told that the other officer, Harris, went off duty at 1:00 AM. Hillman tells Johnny that Mrs. Gregory denies making the call to the beach house. Suddenly Johnny thinks of something. Johnny checks everyone's watches and all of them read 12:50, but according to the Sgt. it is after one AM. Johnny goes to his car and looks at the clock in his car where it reads 1:10. Johnny sees a gun and knows he had found the answer. Hillman tells Johnny that he had a foolproof plan until Johnny locked his car. Johnny tells Hillman that he had knocked him out, killed Appleton, reset all the clocks and woke Johnny up 15 minutes later as the clock was chiming. Johnny was only out for 15 minutes. Johnny hits Hillman with the car door and holds him for the sheriff. Hillman was not too happy to see them.

Remarks: Hillman's motive was money of course. It was he who had taken the $50,000 from Appleton's agency.

## NOTES:
- THE AFRS PROGRAM I HAVE INCLUDES A MINI-SERIAL ABOUT A MILITARY FAMILY, THE BELLWETHERS, AND ENDS WITH AN ORGAN SELECTION REMINISCENT OF EDDIE DUNSTEDTER.
- THE ANNOUNCER IS DAN CUBBERLY

Producer:  Jack Johnstone        Writers:   Robert Ryf
Cast:          Eleanor Audley, Paula Winslowe, Larry Dobkin, Will Wright, Ben Wright, Harry Bartell

◆ ❖ ◆

| SHOW: | THE FIRE IN PARADISE MATTER |
|---|---|
| SHOW DATE: | 1/26/1958 |
| COMPANY: | FOUR STATE FIRE & CASUALTY INSURANCE COMPANY |
| AGENT: | FRED HANLEY |
| EXP. ACCT: | $241.28 |

SYNOPSIS: Fred Hanley calls Johnny, and he has a routine case for Johnny in Paradise, New Jersey. Johnny is told to go to Philadelphia, rent a car and find out how much insurance is due to Joshua Trimmings, who was hurt in a fire.

Johnny flies to Philadelphia, rents a car and drives to Paradise, while commenting on the drab colors of southern New Jersey in January. In Paradise Johnny meets Sheriff Luther Hopkins and he tells Johnny that Joshua might have been hurt, but how bad is something else. Johnny is told that the fire started on Friday and burned too fast to save the house. Joshua jumped from a window, and the sheriff is sure that the old skinflint did it for the money. Johnny learns that Joshua is retired, but that he spends his money somewhere else. Johnny gets directions to Joe Pasquale's house and drives to the fire scene, where he sees some interesting things.

Johnny goes to Joe Pasquale's house where Johnny meets the doctor. The doctor tells Johnny that Joshua is staying there because he loaned Joe money for seeds and fertilizer, and that he told Joe he might lower his fees on the loan if he could stay there. Johnny is told that Joe had to give Joshua free produce last year, and that no one likes him. Johnny is told that Joshua fights with everyone, and that his house was a dump. Johnny is also told that Joshua charges 10-20% interest on his loans, but there is never anything in writing. Johnny goes in to meet Joshua, who tells the doctor that he will pay him for once, and he tells Johnny that the policy is unique, it requires payment if Joshua is incapacitated. Johnny leaves with the doctor and he tells Johnny that there is nothing wrong with Joshua. The doctor tells Johnny that Joshua calls the sheriff at all hours and even makes him clean up the trash around his house, and that the sheriff is fed up with him. Johnny is told that the fire started in several places, and that maybe he was burned out. Doc tells Johnny that the sheriff is a good man though, and has a sense of duty for everyone, even Joshua.

Johnny goes to the local store and buys a loaf of bread and goes to the fire scene while it is raining. Johnny finds some bills in the mailbox that provide clues to arson. Johnny calls Fred to learn what Joshua had done for a living and then goes to Pasquale's house with the sheriff after learning that this was not Joshua's first fire. Johnny tells Joshua that he has been investigating the fires, and Joshua accuses Luke of setting the fire. Johnny tells Joshua that the unpaid bills in the mailbox were a sure sign of planned arson. Why pay the bills if the house were going to burn? Johnny tells everyone that Joshua ran a business that made celluloid dolls, and that his business had also burned. Johnny tells them that celluloid was used to burn the house. Joshua stands and tells Johnny that he is ready to be arrested. Johnny tells him that he was just guessing.

NOTES:
- THE ANNOUNCER IS DAN CUBBERLY
- STORY INFORMATION OBTAINED FROM THE KNX COLLECTION IN THE THOUSAND OAKS LIBRARY

| | |
|---|---|
| Producer: | Jack Johnstone     Writers     Jack Johnstone |
| Cast: | Vic Perrin, Forrest Lewis, Virginia Gregg, Will Wright, Parley Baer |

◆   ❖   ◆

| | |
|---|---|
| SHOW: | THE PRICE OF FAME MATTER |
| SHOW DATE: | 2/2/1958 |
| COMPANY: | FOUR STATE MUTUAL INSURANCE COMPANY |
| AGENT: | |
| EXP. ACCT: | $2,341.00 |

SYNOPSIS: Vincent Price calls Johnny from Hollywood, and Johnny is sure it is a crank call. The Vincent Price? Vincent tells Johnny that he has a problem with one of his paintings that is insured for $100,000. The painting has disappeared and Bert Parker the Four State Mutual agent is never there. Vincent has learned that no one knows where Bert is. Johnny will grab the first plane.

Johnny flies to Los Angeles, California on a Constellation. In the airport Johnny spots Vincent in a crown of autograph seekers. Vincent tells the crowd that this is the great Johnny Dollar and Johnny is beset by the throng of autograph seekers. Johnny finally gets out of the airport and goes with Vincent to his home in Beverly Hills where the house is filled with fine art. Vincent shows Johnny a Goya called the "Man in Red," and a McManner called "Fright," and "Nightwind" by Jean Baptise, which is not lighted like the others. Vincent tells Johnny the lack of light is to accent the somber mood and has allowed the thief to make a substitution. Vincent discovered the substitution when he came back from a tour, and has not contacted the police, that was Bert's job. Vincent tells Johnny that only a few friends knew of the painting, the house was not broken into and visitors were tracked while he was away. Johnny sees the list of visitors and spots Bert Parker's name on the list twice. Vincent does not know Bert very well and Johnny tells him the company will cover the loss.

Johnny and Vincent go to Bert's office and are told that he has not been seen there for two weeks. Johnny gets the address and Vincent offers to drive Johnny there. At Bert's apartment, the landlord lets Johnny into the apartment, and they discover that Bert is gone. Vincent finds a travel folder for Paris, France in a desk drawer. Johnny and Vincent go to the travel office and learn that Bert has traveled to Paris, first class, and is staying at the Hotel du Louvres. Bert had wanted something close to the Montmartre. Vincent tells the agent to make the same reservations for him and Johnny.

Johnny and Vincent fly to Paris, France and check into the hotel where the manager tells them that Mr. Parker has left after a disagreement with the management. "You mean he ran out of money?" Johnny asks only to get a shrug of agreement. Johnny is told that Bert had been at the Montmartre most of his time. Vincent tells Johnny that paintings are often sold in strange ways and tells Johnny that he will see what he can dig up.

Gay romantic Paris, and Johnny is waiting in his room. Vincent comes in later with some packages containing props for Johnny. Vincent gives Johnny a ten-gallon hat, and tells Johnny he is in oil and his name is Matthews. Johnny ends up all dressed up and is told he will go to the Bal Macabre. Remember you made your money in oil, and Johnny is put in a cab.

At the Bal Macabre Johnny sees a lot of dirty people screaming at each other. A sly man comes to the table and tells Johnny that he is "les char gris," the gray cat. He asks if Johnny likes the nightlife, and Johnny tells him he wants to buy some paintings, like a Baptise. Les char gris tells Johnny that he has friend who can help him, and tells Johnny to wait at the corner for a cab. Johnny goes out and the cab takes Johnny to a disreputable apartment where Johnny is to meet a dealer. Les char gris tells Johnny that he only will ask for 10% of what Johnny pays for the painting. At the door, les char gris knocks and Bert Parker opens the door to find Johnny standing there. When les char gris hears that Johnny is an investigator, he remembers someone waiting for him elsewhere. Vincent arrives just as les char gris leaves. Bert offers to give the painting back, and Vincent tells Johnny that he has a secret; les char gris was the one who got him the painting in the first place, but he only paid $300 for it. Johnny asks Vincent why he is not an investigator and Vincent asks Johnny why he is not an actor. Um, er, ah . . . let's get out of here.

The disposition of Bert Parker is up to the company. Vincent, now that he has the painting back does not care one way, or the other. However from the company's standpoint, this is not the kind of black eye that is good for you.

Remarks: To Vincent Price my eternal thanks not only for the help on this case, but most of all it has given me a chance to really know him.

## NOTES:

- THE COPY OF THIS PROGRAM I HAVE IS HARD TO HEAR AT TIMES, AND HAS NO CREDITS AT ALL.
- CAST CREDITS ARE FROM RADIOGOLDINDEX.
- THE ANNOUNCER IS DAN CUBBERLY
- MY FRENCH, COMBINED WITH THE BAD QUALITY OF THE PROGRAM, MAKES TRYING TO IDENTIFY LANDMARKS VERY DIFFICULT, ALTHOUGH THERE IS A HOTEL DU LOUVRE, AND AN AREA CALLED MONTMARTRE WHICH IS SORT OF THE FRENCH GREENWICH VILLAGE.

**Producer:** Jack Johnstone      **Writers:** Jack Johnstone
**Cast:**     Vincent Price, Virginia Gregg, Howard McNear, Junius Matthews, Forrest Lewis, Tony Barrett

| SHOW: | THE SICK CHICK MATTER |
|---|---|
| SHOW DATE: | 2/9/1958 |
| COMPANY: | STAR MUTUAL INSURANCE COMPANY |
| AGENT: | |
| EXP. ACCT: | $0.00 |

SYNOPSIS: Ben Pringle calls Johnny. Ben has retired and is running a poultry farm in Vineland, New Jersey. Things are going terrible. Someone is trying to put him out of business. Ben wanted to make sure Johnny was available before calling Star Mutual.

Johnny travels to Philadelphia and rents car for the drive to Vineland, New Jersey. Johnny gets directions to Ben's farm at a Mobil station. After searching an area full of chicken farms, Johnny pulls into a farm house to get further directions, and he ends up next door to Ben. The neighbor, Mrs. Renzulli tells Johnny that Ben does not know anything about raising chickens. He should sell and move out. He is like all the other city people who retire, buy chickens and lose their money. Mrs. Renzulli tells Johnny that they buy up all the places that go out of business. Johnny asks if Mrs. Renzulli would benefit from Ben going out of business, and Johnny is thrown out. Johnny gets to Ben's farm, and learns that Ben has spent $40,000 so far. He has lost almost all his herd to bugs, and diseases and other things. Ben feels that the birds are being poisoned by someone who wants to see him go out of business. He is right next door—Joe Renzulli.

Ben tells Johnny he has the sickest herd of chickens anyone has ever seen. He has talked to the vet who has cured the chickens of all sorts of diseases. The vet gave Ben a book so Ben would know how to care for his chickens, and feed them. Ben has looked in the book for the latest problem, and there is nothing in there. In the chicken house Johnny sees a bunch of sad looking chickens staggering around. Johnny asks if Ben had been spiking the water with some of his private stock. Ben shows Johnny the feed he bought from Jake Romanov. Ben tells Johnny that Renzulli had helped him, and Ben has seen Renzulli spread something on this yard at night. Johnny goes to talk to Joe Renzulli, who is building an elevated cage for his chickens. Joe tells Johnny that he tried to help Ben by throwing vitamin supplements to his chickens. Johnny asks about poison, but Joe gets defensive when Johnny mentions the police. Johnny gets a sample of the vitamins to have analyzed. Joe tells Johnny that he has to be on good terms with his neighbors, and Joe tells him to find out for himself, because he does not live here. Johnny wonders if he has stumbled into something more than sick chicks.

Ben makes dinner for Johnny and the canned beans look, um, interesting? Ben tells Johnny that if neighbors tell on their neighbors they are outcasts. Johnny asks about Ben's other neighbor, the one with the new Lincoln out front. Ben tells Johnny that he is John Culpepper, who came up from the south, a real nice young man. He has a lot of parties and women. Ben has been there, but

Culpepper just gives him a bottle and tells him to enjoy it at home. There is big barn out back, but Culpepper does not keep horses or other livestock. Ben also tells Johnny that he has heard trucks going in late at night. Johnny asks for a flashlight and goes exploring.

Johnny see Ben's chickens hanging out by the fence, and there is a path from the fence to the barn. Johnny climbs the fence and goes to the barn and notices a faint piercing odor he first smelled in Kentucky. Johnny looks into the barn and sees cases of bottles and a copper still. Culpepper comes up on Johnny with a gun and accuses him of being a revenuer. Culpepper looks at Johnny's ID and Johnny tells him that he is only interested in what is happening to Ben's chickens. Johnny is able to get the gun away from Culpepper, who offers Johnny money to go away. Johnny realizes that whiskey is made from mash, and Culpepper tells Johnny that he has been dumping his mash over the fence, and Johnny realizes that Ben's chickens are just drunk. Ben and Culpepper talk, and Culpepper agrees to pay Johnny's expenses, Ben's veterinary bills, and to move out of the county. Johnny should have turned him in, but that is a job for the company. And you know something? The stuff that Culpepper's was turning out in that barn wasn't half bad.

NOTES:
- THIS PROGRAM CONTAINS ANOTHER "BELLWETHERS" SERIAL AND THE SAME ORGAN SERENADE AT THE END.
- THE ANNOUNCER IS DAN CUBBERLY

Producer:   Jack Johnstone          Writers:   Jack Johnstone
Cast:       Lucille Meredith, Howard McNear, Gil Stratton, Jack Moyles, Sam Edwards

◆   ❖   ◆

SHOW:       THE TIME AND TIDE MATTER
SHOW DATE:  2/16/1958
COMPANY:    UNIVERSAL ADJUSTMENT BUREAU
AGENT:      PAT MCCRACKEN
EXP. ACCT:  $403.50

SYNOPSIS: Pat McCracken calls Johnny, and Johnny asks him what is new. Pat tells Johnny that Edward J. Rollins, III is new. One of Pat's companies has a hefty policy on his life. Rollins requested a change to his policy, and then disappeared. "And you want me to go looking for him?" "That's the general idea." "Look Pat, you could be wasting dough sending me, chances are he will pop up again by himself." "I know, of course it involves a little trip to the Caribbean, but if you're not interested." "Caribbean! I'll be right over."

Johnny cabs to Pat's office. Pat tells Johnny that six months ago Rollins decided to marry a girl named Virginia Blake and took out the life insurance policy. Apparently he has changed his mind. He called from Nassau asking to remove

Virginia from the policy. He was supposed to go to Miami to sign the papers but never showed up. He was in Nassau on his cabin cruiser with three of his friends, and Virginia Blake is among them.

Johnny travels to Nassau, Bahamas and finds a man who had refueled the boat and remembers hearing them mention Crooked Island. Johnny charters a plane, flies to Crooked Island and spots the boat in a cove. The plane sets down and Ed Rollins comes out to meet Johnny in a skiff. Johnny tells Rollins about not meeting the agent in Miami, and he tells Johnny that he changed his mind. Johnny asks Ed about taking out the policy and changing his mind. Ed tells Johnny that he has just changed his mind. He tells Johnny that he thinks Virginia has been two-timing him. He has not asked her because he might not like the truth. Rollins invites Johnny to come along with them to Jamaica. On the boat are Virginia, Bill Winslow who handles the boat and Tony Atherton, who introduced Ed to Virginia. Johnny tells Rollins to introduce him as an old friend. Johnny describes Bill as a man who looks at home on a boat, and Tony as someone who looks at home with a drink in his hand. Virginia, well one look at her and you forget where home is. Johnny waits on deck with Tony and Virginia while the others skin dive. No matter what Tony says to Virginia, she tells him to lay off. Ed and Bill finally surface and Ed is in trouble. Ed tells them that there is something wrong with his air supply. Johnny finds a scraped spot on the air supply, and Ed says he must have scrapped it on something.

Ed considered the event an accident, so Johnny did too. That night Johnny goes up on deck for a smoke and sees Virginia kissing Bill. Ed comes up and tells Johnny about cutting Virginia out of the policy; he has decided to marry her, as he cannot live without her. Ed sees Virginia up with Bill and figures she is navigating. Ed tells Virginia to turn in and takes over the helm. Johnny asks Virginia why Tony feels she did not want to make the trip and she just says that she has known Tony for a long time. Bill tells Johnny that they should reach Jamaica the next night. Bill tells Johnny that he belongs on a boat, and Tony is just a passenger type. Virginia, well she can handle anything.

In Jamaica Johnny calls Pat to have him check up on the three passengers on the boat. After dinner Bill goes to the boat and Tony goes bar hunting. Virginia is edgy and talks to Ed on the terrace. Pat returns Johnny's call and tells him that Virginia has been sending regular $1,200 checks to Tony Atherton. Johnny goes to the terrace and then looks for Atherton in some nearby bars. Back on the boat, Johnny wakes up Tony and asks why he is blackmailing Virginia. A policeman comes on board and tells them that Ed has been slugged and robbed. He may not live.

Johnny is taken to the location of the assault and learns that Ed had been hit with a piece of pipe and his wallet and valuables were gone. Next morning on the boat Johnny asks Tony again why he was blackmailing Virginia. Tony tells Johnny that she was helping him with some bad investments. Tony points to the porthole and tells Johnny he saw Ed walking on the pier with someone following him, Bill Winslow. Johnny questions Bill, who tells him he was just taking a walk and did not see Ed. Johnny mentions him and Virginia, but Bill insists he did not see Ed. Johnny talks to Virginia and she tells Johnny that she and Ed just walked around after dinner. Ed had business so she went back to the boat in a cab and went to bed. She tells Johnny that Ed had talked to her about his doubts about her, and that he still wanted to marry her. She told him that he had to know some things about her. For one, she was once attracted to Bill, but it did not work out. She also told Ed that Tony had been blackmailing her. She had a roommate once who was stealing and went to jail because she could not prove she was not involved.

Johnny walks around for a while and looks at the boat sitting low in the water and gets an idea. Johnny goes back to the boat and checks the tide table to confirm that it was now low tide, and looks up the previous low tide; yeah! Johnny goes to talk to Tony and he confirms that Virginia has been paying him to keep quiet. Johnny tells Tony that Ed's business was to take care of Tony. Tony spotted Ed on the pier and hit him and probably figured you had killed him. Tony recounts how he saw Bill following Ed, and Johnny tells Tony that he just hung himself. Johnny tells Tony to look out and Tony can only see the pilings. Johnny tells Tony he was lying and could not have seen over the pier last night. Tony tries to run and Johnny slugs him. Johnny tells him that Shakespeare is more right than he knew, "There is a tide in the affairs of man which sometimes leads to fortune." In your case, brother you missed.

Remarks: Tony Atherton is in jail where he belongs. Bill Winslow is on a boat, where he belongs. Ed Rollins pulled through and he and Virginia will get married next month.

## NOTES:
- CAST CREDITS FROM RadioGOLDINdex.
- THE ANNOUNCER IS DAN CUBBERLY

| | | | |
|---|---|---|---|
| Producer: | Jack Johnstone | Writers: | Robert Ryf |
| Cast: | Virginia Gregg, Tony Barrett, Lawrence Dobkin, Herb Ellis, Frank Nelson, Ben Wright | | |

◆  ❖  ◆

| | |
|---|---|
| SHOW: | THE DURANGO LARAMIE MATTER |
| SHOW DATE: | 2/23/1958 |
| COMPANY: | FLOYDS OF ENGLAND |
| AGENT: | GEORGE REED |
| EXP. ACCT: | $1,460.00 |

SYNOPSIS: George Reed calls and asks if Johnny remembers Durango Laramie Dalhart. Johnny asks if Durango has ever forgiven George for thinking he was counterfeiting money. George tells Johnny that Durango had written to say that he would be in the office on the 10th of last month to pay his $4,500 premium. That was six weeks ago and he has not shown up. George has wired and written and is afraid that something may have happened because of the way Durango flashes around all his cash. Johnny tells George he will let him know what he finds out in Bum Spung.

This case from George looks like serious business. Johnny travels to Enid, rents a car and drives to Bum Spung, Oklahoma. When Johnny arrives at the broken down shack he gets shot at. Johnny yells out to Durango and a voice tells Johnny that Durango is not there, and to go away. More shots are fired and Johnny notes that the man has shot out one of his tires. When the man comes out to look at the tire Johnny gets his gun from him. The man is Sidewinder Wilson and Durango had sent him a telegram telling him to take care of the ranch for him. Sidewinder is an old friend of Durango's. Sidewinder tells Johnny that Durango left the house unlocked when he left; and no food was left for the animals and the tractor was left in the field, and that is funny. Sidewinder knows that Durango was loaded with money when he left, and his not showing up means that Durango was waylaid somewhere.

Sidewinder tells Johnny that he has not heard from Carol. Sidewinder helps fix the tire so that Johnny can drive back to Enid to see Carol Dalhart, when sidewinder spots Carol's convertible coming up the road. Carol drives up and grabs Johnny and gives him a great big hug and a kiss while Sidewinder just laughs. Carol tells Johnny that Durango has gone to Hartford, and has $50,000 with him. She got a postcard from Chicago, which is not like him as he usually goes straight to Hartford. Sidewinder mentions a real estate man from Chicago who had been there. The card said the Durango was going to look at Ong's Hat. Johnny drives to Enid and calls Phil Avery, an old wire service friend, to see if the wires had picked up anything on Durango, but Phil has heard nothing. Johnny mentions Ong's Hat and Phil laughs.

Phil stops laughing long enough to tell Johnny that Ong's Hat is a town in southern New Jersey. Johnny and Carol grab a flight to Chicago to visit J. Harry Cramlan, the real estate promoter, who admits selling Durango some property in New Jersey for $35,000. Durango bought the property because he thought there was oil on the property. Johnny warns Cramlan that if Durango has been swindled, he is in trouble.

Johnny and Carol fly Philadelphia where Johnny rents a car and drives to Mount Holly where they stop for lunch. Johnny notices a local newspaper article about an oil development in Ong's Hat. Johnny drives to Ong's Hat and finds a large number of cars and people surrounding Durango and yelling at him. Johnny also notices two oil derricks. Johnny fears for the worse as he gets Durango's attention. Durango asks Johnny if he has snuck out to Enid and married Carol, which he had been hoping for. Johnny tells Durango that he is on business. Durango accuses Johnny of transporting Carol across state lines, which means that they have to get married, and his six-gun will see to it. Johnny tells Durango that he has been swindled, but Durango laughs and tells Johnny that he knows the area is not oil land. He tells them that as soon as the locals heard that he was an oilman they have been demanding that he sell them land even though he tells them that there is no oil there. So far he has made $65,000. Durango asks if Johnny is there to buy land or marry Carol? Johnny starts to backpeddle and

Durango tells him it better be both.

Expense account item 7, $1,000. The company now owns a small piece of land in Ong's Hat, New Jersey. As for Carol, that ever loving doll, well someday.

NOTES:

- THERE IS AN ONG'S HAT IN THE PINE BARRENS AREA OF SOUTHERN NEW JERSEY
- CAST INFORMATION FROM RadioGOLDINdex.
- THE ANNOUNCER IS DAN CUBBERLY

Producer:   Jack Johnstone        Writers:   Jack Johnstone
Cast:       Virginia Gregg, G. Stanley Jones, Junius Matthews, Alan
            Reed, Frank Nelson, John McIntire

SHOW:        THE DIAMOND DILEMMA MATTER
SHOW DATE:   3/2/1958
COMPANY:     MASTERS INSURANCE & TRUST COMPANY
AGENT:       BERT MAJOR
EXP. ACCT:   $284.30

SYNOPSIS: Bert Major calls and asks Johnny if he knows anything about spacemen. Bert knows someone who thinks they have contacted him. The company is betting $2,000,000 that the man is either a liar, or pulling one of the biggest hoaxes in history. Conrad Billing; ever hear of him? Billing, the Texas oil man and one of the richest men in the country? Right, and presently living in a mountaintop ranch in California minus $2,000,000 in diamonds he took up there with him. The diamonds were "insured against theft by persons or things unknown on this earth." "You're serious aren't you?" "You bet I'm serious." "Alright, I'll see you in your office."

Johnny cabs to Bert's office and Bert is really excited over this thing. Bert tells Johnny that it is impossible for diamonds to disappear, but it has happened. Billing is staying in his mountain top lodge, and the police verify that no one could have gotten to the stones. Conrad Billings called two weeks ago and wanted the diamonds insured immediately. Bert is sure it was Billing as he had the call traced. Billing called Bert because he had done some business with a friend of his in Dallas. Billing had the diamonds with him, and he lives in one of he most isolated spots on earth. Billing loves diamonds and plays with them like they are marbles, and he can afford to. Johnny tells him that an amateur could get to the diamonds. Bert recounts that he had insured the diamonds against theft by persons or things unknown on this earth. So, if a person took them prove it. Bert tells Johnny that Billing must be in his right mind to run his empire, so they insured the diamonds. Johnny is to go out and make sense of this. Johnny gets the contact names and leaves.

Johnny flies to San Francisco, California and meets with Norton Shields at the Billings company headquarters. Norton has been with Billing for 10 years, except for Korea and he tolerates Billing. Norton tells Johnny that Billing has foibles, like diamonds. Norton saw Billing put the diamonds in a bag to be taken to his lodge before they disappeared. Norton tells Johnny he will have a plane ready for him in the morning.

Next morning a plane takes Johnny to Clear Lake, California where he is met by a car and driver that takes him to Billing. The driver tells Johnny that he waits for Billing when he is not busy, and that no one lives at the lodge but Billing. After passing through a series of gates and "Private Property" signs, Johnny is delivered to a wire gate. Johnny gets out and the car vanishes back down the mountain. A voice tells Johnny that he will be electrocuted if he touches the gates. If he is Mr. Dollar, the voice wants to know where he was yesterday, and Johnny tells him he was with Bert Major, and the gate opens. Johnny is told to drive a car up the road to the lodge. At the top Johnny is met at the lodge by Billing who is sort, bald and dressed in baggy clothes and is hard of hearing. Johnny is shown the view from the lodge and he tells Johnny that he wants to collect on the diamonds. On a control panel, Billing shows Johnny how electronic devices monitor the whole property with video monitors. Fences and sensors, that allow Billing to detect anyone who comes in, surround the whole mountaintop. Billing tells Johnny that he leaves nothing to chance, and that diamonds would be invaluable to other civilizations. Billing defies Johnny to find how the diamonds were stolen. Billing has a direct line to Andy Prentice, the sheriff if Johnny needs it.

Johnny drives down the mountain and sees no loopholes in the security setup. In Lakeview, Johnny is expected in the sheriff's office. Sheriff Prentice gets into the car and tells Johnny to drive to the lake so they can talk privately. Johnny tells him that he does not believe aliens took the diamonds. Johnny notes that Billing does not wear a hearing aid, and Andy tells him he does not need one—he just turns up the volume on the equipment. Johnny asks about a parachutist landing there, but no one could get out, and they found no signs of entry or exit when they searched. Andy has no ideas how it happened. Johnny suggests a plane ride over the mountain and Andy goes along.

Johnny asks the pilot to fly around the mountain between the two fence lines, and he gets an idea. Johnny goes to San Francisco airport, talks to the captain of the airport police and at dusk he is where he wants to be, walking towards the Billing lodge. At the front door, Johnny surprises Billing who cannot understand how he got there. Johnny tells him that the sensors are in the wrong place as there is one spot that is not covered by sensors; and Johnny has a helicopter waiting there. They landed below the line of sight and hearing, so no aliens took the diamonds. Billing confirms that Norton Shields was a pilot while in Korea, and flew rescue missions in helicopters.

"You know, in some ways I felt sorry for him. He'd spent millions of dollars to insure his diamonds and his privacy. Came a real showdown and it turns out he had neither. Oh, he will get his diamonds back sure, and will probably buy more. But privacy is a pretty hard thing to come by, at least in this man's world."

NOTES:

- THE FIRST COMMERCIAL BREAK IS AN AFRS SPOT ABOUT FRANK LUKE DURING WORLD WAR I
- THE SECOND COMMERCIAL BREAK IS AN AFRS SPOT ABOUT THE FLAG OF SOUTH CAROLINA
- THE FINAL COMMERCIAL BREAK IS AN AFRS SPOT ABOUT THE HEROISM OF ROBERT E. COX, USN
- THE ANNOUNCER IS DAN CUBBERLY

Producer: Jack Johnstone     Writers: Allen Botzer
Cast:     Edwin Jerome, Paul Dubov, Frank Gerstle, Junius Matthews, Marvin Miller

◆   ❖   ◆

SHOW: THE WAYWARD MOTH MATTER
SHOW DATE: 3/9/1958
COMPANY: TRI-STATE LIFE & CASUALTY INSURANCE COMPANY
AGENT: EARLE POORMAN
EXP. ACCT: $204.00

SYNOPSIS: Earle Poorman calls and wants Johnny to come down over a $2,000 claim. Johnny wonders how Earle can afford for Johnny to come down, and Earle tells him that sometimes more is required than just paying off a claim. Earle tells Johnny that national security is involved in this case. Johnny will grab the first plane.

Johnny flies to Sarasota, Florida where Earle meets him at the airport. Earle has another new car with all the options. Earle tells Johnny that he cannot talk about the security issues here, and Johnny hopes Earle got him down here to go fishing. Earle finally tells Johnny that he has insured the chemical plant of Dr. John C. Allworth at the request of Todd Swam of the Chamber of Commerce. Earle does not know what kind of chemicals Allworth is involved with. Earle does not know where the plant is, and took Todd's word that the claim was valid. Earle takes Johnny to Todd's office and leaves the keys to his car with Johnny. Inside Todd tells Johnny that he knows all about Johnny, and he knows that Johnny has worked with the FBI. Todd tells Johnny that he works with the Chamber of Commerce and also to be of service to the people. Dr. Allworth is a retired chemist and has developed a key rocket fuel ingredient in his hidden chemical plant. He and an assistant work alone and Todd thinks the accident was sabotage.

Todd and Johnny drive in separate cars to the Everglades and the Cypress Swamp area. At the end of a dirt road, an Indian with a rifle meets Johnny. The man lowers the gun when Todd gets there. Todd introduces Johnny to Ben Osceola. Todd tells Ben that Johnny is to be allowed there anytime he wants. Ben drives Todd and Johnny in an airboat to the site of Allworth's lab. Johnny meets Dr. Allworth and he takes them to the lab vault, which is where the accident occurred. Todd is sure that an enemy agent is responsible. In the vault Allworth keeps the finished rocket fuel component and an apparatus to finish the production process. No one has ever seen the apparatus, which was ruined by the explosion. In the vault the highly corrosive rocket fuel covers the floor. The secret apparatus has been destroyed and is lying on the floor. Allworth tells Johnny that the glass flagon holding the rocket fuel was on a marble slab ready to be shipped to, well to its destination. The flagon exploded yesterday morning. Todd asks where his assistant Leon Salkoff is. Johnny notes that an infamous man named Salkoff was involved in a series of industrial bomb plots, and Allworth tells Johnny that he is the same man, but he was cleared in the trials. Besides, Allworth tells Johnny that Salkoff does not know the combination to the vault. Allworth tells Johnny that Salkoff has gone to Ft. Meyers for supplies, but has not come back. Todd is sure that Salkoff has kept on going. Johnny asks about the windows to the lab and if a gun could have been used to break the glass flagon, but the windows are all in place and not damaged. Johnny goes outside to check to see if the windows could be removed from the outside and is stopped by a man with a gun.

Johnny tries to identify himself when Dr. Allworth comes out and tells Leon that Johnny is ok. Leon tells Johnny that he took so long because he was puzzling over how the flagon exploded. Johnny mentions Salkoff's conduct during the war, and Leon hopes he will be forgiven for what he was forced to do. He hopes working for this country will help him make up for what he did. Leon had phoned the glass company and there is a way the glass could have crystallized. The formula from the company has given him the answer to the puzzle. They have a lot of work to do before morning.

The vault is cleaned thoroughly, and a new flagon is placed in the vault, and everyone waits. Early in the morning Johnny notices the rays of the sun coming through the window toward the flagon. Allworth holds a piece of paper in the light, and it bursts into flames. Allworth tells Johnny that the light could have caused the glass to crystallize, but it should have occurred by now. Todd is positive that Leon is guilty until Allworth notices a tiny moth attracted to the light on the flagon. The moth circles and finally dives at the flagon and sets off an explosion. Todd is forced to apologize.

Yep, a tiny moth triggered the reaction that disintegrated, crystallized that bottle into a million tiny grains, like sand. And simply because of the difference in temperature of his little body. Seems impossible, but it happened.

Remarks: Pay up on this claim in a hurry. The more help we can give to people like Dr. Allworth and Leon Salkoff, the better.

## NOTES:
- MY PROGRAM IS AN **AFRS** COPY WITH NO CREDITS.
- CAST INFORMATION FROM THE **KNX** COLLECTION AT THE THOUSAND OAKS LIBRARY.
- THE ANNOUNCER IS DAN CUBBERLY

Producer:     Jack Johnstone          Writers:   Jack Johnstone
Cast:         Vic Perrin, Herb Ellis, Paul Richards, Lou Merrill, Leon
              Belasco

◆   ❖   ◆

SHOW:          THE SALKOFF SEQUEL MATTER
SHOW DATE:     3/16/1958
COMPANY:       TRI-STATE LIFE & CASUALTY INSURANCE COMPANY
AGENT:         EARLE POORMAN
EXP. ACCT:     $0.00

SYNOPSIS: Johnny is paged in the airport and takes the call in the office. Todd
Swam is calling to tell Johnny that he has to come back there to Sarasota, Florida.
Johnny tells Todd that the company will pay the claim on the lab, but Todd asks
if the company will pay a claim on Salkoff? Todd tells Johnny that it looks like
murder.

Johnny expenses the no-show penalty on his flight to Hartford and Earle picks
him up at the airport. Earle tells Johnny that Salkoff has just disappeared, and it
looks like murder. Earle tells Johnny that Salkoff was involved in subversive
activities during the war, but has been given a clean slate. But some of his old
pals knew he was working for us, they would probably try to catch him, torture
him for the formula and kill him. The details will have to come from Todd. At
the Chamber of Commerce building Johnny meets Todd, who gives him his car
and tells him to go the lab. Todd has called the FBI, and they are going to send
someone to assist Johnny. Johnny drives to Ben Osceola's shack and Ben takes
Johnny back out to the island and Dr. Allworth is there. Allworth takes Johnny
inside and updates him. After Johnny had left, he and Leon worked to make the
fuel additive lost in the accident. Leon had mentioned a man he had seen in Ft.
Meyer the day before, someone he had known in Europe who would like to
sabotage our effort. Johnny is shown Leon's room, which is torn up from a
struggle and Johnny spots blood on the floor. Allworth had heard voices in
Leon's room and heard him call for help. He tried to open his door, but a chair
blocked it. Allworth heard shots and the sound of Leon's body being drug out of
the building. Allworth got out of his room by bracing his bed against the door
and forcing the door open. Allworth chased after the men but they were gone,
and they took Leon's airboat. Allworth rushes off on his airboat to call the FBI,
but he cannot hear Johnny tells him that they already on the way. Johnny looks
around the island and finds nothing. Johnny notices that the front door is closed,
but he had left it open. Johnny walks in and is knocked out.

Johnny wakes up in Allworth's bed and plays possum while watching a man
go through Allworth's files. Johnny pegs him as a subversive and starts to wonder
about Allworth's story. Johnny groans and the man calls him by name. They tell
him they are concerned about him, and did not know who he was until they
searched him. He is Walter Bremman of the FBI. They had hoped that Johnny
was one of the men they were looking for. Bremman tells Johnny that Salkoff is

not dead. Bremman reminds Johnny of the Parley Barron case where a scientist had disappeared. Johnny remembers that the reports of his death were to throw off their pals behind the iron curtain and now they have done the same thing with Salkoff. His partner Mike Kruschen is searching the lab. Bremman tells Johnny that there are two groups, agents from behind the iron curtain, that want to get to Salkoff either to get the secrets or to kill him. By reporting him dead, both will think the other did it. Allworth does not know so do not tell him. Drag out your investigation to help us. Bremman tells Johnny that the agents probably already know about Salkoff. Kruschen comes in and tells Bremman that he found nothing in the lab. Mike and Walt leave and tell Johnny he that knows what to do if anyone shows up. Also, tell Allworth that they have been there and will be back. Johnny is confused and then hears their airboat leave, but not by the normal channel, there is something wrong here. Johnny checks his gun but it is empty, and his airboat will not start. Johnny hears another airboat and sees Mack McLaughlin of the FBI and Dr. Allworth. Johnny tells Mack his boys had been there, and Mack gives a description of the two men. Mack tells Johnny that they are the ones who kidnapped and killed Salkoff. Their real names are Bremenoff and Kruchinski, spies and killers from you know where.

Mack gives Allworth a gun and tells him to shoot anyone he does not know. Johnny and Mack take off in the airboat and Johnny tells him what had happened. Mack tells Johnny that the men have not killed Salkoff because they do not have the formula. They did not kill Johnny because they need every option they can get. They left because they could not find the formula and are going back to Salkoff to get it from him. Johnny tells Mack that they even knew about the Parley Barron case, and Mack reminds him that Johnny broadcast it on his radio show. Mack tells Johnny to keep quiet about this case until the space boys can launch a satellite successfully. Back at Ben Osceola's shack they take Mack's well-armed car to chase after the two men. On the road heading south Johnny sees a police car going north and notices the two men are driving it. A fast U-turn and Mack is after them at over 100 MPH. As Mack pulls up, there are shots and Johnny is told to use the tommy gun rather than his lemon squeezer to shoot the tires. Johnny fires and the car hits some cypress trees and the men are dead.

Leon Salkoff, well I am afraid that he gave more than his skill and effort to the country he loved, that had taken him under its wing. His body was found trussed up and floating face down in the bayou from which Bremenoff and Kruchinski had launched the airboat. Dr. Allworth? Now that a US space satellite is carrying out its mission, he is safely and officially working in a government laboratory. Expense account total including incidental and the trip back to Hartford, ah, forget it. If in any way it helped to get the Explorer out in space in orbit, it's on me.

## NOTES:
- CAST INFORMATION FROM RadioGOLDINdex.
- ONCE AGAIN JOHNNY IS USING HIS "LEMON SQUEEZER."

- THE ANNOUNCER IS DAN CUBBERLY
- THE U.S. ARMY PUT AMERICA INTO SPACE BY LAUNCHING THE EXPLORER 1 SATELLITE INTO ORBIT ON JANUARY 31, 1958, SIX WEEKS BEFORE THE JOHNNY DOLLAR STORY. TALK ABOUT FAST WRITING! THE SATELLITE CARRIED A SET OF GEIGER COUNTERS THAT DISCOVERED A ZONE OF RADIATION AROUND THE PLANET KNOWN NOW AS THE VAN ALLEN BELT.

Producer:    Jack Johnstone          Writers:    Jack Johnstone
Cast:        Herb Ellis, Lou Merrill, Stacy Harris, Jack Kruschen, Vic Perrin, Harry Bartell

◆    ❖    ◆

SHOW:          THE DENVER DISBURSAL MATTER
SHOW DATE:     3/23/1958
COMPANY:       PARAMOUNT INSURANCE ADJUSTERS
AGENT:         PERRY JAIMERSON
EXP. ACCT:     $391.80

SYNOPSIS: Perry Jaimerson calls and Johnny accuses Perry of neglecting him. Perry tells Johnny that Four State in Denver has had a lot of large claims on young policies. $60,000 on one policy, $35,000 on another, $70,000 and a cool $150,000. The beneficiary has been the same man. Johnny tells Harry to leave the door open; he is on his way.

Johnny cabs to Perry's office where the door was wide open. Perry has reservations for him on TWA at 6:00 PM and Johnny is to charge is expenses to Paramount. The local agent is William Whitney. Johnny asks how well Perry knows Whitney. Perry tells Johnny that Whitney is a mild type and is not in with Don Ricardo, who was the beneficiary on the policies. Also, Whitney's wife is an ex- chorus girl who probably thought he had more money that he does. Perry is suspicious and is willing to pay Johnny to find out what is going on.

Johnny flies to Denver, Colorado and cabs to the Brown Palace. Johnny calls Pete Packer at the Denver Post newspaper and Pete is ready to help Johnny tie one on. Johnny asks Pete if he knows Don Ricardo. Pete tells Johnny that he does not want to say anything without reason, but Don Ricardo was involved with Capone back in Chicago. Johnny goes to get a drink and gets more information from the bartender about Ricardo. Johnny is told that Ricardo lives well and gives a lot of parties for people from out of town. The bartender spots a well-dressed man and clams up. Johnny leaves and notices he is being watched.

Next morning, Johnny looks up the Four States office on Broadway and meets Whitney. Johnny tells Whitney that the adjusters are concerned about the policies he has paid on. Johnny is told that the policies were issued to some old miners who paid the premiums. Johnny gets the names of the miners and Whitney tells him that clearing up this matter will take a load off of his mind. Whitney has only seen Ricardo when he gave him the checks. Johnny reviews the files, and then takes a cab to Golden. Johnny notices a foreign car following him, but it disappears. At an old frame house Johnny knocks on the door as the cab driver yells to him that the place looks deserted. The door opens and Johnny walks in only to be shot at twice.

The cab driver runs up and sees that Johnny is hit, but it is only a flesh wound. Johnny tells him to get out of the line of fire. A car drives off and the cabby spots it as a black foreign car. Johnny tells the cabby to take him to Millville and the home of Don Ricardo. The cab drops Johnny off at the front gate and drives off. Johnny meets Don Ricardo and introduces himself. Ricardo has been expecting someone like Johnny to call because of his good luck lately. Johnny asks him who paid the premiums on the policy, and Ricardo tells him that the miners did. He had grubstaked them, and they made him his beneficiary. The miners were in their late 60s, and died in mine accidents. Johnny tells Ricardo he was shot at in Golden, and tells Ricardo that "you are a lousy shot." Johnny tells him about the dust on his small car and Ricardo tells him he might be right and pulls a gun on him and they struggle. The police rush in with Pete who tells Johnny he brought the police because he was sure Johnny would find something on Ricardo. Johnny tells him they will go out on the town when he finishes this job.

Johnny and Pete search the house and find the cancelled checks. Johnny "borrows" a car from Ricardo and drives to a house in the south end of town. Johnny gets out and at the front door Johnny hears loud voices and goes to a bedroom window to listen to the Whitneys getting packed to move out. Whitney tells his wife that she would still be in Ricardo's clubs if it were not for him. Back at the front door Johnny knocks and Whitney opens it. Whitney is glad to see Johnny. Johnny notices the bags and Whiney tells Johnny that he had investigated Ricardo, and he is a gangster. He knew that Ricardo would know that Whiney had Johnny investigate him, and he is scared. He is leaving until this thing blows over. Whitney tells Johnny that he is going where Ricardo cannot find him and Johnny adds, "To where I could not find you?" and Whitney says yes. Johnny remembers Whitney leaving him alone earlier, probably to call Ricardo, and shows Whitney the cancelled checks that show that 20% of the insurance policies were paid to Whitney one day after he paid Ricardo. Whitney struggles with Johnny and loses. Johnny tells him his milquetoast behavior may have sold insurance, but it has not sold Johnny.

"Oh, I guess you find them in every trade, but that doesn't justify them being alive though. Fortunately in the insurance business they never get away with it for long, even a team like Whitney and Ricardo. I wonder if they are sharing the same cell?

Expenses include a doctor's bill, and a night on the town with Pete Packard, and a gift to the cab driver.

NOTES:
- JOHNNY IS SHOT FOR THE 8TH TIME
- THE FIRST COMMERCIAL BREAK IS AN AFRS SPOT ABOUT THE FLAG OF VERMONT

- THE SECOND COMMERCIAL BREAK IS AN **AFRS** SPOT ABOUT THE HEROISM OF CPL. RONALD ROSSER IN KOREA
- THE FINAL COMMERCIAL IS ANOTHER **AFRS** SPOT ABOUT THE FLAG OF IDAHO
- THE ANNOUNCER IS DAN CUBBERLY

Producer:   Jack Johnstone        Writers:   Jack Johnstone
Cast:       Virginia Gregg, Forrest Lewis, Barney Phillips, Edgar Barrier, Frank Gerstle, Peter Leeds

◆   ❖   ◆

SHOW:        THE KILLER'S LIST MATTER
SHOW DATE:   3/30/1958
COMPANY:     INTER ALLIED LIFE INSURANCE COMPANY
AGENT:       PAT CUMMINGS
EXP. ACCT:   $146.50

SYNOPSIS: Pat Cummings calls and asks if Johnny has heard of Everett Benton, the New York investor. Pat has a $100,000 policy on him. Last night he fell from a 14th-story window, and Pat thinks he was pushed.

Johnny cabs to Pat's office where Pat tells Johnny that something does not smell right with this case. Benton had been doing well, his company is successful, and now he falls, or is pushed from a window. The beneficiary of the policy is his wife, who is a redhead 12 years younger than Benton.

Johnny travels to New York City and the expensive Benton apartment. Mrs. Benton fixes a drink as they talk. Johnny notes that she is bearing up well. She tells Johnny that they did not have an ideal marriage and she knows that Everett committed suicide. He had no enemies, and will file a claim on the policy in the morning. And, she has an alibi for the other evening, and it is airtight.

Johnny goes to see Lt. Tovich at the police to discuss the case. Johnny is told that the company finances seem to be ok, and Benton was worth a lot of money. Benton had let himself into the office with his own key, and Mrs. Benton was with Larry Santos at his supper club.

Johnny goes to see Santos who is not too friendly. Santos tells Johnny that Mrs. Benton was in his office all night, and that she did not kill Benton. Johnny tells him that maybe Santos killed Benton, and is told to let the matter drop, as publicity is bad for business. Johnny is told he has a nose problem and better get over it; it could be fatal.

Johnny visits Lt. Tovich again and recounts the conversation with Santos. Lt. Tovich tells Johnny that they found a cigarette butt in the office that was different from Benton's. The phone rings and Lt. Tovich is told that Arthur Mayfield has been killed. He fell out of a 10th floor hotel room. Johnny goes to the hotel and nothing was in the room to indicate anyone was with him. Johnny goes to see Mrs. Benton who tells Johnny that she does not know anyone named Mayfield. Mrs. Benton has an alibi for last night too, she was with Larry Santos. Lt. Tovich and Johnny discuss the similarities of the deaths, but there is nothing to connect the two men.

Johnny mulls over the case when someone knocks on his door. A man is there and asks if Johnny is the one investigating the two murders. He tells Johnny that he is Alvin Whiting, and he has information for Johnny. Alvin looks out the window and tells Johnny that three men had bought an oil lease from a man named Tom Nolan. Nolan was eccentric and needed money so he sold the lease to Mayfield and Benton. Whiting feels that the killer is Nolan and he is getting revenge. Oil has just been discovered on the land and the property is worth millions and Noland feels he has been cheated. Whiting was in on the deal; he was the third man, and he is certain he is next.

Johnny takes Whiting to see Lt. Tovich where he tells his story. Lt. Tovich confirms the lease and tells them that Nolan has served time recently. The phone rings and Lt. Tovich gets the hotel where Nolan has been staying. At the hotel the clerk tells Johnny that he has not seen Nolan since he rented the room. They open the door and the room is empty. A cigarette butt is found that matches the one found in Benton's office. The room clerk describes Nolan as a man with a wild look to him. A guard is posted and Johnny reviews Nolan's records. Johnny notices an item in the files and goes back to see Santos. Johnny tells him of the oil lease and Nolan's revenge. Johnny asks Santos why he put up bail for Nolan when he was arrested last. Johnny learns that Nolan is Santos' uncle, and is supposedly harmless. Santos had arranged the lease to get money for his uncle, who was broke. Noland has been living in Coopersville and Santos has not heard from his uncle for six months. Johnny calls Lt. Tovich and learns that Whiting has disappeared. Johnny goes to Coopersville and locates a woman who recognizes the picture of Nolan, but she tells Johnny that the man's name is Niles. He had been living there until last week when he left us. Johnny thinks that is when Nolan went to New York, but the landlady tells Johnny that he left them, he died. Johnny realizes what has happened and goes to the graveyard to find the grave of Tom Niles, right where he had been. A shot rings out and hits Johnny's flashlight. Johnny fires back and hits Alvin Whiting. Alvin tells Johnny that he had to have the money as he was in debt and was desperate. Johnny tells him that he rigged the story to get the money from the lease. Too bad Noland was dead.

Remarks: I turned Whiting over to the police and he made a full statement. Yeah, his motive was money. He was in the hole, gambling debts and bills; the high cost of living you might say. I guess he knows now that it is a real bargain compared to the high cost of dying.

NOTES:
- CAST INFORMATION FROM THE KNX COLLECTION AT THE THOUSAND OAKS LIBRARY.
- THE ANNOUNCER IS DAN CUBBERLY

Producer:  Jack Johnstone          Writers:   Robert Ryf

**Cast:**   Jack Edwards, Virginia Gregg, Jack Moyles, Tony Barrett,
Parley Baer, Carleton G. Young, Lillian Buyeff

◆   ❖   ◆

SHOW:          THE EASTERN-WESTERN MATTER
SHOW DATE:     4/6/1958
COMPANY:       TRI-STATE LIFE & CASUALTY COMPANY
AGENT:         EARLE POORMAN
EXP. ACCT:     $207.00

SYNOPSIS: Earle Poorman calls and Johnny tells him he is ready to grab his fishing rod and come to Florida. Earle tells Johnny to grab his Levis, boots, a saddle and his six-guns. Earle tells Johnny that the freezing weather has hit the cattle ranchers really hard. A rancher has just hit Earle with a $78,000 claim on his entire herd.

Johnny flies to Sarasota, Florida and Earle drives Johnny to the ranch of Bart Trimble. Along the way, Johnny notices how the vegetation is brown and withered. On the ranch Johnny sees dead steers, 525 head in total, rotting in the sun. Earle called Johnny because Trimble had waited a month after the other claims to file his. In the new tidy ranch house Johnny and Earle meet Betty Trimble and Bart, who is expecting a big check from Earl. Bart recognizes Johnny as an insurance investigator, and asks Earle of they suspect him of killing off his herd. He does not like it, and tells them so. Earle tells Trimble that Johnny has to approve the claim before it is paid, and Trimble gets upset. He tells Johnny to poke around all he wants and not to tell him he is a crook. A man named Shorty comes in and tells Bart that the truck for the hides is there, and Bart leaves with Shorty. Mrs. Trimble tells Johnny that Bart had waited so long to file the claim because he was trying to salvage as much as possible. Johnny gets the name of their vet and tells her that the vet will have to look at the animals.

Bart changes his tone at dinner and apologizes for this comments. He had lost so much that he was just angry. Bart tells Johnny that during the last cold spell, he had been trying to get feed for the cattle. They were all bunched up along the fence and would not move. The next morning they were dead. Earle comments that he has seen Shorty somewhere. Johnny is told that Bart and Betty have put everything they had into the ranch, even Betty's money from nursing, and have lost everything. All the hands are gone except Shorty. Johnny asks if they had thought of leaving and Bart tells him that they had thought of going to California and farm there with relatives.

Johnny goes to bed and listens to Earle snoring. Johnny puts a pillow over his head, which almost turns out to be a deadly mistake. Later that night Earle wakes Johnny up and tells him to breath, and the odor of chloroform is all over the pillow. Someone had come in and poured it on Johnny's pillow. Earle recounts to Johnny how he had fallen out of bed and saw someone leaving, and smelled the chloroform and threw Johnny's pillow outside. Earls tells Johnny that he had seen Shorty on a chain gang and remembers him throwing mud on his new 1958 Cadillac. Earle is sure that it was Shorty who put the gas on him. Johnny tells Earle he will handle things. At breakfast the Trimbles are upset over what has happened. They go to the bunkhouse, but Shorty is gone. Betty tells them she never did trust Shorty but Bart says that he was the only one that stayed on when wages his could not be paid. Bart thinks that the chloroform came from a locker in the barn; they had used it to put an old sick horse down. Betty finds a note that Johnny reads; "I'm tired working for no pay. I will leave you know where to send my pay when you collect on that there insurance. Shorty." Bart mentions that Shorty thought that he would collect his pay if he poisoned the herd. Johnny asks if it was poison, now that he has someone to pin it on.

The vet arrives and Johnny, Earle and Bart go out with the vet to inspect the cattle, but they are too badly decomposed to tell anything. The vet notices a pale purple line on a water trough. The vet tastes it and tells them that someone used penorphic acid to kill the herd. The poison is used almost exclusively in laboratory experiments. Johnny goes to the house to call the state police to round up Shorty Skinner. Johnny then calls the local police, and in Lake Wales the police and they have Shorty in their jail. They picked him up last night for vagrancy, and he put his "X" on the police blotter. Johnny sneaks into Mrs. Trimble's bedroom and finds letters from the relatives urging them to come out to California. The letters were addressed to only one of the Trimbles. As Johnny notices a diploma from the Lippenwald School of Nursing, Mrs. Trimble walks in and Johnny tells her that Shorty has served time, and she is sure that he had poisoned the herd. Johnny asks how she is certain now that the herd was poisoned, and she tells Johnny that it was just understood. In response to Johnny's question, Betty tells Johnny that Shorty had given them a home address when he came to work for them. She shows Johnny the paper and Johnny tells her that Shorty cannot write, and the handwriting on the notes matches the handwriting on the return address note. Johnny tells her that she learned of the poison in Nursing School and used the chloroform to try and kill Johnny to blame it on Shorty. Johnny tells her that Shorty was picked up before he had gone to bed. Bart walks in and asks Betty if she killed the herd, and she tells him that she hated this place. Bart would not do anything, so she did, and she failed.

Expense account item 3, $50 to a lawyer at the county seat who took my deposition. It will be used in the trial against Betty Trimble. As for Bart Trimble, well I'm sorry for him.

NOTES:
- CAST INFORMATION FROM RadioGOLDINdex.
- THE ANNOUNCER IS DAN CUBBERLY

| | |
|---|---|
| **Producer:** Jack Johnstone | **Writers:** Jack Johnstone |
| **Cast:** | **Virginia Gregg, Marvin Miller, Herb Vigran, Jack Moyles, Vic Perrin** |

◆ ❖ ◆

| SHOW: | THE WAYWARD MONEY MATTER |
|---|---|
| SHOW DATE: | 4/13/1958 |
| COMPANY: | NORTHEASTERN INDEMNITY ASSOCIATION |
| AGENT: | FRED NORWOOD |
| EXP. ACCT: | $104.70 |

SYNOPSIS: Fred Norwood calls and he has a case for Johnny in Baltimore. Johnny just loves the thought of all that Chesapeake Bay seafood. Fred tells Johnny if he can get them him off the hook on this one, he will approve the expense account blind. Over $100,000 is missing from a safe at the Trillingham Tobacco Company.

Johnny travels to Baltimore, Maryland and the Sheraton Belvedere hotel. Johnny calls Mr. Trillingham, who will see him. Johnny cabs to the company on Charles Street and meets Trillingham. He tells Johnny that someone opened the office safe and took the money. Johnny is told that they keep large amounts of money on hand because the farmers who sell their tobacco demand cash for payment. Also, Johnny is told that business is not as good as Trillingham would like. Trillingham knows who opened the safe. It was Elmer Cockerley the bookkeeper. Johnny is told that Trillingham has just bought the company, and that he made his money in Florida real estate. Trillingham describes Cockerley as a mild, timid man who has been there for 30 years. At tax time Cockerley discovered that some of the records were missing. During that time Cockerley had his house painted, and bought a new car. Johnny tells Trillingham that he should have been called then, but Trillingham tells Johnny that by the end of the year things seems to work out. Johnny learns that Cockerley has not come in today, and did not go home last night. Johnny rents a car and drives to Cockerley's home and discovers a reason why he might have disappeared.

At the front door Johnny is met by Mrs. Cockerley. She is very gruff, and tells Johnny that she has not filed a claim yet, but she will. When she gets the insurance money she will not have that worthless worm under foot anymore. Johnny asks if she knew that the money was missing and she tells Johnny that they are just making due, and if it were not for Beneficial Finance they might not have made it. She had told Elmer if he was not so worthless he would have helped himself to some of that money, but he would just scream like a baby. He had given her the combination to the safe and told her to go ahead and take the money. She tells Johnny to try and put the robbery on her. She shows Johnny a picture of Elmer and calls him a baby. Johnny tells her that there is something behind her gruffness, and that she is trying to cover up for her husband. He needed her to take care of him and make him toe the line, and she liked it. She tells Johnny that she does not know where Elmer is. Johnny is told to ask August Trillingham where he is; they used to go fishing together. The phone rings and Sgt. Macklin is calling for Johnny. Sgt. Macklin tells Johnny that they have found Elmer Cockerley and what is left of the money. Johnny is told to go to Hance's Bridge, about 9 miles north of town so he can identify the body.

Johnny drives to the bridge to meet Sgt. Macklin and wonders, which he always does when there is only one suspect. The wife tried to confuse him, and then here was Trillingham. Sgt. Macklin tells Johnny that most of the money must have floated down the creek, and that Cockerley was driving too fast making his getaway and went into the creek. Johnny identifies the body and notices a scrap of paper in one of Elmer's pockets that says "night Hance cat." Johnny also notices a bruise on Elmer's head, a bruise left by only one thing. Johnny tells Sgt. Macklin to call the coroner and leaves.

At Trillingham's office, he tells Johnny that the money was too much of a temptation for Elmer. Johnny tells him that it was a temptation for any man, including him. Johnny now remembers that Trillingham had sold a lot of swampland in Florida, and is still a crook and a killer. Johnny mentions the note asking Cockerley to go fishing for catfish with him. Johnny tells Trillingham how he met Cockerley there at the bridge, hit him, put him in his car and pushed it into the creek. Johnny tells him about the bruise on the back of Elmer's head from a .38 Special, which Trillingham pulls from his desk. Mrs. Cockerley comes in and accuses Trillingham of killing her husband. Trillingham goes to close the door, and Johnny slugs Trillingham and tells Mrs. Cockerley that Trillingham will pay for it.

Well, so ends another chapter in the dirty history of crime. I hope that the insurance on Elmer makes up in some small way for Mrs. Cockerley's loss of her, well I was going to say husband. But I guess Elmer was kind of a baby to her. To manage, to brow beat, and to love.

NOTES:
- THE FIRST COMMERCIAL BREAK IS AN **AFRS** SPOT ABOUT THE NEED FOR WORK, AND THE BRAVERY OF CAPT. DOUGLAS T. JACOBSON
- THE SECOND COMMERCIAL BREAK IS AN **AFRS** SPOT ABOUT THE FLAG OF ALASKA
- THE FINAL COMMERCIAL BREAK IS AN **AFRS** SPOT ABOUT THE BOXER REBELLION
- THE ANNOUNCER IS DAN CUBBERLY

| | | | |
|---|---|---|---|
| **Producer:** | Jack Johnstone | **Writers:** | Jack Johnstone |
| **Cast:** | Virginia Gregg, Edgar Barrier, Alan Reed, Vic Perrin, Frank Nelson | | |

◆    ❖    ◆

| | |
|---|---|
| **SHOW:** | THE WAYWARD TROUT MATTER |
| **SHOW DATE:** | 4/20/1958 |
| **COMPANY:** | UNIVERSAL ADJUSTMENT BUREAU |

| AGENT: | PAT McCRACKEN |
|---|---|
| EXP. ACCT: | $815.00 |

**SYNOPSIS:** Pat McCracken calls and tells Johnny he has done a magnificent job for the company, and has saved them a lot of money. He wants Johnny to a take a vacation, at company expense, at Lake Mojave Resort where Johnny loves to fish. Johnny will grab the first plane, but tells Pat to wait until he sees the expense account, because if Johnny ever smelled a rat, it is now!

Johnny flies to Las Vegas, rents a car and drives to Lake Mojave Resort. Johnny muses over the travails of the early explorers as he drives a long at 60 MPH. Johnny arrives and meets Buster Favor, who tells Johnny that the fish are really biting. Johnny is rooming next to Gordon Hatch, an old time confidence man who was never nailed for doing anything big. Buster tells Johnny that he and Ham would have told Hatch they were full up, but figure they are doing a public service by having Johnny come here. Buster got a call on Tuesday from some wealthy folks from Los Angeles, and Tuesday afternoon Hatch came busting in. The people from Los Angeles have been here before, and their wives always bring a lot of furs and jewelry. They also bring a lot of cash so they can go up to Vegas to gamble at night. One of the guests is a lawyer who got Hatch sent up. Hatch swore he would get even, but Buster does not think he would do anything rough. There is no insurance angle unless some of the jewelry disappears. Gordon Hatch walks in and tells Buster about the 10 pound fish he caught and is keeping in a live box. Even the worst crook in the world would not touch another man's catch. Hatch invites Johnny to come to his room for a drink and Johnny tries to beg off but goes to the room to size up Hatch and talk about fishing. Hatch does tell Johnny that his past is past and that he is trying to make amends. Johnny drinks a nightcap and goes back to his room and passes out, victim to the oldest trick in the world, and anything could happen before he wakes up.

Johnny wakes up in the morning when Buster pounds on his door at 9:00. Buster tells Johnny that Hatch is out fishing, and the guests have arrived. Johnny tells Buster that Hatch claims to have turned over a new leaf. Buster tells Johnny that Hatch may not be after Mr. Fellers after all. Johnny has a bad headache from a Mickey the night before, but goes to join Buster in the café for breakfast where the other anglers are bragging about their morning exploits. Mrs. Feller rushes in and tells Buster that all their jewelry has been stolen, along with their money. Someone broke into the cabins and stole everything. Ham Pratt walks in and learns of the thefts. Johnny tells Ham to search Hatch's room and car while he and Buster go for a boat ride.

Johnny and Buster take a boat and find Hatch in a deep cove. Buster sees Hatch doing something near his boat. When they beach their boat, Johnny and Buster are told by Hatch that he has moved his live box. In the box, Johnny sees a bunch of bass and a dead trout on the bottom. Hatch tells Johnny that he is going to leave later to get the trout mounted in Los Angeles. Johnny want to talk to Hatch, but Hatch tells Johnny that he wants to keep their fishing date, so Buster loans Johnny a rod and reel. They walk back to Buster's boat and Buster tells Johnny that there is nothing in Hatch's boat. Suddenly Johnny has an idea, and wants another look at the trout. Johnny wonders why the trout is not floating on the surface belly-up. Johnny pulls out the 10-pound trout, and it must weigh 20 lbs. because the trout is stuffed full of jewels and cash! Hatch pulls a gun and tells Johnny to put the jewels in his boat, so Johnny offers Hatch the whole fish and slugs him with the wet trout.

The expense account includes the cost of five days of really great fishing.

NOTES:
- THIS STORY MENTIONS FAST STRIKE MINNOW HOOKS, WHICH WERE INVENTED BY JACK JOHNSTONE
- THIS IS AN AFRS PROGRAM WITH NO COMMERCIAL BREAKS OR CREDITS
- CAST INFORMATION FROM THE KNX COLLECTION AT THE THOUSAND OAKS LIBRARY.
- THE ANNOUNCER IS DAN CUBBERLY

Producer:  Jack Johnstone          Writers:  Jack Johnstone
Cast:      Lawrence Dobkin, Alan Reed, Russell Thorson, Edgar Barrier, Junius Matthews, Barney Phillips, Eleanor Audley

◆  ❖  ◆

SHOW:        THE VILLAGE OF VIRTUE MATTER
SHOW DATE:   4/27/1958
COMPANY:     CONTINENTAL INSURANCE COMPANY
AGENT:       BEN ORLOFF
EXP. ACCT:   $100.00

SYNOPSIS: Ben Orloff calls and asks if Johnny has ever heard of a place called Virtue. "Do you mean Virtue, South Carolina? You want me to go down there?" "Yes, if you will." "Do you have a bulletproof vest and a couple of extra handguns I can take along?" "My one suggestion is that you do not take along any firearms. Our agent has an office in Georgetown. His name is Joseph Picatello." "Smokey Picatello, the guy that was linked with Murder Incorporated a few years back? I tell you this, Mr. Orloff, if you do not have to pay off on my insurance policy before I'm through, well mister this is going to cost you a whopping big expense account."

Johnny travels to Georgetown, South Carolina and goes to see Joe Picatello. Joe tells Johnny that he used to be a bright young punk and studied law, but gave up law when Dewey took over New York and broke up the rackets. Joe tells Johnny that in spite of his past, he is clean. Joe tells Johnny that he better be careful with his clients or he could be plain wrong, or dead wrong. Joe tells Johnny that some of the boys saved their money and leased the old Caraway plantation near Virtue on the Pee Dee River. They all went respectable, and it has been 20 years now. Joe signed up with the insurance company and talked the boys into buying insurance and has policies on everyone, including the town. The problem is that Buddy McGoon had his fishing boat stolen. Mr. Avery, who runs the general store, had his boat stolen too. Ever since then somebody has had something stolen every day. The people blame the boys, and the boys blame the people. Joe tells Johnny that there is going to be civil war unless you can stop this and the company will be in trouble with the losses, so he sent for Johnny. Joe tells Johnny to take off his lemon squeezer and they will go to Virtue to check out the situation.

Joe and Johnny drive to the Caraway plantation, which is full of flowers and a fine old mansion. Johnny and Joe are shot at and Joe yells at the boys so he can identify himself. Joe introduces Johnny to "Bull" McGoon, "Lefty" Stemper and "Flippy" Lacavitch who takes Johnny's gun. Lefty does not want Johnny there and tells him they will find their own stuff, like in the old days. Johnny asks for his gun back, and Flippy threatens Johnny, so Johnny puts a judo flip on Flippy and gets his gun back. Johnny tells them he will try to stop what is going on, and will bring in the police if necessary. Lefty tells Johnny that the boys are nervous after what has been going on. Lefty tells Johnny that they only have their hunting weapons, and Johnny tells them that the police will be there if anything happens to him. Johnny tells them he will have them thrown off of the plantation, and they start to cooperate. Johnny is told that the boys all love the plantation, and have been straight. But now after 20 years the people are after them. Johnny is told that Mr. Caraway, who owns the plantation, is the mayor of Virtue and the chief of police. Joe and Johnny leave to visit Caraway. In Virtue Johnny finds a quiet town, with no hint of hostility. Johnny tells Joe that he hopes the boys continue to believe that he has protected himself.

Johnny finds Parley Caraway, the mayor, who is police chief, and who has not found out who is stealing the things, but he is sure that the gangsters on the plantation are responsible. He tells Johnny and Joe that he will have to evict them if the trouble does not stop. Johnny is told that the boys have started making the plantation a paying proposition. Johnny notices a diamond ring and a new car outside, which belong to the mayor. He tells Joe that he tries to have a new car every year. Caraway tells Johnny that he can take care of things by himself. Johnny notes that he has made lot of money from the plantation, and Caraway slips and tells Johnny that he has been offered $124,000 for the plantation. Johnny now knows that the mayor has been robbing the people to rile everyone up so that he can have the boys thrown out. Johnny threatens to call the state police and have Caraway locked up and to have Joe bring fraud charges. Caraway tells Johnny that all the stolen property is safe and stored away, and Johnny tells him he will call in the police unless Caraway returns the stolen goods and lets the boys continue their lease. Johnny leaves to go to the plantation to have a drink with some "respectable" people.

"Yea, this insurance business really has some funny ones. And I guess it is the funny ones that balance out the bad, tragic cases. Anyhow, I like it. Expense account total including the trip back to Hartford, uh call it $100 even. And in view of our little secret Joe, maybe you better pay it out of petty cash! And those pals of yours, you better drop in on them to make sure that they say on the straight an narrow, as well as that old coot Caraway."

NOTES:

- THERE IS ANOTHER REFERENCE TO JOHNNY'S "LEMON SQUEEZER," CARRIED IN A SHOULDER HOLSTER
- THE ANNOUNCER IS DAN CUBBERLY

Producer:    Jack Johnstone          Writers:    Jack Johnstone
Cast:        Frank Nelson, Billy Halop, Jack Kruschen, Peter Leeds,
             Gil Stratton, Will Wright

◆    ❖    ◆

SHOW:           THE CARSON ARSON MATTER
SHOW DATE:      5/4/1958
COMPANY:        WORLDWIDE MUTUAL INSURANCE COMPANY
AGENT:          JIM PARIS
EXP. ACCT:      $56.90

SYNOPSIS: Jim Paris calls and Johnny tells him he can smell the smoke from his apartment. Jim tells Johnny that the Cash and Save Market has burned. Jim wants Johnny to look closely at the store, it is part of a chain, and this is the fourth store to go up in as many weeks. The owner is John Wakefield Carson.

Johnny cabs to Jim's office in Hartford, Connecticut but learns little, other than getting a list of the stores that have burned. The coverage is for $106,000 on the latest store. Carson has his office in Boston, and his latest store is there also. Johnny cabs to the scene of the fire, and the building is a total loss. Johnny notes that the store is as far as possible from a fire station. Johnny meets Hal Gibbons of the arson squad who tells Johnny that something inflammable had been used to start the fire. Hal tells Johnny that the other stores were far from a fire department as well. Carson has never showed up at any of the fires, he just files a claim. Carson is a millionaire who likes to quote from the classics.

Margaret Carson shows up and is introduced to Johnny who she recognizes by name. Margaret introduces Walter Smitten, the company lawyer who wants nothing to do with the grocery business. He feels that someone is trying to put Carson out of business. Margaret leaves to file a claim, and Johnny wonders about Walter's intentions to marry Margaret and get to her money.

Johnny calls Jim Paris to get information on the policies. Jim calls back and Johnny gets a list of the markets and the store with the next largest coverage, which is in Salem. Johnny cabs to his apartment and drives to Salem, Massachusetts and the local Cash and Save Market. At the store Johnny spots a man in the back of the building. Johnny hears someone enter the building and follows him into the storeroom. Johnny turns on the lights and calls to the man and is hit by a falling object.

Johnny wakes up in the Salem police department and learns that he was hit with a gallon jug of pickles. Johnny learns that Mr. Carson was the man who hit him, and brought him to the police.

Johnny drives to the Boston office and meets with Carson. He tells Johnny that the fires were set in the order of value, and he had been at the Salem store to inspect the store to prevent spontaneous combustion. Johnny tells him that the fires were set, and Johnny thinks Carson had them set. Johnny asks if Carson is going to rebuild his stores in areas more convenient to the new real estate developments. Carson tells him that he will do what he wants with the insurance money. Johnny tells Carson that he knows who set the fires and leaves.

Johnny calls Hal Gibbons, who tells Johnny that the Hartford fire was arson started by an amateur, as were the other fires. Hal tells Johnny that Walter Smitten could not have started the fires, or Margaret the stepdaughter. Johnny tells Hal to send the police to Carson's office and goes there to try a bluff.

In the office, Johnny tells Carson that he will be taken to court unless he talks. Carson tells Johnny that he likes Walter Smitten like a son. But, he has a stepdaughter, and he had promised his wife that all money from the business is to go to Margaret, and he regrets that promise. Margaret has made too many monetary demands of him since becoming of age. Carson would distrust her every move were it not for Walter. She demands that he be in love with her to use his legal skills to take the stores away from him. Johnny tells Carson that he has proof that Margaret has started the fires, and Carson is relieved. Margaret comes in with a gun and tells Johnny that he should make a deal with her. Johnny tells her that a man from the police is behind her but she tells Johnny that it is a bluff, until the police shoot the gun from her hand.

"Yeah, the company will not have to pay on the four markets, and the courts will have to deal with Margaret. I am sure they will. And next time, well give me something clean to work on, I hate this kind of stuff."

NOTES:
- CAST INFORMATION FROM THE KNX COLLECTION AT THE THOUSAND OAKS LIBRARY.
- THE ANNOUNCER IS DAN CUBBERLY

Producer: Jack Johnstone       Writers: Jack Johnstone
Cast: Byron Kane, Harry Bartell, Virginia Gregg, Jack Edwards, Joe Kearns, Forrest Lewis

◆ ❖ ◆

SHOW: THE ROLLING STONE MATTER
SHOW DATE: 5/11/1958
COMPANY: UNIVERSAL ADJUSTMENT BUREAU
AGENT: PAT MCCRACKEN
EXP. ACCT: $146.00
SYNOPSIS: Pat McCracken calls Johnny and he has $75,000 on his mind. Have you ever heard of the Savalla Diamond? "Yeah, matter of fact I have." It is a pink Diamond." Pat tells Johnny that the owner is trying to sell the diamond, but it was stolen last night.

Johnny cabs to Pat's office where Pat updates Johnny. Johnny then travels to New York City and the apartment of Joseph Wentworth, the owner of the diamond. Wentworth tells Johnny he had been hit on the head and had borrowed heavily to get the stone. The insurance will barely cover the loans, as the diamond was not insured for its full value. Wentworth had a customer who was going to pay $100,000 for it. Eloise Barns, his fiancée, had come by for dinner and Wentworth was putting the diamond into his safe when he was hit. Eloise came back up to the apartment and woke him up. Wentworth has known Eloise for a year. Johnny cabs to Eloise Barns' apartment, where she looks more expensive than the diamond. Eloise tells Johnny that she was looking for a cab when Wentworth was hit. She does not care for diamonds, only money or mink. Eloise tells Johnny that Wentworth is not her fiancé as she is not the "engaged" type. It interferes with her hobby, having fun, and she hopes Johnny finds the diamond real soon.

Johnny goes to see Gerald Mantel, the customer for the diamond. Mantel tells Johnny that he was stalemated over the price and knows what the diamond is worth. He wants the diamond recovered by Friday because he is leaving for Europe on an impulse. Anything wrong with that?

Johnny reviews the case in his room and is called by a man who asks if he is looking for the Savalla Diamond. He knows where it is, and wants money for the information. He will show Johnny it's case to prove he knows where the stone is. Johnny goes to Antonio's Bar and waits for the caller to arrive, when Eloise comes in. Johnny sits with Eloise and then Mr. Mantel arrives. Johnny is told that they have been friends for years, and Eloise is the one who told Mantel about the diamond. The waiter signals for Mantel and he leaves. Eloise tells Johnny that she is only having a drink with Mantel while she waits for Wentworth. She tells Johnny that Mantel is very impulsive and she thinks they both have been stood up. Johnny starts to leave when Wentworth comes in. As Wentworth tells Johnny that he has spent too much time with Eloise, Johnny is paged and the waiter gives Johnny a package that was given to him by a stocky man in a gray suit. The note on the package tells Johnny "Couldn't take a chance contacting you, someone was following me. Contents of the package will show you I know what I am talking about. Will contact you later." In the package is the empty case that Wentworth had kept the diamond in. On the way to the corner for a cab Johnny spots a body in an alley; it is Mantel.

Johnny slaps Mantel awake and he tells Johnny that a cab driver was waiting for him. He went out and no one was there. Johnny suggests that Mantel had stolen the diamond and someone was trying to get it back from him. He swears he does not know where the diamond is. Johnny goes to his hotel to think when Wentworth comes to his room. He apologizes for flying off the handle about Eloise. A man had called Wentworth at this apartment and would tell him where the diamond is for a price. Wentworth tells Johnny that he heard an operator say "Hotel Maysfield" in the background.

Johnny goes to the Hotel Maysfield and learns that the man was named Krause but he had left. Johnny looks in the room and finds a note pad with the imprint of the Cathcart Hotel on it. Johnny goes to the hotel and goes to Krause's room. Johnny tricks him into admitting that he had talked to Wentworth, and Johnny figures that the robbery was staged and Wentworth was using Johnny to find Krause. Wentworth comes in and mentions blackmail. Johnny tells them that Krause was supposed to turn the stone over, but instead tried to blackmail Wentworth about the fake robbery and called Johnny to frighten Wentworth. Wentworth tells Krause he made a mistake blackmailing a desperate man, as he has no money. He needed the money for Eloise to hold on to her. He is willing to add murder to keep Eloise. Johnny tells Wentworth that Eloise only wants mink and money and takes the gun from Wentworth. Wentworth tells Johnny that he was right about him.

Remarks: Krause handed over the diamond. He and Wentworth are both in custody. It was Wentworth who beat up Mantel for hanging around Eloise. An Eloise, last I hear she was going her merry way, having fun she called it. I never did accept her offer to join her after the diamond was recovered and I am not about to.

NOTES:
- THE PROGRAM I HAVE IS SPLICED OVER ITSELF SEVERAL TIMES WITH NO CREDITS AT THE END.
- CAST INFORMATION FROM THE KNX COLLECTION AT THE THOUSAND OAKS LIBRARY.
- ROY ROWAN IS THE ANNOUNCER

Producer:   Jack Johnstone        Writers:   Robert Stanley
Cast:       Lawrence Dobkin, Forrest Lewis, Virginia Gregg, Edgar
            Barrier, Don Diamond

◆   ❖   ◆

SHOW:          THE GHOST TO GHOST MATTER
SHOW DATE:     5/18/1958
COMPANY:       STATE UNITY LIFE INSURANCE COMPANY
AGENT:         OSCAR M. TRIMLEY
EXP. ACCT:     $31.50

SYNOPSIS: Art Price calls Johnny very early in the morning. Art has received a call from an insurance man who wanted Johnny's phone number. He said it was a big emergency and probably called the first person he thought of.

Johnny is called by Oscar M. Trimley, who is in Lake City, New Jersey. He is upset and wants Johnny to come there right away. Ian McAndrews, the man who founded Lake City is dead, or rather he isn't. Anyway, he died five years ago. The $55,000 life policy was paid off, but you have to come here. Ian McAndrews has come back, or his ghost has come back. Johnny tells Trimley he will think about it, and starts making plans to travel to Lake City so he can catch the ghost off-guard. Johnny calls Art and updates him. Johnny then calls Nancy Turner, who investigates the supernatural. Nancy tells Johnny that she has given up the supernatural. Johnny tells her that he has to go to New Jersey to investigate a haunted town, and Nancy tells Johnny that she is going with him. Johnny and Nancy travel to New York City and rent a car for the drive to New Jersey. Nancy talks the whole way about her studies about the supernatural, and Johnny is almost convinced.

Lake City is a small quiet has-been town in northern Jersey, which was based on a mill that has closed. Johnny locates Trimley's office where Johnny and Nancy are introduced to Charlie Reed, Bill Foster and Tony Greg who are members of a businessmen's club in town. They tell Johnny that they are worried about this thing. Johnny is told that he will have to see and hear what is going on at midnight. Charlie fixes up Johnny and Nancy with a boat and fishing equipment, while Charlie goes to get rooms for them. Everyone is mum about what is going on and Johnny thinks that there is something screwy going on.

After an afternoon of fishing, Johnny and Nancy meet with the others for dinner at the hotel where the talk is about Johnny's fishing. Later, Tony drives Johnny and the others to the middle of town where the things are about to happen. As the clock chimes, Johnny is told that old McAndrews died at midnight. Suddenly the lights dim, bats fly from the clock tower and the town is filled with an eerie wail as the clock chimes 13.

Johnny goes to the McAndrews' house where the open door slams in their faces. Johnny goes in with a flashlight and hears footsteps and all sorts of noises. Suddenly they see a green light moving outside and a rocking chair rocking. Johnny looks at the chair and finds no wires or strings and the noises stop. Johnny tells everyone that he wants to investigate in the daylight.

The next day Johnny is helped by the others as he inspects everything and finds nothing other than the town being mobbed with people. A man takes a picture of Johnny and Johnny recognizes him as a New York reporter. Johnny tells them that he is leaving and drives out of town to wait for nightfall. Johnny sneaks back to Oscar's office where they are all talking about notes inviting them to Oscar's office. Johnny is spotted and tells them that too much help was handicapping him. They tell Johnny that they just wanted to make sure that Johnny did not overlook anything. Johnny tells them that the ghost is no more and that it is one of them. Johnny tells them that he has found the sub-cellar in the McAndrews house with all of the complicated electrical equipment that was making the sound effects. Bill admits to making the equipment. Johnny tells them that it was a wonderful stunt, especially after the press was notified and everyone would benefit from the publicity. Johnny tells them that he will not give them away as long as the ghost of Ian McAndrews never walks the streets again.

"I don't know. I suppose I ought to really hit you over the head with this expense account. But, uh, after all the cause was a kind of a worthy one. So I will be honest with it for a change. And it was fun to have Nancy Turner along."

NOTES:

- THE FIRST COMMERCIAL BREAK IS AN **AFRS** SPOT ABOUT THE FLAG OF KANSAS
- THE SECOND COMMERCIAL BREAK IS AN **AFRS** SPOT ABOUT THE WILLIAM B. HALLITBURON'S ACTIONS ON OKINAWA DURING WORLD WAR II
- THE THIRD COMMERCIAL BREAK IS AN **AFRS** SPOT ABOUT THE FLAG OF NORTH DAKOTA
- CHARLIE MENTIONS "FAST STRIKE" HOOKS, WHICH WERE AN INVENTION OF JACK JOHNSTONE.
- NEXT WEEK'S PROGRAM IS BILLED AS THE MOST DANGEROUS, EXCITING INCIDENT IN JOHNNY'S CAREER.
- THE ANNOUNCER IS ROY ROWAN

Producer: Jack Johnstone    Writers: Jack Johnstone
Cast:    Virginia Gregg, Forrest Lewis, Joseph Kearns, Russell Thorson, Sam Edwards, Bob Bruce

◆ ❖ ◆

SHOW:    THE MIDNIGHT SUN MATTER
SHOW DATE:    5/25/1958
COMPANY:    NORTHWEST SURETY COMPANY
AGENT:    BILL CHADWICK
EXP. ACCT:    $600.00

SYNOPSIS: Bill Chadwick calls from Seattle and asks if Johnny has ever fallen under the spell of the Yukon. Bill has a mine that he would like Johnny to take a look at. It is a gold mine in Alaska. Come on out and bring your gun.

Johnny flies to Seattle, Washington on a Mainliner and goes to Bill's office. Bill tells Johnny that the men who moil for gold are a pretty tough bunch. Even the management at the Universal Consolidated Mining Corporation can be tough. Universal is located north of Fairbanks, above the Arctic Circle. The mine is located at the foot of a glacier, and the glacier is changing its course. They seem to think that the glacier is going to sweep over the mine and town and leave the company with a big claim. Bill wonders if the company might be causing the glacier to change course because the gold has run out. Johnny thinks that it is a far-fetched theory, but Bill wonders why the glacier would change course all of a sudden and head for some well-insured property. Johnny arranges to fly out the next morning on a company plane, a two-engine Speedcraft Transport. Johnny gets a room at the Benjamin Franklin hotel, and after a night on the town Johnny goes to a tiny airport and wonders why there is no one on the plane but him and the pilot. Yup, he should have wondered.

Johnny goes to the airport and meets Cliff Murray and they take off and Johnny learns he is the co-pilot. Johnny notes that the only things he has flown since the war have been piper cubs. Cliff tells Johnny that these planes are really easy to fly. They took off from the remote airport because of the cargo and to save time. The miners are worried, and there have been some ice quakes this spring. The engineers think they can change the glacier, and Cliff is carrying the TNT for the job. Johnny flies the plane for a while and they land at Anchorage for food. After taking off again Cliff starts to experience pains in his stomach. Cliff calls the mine airstrip and alerts them of their course. As the pains grow worse, Cliff tells Johnny to take over. Cliff tells Johnny that he will have to land the plane, and he can do it.

Johnny is too busy to make notes on the rest of the flight, so the airport records make up the rest of the report.

2:35—Johnny calls the tower and tells them that Cliff is sick. Cliff manages to tell them that they cannot dump the TNT because Johnny cannot leave the controls. The tower gives Johnny heading instructions from the Snake River marker, and they will wait for the plane. Johnny calls for an engineer and tells Paul Foster that the landing gear will not come down. Johnny will try to use centrifugal force to get it to come down, and might have to make a belly landing. Charlie tells Johnny that during a fly-by he saw that the landing door is partially open and Johnny is told to fly off the fuel.

2:41—Paul asks Johnny if he has tried to shear the lock pin on the gear, and Johnny has not tried that, and has full hydraulic pressure. Paul tells Johnny that he might have to go to Fairbanks if he needs to make a belly landing, but Cliff has told Johnny that they would not want him to go there because of the cargo.

2:50—Don Wilkins the chief engineer asks if Johnny has tried cycling the gear handle, and Johnny tells him he has. Don tells him to continue trying.

3:00—Paul asks about the fuel, and Johnny still has 950 pounds, and Fairbanks is backed up and cannot take him. Don tells Johnny to feather the #2 engine and try to snap the gear down as he un-feathers it, but Johnny has tried that. Paul tells Johnny that they will ready the strip for a belly landing. Don asks Johnny to unload the hydraulic system and free fall the landing gear, but Johnny has tried that.

3:28—Paul tells Johnny that they are going to foam the runway to reduce the friction and prevent fire. Johnny is told to make a pass over the runway to get the feel of it.

3:31—Don asks Johnny to raise the gear handle and then slam it down and hold it there.

3:46—Johnny is told they are laying foam and he should be ready to land at 3:55.

3:51—Paul asks Johnny how things are and Johnny asks if there is a doctor for Cliff. Johnny is told not to feather the engines when he sets down. Johnny tells them that he will make a final pass and Don tells Johnny that Paul will talk him down.

3:54—Johnny makes a wheels-up landing. The doctor reports that Cliff had a successful appendectomy.

A hard-bitten bunch of miners did you say? Those boys up in that lonely outpost are the salt of the earth. And as for trying to pull something on your insurance company, well you should have seen how just one good load of TNT put that glacier back on its course. Yes sir, I hope that the vein of gold never runs out for those boys.

Expenses include gifts for the boys in the tower.

NOTES:

- THE FIRST COMMERCIAL BREAK IS AN **AFRS** SPOT ABOUT THE FLAG OF LOUISIANA
- THE SECOND COMMERCIAL BREAK IS AN **AFRS** SPOT ABOUT THE NATIONAL FLAG AND THE CONGRESSIONAL MEDAL OF HONOR, AND WHAT THEY STAND FOR
- THE FIRST COMMERCIAL BREAK IS AN **AFRS** SPOT ABOUT THE FLAG OF OREGON
- THIS STORY IS BASED ON A REAL EVENT, AND WAS DRAMATIZED BY JACK JOHNSTONE FOR A CONVENTION OF AIRLINE PILOTS WITH JIMMY STEWART PLAYING THE PART OF THE PILOT
- THE ANNOUNCER IS ROY ROWAN

**Producer:** Jack Johnstone     **Writers:** Jack Johnstone
**Cast:** Jean Tatum, Frank Nelson, Russell Thorson, Barney Phillips, Harry Bartell, Forrest Lewis

◆  ❖  ◆

**SHOW:** THE FROWARD FISHERMAN MATTER
**SHOW DATE:** 6/1/1958
**COMPANY:** CONTINENTAL INSURANCE & TRUST
**AGENT:** CLARK THORNESS
**EXP. ACCT:** $181.00

**SYNOPSIS:** Clark Thorness calls Johnny from Fort Wayne, Indiana, and he wants Johnny to come and see him. Clark asks Johnny if he knows Bertram R. Halsworthy, the fisherman. He has disappeared and a claim has been filed on his $160,000 policy. Clark wants Johnny to find him.

Johnny catches a mainliner to Fort Wayne and goes to Clark's office. Johnny is told that Bert Halsworthy lives in Angola, near Lake James and invented some fishing tackle. Johnny asks if it was the Fast Strike hook, and is told that some guy on the East Coast invented that. Johnny is told that Bert left in February for the Gulf of Mexico and came back in April, only to leave again. The police have investigated and have learned nothing.

Johnny drives to Angola to see the widow and she is sure that Bert is dead. He loved to fish in salt water, and they were not happy. Johnny is told that Bert took about $1,000 with him when he left in February. He sent postcards and came back once to get more money and left a note on the freezer.

Johnny goes to see Lt. Bascomb in Ft. Wayne and sees the note: "Be home one of these days, maybe. Meanwhile, going back to get more of these beauties. You will be happier with me away, Martha, so will I. Bert." Johnny learns that the fish were stripped bass, but the season is too early for them, and Lt. Bascomb has checked everywhere. He is sure that Martha killed Bert. Johnny tells Lt. Bascomb that strippers are running now in California, so Lt. Bascomb will check there. Johnny talks to the family attorney who tells Johnny that Bert was a froward fisherman, and maybe it was his wife's fault. Johnny checks on the wife, and is sure that she is not guilty of killing Bert. Johnny checks with Lt. Bascomb who tells him that the fish are the only clue, but strippers are not running now. Lt. Bascomb tells Johnny that Dr. Kindle at the University could probably tell them how long the fish had been in the freezer.

Johnny leaves and runs into Emmett Gowan, a sports writer who is looking for Lake James. Emmett tells Johnny that he met Bert last winter, and that he was a real non-conformist; he would use the wrong bait in the right place and catch fish.

Johnny drives through the night to get to Lake Moultrie in Columbia, South Carolina. At the lake Johnny meets an old man with a load of fish. The man tells Johnny that strippers have been released into two lakes in South Carolina, Moultrie and Monroe, and that soon everyone will know about them. The man tells Johnny that he just like to do things differently. Bert tells Johnny that his wife henpecks him too much. He thinks that if he makes her worry, she will be more tolerant of him, and maybe they can be happy like they used to be.

Johnny sees Mrs. Halsworthy in a fishing magazine, holding a 9-pound pike she caught in Lake James.

NOTES:
- THE ANNOUNCER IS ROY ROWAN
- EMMETT GOWAN IS ALSO IN "THE LUST FOR GOLD MATTER" AS A RETIRED FISHING GUIDE.
- FROWARD IS DEFINED AS STUBBORN OR CONTRARY.
- THIS STORY IS COMMONLY AND INCORRECTLY CALLED "THE FORWARD FISHERMAN."
- ANGOLA, INDIANA IS IN EXTREME NORTHEAST INDIANA, AND LAKE JAMES IS ALMOST ON THE MICHIGAN BORDER.
- STORY INFORMATION OBTAINED FROM THE KNX COLLECTION IN THE THOUSAND OAKS LIBRARY

| | | | |
|---|---|---|---|
| **Producer:** | Jack Johnstone | **Writers** | Jack Johnstone |
| **Cast:** | Byron Kane, Virginia Gregg, Harry Bartell, Will Wright, Forrest Lewis, Howard McNear | | |

| | |
|---|---|
| SHOW: | THE WAYWARD RIVER MATTER |
| SHOW DATE: | 6/8/1958 |
| COMPANY: | CONTINENTAL INSURANCE & TRUST COMPANY |
| AGENT: | LEE HARKINS |

EXP. ACCT:     **$100.00**

**SYNOPSIS:** Lee Harkins calls and Johnny wonders if he is still in Ohio, and wonders if the fishing is as great as he remembers. Lee tells Johnny that the Ohio is on the rampage and it is still raining hard. Lee needs Johnny to come out, but any fishing will be for the bodies of people.

Johnny travels to Cleveland in the rain and is met by Lee in the airport. They are on the way to Carterette, Ohio and Lee tells Johnny it has been raining for four weeks. Lee tells Johnny that he is from Carterette, and has sold a lot of policies to the shopkeepers there, but you never hear about the small communities in the news. Carterette has been lucky so far as the rains were elsewhere, so the flood control project has not been handled properly. Carterette is in a valley on the Crooked River, and some of the town is below the river. If the levees break, the town will be lost. Lee received a call from Fred Norlock, and he will lose everything unless the river goes down.

Johnny notices how the streams are all over the banks and it starts to rain as they get to Carterette, where everyone is working to build up the levee with sandbags. Johnny describes how the river, full of flotsam and debris, is ready to tear everything apart. Johnny notices how a railroad trestle is clogged by debris and causing the river to back up. But how to break up the dam?

Johnny asks Lee about getting dynamite and Lee tells him that Fred Norlock has it. Norlock is the only one working on his own property and Lee tells Johnny that Norlock has opposed the flood control program. Johnny goes to the hardware store and Lee tells Norlock that he should be working on the levee. Lee asks for dynamite and Norlock tells Johnny he is crazy. Norlock will not give Johnny the dynamite, so Johnny pulls his gun and demands the explosives. Norlock relents and Johnny gets what he needs.

Lee and two workers go with Johnny to the trestle. Johnny elects himself to go out on the trestle and plant a case of dynamite on it. The job is done and the dynamite is set off and the trestle goes up and releases the water and saves the town.

The dam is broken, the town is saved, the people go home, and the rain stops in defeat. Johnny and Lee go back to town and rest in the local hotel. Johnny cannot sleep but worries and frets over why one person had worked so hard to save his own things and not help the town. Johnny wakes up Lee and asks about Norlock's business, and Lee tells Johnny that Norlock has $100,000 in coverage. Johnny tells Lee that $100,000 is too much for a town the size of Carterette. Johnny is convinced that Norlock knew about the dam and went through the motions to save his property. And why did he fight them from getting the dynamite? Johnny is convinced that Norlock wanted the levee to break. Johnny goes to look for Norlock and finds him by the river with a case of dynamite. Johnny tells him that the river did not do what he wanted it to, and Norlock tells Johnny he will kill him if he comes closer. Norlock is going to set off a small charge to break the levee and destroy the town. Johnny is told to walk to the river and Lee calls him. Norlock shoots, but Johnny fires back and Norlock is thrown into the river and disappears.

"Norlock's body was never recovered. He'd lived alone, he died alone. A crooked man in the Crooked River. Nor was he mourned in the little town he tried to destroy."

NOTES:
- THE FIRST COMMERCIAL BREAK IS AN **AFRS** SPOT ABOUT THE BELLWETHERS, WHICH TALKS ABOUT SAFETY AND CAR ACCIDENTS
- THE SECOND COMMERCIAL BREAK IS AND **AFRS** SPOT ABOUT EINSTEIN AND HIS DISTRUST OF HITLER
- TOM HANLEY AND BILL JAMES ARE MENTIONED FOR THEIR SPECIAL SOUND PATTERNS.
- THE ANNOUNCER IS ROY ROWAN

**Producer:** Jack Johnstone        **Writers:** Jack Johnstone
**Cast:**       Chet Stratton, Frank Gerstle, Bob Bruce, Parley Baer

◆  ❖  ◆

**SHOW:**       THE DELECTABLE DAMSEL MATTER
**SHOW DATE:** 6/15/1958
**COMPANY:**    MONO GUARANTEE INSURANCE COMPANY
**AGENT:**      RALPH SINGLE
**EXP. ACCT:**  $230.00

SYNOPSIS: Ralph Single calls from Hollywood and asks if Johnny knows who Hildegard Ransom is? Johnny recognizes her as a debutante and asks if Ralph was not going with her sometime back. He was, but he threw her over because of her crazy antics. Want a date with her? Come on out here and you can have a date with her, at company expense.

Johnny flies to Los Angeles, California on a DC-7 Mainliner. Single is a good name for Rip, who has a knack for meeting wealthy important people, particularly women and then sells them insurance. Johnny is not surprised that Rip knows Hilde Ransom, heir to a fortune, but he has not mentioned why he wanted Johnny to meet her. Rip tells Johnny that he can live off the premiums on Hildegard's account. Rip drives Johnny to the hotel in his little old truck, a brand new El Dorado Biarritz, with gold fittings and all the accessories, including a bar. Rip asks Johnny if he has ever heard of the Cape Star, an emerald in a gold brooch with diamonds worth $300,000. Hildegard has reported it stolen and wants Rip to come to see her. Rip does not want to see her after she had a fireplug blown up because she did not like the looks of it, and ended up flooding most of the Bel Aire Estates. Rip gets a call on the phone in his truck and it is Hildegard who wants to know where he is. Rip tells her that he has told the police and she gets angry and threatens to cancel her other policies. Rip gives the phone to Johnny and Hildegard is happy that Johnny is on his way. Rip takes Johnny to an airpark where he keeps his plane to fly Johnny to Balboa, where he will go out to Hilde's yacht.

Rip flies Johnny to Balboa and learns that Rip got some of his money from a rich uncle. Rip tells Johnny that Hilde took the Cape Star with her on a trip and discovered the emerald missing that day. At the dock are a number of boats but the captain of the cruiser does not want to take Johnny out there, he will only take Rip. Johnny tells him to radio the "Hildemora" and straighten things out. Rip leaves and the captain tells Johnny that he is ready to sail.

At dawn the next morning Johnny gets to the Hildemora, and a beautiful Hildegard Ransom, "Rowf!" Hildegard welcomes Johnny and mentions that the "old tub" had been shot at off of Formosa. She was there just cruising around and wanted to visit Chou en-Lai. Hilde tells Johnny that he is more handsome than she had heard and wants to find out if he is as much of a wolf as Rip says he is. While walking along the deck Johnny notices one of the crew duck out of the way, and Johnny remembers his eyes looking at Johnny over the sights of a gun sometime in the past.

Hilde tells Johnny that she will have to go through customs and notices a drawer open with the Cape Star back where she had kept it. Johnny asks if this is a gag, and she says no. So now they can have some fun, as she is tired of the other guests. Johnny wants to meet the guests and the crew. The captain comes in and tells her that one of the men, McCarty, has appendicitis, and was sent ashore in the cruiser. Johnny wants to see the man McCarty and radios the cruiser and gets no response. Johnny notices a speedboat and takes it to follow the cruiser with the first mate. The mate spots McCarty on the bridge shooting at them. Johnny is shown a berry pistol used to shoot up flares. The mate swerves in and Johnny shoots the flare gun at him and hits McCarty who crashes his boat into them.

Johnny pieced things together after the Hildemora picked him up. By sheer luck, his shot with the flare gun had hit McCarty full on and he was badly burned. And after the smash up the mate had pulled Johnny out of the drink. By then the yacht has caught up with them. Hilde tells Johnny that McCarty was smuggling narcotics and had stolen the Cape Star long enough to get the cruiser to come out to the yacht and then played sick to get back to shore. If they did not have to get him back to a doctor they could just cruise around for a few days. Three days. And what a three days!

Remarks: "Heh, heh, It's funny isn't it. You never know what you are going to get into when you take on even the most routine kind of case."

## NOTES:
- THE FIRST COMMERCIAL BREAK IS AN **AFRS** SPOT ABOUT THE FLAG OF MISSISSIPPI
- THE SECOND COMMERCIAL BREAK IS AN **AFRS** SPOT ABOUT THE IMPORTANCE OF THE CODE OF CONDUCT OF AN AMERICAN SOLDIER AND HOW IT EFFECTED SGT. THOMAS A. BAKER ON SAIPAN IN WORLD WAR II
- THE THIRD COMMERCIAL BREAK IS AN **AFRS** SPOT ABOUT THE FLAG OF IOWA
- CHOU EN-LAI WAS THE "RED" CHINESE FOREIGN MINISTER DURING THE 1950s.

- FORMOSA WAS THE SITE OF THE GOVERNMENT OF CHIANG KAI-SHEK AND IS NOW CALLED TAIWAN.
- THE ANNOUNCER IS ROY ROWAN

Producer: Jack Johnstone      Writers: Jack Johnstone
Cast: Virginia Gregg, Chet Stratton, Barney Phillips, Jack Moyles, Frank Gerstle

◆ ❖ ◆

SHOW: THE VIRTUOUS MOBSTER MATTER
SHOW DATE: 6/22/1958
COMPANY: CONTINENTAL INSURANCE COMPANY
AGENT: BEN ORLOFF
EXP. ACCT: $174.00

SYNOPSIS: Lefty calls Johnny—you know Lefty Stemper from Virtue, South Carolina. Lefty is not having trouble with old man Caraway, they bought him out and now own the plantation. The place is fixed up now and they need insurance. Johnny tells him to go to see Joe Picatello. Lefty tells Johnny that he talked to Joe but he never comes over, and is never in his office. Lefty wants Johnny to come down and figure out what is wrong.

Johnny travels to New York City and talks to Ben Orloff. Ben complements Johnny on his previous report on the Village of Virtue Matter. Johnny asks Ben if he has heard from Joe Picatello, but Ben tells him that Georgetown, South Carolina is a small office with little business. Ben tells him that he has not heard from Joe in some time. Johnny suggests that he go down to see if all is well with Joe and Ben tells Johnny to let him hear from him.

Johnny travels to Georgetown, South Carolina, rents a car and drives to Joe's office, which is dark. Johnny gets no answer when he knocks, but hears a door open inside. A voice sounding like Joe asks who is there and reluctantly opens the door and Johnny tells him who he is, you know, Johnny Dollar, the investigator. Joe is very quiet until "Willie" attacks Johnny and punches him out. Joe hears a car coming and they leave. Lefty and Flippy come to the office and trip over Johnny on the floor. Lefty hears a car leave and wakes Johnny up. Johnny tells Lefty that Joe and Willie hit him. Lefty recognizes the name Willie as "Willie the Lump" who was a former partner of Joe. That means the Joe has gone back to the old ways. Joe walks in and Lefty is ready to blast him.

The atmosphere is tense in the office as they discuss how Joe has gone back to the old ways when Joe walks in. Joe asks Johnny what happened and Flippy tells Joe that he has gone back to working with Willie the Lump. Lefty reminds Joe of their deal to take out anyone who goes back to the old ways. Johnny demands Lefty's gun and tells him it was not Joe who worked him over. Look at his hands. Lefty remembers "The Twin," Shep Larco. The law called Joe and Shep the twins because they talked and acted like each other. Joe cannot tell them where he has been and Lefty is still suspicious. Finally Joe tells Johnny that the Secret Service knew that Shep and Willie had pulled a job in Baltimore and could not find them. So they spread the word that Joe knew where they were so that Shep and Willie would look for them. Joe tells Johnny that he has been hiding in Washington. The feds sent Joe to the office as living bait. They all agree to stay with Joe when Shep and Willie come in. Shep thinks that Johnny is with the Secret Service. Willie is told to shoot Joe when shots break out and Johnny has gotten them both with Lefty's gun. Johnny asks if anyone knows a good doctor.

Yeah, I've said it before, and I'll say it again. In this insurance business, you never know what you'll run into."

## NOTES:

- THE FIRST COMMERCIAL BREAK IS AN **AFRS** SPOT ABOUT THE FLAG OF DELAWARE
- THE SECOND COMMERCIAL BREAK IS AN **AFRS** SPOT ABOUT THE IMPORTANCE OF THE CODE OF CONDUCT OF AN AMERICAN SOLDIER AND HOW IT EFFECTED LT. EDWARD V. M. ISAAC IN WORLD WAR I, WHO WAS AWARDED THE MEDAL OF HONOR
- THE THIRD COMMERCIAL BREAK IS AN **AFRS** SPOT ABOUT THE FLAG OF CALIFORNIA
- JOHNNY IS SHOT FOR THE 9TH TIME.
- THE ANNOUNCER IS ROY ROWAN

Producer: Jack Johnstone    Writers: Jack Johnstone
Cast:    Jean Tatum, Jack Kruschen, Les Tremayne, Billy Halop, Frank Gerstle, Gil Stratton Jr.

◆   ❖   ◆

SHOW:    THE UGLY PATTERN MATTER
SHOW DATE:    6/29/1958
COMPANY:    MASTERS INSURANCE & TRUST COMPANY
AGENT:    BARRY WINTERS
EXP. ACCT:    $101.00

SYNOPSIS: Barry Winters calls Johnny, and tells him that he has a problem with an account. Simplex Tackle, a small outfit in Danbury, Connecticut. They are a small partnership owed by nine people. The employees are covered by a group life insurance policy and they have had to pay off on three policies, and they all were murders.

Johnny cabs to see Barry Winters who gives Johnny more than he thought. The police think that one man is responsible because each of the people worked for the same company, died within a month of each other and died on the same day of the week, Wednesday. There has been no apparent reason for any of the murders. The first was Adams, a Vice President who was run over by a car. The second was John Bowers who was strangled. Frank Dalver was shot in his own house. Hanley Thomas the president thinks that more is involved. Johnny gets a list of the officers and their salary, and a list of the employees. There are six officers left.

Johnny goes home and then drives to Danbury and the Simplex plant. Johnny meets with Hanley Thomas who agrees that there is a pattern; someone knew the habits of their victims. All of the employees were talked to, as they all knew the habits of the officers. There have been some hotheads who do not like the top-heavy management, and profits have been good lately. Johnny notices from his list that the three men were killed in alphabetical order but the real pattern is by salary. Adams made $12,000; Bowers made $13,500 and Dalvers made $15,000. So the next to go would be James Williams or Charles Hart who both earn $16,500 and ultimately Thomas. Johnny is told that Williams is on vacation and has not been heard from. Sgt. Dennis calls and tells Thomas that another partner is dead. John Williams has been murdered at Parvin's pond.

Johnny drives to Parvin's Pond and meets Sgt. Dennis who tells Johnny that Williams came up last Monday alone. They think that Williams had just come in from fishing and was bludgeoned to death with an oar. An old lady next door found him. The police think that he came in on Wednesday night. Sgt. Dennis thinks that the murderer is an employee, because the employees are not paid very well because of the recession even though the company was making money. Sgt. Dennis has talked to everyone and the officers are all fine men. According to Johnny's list the next one will be Charles Hart, and Johnny asks Sgt. Dennis to put a watch on him. Johnny drives back to the office of Charles Hart, and talks to his secretary, Miss Gregg. She tells Johnny that Hart has not been in since last Wednesday. Thomas comes in and tells Johnny that Hart often goes on sales trips. Miss Greg tells Johnny that Hart was the one who built up the company and developed and sold all of the products that made the money along with Mr. Adams, until Thomas came in with all of his relatives. Thomas tells Johnny that Hart and Adams did start the company and brought in some partners who decided on the expansion. They came to Thomas for financing which made the expansion possible. Johnny asks what happens to the shares of the dead partners, and is told that the other partners absorb it.

Johnny feels that Hart has plenty of motives and knew about the habits of the others. Johnny drives to Hart's address but no one answers. The super comes up and tells Johnny that Hart is at the factory. A $10 bill gets Johnny into the apartment where he looks through the desk and finds a list of the officers. Hart comes from behind the door with a gun. Johnny asks if the gun was the same one that killed one of his partners and Hart says no. He had realized the pattern from the list and he knows that he is next. Johnny asks about Hanley and the others coming in and he tells Johnny that they deserve to be at the top. He is not an executive, just a worker and he is content with the others bring in charge in spite of the prodding of his secretary. Johnny tells Hart to stay put and leaves to follow a hunch. Johnny picks up Sgt. Dennis and goes to the plant. With Sgt. Dennis' handcuffs, Johnny goes to see Thomas and tells him he is under arrest. Johnny asks if he was going to kill off his relatives also. Too bad he covered up the evidence, except to the oar he used to kill Williams, because he left prints on it. Johnny tells Thomas that he has found the gloves and his wife has told Johnny that he was not at home during any of the murders. Thomas blurts out that his wife helped to plan the whole thing. Johnny tells him he was bluffing and Thomas pulls a gun and tells Johnny that no one will know when he gets rid of Johnny. Sgt. Dennis comes in and tells Thomas that he has heard a clean confession. Thomas tries to shoot Sgt. Dennis, who shoots him. Johnny comments to Sgt. Dennis that "Sgt., I haven't seen that fast a draw except on TV" and Sgt. Dennis tells Johnny "That's where I learned it."

"There will be a lot for the courts to work on, about who else was involved with Thomas. The Sgt.'s bullet killed him by the way, and I'd call it good riddance. Or at least quick justice."

Remarks: Why bother?

## NOTES:

- THE FIRST COMMERCIAL BREAK IS AN **AFRS** SPOT ABOUT THE FLAG OF MASSACHUSETTS
- THE SECOND COMMERCIAL BREAK IS AN **AFRS** SPOT ABOUT THE IMPORTANCE OF THE CODE OF CONDUCT OF AN AMERICAN SOLDIER AND HOW IT AFFECTED SSGT. JOHN W. MINNICK DURING WORLD WAR II.
- THE THIRD COMMERCIAL BREAK IS AN **AFRS** SPOT ABOUT THE FLAG OF ALASKA
- THE ANNOUNCER IS ROY ROWAN

Producer:   Jack Johnstone      Writers:   Jack Johnstone
Cast:        Virginia Gregg, Les Tremayne, Forrest Lewis, Herb Vigran, Junius Matthews, Frank Gerstle

◆  ❖  ◆

SHOW:         THE BLINKER MATTER
SHOW DATE:   7/6/1958
COMPANY:    SURETY MUTUAL LTD.
AGENT:       FRED WILLS
EXP. ACCT:   $434.50

SYNOPSIS: Fred Wills calls Johnny and San Francisco is on his mind. Andrew Foreman is an importer there, and Fred has a $50,000 policy on him. Fred asks if Johnny has ever heard of an importer being exported? Last night he disappeared.

Johnny flies to San Francisco, California and studies the file on the flight. Foreman is 51 and has a good business. His wife Martha is 35 and the sole beneficiary. Johnny goes to the Foreman apartment and Martha looks at home in the expensive apartment. Johnny notices Alcatraz across the bay and thinks of the people he has sent to that exclusive club. Martha tells Johnny that she has filled out the police paper work, and a missing persons report has been filed. She tells Johnny that Andrew was visited the other night by a stranger dressed in rough clothes, like a seaman. The name he gave was Blinker, because he kept blinking his eyes. He was shown into the library, and then Andrew said he was going to drive Blinker downtown to find a hotel. He was gone the next morning and has not been to the office. Andrew had never mentioned Blinker before, and Johnny gets a detailed description of Blinker. Johnny asks what if Blinker had nothing to do with the disappearance? Did Foreman have any reason to disappear? The answer was a certain no, maybe too certain.

Johnny cabs to see an old friend Det. Lt. Scapella who tells Johnny that they have covered all the hotels. Maybe there is no Blinker and Lt. Scapella notes that Martha's story was strange. She had too good of a description of the man and maybe the story was a fake. Johnny mentions the insurance and Lt. Scapella gets a call from Wayne Arnold, Foreman's attorney who received a phone call that morning from someone interesting, a man named Blinker.

Johnny has to back up and rethink the case. Johnny cabs to see Mr. Arnold as he is leaving for an appointment. He heard from Blinker just a little while ago. Blinker had wanted $10,000 and hung up. Arnold thinks that Blinker is holding Foreman for ransom. Arnold has been Foreman's attorney for 3 years and knows of no reason why Foreman would want to disappear. Johnny buys cigarettes on the street and watches Arnold leave. Johnny follows in a cab to Golden Gate Park where a woman gets into the car and kisses Arnold. The woman was Marsha Foreman. Johnny goes to wait for Marsha Foreman and when she comes home, he tells her that she and Arnold made up the story of Blinker. And what about you and Arnold? Did you enjoy your visit with him? She tells Johnny that she is in love with Arnold, and Andrew would not have cared. She tells Johnny that she did not make up the story and her husband has not been killed. "Killed? Who said anything about him being killed?" asks Johnny. Johnny asks why her husband has disappeared, and she tells Johnny that maybe it is related to his business. He imports trinkets and curios from the orient, and has made a lot of money. Johnny gets a key to the office and looks over the papers where a shipment has just come in on the Indian Princess. Johnny goes to find the ship, but it has left, so Johnny goes into Gus's Cafe and talks to Gus, Gussie for short. Johnny asks her about the ship and she knows all the crew, and she knows a sailor named Blinker. Gussie tells Johnny that Blinker has disappeared.

Gussie tells Johnny that Blinker was mixed up in something. He had come in for coffee and seemed pleased with himself and said he was in to something good. He showed Gussie a carved elephant that was going to make him a lot of money. Johnny thinks that maybe the elephant of part of the reason for Foreman's disappearance. Gussie tells Johnny that Blinker has his stuff stored in her back room. Johnny goes through Blinker's sea bag and finds an elephant with a hollow leg filled with an envelope containing white powder. Johnny goes to the pier and Gussie stops Johnny to show him a body, Blinker. Johnny rushes to the warehouse and thinks he is being followed. In the warehouse Johnny locates the shipment and the elephants have the same hollow leg with powder in it. A shot rings out and Johnny ducks and waits for 10 minutes. A shadow comes to the crate and they fire at the same time. Johnny hits Andrew Foreman and Johnny tells him that Blinker had discovered what Foreman was importing and was trying to blackmail him. Foreman caught up with him and he killed him. Foreman tells Johnny that the narcotics were put there without his knowledge. Johnny tells him that Blinker's body has been found, and Johnny bets the slugs came from Foreman's gun. Foreman tells Johnny that he did not have any choice.

Remarks: Andrew Foreman made a complete statement to the police. The murder case against him is open and shut. So, it looks like he is going to beat the narcotics rap after all. The hard way.

NOTES:
- MY PROGRAM IS AN **AFRS** PROGRAM WITH THE COMMERCIAL BREAKS CUT OUT, AND AN ORGAN SERENADE AT THE END
- THE ANNOUNCER IS ROY ROWAN

**Producer:** Jack Johnstone      **Writers:** Robert Stanley
**Cast:**      Paula Winslowe, D.J. Thompson, Harry Bartell, Stacy Harris, Vic Perrin, Bob Bruce

◆ ❖ ◆

| | |
|---|---|
| **SHOW:** | THE MOJAVE RED MATTER—PART 1 |
| **SHOW DATE:** | 7/13/1958 |
| **COMPANY:** | GREATER SOUTHWEST INSURANCE & LIABILITY COMPANY |
| **AGENT:** | JAKE KESSLER |
| **EXP. ACCT:** | |

**SYNOPSIS:** Johnny gets a collect call from Lake Mojave Resort. Red is calling, Red Barrett the fishing guide. The fishing is great but he cannot tell Johnny what the problem is over the phone. Johnny ought to come out as soon as possible. Johnny tells Red that he usually travels for an insurance company, and Red tells Johnny that Greater Southwest insured him. Hmmm?

Johnny calls Jake Kessler to investigate what is going on there. Jake tells Johnny that there is nothing going on there in Kingman. Johnny asks about an accident at Lake Mojave and Jake tells Johnny that the claim was legitimate, but Johnny is convinced that there is something wrong. Johnny flies to Las Vegas with his usual description of the night-lights of the southwest. Jake meets Johnny at the airport and agrees to tell Johnny all about the Hobbes matter. Jake tells Johnny that he will tell him all about the matter and then he can head on home at his own expense. Elmer P. Hobbes was a real estate developer from Los Angeles who spent a few days fishing at Lake Mojave with Red Barrett. Elmer went out alone one day and was caught in a windstorm and his body was found the next day on the Nevada shore. A claim has been filed by one of his two business partners, Stuart Manly. The police investigated and the verdict was accidental death by drowning. Jake tells Johnny that he can just head back to Hartford, but Johnny wants to stick around. Jake feels that there is no reason for Johnny to be there but Johnny feels that at least he can go fishing and asks Jake to drive him to the resort. Jake asks if Johnny knows something and asks Johnny how he wants the crow fixed that he is going to eat?

Johnny is sure that something is wrong, based on the call from Red Barrett. Jake drives Johnny to the resort and goes back to Kingman. Johnny goes to the dock and boathouse where Ham Pratt meets him. Johnny tells Ham that Red usually sleeps on the dock, but Ham tells Johnny that Red has not come back in yet, and it is after midnight. He and Buster were about to go out looking for Red. He pulled the same thing two days ago, and has been doing some strange things since Mr. Hobbes died. Buster Favor tells Johnny that he did not believe that the death was an accident either. Red has been looking for the boat, and Johnny notes that the rental boats have flotation tanks and should have been easy to find. Johnny, Ham and Buster take a boat out to look for Red in the darkness. Buster spots a fire on the beach and they head for it. Red tells them it took long enough to bring Johnny there. Red tells them that he needs Johnny's help to prove that Hobbes was murdered.

Buster is sure that Red must have a good reason for thinking it was murder. Red is sure that Hobbes would never have let himself be caught on the lake with a high wind blowing. Red wants Buster and Ham to leave in case he is wrong. He does not want to be embarrassed by too many people. Buster and Ham leave and Red tells Johnny to get some sleep and that he will show him things in the morning. In the morning Johnny wakes up to frying bacon and eggs and sourdough pancakes. Red takes Johnny up the lake to a rocky cove where there are signs of someone climbing up the rocks and footprints going out into the desert. In the water is a sunken boat, the one used by Hobbes. Johnny dives down to the boat and sees that Red is right. Johnny sees where the flotation tanks were slashed, but Hobbes did not have an axe to slit the tanks, so somebody must have done it. Johnny is convinced that Elmer Hobbes was murdered. Johnny still has to find out who killed Hobbes. Expenses are for the case so far, $159.20 including the shooting and retrieving of one crow. Jake, how do you want it cooked?

NOTES:
- THE FIRST COMMERCIAL BREAK IS AN **AFRS** SPOT ABOUT THE FLAG OF VERMONT
- THE SECOND COMMERCIAL BREAK IS AN **AFRS** SPOT ABOUT DUTY, AND THE HEROISM OF CAPT. JOHN PHILLIP CROMWELL DURING WORLD WAR II
- THE THIRD COMMERCIAL BREAK IS AN **AFRS** SPOT ABOUT THE FLAG OF OKLAHOMA
- THE ANNOUNCER IS ROY ROWAN

**Producer:** Jack Johnstone      **Writers:** Jack Johnstone
**Cast:** Lucille Meredith, Forrest Lewis, Parley Baer, Alan Reed, Barney Phillips

❖   ❖   ❖

| | |
|---|---|
| SHOW: | THE MOJAVE RED MATTER—PART 2 |
| SHOW DATE: | 7/20/1958 |
| COMPANY: | GREATER SOUTHWEST INSURANCE & LIABILITY COMPANY |
| AGENT: | JAKE KESSLER |
| EXP. ACCT: | $307.00 |

SYNOPSIS: Johnny calls Jake Kessler at his office, but Jake thinks Johnny has gone home and could not prove that Elmer Hobbes did not die from an accident. Johnny asks if the claim has been mailed, but Jake tells Johnny that he still has it. Johnny tells Jake to tear up the claim, as Hobbes was murdered.

Johnny tells Jake that Hobbes was murdered, but Jake tells Johnny that the police could not find anything. Johnny tells him that he had found the boat with the evidence of sabotage to the floatation tanks. Johnny talks to Buster and Ham, and updates them. Everyone agrees that they should have been suspicious. There is no real suspect, as Elmer did not really mix with the others. All of the boats from Lake Mojave were back in at the time of the storm, so the killer must have come from another landing up the lake. Johnny relates how he found the anchor rope coiled like it had been wrapped around the body to keep it there. So far, everything is circumstantial. Johnny wonders about the motive. Red tells Johnny what Hobbes had in his boat, but Johnny asks again about motive, but Red knows of no one who would want to kill Hobbes. He was one of Red's best friends. Johnny takes Buster to the office to call Jake, and tells him that he has an idea that he does not like. Buster tells Johnny that Red and Hobbes were usually always fighting when they were together and Red was alone when he found the body. Johnny calls Jake and asks about the beneficiaries. There are two beneficiaries on the policy; Manly is one, and the other is Red Barrett.

Buster is not convinced that Red had any part in Hobbes death but Johnny wonders if Red's actions were to cover things up. Ham comes to the office and asks if Buster told Red to go somewhere, as Red was rushing out in a hurry. Johnny borrows Ham's car and Ham tells Johnny that Red had a new Silaflex rod and Mitchell reel in his room, the same outfit that Hobbes had. Johnny tells Buster and Ham not to say anything to Red and leaves to drive to Los Angeles.

Johnny goes to the home of J. Stuart Manly and slips the lock to get inside. As Johnny looks through the house he senses that someone is there in the den. Johnny goes to the den and is attacked, by Red Barrett! Johnny tells Red that common sense told him that Red and Manly were in cahoots. Red tells Johnny that Hobbes gave the rod and reel found in his room to him so they would have matching rigs. Red has found Hobbe's rod in the closet all set up the way it was at the lake. The rod has the initials "EH" engraved on it. In the closet Red has also found the ax used to slash the flotation tanks. Red had rushed there to look for these items. Red tells Johnny that Hobbes had told him that he never really trusted Manly. Red had called Manly to tell him that Johnny Dollar was working on the case, and he should go to Lake Mojave to clear up any evidence he might have left there. Red attacked Johnny because he though Johnny was Manly, and had had come back. Manly walks into the den and tells Red he was right, and introduces them to his wife who tells Manly to kill them as burglars. She accuses Hobbes of fishing all the time and taking the money. Now they will have the money and the business. Johnny tells Manly that he was foolish to leave the evidence there. Manly tells Johnny that since he has a gun, that he will be shot first. Red asks Manly if he can shoot as well as Red can cast, and Red buries a lure in Manly's hand. Mrs. Manly is upset at that silly redheaded old man for hurting her husband. Red tells Johnny that he hopes that the fishing is real good up where Elmer is now.

"Manly and his wife, yeah, Red had figured right. The morning of the day Hobbes was killed, they had rented a boat out of Cottonwood Landing a few miles up the lake, and then ambushed him there in the big basin. Bob Cole at Cottonwood had noticed the new rod and reel when they came back off the lake just before the big storm, and had noticed the ax too, and had wondered about it. Now he knows. So from here on in, it is up to the Sheriff's office and the courts."

NOTES:
- THE FIRST COMMERCIAL BREAK IS AN **AFRS** SPOT ABOUT THE FLAG OF ILLINOIS
- THE SECOND COMMERCIAL BREAK IS AN **AFRS** SPOT ABOUT MANHOOD, AND THE ACTIONS OF WILLIAM H. HORSEFALL DURING THE CIVIL WAR
- THE THIRD COMMERCIAL BREAK IS AN **AFRS** SPOT ABOUT THE FLAG OF NEW MEXICO
- THE ANNOUNCER IS ROY ROWAN

| | | | |
|---|---|---|---|
| Producer: | Jack Johnstone | Writers: | Jack Johnstone |
| Cast: | Virginia Gregg, Parley Baer, Forrest Lewis, Barney Phillips, Alan Reed, Russell Thorson | | |

◆ ❖ ◆

| | |
|---|---|
| SHOW: | THE WAYWARD KILLER MATTER |
| SHOW DATE: | 7/27/1958 |
| COMPANY: | CONTINENTAL INSURANCE & TRUST COMPANY |
| AGENT: | PAUL HEMPLE |
| EXP. ACCT: | $315.17 |

SYNOPSIS: Paul Hemple calls Johnny, and Johnny tells Paul that he was beginning to think that they had hired someone else. Paul tells Johnny that they have hired some staff investigators, but Paul needs Johnny to work on this one. Paul R. Welton has had his life threatened. Johnny tells Paul that it is ok to hire someone else when there is a life at stake, so Paul tells Johnny that he will call Lt. Randy Singer and tell him the deal is off. Singer has told Paul that if they send Johnny, he will cooperate; send anyone else and he will not. Johnny is told that there is a $2,000 fee if he keeps Welton alive.

Johnny travels to New York City and goes to the office of Lt. Randy Singer. Randy tells Johnny that there is nothing he can do. Welton was a witness to the murder of a bookie, and there are no other clues. On Tuesday of last week, Welton was walking his dog around 2 AM. He passed an alley, saw two men struggling and heard a shot that frightened his dog. The dog ran around in circles and tied up his legs with the leash. The killer came out of the alley and tripped over Welton who got a good look at the man in the street light. The killer slugged Welton, and the dog got a piece of the man's pants before he ran away. The dog kept howling until a patrolman came and found the bookie dead in the alley. Randy has not found the gun used and Welton has been shown the mug files. A reporter wrote up the story that Welton had seen the man, and could identify him. When Welton connected the man in the alley to the bookie, he became afraid. Johnny thinks that maybe the mob is involved in this case, and Randy tells Johnny that he is going to post a guard on Welton's apartment. Officer Conroy comes in and Johnny goes with him to Welton's apartment. At the apartment they find a crowd gathered and several policemen there. On the sidewalk is Welton.

Johnny finds Welton sprawled on the sidewalk, but he is still breathing. Johnny is told that some kids heard some noise in the building, like a fight, with Welton yelling for help. Welton then comes flying out of the window. The apartment is a mess and the assailant made his escape out the back of the apartment. The doctor arrives and Welton is taken to the apartment where the dog is yelping. Welton is sedated and Johnny is told that he can talk to him later. Randy arrives and goes over the crime scene. Johnny goes to the alley and is glad he did, because there is a work crew there. Johnny calls an old friend that Randy would like to put in jail, "Smokey" Joe Sullivan, a man who has been picked up on more petty charges than you can name. In a city with an underworld like New York, Smokey was a good person to know, on occasion. Johnny offers Smokey $100 on the phone and arranges to meet him at the Lexington Hotel. Johnny cabs to the hotel and waits for Smokey, who does not show. Johnny realizes that someone important is there in the hotel as a police car is out front. Johnny walks to 3rd Avenue and spots Smokey at a newsstand. Johnny asks Smokey if he is betting on the horses and using the syndicate. Johnny asks Smokey something that is muffled by a truck pulling away. Johnny tells Smokey he will double the money if the information exists.

Johnny goes back to Welton's apartment where Randy has found nothing. Randy tells Johnny that he has found the gun in a storm drain, and has to push the dog off. Welton wakes up and Johnny goes to make a call. Welton tells Randy that the same man he had seen in the alley had attacked him. Johnny talks to Smokey and mentions $23,000, which gets Welton's attention. Johnny then tells Randy he can make an arrest. Johnny gets the dog and tells Randy that the dog deserves the credit. On the night of the killing the dog supposedly chewed up the killers' pants, but he killer did not shoot the dog. Also the dog did not fight off the attacker earlier because there was no one to fight off. Johnny accuses Welton of faking the attack. Johnny tells him that the electric company has finally fixed the streetlight where the bookie was shot after having been out for three weeks. Johnny's phone call proved that Welton was in hock to the bookie for $23,000. Welton blurts out that the bookie had threatened him, so he had to kill him.

Johnny and Randy take a night on the town; Randy needed a break. Oh, don't forget the $2,000. Welton is still alive, for a while at least.

NOTES:
- THE FIRST COMMERCIAL BREAK IS FOR THE NATIONAL HEART INSTITUTE ABOUT THE HEART-LUNG MACHINE
- THE SECOND COMMERCIAL BREAK IS AND AFRS SPOT ABOUT THE WRIGHT BROTHERS AND THE GAINS IN AVIATION TECHNOLOGY
- MY PROGRAM HAS AN AFRS ORGAN SERENADE AT THE END
- SMOKEY SULLIVAN MAKE HIS FIRST APPEARANCE IN THIS PROGRAM
- THE ANNOUNCER IS ROY ROWAN
- SGT. RANDY SINGER HAS BEEN PROMOTED TO LIEUTENANT IN THIS PROGRAM

| | | | |
|---|---|---|---|
| **Producer:** | Jack Johnstone | **Writers:** | Jack Johnstone |
| **Cast:** | Edgar Barrier, Herb Vigran, James McCallion, Paul Dubov, Lawrence Dobkin, John Dehner, Bill James, Vic Perrin | | |

◆   ❖   ◆

| | |
|---|---|
| **SHOW:** | THE LUCKY 4 MATTER |
| **SHOW DATE:** | 8/3/1958 |
| **COMPANY:** | TRI-STATE LIFE & CASUALTY INSURANCE COMPANY |
| **AGENT:** | EARLE POORMAN |
| **EXP. ACCT:** | $224.95 |

SYNOPSIS: Earle Poorman calls and asks if Johnny remembers the Lucky 4 Ranch where he and Ray Smishney had investigated the death of the concert pianist, and did some really good fishing. Remember the private lake behind the ranch owned by Bill Cherry? Well it is not there anymore, nor is Old Bill. According to the available information he was killed when the dam broke and sent the lake crashing down onto the valley. Earle has the policy and will send it to Johnny at the Lucky 4. Ray has called and he thinks the breach of the dam was no accident.

Johnny calls Ray to tell him he is on the way. Johnny flies to Colorado Springs, Colorado where Ray meets Johnny at the airport. Ray tells Johnny that they were poaching on Cherry Lake when they were fishing there. Bill was kind of ornery, and the creek used to water some pasture before he put in the dam. Because of the altitude, the lake fills lake with summer snowmelt. During a heavy summer rain the dam burst like an explosion. Ray takes a shortcut to his ranch and tells Johnny that he originally thought that the lake gave way naturally, but he has been poking around and found some things. Also, Ray had opened the package from Earle and had seen that the beneficiary was a worthless nephew of Bill's. Ray's car starts acting up and he pulls over. When the hood is raised Johnny spots a lot of wiring and they hit the deck just as a bomb goes off. Somebody must have seen Ray poking around and knows that he sent for Johnny and did not like it.

A moving van driver takes Johnny and Ray to town where Johnny rents a car and drives to the Lucky 4 ranch. Johnny and Ray take a jeep up to the lake site, and Ray shows Johnny a sample of the wiring that came from the car. Ray shows Johnny the flow of the creek is just like it was before the dam went in, and notes that he does not need the water as much as Ralph Kimble. Kimble is a neighbor and is a retired professor who keeps to his self and is ornery just like old Bill. Ray tells Johnny that Bill was found with a package of El Parro Cuban cigarettes in his hand, but Bill never smoked. Ray thinks Bill found someone snooping around the dam. Johnny sees the remains of the concrete dam, and evidence of dynamite used to build it. Ray tells Johnny that Bill did not use dynamite to build the dam, he was afraid of it. Ray shows Johnny a piece of dynamite label plastered on a rock: "Titan Super IXL Dynamite." That brand is only sold in one store in Denver, and Bill never went to Denver, as he hated the place. Johnny and Ray go to Colorado Springs to find Tommy Walker the nephew. At the Ace High Radio Shop, where Tommy was last working, Johnny asks the manager for Tommy and is told that Tommy has not been there for two days. Tommy was supposed to know all about electronics but could only turn on a radio, and the music he listened to! He was so dumb he could not attach wires to a plug correctly. All he wanted was a place to sit and smoke those smelly Cuban cigarettes. Johnny shows the manager the wires from the car bomb and asks for some, but he does not carry that type of wire. Johnny goes back to the ranch to play a hunch.

Back at the ranch Johnny has lunch and reviews the policy from Earle in which Tommy would only get $1,000. Ray tells Johnny that no one liked Bill putting in the dam, but Ray has plenty of water now that he put in the pumps. Ray has used dynamite before, but not that brand. Besides everybody knows where to get it. Everybody? Including Ralph Kimble next door? Ray's wife tells Johnny that the Kimbles are not home as Mrs. Kimble had told her that they were going to Denver. Johnny goes over to look around with Ray. Johnny searches a work shed and Ray finds a case of the Titan dynamite, a rock drill, some of the same type of wire used on the bomb, and the Cuban cigarettes. Ray thinks that the evidence is circumstantial, but Johnny reminds Ray that Kimble was a physics professor. Ray tells Johnny that Kimble knew about the shortcut from the airport, and knew that Johnny was coming. Ray notices mud on a pair of boots, and that mud only comes from around the lake. Johnny mentions that the law needs "seven points of similarity" for the evidence to stand up. Johnny quotes the odds of that happening as 1 in 38,000,000. Mr. Kimble comes in with a gun and tells Johnny to pray fast. Mrs. Kimble calls and tells him that Ray's wife is on her way over with a shotgun, and Johnny slugs Kimble.

"Well, it's up to the authorities now, the courts. And I don't think that there is much doubt as to the outcome. Kimble's attempt to kill us was the clincher. As for Tommy Walker the heir, you will have to pay him off on old Bills' policy."

NOTES:

- MOST CATALOGS LIST THIS AS THE LUCKY FOUR MATTER. I HAVE CHANGED THE NAME OF THIS PROGRAM TO REFLECT THE NAME ON THE SCRIPT TITLE PAGE.
- AFTER THE EXPLOSION, JOHNNY NOTES THAT HE STOWED HIS LUGGAGE IN A CABIN AT THE RANCH. THE BOMB MUST NOT HAVE BEEN STRONG ENOUGH TO DESTROY THE CAR.
- JOHNNY MENTIONS "SEVEN POINTS OF SIMILARITY" CONCERNING THE EVIDENCE. THIS SEEMS TO HAVE SOME BASIS IN FINGERPRINT EVALUATIONS, OR AT LEAST ONE CASE I HAVE FOUND WHICH TRIED TO REFUTE THE STANDARDS. I REALLY CANNOT TELL WHAT THE BASIS FOR THE COMPARISON IS IN THIS STORY.
- THE FIRST COMMERCIAL BREAK IS AN AFRS SPOT ABOUT THE CODE OF CONDUCT AND LT. EDWARD V. M. EZZACK IN WORLD WAR I
- THE SECOND COMMERCIAL BREAK IS AN EPISODE OF THE BELLWETHERS ABOUT WINDSHIELD WIPERS
- CAST INFORMATION FROM THE KNX COLLECTION AT THE THOUSAND OAKS LIBRARY.
- ROY ROWAN IS THE ANNOUNCER

Producer:    Jack Johnstone        Writers:    Jack Johnstone
Cast:        Ken Christy, Vic Perrin, Larry Dobkin, Virginia Gregg,
             Will Wright, Shirley Mitchell

◆  ❖  ◆

SHOW:           THE TWO-FACED MATTER
SHOW DATE:      8/10/1958
COMPANY:        NORTHEASTERN FIDELITY & BONDING COMPANY
AGENT:          NICK WALTERS
EXP. ACCT:      $9.80

SYNOPSIS: Nick Walters calls and tells Johnny that the problem is $58,000. Ever hear of Old Lang Syne Furniture? It is located up north, is run by a bunch of real characters, and produces some of the finest furniture in the world. Oh, and wear a dark suit, white shirt and dark tie and suspenders when you go there.

Johnny cabs to Nick's office in his most funereal clothes. Nick tells Johnny that the craftsmen at the factory are old-world types and the furniture is top rate. One of their lads has run off with company funds, $58,433 to be exact. The police were never called in, and the theft occurred sometime in the past three and a half years. They discovered the theft last month and just let Nick know. When Johnny brings up the timeliness of the claim Nick tells Johnny that he had waived a 60-day notification clause from the policy because the owners do not like to be rushed. Go talk to J. Worthington Keesley, the senior member of the organization; they do not have officers. Johnny is going up, on expense account of course, to take a look at these crazy characters.

Johnny takes a bus to Weldon, Vermont where the plant looks like it had been there since year one. On the walk up the drive Johnny notices horses and carriages parked besides the building. Inside Johnny meets Mr. Keesley who looks like one of the Smith Brothers sitting behind his roll-top desk. Keesley tells Johnny that all the workers wear beards, as did their fathers, so that they can continue the tradition of craftsmanship. The horses were good enough for their grandparents, so they are good enough for them. Keesley suspects Roscoe J. Twiller of the theft. Johnny is shown a picture of Twiller in a group photo from 1941. Keesley should have known when Twiller bought a motorcar, that he was not one to keep the traditions. Twiller was the one who took off with the $58,433.41. Keesley is sure beyond a shadow of a doubt, as Twiller was the only one who had a key to the vault where the building funds were kept. When he suddenly left them 3 years, 5 months and 16 days ago, Keesley should have known then. On June 21 at 10:04 when Keesley went to the vault to put some extra money in the vault, he found a note that said, "Good luck, suckers, signed Twiller." Johnny asks where to start after three years, but Keesley tells him that is up to Johnny unless the insurance company is going to pay the claim.

Johnny agrees that Twiller is the thief, but is sure that the money has been spent by now. Keesley did not know where Twiller lived, as that was none of his business. Maybe Mr. Bottomly, who is working on a Hepplewhite table would know where Twiller lived. Johnny walks through a shop equipped only with hand tools used by old men with long beards. Johnny meets Mr. Bottomly, who tells Johnny that he must find Twiller, who was his neighbor. Twiller drove Bottomly to work in his buggy until he bought the motorcar, at which time Bottomly bought a bicycle. Twiller lived on Peach Avenue in East Weldon. When Johnny mentions that he will talk to the police, the shop is full of upset men who are worried about the blot on their name. Johnny tells them that he will use the police only if necessary. Bottomly tells Johnny that the chief of police is the mayor, John Kenworthy Wilkins, but they have never dealt with him as he is not of their sort and they do not go into town. Bottomly has a picture of the mayor he found in his carriage, he is running for reelection. When the picture is shown, all the men howl their disgust at the disgraceful image, as the mayor is bald and clean-shaven. But how to find Twiller?

Johnny finds the mayor, John Kenworthy Wilkins, on his porch, sipping a gin and tonic. He tells Johnny that he had heard a rumor when he got to town, but did nothing, as a report had not been filed, and that Twiller was gone before he got there. He was elected mayor when the townspeople found out about his record of police work in Ohio. Johnny tells him that the factory has no idea where Twiller might be. Johnny walks across town and meets a boy playing "cowboy." He is Jimmy Carter and asks Johnny if he wants to see his "artistical" drawings, and Johnny admires a beautiful moustache on a girl advertising cigarettes. Jimmy tells Johnny that he needs a paint set. Jimmy shows Johnny what he has done to the mayor's reelection poster by adding hair and a beard, and Johnny realizes how to solve the theft. Johnny takes the poster and tells Jimmy he does not know how good he is. Johnny goes back to the mayor and asks him to make an arrest. He knows who took the money. Johnny tells Wilkins that he showed up just after Twiller left town. Twiller had a thick beard, and you have none. Johnny should have recognized from the red tint on his scalp that he had been using hair remover and accuses him of being Twiller. When Johnny tells him a search of his house would turn up the key to the vault, Wilkins blurts out that he threw the key away.

"I don't know why Twiller gave up so easily, I guess it was because I caught him completely off guard. He even signed a confession and promised to pay back what he could. So from here on in it's up to the courts. And all thanks to a little kid who liked to draw moustaches on billboards. Expense account total, including the finest paint set I could find for my little pal Jimmy, oh, wait, I gotta pad this, it only comes out to $9.80!"

NOTES:
- THE SMITH BROTHERS REFERS TO THE BEARDED SMITH BROTHERS WHICH WAS THE LOGO FOR LUDEN'S "SMITH BROTHERS COUGH DROPS"
- GEORGE HEPPLEWHITE WAS AN 18TH CENTURY ENGLISH CABINETMAKER
- THE FIRST COMMERCIAL BREAK IS AN AFRS SPOT ABOUT HOPE IN THE FACE OF GREAT ODDS, AND THE ATTACK ON PLOESTI
- THE SECOND COMMERCIAL BREAK IS AND AFRS ABOUT THE CHANGES IN WARFARE
- THE ANNOUNCER IS ROY ROWAN

Producer:  Jack Johnstone          Writers:   Jack Johnstone
Cast:      Will Wright, Herb Vigran, Forrest Lewis, Edgar Barrier, Richard Beals, Bill James, Gus Bayz

◆   ❖   ◆

SHOW:        THE NOXIOUS NEEDLE MATTER
SHOW DATE:   8/24/1958
COMPANY:     WORLDWIDE MUTUAL INSURANCE COMPANY
AGENT:       WALDO R. WESTBURY
EXP. ACCT:   $61.20

SYNOPSIS: Waldo Westbury calls Johnny to investigate the death of a client, J. Lamont Scofield, the theatrical producer who was world famous for the beautiful girls in his productions. He died yesterday of "natural causes," but Waldo has doubts, based on the beneficiary of the $750,000 estate. Please come over and see me.

Johnny cabs to the office of Waldo Westbury and is shown the policy that provides $750,000 on Scofield's life. The beneficiary has constantly been changed. Goldie Laverne, an old Burlesque queen, Toodles Tempest, Baby Boodles Baker, Bubbles Jones, Pepper Caprice Carstairs, and Cupcake Delond are listed as former beneficiaries on the riders. Mary T. Smith is the current beneficiary; the T. stands for "Torso." Waldo thinks that Scofield was killed, bumped off. At the time of his death, Mary Smith was his nurse. Johnny is asked to prove that Mary Smith killed Scofield. Johnny is also told that, because of the amount of the policy, there will be no questioning of his necessary expenses, not matter how high! Scofield died in Cranford, New Jersey, and Mary Smith is still there. She used to be a showgirl before becoming a nurse. Westbury knows nothing about the doctor, Leonard Foote.

Johnny travels to New York and rents a "drive your own" car for the drive to Cranford and the office of Dr. Foote. In Dr. Foote's office, Johnny is told that Scofield had a heart condition which required digitalis and intravenous injections of sadilinid. His nurse gave him the injections under his orders, and Mary is a registered nurse. Dr. Foote tells Johnny that his tentative opinion is natural causes. When Johnny tries to infer that Mary could have injected something to hasten death, Dr. Foote questions Johnny's tactics and wants an apology, but Johnny is insistent that Dr. Foote might be involved in a possible cover up or conspiracy. Dr. Foote tells Johnny that he learned this morning that Mary is the heir to the estate, which he did not know before, and he has held the body for an autopsy. Johnny is forced to apologize to Dr. Foote, who offers a towel to Johnny to wipe the egg off of his face.

Dr. Foot tells Johnny that he has realized that it is possible that Mary Smith might have hastened the death of Scofield. Dr. Foote thinks that Scofield could have lived for many years. Dr. Foote has called in Dr. Stanley, a toxicologist to examine the body. Dr. Foote tells Johnny that the police have found no poisons, and the autopsy is because the most possible cause of death would be an overdose of medication.

Johnny goes to Scofield's house and meets Mary Smith, a very young Mary Smith. There was only one word that did Mary justice: WOW! Johnny tells Mary who he is, and she has heard of Johnny and asks him in. She wonders why Johnny is there and Johnny tells her that it is a routine investigation. Mary pours drinks and tells Johnny that she is not grief stricken. Mary asks if Johnny has any money, and tells him that she knows she was the heir to the estate. She has been on 24 hour duty for 2 solid years, and there were time she thought Monty would live forever, even times when she wished she could help him out of this world. Johnny tells Mary he thinks she killed Scofield and is there to make sure she does not skip out when the autopsy report comes in. Mary utters an "oh," and Johnny asks if that concerns her. Johnny tells her that someone with an attitude like hers is either completely innocent, or guilty as the devil. She tells Johnny that she wanted Monty dead and wanted his money. When Johnny mentions an overdose, she tells him that an overdose or poison would be stupid, as no one had been with Monty for a week except her and Dr. Foote. Mary offers to sign a confession if it will confuse Johnny. The phone rings and Dr. Foote calls to tell Johnny that the autopsy showed no signs of poison or overdose. "I guess you cannot build a case out of thin air," she tells Johnny and hands him the "confession." Johnny thinks about the phrase "thin air" and has an idea and thanks Mary for saying that.

Johnny calls his own doctor in Hartford and talks about some ideas he has for the "perfect crime" and gets some enlightening ideas. Johnny drives to the coroner's office and talks to Dr. Stanley and asks if Scofield could have died of an embolus in the brain, and asks Stanley to check on it over Dr. Foote's objections. Later Dr. Stanley tells Johnny that he was right, an embolus in the brain killed Scofield. Dr. Foote has the medical kit used to give Scofield his injections. Dr. Foote tells Johnny that only the small needle was used and the others never contained anything but air. Dr. Stanley tells Johnny that 50 cc of plain air could cause an embolus, and Johnny asks him to look for traces of tissue on the other needles.

"Yes, the microscope showed that needle had been used on J. Lamont Scofield recently. Pretty slim evidence I know, but when Mary was faced with it, well I am still not quite sure why, maybe we scared her, but she broke down and confessed the murder. Yeah, she had been wrong, sometimes you can build a case on nothing but thin air.

NOTES:
- AN EMBOLUS IS AN AIR BUBBLE IN A VEIN OR ARTERY.
- THE FIRST COMMERCIAL BREAK IS AN AFRS SPOT ABOUT HOPE IN THE FACE OF GREAT ODDS, AND THE ATTACK ON PLOESTI
- THE SECOND COMMERCIAL BREAK IS AN AFRS SPOT ABOUT DAVID BUSHNELL AND THE "TURTLE" SUBMARINE AND THE NAUTILUS
- THE ANNOUNCER IS ROY ROWAN

Producer:    Jack Johnstone       Writers:    Jack Johnstone
Cast:        Virginia Gregg, Bartlett Robinson, Marvin Miller, Junius Matthews

◆    ❖    ◆

SHOW:         THE LIMPING LIABILITY MATTER
SHOW DATE:    8/31/1958
COMPANY:     UNIVERSAL ADJUSTMENT BUREAU
AGENT:        PAT MCCRACKEN
EXP. ACCT:     $1,020.20

SYNOPSIS: Johnny gets a collect call from Smokey Sullivan, and reminds him of all the cases he has helped Johnny with. Smokey has information about an insurance racket, but they do not even know that they are being taken. Smokey wants Johnny to come down to New York

Johnny addresses this case to the Universal Adjustment Bureau, even though he has not been assigned to it, but he is sure that they will ok the expense account, and Johnny describes Smokey's checkered past.

Johnny goes to New York City and meets Smokey by a newsstand near the Lexington hotel. Smokey wants Johnny to go to a bar and talk, but Johnny threatens to get Randy Singer involved. Smokey tells Johnny that Jake Fortina is paying drunks to have accidents, and gives him the details. Johnny calls Pat McCracken and tells Pat that Fortina puts up the rum, gives the drunks money and insures them and then kills them after they get he gets the money. Fortina will break an arm or a leg, and then take the drunk to a department store and fake an accident and threaten to sue. Pat tells Johnny that he has noticed a series of unrelated accidents from different insurance companies. Pat tells Johnny that Fortina is smart, so be careful.

Smokey and Johnny go outside to think and Smokey tells Johnny that while he was on the phone a man came in, saw Johnny and ran out. Smokey tells Johnny that he had made a deal with Fortina to break his leg to keep him interested. Smokey called Johnny because he has been playing it straight and has helped Johnny before. Smokey tells Johnny that he will go back and talk to the bartender, who knows Fortina. Smokey gives Johnny his room key at the Brakeley Hotel and tells Johnny to wait for Fortina to come there.

Johnny goes to Smokey's room and finds Fortina waiting for him with a .38 automatic and a huge man named Benny McGurn who tells Johnny that Johnny had sent his brother to prison. Johnny is sure that it is a double-cross, and Benny is ready to kill Johnny and break his bones. Benny tells Johnny that they are there because he saw Smokey talking to Johnny in the bar. Benny grabs Johnny's leg and tries to break it. Johnny jumps up and grabs Benny, only to be squeezed in a bear hug. The door bursts open and there are shots. Randy Singer walks in and tells Johnny that Smokey had called him and brought him there.

Johnny adds $1,000 for Smokey on the expense account.

**NOTES:**
- THE ANNOUNCER IS ROY ROWAN
- STORY INFORMATION OBTAINED FROM THE **KNX** COLLECTION IN THE THOUSAND OAKS LIBRARY

| | | | |
|---|---|---|---|
| **Producer:** | Jack Johnstone | **Writers** | Jack Johnstone |
| **Cast:** | Virginia Gregg, Vic Perrin, Tom Holland, Larry Dobkin, Jack Moyles, Shep Menken, Herb Vigran | | |

| | |
|---|---|
| **SHOW:** | THE MALIBU MYSTERY MATTER |
| **SHOW DATE:** | 9/7/1958 |
| **COMPANY:** | WESTERN MARITIME & PROPERTY INSURANCE COMPANY |
| **AGENT:** | PETER HANLEY |
| **EXP. ACCT:** | $101.50 |

**SYNOPSIS:** Peter Hanley calls Johnny at 4 AM. He had to call all the way across the country only to discover that Johnny is right there in Beverly Hills. Johnny is ready to head back to Hartford, but Hanley wants Johnny to work on a claim for him. The claim is for $150,000 to $250,000 for the loss of a yacht. Hanley will meet Johnny at the Malibu Pier.

Johnny has breakfast and rents a car to go to Malibu, California. Johnny notices that cars are lining the road to the pier and parks where an ambulance has pulled out. Hanley meets Johnny and shows him the accident. The Coast Guard is circling where the $150,000 diesel yacht has blown up. Mr. and Mrs. Merrill and the steward and deckhand escaped, but the skipper went down with the boat. Johnny is introduced to Capt. Rollins of the Coast Guard, who has found no sign of the Tatus, and it seems that the boat just blew up. The explosion was about 2 hours earlier, and someone along the beach notified the Coast Guard. Hanley confirms that the Merrills are ok, but Johnny wants to talk to them. The claim could be much higher than just for the boat because of the jewelry Mrs. Merrill had on board. Hanley tells Johnny that he had been notified of the explosion by a friend.

Johnny follows Hanley to the home of the Merrills. Mr. Merrill tells Johnny that he had sold his plastics business and bought a smaller house in a less fashionable neighborhood, as they do not do a lot of entertaining anymore. Mr. Merrill was thinking of selling the Tatus for economic reasons. Mrs. Merrill tells Hanley that the jewels are safe; they were the first things she grabbed when the engine started making noises. Johnny looks at the jewels and then gets the story of what happened. The engine was making noises and the skipper ordered them off while he looked into a fuel problem. Then the boat exploded. While playing with the jewels Johnny discovers that this case needs investigating, and needs it bad.

Johnny recalls how mercury could coat gold and make it look like silver, and how a diamond would scratch class. While listening to the Merrills talking Johnny was toying with the jewels and dragged them across the glass coffee table, and they did not cut the glass. The jewels are fakes! On the way out Mr. Merrill tells Johnny and Hanley that he needs the money, but would never sell the jewels. Johnny drives back to Malibu and tells Hanley that the jewels are fakes. Hanley tells Johnny that Merrill was quite a promoter and bit off more than he could chew with the plastics plant. Johnny drives to the Coast Guard for a navigation chart and a topographical map of the area, and hires a surveyor named Bartley. Johnny goes to the house of Mr. Dobkin, Hanley's friend, who tells them that he heard the boat's whistle in the fog and then heard the explosion and shows Johnny where the explosion was. Bartley takes a bearing and plots the line on the map. Dobkin thinks that the neighbors would have heard the explosion also.

Johnny and Hanley continue to interview Mrs. Grey, and Mr. Phillips and another woman, who saw the explosion while Bartley plots the lines. Johnny goes to the Coast Guard with his maps to tell them that the boat went down in a different area where it is accessible to divers.

Johnny waits in his hotel until then the Coast Guard calls to tell him that the wreck of the boat was not found, but something that looks like a raft was found, a raft with explosives and oil to make it look like the boat went down. Johnny tells the Coast Guard to search the ports along the coast for the Tatus, and goes to see the Merrills.

Johnny tries a bluff on the Merrills. Johnny tells Mr. Merrill that the Coast Guard has found the remains of the skipper and there are signs that they killed him. Mrs. Merrill blurts out that the skipper is still alive. She tells Johnny that the skipper is in Mexico with the yacht. Mr. Merrill calls his wife a fool. Johnny tells Merrill that his wife's fake jewelry tipped him off. Mr. Merrill tells Johnny that he will fight the insurance company, but Johnny tells him that he will not get to first base.

"Yeah, when a crook tries to pull a fast one on an honest insurance company, well, you'll see when the courts get through with Merrill and his wife."

**NOTES:**

- THE FIRST COMMERCIAL BREAK IS AN EPISODE OF THE BELLWETHERS ABOUT WINDSHIELD WASHERS.
- THE SECOND COMMERCIAL BREAK IS AN **AFRS** SPOT ABOUT THE OLD DAYS AND WARFARE
- INTERESTINGLY LAWRENCE DOBKIN AND BARNEY PHILLIPS PLAY CHARACTERS WITH THEIR OWN NAMES IN THIS PROGRAM.
- THE ANNOUNCER IS ROY ROWAN

| | | | |
|---|---|---|---|
| Producer: | Jack Johnstone | Writers: | Jack Johnstone |
| Cast: | Paula Winslowe, Eleanor Audley, Jean Tatum. Ben Wright, Harry Bartell, Will Wright, Lawrence Dobkin, Barney Phillips | | |

◆ ❖ ◆

| | |
|---|---|
| SHOW: | THE WAYWARD DIAMONDS MATTER |
| SHOW DATE: | 9/14/1958 |
| COMPANY: | WESTERN MARITIME & PROPERTY INSURANCE COMPANY |
| AGENT: | PETER HANLEY |
| EXP. ACCT: | $218.00 |

SYNOPSIS: Peter Hanley calls Johnny again and is returning Johnny's call. Johnny tells him how he is enjoying Malibu, California on expense account. Hanley tells Johnny how Merrill has agreed to plead guilty, but Johnny tells him that he will change his mind. Johnny reminds Hanley that it was the fake jewelry that tipped Johnny off, and Mrs. Merrill is not being held because her husband signed a statement saying that she was not involved. Now she is on the loose. A worried Hanley will come right out to pick Johnny up.

Johnny buys drinks for himself and Hanley who tells Johnny that he had forgotten about the fake jewels. Johnny tells Hanley how he discovered that the jewels were fakes by dragging them across the coffee table. Hanley wants to call in the police but Johnny is sure that the diamonds have not been sold yet, and the Merrills still have them. Johnny is sure that Mrs. Merrill will sell the diamonds to pay for the legal fees. Johnny tells Hanley that he is having Mrs. Merrill tailed to figure out how she will dispose of the jewels. Johnny reminds Hanley of how proud Mrs. Merrill was to show them the fake jewels to get their minds off of them. Johnny gets a call from the detective who has been knocked out by Mrs. Merrill, who is gone.

Johnny and Hanley drive to the Merrill home and are let in by Sam, the detective. Sam tells Johnny that he was casually walking up and down the street all morning and saw Mrs. Merrill go out to the garage. Mrs. Merrill got into the car and ran Sam down in the driveway and got away. Sam does not know what kind of car she was driving, and got into the house to phone Johnny by climbing into an open window. Johnny fires Sam and tells him to get out. Hanley calls his office to get the information on the Merrill car and Johnny searches the house. In a desk, Johnny finds a bill from a jeweler that could have covered the substitution of the jewels. Johnny sends Hanley to the police to have them issue an APB, and then heads to the jeweler.

Johnny drives to Howard's Hillcrest Jewelers and asks for the owner, but is told by a sales clerk that Mr. Howard is busy with a very important client. While the clerk is distracted by another client Johnny searches the back rooms to find Mrs. Merrill talking with Mr. Howard about putting the real jewels back into the mountings. She tells Howard that she must go through the motions of getting a lawyer for her husband. When Mrs. Merrill mentions that Johnny Dollar is working on the case, Mr. Howard is alarmed because he knows about Johnny. Howard tells her that he has already disposed of the jewels and mentions other cases where he has helped people cheat their insurance companies. Howard tells her that he knew the boat thing would not work. Mrs. Merrill is sure that no one else knows that the jewels were fakes. Howard tells her that now he must get rid of Johnny and gets his gun. Johnny walks in and Howard threatens to kill Johnny there. When Johnny tells him that there are customers out front, Howard tells Johnny to go to a private vault in the back of the store. While Johnny is trying to stall for time the clerk pounds on the door and tells Howard that the police are there. Johnny grabs the gun from Howard and slugs him after shots are fired. Hanley comes in with the police who tell Johnny that they have been trying to catch Howard for years.

Expense account item 2, $50 in legal fees to make a deposition, so I won't have to hang around for a trial for two or three. And I have a sneaking suspicion that Howard, Merrill and his wife are going to have a long, long time to think things over.

NOTES:
- THIS PROGRAM IS AN ARFS PROGRAM, BUT THE AUDIO FIDELITY IS ABSOLUTELY WONDERFUL.
- THE FIRST COMMERCIAL BREAK IS AND AFRS SPOT ABOUT PVT. ROBERT VON SCHLICK, WHO WON THE MEDAL OF HONOR DURING THE BOXER REBELLION
- THE SECOND COMMERCIAL BREAK IS AN AFRS SPOT ABOUT THE FLAG OF KENTUCKY
- THE THIRD COMMERCIAL BREAK IS ABOUT THE HEROISM OF LT. FRANK LUKE IN WORLD WAR I.

• THE ANNOUNCER IS ROY ROWAN

Producer:   Jack Johnstone          Writers:   Jack Johnstone
Cast:       Paula Winslowe, Ben Wright, Jack Kruschen, Jack Edwards,
            Marvin Miller, Joseph Kearns

◆ ❖ ◆

SHOW:        THE JOHNSON PAYROLL MATTER
SHOW DATE:   9/21/1958
COMPANY:     UNIVERSAL ADJUSTMENT BUREAU
AGENT:       PAT MCCRACKEN
EXP. ACCT:   $526.50

SYNOPSIS: Pat McCracken calls and tells Johnny he has been working too hard, and needs an all expenses paid vacation in southern California. Johnny tries to turn Pat down, but Pat tells Johnny that the job is really simple. All he has to do is go out to the coast and bring back $100,000.

Johnny cabs to Pat's office and gets the details of the case. Pat tells Johnny about the Johnson Payroll robbery in New York, and that the payroll was insured by one of Pat's companies. One of the robbers was wounded and told them that the others were going to split the money elsewhere. Pat has received a call from a man in Los Angeles who could give them a lead, for a price. Pat wants the money and tells Johnny that the man will contact him at his hotel.

Johnny flies to Los Angeles, California and cabs to the Hotel Nestor where he has been told to go. When the cab arrives a woman gets into the cab and falls onto Johnny. Johnny wants to give her the cab but she leaves. Johnny goes in to register and has a message from the informant to drive to Corrado Beach and meet him on the pier, so Johnny rents a car, drives to Corrado Beach and gets a motel room. The next morning Johnny goes to the pier and talks to a man who tells Johnny that the fishing has been fine lately. Johnny tells him that he is supposed to meet someone and the man points to a man next to a boat on the pier. They walk out to the boat as the first man tells Johnny the bass fishing has been fine. As they get to the second man, they discover that he is dead.

Johnny searches the man but finds no identification and the police are called. The police arrive and they know nothing either. Johnny waits in a local bar and then calls Pat McCracken to update him. Johnny tells him that he got the mug shots that Pat had sent and then sees someone at the bar. Johnny walks over to the woman who had gotten into his cab and wants to go out and talk. As Johnny holds her elbow, the bartender comes over and tells Johnny to let go of the girl, and she walks out. Johnny leaves and looks around for the girl and discovers that there is a key in his coat pocket, but not to his room. Johnny goes to the motel and opens the door, to discover a gun in his back. Johnny is ushered into the room by one of the men in the mug shots, a man named Slattery. Slattery tells Johnny that Blake was the one who killed the man on the pier, and that he has the payroll dough. Slattery knows that Blake's girlfriend got into Johnny's cab in Los Angeles and probably slipped him the key. Slattery wants the money or he will kill Johnny.

Slattery searches the room and does not find the money and slugs Johnny to find out where the money is. Johnny tells him that a man had called from Los Angeles, and Slattery tells Johnny it was Hollis, the dead man on the pier. Slattery tells Johnny that Blake engineered the robbery, and then ran out on him and Hollis, and Johnny is in league with him. Johnny tells Slattery that he does not know anything about the girl or where the money is. Johnny manages to slug Slattery and runs out of the room with Slattery in pursuit. Johnny gets back to his car and goes to look for the girl. Johnny finds a Myrna Grant in the register of the third motel in town, and goes to see her in room 8. The girl tells Johnny to leave and he tells her about the key, the robbery and the double-cross. She tells Johnny that she did not know Blake that long, but he had told her he was in trouble and that he had told her to put the key in Johnny's pocket and the meet him at the beach. She did not know that Blake was a criminal, and agrees to help Johnny find Blake. Johnny and Myrna go back to the bar and Johnny asks the bartender if he knows Fred Blake. The bartender does not know Blake. When Johnny mentions that fishermen must come in here, the bartender mentions that there has been no fishing here for months because of a chemical plant nearby. Johnny realizes that the man at the pier was Blake. Johnny goes to the pier, with a car following him with its lights out. At the pier Johnny gets the drop on Blake and tells him that he killed Hollis and hid on the pier. Slattery arrives with his gun and wants the money. Blake pulls a gun and is shot by Slattery, and Johnny slugs Slattery.

Remarks: The payroll money is back where it belongs and Slattery and Blake are back where they belong, with Blake facing a murder rap to boot. Funny, I probably wouldn't have nailed him if he had not told me that phony story about the fish biting near the pier. Teaches me a lesson, Pat. I'm not going to tell anymore fish stories, they can kill ya.

NOTES:
- THE FIRST COMMERCIAL BREAK IS AN **AFRS** SPOT ABOUT THE FLAG OF GEORGIA
- THE SECOND COMMERCIAL BREAK IS AN **AFRS** SPOT ABOUT HEROISM AND THE ACTIONS OF CPL. RAYMOND ROSSER IN KOREA.
- THE THIRD COMMERCIAL BREAK IS AN **AFRS** SPOT ABOUT THE FLAG OF OHIO
- THE ANNOUNCER IS ROY ROWAN

**Producer:** Jack Johnstone      **Writers:** Robert Stanley
**Cast:** Virginia Gregg, Lawrence Dobkin, Forrest Lewis, Shepard Menken, Frank Gerstle

◆ ❖ ◆

| | |
|---|---|
| **SHOW:** | **THE GRUESOME SPECTACLE MATTER** |
| **SHOW DATE:** | **9/28/1958** |
| **COMPANY:** | **TRI-STATE LIFE & CASUALTY INSURANCE COMPANY** |
| **AGENT:** | **ED BARRETT** |
| **EXP. ACCT:** | **$148.00** |

**SYNOPSIS:** Ed Barrett calls and is sick. He tells Johnny that he was going to go to a fishing lodge of a friend, Tommy Hargrave, and had just received word that a car rolled over on to Tom and killed him. Since the policy was for $70,000 double indemnity and an accident was involved, Ed has to order an investigation. His wife Mary was the beneficiary but they did not get along. The place is called Shadow Hill and is near Bethel, New York. The police department is a man named Skinner, and he had notified Ed.

Johnny travels to New York City and rents a car to drive to Bethel, gets a room in the hotel and then goes to Shadow Hill. On the way up the long driveway, Johnny stops at the accident scene and a man levels a 30/30 at him. Johnny is told to get out of the car but slams the door into the man and gets the gun from him. Johnny is told he will be locked up, as the man is Amos Skinner, the Chief of Police. Johnny tells Skinner that he has come to see him. Are you "the Johnny Dollar?" he asks. Amos shows Johnny the wreck site and tells Johnny that he had called the insurance company for Mrs. Hargrave. Amos thinks that Hargrave took the turn too fast and the car rolled over and killed him. Amos has just come from Doc Walton's and he is worried as to why Hargrave would have an accident on a road he knew too well. Johnny notices that the sedan has the windows closed yet Hargrave was under the car. Amos realizes that Hargrave was murdered. Now to discover who did it and why.

Amos tells Johnny that he learned of the accident from Mary while he was at the gas station talking about the Hamiltonian and how much money Barney Martin has made taking bets on the race. Johnny is flabbergasted that there is a bookie in town. Mary had just driven back from New York, drove back to the gas station and told Amos what had happened. Amos and Johnny go down to the car and realize that the keys are in the ignition, which is turned off. Johnny puts some fine dust on the steering wheel, but there are no fingerprints there. Johnny asks if Hargrave wore glasses and Amos tells Johnny no. Johnny wants to see the body now and goes to see Doc Walton. In the Doctor's office Johnny is shown how the clothes were torn like there had been a struggle, and the mark at the base of his skull. Johnny recognizes the mark as coming from a .38 automatic, of which he has seen plenty. Everyone agrees that Hargrave was murdered. Doc Walton tells Johnny that Mary Hargrave wears glasses, and shows him a pair that he had found in the car. Doc agrees that they could be Mary's, and Johnny wants to see Mary Hargrave.

Johnny, Amos and Doc drive to the Hargrave home, where the evidence points to her. Mary answers the door and is introduced to Johnny, who is expected. She tells Johnny that she was slow to answer the door because she has misplaced her glasses, and the old pair she is wearing is hard to see through. She tells Johnny that she mislaid her glasses a few days ago. Johnny notes that Mary is not grieved and she tells Johnny that all Tommy cared about was fishing and betting on the horses. She is going to sell the house and go to the city. Mary notices the glasses Doc is holding, but Doc realizes that the glasses are not Mary's as the lenses are wrong. Mary tells Johnny that Tommy had been playing the horses while they were there, and had been bragging about the big killing he had made. Johnny takes the glasses and looks at the optometrist's mark. Johnny leaves and tells the others to stay put, and tells Amos not to arrest anyone, as he might be sorry.

Well, that really is just about all there is to this case. Oh, except for the fact that the optometrist in Monticello had no difficulty at all in matching the glasses I had found with the prescription of, yeah, you guessed it. They had belonged to the bookie chief Skinner had told me about, Barney Martin. Of course Barney wanted to put up a fight when we faced him with the facts, but then he couldn't seem to explain the various sundry bruises he was carrying around until we reminded him of the fight he had had with Tommy Hargrave. Yeah, he'd killed him and pushed the car over on top of him. The reason for it all was simple. Tommy had won a cool $25,000 from him, had threatened to put him out of business if he didn't pay, which he couldn't. So Barney killed him and tried to fake the accident, and you know something? I have a sneaking suspicion chief Amos Skinner isn't going to stand for any bookies operating in Bethel, New York from here on out. Oh, and Mary found the glasses she had mislaid.

NOTES:
- DAN CUBBERLY IS THE ANNOUNCER

| | | | |
|---|---|---|---|
| **Producer:** | Jack Johnstone | **Writers:** | Jack Johnstone |
| **Cast:** | Virginia Gregg, Harry Bartell, Junius Matthews, Joe Kearns | | |

◆ ❖ ◆

| | |
|---|---|
| **SHOW:** | THE MISSING MATTER MATTER |
| **SHOW DATE:** | 10/5/1958 |
| **COMPANY:** | UNIVERSAL ADJUSTMENT BUREAU |
| **AGENT:** | PAT MCCRACKEN |
| **EXP. ACCT:** | $0.00 |

**SYNOPSIS:** Jack Johnstone, the writer who dramatizes Johnny's cases calls. He tells Johnny that he sent a copy of the latest report to Mary Ann Hooper, his secretary. Jack tells Johnny that she went to Hollywood, but never got there. Now there is no material for the show. Jack wants Johnny to come out and look for the script and Mary Ann.

Johnny makes reservations to fly to Hollywood, and on the way out meets

Pat McCracken at his front door, and Johnny tells him that he has a problem with his radio program and is in a real hurry to get to the airport. Pat tells Johnny that his program is very important to the insurance industry, as it discourages insurance fraud and false claims, etc. Pat tells Johnny that he wants Johnny to get out to California. Pat has his car, so he drives Johnny to the airport, and gets a speeding ticket on the way.

Johnny flies to Los Angeles, California and calls Jack's office at the airport, and Mary Ann Hooper answers the phone. Mary Ann knows nothing about the script, and tells Johnny that Jack had called her, but now he has disappeared. Johnny cabs to Jack's office and runs into Joan, the receptionist, who tells Johnny that Mary Ann has not been in the office for several days. Now two people are missing. Johnny is taken to the phone switchboard and is introduced to the girls. One of the operators remembers talking to Mary Ann recently, but she has not been there for several days. Johnny is told that Mary Ann works at home until the scripts are ready, and has phone calls routed to her home. She calls Mary Ann, but there is no answer. Johnny calls Pat McCracken, but he is in a conference. Johnny calls his home later, but he is not there. At 10:00 PM, Mary Ann arrives and she tells Johnny that she is not sure where Jack is. Jack had told her on Tuesday that he would have a script for her, but she has not seen it. Johnny realizes that things do not add up.

Johnny flies back to Hartford and goes to the garage behinds his apartment house to get his car, but it is gone. Johnny cabs to Pat McCracken's office and he is told that he is expected. Johnny goes in to find Jack Johnstone in Pat's office. Jack explains to Johnny that his programs help the insurance companies to save money, and they are grateful for his three years of service via his programs. Pat tells Johnny that they had to get him out of town so that they could reinstall his two-way radio. Pat takes Johnny to the window where he shows Johnny a brand new yellow hardtop, with air conditioning and all the accessories, including his two-way radio. The car is a gift of gratitude from all of the insurance companies. Jack wishes Johnny a happy anniversary, and tells him to drive the car in good health.

Johnny thanks all of the many people who help to make this program possible.

NOTES:
- THE ANNOUNCER IS DAN CUBBERLY
- THE SCRIPT SECRETARY FOR THIS PROGRAM IS MARY ANN HOOPER
- THIS IS THE ONLY REFERENCE TO A TWO-WAY RADIO IN THE SERIES
- STORY INFORMATION OBTAINED FROM THE KNX COLLECTION IN THE THOUSAND OAKS LIBRARY

**Producer:** Jack Johnstone        **Writers**    Jack Johnstone
**Cast:**       Jack Johnstone, Larry Dobkin, Virginia Gregg, Jean Tatum, Shirley Mitchell, Forrest Lewis

| SHOW: | THE IMPOSSIBLE MURDER MATTER |
|---|---|
| SHOW DATE: | 10/12/1958 |
| COMPANY: | TRI-WESTERN LIFE & CASUALTY COMPANY |
| AGENT: | WALT BASCOMB |
| EXP. ACCT: | $516.25 |

SYNOPSIS: Walt Bascomb calls Johnny from Los Angeles, and has a case for him. The case is either an accident or murder. The victim is Paul W. Ranken, who was insured for $100,000, double indemnity. Walt suspects murder, but if Ranken died as reported, it is impossible.

Johnny flies to Los Angeles, California and goes to Walt's office where Johnny is told that Paul W. Ranken was a real estate promoter, and the beneficiary is his wife Grace. Ranken was on vacation with his business partner in the Sierra Nevada mountains, and had gone to Forrest Lewis' fishing camp. Ranken had packed in to Lone Horse Lake, and was supposed to be picked up by a guide named Shorty in three days. When Shorty went back, Ranken was dead. Walt had been asked to change the beneficiary on the policy because Ranken had discovered that his partner, Al Warren, had been seeing his wife on the sly. The details of the murder are impossible, so Johnny will have to go there and see for himself.

Johnny flies to Forrest Lewis' camp and learns that Grace and Al were openly in love with each other, even in front of Ranken, who did not approve. Forrest tells Johnny that Ranken had brought them up here so he could leave them alone together without any luxuries. Johnny talks to Grace and Al, who tell Johnny that they are glad, as it will be better for both them and the business. Johnny is told that Ranken was a crook and ran phony real estate promotions, and had gotten letters from his victims. Johnny is told that the body is at the coroner's office in Big Pine, and that they are staying until the autopsy.

Johnny goes to his cabin to discover that someone had searched his bags. Johnny then rides up to the campsite at Lone Horse Lake. Johnny is shown where the tent was, and the footprints that led to the body. Johnny is told that Ranken was found in the snow, and had been hit with a blackjack and there were no other tracks there. Johnny returns to the camp and tells about his bags being searched. Dr. Wilson arrives and tells Johnny that the murder was caused by just one mark on Ranken's head, and that Forrest provided all of the evidence. Johnny gets everyone together and goes over the reasons why Grace and Al would benefit from the death of Ranken, but Johnny is told that everyone was in camp the whole time. Shorty tells Johnny that he has to leave to feed his mules. When Johnny hears mules, he gets a hunch. Shorty tells Johnny that he came from Missouri and is a muleskinner who uses a long whip. Johnny is sure that Shorty used the whip to kill Ranken. Shorty cracks his whip and tells Johnny that Ranken had stolen his father's money. Shorty tells Grace to move away from Johnny, and then hits both her and Al. Johnny gets to Shorty and slugs him.

Johnny reports to Walt that the death was not an accident.

NOTES:
- THE ANNOUNCER IS DAN CUBBERLY
- FORREST LEWIS' CAMP ALSO FIGURED IN "THE GLACIER GHOST MATTER"
- STORY INFORMATION OBTAINED FROM THE KNX COLLECTION IN THE THOUSAND OAKS LIBRARY

Producer:   Jack Johnstone          Writers   Jack Johnstone
Cast:       Edgar Stehli, Forrest Lewis, Virginia Gregg, Jimmy McCallion, Bart Robinson, Vic Perrin

◆   ❖   ◆

SHOW:        THE MONOXIDE MYSTERY MATTER
SHOW DATE:   10/19/1958
COMPANY:     PHILADELPHIA MUTUAL LIFE & CASUALTY INSURANCE
AGENT:       CLARKE BENDER
EXP. ACCT:   $74.65

SYNOPSIS: Clarke Bender calls Johnny and tells him that he got a call form Saticoy City, Pennsylvania from Mrs. Abbey Norton, who cared for Rufus W. Harper, her brother-in-law, and is the beneficiary of his $25,000 policy. Mrs. Norton found Rufus in his car, dead, and the death was called suicide, but she is not convinced.

Johnny flies to Philadelphia and goes to see Clarke who tells Johnny that on the first call Abbey was told about the suicide clause in the policy, and later Clarke was told that the death was not a suicide. Clarke tells Johnny that he will get a fee of $1,500 if Abbey is right and $1,000 if she is wrong. When Johnny asks if the fees are not reversed, Clarke tells Johnny that he is concerned about providing good service to his customer.

Johnny rents a car and drives to Saticoy City and goes to see Abbey who tells Johnny that the body is with the coroner, who is also the local carpenter and coffin maker. Abbey tells Johnny that she wants the money from the policy. She also tells Johnny that Rufus had just sold a lot for $1,600, and the money was gone from his pockets and warns Johnny to be careful. Johnny calls on Dr. Lehman, but he is not in. Johnny then goes to see the coroner, who tells Johnny that Tim Otis, the police in the town, is in bed with a hangover. Johnny is told that when the body was found, the car door was open. Johnny looks at the body and Dr. Lehman arrives. Johnny asks the doctor if the face and neck were cherry red, which is typical of carbon monoxide, and is told that they were not. Doc Lehman also tells Johnny that there was evidence that Rufus was hit on the head with a bottle, either at Paddy's or on the way home. Johnny is also told that Jake Quest has $1,600.

Johnny and Doc Lehman go to see Tim Otis, who is in bed with a headache. Tim tells Johnny that Rufus was at a party at Paddy's and was buying drinks, and that the Durkin boys were also there. The Durkins are Paddy's nephews, and local troublemakers. They tried to get Rufus to gamble with the money he had, and Doc tells Tim that Rufus was murdered. Johnny goes to Paddy's, and Doc Lehman insists on coming with him and tells Johnny that Paddy's is closed tonight. When they get there, Johnny sees a light on inside, and hears the Durkins inside. Johnny goes to the door to listen and hears Bo tell Paddy that he slugged Rufus, and the he is afraid of an investigation. Bo hears a noise and they grab their guns and go outside and find Johnny. While they are threatening Johnny, Doc Lehman uses his voice to create the presence of other police officers. Bo drops his gun, and Johnny drives Bo to the jail from the back seat of Bo's car.

The State Police are called and the insurance is to be paid to Abbey. And, Johnny will be paid more!

## NOTES:
- THE ANNOUNCER IS DAN CUBBERLY
- STORY INFORMATION OBTAINED FROM THE KNX COLLECTION IN THE THOUSAND OAKS LIBRARY

| | | | |
|---|---|---|---|
| **Producer:** | Jack Johnstone | **Writers** | Jack Johnstone |
| **Cast:** | Russell Thorson, Virginia Gregg, Lawrence Dobkin, Harry Bartell, Lillian Buyeff, Forrest Lewis, Alan Reed, Billy Halop | | |

◆　❖　◆

| | |
|---|---|
| **SHOW:** | THE BASKING RIDGE MATTER |
| **SHOW DATE:** | 10/26/1958 |
| **COMPANY:** | EASTERN TRUST & INSURANCE COMPANY |
| **AGENT:** | STUART SMITH |
| **EXP. ACCT:** | $29.55 |

SYNOPSIS: Stuart Smith calls Johnny from New York, and tells Johnny that David Rockwell Winters lives in Basking Ridge, New Jersey, and collects fine art. Winters has reported that the Victoria Rudy has been stolen, and is afraid he will lose something else, his life.

Johnny drives to Basking Ridge and meets Winters, who is glad that Johnny got there before he was murdered. Winters tells Johnny that he has sold his art collection, and that the money is in a vault in the basement, and that there is only one key. Winters also tells Johnny that his nephews and niece want his money, but he does not want them to get it because it will spoil them. Winters tells Johnny that his nephews are Ronald and Bill Tatum and their sister Bettina. When Johnny asks why Winters did not just change his will, he tells Johnny that he never thought of that. Johnny tells him that he will stay until the changes are made. Winters tells Johnny that several attempts have been made on his life, and that they started two weeks earlier. The relatives had come in a green car to visit and ask for money, and Winters threw them out. Then Winters found a loose step, ground glass in this sugar, and was almost hit by a green car.

Johnny goes to nearby Bernardsville to visit the relatives and finds a green car outside the house. Johnny meets Bettina, who is really cute, and Ronald. Both think that their uncle is crazy and want Johnny to look into the insurance for them. Al arrives and they tell Johnny that Winters had promised them an education, and that Bettina has become a nurse, and Ronnie and Al were told that they could go to Rutgers, but now they are living off of Beneficial Finance. Johnny agrees that something is wrong, and that the kids seem to make sense.

Johnny goes back to Winter's home and finds him groaning on the floor. Johnny gives him a brandy and he tells Johnny that he was hit just after Johnny left. The vault key is still in his pocket, but they go to the vault and open it to find the money gone. Johnny finds footprints and calls the police. Johnny makes some calls and then goes to a gun shop and makes a purchase. Johnny then goes back to Bernardsville where Bettina is home and the boys are gone. Johnny draws the blinds and places his gun on a table and talks to Bettina. Johnny tells her that he found her footprints in the basement and asks her why she did it. Bettina grabs the gun and tells Johnny that their uncle was cutting them out of the will, and so she stole the money. She shoots Johnny three times, but the gun contains blanks. Johnny determines that the brothers are not involved.

NOTES:

• THE ANNOUNCER IS DAN CUBBERLY
• BASKING RIDGE IS IN NORTH CENTRAL NEW JERSEY, SOUTH OF MORRISTOWN.
• STORY INFORMATION OBTAINED FROM THE KNX COLLECTION IN THE THOUSAND OAKS LIBRARY

**Producer:** Jack Johnstone      **Writers**   Jack Johnstone
**Cast:**      Frank Gerstle, Will Wright, Jeanne Tatum, Sam Edwards

**SHOW:** THE CRATER LAKE MATTER
**SHOW DATE:** 11/2/1958
**COMPANY:** NORTHWEST INDEMNITY ALLIANCE
**AGENT:** PETER WILKERSON
**EXP. ACCT:** $495.60
**SYNOPSIS:** Peter Wilkerson calls Johnny from San Francisco and tells Johnny that he has a claim on a $300,000 life policy. Johnny is on his way.

Johnny flies to San Francisco, California and goes to the Huntington Hotel and then to Pete's office. Pete asks Johnny if he knows Sam Arnold, the man who writes for all of the pulp magazines. Pete sold Arnold his first policy in 1939 and he has regularly increased his coverage. The beneficiary of the current policy is Vonnie Revell, the stripper. Three months ago Arnold increased the coverage to $300,000. Arnold recently went to Crater Lake and rented a boat and disappeared. The body was found, but was only a skeleton, and his wife based the identification on a ring, but Pete is suspicious of the wife.

Johnny flies to Klamath Falls, Oregon and goes to Crater Lake to talk to the park ranger, who is sure that Arnold was murdered. Johnny is told that the body was found in 1960 feet of water while they were taking depth soundings. Joe thinks that Arnold was on the lake when a big wind came up, and he was thrown overboard and caught his foot in a rope and was pulled down with the boat. Johnny looks at the rope from the body and is sure that Arnold was murdered because the rope is knotted and there is cloth in the knots. Johnny is told that Gimpy Joe Larson, a bad character from San Francisco was at the lake at the same time Arnold was there, and he disappeared at the same time, leaving his camping gear. Joe wonders if Arnold was murdered for something he wrote.

Johnny goes back to San Francisco and meets with Vonnie, who is upset. She tells Johnny that she met Arnold when she was in burlesque, and gets upset when Johnny suggests that she had him killed. She also tells Johnny that she does not know anyone named Gimpy Larson. She tells Johnny that she is going away as soon as she gets the money, which gives Johnny a hunch. Johnny goes to see police Lt. Dubov and learns that Gimpy is not in town. Johnny gets a photo of Gimpy, and he is a dead ringer for Sam Arnold. Johnny leaves and buys some old magazines with articles written by Arnold in them. Johnny then goes to see a man named Ah Lee, who is suspected of selling fake passports. Ah Lee denies making fake passports but for $100 he agrees to help Johnny by telling him where to look for a special forger's mark on fake passports. Johnny calls Vonnie and arranges to have dinner with her. Johnny then goes to Vonnie's and breaks in after she leaves. Johnny searches and finds Vonnie's passport and a fake passport under another name with Sam Arnold's photo on it. The door opens and Arnold walks in with a gun. Johnny tells Arnold that he had built up his insurance so that he could disappear. Johnny tells Arnold that he killed Gimpy and put the body where the rangers were going to do depth soundings so that it would be found. Vonnie comes in and tells Arnold to kill Johnny. Arnold pulls at Vonnie and Johnny slugs him.

## NOTES:

- THE ANNOUNCER IS DAN CUBBERLY
- BOB BAILEY WELCOMES STATION WABI IN BANGOR, MAINE TO THE CBS NETWORK
- STORY INFORMATION OBTAINED FROM THE KNX COLLECTION IN THE THOUSAND OAKS LIBRARY

Producer: Jack Johnstone     Writers  Jack Johnstone
Cast:      Peter Leeds, Barney Phillips, Virginia Gregg, Herb Vigran, Lawrence Dobkin

◆  ❖  ◆

SHOW:       THE CLOSE SHAVE MATTER
SHOW DATE:  11/9/1958

COMPANY:     UNIVERSAL ADJUSTMENT BUREAU
AGENT:     PAT MCCRACKEN
EXP. ACCT:     $383.20

**SYNOPSIS:** Pat McCracken calls, but Johnny tells Pat that he is going on vacation. Pat tells Johnny that he has a case for him at Lake Mojave. Johnny cabs to Pat's office and is told that Jim Barker from Western Maritime had called about his client Jules Maitland, who is insured for $250,000. Pat wants Johnny to go to Lake Mojave and investigate.

Johnny flies to Lake Mojave Resort and gives his usual description of the desert area as he goes to meet with Buster Favor. Buster tells Johnny that Maitland is worried that he is about to be murdered for his insurance money. Maitland's beneficiary is his wife Betty Jane, who lives on their ranch. Their stepson Charles Warren is no good, and would kill Betty to get the money. Buster tells Johnny that Maitland has letters with him threatening his life. Johnny goes out and sees a new car in the parking lot, and is sure that Charles is there. Johnny meets Charles, who knows who Johnny is, and tells him that his stepfather told him that the letters are gone. He tells Johnny that he came to the lake to ask for money to go to school. Buster notes that Charles seems to ok, and that the threats must be all talk. Johnny remembers a newspaper article about a car used in a robbery in Los Angeles, and the license plate number is similar so Johnny raises the hood and adjusts a valve on the engine.

Johnny goes to see Maitland and tells him to stay in his room and then calls Sgt. Hacker at the Los Angeles police and is told that the car matches except for the license plate number. Johnny goes out and sees that the car is gone. Johnny goes to see Maitland, who has just finished shaving. Johnny fixes them a drink and then Maitland starts to stagger. Johnny calls Buster who gets a doctor who is staying at the lodge. The doctor examines Maitland and finds that he was poisoned with potassium peyotin. Maitland tells Johnny that Charlie had given him a new shaving soap to use. Maitland tells Johnny to follow Charles, but Johnny does not have to. He tells Maitland and Buster that he had opened the drain valve on the engine, and Charles' radiator should be empty by now.

The police are called and they pick up Charles on the road and find the poison in his car.

NOTES:
- THE ANNOUNCER IS DAN CUBBERLY
- STORY INFORMATION OBTAINED FROM THE **KNX** COLLECTION IN THE THOUSAND OAKS LIBRARY

Producer:    Jack Johnstone       Writers     Jack Johnstone
Cast:        Larry Dobkin, Barney Phillips, Ralph Moody, Carleton G. Young, Jack Edwards

| SHOW: | THE DOUBLE TROUBLE MATTER |
|---|---|
| SHOW DATE: | 11/16/1958 |
| COMPANY: | TRI-STATE LIFE & CASUALTY COMPANY |
| AGENT: | EARLE POORMAN |
| EXP. ACCT: | $178.70 |

SYNOPSIS: Earle Poorman calls Johnny and tells him he is moving to California to get away from the insurance business. He has a wild case trying to get rid of $65,000, which Albert Schuyler Kingman left to his only son, Henry. The trouble is, Earle has found two sons.

Johnny travels to Sarasota, Florida and goes to Earl's Office. Earle tells Johnny that Kingman was a widower who lived in North Carolina, and the company has waited 20 years to settle the policy. Kingman was killed during a hurricane in 1938 when Henry was 10 years old. After the storm, Kingman's body was eventually found, but Henry disappeared. The insurance case is still open and they are waiting for the beneficiary. The company had advertised for the beneficiary, and two men have claimed the policy. They are staying here in Sarasota, and both seem to have iron clad stories. Earle gets the file on the father and the family for Johnny to review. Johnny and Earle drive to Earl's house for dinner. Johnny reviews the folders and thinks he knows how to expose the phony claimant.

Johnny goes to a motel to question Henry #1, but gets nowhere. Henry #1 tells Johnny all about his buddy Obie O'Brien, and evades a trap about Miss Albertis the supposed Sunday school teacher. Johnny thinks that Henry has too good of an alibi. Henry tells Johnny that he did not have too much education and wandered around after the storm. He saw the ad and thought it would be a chance to get an education. Johnny is unable to trip up Henry #1.

Johnny drives to another motel to see Henry #2, who answers all of Johnny's questions. He tells of being adopted by a family named McGovern after the hurricane. His parents knew who he was but never told anyone. Henry #2 was told he was adopted on his 21st birthday, and his foster parents died about seven years ago. Unfortunately Bridgeton, where he lived, was destroyed by a storm, and no one is there to tell Johnny who Henry #2 is.

Over dinner, Johnny tells Earle and Gertrude about his lack of progress. Earle wonders if the men knew each other, but they each deny knowing of the other. Johnny has an idea, and goes to see Doc Crutcher, an old friend of Earle and Johnny. On the way Johnny is slugged by a man who comes from behind a tree.

Earle is talking to Doc Crutcher as Johnny is given smelling salts. Gertrude brings a cup of tea for Johnny, but Doc suggests brandy, and Johnny changes the order to scotch. Johnny tells Earle to get the two Henrys and bring them there while Johnny asks Doc about heredity.

Johnny talks to the two Henrys, who Earle had found in the same hotel room. Johnny looks at their hands and Henry #1 has bruised knuckles, but Doc notices that Henry #2 also has bruises. Both claim they were hurt opening a window. Johnny tells them that he has realized that the laws of heredity can solve this case. Johnny tells Earle about talking with Doc Crutcher and checking the insurance records, where he learned that both parents had brown hair and brown eyes. Johnny tells them that when parents have the same hair and eye colors, the offspring will as well. When Johnny tells them of their varying hair and eye colors Henry #1 tells Henry #2 the he was a crazy fool and knew it would not work. But Henry #2 is afraid that Henry #1 would cheat him out of the money. Henry #2 pulls a gun and Johnny out draws him and shoots him after Gertrude hits Henry #1 with an old vase.

"Yeah, my heredity gag was just that, a gag. But it certainly brought things to a head in a hurry. How did they know so much about the real Henry Kingman? Well Listen. As soon as we locked them up, I called the national press services and had them put the story of this attempted fraud in the headlines all over the country. Result: a phone call from the head of an orphanage where the real Henry had been taken in as a child, where he still lived. And yeah, the phonies were a couple of kids who had run away from that orphanage after he palled around with them, told them all about himself. As for why they both appeared to make the claim? Sure, each of them saw the company's ad and tried to get in ahead of the other. Well they are in all right. For a long time."

NOTES:
- THE FIRST COMMERCIAL BREAK IS AN EPISODE OF THE BELLWETHERS AND THEIR AUTO INSURANCE
- THE SECOND COMMERCIAL BREAK IS AND AFRS SPOT ABOUT PVT. ROBERT VON SCHLICK, WHO WON THE MEDAL OF HONOR DURING THE BOXER REBELLION
- THE THIRD COMMERCIAL BREAK IS ABOUT THE NEW AMERICAN WARRIOR WHO USES TECHNOLOGY TO DO HIS JOB
- THE ANNOUNCER IS DAN CUBBERLY

Producer: Jack Johnstone     Writers: Jack Johnstone
Cast: Virginia Gregg, Vic Perrin, Sam Edwards, James McCallion, Parley Baer

◆ ❖ ◆

SHOW: THE ONE MOST WANTED MATTER
SHOW DATE: 11/23/1958
COMPANY: TRINITY MUTUAL INSURANCE COMPANY
AGENT: BOB TANK
EXP. ACCT: $3,995.00

SYNOPSIS: Bob Tank calls and tells Johnny that he will put him on the map with all the publicity from this case. Johnny tells Bob that he has another more important case, but Bob tells Johnny that Pat McCracken had given him Johnny's number. Johnny calls Pat, who tells Johnny that he has never heard of Trinity Mutual, but tells Johnny to look into the matter. Johnny goes to meet Bob Tank, who offers Johnny a drink and tells Johnny that he used to work in advertising but inherited the company from his father. Bob tells Johnny that a policyholder died and left $25,000 to his son Albert Siedel. Johnny recognizes Albert as Skippy Siedel, who is on the ten most wanted list and is wanted for arson, murder and bombings, although Bob insists that he is only wanted in six states.

Johnny calls the police all over the country and learns that Skippy's wife is living in Palmdale, California. Johnny goes to the airport and sees a headline in the papers "Famous Insurance Investigator on Siedel Case." Johnny calls Bob and accuses him of tipping Skippy off, but Bob tells Johnny that is it just local publicity. Johnny flies to Los Angeles and goes to the police and then to Palmdale, north of Los Angeles. On the way Johnny spots a stopped train and a crowd of people around an ambulance. Johnny stops and learns that the train had hit a man, who turned out to be Skippy Siedel. Johnny talks to the state police who are sure the man is Skippy, because the car was stolen in Reno by Skippy.

Johnny goes to see Skippy's wife Sandra, who is in seclusion but agrees to talk to Johnny. Johnny gets in and Sandra is so beautiful that Johnny can only stare. Sandra tells Johnny that she runs a beauty shop and is glad that her husband is dead. Skippy had wanted to hide there but she had told him no, so he was going to leave the state. Johnny asks about a local motel, and Sandra suggests McKenny's Ranch Motel, but insists that Johnny have dinner with her. After dinner Johnny leaves, buys gas and a local paper that has an article about a prospector who has disappeared. Johnny drives to the motel over a very remote road. The car starts to cough and Johnny opens the hood to find a bomb. The car explodes and Johnny realizes that Sandra was only a diversion while Skippy planted a bomb in the car. A car drives up with Sandra and Skippy in it. Johnny hides and hears Skippy mention killing the prospector as he starts to burn the car. Johnny surprises Skippy and hits him.

Johnny wonders if Bob got his publicity as he adds the cost of the rental car to the expense account.

NOTES:
- THE ANNOUNCER IS DAN CUBBERLY
- STORY INFORMATION OBTAINED FROM THE KNX COLLECTION IN THE THOUSAND OAKS LIBRARY

**Producer:** Jack Johnstone          **Writers**    Jack Johnstone
**Cast:**          Jerry Hausner, Lawrence Dobkin, Tom Hanley, Bill James, Virginia Gregg, James McCallion

◆ ❖ ◆

| SHOW: | THE HAIR RAISING MATTER |
|---|---|
| SHOW DATE: | 11/30/1958 |
| COMPANY: | STAR MUTUAL INSURANCE COMPANY |
| AGENT: | FRITZ MELCHIOR |
| EXP. ACCT: | $47.50 |

SYNOPSIS: Fritz Melchior calls Johnny, who is glad to hear from Fritz, as his cases usually put a lot of money in his pocket, and he needs a few extra bucks, quite a few. Fred was not thinking about a fee on this case, but will pay Johnny's expenses. John Wakefield Edwards is a retired businessman who lives outside of Albany. Nothing has happened yet, but he has a lot of insurance, and his wife died a few years ago. His beneficiary is his adopted daughter Marylyn, who lives in Troy. Edwards had called last night and demanded that Fritz send Johnny over and not to tell Marylyn. Johnny tells Fritz he will go over first thing in the morning.

Johnny decides to drive to Albany, New York that night and calls Mr. Edwards from the hotel. Edwards tells Johnny to see him first thing in the morning, as nothing will happen in the meantime. "Be here at seven sharp for breakfast" Johnny is told. Johnny leaves the next morning and drives to the Edwards mansion. Johnny sees a new sports car in the driveway with a pretty girl getting in. Johnny introduces himself, and Marylyn Edwards recognizes who Johnny is. She tells Johnny that she thought daddy would call someone like him. She is a model she tells Johnny as they go into the house. Marylyn calls for daddy and then Durkin, the housekeeper. Durkin comes in and tells Marylyn that she has rung for breakfast three times but Mr. Edwards has not come down. Johnny and Marylyn go upstairs and knock on the bedroom door. Johnny thinks he smells cordite, and they open the door to find Edwards dead.

Johnny finds the body with Marylyn and calls the police. Sgt. Christy and Dr. Lincoln arrive, and examine the body. Durkin tells them that Edwards has not been sick, and the doctor thinks it was a heart attack. Marylyn does not want an autopsy, so the doctor calls the cause of death "natural causes." As Durkin closes the windows, the doctor goes back to the morgue. Johnny thinks that something is wrong, and wonders why the windows were open. Did Marylyn really just arrive? And what about Durkin? The undertaker gets the body around noon, and Johnny questions Marylyn and Durkin. Marylyn tells Johnny that no one else would benefit from her father's death, but Durkin tells Johnny that he left her some money in his will, and a codicil in the will says that Marylyn has to share the insurance money with her, if she collects. Durkin tells Johnny that Marylyn and her foster father did not get along, and Marylyn had not seen him for several years. Johnny goes to search the room and only finds a few bottles of hair tonic, and a funny looking hat stand on the dresser. Marylyn rushes in with a .38 she found in a myrtle bush. She gives the gun to Johnny, so now the gun is covered with her prints and Johnny's. Suddenly Johnny has an idea.

Johnny is sure his hunch is right. He tells Marylyn and Durkin to stay at the house and goes to see the undertaker. The undertaker takes Johnny to the body, and Johnny examines the body. Johnny pulls up a hairpiece that covers a small bald spot. Johnny realizes that the stand was for the hairpiece, and that no one probably realized he had used one. Johnny gets a solvent to remove the hairpiece and finds a bullet hole.

Back at the house Johnny questions Marylyn and tells her that her father was murdered. Johnny asks about the stand, and Marylyn tells her that it was a hat stand she played with as a girl. Johnny asks her how long her father had worn a toupee, and Marylyn replies "never" as he was proud of his hair. Johnny tells her of the hairpiece and the bullet wound. The attention turns to Durkin and Johnny decides to try a bluff. Durkin comes in and Johnny tells her of the line click he heard on the phone when he talked to Edwards the previous night. Johnny tells Durkin that he was at police headquarters checking her prints from a water glass against the prints he found on the .38. Johnny tells her that the fingerprints match, but Durkin says it is a lie; she had wiped off the gun. She confirms she opened the windows to get rid of the gun smoke, and wiped of the prints. At least she thought she did.

"Don't worry. There will be no part of the insurance or any other money for Durkin. The courts will take care of that and probably with vengeance. And for Marylyn, well you know something, there is a gal I think I would like to see again, and I do not mean because of her fortune."

NOTES:
* THE ANNOUNCER IS DAN CUBBERLY

**Producer:** Jack Johnstone     **Writers:** Jack Johnstone
**Cast:** Virginia Gregg, Shirley Mitchell, Jack Edwards, Ralph Moody, Junius Matthews, Parley Baer

◆ ❖ ◆

**SHOW:** THE PERILOUS PARLEY MATTER
**SHOW DATE:** 12/7/1958
**COMPANY:** UNIVERSAL ADJUSTMENT BUREAU
**AGENT:** PAT MCCRACKEN
**EXP. ACCT:** $8.00

**SYNOPSIS:** Johnny gets a call from Sam Hodge who asks what is wrong, isn't $10,000 enough? The deal was for $5,000 if the job was done today, but it wasn't. Sam will give Jimmy one more day to take care of Parley. When Johnny says "Huh?" the caller hangs up.

Johnny wonders who Sam is, and what kind of parley is involved, maybe a parley at a racetrack? Pat McCracken calls Johnny and tells him that he has Johnny's check for The Love Shorn Matter, and is going to add an additional $500. Johnny tells Pat about the strange call he got, and Pat tells Johnny that he is going to send the check by messenger, so don't parley it on the horses. Later there is a knock at the door with a special delivery package. Johnny opens the door and falls instinctively when he sees the gun. Johnny wakes up in the hospital where Pat McCracken tells Johnny that he was shot, but the bullet just creased his arm. A police sergeant comes into the room and tells Johnny that they do not know who shot him. Johnny mentions the call about the parley and is told to come to Hartford, Connecticut headquarters when he is able. Johnny tells Pat all he knows and then goes to see the police. When Johnny mentions the call and Jimmy, he is told that the police just closed a case on Jimmy Waller, a hood from Chicago and New York, who just left town. Johnny goes to see Pat who tells him that they have a policy on Parley Barnes, who is a retired businessman who runs the "Clean Business Association." Johnny wonders who is trying to kill Barnes.

Pat tells Johnny that Barnes came from Corpus Christi, New Orleans and Memphis where he had been plugging his business. Johnny goes to the police and tells them to send an officer to 14325 Euclid Ave to protect Barnes. Johnny calls Wayne Stockseth, an old friend in Corpus Christi, and Wayne tells Johnny that Barnes was following a boiler room operator named Samuel Truesdale Hogerston. Johnny gets an address for Sam Hodge and calls the number and gets the same voice as the previous call. Johnny calls the police and then calls again acting as Jimmy. Sam takes the call and yells at his secretary for confusing Jimmy Waller with Johnny Dollar. Sam asks if Parley is dead and tells Jimmy to leave town. Hodge is arrested in his office and Jimmy is arrested at Barnes home.

Johnny wants a fee on this case!

NOTES:
* THE ANNOUNCER IS DAN CUBBERLY
* JOHNNY IS SHOT FOR THE 10TH TIME.
* THE PREVIOUS CASE WAS THE HAIR RAISING MATTER, BUT THE SCRIPT MENTIONS THE LOVE SHORN MATTER, WHICH WAS RECORDED ON THE SAME DAY.
* STORY INFORMATION OBTAINED FROM THE KNX COLLECTION IN THE THOUSAND OAKS LIBRARY

Producer:  Jack Johnstone          Writers    Jack Johnstone
Cast:      Virginia Gregg, Alan Reed, Lawrence Dobkin, Frank Gerstle, Tony Barrett

◆　❖　◆

SHOW:       THE ALLANMEE MATTER
SHOW DATE:  12/14/1958
COMPANY:    GREATER SOUTHWEST INSURANCE COMPANY
AGENT:      FRED BRINKLEY
EXP. ACCT:  $341.10
SYNOPSIS: Johnny is called by Myrna Dodd. She tells Johnny that she has tried

to call Fred Brinkley at Greater Southwest, but he has not returned her call. Myrna tells Johnny that she has been robbed, and Johnny must come to Corpus Christi and she will pay his expenses if necessary.

Johnny flies to Corpus Christi, Texas where Myrna, a living doll, meets Johnny at the airport. Myrna tells Johnny that her husband Al is out fishing on the Gulf of Mexico as she drives Johnny to their home. Myrna tells Johnny that the robbery occurred on their boat, the Allanmee, which is a 52-foot cruiser. They have a guard, but the jewels and the guard were gone when they returned from a trip. She also tells Johnny that the Allanmee's crew usually comes from her husband's shrimp boats. On the boat Johnny finds that it has been torn apart, and the jewels are gone. Johnny also finds a secure compartment where a metal strongbox has been pried open. Johnny tells Myrna to call the insurance company and she leaves. Al Dodd returns and hits Johnny and accuses him of robbing them. Myrna returns to the boat and explains to Al who Johnny is, and Al apologizes. Myrna tells Al what has happened and that Toby Rich, the guard, is gone. Al tells Johnny that he does not want to call the police, and that he will buy his wife new furs and jewelry, and that no claim will be filed, and that he will pay Johnny's expenses. Al offers to take Johnny fishing, but Johnny declines the offer.

Johnny is suspicious and calls Fred from the airport. Fred tells Johnny that the jewels were insured for $7,000, but the furs were not insured. Johnny calls police Lt. Culpepper who tells Johnny that they have nothing on Al Dodd who works as a deck hand on a fishing boat. Al does have a boat with twin diesel engines and usually fishes in Mexican waters. Johnny tells Lt. Culpepper about the robbery and learns that Toby has been arrested in East Humble, Louisiana. Johnny flies to East Humble and inspects the car driven by Toby. In the trunk Johnny finds the furs and the jewels along with a bag containing $320,000.

Johnny returns to the Dodd house to find the boat pulling away from the dock. Johnny jumps on and slugs Al. Myrna tells Johnny that Al told her to leave without packing. Johnny tells Myrna and Al that he has located Toby, and about the jewels, furs and money in his car. Johnny tells Al that he is really smuggling heroin from Mexico, and Al offers Johnny a bribe.

Al is arrested and charged with smuggling and tax evasion.

NOTES:
- THE ANNOUNCER IS DAN CUBBERLY
- STORY INFORMATION OBTAINED FROM THE KNX COLLECTION IN THE THOUSAND OAKS LIBRARY

Producer:    Jack Johnstone           Writers    Jack Johnstone
Cast:        Virginia Gregg, Russell Thorson, Harry Bartell, Sam Edwards

SHOW:        THE TELLTALE TRACKS MATTER
SHOW DATE:   12/28/1958

COMPANY: CONTINENTAL INSURANCE & TRUST COMPANY
AGENT:
EXP. ACCT: **$0.00**

SYNOPSIS: Alvin Peabody Cartwright calls Johnny, addled as usual, and tells Johnny that he has been robbed. Johnny is told to come there or he will cancel all of his insurance.

Johnny drives to Lakewood, Connecticut on Christmas day. When Johnny gets to Alvin's house Alvin gives Johnny his present, a diamond studded watch and wishes Johnny a happy new year as he escorts Johnny to the door. When Johnny mentions the robbery, Alvin takes Johnny to see his tree and explains that his niece and her two children came to see the tree, but all the presents were gone. Johnny is told that a mink coat, some jewels and toys and an envelope with $25,000 were taken. Alvin shows Johnny the window the burglar used, and tells Johnny that the police have not been called. Alvin tells Johnny to follow the footprints in the snow and get his presents back. Johnny follows the tracks, but notes that he would not have, if he had known.

Johnny follows the tracks to a shack where he sees a girl sick in bed taking some medicine, and a boy wearing some fancy clothes. Johnny also sees a woman in a tattered dress, wearing a mink coat and wearing a jeweled watch as she counts the money. Johnny goes into the shack and asks for directions to Alvin's house, and the woman offers Johnny some hot cider. She tells Johnny that she is Betty Rogan, and that her daughter will recover. She tells Johnny that her husband Ricky left for New York and eventually moved all over and had stopped writing. She tells Johnny that she and her daughter Nancy got sick, but now they will be all right because Ricky came home last night and left a note for them. The note said that things never work out, but he had left the gifts, and this is the last time he would say goodbye.

Johnny goes back to Alvin's house and remembers who Ricky Rogan is. Johnny calls Randy Singer to get information on Rogan, and Alvin tells Johnny that his desk was also broken into, and one piece of paper was taken. Randy calls back and tells Johnny that Ricky Rogan is really Rick Marengo, who is a sneak thief and burglar. Rick had pulled a bank job in New York and killed a bank guard and was also injured. Johnny gets a flask and a flashlight and follows a set of footprints leading away from the shack. Johnny finds Rick in the snow, takes his gun and gives him a drink. Rick tells Johnny that he had stolen the things for his family from the house, and Johnny tells him that he knows what happened to him. Rick tells Johnny that he saw the situation of his wife and kids, and that he never did right by her. Rick tells Johnny that he stole the things that mean nothing to that rich man, but mean the world to his wife. Rick dies and Johnny goes to the police and tells them where to find his body.

Johnny mentions the recovery of the goods to Alvin who decides that he will get Betty a decent place to live, and will give her a job, maybe as her housekeeper.

NOTES:
* THE ANNOUNCER IS DAN CUBBERLY

• **STORY INFORMATION OBTAINED FROM THE KNX COLLECTION IN THE THOUSAND OAKS LIBRARY**

| | | | |
|---|---|---|---|
| Producer: | Jack Johnstone | Writers | Jack Johnstone |
| Cast: | Howard McNear, Richard Beals, Virginia Gregg, Herb Vigran, Harry Bartell | | |

◆   ❖   ◆

| | |
|---|---|
| SHOW: | THE HOLLYWOOD MYSTERY MATTER |
| SHOW DATE: | 1/4/1959 |
| COMPANY: | EASTERN LIABILITY & TRUST COMPANY |
| AGENT: | HAL SPIDLE |
| EXP. ACCT: | $0.00 |

SYNOPSIS: Parley Baron calls from Hollywood. He knows that Johnny handles all investigations for the Eastern Liability and Trust. Baron is sure that Eastern will be calling Johnny about a $10,000 embezzlement from the Berkley Furniture Manufacturing Company in Hartford. Check with Berkley and the insurance company. "When you have learned the facts, you will realize it is of the utmost importance to contact me." Baron tells Johnny.

Johnny calls Hal Spidle, his usual contact at Eastern, and Hal has not received a claim yet. Johnny is put on hold by Hal only to find that he has an assignment with Berkley Furniture; they just found out about the embezzlement. Johnny realizes that the informant knew something.

Johnny goes to the Berkley Company in Hartford, Connecticut and meets with the president, Mr. Berkley. Berkley tells Johnny that he wants the money back. It was taken by a bookkeeper that had been with them for 30 years. The man earned $65 a week, which was plenty of money. The bookkeeper was not married, and could not afford a wife. Johnny realizes that the man was paid as little as Berkley thought he could get away with. Berkley tells Johnny that the man went to see his doctor yesterday, and this morning Berkley discovered $9,984.75 missing from the safe. Berkley called the apartment of the bookkeeper to discover that the man had left the previous afternoon. So far the police have not been notified. Berkley will not prosecute; he only wants the money. Johnny gets the address of the bookkeeper. Johnny tells Berkley how an informant had called him on the phone. Berkley tells Johnny that the bookkeeper was Parley Baron.

Johnny cabs to the apartment of Baron and runs into a woman leaving who takes the taxi Johnny had come in. Johnny meets the manager who tells Johnny that Baron left the previous day. Johnny is taken to the apartment and is assured that a nice quiet old man like Baron could not do anything wrong. Baron never had any excitement, except when his niece Virginia Lockhart came to visit. She looks in on him and cooks for him once in a while. In the apartment Johnny sees signs of a hasty departure. The manager tells Johnny that Virginia just left the apartment and shows Johnny a photo. Johnny spots a note that tells Virginia that Baron has less than a week to live and he is going to really live it up to make up for the things he has missed over the years, and for her to not try to follow him. The manager calls Johnny a cab and Johnny goes to the airport just in time to see Ginny Lockhart heading for New York. Johnny catches a flight to New York and sees Ginny getting on a plane. Johnny dashes on the plane and uses his credentials to keep from being thrown off. The stewardess tells Johnny that his plane is going to Miami, Florida—not to California.

Johnny goes to the cabin and fumes over the rest of the flight. Johnny finds the only open seat is next to Ginny Lockhart. Johnny introduces himself to Ginny and tries to start a conversation, but she does not want to talk. She tells Johnny that she is going to try and save someone's life but does not want to talk about it. In Miami Johnny takes a cab and follows Ginny to Hollywood, Florida and a hotel. Johnny overhears Ginny getting a room number and beats her to the room where Johnny thinks Parley Baron is. At the door Johnny tells Ginny why he is there and about what Parley did. Johnny tells her how he hates this assignment because of the way Parley has been taken advantage of by Berkley. Ginny tells Johnny that she will give him the money her uncle has spent if he will not arrest him. She tells Johnny about the new doctor Baron went to, and how the doctor had told Baron he only had a week to live. The doctor later discovered that the lab reports had been mixed up and called Ginny after being unable to talk to Baron. She has been trying to find her uncle because he will be all right. "Well let's tell him the good news." Johnny tells her.

"Oh, I don't know. Maybe I am just a sucker for a good-looking girl. And, uh, maybe this makes me an accessory to the crime. But you know something, and you can blame it on the holiday season or anything you like, I don't care. Expense account total, including the trip back to Hartford, well a happy New Year to you too."

NOTES:
- BILL BAILEY MENTIONS ANOTHER FLORIDA STORY IN THE FEBRUARY 1959 COPY OF HARPER'S BAZAAR, JUST OUT.
- A SALARY OF $65 IN 1959 IS EQUAL TO ABOUT $418 IN 2004, LESS THAN $22,000 PER YEAR.
- THE ANNOUNCER IS DAN CUBBERLY

Producer:  Jack Johnstone     Writers:  Jack Johnstone
Cast:  Virginia Gregg, Jean Tatum, Parley Baer, Forrest Lewis, Junius Matthews, Frank Gerstle

◆ ❖ ◆

| SHOW: | THE DEADLY DOUBT MATTER |
| SHOW DATE: | 1/11/1959 |
| COMPANY: | UNIVERSAL ADJUSTMENT BUREAU |
| AGENT: | PAT MCCRACKEN |
| EXP. ACCT: | $41.00 |

**SYNOPSIS:** Carol Carson calls Johnny at 1 AM and she tells Johnny that Bud Ralson had suggested she call Johnny's at his hotel. She tells Johnny that maybe he can help, as she is in real trouble. She is at the apartment of Everett Reed, and she thinks she has killed him.

Johnny cabs to the New York City apartment of Everett Reed and Carol points to the body. Carol thinks that she is the one who killed him, and she feels lightheaded and confused. She tells Johnny that she came to see Everett around 11 because he sent for her and she had to come. He told her to have a drink and that is when she started feeling lightheaded and dizzy. She left the apartment around 11:30 and walked the streets. She came back and does not remember anything else. When she woke up she saw the body and the gun and called Johnny. Johnny tries to get her to remember where she was, and she remembers getting a cup of coffee near neon sign on Third Avenue. She remembers someone following her and he told her his name: Tom.

Johnny calls Lt. Tovitch of homicide and then goes to get a drink and think about her story; it sounded so phony it might be true.

Johnny calls Pat McCracken and learns that Reed was insured by one of their companies. Johnny starts checking the local eating places, and at Eddies' Bar and Grill a man remembers seeing Carol around midnight. He also remembers seeing a man in the doorway. She was given the coffee and just left. She was in the bar for a minute. Johnny goes to see Lt. Tovitch and updates him. Johnny is told that the Medical Examiner says that Reed died between 11:30 and 12:30, and she called Johnny at 12:00. So far her story only covers 5 minutes. Johnny tells Lt. Tovitch that Carol will not explain why she was at Reed's apartment, or how she got the lump on her head. Lt. Tovitch tells Johnny that Reed was a big time gambler who had been winning lately. Reed had been running around with Jack Vissel and that crowd. Larry Bowman comes in and asks Lt. Tovitch what is happening with Carol, his fiancé. He does not know why she went to see Reed and Larry can prove that he was with her while she was walking the streets. She did not mention that Larry was with her because she was confused. The story he gives to Johnny is all wrong, but Larry is sure Carol did not kill Reed.

Johnny buys coffee for Larry and he tells Johnny that he cannot stand by while nothing happens. Johnny then goes to see Jack Vissel, who tells Johnny that he had no reason to kill Reed. Vissel tells Johnny that he did owe Reed money, two bits. Johnny canvasses the area again and goes to his room. A man knocks at the door and tells Johnny that he is the man Carol had mentioned, Tom. Tom tells Johnny that he had followed her for an hour and gave up trying to meet her. He was with her from 11:30 to 12:30. Johnny takes Tom to police headquarters where he gives his story to Lt. Tovitch and Carol identifies him. After Carol is released, she thanks Tom, and tells Johnny she will call Larry from her apartment. Carol gets a cab and Johnny notices another cab following hers with Tom in it. Johnny goes to Carol's apartment and discovers Carol paying off Tom. Tom tells Johnny that he had seen someone going down the fire escape and followed him. When the story came out, Tom figured he could make some money on it, but only after Carol got out of jail. Carol screams "Larry:" and Johnny turns, deflects the gun as Larry shoots and then Johnny slugs Larry Bowman. Carol tells Johnny that Larry had been gambling with Reed and losing. She went to see Reed to square the deal and Reed drugged her. Larry killed Reed while she was gone, slugged her when she came back and planted the gun on her. She was not sure until Tom told her what he had seen.

"Yeah, Larry Bowman's gambling was a big fat mistake. First with Everett Reed, and then trying to frame Carol. I guess that's the trouble with gambling, you push your luck too far, and sooner or later you are bound to loose."

NOTES:

- STATION **KRMG** IN TULSA, OKLAHOMA IS SALUTED AS THE NEWEST **CBS** STATION
- THE ANNOUNCER IS DAN CUBBERLY

| Producer: | Jack Johnstone | Writers: | Robert Stanley |
|-----------|----------------|----------|----------------|
| Cast: | Virginia Gregg, Junius Matthews, Paul Dubov, James McCallion, Alan Reed, Frank Gerstle | | |

◆　❖　◆

| SHOW: | THE LOVE SHORN MATTER |
|-------|----------------------|
| SHOW DATE: | 1/18/1959 |
| COMPANY: | UNIVERSAL ADJUSTMENT BUREAU |
| AGENT: | PAT MCCRACKEN |
| EXP. ACCT: | $377.00 |

SYNOPSIS: Pat McCracken calls Johnny and wants him to play a long shot for the insurance companies that have become part of a racket.

Johnny goes to Pat's Hartford, Connecticut office where Pat reminds Johnny that insurance companies use the Universal Adjustment Bureau to process difficult claims. Pat reviews the case of Mrs. Dorothy Conrad Shaw who died in an accident when she lost control of her car. Her new husband was Jeremy Alcot Shaw. Pat reviews several other cases where the beneficiary had the initials JAS, the policyholder had a new husband and died in an accident.

Johnny calls a number of insurance companies and alerts them to beware of changes in policies to widows with new husbands, and to report those changes to Johnny. Johnny gets his telephone service to take any calls and then goes to Danbury Connecticut to see an elderly woman. She tells Johnny that Mrs. Conrad lived there until she got married to a young man around fifty. Johnny is shown a photo of Mr. Shaw and learns that Mrs. Conrad placed a lonely-hearts ad that read, "Charming middle aged wealthy family. Would like to meet younger man." Before Mrs. Conrad got married, her insurance was to go to a charity, but she changed it before she was married.

Johnny takes the photo and visits the cities of the cases Pat had reviewed with him. Johnny learns that all of the women ran personal ads. Johnny calls Pat and arranges for the photo of Shaw to be mailed to companies all over the country.

Johnny checks his message, but has no leads. Johnny gets a call from Sam Nelson at Masters Insurance. He tells Johnny that he got the photo, and one of his policy holders asked to change her policy; her prospective husband is the man, Jason Arthur Sharpless!

Johnny goes to the address and meets Dora Merrill and tells her about the aliases when Sharpless drives up. Sharpless comes in and Johnny tells him that he answered the personal ad, and is after Mrs. Merrill's money. Sharpless pulls a gun and when Dora comes in to tell him that she had heard what was said, Johnny slugs him.

The courts will take care of this matter.

NOTES:
• THE ANNOUNCER IS DAN CUBBERLY
• STORY INFORMATION OBTAINED FROM THE KNX COLLECTION IN THE THOUSAND OAKS LIBRARY

Producer: Jack Johnstone      Writers    Jack Johnstone
Cast: Lawrence Dobkin, Frank Nelson, D. J. Thompson, Jeanne Tatum, Shirley Mitchell, Forrest Lewis, Virginia Gregg, Marvin Miller

◆ ❖ ◆

SHOW: THE DOTING DOWAGER MATTER
SHOW DATE: 1/25/1959
COMPANY: FLOYDS OF ENGLAND
AGENT: GEORGE REED
EXP. ACCT: $17.80

SYNOPSIS: George Reed calls Johnny and tells him things are really good at Floyds. But George has a problem though with a small statuette owned by Dora Harkness Balin, a very wealthy but very eccentric woman. The statuette has disappeared. It is only insured for $26.50, but Miss Balin carries hundreds of thousands in other forms of insurance. George tells Johnny that the owner has placed particular value to the statuette. George is afraid she will take her insurance elsewhere, so Johnny tells him he will be in touch.

Johnny travels to New York City and goes to the Balin residence, an old Brownstone. Inside, the house is full of Victorian era furniture and art works. Higgins the butler takes Johnny to the library where Hal Winters, the nephew asks Higgins about the mail, and Higgins goes to check on it. Hal tells Johnny that his aunt likes the pot-metal statue because it looks like her grandfather, because he was the only Balin who did anything on his own. Hall suddenly recognized who Johnny is, and gets nervous and tells Johnny to forget the case. Johnny asks Hal about the statue, the servants, guests, etc., but gets no information. Miss Dora Balin comes in and tells Johnny that he better recover the statue or she will cancel all of her insurance. Dora asks if the mail has come and Hal tells her is was going out to check on it, but is told to let Higgins do it. Hal wants to leave but is told to sit down. Dora tells him he was going to call that girl, that Nancy Gavin, who is trying to take him away from her. Dora likes Nancy but will not let her take Hal from her. Johnny is told to leave no stone unturned just as Higgins comes back in with the mail. There is a letter with no postmark addressed to Dora. The letter is a ransom note for the statue, and the thieves want $75,000.

Everyone is surprised at the ransom. Dora accuses Hal of thinking that the ransom would mean less for him to inherit. Dora is prepared to pay the ransom, and has the money in the safe. The note tells her to give the money to Hal, who will be contacted. If the police are brought in, the statue will be destroyed. Dora tells everyone to stay in the house except for Harold who will do what the kidnappers tell him. Johnny is told to do as he is told. Nancy Gavin arrives and gives Hal a big kiss. Johnny is introduced, and Nancy also knows who Johnny is. Nancy is told of the ransom, and glibly tells Dora to pay it. Nancy asks Dora when she will let Hal marry her and get out on his own. Dora tells Nancy that her precious Harold would not do that. Johnny asks Hal what he would do, and is told to stay out of the matter. Johnny tells Dora that he is on the right track and asks Hal again if he would leave. Johnny is sure Hal's answer will solve the case, but he is dead wrong.

Hal tells Johnny that he would leave his aunt if he could, and Nancy concurs. Dora tells Nancy that Hal needs her, but Nancy tells Dora that Hal needs a break and the chance to show what he can do. Hal tells Dora that he would leave if he could, and that Dora did not know that because Dora only cared for herself. Johnny is sure that he knows where to look for the statue as Hal and Nancy leave. Dora tells Johnny that she had not called the insurance company; Higgins had called. Johnny tells her that the note was poorly written and probably came from within the house. Dora tells Johnny that she had hoped that Hal would make a move to break from her, but it would have to be on his initiative. She tells Johnny that the cheap statue was chosen for the experiment. She pumped up the value of the statue so that Harold would think she would do anything to get it back. He finally got up the nerve to do something, and she is tickled pink that he did. Johnny tells her that she is happy that she has made a thief of Harold. She tells Johnny that in the instruction note she will write she will tell Harold that she hopes he and Nancy will be happy, and will even throw in a few extra thousand dollars as an extra wedding present. Also, she does not want Harold to bring that monstrosity back here! Harold comes back in and asks if Johnny has determined how he will proceed. Johnny tells Hal he is going to give up the case and leaves. Johnny tells Dora to call the insurance company about the extra fee he is to get on the case, and she tells Johnny that she already has. As Johnny leaves Hal shows him the instruction note and asks if it is ok. Johnny realizes that Hal knew what was going on. Hal tells Johnny that Dora was just being her eccentric self, and could not just tell Harold and Nancy to get married, that would ruin her reputation. Hal offers to send Johnny the statuette when this is all over.

"Believe me, I have handled some pretty wacky cases over the years, but this was by long odds the wackiest. And yet, why complain, when it's a good living."

**NOTES:**

- JOHNNY BEMOANS THE LOWLY $17.80 ON THE EXPENSE ACCOUNT, BUT DOES NOT MENTION THE GENEROUS FEE HE WILL GET.
- THE ANNOUNCER IS DAN CUBBERLY

**Producer:** Jack Johnstone      **Writers:** Jack Johnstone
**Cast:** Virginia Gregg, Eleanor Audley, G. Stanley Jones, Eric Snowden, Sam Edwards

◆ ❖ ◆

**SHOW:** THE CURLEY WATERS MATTER
**SHOW DATE:** 2/1/1959
**COMPANY:** MASTERS INSURANCE & TRUST COMPANY
**AGENT:**
**EXP. ACCT:** $0.00
**SYNOPSIS:** Curley Waters calls Johnny and tells him that he has busted out of prison and will come and get Johnny.

Johnny wonders if the call really was from Curley Waters, who Johnny had nabbed for the Mailey's Department Store job when Johnny found him asleep, but without the $84,000. Johnny gets a paper and sees the story about Curley escaping. Johnny goes back to his Hartford, Connecticut apartment to make a phone call, and Curley tells Johnny to drop his gun. Curley empties the gun and gives it back to Johnny and tells Johnny that he came in the rear window. Curley shows Johnny a priest's outfit and tells Johnny that he is going to help Curley get the $84,000, or he will die. Johnny tells Curley that he has a date with Betty Lewis and Al Matthews, but Curley shows Johnny a .257 Roberts Winchester 70 rifle with a 4X scope. He is going to change clothes and drive to Myrtle's Steak House where Johnny is to go in with a note for Gimpy Taylor, Myrtle's husband. The note will be an order for 1 dozen hamburger rolls, 3 cartons of coffee and a broken thermos that has the money in it. Curley warns Johnny that he will be watching, and will shoot Johnny if he does not cooperate.

Curley changes clothes and calls Gimpy to inform him of the plan. They drive to Myrtle's and Johnny goes in and sees a policeman sitting at the counter. Johnny gets the order and goes to the car and returns to his apartment with Curley, who tells Johnny that he is going to dye his hair, when the phone rings. Johnny answers and tells Betty that he must cancel their dinner plans, and asks her to apologize to Al and Bernice Matthews. Curley bleaches his hair and is ready to shoot Johnny when the police bust in and Curley is shot. Betty rushes in and Johnny tells her that he is glad that she caught the clue; Mrs. Matthews is Marry Ann, not Bernice.

Curley Waters is behind bars, and there is no expense account, but what about a fancy fee on this one?

## NOTES:

- THE ANNOUNCER IS DAN CUBBERLY
- STORY INFORMATION OBTAINED FROM THE KNX COLLECTION IN THE THOUSAND OAKS LIBRARY

**Producer:** Jack Johnstone      **Writers**    Jack Johnstone
**Cast:** James McCallion, Forrest Lewis, Lucille Meredith, Tom Hanley, Bill James, Bert Holland

◆ ❖ ◆

**SHOW:** THE DATE WITH DEATH MATTER
**SHOW DATE:** 2/8/1959
**COMPANY:** MASTERS INSURANCE & TRUST COMPANY
**AGENT:** BERT WELLS
**EXP. ACCT:** $47.00

**SYNOPSIS:** Johnny dials a number on a phone and hangs up only to have the phone ring with Betty Lewis on the extension phone. Johnny explains to her how to check the extension by calling the number and hanging up. The phone rings again and reluctantly Johnny answers. Berton Wells has to see him in the office. Bert tells him that unless Johnny gets to the office, he will have a date with death.

Johnny leaves Betty with instructions not to leave and goes to Bert's Hartford, Connecticut office. Bert tells Johnny that the problem is Curly Waters. Johnny recounts how Betty Lewis should get credit for catching Curly after he escaped. Bert tells Johnny that Curly was wounded but has escaped from the hospital. Lt. Howie Daily arrives and tells Johnny that with the help of Gimpy Taylor, Curly Waters has escaped from the hospital, even with three good men watching him. Lt. Daily tells Johnny that he is having a bodyguard assigned to him until Curly is picked up. When Bert mentions Betty, Johnny calls Betty's apartment but gets no answer. Johnny and Lt. Daily drive to the apartment, going up a one-way street the wrong way in the process, and climb the stairs to the apartment. The door to Betty's apartment is open and Johnny searches the apartment to find it empty. The apartment is searched and no trace is found except for a coat hanger on the floor where a coat was taken. The phone rings, Johnny answers and officer Riley wants to talk to Lt. Daily, who is told that Gimpy Taylor has been caught. He plowed his car into a tree and survived. The police know that two men stole the car, but Betty was not in the car. Johnny thinks that Curly is still in town and using Betty to get to Johnny. Betty comes in to her apartment and tells Johnny that she got a call from the hospital telling her that Johnny had been shot by Curly Waters. Johnny tells Lt. Daily that Curly is smart and only Johnny can bring Curly into the open. Johnny is going to go to his apartment and wait. Johnny goes to his apartment and waits. At 12:30 there is a knock at the door and Lt. Daily is there; he is just checking up and tells Johnny that he is taking too much of a chance. Lt. Daily leaves and Johnny brews a pot of coffee. There is a knock at the back door and Johnny hears Betty there. Johnny lets her in and she tells Johnny that she was worried and had to come and see Johnny. There is a knock at the front door, so Johnny sends Betty to the bedroom and a voice tells Johnny that is it "Howie." Johnny opens the door to find Curly Waters there. Johnny is forced to drop his gun and Curly tells Johnny he has been waiting in an empty apartment across the hall. Curly is sure there are no cops in the area, and Gimpy Taylor's wife is spotting for him, and will call if the cops show up. She will shoot into the alley to distract the police. The phone rings and Myrtle Taylor tells Curly that Johnny is not alone. The woman tells Curly to shoot if the bedroom door opens. Curly goes into the bedroom, the door bursts open, Curtly shoots, and Johnny slugs Curly with the phone. Johnny thanks Betty for remembering how to make the phones ring. Betty makes Johnny hold her when Johnny shows her where a bullet had nicked her arm.

"Yeah, Curly is back in the clink, and this time to stay. When the necessary papers were signed, I hauled him over to the state pen myself. So expense account total, including transportation, $47.00 even. Betty? Betty Lewis? Well I tell you this, if I were the marrying kind, believe me . . .'"

### NOTES:
- THIS IS AN **AFRS** PROGRAM WITH AN ORGAN SERENADE AT THE END
- THE ANNOUNCER IS DAN CUBBERLY

**Producer:** Jack Johnstone     **Writers:** Jack Johnstone
**Cast:** Lucille Meredith, James McCallion, Russ Thorson, Sam Edwards, Herb Vigran

◆  ❖  ◆

**SHOW:** THE SHANKAR DIAMOND MATTER
**SHOW DATE:** 2/15/1959
**COMPANY:** PROVIDENTIAL LIFE & CASUALTY INSURANCE COMPANY
**AGENT:** STEVE KILMER
**EXP. ACCT:** $50.00

**SYNOPSIS:** Steve Kilmer calls and asks if Johnny would like to attend a wedding. Johnny says sure, as long as it is not his. Steve tells Johnny that he knows what Johnny means. Steve would be a bachelor too if it were not for a wife, four kids and a couple of grandchildren. Steve asks if Johnny remembers Martha Mayfield Merryman in New York City? Johnny reminds Steve of how Johnny helped clear up a report of her death in 1957. Steve tells Johnny that her son Edgar is getting married, and she insists that Johnny be there. Johnny agrees to take the case.

Johnny travels to New York City and the Merryman brownstone. Martha tells Johnny that her sprout is finally getting hitched, so what about you Johnny? Johnny politely turns her down, but Martha says she will wait, unless Betty Lewis is making time behind her back. She tells Johnny that she heard the broadcast about the Curly Waters case. Martha tells Johnny that she has a lead because she has already proposed to Johnny, and if she were a couple years younger she would run Johnny ragged. Johnny reminds her of a night on the town after the last case. Martha calls Larkin the butler to get them a drink, and accuses him of snooping in the hallway. Larkin is told to open the safe and bring her the ring. Johnny is amazed that Larkin has the combination to the safe. Martha tells him that there is not much in the safe. The ring is the Shankar Diamond, which is worth a million and supposed to bring good luck. Edgar is going to marry Mary Luann Melanie Beaufort Examun Culpepper, and maybe it will bring them luck. Martha tells Johnny that he is going to escort her to the wedding in Greensboro, North Carolina. They will take a company plane together after Johnny goes home to get the proper clothes for a wedding. She is sure someone will try to take the diamond. Larkin brings in the Shankar Diamond, all 34 carats of it, and Johnny feels that someone wants that stone bad, and might even kill for it.

Johnny goes home for his clothes and then back to Martha's, where the chauffeur takes them to the airport and flies them to North Carolina with the Shankar Diamond in Johnny's pocket. Johnny accuses Martha of not leveling with him. She tells Johnny that she feels her chauffeur Eric Chatterly took the job to get close to her. Eric is a distant relation of Larkin the butler. Larkin is retiring soon and did not know much about Eric. Martha has discovered that Eric's father is still serving time in England for jewel theft. Johnny remembers reading about him and his unsuccessful three year plan to get to the crown jewels. She had found Eric alone in the study once and thinks that he was casing the safe. Johnny tells Martha that no one is to know that Johnny is carrying the diamond. At the Culpepper mansion, the place is crowded and Johnny wonders if some of the guests might have designs on the diamond. Johnny is surprised when the local police hire Eric as a special guard. The wedding take place without a hitch and the reception starts at 8:00 and Johnny dances with a number of lovely ladies. Johnny spots Eric outside a window and leaves Martha to investigate when the lights go out and Martha screams. Johnny gets back to Martha and the diamond is gone from her finger.

Martha is taken upstairs and examined by a doctor. Johnny has Eric taken into town by the police, and investigates the window to find a fuse box, which was used to turn out the lights. Johnny drives to police headquarters and is told that Eric does not have the diamond and is going to be released. Johnny asks where the nearest hospital is and an x-ray of Eric Chatterly's torso shows the diamond in his stomach without the mounting. But Johnny tells the police that the stone is not the Shankar diamond. Erick admits taking the stone, but Johnny tells him that it was an imitation. Eric tells Johnny that he was told Martha had the real stone when he wrote him to come over and apply for the job, then Eric clams up. Back at the mansion, Martha tells Johnny that she is sure that Eric did not have the combination to the safe, and that she last wore the diamond last spring. Johnny and Martha fly back to New York and tell Larkin the butler about the theft. Johnny goes to Larkin's room where he is packed for his trip to England. Johnny tells Larkin he will search all of his bags until he finds the diamond. Johnny tells Martha that she had forgotten that Larkin was also related to Chatterly and even gave Larkin the combination to the safe. Johnny tells her that Larkin had an imitation made from strass, a highly leaded glass that looks like a diamond. Larkin conceived the plan to have his distant cousin Eric steal the fake diamond. If Eric were successful, he would settle with him later. If Eric were caught, Larkin would just leave. No matter what happened, Larkin would be clean. Larkin agrees to give Johnny the diamond. Johnny tells him that the x-ray told Johnny that the diamond was a fake; a real diamond is invisible to x-rays.

"So the diamond is safe and sound, and Larkin and his dearly beloved cousin are in the clink. Martha was a bit upset about what Larkin had done, but she will get over it. Yeah, and I sure hope I get over this headache. That brawl she threw for me by way of a celebration was a dilly."

NOTES:
- THE FIRST COMMERCIAL BREAK IS AN EPISODE OF THE BELLWETHERS ABOUT AUTO SAFETY
- THE SECOND COMMERCIAL BREAK IS ABOUT HERBERT HOOVER AND THE IMPORTANCE OF FREEDOM OF THE PRESS
- STRASS IS A BRILLIANT PASTE, OR FAKE JEWELRY, MADE OUT OF LEAD GLASS AND USED TO SIMULATE VARIOUS TRANSPARENT GEMSTONES. IT IS NAMED AFTER GEORGE FREDERICK STRASS (1701-1773) WHO WAS BORN NEAR STRASBOURG, FRANCE.
- MARTHA MAYFIELD MERRYMAN WAS ALSO IN THE GOLDEN TOUCH MATTER AIRED ON 2/17/1957

Producer: Jack Johnstone        Writers:   Jack Johnstone
Cast:       Lillian Buyeff, Jack Edwards, Barney Phillips, Forrest Lewis, Eric Snowden

SHOW:           THE BLUE MADONNA MATTER
SHOW DATE:     2/22/1959
COMPANY:       FLOYDS OF ENGLAND
AGENT:          GEORGE REED
EXP. ACCT:      $620.00

SYNOPSIS: George Reed calls, and Johnny is glad to talk to him, because of the fees he gets from Floyds. George tells Johnny that he just got a transatlantic call for Johnny from a man in France that only identified his self as "les char gris." Johnny tells George that he knows him and his real name is Du Marsac, and that Du Marsac knows more about the dark side of Paris than anyone else. George tells Johnny that Du Marsac mentioned the Blue Madonna by Bardeau. Kingsley Holland, who lives in Philadelphia, owns the paining, which hangs in the Gavin gallery, and is insured for $12,000. Du Marsac has some interesting news about the painting. Johnny tells George that he should be willing to pay Johnny's expenses and pay him a big fat fee. Johnny is willing to bet 10 to 1 that the painting in the gallery is a fake.

Johnny calls Du Marsac in Paris to talk about the painting. Du Marsac wants $1000 but Johnny offers $50. Du Marsac counters with $900 and Johnny with $75, then $750 and $100, $500 and $200 then $400 and $300 and finally Du Marsac offers $200 which Johnny accepts. Fooled again! Du Marsac tells Johnny that the Blue Madonna is now in the shop of Dubisaint, who is a crook, but an honest one. He is going to wait until the real Madonna is found missing before he raises his price. Johnny calls his old friend Foster Harmond in Florida and arranges for him to go to Philadelphia and meet Johnny at the Belleview Stratford hotel. Johnny travels to Philadelphia and dines with Foster. Johnny arranges to go to the Gavin Gallery in the morning and look at the paining. Johnny cabs to Kingsley Holland's apartment and Holland asks if Johnny wants to buy the painting. Holland offers Johnny the painting directly for $12,000 to save the commission to the gallery. Holland wants to go back to Paris and would be there except he had run out of money. Holland tells Johnny that his uncle had left him the painting and tells Johnny that the people in the gallery are crooks, but the Blue Madonna is real.

Johnny thinks that Holland has recognized his name. Next day Johnny and Foster go to the gallery and meet Mr. Gavin, who tells them that the price for the painting is $20,000. Johnny convinces Foster to leave and outside Foster tells Johnny that the painting is a fake. A man on the sidewalk asks Foster if the painting really is a fraud. The man is a Rup Alloway, a reporter who also knows who Johnny is. Foster tells Johnny that the copy is exactly the style of Bardeau. Johnny tells Foster that Holland knows who Johnny is, and what he is doing. Johnny wonders if a switch was made before or after the painting was put in the gallery. Johnny tells Foster that both Holland and Gavin know what hotel Johnny is in, so he is going to go and wait to see who shows up.

Johnny sends Foster back to Florida and calls Sgt. Jerry Hawkins at police headquarters. Later Sgt. Hawkins calls Johnny back and tells Johnny that Holland is a lazy kid trying to live off of his parents, and that Gavin seems to be ok. Also, the story of the fake painting has hit all the wire services and papers. Johnny has an idea what has happened, and is going to play a hunch, and tells Sgt. Hawkins to read tomorrow's paper. In the evening paper, Johnny sees that the prices for Bardeau paintings are going through the roof. After Johnny places a call for Du Marsac, Mr. Gavin comes to Johnny's room and is very angry because the police have closed his shop. He has had offers for all his Bardeau paintings, and has wired Bardeau to paint more. Holland bursts in an accused Gavin of starting the whole thing, but Gavin says did not know that the painting was a fake until this morning. Holland tells Johnny that his grandfather had smuggled the painting into the country. Du Marsac calls Johnny back, and Johnny will have to pay him a vast sum of money, but Johnny tells him that he was going to tell Du Marsac that Bardeau himself smuggled the painting into

Paris. "How did you know?" Du Marsac asks disappointedly. Johnny offers Du Marsac $200, to learn that Bardeau is on his way to Philadelphia with the real Madonna. Johnny calls Sgt. Hawkins to have his boys pick up Bardeau at the airport. Johnny is sure that Bardeau has painted two of the Madonnas for the publicity, and anything he paints now will only make him a fortune. Johnny tells both Gavin and Holland that they will both benefit, and Johnny wonders if "les char gris" was in on this from the beginning?

"Sure, sure he was in with Bardeau. And probably collecting plenty from him. Anyhow, the insurance company is not out anything. But I hope they will be a lot more careful the next time they insure a painting, any so-called original."

**NOTES:**
* **THE ANNOUNCER IS DAN CUBBERLY**

| | | | |
|---|---|---|---|
| **Producer:** | **Jack Johnstone** | **Writers:** | **Jack Johnstone** |
| **Cast:** | **G. Stanley Jones, Forrest Lewis, Harry Bartell, Joseph Kearns, Bert Holland, Byron Kane** | | |

◆   ❖   ◆

| | |
|---|---|
| **SHOW:** | **THE CLOUDED CRYSTAL MATTER** |
| **SHOW DATE:** | **3/1/1959** |
| **COMPANY:** | **TRI-STATE LIFE & CASUALTY COMPANY** |
| **AGENT:** | **EARLE POORMAN** |
| **EXP. ACCT:** | **$168.50** |

**SYNOPSIS:** Earle Poorman calls Johnny from Sarasota, Florida and tells Johnny that he has received a lot of claims for stolen property that were cancelled when the goods were found. Earle wonders if this is some sort of racket, so come on down.

Johnny flies to Sarasota, Florida where Earle meets him at the airport. Johnny is told that he has a date with Miss Betty Charlene Churchill, and that he will also see Dolly Mae Winston, Edith Ann Devere and Linda Carol Keene, all of which have placed claims that were cancelled. The losses range from $7 to $150 and were for wristwatches, handbags and rings, and all of the women know one another. Johnny goes to Earle's office and meets Mrs. Valerie Hatch Kenworthy Froelick Tinsdale Dawson, who tells Johnny that she had a compact stolen from her car. She tells Johnny that Edith had her purse stolen from her home, and he told them where to find the items. He is Shanu Yarba, a swami who uses his crystal ball to locate the stolen items. Johnny is told that Yarba lives behind a hardware store, but Valerie does not want Johnny to tell him that she told Johnny about the swami.

Johnny visits the other women and gets an idea that will use Mike Poorman as bait. Johnny wants Earle to stay with a neighbor while Mike poses as a wealthy widow who will go to the swami to ask his advice on investments. Mike goes to the swami posing as Gertrude Mary Anastasia Conroy and then goes to the beauty parlor where her purse is stolen. Johnny watches the shop, and only sees another woman leave. Mike goes to see the swami and notices that his suitcases are packed. The swami tells Mike where to look for the purse and invites the others to a séance. Johnny watches the store while Mike is with the swami. Mike is told that the crystal ball senses some psychometric paramagnetic radiation and he invites Mike to a séance. Johnny is at Mike's home when the swami opens the front door and does something. A woman named Dora comes to the house and tells the swami not to go in because Johnny Dollar is there. Johnny comes out of the house and slugs the swami and Dora, his wife. Johnny relates that Dora Duggin was a pickpocket and a thief who used wax impressions of the house keys to get into their pigeon's homes.

NOTES:
- THE ANNOUNCER IS DAN CUBBERLY
- STORY INFORMATION OBTAINED FROM THE KNX COLLECTION IN THE THOUSAND OAKS LIBRARY

Producer: Jack Johnstone          Writers   Jack Johnstone
Cast:        Vic Perrin, Paula Winslowe, Peggy Webber, Shirley Mitchell, Don Diamond

◆   ❖   ◆

SHOW:          THE NET OF CIRCUMSTANCE MATTER
SHOW DATE:   3/8/1959
COMPANY:     TRI-STATE LIFE & CASUALTY COMPANY
AGENT:          EARLE POORMAN
EXP. ACCT:     $151.50

SYNOPSIS: Earle Poorman calls Johnny, and Johnny tells Earle that he just left him. Earle tells Johnny to bring his expense report with him. Earle tells Johnny that after Johnny had gone, Earle got a call from Bill Hall, who runs a Men's clothing store called Webb's. Earle has insured both the clothes and the night watchman, and the police think the watchman was murdered. Johnny will catch the first plane.

Johnny flies to Tampa, Florida and is met by Earl. They drive straight to Bill Hall's store where Bill is trying to clean up. Bill estimates that over $9,000 in clothing and accessories had been stolen. They think that the watchman, Jimson Cooley may be dead, as there are signs of a struggle out back. Bill tells them that more than one person was involved because the robbery happened between the regular police patrols. Also, three men had robbed the store last year. Two of the robbers were identified, and that is when Jimson was hired as night watchman. Johnny wonders about the third man. Bill tells Johnny that Jimson was an old man, and he had given him the job to help him out. Jimson used to run a shrimp boat, but is too old for that now. Sgt. Drummond arrives and tells them that they have new clues about the robbery. A drunk was picked up last night who remembers seeing something at around 2 or 3 AM. The drunk saw a car come out from behind the building that he recognized, a pickup truck that was loaded down with something under a net. It was a 1930 model truck belonging to Jimson Cooley.

Everything seemed to point to murder until the truck belonging to Cooley was seen. All the police in the area have been notified, but Jimson's house has not been searched yet. Johnny goes out back of the store and gets a sample of cloth and goes to visit some friends. First Johnny goes to see Doc Crutcher and gives Doc the cloth to examine. Johnny and Earle then go to see the Cooley home, a real broken-down shack surrounded with chickens. Mrs. Cooley wants to know if they have found Jim yet, and is anxious to get the insurance he has. He was a lazy bum and it was her chickens that made any money. She saw a missing net and thought Jim was out shrimping or had sold it for booze. She thinks that the gang that robbed Hall's store did it, as Jim had seen one of the members around town lately. Johnny asks Mrs. Cooley to sell him a chicken, and he gives her a dollar for it, and only takes the head. Back at the Doc's Johnny gives him the chicken head to use as a comparison.

Sgt. Drummond calls Johnny to tell him that Jimson Cooley has been found, and is ok. He told them that a man made him open the store, beat him, and left him in the woods. Johnny goes to headquarters and talks to Cooley, who was a disagreeable sort who had some cuts and bruises. Johnny goes to see Doc Crutcher who tells Johnny that the blood behind the store was not chicken blood. Doc discovered that there was human blood on the cloth, but not Cooley's. Johnny thinks that there was a fight, but Jimson did not lose the fight. Johnny thinks that Cooley was helping the man who robbed the store and now they need to find the other man's body. Johnny suggests that he and Earle go fishing, to let their minds clear. Earle takes his boat out to Humpback Bridge and City Island and Johnny starts to troll. Johnny has Earle troll very slowly in the area where Jimson used to run his shrimp boat. Finally Johnny snags something and pulls up a net with a body in it.

"When Jimson was faced with the man's body wrapped in the net he had sunk, out there in the bay, he broke down and told us what had really happened. Even told us where the stolen stuff was hidden. Yeah, the dead man was one of the gang who had robbed the store a year ago. He persuaded Jimson to help him do it again, and offered him a hundred bucks. But when he had the stuff, he tried to run out without paying off, so Jimson had killed him. Now the courts will have to take over. Incidentally, I hear that Webb's is installing a foolproof burglar alarm system.

NOTES:
- THE FIRST COMMERCIAL BREAK IS AN **AFRS** SPOT IS A BELLWETHERS STORY ABOUT HOUSEHOLD ACCIDENTS.
- THE SECOND COMMERCIAL BREAK IS AN **AFRS** SPOT ABOUT DANIEL WEBSTER AND THE VALUE OF FREEDOM AND PROTECTIVE LAWS.
- THE STORY MENTIONS RADIO STATION **WSPD**.
- THE ANNOUNCER IS DAN CUBBERLY

Producer:    Jack Johnstone          Writers:    Jack Johnstone
Cast:        Lillian Buyeff, Vic Perrin, Harry Bartell, Barney Phillips,
             Bartlett Robinson, Bill James

SHOW:        THE BALDERO MATTER
SHOW DATE:   3/15/1959
COMPANY:     WESTERN MARITIME & PROPERTY INSURANCE COMPANY
AGENT:       ARTHUR ARTHUR
EXP. ACCT:   $0.00

SYNOPSIS: Johnny receives a call from Pat McCracken while he is in Sarasota. Pat wants Johnny to go to the West Coast and See Arthur Arthur in Beverly Hills. Piracy is the problem. Piracy? Johnny does not believe it, but will go investigate.

Earle drives Johnny to the airport for his flight to Los Angeles, California and Earle tries to convince Johnny that piracy is still an issue. In Los Angeles, Johnny cabs to the Beverly Hilton and then goes to see Arthur Arthur. Arthur tells Johnny that Mr. Balderston was cruising around near Mexico on his yacht the Baldero, which is over 100 feet long. The boat is kept in Balboa. The guests on the boat included Mrs. Balderston, Mr. and Mrs. Hooper, Richard Spidal and Lee Willway. They were going to cruise up to San Francisco for a charity ball, which is why they all had their finest clothes and jewels with them. Arthur tells Johnny that $394,000 in jewelry was stolen, along with some other things, and that the robbery was reported by one of the guests. The pirates pulled up in the night, came on board with guns and took the jewels. Arthur is not sure where it happened, as Balderston was kind of vague. Johnny rents a car and drives to the Balderston home. In the driveway Johnny spots a sports car and a larger car with a man getting out. Mr. Balderston greets Johnny, recognizes who he is, and takes him in for a cocktail with Mrs. Balderston. Balderston tells Johnny it took almost 12 hours to cruise back to Balboa. Johnny does not learn much other than the men came on board at night, held the passengers in their cabins and wore disguises. Only Lee Willway had seen the boat that was used. Balderston never did say exactly where it happened and Johnny grows more suspicious of Balderston.

Balderston is not sure where he was and was just killing time until it was time to head for San Francisco. They did not take a position sighting because they were just going to follow the coast back to San Francisco. Lee said it was a long black speedboat. After the pirates left, they started the boat and motored back. They tried to call the Coast Guard, but the radio did not work. Johnny is sure that there is something funny about this case. Johnny checks with the Hoopers, whose story matches Balderston's except they do not think it took 12 hours to get back to port. Johnny goes to see Lee Willway, who is a real doll. Charles of the Ritz would have been proud of this one, but Johnny does not see her being on a cruise with the Balderstons. She tells Johnny that she saw a long black boat and then went to the radio but it did not work. She had been at the radio earlier, but just to listen. Lee tells Johnny that Richard Spidal could have stopped them, as his was the only cabin the pirates did not go into and there was a rifle right outside his door. Lee tells Johnny that the sports car he saw at the Balderston's belongs to Larry Balderston. After turning down an offer for more drinks and dinner with Lee, Johnny goes to see Richard Spidal. As Johnny gets out of his car another car rushed up, a man gets out and slugs Johnny.

Johnny recognizes the lights from his attacker's car as belonging to Larry Balderston. When Johnny wakes up, he is in his car with 5 $100 bills on the seat and a note that says "Take this money and get out of town. You have no case anyway, because the things that were stolen off the yacht have been returned. So you may as well leave while you have your health." Johnny goes in to see Richard Spidal, who gives Johnny a drink. Richard tells Johnny that the only reason Mrs. Balderston had brought Lee along, and Richard was to be her escort, was to shame the ladies at the charity ball. Lee is a beautiful, but a common person. Mrs. Balderston hoped that by taking her to the charity ball, Lee would see that she had no place with them, and she would break off the romance with Lawrence Balderston. Larry probably found out and staged the piracy bit to keep the plan from being carried out; he was always doing crazy things like that. When Richard heard the noise he just locked himself in his cabin. Richard thinks that Lee was in on it and was using the radio to guide Larry to the yacht. Johnny goes to see Mr. Balderston and is told that the jewels have been returned. Johnny asks for Larry and goes to see him in the study. In the study Johnny slugs Larry while he is talking to Lee. Larry admits to Johnny that he rigged the whole thing because he was fed up with the way his mother was trying to run his life. But maybe she was right about Lee. Larry tries to hit Johnny for hitting him, but Johnny gets the upper hand. Johnny apologizes to Mr. Balderston, but he tells Johnny that he had hoped someone would do that to Larry for a long time. He admits spoiling Larry, but did not know he would go as far as he did.

"Fee on this case? Forget it. The $500 that Larry mistakenly tried to bribe me with, plus a nice fat check from Mr. Balderston, well much as the thought of it hurts me, lets forget the expense account too. Ok? Ok."

NOTES:

- THIS PROGRAM CONTAINS THE FOLLOWING COMMERCIALS: WILLIAM BENDIX DOES A FOUR-WAY COLD TABLET COMMERCIAL ($.29 AND $.59); THERE IS A FITCH DANDRUFF REMOVER COMMERCIAL; A FRAM COMMERCIAL ABOUT NUMBERED FRAM OIL FILERS; A TUMS COMMERCIAL (ROLLS $.10 OR 3 FOR $.25 OR 6 ROLL PACK FOR $.49; A KENTUCKY CLUB PIPE TOBACCO COMMERCIAL FOR THE THOROUGHBRED DERBY CONTEST.
- BOB BAILEY OFFERS BELATED CONGRATULATIONS TO STATION WJLS IN BECKLEY, WEST VIRGINIA ON ITS 20TH ANNIVERSARY.
- THE ANNOUNCER IS DAN CUBBERLY

Producer:    Jack Johnstone          Writers:    Jack Johnstone

Cast:   Virginia Gregg, Eleanor Audley, Vic Perrin, Howard McNear,
        Larry Dobkin, Will Wright Carleton G. Young, Jack Edwards

◆   ❖   ◆

SHOW:       THE LAKE MEAD MYSTERY MATTER
SHOW DATE:  3/22/1959
COMPANY:    UNIVERSAL ADJUSTMENT BUREAU
AGENT:      PAT MCCRACKEN
EXP. ACCT:  $196.45

SYNOPSIS: Pat McCracken calls Johnny. "Greetings Master" is Johnny's reply. Pat gently asks about Johnny's trips to Sarasota, and the lack of fishing while he was there. Johnny tells Pat that he has been dreaming of Lake Mojave and its lunker bass. Pat asks what about Lake Mead just outside of Las Vegas? Pat wants Johnny to go fishing at Lake Mead for a slight case of murder.

Johnny is told to contact Roscoe Trimmer in Las Vegas who has all the details on the $20,000 double indemnity policy. Johnny cabs to the airport and travels to Las Vegas, Nevada. Johnny marvels at the nighttime glow of Las Vegas. Johnny gets a room at the Flamingo and accidentally finds the casino. Johnny manages to win so much he will not expense the room and food. Johnny meets Roscoe Trimmer the next morning and is told to take a rental car to Overton where a client, Thomas Mayfield Thomas came from Chicago and retired last year. A week ago Thomas and a friend went out fishing with a local guide, Hob Fulton. They stayed over and went out the next day and were caught in a big east wind. They did not get off the lake quick enough and Hob found their boat and the friend the next morning, but Thomas supposedly went overboard when the wind hit them. Roscoe tells Johnny that the friend was Charlie Wentworth, who came from Chicago two weeks ago. He just hangs around the gambling joints, and supposedly is illegally making book. There is a lot of worry about people coming from Chicago, especially when they do not work and hang around the gambling joints. The police have looked for Thomas' body and they are not holding Wentworth. Roscoe thinks Johnny ought to investigate, and so does Johnny.

Johnny is suspicious of Charlie Wentworth. Johnny calls his friend Ken Bugby, a reporter in Chicago, to get information on Thomas and Wentworth. Ken tells Johnny that Thomas was a mouthpiece for the old Moretti mob. When they started the clean up some years ago, Thomas couldn't or wouldn't get them off the hook, and they all did time and Thomas retired to Elmhurst. A year ago he moved out west somewhere. Charlie Wentworth was a triggerman, "Casual Charlie" they called him. Wentworth is in Joliet; no wait, Wentworth and Snooty Wilson were released about the same time Thomas moved. Johnny goes to the library and looks up the Moretti mob. Johnny is sure that Charlie was getting even, but how to prove it without a corpus delicti. Johnny rents some equipment from a sporting goods store and goes to Overton. Johnny arranges to meet Hob Fulton and goes out on the lake. Hob is sure Johnny does not need the stuff he has brought, but Johnny just wants Hob to take him to the same places where he took Thomas. Hob tells Johnny that Thomas did not seem any too happy, and Charlie kept saying, "let bygones be bygones." Hob mentions that their tackle boxes got thrown over, even Charlie's, which was really heavy. At the Glory Hole (a tree and a half deep) Johnny starts to dive. Two hours later Johnny tries a hole by Goat Island that is five trees deep. Johnny dives, comes back up for a rope and pulls up the body of Thomas Mayfield Thomas with a bullet hole between the eyes.

Johnny takes the body to the Las Vegas police and learns that Thomas was shot with a .38. Johnny searches the gambling joints and finds Charlie Wentworth. Johnny introduces himself and Charlie tells Johnny that he is really sorry about Thomas. Charlie asks Johnny to go up to his room where Johnny accuses Charlie of killing Thomas, but Charlie tells Johnny that he is through with crime and is clean. Johnny tells Charlie that he hated Thomas's guts and Charlie agrees, but he got over it. Johnny asks Charlie why he killed Thomas, and Johnny is told that he cannot prove it. Johnny tells Charlie he as absolute proof; Johnny has Thomas's body with the bullet hole in it from Charlie's gun. Charlie pulls a gun and shoots, but Johnny nails him and takes his gun, the proof he needed.

"Down at headquarters, the ballistics team took less than an hour. Yup, the bullet they found in Thomas Thomas' body came from the same gun Charlie had tried to kill me with. So it is back to prison for him, for a long, long time. Oh, and the company will not have to pay double indemnity for accidental death."

NOTES:
- COMMERCIALS INCLUDE JOAN BENNETT FOR FOUR-WAY TABLETS; FITCH DANDRUFF REMOVER SHAMPOO; A FRAM FILTER COMMERCIAL FOR NUMBERED FILTERS WORTH $1,000; A PEPSI COMMERCIAL—"BE SOCIABLE!"; THE RAMBLER AMBASSADOR COMPACT LUXURY CAR.
- THIS PROGRAM IS FROM WRTW IN ALBANY, AND APPARENTLY WAS RECORDED ON THE AIR.
- THE ANNOUNCER IS DAN CUBBERLY

Producer: Jack Johnstone     Writers: Jack Johnstone
Cast: Larry Dobkin, Bartlett Robinson, Frank Nelson, Harry Bartell, Gil Stratton Jr.

◆ ❖ ◆

SHOW: THE JIMMY CARTER MATTER
SHOW DATE: 3/29/1959
COMPANY: AMALGAMATED LIFE ASSOCIATION
AGENT: WALDO BOTTOMLY
EXP. ACCT: $117.00
SYNOPSIS: Jimmy Carter calls Johnny from East North Weldon, Vermont. Jimmy saved the money from his newspapers to make the call. Jimmy tells Johnny that

he helped Johnny solve the robbery case. Jimmy can help Johnny solve another case of murder.

Johnny recounts how he had gone to East Weldon the previous fall to recover some money stolen from a furniture factory by the baldheaded mayor. Jimmy tells Johnny that he can help solve a murder. Jimmy saw someone throw Mr. Andrew Parkinson off of a bridge, but everyone thinks he just had an accident. Jimmy's time runs out for the call before Johnny can get the name of the man Jimmy saw. Johnny calls the auto club for route information and then calls Pat McCracken and asks him to look up Andrew Parkinson's policy and find out who his company is, and Johnny will call him back. Johnny buys gas and drives to Fitchburg and, after an argument with a highway policeman, Johnny calls Pat to get the name of the company, which Johnny learns does a lot of rural business. Waldo Bottomly issued the policy. The death was the day before yesterday and was called an accident. Lucius Weatherby, the beneficiary, has filed a claim. Johnny drives on into East Weldon and stops at the general store. Johnny asks a local man about where Jimmy Carter is, but he does not know where Jimmy is. Johnny is told that Jimmy lives on North Spruce Street, and Johnny asks the man to tell Jimmy that Johnny is looking for him. At the Carter house Johnny meets Jimmy's mother who wants to know where Jimmy is. She tells Johnny how Jimmy was agitated and had not gone to school or picked up his newspapers. She is sure that something has happened to Jimmy!

Jimmy is gone, disappeared, and his mother wants to know where he is. Johnny tells Jimmy's mother that he has not seen Jimmy. Mrs. Carter tells Johnny that Jimmy idolizes him, and has been upset ever since Mr. Parkinson fell off the bridge. Johnny reassures her and goes out looking for Jimmy. Johnny goes to the drugstore and talks with Waldo Bottomly, the proprietor, who has heard of Johnny. Waldo tells Johnny that he is also the coroner, and that the policy claim has been sent in. Waldo tells Johnny that Parkinson was an old man who had many problems, and fell from the bridge. Bottomly tells Johnny that he saw Jimmy that morning when he made change for him. Waldo tells Johnny that Lucius Weatherby, the town drunk might have seen Jimmy, as he usually sits on the front step by the phone booth. Waldo tells Johnny to take Lucius a bottle of medicinal brandy (That'll be $3.75 please) if he wants any information from Lucius, but Johnny prefers to the use the "pick him up by the lapels and yell" method. Lucius tells Johnny that Jimmy went off in a car, and Lucius could remember the name if he had a drink. Waldo comes out with the brandy and Johnny is forced to use it, and pay Waldo for it.

Lucius gets a long drink and remembers Jimmy being forced into the car of Harvey Willman, who is not one of the more respectable people in town, and was distantly related to Parkinson. Harvey lives on the old farm out on Winter Avenue. Johnny drives to the farm and realizes he does not have his gun. In the front yard is a lot of new Allis Chalmers farm equipment. Johnny spots an old sedan outside as he bangs on the door. Jimmy yells and Johnny breaks down the door. Once inside Willman is behind Johnny with a gun, and Jimmy tells Johnny that he will kill them. Willman searches Johnny and fires once when Johnny uses jujitsu to throw him to the floor. Jimmy picks up the gun and starts to cry in fright as Johnny comforts him. Johnny tells Jimmy that he is a real hero for trapping the killer for Johnny.

"Item 6, $48.50 for a new sports jacket without holes in it. Yeah, Harvey Willman had managed to get off that one shot. Item 7, $67.00 for a brand new bike for Jimmy. Why? Because he saved the company from having to pay double indemnity. Expense account total $177.00, unless you would like to tack on a little extra fee."

## NOTES:

- THE FIRST COMMERCIAL BREAK IS ANNOUNCEMENT ABOUT THIS STATION BEING A CBS AFFILIATE, AND THE BENEFITS THEREOF.
- THERE IS ALSO A FRAM OIL FILTER COMMERCIAL FOR THEIR SILVER ANNIVERSARY; A PEPSI COMMERCIAL; AND A PUBLIC SERVICE ANNOUNCEMENT FOR THE NEW SHORTER FORM 1040-A FOR INCOMES BELOW $10,000.
- THE ANNOUNCER IS DAN CUBBERLY

| | | | |
|---|---|---|---|
| Producer: | Jack Johnstone | Writers: | Jack Johnstone |
| Cast: | Virginia Gregg, Dick Beals, Larry Dobkin, Forrest Lewis, Edgar Barrier, Jack Kruschen | | |

◆　❖　◆

| | |
|---|---|
| SHOW: | THE FRISCO FIRE MATTER |
| SHOW DATE: | 4/5/1959 |
| COMPANY: | GREATER SOUTHWEST INSURANCE COMPANY |
| AGENT: | |
| EXP. ACCT: | $923.91 |

SYNOPSIS: Smokey Sullivan calls Johnny at 5:00 AM. He is living in Frisco now, and wants to know if Johnny has heard of the Barnwell warehouse fire that is still burning. Smokey knows who did it. Johnny tells Smokey that he will stay in the Huntington Hotel. That is too nice a place or Smokey, so he will call Johnny.

Johnny calls Pat McCracken to get some facts and figures. Pat calls Johnny back and confirms the fire at the warehouse of Peter H. Barnwell who has an office in town. The warehouse is insured for $340,000. Johnny never gets an official ok, but flies to San Francisco on a jet flight on American. Johnny gets a paper at the airport and then goes to the Barnwell office. The receptionist is turning away all the reporters but Johnny gets in when he shows her his card. The other reports want to know what paper Johnny is with, and he tells them he is with the Bigsville Bugle near Bum Spung, Oklahoma. Johnny goes into the office and meets Mr. Barnwell who is not upset at the loss. The building has been a loss for years, but he has kept up the insurance on it, so now he will be able to collect on it and be sitting pretty. The police have found no proof of arson, and neither will Johnny. Johnny recounts how Smokey Sullivan had been an arsonist once, but had gone straight after helping Johnny with a case several years ago. Johnny is sure that Barnwell had the fire set so he cabs to see Bill Mullen at the Arson Squad. Bill is glad to see Johnny, but tells Johnny that a derelict named Stumpy Moran slept there on an old mattress, got drunk and set the place on fire with a cigarette. No more mattress, no more warehouse, no more Stumpy. Bill is positive based on the evidence he has seen. Bill wants Johnny to call the papers and get them to get off of the police's back by telling them is was not arson. Johnny leaves for his hotel and waits for Smokey to call. Smokey calls and tells Johnny that Stumpy was a friend of his. He knows Stumpy did not do it as Stumpy neither drank nor smoked. Johnny is told to go to the Hungry Angel Bar and go to their phone booth to meet Smokey. Smokey knows who did it, the only man who could do the job and not leave a trace, "Touchy" Thompson. The police will not question Touchy because he has been straight. He lives in a nice house on Aldea drive, but he is not there because he has gone fishing. Smokey tells Johnny that he is the only one who knows what to look for and will show it to Johnny. There are shots and the line goes dead.

Johnny goes to the phone booth to find the police going over it. Johnny is told that Smokey is in the hospital and will not live. The police tell Johnny that if the warehouse was arson, the only one who could have done it was Smokey, so good riddance. They have all the other firebugs nailed down so it had to be Smokey. At the hospital the doctor is amazed that Smokey will live, even though his heart was nicked. Johnny talks to Smokey who tells Johnny that he did not talk to the cops. He did not see who shot him, but it must have been Touchy. Smokey tells Johnny that Touchy used special chemicals that did not leave a trace. You need a gas mask, and that is what killed Stumpy Moran. Johnny now has to find Touchy, and Smokey tells him to be careful.

Johnny cabs to Touchy's home, but no one is there. Johnny goes to see an old friend, Maury Webster at KCBS radio. Johnny cabs to the studio and Maury tells Johnny all about their 50th anniversary celebration; they were the first radio station in the country and are proud of it. Johnny asks Maury about their news broadcasts and Johnny scribbles a news item to read on the air. The news announcement is read "Dollar has proof that the fire was set by an old hand at that business, Smokey Sullivan, his reason to kill another man named Moran, whose body was found buried in the embers. Incidentally, Sullivan himself has just died." Johnny tells Maury that he is going to stake out the house of Touchy Thompson. Johnny goes to watch Touchy's house and waits for Touchy to come home. When Touchy comes home, Johnny confronts him with the fire, but Touchy shows Johnny some trout he caught at Mono Lake. Johnny knows that trout cannot live in Mono Lake because of mineral deposits. Touchy gets nervous when Johnny mentions the use of special chemicals and Barnwell walks in and tells Touchy that maybe Johnny does have proof. Barnwell tells Touchy that he fell for the fake news story, and thanks Johnny for setting the stage for him. Barnwell tells Johnny he came here because he suspects Touchy, and the police will find that they have killed each other. As Barnwell starts to shoot, Bill Mullen breaks in with reinforcements. Johnny asks what caused Bill to come here, and

Bill tells Johnny that Smokey Sullivan called him from the hospital because he was worried about Johnny. Do you mind? No, not a bit!

"Yeah, they were both in it up to their ears. Each, in trying to defend himself, just put the other in that much deeper. By the time the courts get through with the two of them they will be sorry they ever lived."

## NOTES:
- THIS SHOW IS A FOUR-ACT PROGRAM FORMAT.
- CAST CREDITS ARE FROM RadioGOLDINdex.
- J. DAVID GOLDIN NOTES THAT KCBS WENT ON THE AIR IN 1909. WHILE DOING SOME INTERNET RESEARCH ON THIS MATTER, IT APPEARS THAT, WHILE KCBS DID GO "ON THE AIR" IN 1909, THE SUBJECT OF THE "FIRST" RADIO STATION IS ONE THAT IS OPEN TO DEBATE.
- THE ANNOUNCER IS DAN CUBBERLY

**Producer:** Jack Johnstone      **Writers:** Jack Johnstone
**Cast:** Virginia Gregg, Gil Stratton, Tony Barrett, Vic Perrin, Lawrence Dobkin, Alan Reed, Paul Dubov, Bartlett Robinson, Donald Mosley

◆ ❖ ◆

**SHOW:** THE FAIR WEATHER FRIEND MATTER
**SHOW DATE:** 4/12/1959
**COMPANY:** FLOYDS OF ENGLAND
**AGENT:** GEORGE REED
**EXP. ACCT:** $203.50

**SYNOPSIS:** Sidewinder Wilson calls Johnny from Bum Spung. He is a friend of Durango Laramie Dalhart. If Johnny should some out to Bum Spung, Sidewinder can show something that will make Johnny's eyes pop out of his head. Come on out and I will tell you when you get here.

Johnny cabs to George Reed's office and tells George Reed about the call from Sidewinder Wilson. George tells Johnny that Durango was there a few days ago to pay the $4,500 premium for Carol Dalhart's policy in fresh $100 bills. George tells Johnny about a robbery-murder case near Enid. A messenger was killed and the securities were returned. Johnny gets George to pay his expenses (within reason) as he runs out the door.

Johnny flies to Enid and rents a car to drive to Bum Spung, Oklahoma and the weather-beaten old farm. Johnny sees an ancient Maxwell parked beside the house as Sidewinder shoots a welcome at Johnny. Sidewinder tells Johnny that Durango went to Hartford to pay his insurance, and then to Washington to pay his taxes. Sidewinder tells Johnny that he called Johnny about the securities robbery. If Johnny can find out who returned the securities, he will have a lead on who killed the messenger. Sidewinder knows who sent the securities back; "It was me," he tells Johnny.

Sidewinder takes Johnny inside to tell him all about the robbery. Sidewinder tells Johnny that he returned the securities and then tells Johnny to stay still as a sidewinder approaches Johnny. Sidewinder shoots the snake and takes the rattles for his collection. That snake is #425. Sidewinder tells Johnny that the man who killed the messenger was the "ben-u-fici-ary" of his insurance policy. Sidewinder knew that because he lived on the Fair Weather with him. He knew that Claude Needles left his insurance to his no-good nephew Barney Gifford. Sidewinder talked it over with Carol and Durango (your kinda sweet on her aren't you) and if Durango finds out you have been here and not married Carol he is going to shotgun you into it! Carol rushes in and gives Johnny a great big kiss or rather a bunch of kisses. Sidewinder gets real antsy about Johnny and Carol smooching, and threatens to call Durango. Carol is really ready to marry up with Johnny this time. Carol tells Johnny that Sidewinder wanted to be a deputy in Fair Weather when Claude Needles was killed, so he could hunt for the killer. The police said no, they did not need him. Sidewinder was sore so they all talked about who could have done it. And that is when Sidewinder remembered that Barney would get the money. Carol arranged a date with Barney so Sidewinder could search his house. Sidewinder found the securities and tied up Barney and put him in a shed and had Old Pete watch him. That is when Durango told Sidewinder to call Johnny and get him out her to see Carol. The phone rings and Sidewinder tells Johnny that Barney has gotten loose, beaten old Pete and is coming there to kill Sidewinder.

Johnny realizes that Sidewinder is scared of Barney, so Johnny suggests that they leave. Johnny sends Carol to go get the police, but she will not leave. Barney bursts in the front door with a rifle. Barney tells them to go outside so he can kill them. Barney searches them and takes Johnny's gun. Johnny asks sidewinder if this is retribution for the killing he did earlier today. Suddenly there is the sound of a rattlesnake and Johnny slugs Barney. Johnny thanks Sidewinder for using his rattles.

"You know, I really hated to leave that place, to leave Carol is what I really mean. But there was another phone call and Sidewinder answered it. Yup, it was from Durango, phoning from Enid. Durango was so tickled to learn I was still around he promised to come to the ranch as soon as he could." 'As soon as he can pick up the preacher' Sidewinder adds." "Well, much as I love that gal . . ."

## NOTES:

- THERE IS A COMMERCIAL FOR CBS, AND IT'S POPULARITY IN A RECENT POLL OF RADIO PROGRAMS
- THERE IS A COMMERCIAL ABOUT POLIO SHOTS AND THE NEED TO TAKE THEM
- THE THIRD COMMERCIAL IS FOR PEPSI
- THE FINAL COMMERCIAL IS FOR LYSOL
- THE ANNOUNCER IS DAN CUBBERLY

**Producer:** Jack Johnstone     **Writers:** Jack Johnstone

Cast: **Virginia Gregg, Junius Matthews, G. Stanley Jones, James McCallion, Bill James**

◆ ❖ ◆

SHOW: THE CAUTIOUS CELIBATE MATTER
SHOW DATE: 4/19/1959
COMPANY: FLOYDS OF ENGLAND
AGENT: GEORGE REED
EXP. ACCT: $1,053.45

SYNOPSIS: George Reed calls Johnny about something that might not even need an expense account. "Come on over to my office, Johnny, and take your time."

Johnny cabs to George's office and is told to go right in. Johnny tells George that he rushed right over because George said not to rush. George seems to fumble over lighting Johnny's cigarette and tells Johnny that he got back from Bum Spung much earlier than expected. "Now what does Bum Spung mean?" George wonders. George notes that Durango would like to have Johnny marry his niece, Carol Dalhart. That, Johnny tells him, is why he left as soon as he could when he heard that Durango was on his way back with a preacher. Johnny tells George that he is a confirmed celibate. He really likes Carol, and George asks Johnny why he does not marry Carol. Johnny tells George that he is not ready to marry right now. George tells Johnny that marrying Carol would help his client relationship with Durango. Durango has asked George to get Johnny into the office and keep him there. Durango comes in the office and Johnny goes out the fire escape trying to outrun Durango's bullets.

Johnny really runs down the fire escape and grabs a taxi to his apartment. Durango being in Hartford means only one thing; Durango is still obsessed with Johnny marrying Carol. Johnny packs his bags and calls George to see what has happened to Durango. George tells Johnny that the police did not even take his six-guns. Johnny tells George that he is leaving and putting the cost on Floyds. Durango gets on the phone and tells Johnny to stay in his apartment. "California here I come!" replies Johnny. Johnny goes to the airport and gets a flight under the name "Bailey," just in case. Johnny puts the $146.85 for the flight to Los Angeles on his American Express credit card, but George is going to pay for it. The stewardess pages Johnny Dollar on the flight and Johnny tells her that Mr. Dollar is a friend of his who missed the flight, but she will not give him the information. When the plane lands in Chicago, Johnny is tempted to call George, but does not. On the flight to Los Angeles Johnny dreams of Durango chasing him. When Johnny tries to grab a cab in Los Angeles, Durango is there with a limousine for them to use. Durango had used a jet flight to catch up with Johnny!

Durango tells Johnny to get into the limo and Johnny uses a diversion to run into the airport and climb onto an airplane headed for Portland, Oregon. In Portland, Johnny spots Durango, who had chartered a plane to get there ahead of him. Johnny runs out and gets a cab and ends up at a private airstrip where the pilot is told to fly ANYWHERE!! Suddenly Johnny gets an idea and travels to a person who is in the same situation he is. Johnny travels to Bum Spung and Carol, that lovely, lovin' Carol Dalhart. After a few dozen welcoming kisses, Johnny tells Carol how Durango had gone to Hartford to get Johnny to marry her. Carol tells Johnny that she is not going to marry Johnny just because Durango wants her to. Durango bursts in and Johnny tells Durango that he is not going to marry Carol. Durango tells Johnny that he chased Johnny, not because of Carol, but because Johnny had kept Sidewinder from getting killed. Now Sidewinder is the sheriff. Since Johnny has been so good to Sidewinder, Durango had gone to Hartford to give him a $10,000 wad of cash. Just enjoy it. "Are you sure you don't want me to get the preacher up from Enid? No, I guess not?" Durango says dejectedly.

"This time I did stay over for a couple of days. Yeah, and it I ever take the leap . . . As for the expense account George, I will still argue with you about it but that's all."

NOTES:
*   JOHNNY MENTIONS USING AN AMERICAN EXPRESS CREDIT CARD FOR THE FIRST TIME.
*   THE ANNOUNCER IS DAN CUBBERLY

**Producer:**  Jack Johnstone        **Writers:**  Jack Johnstone
**Cast:**            Virginia Gregg, Jean Tatum, John McIntire, G. Stanley Jones

◆    ❖    ◆

SHOW:              THE WINSOME WIDOW MATTER
SHOW DATE:      4/26/1959
COMPANY:         GREATER SOUTHWEST INSURANCE COMPANY
AGENT:             HERB SHILLING
EXP. ACCT:        $250.00

SYNOPSIS: Long distance calls Johnny with a call from Pat McCracken. Pat asks about his message and Johnny tells Pat he is in Los Angeles to confab with Jack Johnstone, the guy that dramatizes the cases he handles and puts them on the radio. Johnny wonders if Pat has anything for him to handle on the West Coast. Pat tells Johnny to call Herb Shilling there in Los Angeles, California. "And, Johnny, do you have a gun with you? Judging by Herb's wire, you may need it."

Johnny cabs to Herb's office and surprises Herb by getting there so soon. Johnny tells Herb that he was in Los Angeles when he got the news. Herb tells Johnny that the matter has to do with a not-so-little liquor store holdup. Herb tells Johnny that bottled goods stores are prone to holdups, and they limit the number and amount of the policies they issue. The store of Willie Layman was opened in 1951 and he was first robbed in 1952. Willie bought some insurance from Herb, and there have been seven attempted robberies. Willie bought a gun, and knows how to use it. Last night $400 was taken, and Layman was killed. Herb has his life insurance too, $30,000. Johnny rents a car and drives to the West Los Angeles police and sees Sgt. Mike Kirby. Sgt. Kirby tells Johnny about all the holdup attempts and that Willie was a good shot and quick on the draw. Just last month he killed one of the men who tried to rob him. Sgt. Kirby thinks that if they find the other man, they find Willie's killer, probably. Sgt. Kirby tried a stakeout, but nothing happened. As soon as the police left, the robberies started again. Sgt. Kirby and Johnny drive to the store and enter with a key. Johnny sees where the body was lying and the broken bottles. Sgt. Kirby tells Johnny how the bullet went into Willie's shoulder and down through his heart. Mrs. Gloria Layman, who is thirty years younger than Willie, comes into the store. Johnny goes to a phone booth and calls Herb to ask who the beneficiary of the policy was. Johnny is told that it is his wife.

Johnny goes back into the store and Mrs. Layman is telling Sgt. Kirby that she is going to sell the store. She tells Johnny that Willie has some insurance for her, but who thought he would die this soon. Gloria tells Johnny that she was upstairs in bed when the robbery occurred. She came down and saw Willie lying there on the floor. She tells Johnny that she married Willie because it made him happy, but what a bore he was; he always wanted to go back to the old country. She likes to have fun, and Willie did not know where she was half the time. Gloria married Willie last September. Sgt. Kirby gets a phone call and then he tells Johnny that they have picked up the man who did the killing. Johnny and Sgt. Kirby go to headquarters to question a wino named Benny, who tells them that he took the money and ran, but did not shoot Willie. He was only carrying a rubber gun. Bennie tells Sgt. Kirby that he would not have gotten caught if he had not gotten drunk and told someone what he did. Bennie tells Sgt. Kirby that Willie reached under the counter and came up empty so he gave Bennie the money. Officer Conroy comes in with a negative paraffin test. The ballistics test is in and the gun Willie had did not have any prints on it. Sgt. Kirby tells Johnny that the bullet that killed Layman and which were in the wall came from Layman's own gun. If Bennie did not kill him, who did? Johnny thinks he better get some proof.

Johnny tells Sgt. Kirby that Bennie was a shaky wino who could not have outgunned Layman or taken his gun. Johnny can get the killer, but he has to get her his way. Sgt. Kirby and Johnny go back to the store where Johnny goes in to see Gloria alone. Gloria asks if Johnny is getting the money for her. Johnny asks how she knows about the $30,000, when she had said she did not know how much insurance Willie had? Johnny thinks that someone would have had to tell others when the police were there, and Willie was too good with a gun, unless he did not have his gun. Gloria shows Johnny where Willie kept his gun, and Johnny puts his gun there. Johnny tells Gloria to get behind the counter and tells her how a man came in and pulled a toy gun. Gloria tells Johnny that Willie would have grabbed is gun, and points Johnny's gun right at him. Johnny tells her that she had taken the gun, and after the robbers left she had come down and shot Willie from the stairs. Gloria tells Johnny that it happened just the way he said, but he will never tell, and she pulls the trigger on Johnny's empty gun. "You tricked me, you dirty double-crossing, lying cheat!"

"Pretty obvious I guess, right from the beginning as I said. But getting proof, or in this case a confession, isn't always so easy."

NOTES:
- THE OPENING OF THIS PROGRAM MAKES REFERENCE TO A MEETING IN HOLLYWOOD WITH JACK JOHNSTONE ABOUT THE RADIO PROGRAMS
- THERE IS A CBS COMMERCIAL WHICH LISTS THE SEVEN WINNING DAILY DRAMAS PUT ON BY CBS: THE ROMANCE OF HELEN TRENT, THE COUPLE NEXT DOOR, MA PERKINS, WHISPERING STREETS, THE RIGHT TO HAPPINESS, THE SECOND MRS. BURTON, YOUNG DOCTOR MALONE
- THERE IS A CBS COMMERCIAL ABOUT THE CBS NEWS DEPARTMENT USING FIDEL CASTRO AS AN EXAMPLE OF THEIR SPEED AND ACCURACY.
- COMMERCIAL BREAK THREE IS FOR PEPSI.
- THE FINAL COMMERCIAL IS FOR SINCLAIR DINO GASOLINE
- THIS PROGRAM CREDITS JACK JOHNSTONE AS WRITER, FRED HENDRICKSON AS PRODUCER AND DIRECTOR AND STARRING MANDEL KRAMER, JACKSON BECK, JOSEPH JULIAN, JACK GRIMES, BOB MAXWELL, PETER FERNANDEZ, AND ETHEL HUBER AS MUSIC SUPERVISOR AND WALTER OTTO FOR SOUND PATTERNS. THESE ARE THE CREDITS FROM "THE TIP-OFF MATTER," THE LAST OF THE YOURS TRULY JOHNNY DOLLAR SERIES.
- CAST INFORMATION FROM THE KNX COLLECTION AT THE THOUSAND OAKS LIBRARY.

Producer: Jack Johnstone     Writers: Jack Johnstone
Cast: Larry Dobkin, Virginia Gregg, Bartlett Robinson, Paul Dubov, Frank Nelson

SHOW: THE NEGLIGENT NEPHEW MATTER
SHOW DATE: 5/3/1959
COMPANY: AMALGAMATED LIFE ASSOCIATION
AGENT: LEONARD TILLSON
EXP. ACCT: $10.50
SYNOPSIS: Richard Coleman calls Johnny and tells him that Amalgamated insures him, and that he needs a witness. Johnny is told that Coleman has a horrible disease and the doctors cannot help him. Coleman says goodbye and there is a gunshot.

Johnny goes to the Amalgamated office where Leonard Tillson tells Johnny that Coleman lives in Hartford, Connecticut, and is insured for around $40,000. Leonard gets the folder and tells Johnny that the policy is for $50,000, and gives

Johnny Coleman's address, and the address of his nephew Bert. Johnny goes to Coleman's apartment and finds a body in a chair with a .32 automatic beside it. Johnny calls the police and looks through the shabby and pathetic apartment. Sgt. Miller arrives and they agree that there is no sign of suicide, which gives Johnny a crazy idea.

Johnny calls Leonard and updates him. Johnny goes to see Coleman's doctor and learns that the case was hopeless even though he had the money to pay for a hospital. Johnny is told that the nephew was told of the condition and did not visit his uncle, because Coleman wanted it that way. Johnny gets the address for Randolph Gifford, Coleman's attorney and the doctor tells Johnny that Coleman's eyes were bad, and he had to use contact lenses, but hated to. Without the contacts, Coleman could not see any closer than five feet. Johnny remembers that Coleman had said that he looked Johnny's name up in the phone book. Johnny calls Sgt. Miller who calls the death suicide and tells Johnny that the body is still in the apartment.

Johnny goes to see Gifford and is only told that the only relatives were two nephews, Paul and Bert Coleman. Johnny goes back to the apartment and the lab men are still there. Johnny looks at Coleman's eyes, and the contacts are not there. Johnny asks the police to see if Coleman's prints are on the phone book and tells them that he is sure that someone else fired the gun, because Coleman was blind as a bat without his contacts. Johnny meets Rich who tells him that he is not sorry his uncle us dead. He had tried to help, and has not talked to Paul for fifteen years. Paul was adopted and his uncle never liked him because he was a black sheep who stole things.

Johnny calls Leonard and is told that the policy had a suicide clause, and the police found a bullet in the wall. Johnny is told that Paul is on his way to the office. Johnny calls Sgt. Miller and goes to Leonard's office to meet Paul. Johnny accuses Paul of murdering his uncle because he knew there was a suicide clause, but Leonard had not been told yet. Paul asks Johnny how he knew, and Johnny tells him that he knew Johnny's name. Paul admits that the hates Rich, who would get the insurance except in case of suicide. Paul pulls a gun, but the police arrive and he drops it and gives up.

**NOTES:**
- **THE ANNOUNCER IS DAN CUBBERLY**
- **BOB BAILEY CONGRATULATES STATION WDBO IN ORLANDO, FLORIDA FOR THEIR 35TH ANNIVERSARY.**
- **STORY INFORMATION OBTAINED FROM THE KNX COLLECTION IN THE THOUSAND OAKS LIBRARY**

**Producer:** Jack Johnstone      **Writers** Jack Johnstone
**Cast:**      Stacy Harris, Carleton G. Young, Herb Vigran, Parley Baer, Will Wright, Sam Edwards

◆ ❖ ◆

| SHOW: | THE FATAL FILET MATTER |
|---|---|
| SHOW DATE: | 5/10/1959 |
| COMPANY: | CONTINENTAL INSURANCE COMPANY |
| AGENT: | |
| EXP. ACCT: | $0.00 |

SYNOPSIS: Ray Connely calls Johnny. There is no problem; Ray just wants to ask if Johnny can come over for dinner. He has a thick steak in the refrigerator. Be there at 6:30. Johnny is suspicious because of what Ray does not tell him.

Johnny feels that there is something funny about Ray's invitation because Johnny was familiar with Ray's problems with ulcers. Johnny cabs to Ray's Hartford, Connecticut apartment and decides to let Ray bring up any problems. Ray pours Johnny a scotch and soda and Ray has one of his pills. Ray wants to tell Johnny something later. Ray tells Johnny that his wife is away and that he had some groceries delivered, including the steak. Johnny and Ray sit down to dinner, and Johnny's steak is overcooked. Johnny goes to the kitchen to make a sandwich. Ray tells Johnny that he does not like being threatened when Ray starts having stomach pains. Ray collapses in pain and asks Johnny for his medicine. Johnny calls for Ray's doctor and after he arrives he calls for an ambulance. On the way to the hospital Ray dies.

Johnny is told by the doctor that Ray died of an internal hemorrhage. Johnny goes back to Ray's apartment and finds nothing. In the kitchen Johnny finds the bag of groceries and a cufflink with "XD" on it. The next morning Johnny goes to talk to Morris Bain the grocer. Bain tells Johnny that Mrs. Connely was in just the other day, and he asked about her husband. Bain gets a list of the groceries that were delivered to Ray's apartment. The only item not on the list was the steak because Bain does not sell meat. Johnny calls Dr. Ransom and asks for an autopsy and goes to Continental Insurance to get a list of people who might have threatened Ray. Johnny is told by the secretary Grace, that there was a man in yesterday who lost a cufflink with "XD" on it. Johnny asks the secretary to find the policy for the man.

Johnny calls Dr. Ransom and is told that Ray's stomach was full of ground glass. Johnny calls Grace to get the name of the man who visited Ray, Xavier Denato. Johnny gets the address and is told that Xavier was the beneficiary on his father's policy, but his father committed suicide. Johnny goes to the address but Denato has gone. Johnny calls Sgt. Jimmy Maxwell at police headquarters and listens to Jimmy yell at him. Johnny updates him with the information he has about Xavier, or "Zavier" and has an idea. Johnny cabs to Bain's grocery store and asks about his clerk Zavier. Johnny finds him and shows him the cufflinks and tells him where he found them. Xavier tells Johnny that he got the steak and put the ground glass in it. He did not think it would kill Connely. He did not run because he is smart; if you run, the cops think you are guilty. He had to get even because of the insurance policy that Connely would not pay. His father killed himself, as did his grandfather and great grandfather because they were off in the head. But Xavier is smart; he gets even with them. But he will not get caught. Johnny takes Xavier to the police.

"Prison, I doubt it, not with a family history like that. But there are institutions for his kind. I am sure he will spend the rest of his life in one of them. And maybe by studying his case, the doctors, the psychologists can learn more about helping such people. Before they go off the deep end. Expense account? Forget it. Ray Connelly was my friend."

## NOTES:
- COMMERCIALS INCLUDE ONE FOR CBS NEWS, ONE FOR LOWELL THOMAS AND PEPSI, AND THE VALUE OF AN EDUCATION AND THE NEED FOR CONTRIBUTIONS TO COLLEGE FUNDS
- GROUND GLASS WAS ALSO USED IN THE FIVE-PART STORY, THE LONELY HEARTS MATTER
- THE ANNOUNCER IS DAN CUBBERLY

**Producer:** Jack Johnstone    **Writers:** Jack Johnstone
**Cast:** Virginia Gregg, D. J. Thompson, Jack Edwards, Marvin Miller, Larry Dobkin, Harry Bartell, Frank Gerstle

| SHOW: | THE TWIN TROUBLE MATTER |
|---|---|
| SHOW DATE: | 5/17/1959 |
| COMPANY: | FLOYDS OF ENGLAND |
| AGENT: | GEORGE REED |
| EXP. ACCT: | $0.00 |

**SYNOPSIS:** George Reed calls Johnny, and George has a client whose life is being threatened. Johnny tells him that he hates these kinds of cases. George tells Johnny that there are confidential matters involved, and George offers to go along with Johnny. The client is George's brother, Adam. Johnny is on his way.

Johnny cabs to George's office, and is told that the client is George's brother Adam. Eighteen years ago Adam came to the states with his wife, and now owns a brokerage firm in New York. He lives in Upper Montclair, New Jersey. Adam had traveled a lot when he first came to the country and met two men, Shockley and Baron in California who offered him a job. It turned out that the men were swindlers who sold worthless stocks. When Adam finally figured out what was happening, he called in the police and everyone, including Adam, went to prison. Now Shockley is out and is threatening Adam. If his clients ever found out that Adam had been in prison it would ruin the business, and Adam's wife is in the hospital with a heart condition. Shockley has demanded $75,000 from Adam to keep quiet and not leak the past to the papers and kill Adam, making it look like suicide to void his insurance policies. He told Adam he had gotten away with it once before, and Adam cannot call in the police or risk his business. Johnny is not sure what to do yet, other than to not pad the expense account. Johnny buys gas for his car and drives to Adam's home. Adam is a complete twin to George except for his accent. Adam has heard from Shockley earlier and had gone to the bank. Shockley is coming here tonight and wants $10,000 as an act of good faith. George tells Johnny he will take care of the matter and wants Johnny's gun. The phone rings and Johnny goes to an extension to listen in. Shockley is on the phone and he tells Adam that he does not trust him. He tells Adam to meet him at Cedar Knoll, at the shack on the top of the hill, and come alone in his car or someone will die. After the call, Johnny discovers that George has taken a gun and driven to Cedar Knoll.

Johnny gets directions to Cedar Knoll and realizes that Shockley will get there before George will. Johnny leaves to drive to Cedar Knoll in heavy traffic and frequent police patrols. Johnny spots the knoll and the shack with Shockley's car out front. Johnny spots a pair of lights in the cabin and tries to cut a rubber tube on Shockley's car. George arrives and Shockley tells George to wait outside. George tells Shockley that he is going to end this thing and to throw down their guns. Shockley realizes that it is not Adam, but his brother George. Baron throws his gun at George and there are shots. George is thrown onto Johnny, who fights with Baron and Shockley and is almost knocked unconscious. The men get into their car and Johnny warns them to not use it. The men drive off and Johnny tells George that he had cut the brake line, as there is the sound of a crash in the distance.

"By the time the highway police got to the scene of the crash there on the back road, and of course their car exploded and burned, they had forgotten all about the gunshots, if they had heard them at all. So George and I were able to leave by the main road unmolested. At the bottom of the hill I picked up my own car without attracting attention. I suppose I will have to make some sort of report to the police, but I do not see any reason why I should have to reveal the name of the man they were out to get, do you? It is certainly too late to need anyone to bring charges against them. As for the expense account, so what is a couple gallons of gas in so good a cause?"

NOTES:
- BOB BAILEY THANKS "TO ALL OF THE GOOD PEOPLE WHO WRITE IN TO SAY HOW MUCH THEY LIKE THE SHOW. IT MAY SEEM LIKE A LITTLE THING TO YOU, BUT IT MEANS A GREAT DEAL TO ALL OF US. BELIEVE ME, I'LL ANSWER YOUR LETTERS JUST AS FAST AS I CAN GET AROUND TO THEM. BUT YOU'LL JUST HAVE TO BE PATIENT IF IT TAKES A LITTLE TIME."
- BOB SUGGESTS THAT FOR THE NEXT SHOW THE AUDIENCE READ "THE CASK OF AMONTILLADO" BY EDGAR ALLEN POE.
- THE ANNOUNCER IS DAN CUBBERLY

**Producer:** Jack Johnstone  **Writers:** Jack Johnstone
**Cast:**  G. Stanley Jones, Alan Reed, Frank Gerstle

**SHOW:** THE CASK OF DEATH MATTER
**SHOW DATE:** 5/24/1959
**COMPANY:** PHILADELPHIA MUTUAL LIABILITY & CASUALTY COMPANY
**AGENT:** HARRY BRANSON
**EXP. ACCT:** $101.20

SYNOPSIS: Harry Branson calls Johnny, and Harry has a case for Johnny involving some important clients. Johnny suggests a nice fee, but Harry tells Johnny that he will pay expenses and commission. There will be no fee, depending on what Johnny unearths. Johnny asks something or someone. Harry means facts. The clients have disappeared, and the police gave up years ago. Johnny tells Harry he is on his way, and to have shovel waiting for him.

Johnny trains to Philadelphia, Pennsylvania and meets "Old Sober-sides" in his office. Harry tells Johnny that in the case of mysterious disappearance, the insured is declared deceased after seven years and the policy is paid. Seven years ago, Mr. Wilbur Davis of Goshenville disappeared. In checking the files Harry has determined that there have been eight disappearances in the same area, the last four months ago. The beneficiaries were all different persons. Johnny gets a list of the people involved and Johnny reviews the list that night. Johnny rents a car and drives to Kirkwood, New Jersey where Charles Moody had disappeared. At the general store Johnny learns that Moody had taken a bus to Philadelphia and disappeared. Moody left the policy and his money to his nephew. All of his property, except his wine cellar will go to the town. If Moody is dead, the wine cellar will go to a man in Philadelphia; he belonged to some sort of gourmet club. Moody had quite a collection of wines in his collection. Johnny checks out all Moody's other friends and learns nothing, but realizes later how much he did learn. Johnny travels to the other cities where the clients disappeared. In Millmay, Pennsylvania, Johnny learns from the lawyer for Frederick Burton that Burton also had a wine cellar, which will be given to Edward Alden Pouley in Philadelphia. Johnny realizes that the others also had wine cellars. The lawyer realizes that the list Johnny has are the other members of the Epicurean club that Burton belonged to. The only missing name is Bradford W. Turner in Alloway. The lawyer is stunned when he learns that all of the others have also disappeared. Johnny drives to the home of Bradford Turner who tells Johnny that the club has not been very active lately. Pouley has a marvelous wine cellar, with some rare Amontillado. Turner has a rare bottle of Medoc to offer Pouley now. Johnny is told that wine is a passion for Pouley. Johnny tells Turner that he will take the bottle of Medoc to Philadelphia. Johnny drives to Pouley's house. Johnny is taken to the library while Pouley eyes the package Johnny has. Pouley tells Johnny that he has to have the best of everything. Johnny notices a large collection of Edgar Allen Poe, who shares Pouley's initials. Johnny shows Pouley the bottle and Pouley must have it, but Johnny tells him he only wants an appraisal. Pouley tells Johnny he has a cask of Amontillado in his cellar, maybe they can swap. Johnny goes with Pouley to the cellar where Johnny is asked if he is a mason. Johnny remembers the story from Poe and realizes that Pouley is living the story. Pouley shows Johnny a vault where the other members of the club are buried. Pouley tries to knock Johnny out to bury him, but Johnny shoots instead.

"The eight men who disappeared, yeah, they were all buried behind the bricks and mortar that walled up eight of the niches in that deep underground vault. Funny, I completely forgot to look to see if there was a cask of Amontillado in that cellar. Edward Alden Pouley? When the courts get through with his case, I am sure that he will be committed to an institution for the rest of his life. Yeah, I told you in the beginning, this was the weirdest case I ever tackled."

NOTES:

- THE CASK OF AMONTILLADO WAS WRITTEN BY EDGAR ALLEN POE IN 1846.
- AMONTILLO IS A TYPE OF SHERRY MADE NEAR MONTILLA, SPAIN, FROM WHICH IT DERIVES ITS NAME.
- THE ANNOUNCER IS DAN CUBBERLY

Producer: Jack Johnstone     Writers: Jack Johnstone
Cast:     Harry Bartell, Forrest Lewis, Bartlett Robinson, Parley Baer, Marvin Miller

◆ ❖ ◆

SHOW: THE BIG H. MATTER
SHOW DATE: 5/31/1959
COMPANY: GREATER SOUTHWEST INSURANCE COMPANY
AGENT: ROY HARKINS
EXP. ACCT: $447.45

SYNOPSIS: Helen Daener calls Johnny from Morro Bay, California. She has a policy with Greater Southwest Insurance Company. Helen tells Johnny that she always listens to Johnny's radio program and is his most loyal listener, which is why she is calling Johnny rather than the police. If the police nab these terrible people, they would know she told them and something terrible would happen. Helen starts to tell Johnny what is going on when the phone goes dead. "Oh, don't be a sucker now, but yet I wonder."

Johnny calls Royal J. Harkins at Hollywood 8-2124 in Los Angeles and tells him he is coming. Johnny asks about Helen Daener and is told she is a spinster who called and demanded Johnny's phone number. Roy had called her back and got no answer. Johnny flies to Los Angeles at 12:30 AM and is met by Roy with his rental car at 6:30 the next morning. Roy tells Johnny that he still cannot get hold of Helen, and Johnny is not sure that anything has happened, yet. Johnny drives to Morro Bay and goes to Helen Daener's house, which has an expensive car parked out front and a decrepit dock out back. Bessie Daener, Helen's sister, answers the door and tells Johnny that Helen is at the market. Johnny leaves and feels there is something funny going on. Johnny drives to the market and learns that Helen is not there, and that the market delivers groceries to her house, as she has not been out of the house in weeks.

Johnny drives back to the house and asks Bessie where Helen is and is told to come in. Once inside Johnny finds Helen tied to a chair and a .38 in Bessie's hand. Bessie takes Johnny's gun and they wait. Bessie takes the gag out of Helen's mouth and Helen tells Johnny that these terrible people are smugglers who are bringing in narcotics from Mexico. A man named Pete had asked to use the dock, and Helen had watched them take out the heroin instead of fish. She had found some spilled on the dock and remembers how Johnny had described it. Bessie tells Johnny that they will use some "H" on Helen to keep her quiet. Pete comes in and tells Johnny that he made a mistake by coming here. Now, they are going to take a ride, Chicago style. Pete tells Bessie that they will have to wait until after dark to get rid of Johnny. Pete will take Johnny to a quarry in Cayucos Beach and leave his body there. Johnny attacks Pete when he hits Helen and is knocked out.

When Johnny wakes up he is in the car with Pete and Bessie. Johnny tries to get a cigarette and crumples the pack to get the tobacco out. Johnny blows it into Bessie's eyes and when she drops the gun Johnny grabs it, knocks Pete unconscious and the car crashes.

"It was a commercial trucker driving one of those big interstate trailer jobs who pulled off the highway to give us a hand. Yeah, somehow those boys are always around when you need 'em. And he used his head. When he found my credentials in my pocket he saw the whole picture in a flash. So he hailed down the first police car that came along and turned both Pete and Bessie over to them. Miss Helen Daener, bless her heart? That spunky old character was tickled pink to be involved in the whole thing. Yeah, she just can't wait to go to court and testify against those two."

Next week is the wildest case Johnny ever got messed up with.

**NOTES:**
- MORRO BEACH AND CAYUCOS ARE NORTH OF SAN LUIS OBISBO ON THE CALIFORNIA COAST BETWEEN LOS ANGELES AND SAN FRANCISCO.
- THE ANNOUNCER IS DAN CUBBERLY

| | | | |
|---|---|---|---|
| **Producer:** | Jack Johnstone | **Writers:** | Jack Johnstone |
| **Cast:** | Peggy Webber, Virginia Gregg, Bartlett Robinson, Joseph Kearns, Russell Thorson | | |

◆ ❖ ◆

| | |
|---|---|
| **SHOW:** | THE WAYWARD HEIRESS MATTER |
| **SHOW DATE:** | 6/7/1959 |
| **COMPANY:** | NEW BRITAIN MUTUAL INSURANCE COMPANY |
| **AGENT:** | AL TURNER |

Exp. Acct:        $10.00

**Synopsis:** Al Turner calls Johnny and tells him that an important client, Mrs. Virginia Haskell wants to get in touch with Johnny; she is an old friend of yours. Before she got married last year, her name was Van Doren. "Ginnie Van Doren! Well that's something else again, and I mean something. She is one of the most delectable bits of female pulchritude I ever ran up against." Johnny tells Al that even he had serious ideas about her after college and marrying into the family fortune. Al tells Johnny that Virginia lives with Gordon Haskell in Bronxsville. Johnny remembers that she had a thing for Paul Snowden, a childhood sweetheart. She made it clear that she needed to see Johnny about the family insurance. Al tells Johnny that the sky is the limit for his expenses.

Johnny drives his car to Westchester County and Bronxville, New York. The Haskell house is old money and neatly kept. Virginia is just as beautiful as Johnny remembers her from college in the mid-west. She tells Johnny that she is worried about Gordon, and Paul Snowden is who has her worried. She loved Paul, and hoped he would marry her. When her father died and she inherited the fortune, Paul stopped seeing her. She had gone to visit him in his factory in Chicago and she proposed to him. She offered to finance his business, but he did not like that. Paul told her he had to work things out on his own, and to find herself a nice husband. She fell in love with Gordon, but not as much as Paul, but in a different way. Gordon does not have as much money as she has, but they get along and she is a good wife to him. She thinks that Paul might kill Gordon, and that is why she sent for Johnny.

Ginnie tells Johnny that Paul has come here to kill Gordon. Paul was angry when he found out and swore he would kill Gordon. She left Chicago to get a way from Paul. She has helped Gordon start an importing business. Ginnie tells Johnny that Gordon's life is insured, and Johnny will have to protect Gordon. Paul has called her from New York and told her that he would come out when Gordon was there and to prepare for the worst. Now, Gordon is in Larchmont, hiding. Johnny agrees to help and tells her to have Gordon come home. Johnny leaves and feels like an advice to the lovelorn columnist. Johnny is stopped at his car and a voice tells Johnny that he knows why Johnny is here, and shows him some papers he has collected. Johnny is hit and Ginnie comes out calling for him. The attacker mumbles "oh, no" and runs away. Virginia recognizes him as Paul and goes to aid Johnny. Johnny has been convinced by Paul's actions how serious the situation is. Johnny mentions how Paul had some papers and photostats and goes back out again to look for Paul and the papers. Johnny drives away and sneaks back into the house. Johnny opens the front door and calls outside for Paul and tells him to come in the front door. Johnny comes back in to see Gordon there with Ginnie. Gordon tells Ginnie to open the safe and give him the money in it. Gordon pulls a gun on Johnny, but Johnny takes it away after Paul shoots Gordon. Paul tells Johnny and Ginnie that Gordon has a police record under a variety of names. He marries wealthy women and takes their money and has killed some of them. Paul apologies for slugging Johnny.

"Well, maybe Paul and Ginnie will finally get together for keeps. I don't know. I do not even know if I care. I am just glad I was not involved, that is anymore than I was."

NOTES:

- THE ANNOUNCER IS DAN CUBBERLY
- THIS STORY IS THE ONLY REFERENCE TO JOHNNY HAVING ATTENDED COLLEGE

**Producer:**  Jack Johnstone        **Writers:**  Jack Johnstone
**Cast:**  Virginia Gregg, Les Tremayne, Sam Edwards, James McCallion

◆  ❖  ◆

**SHOW:**  THE WAYWARD SCULPTOR MATTER
**SHOW DATE:**  6/14/1959
**COMPANY:**  UNIVERSAL ADJUSTMENT BUREAU
**AGENT:**  PAT MCCRACKEN
**EXP. ACCT:**  $26.15

**SYNOPSIS:** Pat McCracken calls Johnny and remarks how he has not had to bleed through one of Johnny's fancy expense accounts for a month. Pat has a funny case now. Come on over and let's talk.

Johnny cabs to Pat's office and comments about Pat's wild cases. Pat tells Johnny that a big problem for him is preventing the prosecution of insurance fraud, and this has been going on for a long time. Pat shows Johnny a case where a company received $520 and a note telling them that the money was taken and now the writer has a clear conscious and signed "detter." Companies get a lot of such payments but this case is different. Johnny sees a list of payments received from the same person: $833.34 on 7/21/56, $833.34 on 8/21/56, same thing on the 21st of the month, every month for several years. There was a note saying that the payments were restitution for monies paid out on someone who will pay the money back if it takes five years. They have all come from the New York area, and Pat wants Johnny to find out who the payments are coming from. Johnny calculates that $833.34 X 60 months comes to $50,000.40. But, $833.333 X 60 is exactly $50,000! Johnny wants Pat to find out who paid out $50,000 in June of 1956. Johnny learns that there was only one policy paid in 1956, to Henry Davidson Pollock, the sculptor. Pat thinks that Pollock did not die, and the wife is paying the money back, but it is still fraud to Pat. Johnny trains to New York City and the address of record for Pollock. The manager of the building tells Johnny that Mrs. Pollock died last fall. He had carried her in after the auto accident, and Dr. Maitland can verify it.

Johnny learns that Henry Pollock lived in the apartment also, and died in a plane crash in the desert. He kept to himself and his wife was younger than he was. "But the money is still coming in" Johnny notes. Johnny calls Pat to update him. Pat agrees that maybe there is no fraud, but Pat wants an answer. Johnny cabs to Dr. Maitland who tells him that the woman definitely was Mrs. Pollock. Johnny checks with Randy Singer who confirms the death. Johnny checks the newspaper morgues and confirms the death of Pollock in the plane crash. Johnny goes to a gallery mentioned by Dr. Maitland that Pollock used as an outlet. The owner, Mr. Bessem tells Johnny that he never met Pollock, as Pollock abhorred the public. His wife always brought in the art works and took the money. Bessem tells Johnny that anyone who saw the work of Pollock wanted to buy it. Bessem has one piece in the gallery and shows it to Johnny. The price is $15,000. Johnny sees another piece similar in style, but is assured that it is not a Pollock. John Wesley Collins, an admirer, has been making artwork in Pollock's style for the past two years.

As he leaves, Johnny watches Bessem make a phone call, so he goes back in to hear Bessem make a call to Henry to tell him about Johnny's visit, and Bessem agrees to leave the door open for him. Johnny leaves and calls Dr. Maitland to ask if Pollock had a scar on the thumb of one hand, which he did. Johnny goes back to the gallery and meets Bessem. Johnny asks Bessem if he wants to write a statement or go to the police. Johnny notes the similarity of the styles of Collins and Pollock. Johnny shows the similarity of thumbprints on the two pieces. Bessem pulls a gun as Henry Collins walks in and tells Johnny that he is giving up. Henry tells Johnny that he wanted to get away from his wife. He was going to fly to the West Coast and disappear. At the last minute he gave the ticket to someone else. Knowing he was thought dead, he decided to disappear in New York. He remembered the insurance money and decided to repay the insurance his wife had gotten. Henry tells Johnny that the works of John Wesley Collins have sold well, and the balance of the policy had been sent to the company that day.

"So Pat, there you have it. And you can take whatever action you think is necessary. Pollock is waiting for the company or the courts, or whomever. And Walter Bessem is too scared to go anywhere. As for the expense account, I am sure the company can afford it."

## NOTES:

* THE ANNOUNCER IS DAN CUBBERLY
* WHEN I CALCULATE $833.333 × 60, I GET $49,999.98, NOT $50,000 AS JOHNNY STATED. MAYBE IT WAS THE NEW MATH BACK THEN.

| | | | |
|---|---|---|---|
| **Producer:** | Jack Johnstone | **Writers:** | Jack Johnstone |
| **Cast:** | Herb Vigran, Edgar Barrier, Carleton G. Young, Will Wright, Lawrence Dobkin | | |

◆  ❖  ◆

| | |
|---|---|
| **SHOW:** | THE LIFE AT STAKE MATTER |
| **SHOW DATE:** | 6/21/1959 |
| **COMPANY:** | CONTINENTAL INSURANCE & TRUST COMPANY |
| **AGENT:** | BILL FERGUSON |

**EXP. ACCT:** $0.00

**SYNOPSIS:** Johnny receives a call from the operator from Hartford. Johnny is connected to Bill Ferguson. Johnny tells Bill he was almost ready to leave New York and head home. Bill asks if Johnny remembers Alvin Peabody Cartwright? Johnny tells Bill how he had cleared up a robbery for him, and Cartwright insisted on giving him a small bonus of $3,000. Johnny is ready, willing and able to help Alvin if he needs help. Bill tells Johnny that Cartwright has a small place there in Los Angeles, and he must see Johnny right away.

Johnny calls "Crestview 3-2121" to speak with Alvin. Johnny has a very confusing call with Alvin, until Johnny tells him who he is. Alvin wants to know how Johnny got there so fast, and hopes Johnny has not been fooling around with rockets. Johnny tells him he was in Los Angeles already. Alvin and Jonathan Peeples both want to see Johnny, so get here right way. Johnny gets an Avis rental car, and on the way out a boy with a hula-hoop caused Johnny to stumble. Johnny wakes up in the dispensary hours later and rushes out to the car. Johnny drives to Alvin's house to find the door wide open. Jonathan Peeples meets Johnny and tells him that Alvin is gone, and based on the evidence, Alvin has been murdered.

Peeples tells Johnny that he had been called by Alvin to come over, and he did not hurry, as Betsy (his car) does not like to be rushed. Peeples tells Johnny that he found the door wide open, but Alvin often left the door open. Peeples tells Johnny that he is not a wealthy man, and relies on Beneficial Finance to keep up the payments on his car. Peeples had looked for Alvin, but could not find him. He saw two men walking out of the garage carrying a tour-robe, which is a big heavy suitcase like a small wardrobe trunk, and it was dripping something all over the driveway. As Johnny goes to look at the driveway Peeples tells Johnny that Alvin kept his tools and frozen foods in the garage. Johnny realizes that the driveway is full of blood. Johnny inspects the garage and the house. Peeples remembers seeing the men's car and he has seen it before. It was a silver and cream sedan with license plates CFU-610. He has seen it at the Malibu docks where Alvin keeps the Alpecar, his yacht. Johnny drives to the docks in Malibu and Peeples sees the car, but the boat is gone. A man named Whitey tells them that the boat left about ten minutes ago, and two men had a boat take them to the Alpecar. Whitey wants to sue them for making a mess on his dock with the drippings from the trunk.

Peeples fears that the men are taking Alvin's body out to sea to dispose of it. Johnny arranges to borrow a boat at the dock that belongs to a Larry Comstock, and has Whitey call the Coast Guard. Peeples and Johnny speed out to the Alpecar, which is just cruising along. Peeples sees one of the men at the wheel, and the other coiling ropes, and Alvin! They have put him back together again! Alvin welcomes Johnny and Peeples, and tells Johnny that he had wanted to take him out for a ride on his nice new boat. He deserved it for all the work he has done for him over the years. He feels that Johnny deserves a nice long cruise. Peeples was invited to come along too. Alvin realized something was wrong as soon as he left the dock. He forgot to wait for Johnny and Peeples. Alvin tells

Johnny that he had also forgotten to take the trunk of thick juicy tenderloin steaks, and had to send Gerald and Harold back to get them. Gerald and Harold are Alvin's new cook and butler. Johnny realizes that all the blood came from the steaks, which had thawed out too much.

"You know something? It's crazy, it's wild. But it does my heart good to get tangled up in something like this sometimes. Helps keep away the ulcers. As for the expense account, forget it. Alvin Peabody Cartwright shoved a check into my hands before I left that would cover the expense account a dozen times over. As for Larry Comstock, the man whose boat I had appropriated? Well when he heard the story of what had happened, he wouldn't accept a penny for it. So, that's that!"

NOTES:
- BILL BAILEY CONGRATULATES STATION WDBJ IN ROANOKE, VIRGINIA FOR THEIR 35 YEARS ON THE AIR.
- JOHNNY MENTIONS THAT HE WAS CALIFORNIA WORKING ON A CASE IN MORRO BAY. THAT WAS THE BIG H MATTER, SO THERE IS SOME MIX-UP IN THE ORDER OF THE PROGRAMS
- THE ANNOUNCER IS DAN CUBBERLY

Producer: Jack Johnstone    Writers: Jack Johnstone
Cast: Virginia Gregg, Jean Tatum, Howard McNear, Forrest Lewis, Joseph Kearns, Paul Dubov

◆    ❖    ◆

SHOW: THE MEI-LING BUDDHA MATTER
SHOW DATE: 6/28/1959
COMPANY: WORLDWIDE MUTUAL INSURANCE COMPANY
AGENT: MARTY BRUCE
EXP. ACCT: $300.00
SYNOPSIS: Marty Bruce calls Johnny and asks if Johnny has ever heard of the Mei Ling Buddha, the most valuable piece of jade in the world. Marty has it insured for $40,000. He does not know if anything has happened to it, or if nothing has happened to it. Come on over and let's talk.

Johnny cabs to Marty's office and is told that Ray Kerner, one of Marty's agents knew that the Buddha was insured, and should have investigated when he saw it in Europe. It was in a dingy old antique shop in Paris and Ray did not even have the sense to get the address of the place. It is supposed to be locked up in the house of Darryl Harcourt in Boston, but there has been no report of a theft. Johnny calls his friend Louis Du Marsac in Paris and tells him he will pay $200 for information on the Buddha. Du Marsac has seen the Buddha that morning; and it had been smuggled in only a few weeks ago. The asking price is 32,000,000 francs, about $80,000. Du Marsac offers to obtain (steal) it, but Johnny tells him he will send a check. Marty tells Johnny that Mrs. Mary Haskell is taking care of

Harcourt house. Only the contents of Mrs. Haskell's room and the study are still there. The study goes to a nephew the day he graduates from Harvard. The Buddha was the only thing of value in the room, and the house goes to Mrs. Haskell.

Johnny rents a car and drives to the Harcourt house in Boston, Massachusetts. Mrs. Haskell meets Johnny and comments on the dismal, desolate house. She will live in the house until the estate is settled. Johnny wants to see the study, but he is told that the room is sealed. Mrs. Haskell tells Johnny that she last saw the Buddha before Mr. Harcourt died two years ago. After assuring Mrs. Haskell that he is authorized to go into the study, Johnny is taken into the study, which is covered with dust. Johnny trips over a fan and goes to a wooden casket on the desk, but the Buddha is gone. Johnny searches the room, but there is no trace of the Buddha. But how could someone get in without leaving a track in the dust? Mrs. Haskell tells Johnny that she has the only key to the room and no one has been in it except the taxman and the appraiser. Mr. Bancroft in town is the attorney. Johnny has the room re-sealed and tells Mrs. Haskell he will be back.

Johnny stops to see Mr. Bancroft and is told that only Mrs. Haskell has access to the study. Johnny is told that Mrs. Haskell was paid very little over the years and that she deserved more. All the valuable things, the collection of tapestries, have been willed to various museums, and they were kept in a hermetically sealed room. When Johnny asks about the hermetically sealed room, Bancroft tells him that both the library and study had very thick doors and sealed windows. That information causes Johnny to wonder about the source of the dust in the study. Bancroft tells Johnny that Charles Curtis the nephew is an admirable man. He is going to be a lawyer and is very wealthy. He plans to donate the Buddha to a museum. Johnny has an idea about the dust and the tapestries and goes to play a hunch. Johnny searches Mrs. Haskell's room and finds a bankbook with a very low balance and a sudden deposit of $21,000. Johnny thinks it is the money from the Buddha. Johnny takes her to the study and shows her that the dust is really fuller's earth, which was used to clean tapestries. Johnny tells her that the fan he tripped on earlier did not have any dust on it because that is what was used to spread the dust in the room. Mrs. Haskell refuses to go with Johnny to the police, and tells Johnny that she deserved more. Now she has money, plenty of money and offers Johnny a bribe of $10,000 or $12,000. Johnny tells her to think of a better way out, and she is going to have plenty of time to think.

"Yeah, I know, the Mei Ling Buddha still has to be brought back from Paris. Maybe I will get the assignment. Maybe it will go to one of our regular foreign investigators. As for Mrs. Haskell, well I am sure Mr. Bancroft will not waste anytime in taking whatever steps are necessary."

**NOTES:**

- **FULLER'S EARTH IS A FINE CLAY-LIKE SUBSTANCE WHICH IS USED TO CLEAN FABRICS, AND AS A CATALYST.**
- **THE ANNOUNCER IS DAN CUBBERLY**

| Producer: | Jack Johnstone | Writers: | Jack Johnstone |
|---|---|---|---|
| Cast: | Virginia Gregg, Paul Dubov, Will Wright, Forrest Lewis | | |

◆    ❖    ◆

| SHOW: | THE ONLY ONE BUTT MATTER |
|---|---|
| SHOW DATE: | 7/5/1959 |
| COMPANY: | EASTERN LIABILITY & TRUST COMPANY |
| AGENT: | FRED WAKELY |
| EXP. ACCT: | $25.55 |

SYNOPSIS: Fred Wakely calls Johnny because he thinks Johnny is the best private eye in the business. He wants Johnny to investigate something that may or may not fall under the heading of insurance. The matter concerns Sarah Balderson Barling, who is an important client. Johnny is told that he will get a $5,000 bonus for handling this case.

Johnny cabs to Fred's office and is told that Mrs. Barling is worried about her daughter, Truda Lynn Barling, who is just over twenty-one and threw herself a birthday party that cost $40,000, including the damage to the hotel. She is young, wealthy and rebellious and does not get along with her mother. Truda packed up and left 5 days ago and left with Harvey Howard, who is a playboy. Lucy Taylor, a "playmate," also left with Truda. Johnny is told to bring Truda back or the company will lose all of its insurance. When Johnny starts to decide against the case, he is offered $10,000 to find Truda.

Johnny finds the taxi driver that took Truda and her friends to the train station where they went to New York City. Johnny calls Randy Singer in New York and he knows who Truda is. She and her friends have been raising cane around the nightclubs, and Truda is staying at an expensive apartment. Johnny trains to New York and goes to the apartment Truda is renting. After getting past the doorman and the elevator operator Johnny notices the door to the apartment is open. Johnny rings the bell several times and gets no answer. Johnny walks in to find the body of Truda, who had been beaten with a bronze candlestick holder, and calls Randy Singer. Johnny searches the apartment and notices a still-smoking cigarette butt. Johnny calls Randy back and tells him to pick up Harvey and Lucy on his way over.

Johnny questions the elevator operator and the doorman and learns that there is only one entrance to the building. Two people had been to see Miss Barling after she had been to see Doctor Thorson across the street. Miss Barling came back and said she was going to leave. Then Miss Taylor came by about ten minutes before Johnny got there and left almost immediately. Then Harvey Howard had come there right after Miss Taylor left. He only stayed a minute also. Johnny leaves to go to see Dr. Thorson, who tells Johnny that Truda had a mild ulcer and was a hypochondriac. She used the doctor as a confidant and came to see him to boost her courage. She told him she was now able to think for herself, and had decided to renounce the two "leeches" that came with her and go back to Hartford. Johnny is sure one of them killed her, but which one?

Johnny is told the police are there when he gets back. Randy has Miss Taylor and Howard locked in the bedroom. Randy calls Miss Taylor a "real looker," and tells Johnny that she was in her hotel room packing, as was Howard. Johnny meets the two friends and questions them. Lucy tells Johnny that she came to see Truda everyday. She admits that Truda called her to tell her that she was going home. When Lucy got there, Truda would not let her in. Howard tells them that he found the door open when he got there to talk to her. He came and knocked, but got no answer. Howard then admits that he came in and found the body, and Lucy tries to get him to admit he killed her. Randy tells Howard that he came in, found Truda sitting in a chair smoking a cigarette, put on his gloves and killed her, but Howard denies it. Lucy tells Johnny that she did not come into the apartment. Johnny tells Randy that he had found a cigarette with lipstick on it, but it was Lucy's cigarette. Truda would hardly smoke a cigarette with an ulcer and her other "illnesses." Howard then tells them that Truda did not smoke. Johnny tells Randy to take Lucy's gloves, where the lab will probably find microscopic traces of bronze from the candlestick she was beaten with.

"Yeah, guilty as sin. But you know something, if that pretty boy Harvey had found her alive when he arrived I am not so sure he wouldn't have done her in. There are times I am glad I am not rich, with a bunch of these leeches around grabbing at my dough. Which reminds me, that nice extra fee you promised me on this case."

NOTES:
• JIM MATTHEWS IS THE ANNOUNCER FOR THIS PROGRAM

**Producer:** Jack Johnstone      **Writers:** Jack Johnstone
**Cast:** Virginia Gregg, Les Tremayne, Herb Vigran, Alan Reed, Frank Gerstle, Jack Edwards, Jack Grimes

◆ ❖ ◆

**SHOW:** THE FRANTIC FISHERMAN MATTER
**SHOW DATE:** 7/12/1959
**COMPANY:** GREATER SOUTHWEST INSURANCE COMPANY
**AGENT:** ROY HARKINS
**EXP. ACCT:** $650.85

**SYNOPSIS:** Buster Favor calls Johnny from Lake Mojave, and tries to bait him to come out and go fishing. Buster tells Johnny to come on out for a few days, as "the days a man spends fishing are not deducted from his life span." Johnny asks if Buster has some insurance problem to bill his expenses to, and Buster thinks that there might be something here, so Johnny relents.

Johnny tells Roy that he had no notion that the company was involved, but the facts will justify paying the expenses, plus a big fat fee. Johnny flies to Las Vegas, and rents a car and drives to Lake Mojave Resort. When Johnny gets to the lake, Buster gives Johnny a room and a new Harnell rod with a Mitchell 300 reel. Buster tells Johnny that the insurance matter is out on the lake and leaves to meet Johnny on the dock. Buster and Johnny take a boat to a narrow cove where another man is fishing with a large saltwater rod. Buster fakes a motor problem and quietly tells Johnny that the man is Otis Hellman from Los Angeles. Buster tells Johnny to watch him when he gets back to the dock. Johnny remembers that Otis has just gotten out of prison, and Buster tells Johnny that he has been at the same cove day after day, and he isn't after fish.

Johnny and Buster fish for a while and watch out for Hellman. Buster leaves to beat Hellman to the dock where Hellman tells them that he had caught nothing. Johnny notices the large treble hooks that Hellman is using. Later Buster tells Johnny that Hellman had told him he was trying to snag carp. Johnny is sure that Hellman is trying to snag something, and Buster thinks that there is a body in the lake, and that is why he called Johnny. Johnny calls Roy Harkins and Roy tells Johnny that Hellman had taken $60,000 from a mine, along with his partner Oscar Kirkman. Kirkman has disappeared and so has the money. Johnny tells Roy he might be able to find Kirkman's body. Johnny prepares to drive to Las Vegas to rent some special equipment when Johnny learns from Buster that that Hellman had been watching Johnny that morning. In Las Vegas, Johnny rents a skin diving outfit and learns that a man had rented some gear a couple years ago from the same store and never brought it back. His name was Oscar Kirkman.

Johnny gets a topographical map and studies it in his room. Johnny shows Buster where the cove is and where a mine called Kirkman's Folly is at the end of the cove, right where Hellman had been fishing. Johnny borrows Buster's boat and goes to the cove as Buster arranges for Hellman's boat to have troubles. Johnny dives into the cove and finds the entrance to the old mine. Johnny removes the boards on the entrance, finds a package of money wrapped in plastic and wax, which he takes it to the surface. Johnny throws the money into his boat and is told "thanks" by Hellman, who is waiting for him. Johnny overturns Hellman's boat and drags him under the water until he faints.

"Buster, bless his heart had been worried when he saw Hellman follow me up the lake. So he had borrowed a boat and was waiting for us there at the end of the cove. Otis Hellman, well that is up to the courts. The money of course, all $60,000 of it, will go back to the company."

## NOTES:
- **THE ANNOUNCER JIM MATTHEWS**

**Producer:** Jack Johnstone      **Writers:** Jack Johnstone
**Cast:** Barney Phillips, Sam Edwards, Bartlett Robinson, Forrest Lewis, Ralph Moody

| SHOW: | THE WILL AND A WAY MATTER |
|---|---|
| SHOW DATE: | 7/19/1959 |
| COMPANY: | GREATER SOUTHWEST INSURANCE COMPANY |
| AGENT: | JAKE KESSLER |
| EXP. ACCT: | $3,280.00 |

SYNOPSIS: Red Barrett calls Johnny from Lake Mojave Resort and tells him to come back out. He had been in Kingman when Johnny was there, and has run into some trouble. When Avery Nicolette died, Red went to take care of his things, including his money. Red discovered that someone had changed the will, and the police agree that the will was valid. Red tells Johnny to come out if he ever expects to see Red again.

Johnny flies to Las Vegas, rents a car and drives to Kingman, Arizona and goes to Jake Kessler's office. Jake tells Johnny that he had written Avery's policy and the beneficiary was to be named in the will, which is highly irregular. They were not sure that Avery had a will until Red showed them where it was. Red was the only friend Avery had, and Red was supposed to get everything but the insurance, all of which amounted to a couple thousand in the bank, his clothes and things. Johnny tells Jake that the will had been tampered with, but Jake tells Johnny that the authorities were sick of Red badgering them about the will. Jake tells Johnny that a man named Louis Marino was supposed to get the money according to Mrs. Turner, a nurse and housekeeper for Avery. She had heard Avery mention Marino. Also, the other witness, Tim Hanson had been killed in an accident. After startling Jake by telling him he is on expense account, Johnny leaves to talk to Red at Lake Mojave. Red tells Johnny that Avery had shown Red the will and Marino was not in it. As Red tells Johnny that Marino got angry when he mentioned calling Johnny, shots ring out.

Buster knocks on the door and tells Johnny the shots came from up on the old mining road. Buster knows that Marino had been living in Vegas and working in a garage. Buster had used Tim from time to time, and tells Johnny that Tim never drank, even though he was supposedly drunk when he was killed. Johnny learns that Avery had come to Kingman in January, and Mrs. Turner became his nurse in March when Avery got sick. The will was also made out in March and Marino came to Vegas in March. Tim Hanson died in April, and Red almost died in April in a car crash when his steering gave out. Johnny leaves to see the surrogate of the will, Lawyer Robins. Johnny sees the will, which leaves the insurance money to Mario. The handwriting seems identical, and the police have examined it. Johnny looks at the paper under a magnifying glass and bets that Marino was an addition to the will. Johnny asks Robins to arrange a meeting with Red, Marino and Turner for the next morning. Johnny leaves to go Lake Mojave, but stays in a motel after his rental car explodes in a bomb blast.

Johnny calls the police and learns from Sgt. Tommy Parker that the police have been suspicious of Marino too. Sgt. Parker tells Johnny that the police in

Vegas had run a check on Marino, and he was recognized as "Louis the Penman," a forger for the mob in Chicago. Parker checked on Mrs. Turner, her real name was Polino, with a string of elderly husbands who died in car accidents. Interestingly, her first husband was Louis Marino. Johnny goes to the meeting with Lawyer Robins and takes Sgt. Parker with him. Johnny arrives just as Red tells everyone that he will give the money to charity, and Marino gets angry. Johnny lets Mrs. Turner know that he knows about her former husbands and Marino tells Johnny that Hanson was drunk, but Johnny tells him that Hanson never drank. Johnny notes that someone could have tampered with the car, and that Louis is a mechanic. Mrs. Turner tells Johnny that she and Hanson had seen Avery write the will. They all signed it, folded it and put it in an envelope. Johnny tells them that the paper is coated, and folding breaks the coating causing ink to bleed, like it has on the will. The part giving the money to Marino was added after Mrs. Turner found the will in the linen closet. Lawyer Robins looks at the paper and is convinced that Johnny is right, at which time Louis pulls a gun.

"Yeah, Louis pulled a gun and started making the normal fool of himself. Then Sgt. Parker quietly walked in and took over. And, you know something? I think that given time with Mary and Louis in the clink for this forgery, he will probably pin those other things I mentioned on him, as he is a good man."

NOTES:
- EXPENSES INCLUDE REPLACEMENT OF THE RENTAL CAR.
- THE ANNOUNCER IS JIM MATTHEWS

Producer:     Jack Johnstone          Writers:    Jack Johnstone
Cast:         Virginia Gregg, Barney Phillips, Forrest Lewis, Parley Baer,
              Jack Moyles, Billy Halop, Byron Kane

◆  ❖  ◆

SHOW:         THE BOLT OUT OF THE BLUE MATTER
SHOW DATE:    7/26/1959
COMPANY:      FOUR STATE MUTUAL INSURANCE COMPANY
AGENT:        HARRY MCQUEEN
EXP. ACCT:    $171.50

SYNOPSIS: Harry McQueen calls from Boston and he has a funny one for Johnny. It seems that someone is threatening the life of Amos Weatherby, a retired sea captain. He lives on Cape Anne, and his niece is the beneficiary of his $50,000 policy. She is worried about her uncle and has asked for Johnny to come up. Harry is sure that the niece is not plotting to get the money. And, Harry assures Johnny, that she is gorgeous.

Johnny drives his car to Annisquam, Massachusetts on Cape Anne (at 10 cents a mile). Johnny arrives at the big frame house that looks over the bay. One corner has a tower with a brass rail and a weather vane. The niece, Thelma Jean, is a real vision who knocks Johnny out with her looks. Thelma tells Johnny that the captain has gone up to the bridge to check on the weather. He usually spends all his free time there, watching the ocean. Thelma tells Johnny that she was engaged to a man named Roger Burton, who the captain never liked. The captain discovered that Roger had been married twice to rich women who died mysteriously. Thelma broke off with Roger and the captain threw him out. Roger threatened to kill the captain, and bragged he could get away with it as he did with a couple of "nosey wives." After Johnny tries to flirt with Thelma, she tells Johnny that Harry McQueen had called Johnny an old, dull, stodgy, pedantic bumbling person. Thelma tells Johnny that after Roger had been thrown out, someone started sneaking around the property at night, and it must be Roger Burton.

Thelma is sure that the prowler is Roger. Thelma tells Johnny that she had seen Roger poking around between the house and an old building called the cell, which was an old jail, but is now used as a transformer station for the house. As a storm builds, Thelma tells Johnny that the captain loves to stay up on his bridge during storms, it reminds him of his sailing days. Thelma tells Johnny that she had found ladder marks by the house that morning. The captain comes down and asks for the location of his sou'wester. Johnny is introduced as an old friend who will stay for the night. Thelma shows Johnny the ladder marks and Johnny finds a lightning rod that has been cut off, and a copper wire leading to the transformer station. Johnny goes to the bridge and finds the copper wire attached to the brass railing the captain was holding on to.

Johnny tells the captain to go below, but he refuses until Johnny slugs him. Johnny carries the captain downstairs and Thelma is upset. Johnny tells her about the cable and tells her to keep the captain off of the bridge. Johnny goes to the transformer house and sees where the doors are open with Roger waiting inside with a .38. Roger tells Johnny how he will kill the Captain, and Johnny can only wait. Johnny sees that the cable on the railing is connected to a 22,000-volt transformer that Roger will use to electrocute the captain. Roger tells Johnny that he will throw the switch when the captain goes out on the deck, and it will kill the captain and melt the copper wire, and everyone will think that lightning killed the captain. Roger points to the captain getting ready to go out and hold onto the rail. Suddenly a bolt of lightening strikes and Roger is electrocuted.

"Yeah, the bolt of lightening had struck the rod high up on the tower, had streaked down the wire into the blockhouse and fairly exploded inside of it. The force had blown me out through the door and it was a couple of hours later inside the house before I was able to move. Burton, holding the switch had been killed instantly. I am glad I hadn't tried to get any closer to him. It was a bolt out of the blue. It was justice in its own strange fashion."

NOTES:
- THE ANNOUNCER IS JIM MATTHEWS

| Producer: | Jack Johnstone | Writers: | Jack Johnstone |
|-----------|----------------|----------|----------------|
| Cast: | Virginia Gregg, Carleton G. Young, Ralph Moody, James McCallion | | |

◆ ❖ ◆

| SHOW: | THE DEADLY CHAIN MATTER |
|---|---|
| SHOW DATE: | 8/2/1959 |
| COMPANY: | CONTINENTAL INSURANCE & TRUST COMPANY |
| AGENT: | BILL FERGUSON |
| EXP. ACCT: | $27.35 |

SYNOPSIS: A very addled Alvin Peabody Cartwright calls Johnny. Alvin is being threatened and he wants Johnny to look into the matter. Johnny is to come to Lakewood before he is killed. If Johnny does not come, and he is killed, Alvin will cancel all of his insurance.

Johnny recounts how Alvin has been taken advantage of in the past as he cabs to Bill Ferguson's office. Bill has heard nothing, but tells Johnny to look into the matter.

Johnny drives to Lakewood, Connecticut in his personal car. Johnny knocks at the door only to have Alvin thank him for the unexpected visit. Inside, Alvin tells Johnny that he will get killed like Hector Kenworthy and Alphius J. Perrim if he does not carry on a chain letter. Alvin reads the letter that promises him money in a dozen-dozen hours (that is six days; Alvin figured it out all by himself!) if he forwards the chain letter. But if he breaks it, dire circumstances will come to him. His two friends broke the chain, and they are both dead.

Alvin tells Johnny that Kenworthy died six days after he broke the letter. Johnny tells Alvin about the nature of phony chain letters that have duped the general public. Alvin tells Johnny that this chain letter goes only to an exclusive group of retired people. Alvin tells Johnny that hit-and-run drivers killed both of his friends on the 6th day after they broke the chain. Alvin tells Johnny that Admiral Parley Baron forwarded the chain letter and came into a fortune, and Adjutant Frederick Melchior was cured of cancer. Alvin tells Johnny that he is supposed to send $100 to a post office box in New York, where the name at the top of the letters will receive it. Two other wealthy people in the area have received similar letters. Johnny is sure that someone has bought a list of rich people and is using it to bilk people. Johnny tries to call the police, but the phone is dead.

Alvin is sure that someone has come to get him. Johnny goes out to look at the phone lines and is slugged by a man. Johnny wakes up in the library with a headache and Alvin offering him a drink of brandy. Alvin tells Johnny that he had followed Johnny and hit the man with a cricket bat, and has him tied up and locked in a closet. Johnny questions the man, who was a "pug-ugly gorilla" who had been hired to beat Alvin and make it look like a burglary. After a night's sleep the phone is fixed and the man is still in the closet. Johnny calls Randy Singer and gives him the address the letter was supposed to be sent to, and asks him to have the box watched. Johnny visits Mrs. Templeton and tells her not to send any money or she could go to prison. Johnny and Alvin visit Mr. Winterbottom and tell him the same thing. Johnny goes back to Alvin's home, where Randy calls to tell Johnny that he has nabbed Daniel Stringer, who has a number of aliases. He was opening a number of chain letters full of money and was getting ready to mail more. Johnny tells Randy he will get a postal inspector to prefer charges.

"Yeah, maybe some of those chain letters, the little ones, are harmless, but again, maybe they are not. And they are all against the law. But there is only one thing to do, avoid them like the plague. Or better still, if you get one, take it right down to your local postmaster. He'll know how to go about helping to stamp out this racket. And believe me, that's all it is, a racket."

NOTES:

- THE FIRST COMMERCIAL BREAK IS A PUBLIC SERVICE ANNOUNCEMENT ABOUT THE ELECTORS OF THE ELECTORAL COLLEGE

- THE ANNOUNCER IS JIM MATTHEWS

**Producer:** Jack Johnstone     **Writers:** Jack Johnstone
**Cast:** Virginia Gregg, Howard McNear, Paul Dubov, Frank Gerstle, Herb Vigran

◆ ❖ ◆

**SHOW:** THE LOST BY A HAIR MATTER
**SHOW DATE:** 8/9/1959
**COMPANY:** WORLDWIDE MUTUAL INSURANCE COMPANY
**AGENT:** FRED STARKEY
**EXP. ACCT:** $162.70

**SYNOPSIS:** Fred Starkey calls Johnny from Columbus, and wants Johnny to come out on a case. Mrs. George Hemingway Tilford is pretty wealthy since her lumberyard burned down. She insists on Johnny coming out to talk to her. Johnny agrees to come, as the company is going to cover his expenses and his usual fees.

Johnny flies to Columbus, Ohio and cabs to the Hilton for the night. Johnny visits Fred the next afternoon. Fred has nothing new to tell Johnny. The lumberyard fire was a total loss, and cost the company $330,000, but it is was under-insured. The yard was near Minerva Park. Her husband left Mrs. Tilford a quarter million in securities when he died several years ago. She is a great admirer of Johnny's. Fred is sure that the visit has nothing to do with the insurance, and bets Johnny $500.

Johnny rents a car and drives to Minerva Park and the Tilford home. Mrs. Tilford meets him at the door, and she is really glad to see Johnny. She tells Johnny that she listens to his program every Sunday on WBNS. She wrote Johnny for a picture a year ago, and wishes she was young again after meeting Johnny. She sneaks Johnny into the library, past the three suspects in the living room. She tells Johnny that she has figured out why the lumberyard burned down. She is sure it was set.

Mrs. Tilford tells Johnny that each of the three suspects could have gained from the fire. She has proof and knows Johnny can figure it out. She is kind of holding out for a big climax, and Johnny is going to help her make sure. Johnny goes in to meet the suspects. First is Harry W. Shelder, the husband's business manager, who is very clever about money. He could have burned the lumberyard down so that it could be replaced by homes and stores, making it worth millions. Second is Michael Tilford, an adopted son, who went to a business college, but did not do very well and has been living at home. He wants to sell the property to a development company. Mr. Tilford's will stipulated that Michael would get half the income from the property if it were sold. Third is Nancy Willis, Mrs. Tilford's niece. Her parents were not wealthy but she is the heir to the bulk of the estate. Mrs. Tilford goes upstairs to wash her hair and Johnny meets the suspects. Shelder tells Johnny that Mrs. Tilford does not have long to live. She can make millions if he manages the property for her. Michael calls Shelder's plans too risky. He wants someone else to take the risk while all we, er, mother has to do is sit by and share in the profits. Neither trusts the other for one second. Nancy tells Michael that she is tired of his plans and to let Aunt Grace handle things her way. Mrs. Haskel is called and told to bring in the portable bar for cocktails. Mrs. Haskel runs back into the living room and tells them that Mrs. Tilford is dead.

Johnny recounts how she had died sitting under the hair drier and knocked it over when she fell. The doctor arrives and he calls the cause of death a heart attack. Harry and Michael continue to argue with each other. Michael tells Johnny how she gave everyone more than they deserved. Even Michael admits he took money from her. Nancy tells Johnny that she took care of her aunt because neither Harry nor Michael had been there for weeks. Mrs. Haskel tells Johnny how Nancy bought the hair dryer, and how much Mrs. Tilford loved it. Johnny remembers a newspaper article about a freak accident with a hair drier just like Mrs. Tiford's, and how it had injured someone a month earlier. A wire had come loose, and there was a big noise about it. Harry tells Johnny that Nancy had bought the drier three weeks earlier as a gift, but she charged it to Mrs. Tilford's account. Johnny inspects the drier and finds the bare wire that electrocuted Mrs. Tilford. Johnny tells them that Harry and Michael had not been there for weeks, and Mrs. Haskel was afraid of it. Johnny tells Nancy that she was there and Nancy pulls a gun and Michael tries to take it from her and is shot. Johnny takes the gun and the police are called.

"So Nancy's wild shot busted one of his ribs, but Mike will recover. Nancy? I don't know what the penalty for murder is in Ohio, but believe me, she will find out the hard way. As for the estate, well that is up to the courts too. No doubt much of what might have been Nancy's share will go to the company for the payment on the fire."

## NOTES:
* **THE ANNOUNCER IS JIM MATTHEWS**

| Producer: | Jack Johnstone | Writers: | Jack Johnstone |
|---|---|---|---|

Cast:     Virginia Gregg, Helen Kleeb, Shirley Mitchell, Ben Wright,
          Sam Edwards, Harry Bartell, Lawrence Dobkin

◆　❖　◆

| SHOW: | THE NIGHT IN PARIS MATTER |
|---|---|
| SHOW DATE: | 8/16/1959 |
| COMPANY: | FLOYDS OF ENGLAND |
| AGENT: | GEORGE REED |
| EXP. ACCT: | $5,878.00 |

SYNOPSIS: George Reed calls Johnny, and tells Johnny that he wishes he was going to France at someone else's expense. George tells Johnny that he has just received a collect transatlantic phone call from Johnny's friend Louis Du Marsac, "les char gris." He wants to talk to Johnny about the Olney diamond, three quarters of a million in diamonds in a necklace that was stolen from the Earl of Olney in the states during a recent visit. George tells Johnny that he will not quibble over the expense account.

Johnny calls "les char gris" and learns, after a promise of $2,000, that he can help Johnny find the diamonds.

Johnny gets $1,000 in American Express traveler's checks and flies to Paris, France. On the plane Johnny sits next to Annette Dubov, a lovely young lady with money of her own. Annette recognizes Johnny's name from the radio and tells him that she has no definite plans, a situation Johnny promises to change. In Paris, Johnny takes a cab to his hotel shaves and goes to meet Louis Du Marsac. At Louis' apartment, Johnny notices that the door is open and goes in.

Johnny notes how the apartment is in a shambles. The phone rings and Johnny answers, only to talk to Louis. Louis tells Johnny to meet him at the Café Chez Macabre, a beatnik place. While Johnny is on the phone a man comes in and slugs Johnny. Johnny wakes up in a chair next to a bottle of cognac and a note nearby saying "je regrete," "I'm sorry." Johnny leaves and goes to the café to meet Louis. The Café is a really dirty place, full of strange people. Louis comes in and sits at Johnny's table. Johnny tells him what had happened and Louis tells Johnny the man must have thought Johnny was Louis, and apologizes. Louis starts ranting something for the benefit of someone else. Louis tells Johnny that Francois Dubisaint, the art dealer, has the Olney diamonds. Johnny remembers that Dubisaint was involved in the Vincent Price painting case and the Blue Madonna case. Louis tells Johnny that he has arranged for Johnny to pay Dubisaint 50,00,000 francs, and that Dubisaint will contact Johnny tonight at midnight. Dubisaint will be looking for Johnny under the name Robert Matthews, a rich man from Texas. Johnny warns Louis about a double-cross, and agrees to pay $3,000 if all goes well. Johnny relates how most crimes are solved, not by detectives, but by informants who must be paid-off.

Johnny arranges for another room and waits to meet Dubisaint at midnight. Johnny realizes his gun is missing just as the phone rings. Dubisaint is on the phone and Johnny tells him to come on up. Johnny is warned that Dubisaint has a gun with a silencer, just in case. Johnny rigs up a dummy in the bed and then waits behind the door. Dubisaint comes in and tells Johnny that he is wise to him. Annette tells Francois that she is sure Johnny is here. Annette realizes that there is a dummy in the bed, and that Johnny has no gun. Johnny throws a light bulb as a distraction and tackles Dubisaint, only to find out that Annette has the gun. Louis Du Marsac comes in and slugs Annette, only to raise his fee to $5,000 for saving Johnny's life.

"Of course there will be some fancy international legal procedure necessary, but I am sure the company can arrange for return of the necklace to the United States. As for Dubisaint, and the lovely but treacherous Annette, well the Paris police are making the arrangements for them, and I am sure that they will not be very pleasant ones. Incidentally, I met a luscious little blonde on that return trip, and she . . . well let's not go into that."

NOTES:
- TWO OTHER CASES ARE MENTIONED IN THIS EPISODE
- THE ANNOUNCER IS DAN CUBBERLY

Producer: Jack Johnstone     Writers: Jack Johnstone
Cast: Virginia Gregg, Forrest Lewis, G. Stanley Jones, Tony Barrett, Bill James, Gus Bayz

◆　❖　◆

SHOW: THE EMBARCADERO MATTER
SHOW DATE: 8/23/1959
COMPANY: FLOYDS OF ENGLAND
AGENT: GEORGE REED
EXP. ACCT: $1,174.00
SYNOPSIS: The night clerk calls Johnny in his Paris hotel room, and George Reed is calling from Hartford, and Johnny has to tell the night clerk to get off the line. George congratulates Johnny for recovering the Olney jewels, in spite of the money spent. Johnny is to contact Maurice Rigot in Paris. Rigot wants help recovering the Cellini Medallion, which has been stolen from the Louvre three weeks ago. Johnny tells George that he has a better idea.

Johnny calls Louis Du Marsac, "les char gris", who tells Johnny that he has made only one small investment with the money he had gotten from Johnny, she was so young and beautiful, so why did she steal from Louis? Johnny offers Louis $100 for information on the medallion, and Louis agrees to bring the information for $200. Louis comes to Johnny's room an hour later, and tells Johnny that the medallion is on its way to San Francisco, hidden in a shipment of wine on the Klemperhol, a freighter out of Le Havre. It will arrive tomorrow, and the medallion is hidden in a bottle of wine. Frank Gerstel, a fence who operates in New York, is supposed to pick up the wine.

The correct case has a circle with a Maltese Cross in it. Johnny pays Louis $200 and questions how he got so much information so quickly. Louis tells Johnny that he helped his friends smuggle the wine aboard the ship and marked the case himself.

Johnny flies to San Francisco, California and goes to the Huntington Hotel. Johnny walks to a restaurant for dinner and walks back to his hotel, only to be followed. The man following Johnny turns out to be Smokey Sullivan, his old friend. Smokey tells Johnny that he has been hanging around the docks and has learned that there is a lot of smuggling going on there, mostly narcotics. Johnny advises Smokey to go to the Feds, but Smokey is concerned about his past. Smokey had seen Frankie Gerstel hanging around the docks waiting for a boat, and Smokey helped Frankie unload a shipment of wine this morning. Johnny and Smokey head for the warehouse where the wine is stored. Johnny pounds on the door for a night watchman, only to find him dead, shot in the head. Johnny wonders if Frankie got there first and has the medallion. Johnny takes the guard's flashlight and goes into the warehouse to look for the medallion. Johnny spots the cases of wine and goes to it in the dark. Johnny spots an opened case and hears a noise. There is a shot and Johnny waits in the dark. Frankie calls to Johnny to give up, and shoots several times. Johnny throws a cinch bar to distract Frankie. Johnny gets a bead on him and fires but misses. Frankie walks to the crates to kill Johnny and is shot by Smokey; he had the night watchman's gun. The police arrive and Smokey wants to run, but Johnny reminds him that he is on the side of the police now.

"The Cellini medallion; in Frankie's pocket. It was pretty obvious that he'd killed the watchman, taken the medallion out of the wine case and was about to leave when we showed up. Smokey's shot had killed him. Had Smokey a bit worried too, when the police barged in on us, but now he is a public hero. Oh, sure, there will have to be some kind of hearing on the whole affair, my deposition is already in. But Smokey is really in the clear, and as for the couple hundred bucks I gave him, well forget it George, it came out of my own pocket."

## NOTES:

- BOB BAILEY WELCOMES STATIONS **KAAB** IN HOT SPRINGS, ARKANSAS, **WRIG** IN WAUSAU, WISCONSIN, **WOMI** ON OWENSBURG, KENTUCKY TO THE **CBS** NETWORK.
- JACK JOHNSTONE USES A PLAY ON THE NAME OF ONE OF THE ACTORS, FRANK GERSTLE AS THE NAME OF THE FENCE, FRANK GERSTEL.
- THE ANNOUNCER IS DAN CUBBERLY

**Producer:** Jack Johnstone      **Writers:** Jack Johnstone
**Cast:** Forrest Lewis, Vic Perrin, G. Stanley Jones, Tony Barrett, Frank Gerstle

◆ ❖ ◆

| | |
|---|---|
| SHOW: | THE REALLY GONE MATTER |
| SHOW DATE: | 8/30/1959 |
| COMPANY: | UNIVERSAL ADJUSTMENT BUREAU |
| AGENT: | PAT MCCRACKEN |
| EXP. ACCT: | $401.05 |

SYNOPSIS: Pat McCracken calls Johnny about Percival Lesilie Verfoot, who is the headman at Tri-Western in Eugene, Oregon. He has $50,000 and wants to give it to the beneficiary of a policy, Mr. Jonathan Doe. Pat wants Johnny to find Mr. Doe, and Johnny wants his expenses and the usual commission based on face value of the policy. Pat tells Johnny that they usually make that deal based on what he is able to save the company. Johnny convinces him to stretch the point and give it to him on this case anyway.

Johnny flies to Portland and then gets a flight to Eugene, Oregon. In the Tri-Western office Les Verfoot welcomes Johnny. Les is a big-mouthed guy who offers Johnny a drink. Les tells Johnny that Harvey Wakeman and his wife and son came here a few years ago to retire. Harvey bought a farm and did wonders with it. He left his insurance to John Doe, but Les does not know who Doe is. Johnny learns that Wakeman died in his sleep, and Doe had a farm just north of Wakeman's, and left Doe the money, but Les cannot find him. The police cannot find him and want to wait. The policy stated that if the beneficiary cannot be proved to be alive, the money goes to the secondary beneficiary after seven years. Les wants Johnny to find Doe, or prove him dead. Johnny is not sure how he will proceed.

Johnny rents a car and drives to the Wakeman farm. At the farm Johnny meets Ben Wakeman, the son. Ben has no idea what had happened to Doe. Mrs. Wakeman is sure that Doe was so broken up about Harvey that he left after Harvey died. After all, Harvey had spent almost all of his time at Doe's farm, and their Allis Chalmers tractor is still there. Mrs. Wakeman wonders if Doe might have been murdered. Mrs. Wakeman has never met John Doe, nor has Ben. No one else in the area knew Doe either. Johnny is sure they are telling the truth. Johnny goes to the police and gets the name of the man who worked the case, Sgt. Conroy. Johnny searches for other sources of information, but can find no trace of Doe, who has never owned a car, and has borrowed the Allis Chalmer tractor from Wakeman. Johnny searches for anything with Doe's name on it and finds nothing. Johnny wonders if Doe ever existed. At City Hall, Johnny is told that Mr. Waverley, the lawyer had signed all of Doe's papers, but Waverley is out of town. The next day Johnny goes to meet Sgt. Conroy, but learns nothing. Sgt. Conroy tells Johnny that Ben Wakeman was just like his father, very quiet. Sgt. Conroy tells Johnny that Ben is the secondary beneficiary on the policy.

Johnny calls Verfoot who tells Johnny that Ben will get the $50,000 if he just waits. Johnny goes to the farm to talk to Ben, who has an answer for everything. Mrs. Wakeman just talks and talks while Johnny is there and threatens to call Mr.

Waverley. Johnny finally leaves to meet with Mr. Waverley. He tells Johnny that Mrs. Wakeman is the reason Harvey Wakeman spent his time on Doe's farm, to get some peace and quiet. Waverley cannot tell Johnny anything about Doe. He tells Johnny that Doe was never alive; he was a fictitious person. Harvey knew he would not live long and arranged for his farm to go to his wife and son. We wanted to do more and arranged for Waverley to write the policy so that the money could not go to Ben until he is old enough. John Doe was a fictitious person for a sound logical reason. Harvey could leave the money to someone without slighting his wife or son, yet have them benefit later. Waverley and Johnny agree it would be best for the Wakemans not to find out for about seven more years.

"So Les, you can just hold this $50,000 payment outside and outstanding for a while. And don't forget to keep up the interest on it. Also, I think you have sense enough to keep your mouth shut about it."

## NOTES:

- THIS IS THE SECOND STORY IN WHICH JACK JOHNSTONE MENTIONS ALLIS CHALMERS FARM EQUIPMENT
- THE ANNOUNCER IS DAN CUBBERLY

Producer:  Jack Johnstone          Writers:   Jack Johnstone
Cast:      Virginia Gregg, Lawrence Dobkin, Marvin Miller, Sam
           Edwards, Junius Matthews, Stacy Harris, Bart Robinson

◆    ❖    ◆

SHOW:         THE BACKFIRE THAT BACKFIRED MATTER
SHOW DATE:    9/6/1959
COMPANY:      UNIVERSAL ADJUSTMENT BUREAU
AGENT:        PAT MCCRACKEN
EXP. ACCT:    $450.00

SYNOPSIS: Johnny is called early in the morning by Betty Lewis, who asks Johnny to marry her, but gets the usual runaround from Johnny. Betty chides Johnny for missing her housewarming party. Johnny tells Betty that he was in Oregon, and is concerned about the sound of shots in the background. Betty tells Johnny that they are backfires. Some kids have a hotrod and do it every morning at eight o'clock. Betty invites Johnny over for breakfast the next day to find out for himself. Maybe Betty can convince him to marry her. "So, why not?"

Johnny knows he has not been assigned to a case, but urges Pat to read on. Johnny drives to Betty's house at 11325 Maple Drive in Hartford, Connecticut amazed at how many people are around early in the morning. Betty's house is a one-story house between two larger ones. Betty is amazed that Johnny is there before 8:00 and greets him with a great big kiss. She tells Johnny that if he had any sense he would marry her, but Johnny raises the same reasons why he cannot, the job, and Betty reluctantly agrees. Betty tells Johnny that Barton J. Robinson lives across the street. Johnny remembers that he prosecuted a big insurance fraud case a few years back. Betty tells Johnny that Robinson is very punctual, and always eats breakfast by the window at 8:00. Johnny tells Betty he is going to warn Robinson to stay away from Betty. The hotrod shows up and the backfires sound off, but Johnny notes how the backfires stop when they pass Betty's house.

Betty tells Johnny that no one knows who the kids are who drive the car. Johnny remembers the tag number, 3CFU160, and calls Jerry Wilson at the Motor Vehicle Office. Jerry tells Johnny that he must have made a mistake. Johnny tells Betty that the license was a phony, and the drivers were not kids. Betty tells Johnny that Robinson has been away for a few weeks and this morning is the first time he has been there to eat his breakfast. Betty tells Johnny that the hot-rodders showed up a week after Robinson left. Johnny is sure that the drivers are casing the place. Johnny leaves a very disappointed Betty with a kiss and a promise to take her out that night and goes to look into the matter of the phony tags and the drivers who were not kids. Johnny inspects tire marks left by the car, and canvasses the neighbors to get information. Later that afternoon the cook at a diner tells Johnny that he has seen the car take the cut-off to Biley's Swamp. Johnny drives there and sees the tire marks he is looking for. Johnny spots the car behind a shack and goes in, only to get slugged.

When Johnny wakes up he hears voices and a man is searching him. A man named Gil throws water on Johnny and a man named Ringer tells Johnny that the police must have given up on finding him after he got out of the clink, and sent Johnny to find him. Ringer tells Johnny that no one can stop him from killing the man who sent him up, Barton Robinson. Ringer tells Johnny that the backfires will cover the sound of the shots, and he only needs one. Ringer tells Johnny that Robinson has the place locked up tight, but tomorrow they will get Robinson as he eats breakfast. Johnny is tied up with wet rawhide thongs as it starts to rain outside. After Ringer and Gil leave, Johnny rolls outside and puts the rawhide into a puddle to loosen the thongs and remove them. Johnny hides behind the door as Ringer drives back, and tells Gil that Robinson was not there at the window, and Johnny Dollar must have warned him. Another car drives up, and it is Betty. Ringer shoots, but Johnny gets loose and slugs Ringer. Betty drives up and hits Ringer with her car. She tells Johnny that when he did not come last night she was worried, and had told Robinson to stay away from the window. Then she followed the car and rescued Johnny. Ringer gets up, but Johnny slugs him as he is kissing Betty to calm her nerves.

"It was Betty Lewis who really saved the life of that insurance attorney. So most of this expense account covers some well-earned entertainment, plus a little gift for her. No, not an engagement ring, but a big jug of My Sin. But I must admit she certainly makes me think of the merits of . . . uh, yeah."

## NOTES:

- ACCORDING TO MAPQUEST, 11325 MAPLE DRIVE DOES NOT EXIST IN HARTFORD.
- THE ANNOUNCER IS JIM MATTHEWS

| Producer: | Jack Johnstone | Writers: | Jack Johnstone |
|---|---|---|---|
| Cast: | Virginia Gregg, Forrest Lewis, Barney Phillips, Tom Holland | | |

◆  ❖  ◆

| SHOW: | THE LEUMAS MATTER |
|---|---|
| SHOW DATE: | 9/13/1959 |
| COMPANY: | WORLDWIDE MUTUAL INSURANCE COMPANY |
| AGENT: | LES WALTERS |
| EXP. ACCT: | $89.50 |

SYNOPSIS: Les Walters calls Johnny and tells him that Elmer Leumas has disappeared, that there is nothing to go on.

Johnny goes to Les' office, and is told to go to Vineland, New Jersey, where Elmer was the owner of the Leumas Glass Company, from which he retired at 59 and lives with his younger wife Lena. Johnny goes to Philadelphia and rents a car for the drive to Vineland, where he stops to see Sgt. Tomasso, who tells Johnny that Mrs. Leumas is not upset. She is a social butterfly but Leumas hated parties. Leumas left 10 days ago and took his luggage and sold his boat. Johnny gets a hotel room and goes to the huge home of Lena Leumas, who is a real dish. She tells Johnny that she saw him in town and knew he would invite himself there. She tells Johnny that she will get the insurance and a lot more money. When Johnny asks if she thinks that her husband was murdered, she asks who would do that? Lena tells Johnny that the boat was sold to Samuel Remle in Tuckahoe, New Jersey. Johnny changes his ploy and tells Lena that she had planned to kill Leumas, and she tells Johnny to leave. On the way out Johnny meets Pete, who is protecting Lena. Pete calls Jerry and Johnny is knocked out. Johnny wakes up later and goes to his hotel.

The next day Johnny goes to the police and gets a hunch. Johnny goes to Tuckahoe and the boat is gone. Johnny gets a description of the owner, who is clean-shaven with short hair. Johnny calls the Coast Guard and learns that the boat is in Cape May. Johnny drives to Cape May and meets the owner of the boat, but is it Leumas or Samuel?

Johnny meets the owner and is told that "Leumas" spelled backwards is "Samuel," and "Elmer" spelled backwards is "Remle." As for Pete and Jerry, they are bodyguards for Lena. Leumas tells Johnny that he is trying to figure out their relationship and does not know where he will go.

Pete and Jerry are arrested, and as for Leumas and his wife, who knows?

NOTES:
- THE ANNOUNCER IS JIM MATTHEWS
- STORY INFORMATION OBTAINED FROM THE KNX COLLECTION IN THE THOUSAND OAKS LIBRARY

| Producer: | Jack Johnstone | Writers | Jack Johnstone |
|---|---|---|---|

Cast:     **Virginia Gregg, Harry Bartell, Paul Dubov, Jack Kruschen, Sam Edwards, Russell Thorson**

| | |
|---|---|
| SHOW: | THE LITTLE MAN WHO WAS THERE MATTER |
| SHOW DATE: | 9/20/1959 |
| COMPANY: | UNIVERSAL ADJUSTMENT BUREAU |
| AGENT: | PAT MCCRACKEN |
| EXP. ACCT: | $12.34 |

SYNOPSIS: Pat McCracken calls Johnny and tells him of 1, 2, 3 in a row, mysterious disappearances in a row Johnny has worked on. First was the case in of John Doe, then Elmer Leumas who disappeared to get away from his wife. This case is in Kerr's Ferry, New York. The charges are perpetrating fraud.

Johnny cabs to Pat's office commenting on the three mysterious disappearances. Pat tells Johnny how Howard L. Edwards insured his life for $50,000, double indemnity, with his wife as beneficiary. The police are not sure he is dead, even though his car was found in the river. The police discovered that Edwards and his wife are stone-broke and living off the finance company. The wife broke down and confessed that they had planned the disappearing act for some time. This type of fraud has been tried before. Johnny tells Pat that if he finds Edwards he will get a nice fat fee, which Pat almost chokes over. "Just find him," Pat asks. Johnny drives to Kerr's Ferry and contacts Sgt. Ben Ringler at the local police department. Sgt. Ringler tells Johnny that the Edwards car was deliberately run into the river. It was after midnight when his wife called and asked them to look for him. The next morning a kid spotted the car's wheels while fishing. Edwards claimed to be an inventor and he had their house up for sale. That way she could leave as soon as she got the insurance money and no one would suspect her. Sgt. Ringler is doubtful that Johnny can get anything out of Mrs. Edwards; he tried and got nothing, so what is Johnny going to be able to do?

Johnny visits Mrs. Edwards, but she does not want to open the door. When Johnny says he is with the insurance company and she lets him in. She hopes Johnny can find Howard, because the police can't. Sgt. Ringler and his son-in-law have been pestering her. She tells Johnny that Howard had been preoccupied with a machine and did not pay any attention to her. She is selling the house, as that is all they have left. The insurance would make up for all the skimping. She needs the money but does not wish her husband dead. Howard finally has found someone who would buy his invention, but everything is gone now. Howard had going to see the buyer but the plans are now lost in the river. She had told Sgt. Ringler, but his son-in law, Peter Barskin, said she was lying about them. Johnny infers that Howard would likely sell the invention and skip out on her, but she strongly disagrees, he would never do that. She told the police that Howard had talked of going away to work uninterrupted and they had told the insurance company. Johnny goes back to police headquarters where Sgt. Ringler and Peter Barskin are playing checkers. Johnny tells them that they have not considered all the possibilities. Johnny is working on the possibility of murder.

Johnny calls Randy Singer and asks him to have a fingerprint expert come up to help him, and Randy agrees to have Marty Levit come up to help out. Marty arrives and they go to look at the car but Marty cannot find any fingerprints, including ones on the steering wheel and gearshift. The car had been wiped clean. Johnny drives Marty to the train and goes to the Edwards house where Mrs. Edwards is very anxious. She shows Johnny how the house has been ransacked, and she had seen a man running out the back door. She tells Johnny that she has not called the police. Johnny searches the house and finds part of a letter from a plastics company in a desk drawer. The letter seems to imply that the local authorities had recommended the man who Howard had gone to see. Johnny realizes that whoever had been there knew the value of those letters. Peter Barskin walks in with a gun and tells Johnny that he will never find out. Johnny tells Pete that "this isn't Gunsmoke" and draws on Pete and shoots him. Pete asks how Johnny found out, and he tells Pete he was not sure until Pete came in with the gun. Sgt. Ringler comes in and tries to arrest Johnny, but he is told to drop his gun or he too will get shot. Johnny is sure that Kerr's Ferry will get a new chief of police, and Ben and Pete might even share the same electric chair.

"Sure, it's up to the courts. But when the State Police came in and found the papers on the invention hidden in Pete's house, oh, that invention now belongs to Mrs. Edwards, to say nothing of the insurance money, $50,000. So Pat, I'll let you of the hook real easy."

NOTES:
- THE FIRST COMMERCIAL BREAK IS AN **AFRS** STORY ABOUT CYRUS W. FIELD, WHO LAID A CABLE ACROSS THE ATLANTIC.
- THE SECOND COMMERCIAL BREAK IS AN **AFRS** SPOT ABOUT THE CONSTITUTION AND THE 17TH AMENDMENT
- THE ANNOUNCER IS JIM MATTHEWS

Producer: Jack Johnstone    Writers: Jack Johnstone
Cast:    Virginia Gregg, Larry Dobkin, Ralph Moody, Gil Stratton, Herb Vigran, Vic Perrin

SHOW:    THE GRUESOME SPECTACLE MATTER
SHOW DATE:    9/27/1959
COMPANY:    TRI-STATE LIFE & CASUALTY INSURANCE COMPANY
AGENT:    ED BARRETT
EXP. ACCT:    $148.00
SYNOPSIS: Repeat—A car crushes a man after rolling on him—with the ignition off—but who left the glasses in the car?

NOTES:

THIS IS A REPEATED PROGRAM, BUT THE PROGRAM FILES I HAVE ALL SEEM TO BE COPIES OF THE ORIGINAL PROGRAM—ALL OF WHICH ARE DISTORTED SOMEWHAT. THEREFORE, I CANNOT REALLY SAY WHAT THE DETAILS OF THE PROGRAM ARE.

Producer:  Jack Johnstone          Writers:  Jack Johnstone
Cast:

◆    ❖    ◆

SHOW:          THE BUFFALO MATTER
SHOW DATE:     10/4/1959
COMPANY:       UNIVERSAL ADJUSTMENT BUREAU
AGENT:         PAT MCCRACKEN
EXP. ACCT:

SYNOPSIS: Pat McCracken calls and Johnny complains about not having an assignment for several days. Pat complains about the expense account from last week, which Johnny cannot clearly remember. Pat reminds him that the $12.30 was enough to make Pat worry that Johnny was sick. Pat tells Johnny that he has convinced the company to add on a $500 fee because he almost got himself killed. Pat tells Johnny to go to Buffalo and contact Edward J. McNair at McNair's Emporium. Someone lifted over $400,000 from the safe over the weekend. Johnny is on his way.

Johnny flies to Buffalo, New York and meets with Mr. McNair who totals the loss at $421,216 and he blames himself for the loss. John Harker had recommended changing the procedure, but he resisted. Every Saturday night each department head would bring the receipts to Harker who would issue a receipt and put the money in the vault. Johnny notes that it would have been better to have an armored car take the money to the bank, and McNair agrees, and that is what Harker had suggested. As Johnny is told that Mr. Ellery was the last to knock on the door, there is a knock on the door and Mr. Harker enters. Harker tells Johnny that Mr. Ellery knocked and told him who was there. Harker went to open the door but it was slammed open and he was knocked unconscious. When he woke up the money was gone from the safe. Ellery had been beaten and bound by the robbers. Ellery had told Harker that the robber was wearing a mask. McNair tells Johnny that Harker is taking his cruiser on a trip with a friend and is leaving that night. Johnny meets with the police and learns nothing. Johnny meets with Mr. Ellery who tells Johnny that the events were just like Harker told the police. He usually had gone up, knocked on the door and given the money to Harker. That night, the man sneaked up on Ellery and threw him into the room. Ellery tells Johnny that Harker is working hard for the company and McNair appreciated it. Harker had been with the company for a year and has lived up to the recommendations from the big department stores. That is why Mr. McNair given him a much higher salary. Johnny wonders at the way Harker was sent out before he could be questioned, and the way the robber would have to know everything about the procedures. Johnny goes to his hotel to unpack and notices his bag was unlocked. He hears a sound he has heard before and throws the bag out of the window before it explodes. Johnny suspects that someone in Buffalo does not want him around. Johnny explains to the police what had happened, and their theory is that the man in the mask planted the bomb. Johnny reviews how only three people knew he was there: McNair, Harker and Ellery. The next morning Johnny goes to the bank and meets an old friend named Barton, who is the Cashier and a Vice President. Johnny asks about the financial conditions of McNair and his store and is told that McNair is worth millions and the store pays cash for everything. Johnny calls Macy's, Gimbels and John Wannamaker's to check up on Harker. Johnny learns that none of the stores had ever heard of John Harker. Johnny goes back to McNair and he has no idea where Harker has gone. Johnny suggests that by encouraging him to take the boat, McNair played into his hands and allowed him to get away with his money. Johnny tells McNair that his friend is probably the man in the mask. Johnny tells him that Harker had said, "he should have known by the tone in his voice that something was wrong" when Ellery knocked. But, Ellery did not know that the robber was there until after the door had been opened! Johnny tells McNair that he was a fool when he hired Harker, because his recommendations were fakes. He trained Harker how to fix the robbery, and helped him get away. Johnny laments how he really needs a stroke of luck now, and luck shows up in the guise of a storm. A big storm is approaching and the Coast Guard has notified all the boats on the lake. Harker responded and told them that they are riding out the storm in Canadian waters. Johnny asks, off the record, if he went out to get the men, would there be anyone who could do it. The Coast Guard remembers a man who has a converted sub chaser who might be able to take Johnny out. Johnny rents the boat and the skipper and relates how the case could have ended, but it will have to wait for the next report.

NOTES:
* THE ANNOUNCER IS JIM MATTHEWS

**Producer:** Jack Johnstone      **Writers:** Jack Johnstone
**Cast:** Lawrence Dobkin, Bartlett Robinson, James McCallion, Dick Crenna, Junius Matthews, Gil Stratton

◆ ❖ ◆

| | |
|---|---|
| **SHOW:** | THE FURTHER BUFFALO MATTER |
| **SHOW DATE:** | 10/11/1959 |
| **COMPANY:** | UNIVERSAL ADJUSTMENT BUREAU |
| **AGENT:** | PAT McCRACKEN |
| **EXP. ACCT:** | $1,800.00 |

**SYNOPSIS:** Pat McCracken calls Johnny and Pat has the expense report Johnny sent in, but why did he add return transportation when he is still in Buffalo? Johnny admits he got a little ahead of himself. Johnny tells Pat that he has not gotten the money back yet, but he knows where is it. It is impossible to get the money because of the storm. Johnny promises Pat that he will get the money back or die trying. Pat tells Johnny that he better get the money back or he will gladly attend the funeral.

Johnny relates how the Coast Guard had prevented him from going out in the sub chaser because of the storm. Johnny was able to get half of the money back, but will credit it to this report as the charge was on his American Express credit card. Mr. McNair visits Johnny in his hotel room. He tells Johnny that he does not want the crooks to get away with his money. Johnny tells him that the Canadians have been contacted, and there could be international problems if Harker does not have the money. McNair tells Johnny he will ride Johnny out of Buffalo on a rail if he is wrong. Johnny is not feeling so good, but gets a call from Murphy at the Coast Guard, and he has a weather report that the storm is subsiding. He can arrange a boat for Johnny once the weather clears. Johnny has an idea. He will be right on top of the crooks when the weather clears. Johnny cabs to the municipal airport and spots what he needs. Johnny rents a helicopter from Tinker Barnham for $300. For $600, Johnny convinces Tinker to take off, even though the weather is not good. Johnny takes his first ride in a helicopter out over lake Erie. Tinker spots the Long Point peninsula and the cruiser. Johnny fastens himself to a wench as he spots Harker on the boat. Johnny realizes he is outnumbered but tries a ruse. Johnny uses a megaphone to tell Harker that McNair has found the man who took the money, but the money is still missing. Johnny mumbles something about Mr. McNair and tells Harker he is coming down. Tinker eases Johnny down onto the cruiser. Johnny is dropped onto the boat and Billy takes his gun from him. Harker tells Billy to shoot Johnny. Harker tells Johnny that he is not a fool, and did not believe anything Johnny told him. Johnny is taken below, out of sight of the helicopter, and Harker signals to Tinker to leave. As Tinker leaves Billy gets ready to shoot Johnny, but Tinker comes back. The boat starts up as Johnny looks at Billy's .38. Johnny is told to move to the front of the cabin and spots a duplicate set of controls as he moves forward. Johnny stumbles and grabs the wheel, causing the boat to weave. Billy shoots, but Johnny slugs him and takes his gun. Johnny goes up but Harker tells Johnny that he has a gun too. The helicopter comes back and Harker shoots at Tinker and Johnny pushes Billy overboard. Johnny fights with Harker and overpowers him. Tinker calls to Johnny to make sure he is ok and then goes after Billy in the water. After all, Tinker had told the tower that this was a sea rescue operation.

"Yeah, like Billy had said, the stolen money, all of it, was stashed away in the forward chain locker. So after tying up Harker with all the line I could find, I started the engine of this beautiful yacht but then suddenly realized, well put it this way: If Tinker and his copter hadn't stayed with me, so help me I never would have found my way back to Buffalo."

The expense account includes $1000 for Tinker.

NOTES:
- SAM EDWARDS APPEARS IN THIS PROGRAM, BUT THE CREDITS DO NOT REFLECT IT. RADIOGOLDINDEX NOTES THAT THE ENDING OF THE PROGRAM HAS BEEN MODIFIED. PERHAPS THE ORIGINAL CLOSING CREDITS INCLUDED THE CORRECT ACTORS.
- THE ANNOUNCER IS JIM MATTHEWS
- JOHNNY NOTES THAT THIS WAS HIS FIRST RIDE IN A HELICOPTER. HOWEVER IN THE STAR OF CAPETOWN MATTER, HE RODE A HELICOPTER OUT TO THE SHIP HE MISSED.

Producer: Jack Johnstone        Writers: Jack Johnstone
Cast:        Lawrence Dobkin, Bartlett Robinson, James McCallion, Dick Crenna, Junius Matthews, Gil Stratton, Sam Edwards

◆  ❖  ◆

SHOW:          THE DOUBLE IDENTITY MATTER
SHOW DATE:     10/18/1959
COMPANY:       UNIVERSAL ADJUSTMENT BUREAU
AGENT:         PAT MCCRACKEN
EXP. ACCT:     $20.00

SYNOPSIS: Johnny gets a call from a woman who tells him that she is home from her vacation, and asks him to come over and propose. Johnny recognizes her as Betty Lewis. Johnny suggests he pop the question and asks, "So, will you marry me, Paula?" Betty wants to know how Paula is, and Johnny has to admit he was joking. Johnny suggests dinner, and Betty agrees to have the cocktails ready at 6:30. The phone rings again, and Randy Singer is on the phone. Randy has to see Johnny right now. Randy arranges for a squad car to pick Johnny up at Grand Central Station.

Johnny tells Pat McCracken that he has not been assigned to the case yet, but read on. Johnny trains to New York City and meets Randy in his office. Randy tells Johnny that "they" are insurance matters, and Johnny should have been assigned to them. One case was Paul R. Brownfield who "committed suicide" by sleeping pills in the fall of 1956. Eastern Casualty and Trust paid $41,000 to his wife of two months, and she disappeared after she was paid off. Franklin P. Ogborn died the same way in September 1957 and Tri Mutual paid off $30,000. Peter William Gerheart died the same way in August 1958 and the widow collected $50,000. Last month William Earl Chadwick died and the company paid off $25,000. In each case the marriage was only a few months old, and the wife was much younger, and the men were married to the same girl. Randy has found the girl, but she is out of his jurisdiction, but not Johnny's. The girl lives at 11325 Maple Drive in Hartford, Connecticut, and goes by the name of Betty Lewis!

Johnny reviews the files and the description of the girls is identical. According to Randy, the girl was Betty Lewis, the girl Johnny knows and almost took seriously. Randy wants Johnny to go back and get friendly with the girl and try to trip her up. Randy tells Johnny that the sleeping pills used in each case were a special prescription. Randy has found a kid who delivered the pills, and the boy had letters telling him to make some more pills. Officer Conroy comes in and tells Randy that the reporter has been sent away. He had told him that Randy was busy with Johnny Dollar about the suicide cases.

Johnny is met at his apartment by Betty, who is anxious after her extended vacation. She is not going to give up on Johnny. Johnny asks how she got into the apartment, and she tells Johnny that the door was wide open. Johnny asks about her vacation, and she tells Johnny that she had gone to several places, including New York. Johnny asks Betty what her hair color used to be, and she gets really irritated. Johnny notices that his desk is all messed up and Betty asks Johnny if he always leaves the window to the fire escape and the front door open. Johnny goes in and finds where the window had been jimmied open, and Betty tells him that it looks just like her mailbox. Betty asks if Johnny's questions have anything to do with the article she saw in the papers about a number of suicides. Johnny is sure that Betty scared off someone when she got there. Johnny realizes she had said her mailbox had been opened, and she tells Johnny that the lock was broken. Today, she came home from the office and there were high-heel footprints in the mud around the mailbox. Maybe someone was using her name and mailbox. Johnny wants a key to her house so he can solve four murders. The next day, Johnny stays in the house after Betty leaves for work. At 10:30, the mailman leaves a package in the mailbox. Johnny goes out to get the package and it is addressed to Betty Lewis. A woman drives up and asks what Johnny is doing poking around her mailbox, and the girl looks a lot like Betty. She asks for the package, but Johnny tells her he needs it to pin the murders of four husbands on her. She pulls a gun and demands the package. Johnny takes the gun from her and puts her in her car for a drive to police headquarters.

"Sure, there is a lot more to be done, only by the police both in Hartford and down in New York. But there is not much doubt about the outcome, especially since the kid who supplied the drugs broke down and said plenty. The insurance companies? Well the money she had left can be prorated among them and that will be that. My problem of course will be explaining things to Betty. But, you know something, that may have its pleasant aspects, too." Johnny calls the expense total $20.00, provided there is a fee on this one.

NOTES:
- JOHNNY NOTES THAT BETTY LEWIS IS A BLONDE
- THE ANNOUNCER IS DAN CUBBERLY

Producer:   Jack Johnstone        Writers:   Jack Johnstone
Cast:       Joan Banks, Lillian Buyeff, Herb Vigran, G. Stanley Jones

| SHOW: | THE MISSING MISSILE MATTER |
|---|---|
| SHOW DATE: | 10/25/1959 |
| COMPANY: | FLOYDS OF ENGLAND |
| AGENT: | GEORGE REED |
| EXP. ACCT: | $0.00 |

**SYNOPSIS:** George Reed calls "John" and asks if he has a security clearance. George cannot discuss the case over the phone, so Johnny goes right over.

Johnny cabs to the office of George Reed, who takes Johnny to an empty office. George tells Johnny that there is a small company in California that operated as the Smithwick Paint Remover Company. It really is a cover up and should be called the Smithwick Missile Company. The government does not recognize them, and Floyds writes the insurance based on orders from the top brass. Smithwick has reported that they have a missing missile. Dr. Smithwick will be waiting for Johnny.

Johnny flies to Los Angeles, California, rents a car and drives to the Smithwick Paint Remover building where Johnny notices a good-looking blond closing a door. She is Gloria Snowden the secretary and knows who Johnny is. She tells Johnny that Dr. Smithwick has gone to Washington, and Gloria was told to have Johnny wait for him. Johnny gets directions to a motel and arranges to take Gloria to dinner. Johnny finds the motel and gets a room. There is a knock at the door and no one is there when Johnny opens it. There are two shots and Johnny groans.

Johnny gets up when the manager, Mr. Barnwell comes back and tells Johnny that he heard shots. Johnny gets up and asks how the manager knew they were shots and not a backfire. The manager tells Johnny that he did not see anyone, only a car pulling away. Johnny tells him not to call the police and arranges for another room without listing it on the register. Johnny waits for a while and then goes back to get Gloria, but she is gone. Johnny sits in his second room and hears someone knocking on the other room. The visitor identifies himself as Bob McKenny, who used to work for CBS and handled his radio program; Bob wants to talk to Johnny. Bob had learned that Johnny was there from Mr. Barnwell, the manager. Bob has a tape recorder with some coded signals that he had recorded earlier that evening. Bob tells Johnny that he has an amateur license, W6BFG, and experiments with high frequency signals. Bob had crossed some wires and discovered signals on a frequency that is not supposed to be used by anyone. Bob recorded the signals and played it back real slow, and determined that it was international Morse code. Johnny listens to the code, and determines that is was not destined for anyone on this side of the iron curtain. Bob tells Johnny that the signal was very strong and probably originated nearby. Bob mentions that Kenny McManus has a direction finder and Bob will get him to help locate the signals. Johnny asks Bob to leave the tape recorder with him. Bob realizes that Johnny also had understood two words in the code: "Johnny Dollar"!

Johnny calls Lt. Harry Golden on the homicide squad and he has Alan Orloff, an interpreter, visit Johnny. Orloff tells Johnny that the tape had a threat against Johnny and secret plans for a missile and someone is holding them for an agent to pickup today. Bob McKenny comes back and tells Johnny that the broadcast station is in North Hollywood. Bob gives Johnny the address, and tells Johnny that there is no outside antenna. Johnny looks at the address and decides to go to the missile plant instead. Johnny drives to the missile plant and Mr. Smithwick tells Johnny he was sure the missile plans were missing, and had urged the government to send someone to look into the theft. The men should be here today. But when he returned from Washington, he found the plans in the proper place. Johnny tells him the plans were stolen for the benefit of one of the big foreign powers. Johnny wants to call Gloria into the office, but Smithwick tells Johnny that the only reason she is there is because she is stupid. Gloria is called in to the office. Johnny tells Smithwick that Gloria was the only one who could arrange to have Johnny attacked and the last one to be suspected of copying the plans. Johnny prepares to play a tape of the signals taken from Gloria's home. Gloria pulls a gun and Johnny throws the tape recorder at her and gets the gun. Johnny hopes the G-men will keep the date with the contact Gloria was supposed to meet.

"The government boys were more than glad to take over, and I hope they can find some way to reward Bob McKenny who really solved this case."

Because this was so good a cause, Johnny waives the expense account.

NOTES:
- JOHNNY MENTIONS TO BOB THAT HE HAD "POUNDED A KEY" MANY YEARS AGO
- BOB MCKENNY IS LISTED AS A TECHNICIAN ON MANY OF THE JOHNNY DOLLAR SCRIPTS.
- BASED ON THE CLOSING PREVIEW IN THIS PROGRAM, IT WOULD SEEM THAT THE ORDER OF THIS PROGRAM AND "THE DOUBLE IDENTITY MATTER" MAY HAVE CHANGED AT SOME POINT, ALTHOUGH MOST CATALOGS PLACE THIS PROGRAM AFTER THE DOUBLE IDENTITY MATTER.
- THE ANNOUNCER IS DAN CUBBERLY

**Producer:** Jack Johnstone      **Writers:** Jack Johnstone
**Cast:** Virginia Gregg, G. Stanley Jones, Forrest Lewis, Harry Bartell, Don Diamond, Bartlett Robinson

| **SHOW:** | THE HAND OF PROVIDENTIAL MATTER |
|---|---|
| **SHOW DATE:** | 11/1/1959 |
| **COMPANY:** | PROVIDENTIAL ASSURANCE COMPANY |
| **AGENT:** | ERNEST L. WHITEMAN |
| **EXP. ACCT:** | $0.00 |

**SYNOPSIS:** Ernest L. Whiteman from Providential Assurance Company calls, and Johnny tells him that he has never heard of him. Whiteman has a case of embezzlement and wants Johnny to look into it. Johnny inquires about the fee over and above his expenses, and is told he can name his own figure, up to $5,000 if he gets the $200,000 back. Johnny suggests that he should pad his expense account.

Johnny cabs to the Hartford, Connecticut offices of Mr. Whiteman where Johnny meets Elwood Sprague who is the owner of the company. Sprague tells Johnny that he made a lot of money in oil and started this company and is getting more money. Mr. Whiteman and Sprague tell Johnny that his company is gaining a reputation by settling all their claims in cash without questioning them. Sprague tells Johnny that they hope to lose money in the business for tax reasons. The money in question was stolen from the office and Tom Hauser was the one who stole the money. He kept the books and had the combination to the safe. Whiteman discovered today that Hauser had been juggling the books and now Hauser is gone. Johnny wonders how they got a license, and Sprague tells Johnny that they do not have one yet. Johnny is told not to worry about it and to catch Hauser. When Johnny warns them of the problems the Insurance Commission and the government can bring, Sprague just looks at it as a tax loss and tells Johnny to find Hauser. When Johnny tells Sprague that he does not worry about being fined millions, but worries over $200,000, Johnny is told that what Hauser did was illegal. Johnny wants to beg off the case and tells them that he will have to notify the commission. Sprague tells Johnny he can do whatever he wants after he catches Hauser. With $5,000 dangling in front of his eyes, Johnny decides to take the case.

Johnny checks the last known address of Hauser and learns from the manager that Hauser left the previous night. Johnny gives the manager a five spot and gets the key to the apartment. At the door, Johnny hears a voice on the phone and realizes that Hauser is still there. Hauser tells the man on the phone that "he can take care of Johnny Dollar." Johnny opens the door and is beaten by Hauser. Johnny wakes up with the manager putting a cold rag on his head. Johnny grabs the lamp he was hit with and cabs to police headquarters and talks to Sgt. Ed Wilson, who takes the lamp to the lab. Johnny goes home and takes a shower only to be called by Sgt. Wilson and informed that Tom Hauser is one of the 10 most wanted. Sgt. Wilson tells Johnny that if Hauser thinks Johnny saw him, Hauser will be back to finish him.

Pat McCracken calls Johnny and Pat wants him to look into a phony insurance company. Pat has a complaint about a small company who is stalling on a claim, and Johnny recognizes what is happening. Johnny tells Pat that he is working for them, and Pat tells Johnny to stay away from them. Pat is told that the Commission is coming the next week to investigate Providential. Johnny is sure that Providential is a scam when Sprague calls Johnny. Sprague wants to see Johnny in his room at the Guilford Hotel. Johnny senses the fear in Sprague's voice when Pat calls back to tell Johnny that he had talked to the police and cannot reach anyone at Providential. Johnny goes to the hotel and meets Sprague in his room. Sprague admits that he never did make any money in oil and has used his whit's to fool people. Whiteman was fooled and convinced Sprague to act as a front man. Whiteman was very good at selling policies, and when a claim came in, they stalled it. They were going to keep at it until the commission investigated. Whiteman brought Hauser in to take the wrap because of his record, but Hauser took all the money. Sprague had heard Whiteman talking to Hauser to split the money and kill Sprague. Johnny starts to take Sprague to the police when Whiteman comes in with a gun. Whiteman tells Johnny that he has killed Hauser and now is going to kill Sprague and Johnny. Sgt. Wilson and Pat McCracken come in behind Whiteman and there is a barrage of gunfire and Whiteman is killed. Sprague agrees to go with the police, real peaceful.

"So the big fat fee that was promised doesn't get paid to me after all, and I am sure I might as well forget the expense account for a change. But you know something? It doesn't matter. Because the important thing was to have had some small part in wiping out this dirty racket. Me? I feel good."

**NOTES:**
*   **THE ANNOUNCER IS DAN CUBBERLY**

Producer:    Jack Johnstone         Writers:    Jack Johnstone
Cast:        Virginia Gregg, Edgar Barrier, Junius Matthews, Jerry
             Hausner, Lawrence Dobkin

◆    ❖    ◆

SHOW:         THE LARSON ARSON MATTER
SHOW DATE:    11/8/1959
COMPANY:      PHILADELPHIA MUTUAL LIFE CASUALTY INSURANCE COMPANY
AGENT:        HARRY BRANSON
EXP. ACCT:    $79.75

SYNOPSIS: John is called by Harry Branson who tells Johnny that they have not had need of Johnny's services for a while. Johnny asks Harry if the problem is murder, mayhem or arson, and Harry tells Johnny it may be all of them combined. Johnny asks if they have been selling insurance to gangsters. Harry tells Johnny that the policy was sold to a former gangster, Bertie Larson. Johnny remembers that Bertie had been up before a special investigating committee, the one that had been on the television investigating narcotics and killings. Johnny tells Harry to cancel the policies and pay Bertie off, but Harry tells Johnny that since the hearings, they have increased the amount of the coverage. In view of the threats on his life and family, Harry needs help. Johnny tells Harry that if Harry wants his help, there is going to be a big fee involved.

Johnny trains to Philadelphia and goes to see Harry. Harry tells Johnny the Herbert James Larson lives in Penfield, Pennsylvania in a nice home insured for $30,000 and his property is insured for $20,000. Larson's life is insured for

$20,000. The beneficiary of all the policies is the wife, Nora. Bertie's life has been threatened over the phone ever since he started testifying. Last week Bertie found a can of gasoline sitting on his doorstep, as threat. Bertie has continued testifying in spite of the threats. Harry is sure the threats must have come from gangsters. Harry wants Johnny to protect Bertie because the police protection is inadequate. Johnny agrees to help Harry.

Johnny gets a rental car and drives to Bertie's house where no one is home, and no policemen are around. Johnny spots lights in a window and walks up to the house. Johnny smells gasoline in the garage and heads there. Johnny remembers smelling the gas before he is slugged and shots ring out.

Johnny wakes up in a hospital room with a police sergeant and another man. The man tells the sergeant that he thought Johnny was one of the men who were threatening him, and the shots were to summon the police. Johnny is told how Bertie found Johnny sneaking around and had slugged him. Bertie tells Johnny that the hospital bill is on him. Bertie tells Johnny that he is going up to the country to make sure his wife is ok. She is staying with friends in the Catskills. Bertie leaves and the sergeant tells Johnny that he is lucky that Bertie did not kill him. The sergeant tells Johnny he should have come to him first. Johnny is told that Bertie is not the man the committee is after, as Bertie was only a messenger. The committee is using Bertie to flush out the others. Johnny is told that Bertie is scared, but he is reveling in the glory, and it is helping his used car business. The threats are only on Bertie's word. Johnny tries to tell the sergeant about the gas, but he just walks out.

Johnny feels that something is wrong with this case. Johnny leaves his room and drives to Bertie Larson's house. Johnny spots a big car in the driveway and sees a man packing it. Johnny surprises Bertie and is told that he had come home to get some things for his wife and he had spotted someone running away. Bertie tells Johnny he had smelled gasoline in the house and takes Johnny in to show him. Johnny notices the house is almost bare and tells Bertie that he would probably put in a claim for everything if the house burnt down. Bertie shows Johnny how gas had been poured in the carpet and Johnny notes that the window screen had been punched out from the inside. Johnny tells Bertie that he had been losing money at the used car business and is using the threats as a cover for the arson he was going to commit. Bertie pulls a gun and Johnny gets the drop on him. Nora Larson comes in and tells Johnny to drop his gun. Bertie tells Nora they can now torch the place with Johnny in it. They will also strip Johnny so the bones will be Bertie's, that's $20,00 more in insurance. Nora tells Bertie she is leaving both of them there and shoots Bertie. The police rush in and shoot Nora. The sergeant tells Johnny that the hospital had called him when Johnny left, and Johnny is mighty glad.

Johnny's expenses include a stay in the Belleview Stratford hotel.

## NOTES:
- THE FIRST COMMERCIAL IS FOR WINSTON CIGARETTES.
- THE SECOND COMMERCIAL BREAK IS FOR OTHER CBS SHOWS INCLUDING

GARY MOORE, ARTHUR GODFREY, ANDY GRIFFITH, BOB AND RAY, ART LINKLETTER, AMOS N' ANDY, THE NEW YORK PHILHARMONIC AND THE METROPOLITAN OPERA.

- THE THIRD COMMERCIAL BREAK IS MONA FREEMAN WITH A COMMERCIAL FOR FOUR WAY COLD TABLETS AND ONE FOR FITCH DANDRUFF SHAMPOO.
- THE FINAL COMMERCIAL IS FOR EXLAX.
- THE ANNOUNCER IS DAN CUBBERLY

**Producer:** Jack Johnstone      **Writers:** Jack Johnstone
**Cast:** Virginia Gregg, Harry Bartell, Don Diamond, Bert Holland

◆ ❖ ◆

**SHOW:** THE BAYOU BODY MATTER
**SHOW DATE:** 11/15/1959
**COMPANY:** TRI-STATE LIFE & CASUALTY INSURANCE COMPANY
**AGENT:** EARLE POORMAN
**EXP. ACCT:** $168.65
**SYNOPSIS:** Earle Poorman calls Johnny from Sarasota. Earle reminds Johnny of how his house is on a bayou. Earle asks how Johnny how he would feel if Earle sold $50,000 of straight life to a man, and then found his body under his dock three days later? Johnny agrees to catch the first plane to Florida, and not to go fishing.

Johnny flies to Tampa, Florida and is met by Earle. Earle tells Johnny that he was called before the police. Earle thinks the man had a heart attack. The man was Ralph P. Carter, and lived four houses up the bayou and used to live in New York. He was 64 and had some heart trouble and retired to Florida with his wife, and Earle knows that they are loaded. Johnny immediately suspects the wife until Earle tells him that she is in her fifties. Earle tells Johnny that Carter owned several other policies, blue chip stocks and bank accounts and that the policy means nothing. Earle tells Johnny that the wife did not know about the policy, and the beneficiary is a former stripper, Mitsey Taylor who lives in New York. Carter told Earle that he knew her rather well before he married his wife three years ago.

While waiting for the autopsy to be conducted by Dr. Phillips, Johnny talks with Sgt. Edwards. Johnny is told that the autopsy is because Carter was alone when he died. Also, Mrs. Carter is not home, and does not know about her husband's death. Sgt. Edwards has checked with Carter's physician, Dr. Foot, and Carter's heart condition was serious. Dr. Phillips, an old friend of Johnny's, tells Johnny and Sgt. Edwards that Carter died from a heavy blow at the base of the skull by a poker the police took from the house. Sgt. Edwards tells Johnny that he will issue an APB for Mrs. Carter.

Sgt. Edwards tells Johnny that the APB is out, and Earle tells Johnny that the Carters did not get along too well. Sgt. Edwards tells Johnny that the neighbors had reported a big fight the previous night. The neighbors also reported that Mrs. Carter was seen leaving about the same time the coroner says Carter died. Sgt. Edwards is sure that Mrs. Carter did it because she was much younger and very attractive. Also, the lab reported finding lint from gloves on the poker. Earle tells Johnny that Mrs. Carter always wore a hat and gloves when she went out. Johnny goes to Earle's for lunch and then walks to the Carter house. Johnny finds a door open and looks around. Johnny spots a locked desk and pries it open. In a folder are a number of checks made out to Mitsey Taylor, but three checks are missing. Johnny goes to Mrs. Taylor's desk and finds the missing checks. Mrs. Carter comes in and Johnny gives her his credentials. She tells Johnny that she was upset and had been at a beauty parlor. Johnny asks her if she left before or after Ralph had died? She is shocked, but not sorry. She tells Johnny that this was her second marriage and had hoped that he would be content with her money and settle down. The only woman he cared about was that horrible girl. She found the checks yesterday, and told him that she was going to divorce him. She tells Johnny that she always wears special gloves made in France. Sgt. Edwards returns and arrests Mrs. Carter for suspicion of murder. Johnny tells Sgt. Edwards that the suspicion may save him from being sued for false arrest.

Johnny is taken to the airport and flies to New York and cabs to the neighborhood of Mitsey Taylor. Johnny phones her and pretends he is Louis. Mitsey tells Louis he should have stayed in Florida, but since he is here, come to the apartment and she will pay him off. Johnny calls Randy Singer and he agrees that the wife would have caught on eventually, but Mitsey could not wait. Johnny arranges for Randy to come over when things are wrapped up. Johnny goes to Mitsey's apartment and forces his way in. Johnny tells her that she will not collect on the $50,000 policy she did not know about. Mitsey tells Johnny he will be floating in the East River the same way Carter was floating in the bayou. Louis comes in from the next room and Mitsey takes Johnny's gun. When Mitsey goes to close the door, Randy is there and Louis is shot. Randy comes in with a very sarcastic "Hi ya, Johnny, fancy meeting you here" remark, and Johnny thanks him for coming over.

"Louis managed to survive, and I understand the way he shot off his mouth in the hospital, well I understand he pretty much cinched the case against both himself and Mitsey."

NOTES:
- COMMERCIAL #1 IS FOR WINSTON CIGARETTES.
- COMMERCIAL #2 IS FOR COLUMBIA STEREO-ONE PHONOGRAPHS.
- COMMERCIAL #3 IS MEL TORME FOR FOUR WAY COLD TABLETS AND A COMMERCIAL FOR FITCH DANDRUFF SHAMPOO.
- COMMERCIAL #4 IS FOR EXLAX AND THE NEED FOR COLD REMEDIES.
- DAN CUBBERLY IS THE ANNOUNCER.

Producer:   Jack Johnstone          Writers:   Jack Johnstone

Cast:        Virginia Gregg, Lillian Buyeff, Vic Perrin, Sam Edwards,
             Barney Phillips, Herb Vigran, Frank Gerstle

◆    ❖    ◆

SHOW:        THE FANCY BRIDGEWORK MATTER
SHOW DATE:   11/22/1959
COMPANY:     TRI-STATE LIFE & CASUALTY INSURANCE COMPANY
AGENT:       EARLE POORMAN
EXP. ACCT:   $200.00

SYNOPSIS: Earle Poorman calls Johnny from Sarasota, and Johnny complains about being called to Florida and only fishing bodies from the water. Earle tells Johnny that maybe he can get some fishing in when Johnny comes down to determine if a policy holder was killed or committed suicide.

Johnny flies to Tampa and then to Sarasota, Florida where Earle meets Johnny in his brand new air-conditioned car. Earle tells Johnny that if suicide is proved, Johnny can save the company $40,000. The insured was a tin-horned gambler named Alfie Garver, and he only paid one premium. Alfie had been losing money at the dog track and is living on handouts. His wife told a doctor that Alfie was in bad shape and might commit suicide. Alfie was out last night and got into a big fight with Luke Thrasher at the track. Luke has had several mysterious murders tied to him, but no one could prove anything. The fight was over a bet that Alfie had welched on and Luke told Alfie to get out of town or he would kill him. Alfie's wife had been at the police at 2 AM asking them to find Alfie. She is the beneficiary and about as worthless as Alfie. Luke was arrested and is being held in jail. As Earle approaches a police car, Earle tells Johnny that the police found Alfie's coat on the bridge and a boat found his hat in the water. Earle stops and they talk to Lt. Dodge, who tells them that they have something to work on. The evidence, including blood on the bridge, points to a struggle. Johnny reviews the evidence and is inclined to agree until he looks at the jacket. Johnny spots a feather, and Johnny thinks that it is a clue that Alfie was not murdered. Johnny asks Earle to take him to Doc Crutcher with a little sample of the blood. Dr. Les Crutcher pours Johnny and Earle a drink and then works on the blood sample. Doc Crutcher tells Johnny that the blood was from a chicken. Earle is now sure that the signs of a struggle were a fraud. Johnny will be sure when they find Alfie. Johnny goes to see Lt. Dodge who tells Johnny that Luke's alibi was airtight. Johnny arranges to borrow a car and act as chauffeur for Luke Thrasher. Johnny takes Luke to a dingy motel but does not get much help finding Alfie. When Johnny tells Luke that he is an investigator, Luke gets out of the car and reminds Johnny that he has killed others.

Johnny muses how his hunches do not always pan out, but he has a couple about Luke Thrasher. Johnny drives to Earle's house and answers a late night phone call from Doc Crutcher. Doc tells Johnny that the blood contains signs of a tripaniosis virus rarely found in the south. He had checked with a vet and discovered the chicken could only have from Andy Polucci on Bee Ridge Road. Johnny goes to see Andy and wakes him and asks if Alfie Garver bough a chicken the other night, and Andy tells Johnny that Alfie's wife bought the chicken, along with Luke Thrasher. Andy threatens to complain to the police, and Johnny tells him to go right ahead. Johnny goes to the motel room of Mrs. Garver and invites himself in. Johnny tells her how she and Luke planned the murder of her husband. Since Luke was winning at the track, they decided to get rid of Alfie, and used the talk of suicide as a decoy. She spilled the chicken blood after Luke's alibi was established so she could collect on the insurance. She tells Johnny that she did not kill Alfie; Luke did it. Luke comes in and she takes Johnny's gun. Lt. Dodge gets the drop on Luke from a window and makes Luke drop his gun. Lt. Dodge tells Johnny that he got a complaint from Andy Polucci for getting him up in the middle of the night.

"Luke Thrasher, in spite of all the pressure they put on him, still refused to talk. So, it was Lena Garver who finally broke down and told the police where hey could dig up Alfie's body. Yeah, the bullets in him came from the gun Luke had held on me. So, it's up to the courts."

Johnny manages to get in some really great fishing with Earle Poorman this time.

NOTES:
- COMMERCIAL #1 IS FOR WINSTON CIGARETTES.
- COMMERCIAL #2 IS STU ERWIN FOR FOUR WAY COLD TABLETS AND A COMMERCIAL FOR FITCH DANDRUFF SHAMPOO.
- FINAL COMMERCIAL IS FOR EXLAX.
- THE VIRUS DOC CRUTCHER MENTIONS, TRIPANIOSIS APPEARS TO BE ANOTHER JACK JOHNSTONE CREATION. THERE IS A VIRUS CALLED TRYPANOSOMIASIS THAT CAUSES CHAGAS DISEASE, BUT I DON'T HEAR THAT MANY SYLLABLES IN THE WORD DOC SAYS.
- THE ANNOUNCER IS DAN CUBBERLY

**Producer:**   Jack Johnstone          **Writers:**   Jack Johnstone
**Cast:**   Virginia Gregg, Vic Perrin, Barney Phillips, Edgar Stehli, Peter Leeds, Frank Gerstle

◆   ❖   ◆

**SHOW:**          THE WRONG MAN MATTER
**SHOW DATE:**   11/29/1959
**COMPANY:**     FLOYDS OF ENGLAND
**AGENT:**        GEORGE REED
**EXP. ACCT:**    $1.00

**SYNOPSIS:** George Reed calls Johnny, and Johnny is glad for the assignment. The man in trouble is John Patrick O'Shea who is retired, lives in Hartford and is confined to a wheel chair. Last night someone broke in and beat him severely. He would have been killed if a neighbor had not barged in and scared the man away. George wants Johnny to pick him up so they both can go over, as George is personally involved in this case.

Johnny cabs to George's office and they drive to the Hartford, Connecticut apartment. George tells Johnny that Harry Marshall, a male nurse, had been sent over to change the beneficiary on O'Shea's policy. The only relative is a neer-do-well nephew in Boston. O'Shea does not have much money, so he bought a policy and named Marshall as the beneficiary. Marshall felt that O'Shea should have made provisions for the nephew and convinced O'Shea to make the changes. Marshall came over to talk to George, but George had gone to a movie with his wife. Marshall left a note in the door saying he had stayed until almost eleven and hoped George and his wife had enjoyed the movie, and asked him to call Marshall in the morning. When Marshall got home, O'Shea had been attacked and the police were there. George and Johnny arrive and ring the bell. Harry answers the door and Lt. Barley is there. Barley shows Johnny a Harris Tweed patch torn from a jacket in the window. Marshall blurts out that he could kill the man who hurt O'Shea. Johnny wants to sit down and talk to Marshall for a while.

Johnny learns that Marshall had left shortly before 10:00 PM and O'Shea was still up watching TV. Marshall waited at George Reed's house, and then returned to find the front door open, Mr. Wakely from next door, and the police in the house. Mr. Wakely walks in and asks if Johnny wants to talk to him. Wakely tells Johnny that O'Shea would be dead if he had not come over. Wakely got here 2 minutes after 11:00. He had been trying to listen to the news, and came over to tell the man to turn down his TV. He does it every night, and had called Marshall to have him turn it down. When he got to the porch, he hears O'Shea calling for help. Wakely broke down the door and found O'Shea on the floor covered with blood and the window open, and then he called the police. Wakely tells Johnny that everybody on the block would be willing to kill O'Shea because of the noisy TV.

Wakely warns Johnny not to accuse him of anything and pulls a gun. Johnny takes the gun from Wakely and it fires once when Johnny slugs him. Johnny tells Marshall to call the police as he goes up to talk to O'Shea. Johnny changes his mind and calls George and asks when he had decided to go to the movie. George tells Johnny that it was after dinner, as he and his wife had no other plans. Johnny checks on O'Shea who is out, and then searches Marshall's room and finds receipts for the rental of a room several blocks away. Johnny leaves and goes to the rooming house and the manager takes Johnny to Marshall's room. In the room Johnny finds a Harris Tweed jacket with a missing piece. Johnny returns to O'Shea's house and Lt. Barley is there. Marshall spots the coat and he is speechless. Johnny tells Lt. Barley how Marshall was smart by adding another beneficiary to the policy, that way not too much would be diverted away. If O'Shea were to die before the change was made, no one would suspect Marshall. Johnny tells Marshall that he had been checking on George very carefully, as the note he left said, "hope you and Mrs. Reed enjoyed the movie." Marshall congratulates Johnny on his skill.

"So George, having saved your company from having to pay off the old man's insurance, well how much is my fee going to be? If it's big enough I'll forget all about the, wait a minute, what expense account? A lousy buck for the trip over to your office this morning? Oh, me."

NOTES:
- THE FIRST COMMERCIAL BREAK IS AN **AFRS** SPOT WITH A MINI-BIOGRAPHY OF WALTER HUNT, WHO INVENTED THE SAFETY PIN AND OTHER THINGS.
- THE SECOND COMMERCIAL BREAK IS ABOUT THEME OF WESTERNS, AND THE ORIGINATOR OF THE WESTERN, SAMUEL COLT.
- THE ANNOUNCER IS DAN CUBBERLY

**Producer:**    Jack Johnstone        **Writers:**    Jack Johnstone
**Cast:**        Virginia Gregg, G. Stanley Jones, Chet Stratton, Sam Edwards, Junius Matthews

◆    ❖    ◆

**SHOW:**          THE HIRED HOMICIDE MATTER
**SHOW DATE:**    12/6/1959
**COMPANY:**      TRI-WESTERN LIFE INSURANCE COMPANY
**AGENT:**         HORACE W. MILFORD
**EXP. ACCT:**     $0.00

SYNOPSIS: The Milford Advertising Company calls, and Horace. W. Milford wants to talk to Johnny. Johnny tells him that if he wants to buy time for his radio show he will have to call CBS. Mr. Milford tells Johnny that this is a personal matter, but that Tri-Western insures his life. Milford tells Johnny not to contact the insurance company, and that he will pay Johnny's expenses. He wants Johnny to help prevent a murder.

Johnny flies to Denver, Colorado and gets a hotel room at the Brown Palace. After getting some sleep, Johnny walks to the office of the Milford Advertising Agency. Mr. Milford tells Johnny that the whole matter must be kept confidential. Johnny must prevent a murder. Milford tells Johnny that after his wife passed away, his daughter and the business have been his only concerns. Until two years ago he did everything at the firm. Then, two years ago he brought in Tony Ferringer, his son-in-law who brought in a major electronics firm as an account. Unfortunately he did it in a rather unethical way and told Milford that he had sensitive information on the company executives. Tony constantly reminded him that he had brought in the account. Tony had courted and eloped with his daughter and bragged how he would take the business away from Milford. Milford tells Johnny that Claire, his daughter, had killed herself because of

Tony. Milford tells Johnny that he hates Tony. Tony has now started his own agency and threatened to take the account away. Two days ago the executives of the account came to Milford and told him that they had heard what Tony had said, and there was no truth in it and they would stand by Milford. Milford tells Johnny that he had hired a professional killer to take care of Tony. He has no way to call the man off until he has murdered Tony.

Milford tells Johnny that he very carefully arranged with an underworld contact named Eric Blinker for a killer to contact Milford. The killer only told Milford that his name was Blackie. There is no way now to call off the killer, because Blinker's body was found in the river yesterday. Milford has never met Blackie and only talked to him from a window. He paid Blackie $5,000 and was told that Blackie would do the job by the end of the week. Milford has not talked to Tony, as that would allow him to bleed Milford dry. But how to stop the killer? Milford tells Johnny that Tony has insurance with some distant relative, not even his wife was named. Johnny gets Tony's address and then Tony enters the room. Tony tells Milford how he has heard that he stole the electronics account from him, and how he will make him pay. Tony leaves and Johnny gets an idea. Johnny gets a cab to follow Tony to his home. Johnny has the cab wait as he walks up to the house. Johnny rings the back door buzzer and then hides. Tony comes out and Johnny slugs him and drags him inside.

Johnny pays the cabby to help him take Tony to a boarding house across town. Johnny pays the manager $10 to tell Tony a cabby brought Tony there. Johnny cabs back to Tony's house to find Blackie there. Blackie has Johnny sit on a piano bench and Blackie tells Johnny that he knows Johnny is not Tony, but Johnny knows too much. Blackie knows Johnny took Tony to the rooming house. Now Blackie has no choice. Johnny tries to bluff Blackie as he prepares to shoot Johnny in the head. Johnny falls from the bench and gets the gun from Blackie and slugs him.

"Nailing Blackie for the murder of Eric the stoolie allowed me to keep Mr. Milford out of the picture completely. Nor did Blackie talk, some code of the underworld, I guess. As for the expense account, in view of the fee that was handed to me, you can forget it. As for Tony Ferringer, he never did figure out what happened to him. Now will somebody please give me a nice clean case to work on?"

## NOTES:

- I HAVE TWO VERSIONS OF THIS PROGRAM, AND ON ONE, BOB BAILEY WELCOMES WKNE IN KEENE, NEW HAMPSHIRE BACK TO CBS, AND WKZT IN BRATTLEBORO, VERMONT IS WELCOMED ABOARD
- THE ANNOUNCER IS DAN CUBBERLY

**Producer:** Jack Johnstone      **Writers:** Jack Johnstone
**Cast:**      Virginia Gregg, Marvin Miller, Lawrence Dobkin, Russell Thorson

| | |
|---|---|
| **SHOW:** | **THE SUDDEN WEALTH MATTER** |
| **SHOW DATE:** | **12/13/1959** |
| **COMPANY:** | **UNIVERSAL ADJUSTMENT BUREAU** |
| **AGENT:** | **PAT MCCRACKEN** |
| **EXP. ACCT:** | **$38.25** |

**SYNOPSIS:** Pat McCracken calls and Johnny tells his "Santa Clause" that all he wants is a million bucks, a new convertible, a bevy of beautiful blondes and two red heads. Pat laughs and tells Johnny that he has a case of pure old-fashioned greed plus a no-good Samaritan. Johnny inquires about the fee, but Pat tells Johnny he may end up being one of Santa's helpers.

Johnny cabs to Pat's office where Pat tells Johnny that some of the clients that Universal Adjustment Bureau handles cater to the farming community and issue annuity policies. Pat tells Johnny that he has received word of a lot of people cashing in their policies and borrowing against their farms to invest in the stock market. The money was given to a stranger who moved into town who promised to double their money in two weeks. Johnny recognizes the scam where the early contributors are paid off by the later ones until the scam artist has enough money to leave town. The latest claims have come from Enterprise, New Jersey. The local authorities cannot do anything because the man is still paying off. Johnny is anxious to look into this, on expenses only, on account of Christmas.

Johnny flies to Philadelphia, rents a car and drives to Enterprise, New Jersey, a small run down farming town. Johnny goes to City Hall and talks to Police Chief Walters. Johnny tells him who he is and Chief Walters recognizes him, and tells Johnny he listens to his programs on WCAU in Philadelphia. Chief Walters tells Johnny that a lot of people have taken money from their policies and in a few weeks the folks will have a lot of money. Mr. Lowry who runs the paper says that John D. Morgan, the man who is putting a lot of money into the town, is a crook. Morgan has told the townspeople that he belongs to the New York Stock Exchange and is related to the Morgans and the "Rockyfellers." Morgan is being so generous because one of his ancestors, Jodiah Morgan, got his start in the town back in the 1800's. Morgan is staying at the Parker House and keeps the money in a safe there in his third-floor suite. Johnny asks the chief to tell Morgan that he wants to see him, under the ruse of a local boy who made good selling on the road.

Johnny goes to see Mr. Lowry at the newspaper, and he tells Johnny that he has tried to tell people that Morgan is a schyster, but then people would not buy the paper. Morgan keeps taking in money, but will leave when he has all the money in town. Johnny suggests a plan to Mr. Lowry, but it will require his money, as they need to convince him that they are on Morgan's side. Johnny wants Lowry to stop the press and print an apology and then call on Morgan with his money to invest. Johnny will try to get some money himself. Once he gets the money, Morgan will try to leave town, and then they will get him. Johnny goes to City Hall and convinces the chief to search the records there, and the chief finds no record of a Jodiah Morgan. Johnny calls the New York Stock Exchange and they have never heard of Morgan. Chief Walters and Johnny go to the local bank to get money to loan to Morgan and Johnny gets the bank president, Mr. Peterson, to cooperate. Johnny calls Pat and gets $10,000 wired to the bank. Johnny gets $1,000 from Peterson's personal account and tells the chief to head for Morgan's room. Johnny gets the location Morgan's car and goes there. In the garage Johnny spots the car and uses an old trick. At the hotel Johnny finds a room full of people and an empty safe. Chief Walters had the safe opened and it is empty. Lowry tells Johnny the people think Johnny is responsible for Morgan disappearing. Johnny runs out the back window and towards the garage with the crowd in hot pursuit. John D. Morgan was sitting in the car with the money and a .38 Colt aimed at Johnny. Johnny tells him he took the distributor cap from the car. Morgan wants the distributor cap, but a crowd gathers and Morgan becomes afraid. He tells Johnny that the money is in the trunk, and agrees to give it back to the people.

"That mob, slowly, menacingly moving in on us was something I won't forget for a long, long time. Matter of fact it was Morgan tossing out the money and shrieking out a confession promising to pay them back that saved me from them. And now, of course, he will be taken care of by the courts, yeah plenty."

NOTES:
- COMMERCIAL BREAK ONE IS A WINSTON COMMERCIAL
- COMMERCIAL TWO IS FOR COLUMBIA STEREO-ONE PORTABLE RECORD PLAYERS FOR $139.95. THEY PLAY 45S, 78S AND THE NEW LP AND STEREO RECORDS.
- COMMERCIAL THREE IS STUART ERWIN FOR FOUR WAY TABLETS AND FITCH DANDRUFF SHAMPOO.
- COMMERCIAL FOUR IS A "SHOP EARLY AND SAFELY AND BUY A GIFT SET FROM YARDLEY" SPOT.
- THE ANNOUNCER IS DAN CUBBERLY

| | | | |
|---|---|---|---|
| Producer: | Jack Johnstone | Writers: | Jack Johnstone |
| Cast: | Lawrence Dobkin, Forrest Lewis, Junius Matthews, Edgar Barrier, Russell Thorson | | |

◆ ❖ ◆

| | |
|---|---|
| SHOW: | THE RED MYSTERY MATTER |
| SHOW DATE: | 12/20/1959 |
| COMPANY: | UNIVERSAL ADJUSTMENT BUREAU |
| AGENT: | PAT MCCRACKEN |
| EXP. ACCT: | $0.00 |

SYNOPSIS: Johnny is called by Red Barrett and told to come out to Lake Mojave Resort. Johnny tells him that he is too busy to come out and go fishing, as he has too much work. Red tells Johnny that Pat McCracken told him to call Johnny. Red tells Johnny that something will happen, and it will be very bad for Lake Mojave Resort. Red does not believe that Johnny would just sit there and do nothing, so Red tells Johnny to catch the next plane and hangs up.

Johnny decides to believe in Red's story and catches a plane to Las Vegas. Johnny opines on the desert sky at night and the lights of Las Vegas. Johnny rents a car and drives to Lake Mojave Resort, commenting on the desert. Buster Favor meets Johnny and tells him that the police have not even gotten there yet, and that Red has disappeared. Buster takes Johnny to Red's room and it has been ransacked. Johnny spots signs of a cooked meal and blood on the floor. Johnny reminds Buster how Red often talks of just leaving, but Buster tells Johnny that he had not said anything to anyone. Buster tells Johnny that Ham Pratt had come to talk to Red after dinner, and he was gone. So, why would someone want to do Red in? Buster can think of nothing that could cause problems for the resort and Ham comes in to tell them that everyone in the area is looking for Red. Ham tells Johnny that he has received a tip that a car like Red's has been seen near Bolder City. Johnny is suspicious that he will have a score to settle with Buster and Ham.

Johnny thinks things are starting to add up, starting with Red calling Pat and the lamp with the unbroken bulb, and the fish scales in the blood on the floor. All very fishy. Johnny looks over the room and notices that something important is missing from Red's room, and his boat is empty as well. Johnny tells Buster that he is going to do nothing until morning, and Buster suggests they go fishing, as Johnny is just a bundle of nerves, and Johnny agrees to go fishing. Johnny recalls that he had been a little feisty, and the fishing did wonders for his disposition. First thing in the morning Johnny recalls not finding Red's tackle and personal clothes, and notes that the blood on the floor was from a bass. The road Red' s truck had been seen on led to a resort called Temple Bar. Johnny drives to Temple Bar and waiting at the dock is Red Barrett, all ready for Johnny with an extra rod and bait. Red tells Johnny a smart man like him could track him down. Red had decided to move on to a different resort, and Ham was in on it too. And the terrible thing that would have happened to the resort? They would lose the best guide in the area! Red shows Johnny a letter from Pat McCracken telling them that Johnny needs some rest and relaxation, on the Universal Adjustment Bureau, and Merry Christmas!

"A very wise man once said that the time a man spends fishing is never deducted from his life span. And you know something? I for one am convinced that he was right. So, Merry Christmas to all of you too."

NOTES:
- COMMERCIAL BREAK #1 IS FOR WINSTON CIGARETTES
- COMMERCIAL #2 IS MEL TORME FOR FOUR WAY TABLETS AND A COMMERCIAL FOR FITCH DANDRUFF SHAMPOO
- COMMERCIAL #3 IS ONE ON FIRE PREVENTION DURING THE HOLIDAYS, AND GIFTS FROM YARDLEY
- THE ANNOUNCER IS DAN CUBBERLY

**Producer:** Jack Johnstone      **Writers:** Jack Johnstone
**Cast:** Forrest Lewis, Barney Phillips, Alan Reed Sr, Lawrence Dobkin

◆   ❖   ◆

**SHOW:** THE BURNING DESIRE MATTER
**SHOW DATE:** 12/27/1959
**COMPANY:** UNIVERSAL ADJUSTMENT BUREAU
**AGENT:** PAT MCCRACKEN
**EXP. ACCT:** $874.20

**SYNOPSIS:** Johnny is called by a man who just says "yeah." The caller turns out to be Pat McCracken who tells Johnny that "yeah" was the conversation during a call he just had. Johnny remembers that a friend in San Francisco talked like that, but Pat tells Johnny that the call came from Los Angeles. Johnny tells Pat to check his records, and he will find a lot of arson claims, and will have to pay his expenses to Los Angeles.

Johnny is sure that the call came from Smokey Sullivan and calls the number Pat had given him. Smokey tells Johnny he has a legitimate job in Los Angeles. Smokey tells Johnny that he has helped Smokey in the past, and now Smokey has a chance to help Johnny. Smokey tells Johnny that there have been a lot of fires in the area, and he has a lead. Smokey is at 322 S. Equity Ave. and Johnny tells him that he will meet Smokey there. Pat calls back and tells Johnny that there have been seven fires covered by seven companies, and the police reports suggest arson.

Johnny flies to Los Angeles, California and cabs to Smokey's address in a beat up industrial area. Johnny knocks on the door of a rooming house and a woman opens the door. Johnny asks for Smokey and the woman asks if Johnny is the man Smokey is expecting. Johnny goes up and pounds on Smokey's door to hear glass breaking inside. Johnny rushes in and finds Smokey lying beaten on the floor. The landlady gets towels, cold water and a bottle of cognac for Smokey. The landlady tells Johnny she thought the other man was the one Smokey was expecting. Smokey comes to and tells Johnny that the man was "The Chimp," a strong-arm man for Mickey Fortina. Smokey tells Johnny that he has to stop Mickey or there will be more fires. Smokey tells Johnny that he had scared off the Chimp when Johnny knocked on the door, and someone had tipped of Forina about Smokey's call to Johnny. Johnny takes Smokey to the Statler Hotel and gets a room and a doctor for Smokey. Smokey tells Johnny that all the fires were set for the insurance, and set by different persons. Fortina is a go-between; he makes deal to torch a place and brings in the people to do the jobs. Fortina had sent for Smokey and asked if he wanted to work for him. Johnny is sure that Fortina knows Johnny was sent for. Smokey tells Johnny that Fortina's office is located at 1025 S. Spring. There is knock at the door and a voice calls out "police." Johnny opens the door to find an old friend, Sgt. Pat Nichols. Sgt. Nichols tells Johnny that the room clerk had reported an injured man being brought in. Sgt. Nichols knows who Smokey is and Johnny tells Smokey to talk to Sgt. Nichols. Johnny convinces Sgt. Nichols that Smokey needs a bodyguard, and then goes to talk to Fortina.

At Fortina's office, Johnny plans on acting like a man who needs a property burned down. Johnny goes into the "Fortina Friendly Loan Company" as Mr. Morris. Through the open door Johnny hears Mickey ask about the Chimp and the hotel. Fortina comes out and Johnny tells him that he owns a shoe store and that business has been bad. Fortina offers a loan and Johnny tells him that he has $180,000 in insurance on the property and wants it torched. Fortina tells Johnny that he needs to make a $10,000 deposit and Johnny tells him just to torch the place, and he will give Fortina $15,000. The Chimp comes in and tells Mickey that he knows who Johnny is and that Husky is on his way to the hotel to take care of Smokey. The secretary warns them that the police are there and Mickey pulls a gun after Johnny slugs the Chimp. Johnny turns out the lights, there are shots and a fight and Johnny gets the best of Mickey just as Sgt. Nichols and Smokey come in. Smokey had told Sgt. Nichols what the deal was after Husky Costalini came to the hotel. Sgt. Nichols took Husky to jail and then he and Smokey came here. Sgt. Nichols is sure that the boys will talk to avoid taking the rap for everything.

"Yeah they talked all right, and as a result the police in a couple of nearby states should have no trouble at all in picking up some of the other of Fortina's boys, his hired torches. Ah, funny isn't it? These stupid jerks just never seem to learn."

### NOTES:

- COMMERCIAL BREAK #1 IS FOR WINSTON CIGARETTES.
- COMMERCIAL #2 IS MONA FREEMAN FOR FOUR WAY AND A COMMERCIAL FOR FITCH DANDRUFF SHAMPOO.
- THIS PROGRAM WAS RECORDED LIVE ON WROW IN ALBANY, AND HAS A LONG AD AT THE END FOR VETERANS BENEFITS.
- THE ANNOUNCER IS DAN CUBBERLY

| | |
|---|---|
| **Producer:** | Jack Johnstone          **Writers:** Jack Johnstone |
| **Cast:** | Virginia Gregg, Jean Tatum, Lawrence Dobkin, Vic Perrin, Paul Dubov, Don Diamond, Frank Gerstle |

◆　❖　◆

| | |
|---|---|
| **SHOW:** | THE HAPLESS HAM MATTER |
| **SHOW DATE:** | 1/3/1960 |
| **COMPANY:** | EASTERN TRUST & INSURANCE COMPANY |
| **AGENT:** | |
| **EXP. ACCT:** | $100.00 |

**SYNOPSIS:** Johnny is called by a man who needs Johnny's help. The man is Walter E. Lynch and Johnny must come out to Manchester and protect him. He implores Johnny that his life has been threatened, but Johnny wants to know what company his insurance is with. Lynch has not called the police and wants protection. Johnny hangs up and Pat McCracken calls and reminds Johnny that he was due in Pat's office for a disposition eight minutes ago at 10:00. Johnny asks Pat to look up the insurance on Walter Lynch.

Johnny cabs to Pat's office, signs a deposition, and Johnny tells him of the conversation with Lynch. The secretary brings in a copy of the policy that Mr. Bartell had located. The policy is for $50,000 with a nephew, Fred Lynch, as the beneficiary. Pat authorizes Johnny to pay Walter Lynch a visit. Johnny drives to Manchester, Connecticut in his car. The Lynch house is a small Cape Cod with two police cars out front. A police sergeant asks for Johnny's ID and then tells Johnny that Lynch is dead, murdered. Johnny goes in and confirms that Lynch had been murdered, and the police doctor shows Johnny where the knife had gone in. Officer Conroy comes in and reports that there were no footprints outside. The police sergeant tells Johnny that a neighbor, Mr. Halsey had called them. Halsey had come over to talk to Lynch about his nephew, saw what happened and then called the police. Johnny learns that Lynch had been awarded custody of a fortune that had been left to Freddy by his mother, and Lynch had spent it all. Johnny is told that the police think that the Lynch tribe is no good. The knife wound troubles the doc. He tells Johnny that it that came from a long, two-bladed knife. Mr. Halsey comes in and recognizes who Johnny is, and tells Johnny that the nephew, Freddy, was a worthless bum who worked in the theater, and that Freddy was there that morning. Halsey does not blame Lynch for not giving Freddy any money, because he was living in New York, that pit of iniquity with all those sinful people, actors, chorus girls and the like! Halsey tells Johnny that Freddy was there from around 9:30 to before 10:00. The doc fixes death at around 10:00. Halsey is sure of the time as he was listening to the radio, and Freddy left just before the WDRC announcer gave time signal at 10:00. Johnny is sure that Freddy did not kill Lynch because Walter was alive after 10:00; Johnny had talked to him at 10:08!

Johnny is sure that he was the perfect alibi for Freddy Lynch who had walked to catch a bus at 10:15. Freddy must have done it, because Halsey had seen no one else come in. Johnny gets the address for Freddy and drives to New York City. Johnny gets into Freddy's room, which is covered with posters, playbills, and costumes. Freddy comes in and Johnny tells him he is Jerry Allen the agent, and that he has been trying to get in touch with Freddy. He has a part for Freddy, but Freddy tells Johnny that he is thinking of giving up show business, but changes his mind when "Jerry" asks if he just inherited a fortune. Jerry tells Freddy that the play is written by Johnstone, who has had a bunch of hits lately. The part is of a young man who ages 20 years in the second act and then is 60 in the third act. Freddy gives Johnny his best shaky old man's voice to prove he can do the part. Johnny gets Freddy to say the same things he had told Johnny over the phone. Johnny tells him that he had killed his uncle and called him from the bus station to get Johnny to come there. Freddy pulls a long, thin Arabian knife and Johnny shoots him in the hand. Johnny didn't think he was that good a shot.

"So now I will have to make another disposition for the sake of another trial. I am sure that hamming it up in court won't keep Freddy from playing out the rest of his life in front of a captive audience."

NOTES:
- COMMERCIAL BREAK #1 IS FOR WINSTON CIGARETTES.
- COMMERCIAL BREAK #2 IS MONA FREEMAN FOR FOUR WAY AND A COMMERCIAL FOR FITCH DANDRUFF SHAMPOO.
- THE ANNOUNCER IS DAN CUBBERLY

Producer: Jack Johnstone      Writers: Jack Johnstone
Cast: Virginia Gregg, Chet Stratton, Lawrence Dobkin, Sam Edwards, Herb Ellis, Ralph Moody, Junius Matthews

◆ ❖ ◆

SHOW: THE UNHOLY TWO MATTER
SHOW DATE: 1/10/1960
COMPANY: TRI-WESTERN LIFE INSURANCE COMPANY
AGENT: JACK PRICE
EXP. ACCT: $287.20

SYNOPSIS: [The intro is missing on my copy of the program.] Johnny flies to Corpus Christi, Texas and gets a room at the Robert Driscol hotel. As Johnny is checking in, he meets Doug Johnstone, who is Jack's younger brother. Doug offers to get together and talk about Jack, and offers Johnny any help he can give. Doug asks if Jack Price called Johnny in, and Johnny confirms it but does not know anything about what case he is working on. Doug has some ideas about old man Peterson. Doug feels that Peterson did not die from a heart attack, but that he was murdered. The next day Johnny goes to see Jack Price, who tells Johnny that he is looking into Sterling Peterson who disappeared just after his uncle died. Sterling did not know that he was the beneficiary of the policy. Paul Peterson, Sterling's half-brother gets everything else. Paul is a stockbroker and Jack does not know what Sterling does, only that he is gone. Jack also has not called the police. Jack confirms that the doctor said death was from a heart attack, and Johnny asks Jack to order an autopsy. Johnny goes to see Doug Johnstone who knows Sterling from his activity at the Merrill Lynch office. Sterling was always trying to get money from Paul, who was working the market by buying penny stocks and other speculative stocks, but he always made money. Sterling needed money to pay off his gambling debts. Doug feels that Sterling was at the point where he would kill to get money. When he found out he would not get the property, he left not knowing about the insurance. Johnny cabs to Paul's apartment and then to the Merrill Lynch office where Paul has not been seen for several days. A friend notes that Paul was out looking at investments. Johnny goes back to Jack's office to learn that the autopsy is finished, and that death was from a drug that had been substituted for the old man's digitalis. Johnny cabs to Sterling's rooming house and learns from the landlady, Mrs. Toomey, that Sterling owed two month's rent. In Sterling's room, Johnny sees that all Sterling's clothes are gone, but the medicine cabinet has all his personal items. Mrs. Toomey tells Johnny that Sterling had waited all day for Paul to come. Paul did call and told Sterling to meet him at a dive. Sterling came back late that night but was gone the next morning. Johnny goes to his hotel where there is a message from Jack telling Johnny that the police are looking for Sterling, and the police want to talk to Johnny. Johnny is visited by Paul Peterson, who is answering Johnny's note to call him. Paul shows Johnny a number of letters from Sterling, mailed from various cities. The typed letters seems to indicate that Sterling was running away. Johnny wonders if Paul had typed the letters and used his business trip to mail the letters. Johnny asks if Paul killed Sterling after he tried to blackmail Paul. When Johnny mentions the personal items left in the medicine cabinet Paul pulls a gun and threatens to kill Johnny. The police come in with Doug Johnstone and Paul gives up.

"So, another day, another dollar, and I'm not talking about myself."

NOTES:
- COMMERCIAL BREAK #1 IS FOR CAMEL CIGARETTES.
- COMMERCIAL BREAK #2 IS MEL TORME FOR FOUR WAY AND A COMMERCIAL FOR FITCH.
- THE FINAL COMMERCIAL IS FOR EXLAX.
- THE ANNOUNCER IS DAN CUBBERLY

Producer: Jack Johnstone     Writers: Jack Johnstone
Cast:     Virginia Gregg, Jack Edwards, Forrest Lewis, Stacy Harris, Gil Stratton, Barney Phillips

◆  ❖  ◆

SHOW:        THE EVAPORATED CLUE MATTER
SHOW DATE:   1/17/1960
COMPANY:     FOUR STATE INSURANCE COMPANY
AGENT:       HENRY BASCOME
EXP. ACCT:   $574.00

SYNOPSIS: Henry Bascome calls and asks Johnny to come down and look into a matter. The investigation is in New York, and the fees will be based on the straight life policy worth almost $200,000. Johnny is on his way.

Johnny flies to New York City and goes to Henry's office. The $189,000 policy is on Jonathan R. Kenworthy, a retired mine owner. Kenworthy was murdered, and the grandson, Carleton M. Kenworthy, is the beneficiary. The police feel that Carleton, who is the sole heir, did it because he has the motive and a perfect alibi. Henry knows that Jonathan Kenworthy had no enemies and Carleton is about as useless as you can get. Carleton does not work, and is generally a playboy. Carleton hangs around with Allen Barker, who is a real leech. The grandfather did not suspect what was going on, and believed his grandson was investing the money he gave him. The murder was last Tuesday, and Randy Singer is handling the case. Johnny leaves to visit Randy. Randy tells Johnny that he is sure that Carleton killed his grandfather, as he was up to his ears in debts. Kenworthy was killed with a poker from the fireplace, but Carleton has an alibi, he was in Alaska.

Randy tells Johnny that Carleton was in Alaska, and Randy has checked out everything. The lab report on the poker comes in and shows fingerprints from both Kenworthys. Carleton comes in and tells Johnny and Randy that he often made the fire for his grandfather. Carleton tells Johnny that he went to Alaska alone. Johnny asks for an address and goes to see Allen Barker. Allen is almost a twin of Carleton, who tells Johnny that he and Carleton like the same things and are called "The Inseparables." Allen tells Johnny that he took a trip while Carleton was gone, and has no idea where he went. Johnny tells him that he could benefit from Kenworthy's death, but feels Baxter is too weak natured to actually do it. Johnny gets an idea, an expensive idea.

Johnny flies to Juneau, Alaska via Seattle. In Juneau, Johnny realizes he should have brought a photograph. Johnny goes to the hotel and gets the same story that Randy had gotten. At dinner in the hotel Johnny gets the clue that will solve the case. Johnny flies back to New York and goes to see Randy and Carleton in Randy's office. Carleton tells Johnny that he was in Juneau when his father was killed. Johnny asks if Carleton ate dinner at the hotel, which he did. Carleton tells Johnny that he paid cash for the dinner of shrimp cocktail, salad, a steak and coffee. Johnny asks Carleton what he had in his coffee, and Carleton tells Johnny that he used the cream and sugar that was on the table. Johnny tells Carleton that Allen went there posing as him. Johnny tells him that the hotel does not use cream, only evaporated milk. Carleton breaks down and tells Johnny and Randy that Allen helped him kill his grandfather.

"Believe me, if I were to put down all I think about the Allen Barkers and Carleton Kenworthys, and all the rest of that rotten . . . ah, why bother."

NOTES:
- COMMERCIAL #1 IS FOR CAMEL CIGARETTES.
- COMMERCIAL #2 IF STUART ERWIN FOR FOUR WAY, AND A COMMERCIAL FOR FITCH.
- COMMERCIAL #3 IS FOR EXLAX
- BOB BAILEY WELCOMES STATIONS WBRK IN PITTSFIELD, MASS AND WKNY IN KINGSTON, NEW YORK TO THE CBS NETWORK.
- THE ANNOUNCER IS DAN CUBBERLY

Producer: Jack Johnstone        Writers:  Jack Johnstone
Cast:        Harry Bartell, Herb Vigran, Carleton G. Young, Herb Ellis, Jack Edwards

✦  ❖  ✦

| | |
|---|---|
| SHOW: | THE NUCLEAR GOOF MATTER |
| SHOW DATE: | 1/24/1960 |
| COMPANY: | FLOYDS OF ENGLAND |
| AGENT: | GEORGE REED |
| EXP. ACCT: | $0.00 |

SYNOPSIS: George Reed calls Johnny and tells him that he is all cleared, and though it is not covered by the insurance, it is ok to go on over. George just got a call from Dr. Paulus Rayburn, who runs Nuclear Processors, on the north end of Hartford, Connecticut. Floyds holds the other insurance, and George needs Johnny to look into something. Dr. Rayburn has reported something missing that is important to the space program, and Johnny is needed to look into it.

Johnny buys coffee and donuts on the way to the Nuclear Processor site. At the main gate three guards inspect Johnny's ID and let him into the plant. Another guard at the main building takes Johnny inside where he meets Dr. Rayburn. Dr. Rayburn tells Johnny that the plant does scientific research, and that time is of the essence. A small quantity of radioactive material has been stolen. Outside of the paramagnetic fields in the plant, the material will become dangerous within hours and can destroy a small city. The chain reaction could start in four to six hours, depending on conditions, which is why he could not wait for investigators from Washington. The time now is 9:34, and the material was stolen at 7:46. It was stolen by Dr. Igor Raminoff who did not know the danger of the material.

Dr. Rayburn tells Johnny that he brought in Dr. Raminoff for another project, and that he stole the materials for a foreign government. Dr. Rayburn had employed Raminoff before a security clearance was obtained. Johnny gets a list of addresses and contacts and tells Dr. Rayburn to call the FBI. Johnny gets a detector that will react to the material that was stolen. The detector is very fragile, so Johnny must take care. Johnny buys gas and heads for town. Johnny goes to Raminoff's address and realizes he does not have a picture or description. Johnny stops at a drugstore, and as he is trying to park he hits a young blonde man who has just gotten off of a bus. Johnny takes the man and his briefcase to the hospital. Johnny leaves the man at the hospital and goes back to Raminoff's with the detector going crazy on the seat; it had fallen to the floor and cannot be turned off.

Johnny goes back to Raminoff's rooming house and knocks at the door. The landlady asks if Johnny is Mr. Parker. She tells Johnny that Raminoff has gone, and that he has rented the whole third floor. Johnny goes up and breaks down the door and enters the dark apartment and is slugged by a man who tells Johnny that he is not Parker. Johnny is searched and the landlady is told to get some towels and water. The man is Stacey Ringler who Johnny knows from the FBI. He tells Johnny that he is with the Nuclear Processors security department now, and that Harry Parker came up from Washington this morning and is working with Stacey. They got into Raminoff's rooms and were waiting. Stacey tells Johnny that the man he ran down at the drugstore is Raminoff. Parker followed Johnny to the hospital and has arrested Raminoff. Johnny wonders if someone in the mob at the drugstore has the material, so they go back to the bus stop. Stacey notices the detector and Johnny tells Stacey how it was clicking, but now the battery is dead. Johnny suddenly realizes that the material must be in the briefcase on the back seat. The time is 11:38 and the material could go off in seven minutes. Johnny floors the car and heads for the plant.

"So, by some miracle we made it. But only seconds before that tiny mass of nuclear destruction was due to become critical. Yeah, we made it, by the skin of our teeth. But after all, what more could you ask. Expense account total, oh so what, I needed a tank of gas anyway."

NOTES:
- COMMERCIAL #1 IS FOR CAMEL CIGARETTES.
- COMMERCIAL #2 IS MONA FREEMAN FOR FOUR WAY COLD TABLETS AND A COMMERCIAL FOR FITCH DANDRUFF SHAMPOO.
- COMMERCIAL #3 IS FOR EXLAX.
- BOB BAILEY MENTIONS THAT THEY ARE GOING TO MISS DAN CUBBERLY, WHO IS THE ANNOUNCER

Producer: Jack Johnstone      Writers: Jack Johnstone
Cast: Virginia Gregg, G. Stanley Jones, Bartlett Robinson, Sam Edwards, Stacy Harris

◆ ❖ ◆

SHOW: THE MERRY-GO-ROUND MATTER
SHOW DATE: 1/31/1960
COMPANY: UNIVERSAL ADJUSTMENT BUREAU
AGENT: PAT MCCRACKEN
EXP. ACCT: $0.00

SYNOPSIS: A glum Pat McCracken calls Johnny and mentions Alvin Peabody Cartwright and tells Johnny that now he has a problem. Johnny tells Pat about all the money he has gotten from Cartwright, and Pat almost gets Johnny to work on the case without expenses because he likes Alvin. Pat tells Johnny to drive up to Lakewood and see Alvin. Pat does not know what is going on, as Alvin tells something different to everybody he talk to.

Johnny notes how doing a job for Alvin is like riding a bunch of carnival rides. Johnny buys gas and drives to Alvin's estate in Lakewood. At the front door Alvin tells Johnny to get inside and not to track up the house, and then he recognizes Johnny. Alvin wishes Johnny a Merry Christmas and then gives Johnny a present, a diamond encrusted money clip. Alvin want to wish Johnny a happy New Year before he leaves, and then Alvin remembers why Johnny is there and tells him that he is in terrible trouble.

Alvin tells Johnny that the problem is his new art gallery. Ever since he went to Paris and saw the Louvre, he has wanted an art gallery. Alvin takes Johnny to a room and shows Johnny an ornate gallery with a marble ceiling. The room is full of paintings, tapestries, sculptures and jewelry. Alvin tells Johnny that he has been robbed. A sacred painting, an icon encrusted with jewels has been stolen. It was worth $90,000. Johnny notes it was small enough to be taken out under a coat. Alvin tells Johnny that he had a guard on duty. He was the first man who answered the ad, but Alvin has fired him. Alvin tells Johnny that only one person was allowed in at a time. The other night a man dressed in rags came in to see the gallery, and another man, Alvin's friend Jonathan Peebles also came to visit and gave Alvin a lecture on security. When the old man left, he tripped on the stairs and the guard helped him up and drove the old man to town. Jonathan then noticed that the icon was missing. The guard was Gummy O'Bannyon. Johnny recognizes the name as an old gangster from New York.

Johnny goes to Gummy's shack and listens outside. Inside Gummy and the old man are drinking beer and counting a stack of money. Gummy mentions that another man had given them money to have the old man fall. His name was funny, like some sort of building. Johnny goes to New York and a fancy apartment house where the doorman has a note for Johnny. The note tells Johnny that Peebles has been trying to contact Johnny, and that he is to see Peebles before he talks to Alvin. The note tells Johnny that the icon is in an urn in the gallery. Johnny drives back to Lakewood to find the door open at Alvin's home. Jonathan and Alvin are arguing with each other at the breakfast table. Jonathan wants Alvin to turn the gallery over to a museum. Also, Jonathan wants Alvin to get some legitimate guards for the gallery, and Alvin agrees that the whole thing is silly. Alvin will do anything to get the icon back. Jonathan tells Alvin that he has the icon and will give it back if Alvin will do as he asks. He tells Alvin that he hid it to pound some sense into Alvin's head. Alvin promises to do as Jonathan asks, and the argument continues.

"And if you think for a minute that was the end of it, you are wrong. Those two wild old men sat there for the better part of an hour squabbling, shaking their fists at each other, and a half dozen times they almost came to blows. But, finally they ran out of breath, put their arms around each other, shed some tears of repentance, and then as they have done so many times before, quietly solemnly swore undying friendship for each other. What a pair!" The expense account? Why bother. After all, by now Alvin has probably forgotten he even sent for me."

NOTES:
- COMMERCIAL #1 IS FOR CAMEL CIGARETTES
- COMMERCIAL #2 IS MEL TORME FOR FOUR WAY COLD TABLETS AND A COMMERCIAL FOR FITCH DANDRUFF SHAMPOO
- COMMERCIAL #3 IS FOR EXLAX
- THE ANNOUNCER IS JOHN WALD

Producer:    Jack Johnstone          Writers:    Jack Johnstone

**Cast:**     Lawrence Dobkin, Howard McNear, Frank Gerstle, Will Wright, Forrest Lewis, Joseph Kearns

| | |
|---|---|
| **SHOW:** | THE SIDEWINDER MATTER |
| **SHOW DATE:** | 2/7/1960 |
| **COMPANY:** | GREATER SOUTHWEST LIFE INSURANCE COMPANY |
| **AGENT:** | JAKE KESSLER |
| **EXP. ACCT:** | $345.40 |

**SYNOPSIS:** Jake Kessler calls Johnny and tells him that a client, Rafe Chisolm, has a cattle ranch, and his cattle are being poisoned. Rafe found out who has been poisoning the cattle and there will be a killing. Can you come out and see what you can do?

Johnny calls Buster Favor to find out about the Circle RC ranch. Buster hopes Johnny can come out before someone is killed. Buster agrees to meet Johnny in Las Vegas. Johnny flies to Las Vegas, Nevada where Buster meets him and drives Johnny to the Circle RC ranch. On his way to the ranch, Buster comments to Johnny about the importance of water in the area to feed cattle. Buster tells Johnny that Rafe is pretty tough, and people call him "The Sidewinder." Local folks were not happy when he got a lease on the good ranch land with all the water on it. Buster feels that an ex-partner, Jerry McCoy, is the one who is poisoning the cattle. Rafe had cheated Jerry out of the money he bought the ranch with, and Buster is sure that Jerry has caught up with Rafe. At the ranch Johnny notices the abundance of water. Mrs. Chisolm meets the car and she tells Johnny that her son Wayne told Rafe that Jerry McCoy was out fooling around with a water trough and he grabbed his gun and a knapsack and rode out after him. Mrs. Chisolm does not know what is in the knapsack. She is clearly worried about Rafe and Wayne has gone out as well. With Rafe mad, he would shoot anyone, including his son. Buster and Johnny borrow horses and ride out to find Rafe.

Buster notices that the hoof prints of the horses indicate that someone is following Rafe. There are shots and Buster and Johnny ride to Block Canyon where Rafe has a windmill and shack. Buster spots a storm coming in and they ride for cover in a cave in Shadow Mountain. The storm starts before they get to the cave, but they make it into the cave on foot. In the cave are a number of animals, all seeking safety from the storm. The winds finally subside only to bring a hailstorm, with hail the size of golf balls. The storm is finally over and the animals leave. Buster notices Wayne lying under a rock in the cave and sees that he has been shot by Rafe.

Wayne tells Buster that he had followed Rafe, and when he spotted Wayne, he shot at him, but did not mean to shoot him as Wayne was hit by some wild shots. Wayne tells Buster and Johnny that he circled back to the shack where Rafe had found Jerry McCoy skinning a calf in the shack. Wayne heard Rafe decide to let Jerry go if he does as he is told. Jerry was told to cut some thongs from the steer hide. Jerry was then told to tie Rafe to a post in the shack with thongs around his ankles and his neck. Rafe tells Jerry that his son will be there soon to let him loose. Jerry was told to leave and gives Jerry his gun. Jerry left and took Rafe's horse just as the storm started. Jerry was told not to touch the knapsack, the same one he used when he was prospecting. Jerry opened the knapsack and screamed. Wayne tells Johnny that there were three sidewinders in the knapsack and that Jerry was bitten and died. Wayne is sent home and Buster and Johnny ride to the feed shack. Johnny finds Jerry's body half buried in the sand. In the shack they find Rafe Chisolm, the rawhide had dried out and shrunk, choking him.

"I don't know, I don't know. And who is to question the ways of justice?"

NOTES:

- COMMERCIAL #1 IS FOR PEPSI (BE SOCIABLE).
- COMMERCIAL #2 IS FOR CAMEL CIGARETTES.
- COMMERCIAL #3 IS STU ERWIN FOR FOUR WAY, AND A SPOT FOR FITCH DANDRUFF SHAMPOO.
- THIS PROGRAM ENDS BEFORE THE CLOSING CREDITS.
- CAST INFORMATION FROM THE KNX COLLECTION AT THE THOUSAND OAKS LIBRARY.

Producer: Jack Johnstone         Writers: Jack Johnstone
Cast: Joseph Kearns, Barney Phillips, Virginia Gregg, Sam Edwards, Junius Matthews, Ralph Moody, Bill James

◆ ❖ ◆

SHOW: THE P.O. MATTER
SHOW DATE: 2/14/1960
COMPANY: MID-EASTERN INDEMNITY CORPORATION
AGENT: HARRY McQUEEN
EXP. ACCT: $397.70

SYNOPSIS: Harry McQueen calls Johnny, and Johnny tells him he can't wait to come to New York and have some fun—on expense account of course. Harry mentions Dan Diamond and Johnny wants to work elsewhere and tells Harry he has another assignment, and wants to live to middle age. Johnny reminds Harry that three people died in the last job Diamond pulled. Harry tells Johnny that Dan has retired and is growing orchids in Long Beach. Dan is in New York and has just lifted $75,000 from a jewelry store. Johnny wants to turn the job down, until Harry mentions the commission on a $75,000 recovery and the unlimited expense account.

Johnny does not want the case, but the bait is too much to resist. Johnny trains to New York City and meets with Harry. Harry relates to Johnny how Diamond robbed the cash from the jewelry store at closing time. The cashier told the police that Dan Diamond identified himself during the robbery. The police have him in jail but are going to release him today for lack of evidence. Harry tells Johnny that Randy Singer is assigned to the case, so Johnny goes over to talk to him. Randy tells Johnny that he is working on the case due to the killings on the previous cases involving "Dapper Danny." Randy tells Johnny that there is no evidence and that Diamond has an ironclad alibi. Randy has found nothing, including the missing money. Randy tells Johnny that Diamond works alone and would not trust the money with anyone short of the government. Randy gets a call and learns that Diamond is on his way home, so Johnny decides to leave for California.

Johnny gets a photo of Diamond from Randy and flies to California only to find out he is sitting next to Danny Diamond, who is holding a dispatch case in his lap. Johnny identifies himself as "Jerry Reynolds," and Diamond tells Johnny that he probably has read about him in the papers. Diamond unsuccessfully tries to fool Johnny into answering to his real name. Johnny tells Diamond that he is going out to visit a friend, Jack Johnstone, who writes for the radio. Dan thinks the name sounds familiar, as he listens to the radio. When Dan goes to the back of the plane to get a drink, Johnny tries to figure out how to get into the dispatch case and gets the latch open. Diamond comes back drink-less and tries to buy a bottle from a fellow passenger. Johnny moves the case and it falls open onto the floor. The case is full of newspaper articles about the robbery. Johnny wonders if the case is a decoy.

In Los Angeles, Johnny rents a car and drives to Long Beach, California and gets a hotel room. Johnny calls Western Union and has a telegram from Randy Singer that tells Johnny to "Make contact with PO. Your man is Sgt. Wyman. Good Luck, Randy." Johnny is sure the "PO" should be "PD" as he drives to see Sgt. Wally Wyman who tells Johnny that he knows all about Dan Diamond, but they can do nothing without evidence. If Johnny can find something against Diamond, the town will love Johnny. Johnny arranges to have the police call Diamond in for a "talk" so that Johnny can search his luggage before he unpacks. The police call Diamond to come in while Johnny "takes a walk on the beach." Johnny drives to the neighborhood and sees Danny arrive in a cab, and then drive away in a sports car. Johnny jimmies the back door and searches the luggage and the house and finds nothing. Johnny feels that the money is still in New York. Johnny remembers Randy saying that Diamond would trust no one but the government, and gets and idea. Johnny goes back to Sgt. Wyman and mentions the "PO," which he thought was "PD." Johnny asks where the closest post office to Diamond's house is and drives there. Johnny finds Danny's car parked out front, and inside Danny is in line behind a wino. The clerk tells Diamond that he has a package from New York for him. As Diamond leaves, Johnny lunges at the package and manages to tear it open exposing the money inside. Danny tries to shoot Johnny, but Johnny slugs him. Johnny tells Danny that now he has him for murder, as his wild shot killed the wino.

"So, from here on in of course, it's in the hands of the law, the courts. As to credit in solving this one, well actually it all goes to simple typographical error. Funny."

NOTES:

- COMMERCIAL #1 IS MONA FREEMAN FOR FOUR WAY, AND A SPOT FOR FITCH DANDRUFF SHAMPOO.
- COMMERCIAL #2 IS FOR CAMEL CIGARETTES.
- COMMERCIAL #3 IS FOR EXLAX
- THE ANNOUNCER IS JOHN WALD

Producer:  Jack Johnstone         Writers:   Jack Johnstone
Cast:      Virginia Gregg, Harry Bartell, Herb Vigran, James McCallion, Stacy Harris, Gil Stratton

◆  ❖  ◆

SHOW:        THE ALVIN'S ALFRED MATTER
SHOW DATE:   2/21/1960
COMPANY:     FLOYDS OF ENGLAND
AGENT:       GEORGE REED
EXP. ACCT:   $0.00

SYNOPSIS: George Reed calls Johnny, hesitantly. George understands that Johnny has handled cases for Continental Insurance and Trust Company. Johnny tells George that the crazy cases Floyds has given him are nothing compared to the ones from Continental, all because of one man: Alvin Peabody Cartwright. Johnny tells George that Peabody told Continental that he would drop them if they sent anyone else. Johnny tells George that, in spite of the crazy cases, he has come to like Alvin and would do almost anything to help him out. George hems and haws and hesitantly tells Johnny that his problem is, you guessed it, Alvin Peabody Cartwright!

Johnny muses how George's cases were bad enough as Johnny he cabs to George's office. George tells Johnny that he had managed to convince Alvin to change companies. George tells Johnny that they should have been more careful, especially on this one policy for Alfred Cartwright, a ward of Alvin's. Alvin has told George that Alfred has been abducted. Also, Alfred is a dog, a female dog. "Oh, No!" cries Johnny.

George tells Johnny that Alfred has life, accident, injury, and mysterious disappearance insurance. Being a ward, Floyds never thought twice about the policy. George tells Johnny to go to Lakewood and find out what has happened. There is no limit on expenses and Johnny can name his fee. Johnny agrees to take the case if George keeps it quiet that Johnny Dollar was searching the country for a pooch! Johnny buys gas and drives to Lakewood where Alvin is too upset to talk and slams the door on Johnny. Alvin finally recognizes Johnny and invites him in. Alvin tells Johnny that he must spare no expense to find Alfred, who was like a child to Alvin. Alvin shows Johnny Alfred's room, which is like a child's playroom, complete with a tree, fire hydrant, model train and a working seismograph. Alvin tells Johnny that some of the toys are his, things he never had as a child.

Maybe he is silly, but now he has the things he wanted as a child. Johnny notes that his parents could not afford to buy him a model train. Alvin feels that the problem with growing up is that people do not enjoy the simple things of life, or that someone would laugh at them if they did. Alvin had searched for a long time before he found the dog at the pound, and is upset at losing his dog. He had hoped for a boy so he named the dog Alfred. Alvin knows that Clarence Brickston, a servant he had fired yesterday, is the only one who could have done it. Alvin had gone to visit the widow Parkinson and no one was home except Alfred. Clarence had a key and came in and abducted Alfred. The police say that Clarence has an alibi, his wife said that he was at home with her. Johnny has a crazy idea and borrows something of Alfred's.

Johnny drives to the address of Clarence Brickston. Mabel Brickston answers the door and Johnny walks in. Clarence tells Johnny to get out and that he is tired of everyone yelling at him for taking the dog. Clarence has scratches on his hands, and they seem to know an awful lot about the dog. Clarence tells Johnny that the dog escaped to get away from Cartwright. Johnny tells Clarence that he had a key, but he forgot about the seismograph, which registered the footsteps while Clarence chased the dog. Johnny shows Mabel and Clarence the tape from the seismograph to prove it. How's that for scientific investigation? Mabel tells Johnny that Clarence took the dog so that they could return it for a reward. Clarence gives up to Johnny, as he is too smart for him.

"Oh sure, modern scientific investigation, but he fell for it. And Mabel brought the dog up from the cellar, and she was kind of a mangy little pooch, the dog I mean. But she meant the difference between keeping or losing Cartwright's insurance account, which reminds me, you can forget the expense account. Cartwright did well by me as usual. And he'll probably break down and take Clarence back. Oh Well."

NOTES:
- COMMERCIAL #1 IS FOR PEPSI.
- COMMERCIAL #2 IS FOR CAMEL CIGARETTES.
- COMMERCIAL #3 IS MEL TORME FOR FOUR WAY AND A SPOT FOR FITCH SHAMPOO.
- COMMERCIAL #4 IS FOR EXLAX.
- BOB BAILEY WELCOMES WATV IN BIRMINGHAM, ALABAMA AND KSOB IN CEDAR CITY, UTAH TO THE CBS NETWORK.
- THE ANNOUNCER IS JOHN WALD

**Producer:** Jack Johnstone  **Writers:** Jack Johnstone
**Cast:** Virginia Gregg, G. Stanley Jones, Howard McNear, Frank Gerstle

| SHOW: | THE LOOK BEFORE THE LEAP MATTER |
|---|---|
| SHOW DATE: | 2/28/1960 |
| COMPANY: | UNIVERSAL ADJUSTMENT BUREAU |
| AGENT: | PAT MCCRACKEN |
| EXP. ACCT: | $9,570.00 |

SYNOPSIS: "Thirty days hath September, April June and November" starts the caller, and Johnny finishes that "all the rest have thirty one, except for February which gets cheated out of a couple days. So who is this?" The caller is Pat McCracken. Pat tells Johnny that being near the end of February has something to do with a case Johnny could not solve almost six years ago. Johnny remembers Bernard Margot, "Barney the Bum," who jumped off the Tri-Borough Bridge. Johnny reminds Pat that the whole thing was a phony so "Big Mike" Killian could collect the insurance. Pat reminds Johnny that he spent several thousand dollars to find Barney, but could not prove it. Pat tells Johnny he can save the company a lot of money if he can find Bernie before March 1.

Johnny cabs to Pat's office. Pat tells Johnny that this is one he would like to close out, and that Continental should not have issued the policy, but Barney had already jumped before they could cancel the policy. A witness claims to have seen Barney jump, but Killian has not been paid the $300,000. Unless Barney is picked up before March 1, the courts will order the policy paid. Johnny bemoans that today is February 27. Pat tells Johnny that the witness, Mattie Prescot just came back from Paris, where she saw Barney Margot. Pat tells Johnny that, with all the diplomatic red tape, they cannot get him back in time. But if Johnny can somehow get him back in time, there is a $10,000 bonus plus expenses. Johnny tells Pat that it is impossible, which is why he is going to try!

Johnny goes to the New York City apartment of Mattie Prescot, who recounts her testimony about seeing Barney jumping from the bridge, but she must have been wrong. She tells Johnny that she saw Barney in Paris, France, in the antique store of Monsieur Dubisaint. She is sure of it. On the elevator, Johnny remembers that Dubisaint is a fence. Suddenly two men stop the elevator. One of them tells Johnny that Big Mike does not like Johnny Dollar messing into things, and they slug Johnny and put him in the basement. Johnny is found by the building super and then goes to then send a wire, book a flight to Paris and then goes to see Randy, who tells him that the men were probably two of Killian's boys. Johnny wants Randy to stay put until he comes back from Paris.

Johnny flies to Paris, France and calls his friend Louis Du Marsac who is not home. Johnny cabs to the shop of Dubisaint who recognizes Johnny from previous cases. Johnny wants information on Margot, but Dubisaint calls for Maurice and tells him to leave and arrange for the funeral of his friend. Dubisaint does not know anything about Margot, and tells Johnny that he is wasting his time. Johnny calls Louis again and the phone is busy so he cabs there. At Louis' apartment, Johnny finds him on the floor. Johnny rushes in and Maurice slugs Johnny.

Johnny knows that his arrival is the only thing that saved Louis from being killed. After some cognac, Louis comes to and he tells Johnny that he has found Barney. Johnny agrees to $350 for the information on where Barney is. Louis tells Johnny that he has Barney, so Johnny tells Louis that he will give him $1,000 if he can deliver Barney to Johnny. Louise asks for $2,000 if he has also arranged for transportation out of France to the States. Johnny agrees if he can get Barney back before midnight. Johnny agrees to $2,500 if he makes it back in time. Louis takes Barney out of his closet and they drive to the airport where a plane is waiting. Johnny manages to get the pilot to fly to the States for $7,000. Johnny calls Randy to get clearance for the plane to land, and Randy agrees, reluctantly. The plane trip was one not to forget. Johnny finally lands and an escort is waiting to take Barney back to jail. In Randy's office, Johnny is yelled at by Randy for what he did, but he keeps falling asleep. Randy tells Johnny that they landed at 12:07 AM, which Johnny says is too late. He had to get Barney back by midnight, now he will have to pay the fees out of his own pocket. Johnny feels like blowing his brains out, but Randy reminds Johnny that 1960 is a leap year. So Johnny got Barney in before midnight on the last day of February!

"You know something, I should have blown my brains out for forgetting that extra day this month, this year. But instead I'll just take that $10,000 in fees. As for the expense account, hold your hat—$9,570!"

## NOTES:

- COMMERCIAL #1 FOR FRITO CORN CHIPS.
- COMMERCIAL #2 IS FOR CAMEL CIGARETTES.
- COMMERCIAL #3 IS STUART ERWIN FOR 4-WAY COLD TABLETS AND A SPOT FOR FITCH SHAMPOO.
- COMMERCIAL #4 IS BURGESS MEREDITH FOR THE SUPER 60 HEARING GLASSES FROM MAKO ELECTRONICS.
- COMMERCIAL #4 IS FOR EXLAX.
- CLOSING COMMENTS: "HERE IS YOUR STAR WITH SOMETHING TO THINK ABOUT. ON ACCOUNT OF IT'S BROTHERHOOD WEEK, JOHNNY?" "JOHN IT IS A THOUGHT FOR THIS WEEK, AND EVERY WEEK, AND IT'S SIMPLY THIS: IN MY JOB I RUN ACROSS ALL SORTS OF PEOPLE, BOTH THE RIGHT GUYS AND THE WRONG ONES. AND THIS MUCH I AM SURE OF, A CROOK IS A CROOK, IN ANY PLACE, IN ANY LANGUAGE, HE'S JUST NO GOOD. BUT AN HONEST MAN, A MAN WHO RESPECTS THE LAW AND THE RIGHTS OF HIS FELLOW HUMANS, REGARDLESS OF HIS HUE, HIS ORIGIN OR HIS ACCENT, WELL BELIEVE ME, THAT ONE IS YOURS TRULY WITH JOHNNY DOLLAR."

**Producer:**    Jack Johnstone      **Writers:**    Jack Johnstone
**Cast:**        Virginia Gregg, Lawrence Dobkin, Forrest Lewis, Frank Gerstle, Herb Vigran, Tony Barrett

◆ ❖ ◆

| | |
|---|---|
| SHOW: | THE MOONSHINE MATTER |
| SHOW DATE: | 3/6/1960 |
| COMPANY: | PROVIDENTIAL ASSURANCE COMPANY |
| AGENT: | CLARK TRACY |
| EXP. ACCT: | $340.00 |

SYNOPSIS: Clark Tracy calls Johnny and asks Johnny to go to Kennett, Missouri. They have the wrong man there, Charles Kingsley St. Clair, a Harvard man who does not know who to deal with the people in that area. They are moving him out and closing the office, but they have one outstanding claim on the death of Casper Crump. The widow Eupha Crump has to be given the $5,000 due her, but St. Claire claims he cannot do it. Can you clear this thing up for us? Clark promises Johnny a fee and no questions on his expense account.

Johnny flies to Memphis and takes a bus to Kennett. St. Clair tells Johnny that he is glad to be getting out of the country. The natives out in the country are poor white trash, ignorant illiterate moonshiners who did not know what they were buying. Mrs. Eupha Crump lives in the 20-mile swamp, which is a nest of moonshiners. A gentleman would never venture in there. The natives say it was murder and the police leave them alone. Johnny rents a car held together by bailing wire and rope and drives out to the swamp. Johnny drives down a road along the swamp, past the sunning snakes and rotting logs. At a shack on stilts Johnny is shot at, loses control of the car and crashes.

When Johnny comes to he does not have his gun, and sees two lanky men walking towards him. They do not think he is a revenuer, but do not know who he is. Johnny gets up and tells Cass Dingle and Morphy Teed that he has a check for Eupha Crump. They tell Johnny that Eupha is a mighty fine woman. They agree to take Johnny to Eupha and notice his missing gun; too bad, as there are people here who will shoot first and find out about you later. People like Dade Wupper. He killed Caper Crump and he will think that Johnny is coming after him.

In Cass Dingle's cabin, a really squalid place, Johnny gets a drink of corn liquor right from Eupha Crump's still. Cass and Johnny take a dugout canoe up the slough. At the Crump cabin Morphy tells Cass that one of Eupha's kids has gone to tell Dade Wupper about Johnny. Johnny notes that Eupha is a nice looking woman of 20 with 4 kids. She takes the money and tells Johnny that most of the money will go to improve the still and buy Cass a new suit of clothes. Morphy rushes in to tell them that Dave is all liquored up and on his way with his shotgun loaded with slugs.

Johnny and Cass leave but Dade is right on their trail shooting at them. Dade shoots and kills Cass. Johnny dives into the water and swims under water towards Dade's dugout. Dade yells at Johnny that he will get him like he got Casper. Johnny goes under and swims to Dade, grabs his legs and overpowers him.

"So maybe those people were pretty much a law unto themselves, but Dade Wupper went back to Kennett. There he will stand trial for two murders. And I will continue to poke along in this soft cozy little job of mine, yeah.

NOTES:

- THIS PROGRAM HAS 5 COMMERCIAL BREAKS IN IT. COMMERCIAL ONE FOR PEPSI—"BE SOCIABLE," THE SECOND COMMERCIAL IS FOR CAMEL CIGARETTES, THE THIRD COMMERCIAL IS MONA FREEMAN FOR 4-WAY COLD TABLETS (29 CENTS) AND FITCH DANDRUFF REMOVER SHAMPOO, COMMERCIAL FOUR IS FOR FRITOS AND COMMERCIAL FIVE IS FOR EXLAX.
- THERE IS A KENNETT, MISSOURI LOCATED IN THE EXTREME SOUTHERN PART OF THE STATE, NEAR THE MISSISSIPPI RIVER NORTH OF MEMPHIS.
- THE COTTONMOUTH WATER MOCCASIN (PISCIVORUS LEUCOSTOMA) IS THE ONLY NORTH AMERICAN POISONOUS WATER SNAKE. IT IS A PIT VIPER AND RELATED TO THE COPPERHEAD AND THE RATTLESNAKE. THE MOCCASIN HAS A REPUTATION FOR BEING AN AGGRESSIVE REPTILE THAT WILL STAND ITS GROUND OR EVEN APPROACH AN INTRUDER.
- JOHNNY MENTIONS SWIMMING TO SOME TULES (PRONOUNCED TOOLEES), WHICH ARE A TYPE OF REEDY GRASS.
- WHEN JOHNNY CRASHES HIS CAR, THE SOUND EFFECT IS THE TYPICAL CAR SCREECHING ON PAVEMENT. TOO BAD HE WAS ON A MUDDY DIRT ROAD.
- JOHNNY MENTIONS GOING UP THE SLOUGH (PRONOUNCED SLU), WHICH IS A CREEK-LIKE CHANNEL IN A SWAMP.
- THE ANNOUNCER IS JOHN WALD

Producer:    Jack Johnstone         Writers:    Jack Johnstone
Cast:        Virginia Gregg, Harry Bartell, Ben Wright, Sam Edwards,
             Vic Perrin, Ralph Moody

◆    ❖    ◆

SHOW:        THE DEEP DOWN MATTER
SHOW DATE:   3/13/1960
COMPANY:     CONTINENTAL INSURANCE COMPANY
AGENT:
EXP. ACCT:   $131.50

SYNOPSIS: [Opening Missing] Ralph calls about Bertram Haskel who owns a copper mine in Michigan. His partner Bert Oliver has been murdered, and Haskel wants Johnny to investigate. It is the insurance on Haskel that is motivating this investigation. Ralph tells Johnny that the country and the people are pretty rough up there.

Johnny flies to Chicago and then on to Houghton, Michigan where he rents a car. Johnny drives to the Haskel mine where there are a number of weather beaten houses and a big hole. Johnny goes to the office where Mr. Haskel is telling a man that he better not throw Mrs. Oliver out of her house. Haskel tells Johnny that Ben Oliver and he had worked together for years, and he is making a fortune. Ben did not want to be a partner, only a scientist. Ben was murdered in the mine exploring an abandoned area. It had to be one of the miners, but not one of the six could have done it as there was only one shot fired in total darkness.

Haskel shows Johnny a map of the mine, and where the ore comes up. Ben was killed 321 feet below the surface in a big room. Haskel take Johnny down into the mine to show Johnny where Oliver was killed. Johnny describes the ride down, past the various stopes in the mine. In the bottom stope, Johnny notices that the lights were on. Haskel tells Johnny that Ben was checking for uranium and had asked for a Geiger counter. Haskel went down with the equipment and six others when the lights went off. When the lights came back on, Oliver was found dead from a pellet-gun wound. There was no sign of a flashlight, and one of the men in the car did it. Johnny thinks he has a pretty big order.

Johnny arranges to stay with Haskel, and over dinner Haskel tells him that the uranium was not worth digging for. Haskel and the police have no clue. The pellet gun was a foreign make, which could have come from anywhere, as there is a big foreign population there. Johnny has a few ideas, and asks to talk to the six men who went down with Haskel. Johnny questions the men and then talks to Mrs. Oliver. She tells Johnny that Bertram was always kind to Ben, but she tells Johnny that if he is going to work for Haskel, to look out and make sure he gets credit for anything he discovers. Ben was easy going and easy to be taken advantage of. She typed the report where Ben was certain that there was uranium with great commercial possibilities in the mine. Mrs. Oliver tells Johnny that in the report, she made Ben say that he wanted to share in the profits; unlike the money he did not get from the copper finds. Mrs. Oliver shows Johnny Ben's equipment that includes a scintillator and a black light. Johnny turns it on and Ben's clothes glow. Johnny is sure that the glow is the solution to the murder. Johnny puts Ben's jacket on under his topcoat, takes the equipment and goes to see Haskel. Johnny gets Haskel to take him down into the mine. Haskel is asked to turn the lights off and Johnny moves to the place where Ben was killed. Johnny removes his topcoat and turns his back to Haskel. Johnny tells Haskel to turn on the black light so he can see the target on the back of the coat Ben was wearing. Haskel shoots at the coat, but Johnny had taken it off. Johnny tells Haskel that he knew there was uranium in the mine and killed Oliver to keep the profits.

"The almost perfect crime. And he was so sure of it that he called me in to back up his story of loyalty to Ben Oliver. So that no one would ever question his taking over the uranium that Ben had found."

NOTES:
- COMMERCIAL #1 IS FOR FRITOS, WITH A FREE PACKAGE OF BURPEE FLOWER SEEDS TO CELEBRATE SPRING
- COMMERCIAL 2 IS FOR WINSTON CIGARETTES
- COMMERCIAL #3 IS MEL TORME FOR 4-WAY AND A SPOT FOR FITCH DANDRUFF SHAMPOO
- COMMERCIAL #4 IS FOR EXLAX

- THE ANNOUNCER IS JOHN WALD

**Producer:**  Jack Johnstone          **Writers:**  Jack Johnstone
**Cast:**  Ben Wright, Virginia Gregg, John Stevenson

◆ ❖ ◆

| | |
|---|---|
| SHOW: | THE SATURDAY NIGHT MATTER |
| SHOW DATE: | 3/20/1960 |
| COMPANY: | SURETY MUTUAL INSURANCE LIMITED |
| AGENT: | PETER H. FILLMORE |
| EXP. ACCT: | $301.01 |

SYNOPSIS: Peter H. Fillmore calls Johnny from Denver, and he has just discovered a racket of grocery store robberies. They occur every Saturday night with most discouraging regularity. Fillmore is certain that a gang is involved, and Johnny should agree once he gets the facts. They will not quibble over the expense account and there is a fee and commission involved, on account of the danger to Johnny's life. Goodbye.

Johnny grabs a box of .38 shells and flies to Denver, Colorado. In his office, Mr. Fillmore tells Johnny that all the robberies did not occur in Denver. But Fillmore has found a pattern. The policies involved are for unlimited loss and have increased his business. Every robbery occurs on Saturday night, eight so far. The robbers enter at gunpoint just at closing time. The two robbers also wear stocking masks over their heads. There has been no police coordination, because of the different localities. Fillmore has just found a pattern. The robberies occur in a pattern of decreasing city population. Fillmore feels that the next robbery will be in Wheat Ridge or Grand Junction; they have equal populations. Johnny must decide on which town. Johnny takes a quarter and flips it; heads Wheat Ridge, tails Grand Junction. "Can you think of a better way?"

Fillmore is worried about paying off on another claim. Albert Berry, Fillmore's assistant comes in and tells Fillmore to cancel the policies, but Fillmore does not want to. Berry tells Fillmore that he would rather leave than continue selling these policies. Johnny tells Berry that, at the flip of a coin, he is heading for, somewhere, but he needs to get busy. Johnny rents a car for the drive to Grand Junction, but stops first at the police department in Wheat Ridge where Sgt. Kiesman tells Johnny that they are watching the store in Wheat Ridge. Johnny is told to talk to Dick Spidel in Grand Junction. Johnny drives on towards Grand Junction. Along the way he spots a number of cold trout streams and thinks of coming back some day to fish. After lunch Johnny is watching the scenery when a car swings into him at a detour and runs him off the road.

Johnny is rescued by a state trooper and taken to a hospital where he is given a hypo and goes out. Johnny wakes up with Dick Spidel in his room. Dick tells Johnny that they know he was run off the road. The same car was used at a market robbery there in Grand Junction. Dick tells Johnny that the owner of the market, Barnaby Shaltus has a record of stock manipulations and phony bankruptcies. Johnny realizes when Shaltus was robbed that he knew he would get the insurance. Dick tells Johnny to stay put and that he is being guarded until the doc says he can get up.

Johnny is out the next day and goes back to Mr. Fillmore. He tells Fillmore that the owners could arrange the robberies themselves and get a part of the robbery. Johnny is sure that someone is running a robbery ring. Fillmore realizes that someone must know who had the policies. Johnny suggests that Al Berry is collecting both ways, by selling policies and arranging the robberies. Berry comes in and tells Johnny that he should not have gone through his files and made it so obvious. Johnny tells him he was sloppy for pulling the robberies in the same order he sold the policies, from biggest to smallest. Berry pulls his gun, and Johnny tells him that the police are there. Berry is sure that he is joking, until a police Sergeant comes in and takes the gun.

"Sure, in the hope it might make things easier for him, Al produced the punks who had been working with him, who had actually pulled the jobs. And then he came up with most of the dough from the robberies. But you know something? I doubt if it will do him any good, nor the store owners who had played along with him." Johnny will leave the wrecked car with Fillmore.

NOTES:
- COMMERCIAL #1 IS FOR PEPSI
- COMMERCIAL #2 IS FOR WINSTON CIGARETTES
- COMMERCIAL #3 IS STUART ERWIN FOR 4-WAY, AND A SPOT FOR FITCH DANDRUFF SHAMPOO
- COMMERCIAL #4 IS FOR FRITOS
- COMMERCIAL #5 IS FOR EXLAX
- THE ANNOUNCER IS JOHN WALD

Producer:    Jack Johnstone        Writers:    Jack Johnstone
Cast:        Bartlett Robinson, James McCallion, Forrest Lewis, Russell
             Thorson

◆    ❖    ◆

SHOW:        THE FALSE ALARM MATTER
SHOW DATE:   3/27/1960
COMPANY:     TRI-STATE LIFE & CASUALTY COMPANY
AGENT:       EARLE POORMAN
EXP. ACCT:   $151.00

SYNOPSIS: Mike Poorman calls Johnny tells him that she heard on WSPB radio about a man who was found dead in his car just off the Tamiani Trail. The radio report said the car was just like Earle's. Mike had called the radio station, and they did not know anything. Johnny tells her to call the station again. Johnny is going to see how quickly he can get there.

Johnny flies to the Poorman home in Sarasota. Mike meets Johnny at the door and tells him that Earle had run out that morning, and that the radio station had called back. They checked with the police in Briscoe Springs, and they had reported the man who was named Jansen, or something like that, had suffered a heart attack. Johnny suggests that maybe he can get Earle to take him fishing, but Earle is not home yet. The phone rings and Johnny answers it. Earle apologizes to Mike for not calling earlier, but he is on a murder case and asks her to call Johnny Dollar and have him meet Earle down here. Johnny asks "Down where?" Earle tells Johnny to meet him at an address near Venice. "Who is this?" asks Earle. Earle does not know who is on the phone because he does not know that Johnny had come down.

Johnny drives to the address given to him by Earle, and it is a huge expensive home. Johnny spots Earle's car and another that belongs to Doc Crutcher. Doc had called Earle to the estate. Johnny learns that Doc Crutcher had been the family doctor for Linda since before she married Frank, but it is a bad marriage. Frank was only out for Linda's money. She had hired a bunch of other old boyfriends, but ended up running the family chemical company herself. Doc shows Johnny the body of Linda on the bed, and even in death she is beautiful. Doc had found the body twisted in pain when they got there, but it looks peaceful now. Johnny suspects cyanide, but Doc says it is something subtler, possibly potassium theramalicilate. PTM initially gives symptoms of cyanide, but later those symptoms are gone. The maid had called and said that Linda was having a heart attack. When they got there, Doc started running tests and found indications of the PTM, but no evidence of it. Doc has checked everything, but cannot find the poison. Johnny wants to question the servants, and they all convince Johnny that they were devoted and loyal to Linda. The personal maid Irene tells Johnny that Linda was sitting at the dressing table and putting on some perfume when she clutched at her heart. Johnny goes back to Doc Crutcher and they look at the empty perfume bottle. Doc runs a test to see if the bottle ever had the poison in it. Earle thinks that Frank Hanson, her husband, is the likely suspect. He went to the plant this morning, but has disappeared. Doc tells Johnny that the poison had been in the perfume bottle. Johnny then remembers Mike telling him earlier that the man found by the police that morning was named Jansen or something like that.

Johnny calls the police in Briscoe Springs and learns that Frank Hanson had been driving along smoking a cigarette and had a heart attack. Huh? Johnny tells them to run tests for the poison. The police call back to say that the poison was found in the cigarettes. Johnny talks to Earle about Linda's love life, and one name comes up, one man who had promised to get even if Linda married anyone else. Johnny asks Doc to concoct something that would make a stain after a few minutes. Doc gets two chemicals which, when mixed, will produce a blue stain. Johnny wants to play a hunch and tells Doc to get the materials ready. Johnny, Earle and Doc drive to the chemical plant and meet the chief chemist, Harry Forester. Johnny shakes hands with both hands and they go into the office. Johnny asks Harry, "If Linda were to die" and Harry interrupts to tell Johnny that he was in love with her at one time.

But Johnny continues that the money would go to her husband Frank. But if Frank were to die, would you not be next in line? And Harry knows where to get hold of PTM, but Harry tells Johnny that he is scared of it and never uses it. Johnny takes out a bottle and spills some of it on Harry's hand. A bluish tinge appears and Johnny says that the stain is proof that he has been handling PTM, that he had put it in Linda's perfume bottle and Frank's cigarettes. Harry admits to killing them both, and he tries to swallow a capsule to get out of going to jail, but Johnny slugs him. Doc thinks the capsule is full of PTM.

"So, it will be up to the courts whether Harry Forester likes it or not. And believe me, I would hate to be in his shoes. Yeah, I keep wondering, why don't they ever learn?"

### NOTES:
- COMMERCIAL #1 IS FOR WINSTON CIGARETTES.
- COMMERCIAL #2 IS A PUBLIC SERVICE ANNOUNCEMENT FOR THE RED CROSS, AND THEIR NEED FOR MONEY.
- COMMERCIAL #3 IS FOR EXLAX.
- THE ANNOUNCER IS JOHN WALD

**Producer:** Jack Johnstone    **Writers:** Jack Johnstone
**Cast:** Shirley Mitchell, Virginia Gregg, Vic Perrin, Lou Merrill, Paula Winslowe, Frank Nelson, Dick Crenna

◆  ❖  ◆

**SHOW:** THE DOUBLE EXPOSURE MATTER
**SHOW DATE:** 4/3/1960
**COMPANY:** MASTERS INSURANCE & TRUST COMPANY
**AGENT:** FREDERICK KEELEY
**EXP. ACCT:** $17.20

SYNOPSIS: Frederick Keeley calls Johnny and he has a problem. One of their claimants has apparently never received a claim check. Johnny tells Keeley to call the bank and stop payment. However, Keeley tells Johnny that the claimant has cashed the check. Johnny thinks that someone may have gotten the check first, which would be forgery. Johnny agrees to look into the case.

Johnny cabs to Keeley's office and is told that a $3,000 claim is relatively unimportant (i.e. small commission for Johnny), but the claimant must be stupid to think that he can get away with it, but Peter Upman is not stupid. Keeley is sure that the case is forgery, that someone else has taken the check. Keeley is sure that this could lead to larger crimes. According to the bank, they have proof that Upman appeared, cashed the check and left with the money. But Upman had signed a deposition that he never got the check. That is why Johnny has been called. Johnny accepts the challenge. Johnny drives to Milford, Connecticut and the Peoples National Bank, which is closed. Johnny gets a hotel room at the Milford Arms, has dinner and visits Mr. Upman, who is a nervous football type. Peter is sure that Johnny has the replacement check and asks for it. Upman repeats his story that he never got the check, but Johnny tells him that they have a receipt. Peter tells Johnny that Alfred Price, the lawyer, took his statement, so ask him. Upman tells Johnny that he is a nervous person, and it might not be healthy to aggravate him. That is not a warning; it is a threat.

Johnny is unable to reason with Upman. Johnny goes to visit Mr. Price who tells Johnny that Peter comes from a wealthy family. He wanted to make something of himself, but his father cut him off. The other family members do not get along with him. Peter owns a small electronics shop, and is the only one in the family who knows the value of money. He could use the money, but Price does not think that Peter would try to cheat the insurance company. But what about the check? Price asks if Johnny has talked to the teller or seen the photograph of the transaction. Price tells Johnny that the bank camera is a very clever device. First thing in the morning Johnny goes to talk to Mr. Oliver. The camera is a clever device, when it works. It takes a picture of everyone who steps up to a teller counter. It really helps stop bad checks. Johnny asks to see the picture and Oliver gives it to him, but it is very fuzzy and could be a double exposure. The camera was an experimental model, and only Oliver and the head teller know that the pictures are fuzzy. The picture could be of anyone. Mrs. Eberhart, the head teller tells Johnny that Mr. Upman cashed the check. Mrs. Eberhart is called to the desk, and Johnny casually pulls his gun and holds it across his chest as Mrs. Eberhart approaches. Johnny now sees things a lot more clearly.

Mr. Oliver is told not to mention the gun as Mrs. Eberhart comes in tripping over things and misidentifying the other employees. She notices that Johnny smokes a pipe too, just like Mr. Oliver. Johnny tells her to take a good look and she finally recognizes that the pipe is Johnny's pistol. Johnny asks when she last had an eye exam and Mrs. Eberhart gets upset. Johnny tells Oliver that she is blind as a bat. Johnny calls Price, has lunch and then goes to Price's office. Price gives Johnny photos of Janet Upman and Edward and Paul Upman, who Johnny mistakes for a young Peter. They dislike Peter because of the hidden bequest in the will that Peter does not know about. Peter gets over a million in a few months, when he turns thirty-five, provided he stays out of trouble. Johnny is ready to try something with Price's assistance. Johnny calls Peter and Price calls the other family members. When they are all assembled in Price's office Peter tells Johnny that he does not like Johnny. Johnny tells them about the check from Aunt Elizabeth and Paul tells them that Peter should be locked up. Johnny tells Paul that is would be easy for him to pick up the check, forge the signature and take the check to half-blind Mrs. Eberhart to cash. Johnny tells Paul that a little machine put the finger on him, a machine that took a picture of him. Janet tells Johnny that the camera in the bank has not worked in years. Her boyfriend is a cashier at the bank and he told her so. Johnny asks Janet "He didn't tell you it has been fixed?" Johnny gives the picture to Price, who agrees that the picture is clear. Peter gets angry and goes after Paul and a fight breaks out. Price is sure that Peter will kill Paul, but Johnny asks Price if he can think of a better way for justice to be done?

"Yeah, Peter paid Paul on this one, but I mean royally. And I must confess it did my heart glad to watch him. And Pete, bless his fighting Irish heart, Yep, he'll be a millionaire one of these days. He's earned it."

NOTES:
- COMMERCIAL #1 IS FOR PEPSI.
- COMMERCIAL #2 IS FOR WINSTON CIGARETTES.
- COMMERCIAL #3 IS FOR EXLAX.
- THE ANNOUNCER IS JOHN WALD

**Producer:** Jack Johnstone       **Writers:** Jack Johnstone
**Cast:**        Ralph Moody, Peter Leeds, Virginia Gregg, Bartlett Robinson, Marvin Miller, Jack Moyles, Eleanor Audley, Sandra Gould

◆　❖　◆

**SHOW:**        THE DEADLY SWAMP MATTER
**SHOW DATE:**  4/17/1960
**COMPANY:**    PROVIDENTIAL ASSURANCE COMPANY
**AGENT:**      CHARLES KINGSLEY ST. CLAIR
**EXP. ACCT:**  $161.60

**SYNOPSIS:** Charles Kingsley St Clair calls Johnny from Kennett, Missouri, and Johnny tells him that he thought he was leaving the company. St Clair tells Johnny that he is a changed man now. Johnny tells him that they make some powerful moonshine down there. Charles tells Johnny that Dade Wupperman has been tried and incarcerated, but his brother Dan'l, or rather Daniel has been making trouble. Charles wants Johnny to come back and help him. Johnny reluctantly agrees to come down.

Johnny flies to Memphis, Tennessee where Kingsley meets Johnny, and to Johnny, he has changed. Charles tells Johnny that he has decided to stay in Kennett. When he got there the swamp people were the only ones he had to deal with, but he has decided to stay. Johnny taught him how to deal with them on his last visit. Johnny has friends there now, and they will help. Charles tells Johnny that there have been a series of murders, and the victims have been relatives of the swamp people. They view the insurance company and Johnny as a protection agency. These cases are not a matter for the local police, as they have no jurisdiction. Charles tells Johnny that Eupha Crump, who Johnny helped on his last trip, was the latest victim. Johnny asks what else he knows, so he can start to work on the case.

Johnny remembers Eupha as a person out of place in the swamp, working hard to care for her family. Now Cass and Eupha are dead. But Charles tells Johnny that Cass is still alive and that he married Eupha. Cass asked Charles to have Johnny help him. Johnny borrows Kingsley's car and drives to the 20-mile swamp. Johnny heads to Eupha's house when he is shot at. Johnny stops and waits on the floor. Cass Dingle comes up and asks for "Mr. Johnny." He tells

Johnny that he shot to make Johnny stop so he could not go to the house. Cass tells Johnny to hide his car at the old cabin. After getting the car out of a mud hole, Johnny does not find Cass at the cabin. Johnny walks to the cabin and goes in. Inside he finds Cass tied up on the floor and Dan'l Wupperman standing there with a very old, large bore rifle. Three other men appear and Johnny gives up, even though he notes he took a course from the FBI on how to disarm a man with a gun in your back, but not four men. Paul Wupperman takes Johnny's "pretty gun" and is told to hold onto it while Dan'l kills Johnny.

Johnny notes he has been in some tight spots before, but never anything like this. The swamp people use their guns for survival, but he notes that survival is not for Johnny today. Dan'l tells Johnny that he is going to kill him for sending his brother to jail. He tells Johnny that he has no business there. Dan'l killed Eupha because Johnny gave her the money, and he knew that Johnny would come back. Cass tells Dan'l that this is all wrong. Paul thinks that if you kill an outside man, the police will come after him. Dan'l cocks the gun, and Cass tells Dan'l to kill him instead. Cass asks Johnny if he talked long enough, and it should be five o'clock by now. Johnny agrees it is about time and starts to whistle his theme. Dan'l wants to know what he meant, and Johnny tells him that if he is not out of the swamp, the state police will come in to get him. Dan'l thinks he is lying. Paul is told to go out and look for any one, along with two of the others. Now there is only one enemy to deal with. Johnny tells him that he has not heard from the others because the police have them. Dan'l starts to look at Johnny's watch to see what time it is and Johnny knees Dan'l and gets his gun and slugs him.

"I knew the sound of the gunshot would bring the others back to the cabin, after all they certainly hadn't found any sign of those mythical State Police out there. So after setting Cass free, I laid down just inside the door looking very dead. And then when John and Paul and Peter came in one at a time, Cass, who was standing back of the door, very quietly and carefully, took care of them, with the help of the butt of Dan'l's gun. So now four more of the swampers have left that region to spend a long, long time behind the bars."

NOTES:
- COMMERCIAL #1 IS FOR PEPSI.
- COMMERCIAL #2 IS FOR WINSTON CIGARETTES.
- COMMERCIAL #3 IS FOR EXLAX.
- THE ANNOUNCER IS HUGH DOUGLAS
- DADE WUPPERMAN'S NAME IN THE MOONSHINE MATTER WAS DADE WUPPER

Producer:    Jack Johnstone       Writers:    Jack Johnstone
Cast:         Ben Wright, Sam Edwards, Roy Glenn, Vic Perrin

| SHOW: | THE SILVER QUEEN MATTER |
|---|---|
| SHOW DATE: | 4/24/1960 |
| COMPANY: | INTER-COASTAL MARITIME & LIFE INSURANCE COMPANY |
| AGENT: | BYRON KAYE |
| EXP. ACCT: | $58.35 |

SYNOPSIS: Byron Kaye calls Johnny and tells him that things are not well in Cod Harbor. Johnny reminds him of the case he had handled for Meg McCarthy and her greasy spoon restaurant. Byron tells Johnny that is it Meg who called him and insisted that Johnny come up to see her. Meg has told Byron that if Johnny does not come up, she will cancel her insurance on the restaurant. Johnny tells Byron that Meg is used to handling things herself, so something must be wrong; the last time she called it was a murder. Byron tells Johnny he will pay the expenses.

Johnny decides to drive to Cod Harbor, and buys a tank of gas. Johnny arrives just after noon, and describes the town and Meg's Palace. Johnny describes the boats tied up in the harbor on his way to visit Meg. In the Palace, Meg is yelling at someone who broke up some dishes while he was drunk. After the man leaves, Megs attacks Johnny who is hiding in the shadows. Then she recognizes her "darlin' Johnny boy." Meg tells Johnny that she has to take care of the boys who come to her restaurant. Over a cup of terrible coffee, Megs tells Johnny about Marty Silver, who owns the Silver Belle. He sailed in several days ago from Gloucester, and wants to sell the Silver Bell. Captain Andy comes in and mentions that several people have made bids on the boat. Meg tells Andy to make sure that no one buys the boat. Meg tells Johnny that if Marty finds out that she sent for Johnny, there will be a murder, hers.

Meg tells Johnny that she had called Tom Lavery in Gloucester, and he has never heard of Silver, and Tom has lived there a long time. Last night Meg took a good look at the boat, and discovered that the boat was originally named the Arctic Queen. Meg called Tom again and learned that the Arctic Queen was supposed to have been lost at sea, with both hands aboard lost, the captain and the first mate Marty Flag. She feels that Silver and Flag are one in the same. Johnny is about to go to the phone booth to call the Coast Guard when she tells Johnny that Silver is going to murder her for snooping around his boat. Meg gets upset because she feels that Johnny is not taking care of her life, and cares more about the boat. Johnny tells Meg that he will let nothing will happen to her and leaves to call the Coast Guard. Johnny calls the Coast Guard who has never heard of Silver. They are sure that Silver killed the captain of the Arctic Queen, painted the boat, and is trying to sell it. Johnny tells them he will watch Silver and do nothing to scare him until they get there. But, Johnny has to break that promise after he hangs up the phone.

Johnny goes back into the café and hears some activity in the kitchen and a door slam. Johnny goes into the kitchen where Meg has been attacked. She is sure that Silver would have killed her if Johnny had not come back in. She tells

Johnny that Silver was hiding in the kitchen. Johnny hears foots steps coming in and Captain Andy rushes in. Andy had seen Silver running from the restaurant and Johnny tells him that Silver had attacked Meg in the kitchen. Andy is ready to kill him, and tells Johnny that Silver has gone back to the Silver Queen. Megs sees the Silver Queen leaving port and Johnny gets Andy to follow him. As they go out to sea they follow the running lights of the Silver Queen. Slowly they pull up on the Silver Queen and Johnny checks his .38 to make sure it is loaded. Johnny realizes that Silver can see them as well and goes to turn off their lights, but Silver has turned off his now. Johnny turns on the spotlight and notices Silver turning to run them down. Johnny shoots and Silver is hurt. Finally, the Silver Queen hits their boat.

"Well, I suppose I ought to make some crack about it being a long swim back to Cod Harbor, but I won't, because it wasn't. The Silver Queen sank like a rock, and with the help of the spotlight we finally managed to find and pick up the body of Marty Silver. Then, with both Andy and me bailing like mad, we slowly limped back to port. And that is about it."

NOTES:
- COMMERCIAL #1 IS FOR WINSTON CIGARETTES.
- FOR COMMERCIAL #2, BOB BAILEY BREAKS OUT OF CHARACTER TO REMIND THE AUDIENCE THAT "HERE IN AMERICA RADIO IS FREE, ITS PRODUCTS ARE TRUTH AND ENTERTAINMENT. BUT TRUTH IS OFTEN MISSING BEHIND THE IRON CURTAIN WHERE SEVENTY-SIX MILLION PEOPLE ARE FED A LOT OF CONTROLLED OPINION PROPAGANDA. WE CAN KEEP FAITH WITH THOSE CAPTIVE PEOPLE THROUGH RADIO FREE EUROPE. THEY ASK FOR MORE, RISK THEIR LIVES TO LISTEN SO THE LEAST WE CAN RISK IS THE TRUTH DOLLAR. SEND IT NOW. SEND ALL YOU CAN SPARE TO THE CRUSADE FOR FREEDOM CARE OF YOUR POST OFFICE. DO IT, WILL YA, RIGHT AWAY.
- COMMERCIAL #3 IS FOR EXLAX.
- JOHNNY MAKES REFERENCE TO HIS .38
- THE ANNOUNCER IS JOHN WALD

**Producer:** Jack Johnstone     **Writers:** Jack Johnstone
**Cast:** Virginia Gregg, Olan Soule, Ralph Moody

◆  ❖  ◆

| | |
|---|---|
| SHOW: | THE FATAL SWITCH MATTER |
| SHOW DATE: | 5/1/1960 |
| COMPANY: | WESTERN LIFE & TRUST INSURANCE COMPANY |
| AGENT: | ART BASCOMB |
| EXP. ACCT: | $386.21 |

SYNOPSIS: Johnny is called very early in the morning. The caller tells Johnny that he has checked the plane schedules, and if he leaves now he can just make the early plane to the West Coast. Johnny asks who is on the phone, and it is Art Bascomb. Art tells Johnny that he has to catch the plane, as this is a case of murder.

Johnny flies to Los Angeles and Art meets Johnny at the airport. They get in Art's car and head for Balboa, California. Art tells Johnny that one of the yachts there, a 42-foot cruiser is owned by Friedbaron Electronics, which is owned by Lester Friedbaron. Friedbaron owns the sales and manufacturing rights to a radio control device. Friedbaron's partner, Edgar Porter, invented the device and owns the patent. Porter took the boat out for a cruise yesterday. Friedbaron called him and during the conversation someone killed him. The Coast Guard is trying to find the boat. Porter was out there alone with no other boats around, but someone apparently killed him. Friedbaron had recorded the conversation over the radio and has the recording. Johnny is confused. The Friedbaron home is smaller than most in the area, and Lester Friedbaron is in his mid-fifties with a much younger beautiful wife. Friedbaron tells Art and Johnny that the Coast Guard still has not found the boat, and that Porter told him that he was alone. Friedbaron plays the tape of the conversation, and tells Johnny that he made the tape recorder himself. On the tape Baron talks to both Mr. and Mrs. Friedbaron and tells them that he is alone. Baron notes that the weather is chilly and Friedbaron tells him to turn on the cabin heater and be sure to open the vent, and then there is a shot. Johnny tells them that it is impossible, except that it happened.

Johnny tells Friedbaron that there is nothing that can be done until the boat is found. Mrs. Friedbaron, who wants to be called Marylyn, notes that Baron had already put on the heater. Mr. Friedbaron tells Johnny that carbon dioxide could build up quickly, but Baron knew that. Johnny is told that Baron was meticulous about the boat, so no one could have stowed away on the boat. Friedbaron tells Johnny that the noise could have been an electrical short, but he doubts it. Johnny is told that Baron was ready to get millions from the invention. The policy was a partnership policy worth $250,000 and all of the patent rights revert to Friedbaron if Baron dies. Marylyn met Baron at a party and asked him to bring the invention to Friedbaron. Johnny is told that Adam Patrick is the contact at the Coast Guard. Johnny borrows Art's car to go visit his old friend, Adam Patrick, who helped him on the Ellen Dear case. Johnny has a handful of ideas and wants to go alone. He will only tell Art that if he can get to the boat before anyone else, he can prove that two plus two equals five.

Johnny meets with Patrick and gets on a cutter with him to go out to the Leslyn, the Friedbaron boat. Pat has told Friedbaron that the boat had been found and gave him the coordinates. Pat knows that the Friedbaron's are quite a team, especially with Marylyn's "assets." Pat tells Johnny that Friedbaron is in debt after building his plant and could use the money from the insurance. They reach the boat and Johnny goes on board with Pat and a doctor to find Baron dead, laying over the radio. The doctor tells Johnny that it appears to be carbon monoxide poisoning. Friedbaron arrives in his speedboat and comes on board. He tells them that it was carbon monoxide poisoning, and opens the vent. Johnny tells him that the vent was open when he got on the boat, which puzzles Friedbaron. Johnny tells them that the carbon monoxide came from some other source. Johnny tells him how convenient it is to get the invention, and how Baron must have had an eye on Marylyn, but his being dead would be even better. Johnny reminds Friedbaron that he had been a chemist, and knows how a crystal that had been heated could produce carbon monoxide. Johnny shows Pat how Barton had to bend over the transmitter to use the radio, and how Friedbaron had mentioned earlier that Baron fell against the transmitter. Johnny tells him that he knew that Baron would be leaning over the radio. Pat finds a small coil on the transmitter, and Johnny tells him that it was used to heat up a crystal that produced the carbon monoxide. Pat agrees that all Friedbaron had to do was call Baron on the radio, and the coil would heat up. "Well, Mr. Friedbaron?"

"Yep, Lester Friedbaron had suddenly run out of answers. And I am willing to bet that the best lawyer in the country can't get him out of this one. Best of all, of course, he won't collect a penny of the insurance on the partner that he murdered."

NOTES:
- JOHNNY NOTES THAT ADAM PATRICK HELPED HIM WITH THE ELLEN DEAR MATTER, BUT IN MY PROGRAM THE COAST GUARD CONTACT IS CAPT. BARNEY THORSON.
- THE ANNOUNCER IS JOHN WALD

Producer:  Jack Johnstone        Writers:   Jack Johnstone
Cast:      Virginia Gregg, Olan Soule, Sam Edwards, Will Wright,
           Hershel Bernardi

◆  ❖  ◆

SHOW:          THE PHONY PHONE MATTER
SHOW DATE:     5/8/1960
COMPANY:       INTERNATIONAL LIFE & CASUALTY INSURANCE COMPANY
AGENT:         ART INGLES
EXP. ACCT:     $1.35

SYNOPSIS: Art Ingles calls Johnny and asks if he is ready for case. Johnny asks if it is murder, fraud or arson, and Art tells him that he does not know. A very important client wants to see Johnny, and no one else. Johnny tells Art that the last time he took a case like this he was slugged, shot at and thrown off a bridge, but he will take the case.

Johnny does not like vague assignments but International has paid him well. Johnny meets Art and they drive across Hartford, Connecticut to Mr. Wendell's office. Johnny is told that Wendell owns Crown Lithograph and that the company is worth millions. Wendell carries half a million on himself and his wife, and Wendell is used to having his own way, and Johnny remembers that he is called "Alimony Wendell." Johnny thought that he had read where Wendell was supposedly through with the gold-diggers. Art tells Johnny that nine months ago he married LaVon Laverne (Yikes! Remarks Johnny) and now she has a ring in his nose and is making a dent in his bank account. In Wendell's huge and lavishly appointed office Johnny is fooled by Wendell's appearance. He is not a doddering old man but a sharp businessman. Wendell is concerned about his wife, but not her insurance, and tells Ingles to leave. Wendell tells Johnny that he has had seven wives and has made a fool of himself. He should not have paid them off. But LaVon is a good wife, but she is afraid of being murdered.

Wendell tells Johnny that she is afraid that someone is going to kill her. Wendell wants Johnny to find out if there are grounds for her fear. Johnny asks if he has called in a psychologist, but Wendell will have no part of that. Wendell wants Johnny to come to their lodge on the Peekabuck River, posing as an old friend. They are going to meet LaVon there for lunch. Wendell calls for his car and Johnny is still not sure what he is supposed to do. Wendell tells Johnny that he has followed Johnny's career for years on the radio, and knows that Johnny knows how to get close to people and inspire confidence. Johnny adds that he also would be handy to have as a bodyguard. Wendell drives Johnny to his apartment where he packs his bags and gets his .38 caliber lemon squeezer. They drive to the lodge and Wendell tells Johnny that he knows of no one who would want to harm LaVon, but her past careen included dancing in some questionable clubs owned by gangsters. They arrive at the 10-room lodge, but LaVon's car is missing. They go in and Wendell pours drinks and calls home. LaVon is there and Wendell tells her that he is worried. He mentions that she has a visitor and then the line goes dead. Wendell tells Johnny that she gave a strange gasp and dropped the phone. Johnny picks up the phone and has the operator connect him with the Hartford police, homicide division.

Johnny and Wendell drive back to Hartford, and the police are at the Wendell home, and Lt. Billy Walker is in charge. LaVon is on the floor with the phone beside her. The police medic had removed a gruesome knife from her back, and Wendell is very upset. Lt. Walker tells Johnny that the knife went through her heart and came from a collection over the mantel piece. Lt. Walker tells Johnny that the servants were off for the weekend, and were too old to have killed her. Also the back door was ajar. Wendell regrets letting the servants off for the weekend. Johnny is told to find the killer. Johnny tells Wendell to call his attorney, who is Harold Spidel, and Wendell tells Johnny that he will call soon, after he is composed. Lt. Walker is on the phone and is told that the only prints on the phone were from LaVon, which is strange unless someone wanted it to appear that way. Johnny agrees and leaves. Johnny borrows Wendell's car and drives to the office of Lawyer Spidel on a hunch, and Spidel will never know how much he did help. Spidel tells Johnny that it is too bad, but it does save Wendell the expense of another divorce. He was certain that the marriage was due to fail. None of his wives was as expensive as LaVon was. Johnny is told that he is the perfect alibi for Wendell, as he heard him on the phone with LaVon. Johnny calls Betty Lewis and she agrees to go along with a little stunt that might solve the case. Johnny goes back to Wendell's home where Wendell has calmed down and tells Johnny that what has happened has happened. Johnny tells Wendell not to call his lawyer, as Johnny is expecting a call, and that he has heard that Wendell was a pretty ruthless businessman. The phone rings and Johnny answers the phone and Betty agrees to hang up. Johnny tells the phone that he will give it $500 if the information is accurate. He ups it to a $1,000 if the caller will come to the house and agree to appear in court. Johnny is "told" that the caller saw him through the side window. He saw him take the knife and open the back door. Wendell tells Johnny to hang up and that the informer will get what Johnny will get, a bullet in the head. Johnny tells Wendell that his name is not Matt Dillon but if the thinks he can out draw him, then Johnny draws his gun and shoots Wendell. Wow!

"Well I hope that Wendell never finds out that my phone conversation with a mythical informer was just as phony as his, his talk with his wife after he had killed her and left her there at the telephone in his home and set me up as his alibi at the lodge. But what is the difference where he is going. Expense account total, $1.35? Let's talk about the fee on this one!"

## NOTES:
- COMMERCIAL #1 IS FOR CAMEL CIGARETTES.
- COMMERCIAL #2 IS FOR THE CBS NEWS BROADCASTS AND THE NEED FOR CANCER CHECKUPS.
- COMMERCIAL #3 IS FOR ExLAX.
- THE ANNOUNCER IS JOHN WALD

Producer:    Jack Johnstone      Writers:    Jack Johnstone
Cast:         Virginia Gregg, Harry Bartell, Marvin Miller, Dick Crenna, Lou Merrill

◆    ❖    ◆

SHOW:          THE MYSTERY GAL MATTER
SHOW DATE:    5/15/1960
COMPANY:       CONTINENTAL INSURANCE & TRUST COMPANY
AGENT:         FRED MELCHIOR
EXP. ACCT:      $0.00

SYNOPSIS: A girl calls and asks Johnny why he doesn't get married to her. Johnny agrees to marry Janet, I mean Carol. The caller is Betty Lewis, and Johnny tells her that he knew it all along. Betty tells Johnny that if it were not for his business, she would trick him into a trip to the altar. "Yes Dear" Johnny answers and hems and haws about her badgering him about marriage. Betty tells Johnny that if he ever gets an honest job, she will marry him. She has called Johnny about insurance, and must see him. She is not at home, and tells Johnny to stay home until she calls him. She cannot talk, and tells Johnny to wait for her call. Hmm, there is something very funny about this.

Johnny feels that there is something strange, as he had the same conversation with Betty a few days earlier. But why stall Johnny when he has another case. Johnny waits an hour and then calls Betty's house and then her office where she has been all morning. Johnny asks Betty why she did not call him back, but she tells Johnny that she had not called him. Betty accuses Johnny of having so many girls on the line and getting them confused. Betty tells Johnny that she did not call. Johnny hangs up and wishes he knew what is going on.

Johnny cabs to Fred Melchior's Hartford, Connecticut office and Fritz tells Johnny that he did not expect Johnny so soon. Fritz tells Johnny that Johnny had called him back and asked if it was ok to be late, and Johnny tells him that something screwy is going on. Fritz tells Johnny that he had called Johnny and he agreed to come over. After a while Johnny had called and told him that he should not waste time coming to the office. Johnny tells Fritz that he did not call. Fritz is certain that Johnny had called and asked for all the details on the case. Fritz had told him everything about the case, but this means that Johnny has not been to see the client on East Maple Drive. Fritz grabs Johnny and they drive out there. Fritz tells Johnny that time is of the essence. Fritz tells Johnny that he had been called earlier by John Sawyer. Johnny tells Fritz that Sawyer lives across the street from a friend. Sawyer had been in the DA's office in New York and had sent up "Andy the Actor" Rinaldi. Johnny recalls how he had a record and the skill to impersonate people. Fritz tells Johnny that Andy had been paroled and is on the loose. Mr. Sawyer was awaked by someone prowling around and feels that it was Andy. Sawyer wants Johnny on the case. Johnny wonders how Andy could impersonate both himself and Betty Lewis. Johnny takes the wheel and they arrive at the Sawyer home. The door is open and there are shots and Fritz sees a body in the doorway.

Johnny discovers that the body was not Sawyer's. Sawyer comes out and gives Johnny a still smoking .38. Sawyer had shot Andy the Actor, who is still alive. Johnny thanks Sawyer for saving his life. Johnny follows the ambulance but Rinaldi does not come too. Johnny goes to his apartment where a man from the phone company is waiting for him. He tells Johnny that there had been a tap on his line, but Johnny would never have noticed it, but they did. Johnny knows who did it and goes in to test the phone with the repairman on the line. Johnny dials Betty and tells the lineman to get off the phone. Betty tells Johnny to come over, but Johnny asks Betty what part of the movie they came in on several nights ago. She tells Johnny that it was right when Jimmy Stuart walked up to the judge. Betty tells Johnny to come out, as she has a big surprise for him, a really important one. She is a really important one. Johnny rushes over and Betty takes him inside. She tells Johnny that she had come home early and saw Johnny and another man drive up, but she was too busy to call out. She went to the back door but it was open. In her living room, hiding behind a curtain was a girl with a gun. She aimed at Johnny and the other man. Betty ruined one of her nicest vases by hitting the woman with it and then tied her up. The girl came too and tried to talk, which is why she put the gag in her mouth. Johnny grabs Betty and kisses her. "Oh, honey, why don't we just get married?" moans Betty as Johnny kisses her.

"Eh, what a gal. And maybe someday, um yeah, expense account total including . . . that's funny. Something or someone seems to have diverted my attention for the moment from anything as trivial as an expense account. Trivial?"

## NOTES:
- COMMERCIAL #1 IS FOR PEPSI
- COMMERCIAL #2 IS FOR CAMEL CIGARETTES.
- COMMERCIAL #3 IS FOR KELLOGG'S ALL-BRAN
- THE ANNOUNCER IS JOHN WALD

**Producer:** Jack Johnstone  **Writers:** Jack Johnstone
**Cast:** Virginia Gregg, Jerry Hausner, Parley Baer, Peter Leeds

◆  ❖  ◆

**SHOW:** THE MAN WHO WAITS MATTER
**SHOW DATE:** 5/22/1960
**COMPANY:** EASTERN LIABILITY & TRUST COMPANY
**AGENT:** TED BESSEM
**EXP. ACCT:** $0.00

**SYNOPSIS:** Ted Bessem calls and Johnny is told that it might be a good time to take another crack at the diamonds. Ted has some new information on Rocky Harrison. Rocky disappeared after his probation, and Rocky is the only who knows what he did with the diamonds. Johnny is on his way to see Ted.

Johnny, and Johnny alone could take credit for Rocky's trip to Sing-Sing seven years ago. But Johnny had not been able to recover the Olney diamonds. The fact he was new in the business was no excuse. Johnny trains to New York City and Ted Bessem's office. Ted tells Johnny that Rocky had admitted everything to get a lighter sentence, and told the jury that the diamonds had been stolen from him. They also believed that the servant accidentally fell down the stairs and was killed, which kept Rocky from being tried for murder. Rocky behaved after probation and got a job and saved his money, which disappointed the police. Now that probation is over he has disappeared. Ted is sure that Rocky is here in New York, the easiest place in the world to get lost. Ted talked to a paid informant named Soder, Whiskey Soder, and he told Ted that Rocky is in town. Johnny gets the address for Soder. Ted tells Johnny that Rocky has changed his appearance, but Soder had recognized him. Johnny is told to be careful. Here is a chance to make up for seven years ago. Johnny cabs to the address and asks the manager for Soder. Johnny is told that he is the second man to ask to see Soder that day. Johnny goes to the room and knocks. Johnny breaks down the door to find Soder dead on the floor.

The manager tells Johnny that she did not hear anything, and Johnny tells her that the man used a pillow to muffle the shot. The manager tells Johnny only that the other visitor had gray hair. Johnny gives her $5 and tells her to call Sgt. Randy Singer and tell him that Johnny was there. The manager recognizes Johnny's name from the radio. Johnny mentions how Rocky had changed his appearance once before, but Johnny used an old trick to catch him. Maybe it would work again. Johnny stops at a drug store for some "goop" to plaster down his hair, some black hair dye, some peroxide to get rid of his suntan, which would take time. After several days Johnny has grown a mustache, which he has dyed black as well. Johnny buys some new clothing including an apron, and a pair of thick glasses, which he can see through, but which give him a headache. Johnny acts the part of a slow-witted waiter at bar and waits for several days for someone to show up. One night a man named Barney calls another one Rocky and is told his name is Tillson, Edward Tillson. Johnny is sure that he is on the right track. The man Tillson had been there for three nights, and Johnny had not recognized him. Rocky has a beard, gray hair, has put on twenty pounds and has had his teeth fixed. The partner must be Bernard Little, a fence known to the police. Johnny stays near them but they clam up when he comes near. Tillson and Barney leave to go to see the owner. Pete Monister had been away when Johnny was hired, and probably knew all about Rocky. Johnny goes to change clothes and leave when Pete comes in and tells Johnny that he is fired, as he is not needed. Johnny leaves and is met in the alley by Tillson, who hits Johnny while Barney tells him not to shoot. Tillson tells Barney he is just going to use the butt of his gun.

Johnny vaguely remembers something hitting him, and then noise and gunshots and sirens. Johnny wakes up in a hospital with a doctor holding a hypo. Sometime later Johnny wakes up and Randy Singer is there. Randy tells Johnny that he will be ok. Randy did not know that it was Johnny who was being jumped. He had been following Rocky ever since Whisky Soder had told Randy where Rocky was. Randy tells Johnny that he had told Randy where to find Rocky seven years ago, at the Purple Hat bar. "Are you the only one who thought he could lead us to the jewels?" asks Randy. Randy does not have the jewels, thanks to Johnny. Both Rocky and Barney are dead. They have searched Rocky's house and found nothing. Johnny has a hunch that he can fake his way into finding the jewels. Johnny goes back to the Purple Hat and barges into Pete Monister's office. Pete recognizes Johnny as the waiter he fired. Johnny tells him that his desk is bugged, and Johnny tells him not to reach for a gun or he will shoot. Johnny tells Pete that he heard Pete tell Tillson when to tell Johnny to go out into the alley, but Pete plays ignorant as the to the reason. Johnny tells Pete that he knows where the jewels are and tells Pete to open the safe. Pete wants to make a deal but Johnny tells him he wants the jewels or he will kill Pete. Pete agrees to open the safe.

"The fee on this one, for recovery of the diamonds, well maybe the department frowns on such things, but half of it goes to Randy Singer, NYPD. Good man. Good Friend. Expense account total, including the ride back to Hartford, well it just about balances with what I made on my job as waiter."

## NOTES:
- COMMERCIAL #1 IS FOR CAMEL CIGARETTES.

- THERE IS A REFERENCE HERE TO JOHNNY HAVING BEEN IN THE BUSINESS ONLY SEVEN YEARS. BUT IN THE BENNET MATTER OF 1956, JOHNNY STATES THAT HE HAD BEEN AN INVESTIGATOR FOR 14 YEARS.
- CAST INFORMATION FROM THE KNX COLLECTION AT THE THOUSAND OAKS LIBRARY.

Producer:  Jack Johnstone      Writers:  Jack Johnstone
Cast:      Marvin Miller, Virginia Gregg, Forrest Lewis, Barney Phillips, Frank Gerstle, Herb Vigran, Peter Leeds

◆   ❖   ◆

SHOW:      THE RED ROCK MATTER
SHOW DATE:    5/29/1960
COMPANY:    GREATER SOUTHWEST INSURANCE COMPANY
AGENT:      JAKE KESSLER
EXP. ACCT:    $496.25

SYNOPSIS: [The opening for this program is missing.] Johnny sends a telegram to Jake Kessler with his arrangements and then flies to Las Vegas. Jake drives Johnny to Kingman, Arizona and tells him that back in '52 Ralph Garrett and Jerry Bisbee were prospecting in these parts. Ralph was ok, but the town had hoped for years that Jerry Bisbee would go somewhere else. They had gone over to Chloride to prospect near Mt. Tipson. A month or so later Jerry came back alone. He said that Ralph had left him to get a job in California. Ralph's wife claimed it was a big lie, and that Bisbee had killed Ralph in the desert. She claims that Ralph had gotten suspicious of Bisbee and did not trust him, and he would not have just left her like that. The police were called in, but no one could find a body. Mrs. Garrett had Bisbee tried, but he got off. Just last year the claim on Ralph's insurance was paid off. Bisbee moved and has not come back. Last week there was a windstorm that uncovered a body in the desert. The papers did not report that the skeleton had a bullet hole in the back of its head. A hole of the same size as the Winchester '94 Bisbee used to carry. Jake tells Johnny that only Doc Blessing can identify the body, and he is waiting in Kingman. When Johnny and Jake get to his office, there is a note from Doc Blessing telling them to wait for him. Blessing had taken over his father's practice along with all the patient records. Doc Blessing comes in and tells them that he has evidence that his father had repaired a broken femur on Ralph's leg with a steel plate back in 1942. On the skeleton is the same stainless steel plate. The skeleton is Ralph Garrett's. Jake tells Johnny to find Bisbee and bring him back to justice, that's all!

Jake tells Johnny that Bisbee left right after the trial and has not been seen again. The Kingman police have notified the state police and bulletins are out. Bisbee was a prospector and worked in some of the mines to feed his drinking. Johnny has an idea and makes a phone call to the Bureau of Mines in Washington. He gets a list of recent claims for Jerry Bisbee, and the last few have been in Nevada. Johnny is told that the Carson City office would have more information. Johnny calls Carson City, and a lady there will not give out any information without the permission of Mr. Harker. Johnny rents an old and under-powered plane to fly to Carson City. Johnny goes into town to see Mr. Harker who is reluctant to give out information until Johnny mentions murder. Johnny rents a car and drives to Virginia City, Nevada.

Johnny describes Virginia City as a fabulous monument to the Comstock Lode. Johnny describes the buildings that still stand and the historical names of the times. Johnny talks to a grizzled old man who tells Johnny that he should stay away from Bisbee, as he is crazy. He is up on Red Rock Pass, but Johnny's car will not make it, he will have to rent a horse. But if Bisbee finds him up there, he will shoot. Johnny rents a horse and heads out for the pass. Johnny finds the shack and no one is there. Johnny follows a trail to a mine and is shot at. A voice tells Johnny to get out. Bisbee tells Johnny that he knows why Johnny is there, but Johnny will not take him in. Bisbee tells Johnny that they tried him once and cannot try him twice for the same crime. Johnny waits and then hears a rattlesnake at his feet and shoots it, but there is nest of them. Johnny runs to another rock and Bisbee tells him that he can get Johnny at any time. As Bisbee approaches he tells Johnny to give up and throw out his gun. Johnny throws out his gun and Bisbee tells him he is going to shoot him. Bisbee runs behind the same rocks Johnny was behind and his bitten by the rattlesnakes.

"By the time I got over to him and hauled him out of that pit of death, half a dozen of the deadly rattlers must have struck him. He died before I could get him back to Virginia City. Yeah, justice again in one of her own inscrutable ways."

NOTES:
- COMMERCIAL #1 IS FOR PEPSI.
- COMMERCIAL #2 IS FOR CAMEL CIGARETTES.
- COMMERCIAL #3 IS DENNIS JAMES FOR KELLOGG'S ALL-BRAN CEREAL.
- TOM HANLEY AND BILL JAMES ARE THE CBS SOUNDMEN, AND ARE NOTED IN THE CAST FOR THE FIRST TIME.
- THE ANNOUNCER IS JOHN WALD

**Producer:** Jack Johnstone    **Writers:** Jack Johnstone
**Cast:** Virginia Gregg, Parley Baer, Harry Bartell, Vic Perrin, John Dehner, Will Wright, Tom Hanley, Bill James

◆   ❖   ◆

**SHOW:** THE CANNED CANARY MATTER
**SHOW DATE:** 6/5/1960
**COMPANY:** PROVIDENTIAL PROPERTY INSURANCE COMPANY
**AGENT:** JACK PRICE
**EXP. ACCT:** $1,121.00
**SYNOPSIS:** Jack Price calls Johnny and he tells Johnny that he is now working for

Providential Property Insurance there in Corpus Christi. He has a claim for $465,000 that Johnny can help them with. Jack offers Johnny a big commission and expenses. Johnny agrees to grab the first flight he can.

Johnny flies to Corpus Christi, Texas and Jack meets Johnny at the airport and starts to take him to the Robert Driscol Hotel. Jack tells Johnny that the case is the Canary Diamonds, the most perfectly matched set of yellow diamonds in the world. The diamonds are set in a necklace, a brooch and a solitaire on a ring. They were stolen from Mrs. Clara Barnes Smithwick Tyson Brownfield. Jack tells Johnny that Mr. Tyson made his money in oil and died a few years ago, leaving his wife a considerable fortune in the stock market. A year ago she married young Augustus Brownfield. He is about forty-five, ten years younger than his wife. Jack is sure that August Brownfield is on the level. He has a small cannery business that handles items for the fancy restaurants. Jack tells Johnny that the diamonds disappeared a few weeks ago. Mrs. Brownfield had gone out that night, and was placing a set of earrings back in the safe when she noticed that the diamonds were gone. But other items were left in the safe. The police found nothing, only that it was a professional job. Only the Brownfields knew the combination. Johnny wants to go visit the Brownfields that evening. Jack and Johnny arrive at the mansion and Mrs. Brownfield is described as a real lady, and Gus a devoted husband. Mrs. Brownfield cannot imagine anyone taking the stones out to be sold. They tell Johnny that they had gone to a party that evening. On the way they passed the packing plant and Gus noticed the lights were on. The party was boring so Gus had gone to the factory for a few minutes to turn off the lights and do a few odds and ends and then went back to the party. Johnny mentions that Mrs. Brownfield had mentioned the stones being broken up, and she refuses to talk to Johnny.

Gus tells Johnny that his business is not profitable and Johnny is told to leave. Johnny tells them that the notion of the stones being broken up has given him an idea. Johnny leaves to play a hunch. The reaction of Gus Brownfield only seems to clear him in Johnny's mind. Johnny also agrees that the job was done by a pro. Later that night Doug Johnstone visits Johnny in his room. Doug had run into Jack Price and learned that Johnny was there, and he just had to stop in and give Johnny a hand. If he didn't, Jack his brother would not forgive him. Johnny tells Doug that he would like drag Jack into the cases so he could help him solve them. Doug tells Johnny that he has figured out the case, and the thief is in the local jail. Doug tells Johnny that Brownie is an old friend and he knows about Gus' cannery and the people who work there, especially one man in the shipping department. Doug had done some digging and found a story about a jewel heist that has a picture the man from the shipping dock. The heist happened fifteen years ago. The man is Les Murdock. Johnny recognizes him as "Fingers" Murdock who went to jail in 1945 for twenty years. Doug tells Johnny that Murdock was paroled two years ago for good behavior. The police arrested him and he finally confessed. Doug has solved the case, but the police do not have the jewels, so Johnny's work is not done, as he has to get the diamonds back.

Johnny visits the jail, but Murdock will not tell him anything. He would rather spend time, get out and then spend the money from the jewels. Johnny remembers Murdock's international connections. Johnny calls Brownfield and learns that a shipment had been made recently to the Imperial Import Company in Paris, and it should arrive today. Johnny calls Louis Du Marsac in Paris and Johnny asks him what he knows about canaries. Louis tells Johnny that they are for the birds. Louis has never heard of the Canary Diamonds. But for $500 he will find out about them. Louis tells Johnny that the smuggler and fence Dubisaint has closed his antiques shop and opened a new produce company, the Imperial Import Company. Johnny agrees to wire Louis $100 if he can tell Johnny where Dubisaint is. Johnny flies to Paris, France and goes to the Imperial Import Company warehouse with a 39-cent solution to the problem. Johnny meets a surprised Dubisaint and asks him to help find some stolen jewels. Johnny wants to look for the latest import of canned goods from the states. Over Dubisaint's objections Johnny goes into the warehouse and finds ten cases of fruit from Corpus Christi. Johnny tosses Dubisaint a can opener and tells him to open the cans until they find the diamonds. Johnny tells Dubisaint that his .38 is all the authority he needs, unless Dubisaint wants Johnny to call the police. Reluctantly Dubisaint shows Johnny which case has the dented can with the diamonds in it.

"Thanks to its Paris representative, the company was able to arrange for getting the stones back to the U.S. As for Dubisaint, well I suspect he was long gone when the police arrived at his place. Expense account total, including the trip home, $1,121.00 and uh, don't forget about my commission on this one."

NOTES:
- COMMERCIAL #1 IS FOR PEPSI.
- COMMERCIAL #2 IS FOR CAMEL CIGARETTES.
- COMMERCIAL #3 IS DENNIS JAMES FOR KELLOGG'S ALL-BRAN CEREAL.
- THE ANNOUNCER IS JOHN WALD

Producer:   Jack Johnstone          Writers:   Jack Johnstone
Cast:       Virginia Gregg, Jack Edwards, Russell Thorson, Stacy Harris,
            Jack Kruschen, Forrest Lewis, Tony Barrett

◆   ❖   ◆

SHOW:        THE HARRIED HEIRESS MATTER
SHOW DATE:   6/12/1960
COMPANY:     INTERNATIONAL CASUALTY & LIFE INSURANCE COMPANY
AGENT:       BERT LARKIN
EXP. ACCT:   $7,604.25
SYNOPSIS: Bert Larkin calls Johnny and he has a $300,000 problem that must be distributed shortly. Johnny tells him just to send the money to him and asks Bert

if he is expecting a policyholder to kick the bucket. Bert tells Johnny that William Makepiece Everly lives in the Piney Woods part of Hartford, Connecticut. His doctor tells Bert that Everly does not have long to live, and Everly wants to see Johnny. Johnny thinks that there is something funny going on here, and Bert agrees.

Johnny buys gas and drives to the Everly estate. Dr. Thatcher meets Johnny at the door and Johnny is taken to Mr. Everly's room. On the way the doctor tells Johnny that he has contacted Everly's nephew but has been unable to find his niece. That is why Everly wants to talk to Johnny. Johnny meets Everly and he tells Johnny that Doc Thatcher does not know what he is talking about, and that he will probably outlive both of them. He has willed everything to his niece. She has been kind and loving and has stood on her own feet. But, Everly does not know where Nancy is, and he wants Johnny to bring her there while he is still alive. Everly tells Johnny that he wants nothing to go to his stepson Alfred Harker, a worthless no-good idle sponge who has even forged checks to get his money. If he finds out that Nancy gets everything there is nothing he would not do. Everly gets upset and tells Johnny that Nancy does not know about Alfred, and Johnny must protect her from him at all cost. Everly is given a shot and goes to sleep. Dr. Thatcher tells Johnny that he had told Alfred that Nancy is the sole heir. But where to look?

Dr. Thatcher tells Johnny that Alfred had kept track of where Nancy is living. Johnny is sure that Nancy is a sitting duck for Alfred. Johnny gets Alfred's address and heads for his apartment. The building super tells Johnny that Harker had packed and left on a trip the previous day. Johnny gives the super a five spot to get into the apartment and it is obvious that Harker left in a hurry. Johnny finds a schedule for flights to Los Angeles and Nancy's address in Philadelphia. Johnny flies to Philadelphia, Pennsylvania and goes to Nancy's apartment, but she is not there, but Mary Ann Hooper is. Mary Ann knows Nancy from the office, and she tells Johnny that Nancy has been transferred to the Los Angeles office of Hardon, Karmon and Fisher, the ad agency. Mary Ann invites Johnny in for a drink, but Johnny runs to the airport to get a flight to Los Angeles, California. Johnny goes to the Hardon, Karmon and Fisher office in Los Angeles, and Nancy is not there and will not come in that day. Johnny gets her address at 1308 Pandora Ave in West Los Angeles and grabs a cab there. So Nancy is in Los Angeles and so is Alfred, so there is no time to waste. At Nancy's address the landlord tells Johnny that she lives there, but left a few hours ago on a trip with a nice young man. They were headed for Los Vegas, probably to get married. Ouch!

Johnny calls the Las Vegas marriage bureau. He asks if Alfred and Nancy have been there and tells the clerk to keep them from being married. The clerk tells Johnny that he needs some legal grounds to not issue a license. Johnny cabs to the Lockheed Air Terminal and charters a plane to Las Vegas, Nevada. Johnny cabs to the license bureau, but learns that Nancy and Alfred have gone. The clerk tells Johnny that they left on foot, so they must have gone somewhere close to get married. Johnny gets a list of nearby wedding chapels and people where the wedding could take place and starts to check them out. Johnny finally finds a wedding in progress for Alfred Harker. Johnny interrupts the ceremony and tells Nancy that Alfred is marrying her for her money. Nancy tells Johnny that she has no money, but Johnny tells her that she will have plenty of money when her uncle dies. "Ask Alfred, as he knows all about it." Johnny tells her. Johnny tells them that Uncle William is leaving Alfred nothing, so the quickest way to get the estate is to marry Nancy. Alfred tells Nancy he can explain everything and Nancy asks why Uncle William would write to Alfred and beg him to marry Nancy? Johnny asks to see the letter, but Alfred has thrown it away. Johnny tells Nancy that the letter was forged, just like the checks Alfred had forged over the years and Alfred admits it. Alfred pulls a gun and tells them that nothing will stop this wedding. Johnny calls him foolish and Alfred pulls Nancy to him. Nancy struggles to get away from Alfred and he shoots at Johnny, but Alfred is slugged by Johnny.

"Pulling his gun was a big mistake. Yeah, the people there in Vegas, the police, just don't go for that sort of thing. As for any charges the company may care to make against him, well that's up to the legal department. The main thing is to keep him away from her permanently. Incidentally, I managed to get her home to see her uncle before he died.

NOTES:
- COMMERCIAL #1 IS FOR PEPSI.
- COMMERCIAL #2 IS FOR FRITO CORN CHIPS.
- COMMERCIAL #3 IS DENNIS JAMES FOR KELLOGG'S ALL-BRAN CEREAL.
- BOB BAILEY WELCOMES STATION KFBK IN SACRAMENTO, CALIFORNIA.
- I FIND IT INTERESTING THAT HARDON, KARMON AND FISHER IS A WONDERFUL PLAY ON HARMON-KARDON, WHICH OWNS FISHER ELECTRONICS. THESE WERE VERY HIGH-END CONSUMER STEREO COMPONENTS DURING THE 1960's.
- THE ANNOUNCER IS JOHN WALD

Producer:   Jack Johnstone        Writers:   Jack Johnstone
Cast:       Virginia Gregg, Jean Tatum, Lillian Buyeff, Marvin Miller, Russell Thorson, Bart Robinson, Forrest Lewis, Sam Edwards, Harry Bartell

◆   ❖   ◆

SHOW:         THE FLASK OF DEATH MATTER
SHOW DATE:    6/19/1960
COMPANY:      WESTERN INDEMNITY COMPANY
AGENT:        PAUL PETERS
EXP. ACCT:    $431.00
SYNOPSIS: Paul Peters calls Johnny from Los Angeles and asks Johnny to come out and help the race to outer space. Johnny demurs on a ride in a space capsule,

but Paul tells him that they have no proof that the deaths were not accidental, but if Johnny can prove otherwise . . . Paul tells Johnny that he is convinced that sabotage is involved.

Johnny flies to Los Angeles and cabs to Paul's office on the "miracle mile." Paul has rented a car for Johnny to drive up to Santa Barbara, California and the Bar-Bar Manufacturing Company, named after Dr. Joseph L. Barrum and Dr. Ralph T. Barnwell. They are top grade scientists who are working up on a capsule that will allow a man to return from outer space. They will make millions if the capsule works. So far two men have died during the testing of the device, but no one knows why they died. The doctors do not want Johnny poking around, but the insurance company insisted, so Johnny is expected. Johnny drives up to the plant and meets Dr. Barnwell who is pulling something from the ocean. He tells Johnny that the test must work this time. The last time the tests were successful, but the man inside died. This time Dr. Barrum is manning the capsule. Barnwell opens the capsule and discovers that Dr. Barrum is dead.

Barnwell tells Johnny that there was nothing in the capsule to kill him. An autopsy will be held, but he know that the result will be death by suffocation. Johnny asks about the possibility of poisonous gas, but Barnwell tells him that any known poison would have been spotted. He tells Johnny that nothing would go into the capsule without them knowing. Barnwell tells Johnny that oxygen is provided in the capsule, and that the tanks have been taken out. Johnny tells him that not knowing how the capsule works will be to his advantage. Johnny tells Barnwell that he has a hunch. "Do you believe in hunches, doctor?"

Johnny's hunch is a long shot. Johnny gets a pass that allows him full access to the plant. Johnny looks at the rooms where the oxygen bottles are kept and talks with Pete Prosser. Pete tells Johnny that he opened the release valves on the capsule to equalize the pressure. Pete tells Johnny that the oxygen bottles come from his storeroom. He does not know who fills up the bottles. They are always full when they are needed. The bottles today were checked, and they were ok. Pete has the bottles ready to empty into the air and opens the main valves on the bottles. Johnny asks Pete to close the valves and offers to empty the bottles for Pete so he can go home. Johnny goes to another lab and gets a couple of white mice and takes them back to the oxygen bottles where Johnny empties the tanks into a cage holding the mice. After a minute the mice keel over and die.

Johnny now knows how the others were killed and remembers the phrase "cui bono;" who benefits. Johnny goes to Dr. Barnwell's office with an oxygen bottle and sets it on his desk. Johnny tells him that the bottle has a leaky valve. Barnwell tells him that too much oxygen is dangerous in the room, but Johnny promises to be careful. Johnny asks if Barnwell got out of the government because the government found something on him. Johnny tells Barnwell that he opened the capsule today to dissipate the poison gas from the tank. Johnny tells Barnwell that now that the capsule works, it is worth millions that will all go to him. Barnwell gets very nervous about the oxygen bottle and wants out of the room. He tells Johnny that the bottle has hydropenoxygen gas in it. Johnny tells

Barnwell that if he moves he will shoot him, and Barnwell tells Johnny that he killed all of the others to get the money from the capsule and stars choking. Johnny tells him to relax, that all the tank has is pure oxygen, I hope!

"I don't know, of course, but I suspect that the government will take over. Maybe they will have something in that space rescue capsule. But as for money, royalties, I am sure that Barnwell won't be able to spend much of it in prison."

NOTES:

- HYDROPENOXYGEN GAS IS ANOTHER JACK JOHNSTONE INVENTION.
- TOM HANLEY AND BILL JAMES ARE MENTIONED AGAIN FOR THEIR SOUND WORK.

Producer: Jack Johnstone      Writers: Jack Johnstone
Cast:        Paul Dubov. Parley Baer, G. Stanley Jones, Forrest Lewis, Tom Hanley, Bill James

◆　❖　◆

SHOW:          THE WHOLLY UNEXPECTED MATTER
SHOW DATE:    6/26/1960
COMPANY:      UNIVERSAL ADJUSTMENT BUREAU
AGENT:          PAT MCCRACKEN
EXP. ACCT:      $0.00

SYNOPSIS: Pat McCracken calls, but Johnny tells him that the answer is NO. His bags and fishing tackle are all packed. He has tickets and the answer is no. There is nothing that cannot wait a week or two until he gets back. "And so help me, if he tries chasing me out to the airport . . ."

Johnny cabs to the airport in a cab that gets a flat tire and almost makes him miss his plane. Johnny gets on his shuttle plane to New York and the stewardess knows all about Johnny from his radio program. Johnny tells Claire that he is going to Lake Mojave to do some fishing. Once airborne, Johnny moves to his assigned seat, right beside Pat McCracken. Johnny tells Pat that in New York, they will part company. "You want to bet on that?" asks Pat.

Johnny switches flights in New York, but Pat gets on at the last minute. Pat tells Johnny that he had checked with the airline to get the flight. Pat is betting that Johnny is going to the Lake Mojave Resort, and has brought his fishing tackle also. They can go fishing together, provided that there is no talk of business. Pat notices a man who looks familiar, and he was on the flight from Hartford also. "Are you sure you do not know him?" Johnny asks Pat. Pat and Johnny get to Las Vegas with the same man on the flight. Pat and Johnny get a hotel room and visit the casinos, and Johnny manages to collect $365 at the dice table. Pat meets up with Johnny and tells Johnny that he has seen the man watching Johnny at the dice tables, but Johnny discounts it; lot of people from Hartford come to Las Vegas.

Johnny and Pat drive to Lake Mojave Resort across the colorful desert. Johnny and Pat get rooms and a promise of their limit every day. Buster Favor tells Johnny that a Mr. Malloy is there from Hartford also. Pat gets a phone call and his secretary calls about the Morley Warehouse fire. She tells Pat that Johnny had told the police how to catch "Scar Face" Maloney. Well, Maloney has escaped and is after Johnny. Pat tells Johnny that he is now on the expense account. "Malloy, Maloney, hmm." wonders Johnny. Buster tells them that Mr. Malloy does have a scar and had asked when Johnny was going to be arriving. Buster tells Johnny that Malloy has gone out fishing. Johnny and Pat go fishing as well. Johnny gets a boat and searches the lake for Maloney. Johnny finally decides to do some fishing in a deep cove. Pat notices a man on the rocks over the cove and Pat sees blue steel aimed right at Johnny.

Johnny rocks the boat to the ledge and tells Pat to act like Johnny is still there. Johnny climbs the rocks up towards the man on the rocks with his gun drawn. Johnny finally spots the man with . . . an old pair of binoculars. Johnny trips and the man spots him. He tells Johnny that he is Franklin J. Malloy, and he did not realize that Johnny was that jealous of his fishing secrets. Malloy tells Johnny to put his gun down and tells him he is a real fan of Johnny's. A lady friend who works for the airline had told him that Johnny was going to Lake Mojave, so he came out to spy on Johnny hoping that he could learn to catch some of the nice big fish out here the way Johnny does. Buster arrives and tells Johnny that the Hartford police have picked up Scar Face Maloney and he is back in the pen. Johnny tells Buster to take Pat out where he can catch an old bluegill or a carp. "Mr. Malloy and I are going out for some real lunkers; a couple of secret spots I know. Ok, Mr. Malloy?" "Bless you, Mr. Dollar," replies a very happy Malloy.

"Well, you sure can't win 'em all especially when there isn't anything to win. And at long last I got in a full week of fishing at Lake Mojave. Expense account total? Well Pat, you add it up, you're paying for it!"

NOTES:
- THE FIRST COMMERCIAL BREAK IS AN **AFRS** SPOT ABOUT THOMAS EDISON AND THE PHONOGRAPH.
- THE SECOND COMMERCIAL BREAK IS AN **AFRS** SPOT ABOUT THE SEVENTH AMENDMENT AND THE RIGHT TO A JURY TRIAL.
- THE THIRD COMMERCIAL BREAK IS AN **AFRS** SPOT ABOUT THE ORBITAL ASPECTS OF THE MOON, AND SIMON NEWCUM'S CORRECTION OF LUNAR ORBITAL DATA ALLOWING A FLIGHT TO THE MOON.
- THE ANNOUNCER IS JOHN WALD

**Producer:**   Jack Johnstone          **Writers:**   Jack Johnstone
**Cast:**        Virginia Gregg, Shirley Mitchell, Larry Dobkin, Sam Edwards, Barney Phillips, Edgar Barrier

◆ ❖ ◆

| | |
|---|---|
| SHOW: | THE COLLECTOR'S MATTER |
| SHOW DATE: | 7/3/1960 |
| COMPANY: | FLOYDS OF ENGLAND |
| AGENT: | GEORGE REED |
| EXP. ACCT: | $371.20 |

SYNOPSIS: George Reed calls and tells Johnny that he is in an embarrassing situation. A very important client of the company is Orson Ogleby Terwilliger. He is a collector and lives near Bethel, New York. Go on down and see him. He wants a change made to his policy for $500,000 double indemnity. George tells Johnny that he is calling from the city jail. He was rushing and was speeding a little and argued with the officer, and his hearing is not until tomorrow. George offers to double the expenses and give Johnny a $100 besides. All Johnny has to do is find out what the change is to the policy. Johnny tells George that every time George gives Johnny a simple assignment, he is lucky to get out alive.

Johnny flies to New York where he rents a car and drives to Bethel, New York at the foot of the Catskills. The town is very small, and Johnny is told how to get to Terwilliger's home by a local man who is interested in buying the property. He tells Johnny that maybe Mr. Terwilliger will show Johnny his gun collection. Johnny drives on up to the estate on a rough road. On the way Johnny spots a wrecked car lying against a boulder by the road. Johnny finds a body, and the driver's license belongs to Mr. Orson Terwilliger.

Another car approaches from the house and a woman rushes to the car and collapses and cries in Johnny's arms. She is Blanche Terwilliger and she knows who Johnny is. She is glad that Johnny found him, because of all the awful things the people say. They drive to the house and call the doctor and the police. Chief Allen and the doctor arrive and go to the accident site. They tell Johnny that it was an unfortunate accident, and that the bruises on the body are all from the crash. Johnny tells them that that one of the bruises, a round one behind the ear, was not made by something in the car. Johnny is told not to let his imagination run away with him. They take the body to the house and the chief asks Johnny if Mrs. Terwilliger is a beautiful woman. Too bad she and Mr. Terwilliger never . . . Blanche calls to make arrangements for the funeral and to have the car removed. Blanch asks Johnny to stay and help to fill out the insurance papers. Johnny wants to get a hotel room, but Blanche tells him to stay and have dinner. Johnny goes to get a room at the Emmers Hotel and calls George, who tells Johnny that Blanche is the only beneficiary. Johnny feels that Terwilliger wanted to change the beneficiary, but the beautiful Blanche played it smart.

Johnny notes that the only things he has to go on are some rumors about the Terwilligers and the mark behind his ear. Johnny buys a flashlight and goes to search the accident scene. Johnny finds something with ordinary fletching and a big stone head. Blanche walks up with a gun and threatens to shoot until she recognizes Johnny. Johnny takes the gun and tells her that there must have been some Indians in the area. After dinner Blanche tells Johnny that she is glad to have him there. Johnny wants to see the weapons collection and tells her that with her figure she must have been an athlete in college. Johnny holds her hand and she tells Johnny that she was a girl athlete. Johnny tells her that her husband must have had to drive slowly on the road, slowly enough so that someone could not have missed him with a peashooter. Johnny tells her that archery was her best event. He could tell by the calluses on her hand, which came from a heavy hunting bow. Blanche admits that she killed her husband, "but if you knew what I had to put up with" she tells Johnny. Johnny tells her that she took a chance on murder to get a million bucks, but she lost.

"And according to the law, no person convicted of the murder of the decedent shall be entitled to any portion of the estate, including the insurance. But just don't forget my commission on that amount. Expense account, including room and board at Emmers, and the trip back to Hartford, $185.60, doubled!"

NOTES:
- COMMERCIAL #1 IS FOR PEPSI.
- COMMERCIAL # 2 IS FOR NO-DOZ.
- COMMERCIAL #3 IS FOR FRITOS.
- COMMERCIAL #4 IS FOR EXLAX.
- THE ANNOUNCER IS JOHN WALD

Producer: Jack Johnstone      Writers: Jack Johnstone
Cast:     Virginia Gregg, G. Stanley Jones, Forrest Lewis, Vic Perrin, Bart Robinson

◆　❖　◆

SHOW:         THE BACK TO THE BACK MATTER
SHOW DATE:    7/17/1960
COMPANY:      CONTINENTAL INSURANCE & TRUST COMPANY
AGENT:        ED BARRENGER
EXP. ACCT:    $25.80

SYNOPSIS: Ed Barrenger calls and he has made reservation for Johnny to fly to New York on the next flight. He will meet Johnny at the airport and give him the details. The reason is to prevent a murder.

Johnny buys gas and drives to the airport where Ed is waiting. Ed gives Johnny the address for Lucien R. Fletcher, who owns an ad agency. Ed tells Johnny that Fletcher had called him just before Ed called Johnny. The agency is a small one, and Fletcher's partner is William Spade. Fletcher feels that Spade is out to murder him. Spade is out of town and is due back today. Fletcher is not the kind to go off half-cocked, so get to New York City. Johnny tells Ed to call Lt. Randy Singer, and Johnny leaves.

Johnny calls the 18th precinct and gets Officer Conroy. Conroy calls Johnny a private eye, and Johnny calls Conroy a copper, terms which neither like.

Conroy tells Johnny that Randy is not there, and he does not know if Randy got any calls. Johnny tells Conroy to tell Randy that he is at 614 East 52nd, and Conroy tries to tell Johnny that Randy has gone there with the police doctor but Johnny cuts him off. Johnny cabs to the address and goes to the Fletcher apartment, only to find Randy there. Randy takes Johnny to the library to see a dead Mr. Fletcher.

Randy tells Johnny that Fletcher was killed with one bullet through the heart. Fletcher must have known who did it to let the man get that close. Ed Barrenger had called, and Randy had tried to call Fletcher but could not get him at the office or at home, so Randy came over and found Fletcher. The doc thinks that death happened around midnight. The bullet was placed just right to penetrate a back support corset for his sacro-lumbar problem. The shot had to be placed just right or the steel ribs would have deflected it. Johnny tells Randy that a .38 packs a lot of wallop, but Randy tells Johnny that it was a .22. Barrenger had told Randy that Fletcher had been expecting problems and who he suspected. Johnny starts to tell him about the partner when there is a knock at the door. Johnny opens the door to find Mr. Spade who has just arrived from Philadelphia with an urgent matter for Mr. Fletcher. Johnny questions Spade about his trip and Spade shoves his plane ticket into Johnny's hand. Randy tells Spade that he was in Philadelphia when his partner was shot. Johnny tells Spade to go to the office to take care of his important matter. Johnny tells him that they will be in touch if they hear anything. Randy wonders what is going on with Johnny, and Johnny tells him that he knew Spade was in Philadelphia, and had checked the plane schedules when he arrived. Johnny is sure that Spade was on the plane. "So it seems that there was no way for Spade to have murdered Fletcher," states Randy. "Wanna Bet?" asks Johnny.

Johnny calls the Fletcher agency and Spade is not there. The operator tells Johnny that Spade had called her from the airport when he arrived. Johnny calls various airline offices and finally talks to the stewardess who remembers Spade because he was always punching the call button claiming he was airsick. Johnny wonders if he was purposely calling attention to himself. Johnny calls the Belleview Stratford hotel and the desk clerk tells Johnny that Spade had come in around ten and gone right to his room. He left at eight this morning and mentioned the importance of catching a plane to New York. Johnny is sure that Spade had murdered Fletcher, but where was he before he checked in? Johnny is sure that Spade went to New York under another name, killed his partner, and came back in time to leave at eight. But how to trick him? Johnny cabs to Spade's office and Spade tells him that he is busy with his new client. The desk is piled up with all the newspapers and Johnny tells him that the papers would only print a story if Fletcher were dead. Spade tells Johnny that they ran the business together, but Fletcher was a difficult person. Spade blames the problems on the pain from Fletcher's back problem. Johnny tells Spade that he had plenty to benefit from by killing Fletcher, and maybe Fletcher even gave him a key to his apartment. Spade tells Johnny that it is bad enough that Fletcher is dead. Johnny corrects him by saying that that is the second time you said Fletcher was dead.

Johnny tells him that no one said that Fletcher was dead. Johnny tells Spade that he should have thought about the corset, and that little .22. Spade tells Johnny that he saw him fall that he was sure he had killed him as he had aimed for his heart. Oh, no. Johnny tells Spade that Fletcher is dead and makes a phone call.

"Ah, it's funny how a man like that can plan a thing so carefully, carry it out so carefully and then when he is caught, lose his head and blab all over the place. Heh, he even made a grab for the little .22 pistol he'd used and had right there in his desk. That will be good as evidence."

NOTES:
- COMMERCIAL #1 IS FOR PEPSI.
- COMMERCIAL #2 IS FOR NO-DOZ STAY AWAKE-TABLETS.
- COMMERCIAL #3 IS DENNIS JAMES FOR KELLOGG'S ALL BRAN.
- THE ANNOUNCER IS JOHN WALD

**Producer:** Jack Johnstone    **Writers:** Jack Johnstone
**Cast:** Virginia Gregg, Jean Tatum, Frank Gerstle, James McCallion, Herb Vigran, Jack Edwards, Forrest Lewis

◆ ❖ ◆

**SHOW:** THE RHYMER COLLECTION MATTER
**SHOW DATE:** 7/31/1960
**COMPANY:** MONO GUARANTEE INSURANCE COMPANY
**AGENT:** FRED PORTER
**EXP. ACCT:** $35.50

**SYNOPSIS:** Fred Porter calls and asks Johnny if he remembers the theft of the Rhymer collection, a set of miniature paintings done on porcelain. Six were stolen and the insurance company had to pay out $20,000. Wilbert Rhymer has contacted Fred and he wants to talk to Johnny. Fred is sure that Wilbert wants to talk to Johnny about the miniatures, as he demanded that only Johnny be brought into the case. Johnny questions why he should get involved and Fred reminds him that the company investigator was Jerry Pitcher, the investigator who was suspected of complicity in some of his cases. The police could never prove anything so the insurance company fired Jerry and warned the other companies. Johnny asks where Jerry is now, and Fred does not know. Johnny will take the first train.

Johnny takes a train to Philadelphia, Pennsylvania and cabs to the Rhymer Gallery, where Mr. Rhymer is described as "very, very British." Rhymer tells Johnny that he had wished Johnny had been assigned to the case originally, as he could have recovered the miniatures, which were vastly under insured. Rhymer is sure that Pitcher was involved with the theft because of the way he handled the investigation. Rhymer gives Johnny a check for $4,050 that he will mail to the insurance company that day. The amount is exactly what the insurance company paid him for one Pellegrini. Rhymer tells Johnny that the Pellegrini has been returned and that Rhymer has a buyer for it, Mr. Charles Cunningham who is a regular customer. The painting was found inside the door under the mail slot tied up in some brown wrapping paper. The Pellegrini is very well known, and Johnny thinks that it might be too well known to sell, so it was returned. Johnny wonders about the black market in Paris, and Rhymer notes that a lot of famous works have been sold there. Rhymer has no idea why the painting was returned, unless the thief was a connoisseur who could not destroy the paintings and realized he could not sell them. Johnny notes that the return rules out Jerry Pitcher. Johnny asks for the string and wrapping paper, but is told that it has been thrown out. Rhymer had called for Johnny hoping that he could return the rest of the paintings. Johnny jokes that he could just sit and wait for the others to be returned. When asks what his next move is, Johnny has no idea.

Johnny cabs to Fred Porter's office and updates him on the return of the Pellegrini. Johnny is told that a complete investigation was done at the time of the theft and Jerry Pitcher was assigned because he seemed to know something about art. Only Rhymer thought that Pitcher was involved in the theft and it was then that the insurance company learned of Pitcher's reputation. Fred is sure that Jerry has skipped the country. Johnny has an idea and calls his old friend Louis Du Marsac, who knows all about the black market. Louis asks for $1,000 but Johnny only asks if Du Marsac has heard of Jerry Pitcher. Louis has never heard of Jerry, but he knows that the Rhymer collection of miniatures was on the black market and for $200 Louis tells Johnny that the paintings were bought 3 years ago for a gallery in the US. For $250 Louis tells Johnny that Mr. Rhymer bought them himself. For $400 Louis tells Johnny that he last saw them six months ago in the gallery of his dearest friend, that scoundrel and crook Francois Dubisaint who could not sell them because they were too hot. Louis does not know who Dubisaint was trying to sell the paintings for. Johnny is sure that Louis knows what the paintings are worth, and tells Fred that that information would really cost. Johnny has an idea and goes to the Museum of Art and talks to Mr. Kingman who tells Johnny that a fool stole the paintings, as they could never be sold without the thief being brought to justice. Kingman tells Johnny that the paintings were originally not worth much. But now that their history is known, they are worth around $200,000. Kingman tells Johnny that a Mr. Cunningham would pay dearly to buy a Pellegrini. Johnny tells Kingman what has happened and gets the address of Mr. Cunningham. Johnny calls Cunningham, but he is out of town. Johnny gets a room at the Belleview Stratford and next morning Johnny calls Cunningham again. Johnny is told that the value of the paintings has gone up recently. Johnny suggests to Cunningham that he could be part of a fraud investigation, so Cunningham tells Johnny that he is going to pay Rhymer $20,500 for the Pellegrini. Johnny suggests he call the bank and stop payment on the check. Johnny cabs to Fred's office and they go to Rhymer's gallery together. Johnny asks Fred about Rhymer's policy premiums and Fred notes that there is a large one slightly over due. Johnny wonders how bad business is and how much Rhymer owes. At the shop Johnny is told that another of the paintings, a Lombardi, has been returned just like the other was. Rhymer has saved the string and wrapper for Johnny, but Johnny tells Rhymer that he was stupid if he did not wear gloves while he wrapped the paining up. Johnny tells Rhymer that he brought Johnny in so that Rhymer would not be suspected. Johnny asks about Rhymer's last trip to Europe and he confirms that it was in June. Johnny wants to look at Rhymer's bank statements for the past year, or would you like to talk to the police? Johnny tells Rhymer that he bought the paintings on the black market and notes that he should have been alarmed when Rhymer noted that the paintings were under insured. Johnny tells him that they were insured before their real value was known. By the time he did know, Rhymer had already pulled the fake robbery and collected the insurance to keep his business going. Rhymer is told he tried to sell the paintings in Paris but they were too hot. He needed money and now he could sell them for $200,000. He made them reappear one at a time and gave the cock-and-bull story about the thief not wanting to be caught. Rhymer asks Johnny if he returned the others and gave a full confession, if the police would be gentler with him.

"Son of a gun, why do they do it? Won't they ever learn? What's the matter with people anyhow, some people that is. Oh, Well. Expense account total including the tip back to Hartford, $35.50. And Freddy don't forget, a nice fee on this one, as well as a check to les char gris over there in Paris."

NOTES:
* THE ANNOUNCER IS DAN CUBBERLY

Producer:   Jack Johnstone          Writers:   Jack Johnstone
Cast:       Harry Bartell, Ben Wright, Forrest Lewis, Junius Matthews,
            Marvin Miller

◆   ❖   ◆

SHOW:        THE MAGNANIMOUS MATTER
SHOW DATE:   8/7/1960
COMPANY:     UNIVERSAL ADJUSTMENT BUREAU
AGENT:       PAT MCCRACKEN
EXP. ACCT:   $0.00
SYNOPSIS: Johnny is called by an addled Alvin Peabody Cartwright, who offers Johnny the position of First Vice President of the Magnanimous Accident Insurance Company. Alvin tells Johnny that it is his new company, and tells Johnny to come to Texas. Then Pat McCracken calls and tells Johnny that he has to go to Corpus Christi, Texas. Come on over, or else!

Johnny goes to Pat's office and is given a drink. Pat tells Johnny that he has a wealthy client named Alvin Peabody Cartwright who is running his own company in Texas, but does not know what he is doing. Johnny is told that Alvin sells a policy and pays off for any accident, and Pat has proof. Pat has a claim to settle a case through the Universal Adjustment Bureau, and he is afraid that the racketeers will be involved soon.

Johnny goes to Corpus Christi, Texas and goes to Alvin's office, which is a madhouse. Johnny closes the office for the receptionist Laura, but Alvin tells her that he is waiting for his new Vice President. Laura tells Johnny that she listens to the cases, and is convinced that Alvin is crazy for selling insurance to people who do not deserve it. No one can argue with Alvin, but it must be stopped. Johnny uses his American Express credit card to wire money to Smokey Sullivan in Los Angeles. Johnny calls Smokey who tells Johnny about a phony racket he used to pull with his trick knee, and Johnny tells Smokey to come to Texas. Johnny gets a room at the Robert Driscol hotel and has dinner. That evening Johnny tells Smokey of his plan.

The next day Smokey buys a $10,000 injury policy. Johnny talks to Alvin who tells Johnny about his philanthropic company. Johnny warns him that crooks will take advantage of him, but Alvin tells Johnny that he is too smart for them and makes a bet with Johnny. If Johnny wins, Alvin will close the company and cancel all of the policies. Later Smokey comes in and tells Alvin that he fell in a building and injured his knee. It is such a sad story that Alvin wants to pay immediately. Smokey signs a release and gets the money. Smokey pops his knee back into place, thanks Alvin for the money and tells him that he will tell all of his friends. Alvin agrees to close the company.

NOTES:
- THE ANNOUNCER IS DAN CUBBERLY
- STORY INFORMATION OBTAINED FROM THE KNX COLLECTION IN THE THOUSAND OAKS LIBRARY

| | | | |
|---|---|---|---|
| Producer: | Jack Johnstone | Writers | Jack Johnstone |
| Cast: | Howard McNear, Lawrence Dobkin, Virginia Gregg, Vic Perrin | | |

◆　❖　◆

| | |
|---|---|
| SHOW: | THE PARADISE LOST MATTER |
| SHOW DATE: | 8/14/1960 |
| COMPANY: | NEW BRITAIN MUTUAL INSURANCE COMPANY |
| AGENT: | AL TURNER |
| EXP. ACCT: | $50.00 |

SYNOPSIS: Al Turner calls and asks how old Johnny is. Johnny tells Al that on his next birthday he will be uh, why? Al thinks that is it time for Johnny to enter a home for the aged. Al wants Johnny to go to the Mackley Rest Home in Frog Mountain, New York. Sudden death is the problem; four in a row and Al covered three of them. The beneficiary for all of them was the Mackley Rest Home.

Johnny buys gas and drives the Kingston area and then to Frog Mountain, New York. Johnny drives by a rest home and stops. A man introduces himself as Justin Perry. He asks if Johnny has some relatives to send to him at the Paradise Rest Home. Johnny learns from Justin's son Eddie Perry that the

Mackley place is a mile up the road. Johnny drives up the road to the Mackley Rest Home, a new place but one lacking in warmth. The guests were just sitting around. In the office Johnny meets Peter Mackley, who knows that Johnny is coming. Johnny notices that the place must have cost a lot of money, and Pete tells Johnny that the place will not pay for itself for years. Johnny tells him that a few more policies will really help in that regard. Pete tells Johnny that he is not the police, so get out!

Pete admits that it was too bad that the four people died. The deaths were unexpected, even by Dr. Nathan Way in Kingston. Pete tells Johnny that Mr. Partley slipped on the porch. The others were natural causes, and Johnny wonders if poison was involved. Dr. Way comes in and Pete tells him that Johnny thinks the deaths were deliberate. Dr. Way tells Johnny that the financial debt is to be expected for a new place. Pete tells Johnny that he and his wife have been in the business for fifteen years, ever since his parents died. He started in Pennsylvania and moved to New York because the air is better and they had to close down, as the buildings were substandard according to some new code. Dr. Way tells Johnny that some of the clients had moved with Pete from Pennsylvania. Dr. Way tells Johnny that he had suggested that people leave the insurance to the rest home, and they thanked him for the idea. Pete tells Johnny that unless he loses his reputation he will do ok. Dr. Way tells Johnny that he did not do autopsies as the victims were up in years. Johnny wants the bodies exhumed and autopsies done; and he is going to check on Dr. Way. Dr. Way leaves to start the process. Johnny drives to Kingston and gets a room and meets with police Lt. Art Connelly. Art is glad that Johnny is looking into the deaths. Mackley is well thought of and Dr. Way is a fine man and the best one to do the autopsies. Johnny tells him that Mackley had a lot of guts to compete with Justin Perry, as a lot of the people in town were partial to Perry. Doc Way comes in and tells Johnny that he can do the autopsies that night and that he will call Johnny when he is finished. Johnny goes to his room and falls asleep. Johnny hears the door close and the lights go out. Johnny is slugged and goes out.

Johnny wakes up the next morning with Doc Way tending a head wound and offering some medicinal brandy. Doc tells Johnny that he has done the autopsies and came to tell him the results. Doc tells him that three of the deaths were from poison and Johnny calls Lt. Connelly. Doc tells Johnny that the only drugs those people got were the ones he prescribed. Lt. Connelly calls and Johnny tells him that Pete Mackley had slugged him that night. Lt. Connelly tells Johnny that he is wrong as Lt. Connelly had Mackley at headquarters all night. Doc tells Johnny that the prescriptions were always made up at Mrs. Peason's pharmacy and they go there. Johnny asks Mrs. Pearson if she stocks a drug called sodium theramelicilate. She tells Johnny and Doc that she keeps a supply for the local vet. Johnny hears a motorcycle pull away outside and Mrs. Pearson tells him that it was the boy makes all the deliveries. She finds the bottle, and a lot of the tablets are missing. Johnny and Doc Way chase after the motorcycle on a winding mountain road. Young Edward Perry finally crashes while looking back. Doc and Johnny rush up to the wreck and Edward tells Doc that he knew they had gotten wise that he was putting the poison in the medicine, and that his father made him do it. If enough people died at the Mackley place they would come to the Paradise and put Mackley out of business.

"Ah, I don't know. I don't know what the courts will do. Ask me, Justin Perry murdered his son just as much as though he had done it with his own two, eh, I don't know."

NOTES:

- THE ANNOUNCER IS JOHN WALD

**Producer:** Jack Johnstone      **Writers:** Jack Johnstone
**Cast:** Virginia Gregg, Harry Bartell, Edgar Barrier, Sam Edwards, Stacy Harris, Junius Matthews, Forrest Lewis

◆ ❖ ◆

SHOW: THE TWISTED TWIN MATTER
SHOW DATE: 8/21/1960
COMPANY: FLOYDS OF ENGLAND
AGENT: GEORGE REED
EXP. ACCT: $196.55

SYNOPSIS: George Reed calls Johnny and asks if the name Franklin P. Franklin means anything. Johnny remembers that he was a World War I fighter pilot, "Franky the Flying Fool." George tells Johnny that Franklin died the other day, leaving $110,000 to be divided between his two sons. Randolph buried his father but George cannot find Phillip. Come on over and I will tell you what I know.

Johnny ponders how Floyds hands him some funny cases that really pay off as he cabs to George's office. George tells Johnny that Franklin was a daring aviator, and flying was an obsession for him. Franklin crashed into a mountain and was injured during the war. If it were not for his family's money, he might have ended up in a mental institution. Franklin was able to recover mentally and physically and raise a family and manage the family money. The mother of the twins died when they were born. Both of the boys inherited some of their father's instabilities. Randolph is a salesman for a machine company, and Phillip is a henchman working for Carlo Frizetti in Chicago. Johnny remembers working on a case concerning Frizetti once. According to Randolph, his brother Phillip died a year ago but no proof has been offered. Johnny is told there will be a commission based on the face of the policy and his expenses, reasonable expenses.

Johnny goes to visit Randolph Franklin in Hartford, Connecticut and the doorman is not sure if Randolph is in or not, as he is always on the road. The doorman tells Johnny that the phone is broken so Johnny takes the elevator up. Randy is in his thirties with shifting eyes and terribly nervous. His head shakes violently and his hands shake and he is constantly adjusting his tie. Randy tells Johnny that Phillip is dead and it was his fault. Phillip worked for Carlo Frizetti and Randolph had gone to Chicago on business and met with Phillip. He told him to come home and get a job or dad would cut him out of the will. Randolph tells Johnny that he has to find Phillip. He tells Johnny that when he thinks about an aircraft accident he gets blackouts and cannot remember things. Randy tells Johnny that the plane ran into a storm and crashed into a mountaintop. It was an accident just like his father's. When Johnny mentions that his father's crash caused him to lose his sanity, Randy tells Johnny that his father was not insane, only terribly scared. Only Randy, the pilot and Phil were able to crawl away from the wreckage of the airplane, each going in a different direction. Randy had been unconscious for several days when he was found. The plane was burned completely so there was no way to find Phillip's body. Johnny tells Randy that he seems to be the sole beneficiary of the insurance. Johnny asks for his employer's name and address and tells him that he has a crazy hunch, a term that Randy hates. Johnny tells him that he is going to continue the search for his brother, so stick around.

Johnny goes to New York City and checks with Randy's employer. Johnny learns that Randy had been a good salesman, but since the accident he has not sold much, and has had long unexplained absences and they were seriously considering dropping him. Thus he seems to have a need for the insurance money. Johnny goes to Chicago, Illinois and meets his friend Smokey Sullivan, who takes him to Carlo Frizetti's hangout. Johnny knocks and Randy opens the door. The man tells Johnny that he is Phil Franklin. Carlo comes in and welcomes Johnny as a friend, for once. Carlo tells Johnny that the man is Phil Franklin. Half the time he is there helping out, half the time the boys are out looking for him. Carlo tells Johnny that a year ago he cracked up in an airplane accident. Phil brings cocktails and Johnny leaves quickly with a highball glass and flies back to Hartford. Johnny drives to Randy's place, but he is not there. Johnny pays the doorman to call him when Randy comes back and to keep his mouth shut. Five days later Charlie the doorman calls Johnny and tells him that Randy is back. Johnny stops at the police lab and picks up Lt. Tim Waverley and gives him the highball glass with instructions. They then drive to Randy's apartment. Johnny tells Randy that he has been away, and he seems confused. Johnny introduces Lt. Waverley and asks Randy where he was. Randy does not know where he was. Lt. Waverley shows Randy the glass and he does not remember seeing it and gives it back to Lt. Waverley. Lt. Waverley looks at the glass and tells Johnny that the prints are identical. Johnny tells Randy that since the crash he has been both himself and his brother Phillip. Randy tells Johnny that he had a blackout after Johnny was there and mentioned the crash, and Johnny tells him that he talked to him in Chicago, and the fingerprints prove it. Johnny struggles with Randy and ends up slugging him. Johnny takes Lt. Waverley's gun and fires five times in Randy's direction until he faints. Johnny and Lt. Waverley take Randy over to see Doc Parsons, the psychiatrist. Johnny confirms with the doctor that it was a guilt complex that brought about the nervous condition. Doc Parson tells Johnny that Randy had built up the complex at the shock of his brother's death in the plane crash, and Randy felt responsible for Phillip's death. During the blackouts' he really felt he was Phil. Johnny is told the shots could have shocked Randy to death, and Johnny tells the Doc that he only did it after he realized what was going on. Doc Parsons tells Johnny that the combination of the gunshots, the pain of being hit and the exposure as Phillip all acted to offset the terror of the plane crash. Dr. Parsons feels that Randy will probably recover with the proper treatment. "And, don't you ever try anything like this again, young man!"

"Yeah, Doctor Parsons was right. After this I'll leave the shock treatment bit to people like him, who really know what they are doing. Expense account total $196.55. There'll be no fee on this one.

## NOTES:
- THE ANNOUNCER IS JOHN WALD

Producer:   Jack Johnstone        Writers:   Jack Johnstone
Cast:        G. Stanley Jones, Frank Gerstle, James McCallion, Jack Moyles, Herb Ellis, Russell Thorson

◆   ❖   ◆

SHOW:           THE DEADLY DEBT MATTER
SHOW DATE:    8/28/1960
COMPANY:      TRI-STATE LIFE & CASUALTY INSURANCE COMPANY
AGENT:         DON BOOMHAUER
EXP. ACCT:     $200.00

SYNOPSIS: Don Boomhauer calls Johnny from Sarasota, and business is booming in the real estate market. Don mentions that Earle has gone to California, and it seems that he might just stay out there. With Earle out of town, Don has been holding down the Tri-State office, and now he has a problem. The client is Thomas Patterson. A few years ago when he was living up in Jacksonville, Thomas was the sole witness to a murder. The killer was tried and sent to state prison. (Uh-oh!) So now the killer is loose, and Don feels that Patterson's life is not worth a hill of beans. Johnny will catch the first plane he can.

Johnny flies to Sarasota, Florida and meets with Don Boomhauer. Don tells Johnny that the policy is for $70,000, and Johnny starts figuring his commission. Young Tommy lived up in Jacksonville and worked as a milkman. One morning in 1951 he saw a man named Casey Carey kill a man named Harker who was busy shooting at him at the time with a .38. The jury did not buy self-defense because there was a feud between them, and Carey did not get life because Harker had a police record, so Carey was sentenced to ten years. It was Patterson's testimony that convicted him, and he swore that he would get even. Patterson has a small family and the threats scared him. Later Tom was left some money and legally changed his name to Thomas K. Patterson and moved to Venice and started the Excellent Dairy Company. In Jacksonville he bumped into a man on the street one day, looked into his face and started running. It was Casey Carey. Tom could not believe it, but he looked into the records and found that Carey had gotten out on good behavior. Tom feels that Carey is out to get him.

Don tells Johnny that Tom was not sure that Carey had recognized him. Tom went home and bought a Colt .32 and got a permit. Don tells Johnny that a couple months ago Carey moved to Venice and got a job at a service station. Tom tried to avoid him, but when they met Carey was the one who avoided Patterson. Johnny wonders if Carey is playing a cat-and-mouse game to build up the suspense and prolong the agony. Don is sure Carey is succeeding. Tom was a nervous wreck when he called and asked for Johnny to come down. Don reminds Johnny that Carey swore he would kill Tom, and Don is sure of it. Johnny borrows a car and drives to Venice to see Tom and the police. Johnny finds Tom in his office and he is beside himself with fear. Johnny takes him to the police and the chief, Brad Younger is cooperative and knows all about Casey Carey. Chief Younger tells Johnny that he had learned all about Carey from his employer, and he had talked with Carey. There was no reason to tell Tom and get him upset. Tom gets excited and tells the police that they should have done something. Tom demands protection when the chief tells him that Carey is ok. Chief Younger asks Tom to turn in his gun and Tom refuses. Johnny won't help him, so he will have to help himself. Johnny promises the chief he will get the gun from Tom. After lunch together, Johnny drives Tom to Carey's house for a showdown. Johnny knocks at the door and a neighbor tells Johnny that there is evil in there. The woman had heard a shot and has called the police. Tom and Johnny enter and find Carey shot through the head with a .32. Chief Younger arrives and arrests Tom for murder.

Tom tells the chief he is wrong, but Chief Younger has Tom's gun. Johnny tells Chief Younger that he had to drag Tom to the house. The chief tells Johnny that a young officer named Billy Barker had given him the gun. It was found beside the road over by Midnight Pass. Barker had stopped to fix a tire and found the gun. Tom is insistent that he had left the gun at home. The Chief Younger tells them that Tom had come over here and killed Carey after he left the chief's office. Johnny tells Chief Younger that Tom had been with Johnny all afternoon. The chief tells them that the bullet and the medical exams will prove that Tom did it. Maybe Chief Younger was right when the report proves that the bullet came from Tom's gun, and the neighbor heard the shot just a few minutes before they pulled up. Johnny decides to play a wild hunch. Johnny calls Don Boomhauer and he tells Johnny that the man Carey killed was named Harker, not Barker. Johnny makes another call to Mike Kirby on the city room of the Jacksonville Times Press. Mike searches the files and finds some revealing information. It seems that the boy was working on the police force there, trying to live down the family reputation. A month or so ago he quit and moved. Johnny is sure that he is still a cop. Johnny goes back to police headquarters and asks the chief to call one of his officers in. The chief calls Billy Barker and Johnny asks him why he changed his name from Harker, and why he moved here after the man who killed his father, Casey Carey, moved here? The man you swore you would get for killing your dad. You worked on the force in Jacksonville, and then moved here when Carey did, biding your time. This afternoon you heard us talking. You got Tommy's gun some how and went to the house and killed him. When Johnny asks Billy to go to Sarasota and take a paraffin test, he pulls his gun, but Johnny is able to get it away from him. Johnny asks the chief to release Tom.

Johnny goes fishing with the chief the next day. Remarks: "The fishing was great."

**NOTES:**
- THE FIRST COMMERCIAL BREAK IS AN **AFRS** SPOT WITH A MINI-BIOGRAPHY OF EDISON AND HIS ELECTRIC LAMP.
- THE SECOND COMMERCIAL BREAK IS AN **AFRS** SPOT ABOUT THE IMPORTANCE OF SILVER OVER GOLD IN MILITARY INSIGNIA.
- THE ANNOUNCER IS JOHN WALD

Producer: Jack Johnstone      Writers: Jack Johnstone
Cast: Virginia Gregg, Russell Thorson, Barney Phillips, Sam Edwards, Bert Holland, Stacy Harris

◆   ❖   ◆

| | |
|---|---|
| SHOW: | THE KILLER KIN MATTER |
| SHOW DATE: | 9/4/1960 |
| COMPANY: | FLOYDS OF ENGLAND |
| AGENT: | GEORGE REED |
| EXP. ACCT: | $0.00 |

**SYNOPSIS:** George calls Johnny and Johnny asks if it is George Reed. Floyds of England? So that's the big insurance company that sent you out to nail Felix Caine a couple months ago? George tells Johnny that the insurance company must have paid him a lot of money to clear up the robbery and nail Felix. Maybe you even got a big bonus because now Felix is dead. That's killing for money isn't it? And his girl, you had someone trick her into telling you where to find him, so she's doing a stretch now because she was in with them. Remember when you tagged Felix and he fell on his own gun and killed himself? Is that the way you said it happened? Nobody could prove otherwise, and you were pretty lucky then. You got away with it because Felix's brother was on the lam on the west coast. They were awful close all their life. Now that Felix is dead, it means that the other one will get even with you. My name is George, George Caine, Felix's brother.

So what if I hadn't killed Felix Caine. It does not make any difference now. But why would George call me to warn me? Johnny calls George Reed and asks if he knows where George Caine is. George Reed does not know where he is. Johnny realizes that George must be in New York City, so he is going to go there and contact Randy Singer. Johnny trains to New York and talks to Randy. The police want George Caine for a charge of assault with intent to kill. Johnny reminds Randy that Felix fell on his gun, but Randy reminds Johnny that he will not convince George, as George is very clever and Randy does not know where he is. With the new direct dialing for long distance you cannot tell where a call is coming from. Randy is glad that Johnny is letting them look for George, now go on back to Hartford, and be sure you do go. Randy threatens to call all the precincts in New York and tell them to arrest Johnny and bring him to Randy if they see him. Randy tells Sgt. Conroy to take Johnny back to Hartford. So be a good little boy. By the way, Conroy is a fan, so you can tell him all about your adventures on the way home.

Sgt. Conroy escorts Johnny all the way to his apartment, at Johnny's expense. Conroy (with a deep Irish accent) asks Johnny to finish a story and calls the office. The phone rings and George tells him that the New York cops will not help him. "You killed my brother and I am going to kill you." Then Betty Lewis, "the girl he is going to marry someday" calls and there is a click on the line. Johnny tells Betty he was out on business, but not with any other girls. Betty asks if Johnny has forgotten about their date in New York tonight? Betty is staying with Nancy Spaulding at 1624 McDougal Alley. The line clicks again and Johnny dismisses it. Johnny tells Betty not to be surprised if they have a police escort. Johnny gets ready to fly to New York when there is a knock at the door. It is Mr. Perry, the building super. He tells Johnny that the young man who rented the room next door left in a hurry, and Mr. Perry has found a wiretap in the room. The man was named John Jones. Johnny gets a description and calls Randy Singer. Johnny promises to call Randy when he gets to the Spaulding apartment. Johnny remembers that Betty had helped him get Felix, so Johnny rushes to get to New York ahead of George Caine.

Johnny flies to New York and cabs to the Spaulding apartment. Johnny knocks and asks for Betty, but Nancy tells Johnny that Betty left with a detective. From the description Johnny realizes it was George Caine. Nancy tells Johnny that they went to meet him. They went east, and the driver was Tommy, who sits at the cabstand on the corner. Nancy spots the cab, back outside and Johnny rushes down to the cab. Tommy tells Johnny that he took them to the Bowery. On the way there a police car stops them for speeding and Johnny tells Officer Tim O'Reilly that he is in a hurry. O'Reilly tells Johnny to get into the squad car, and Randy is there waiting for him. Randy tells Johnny that everything is under control. George is not taking Betty anywhere. They had followed the cab and nabbed him at a boarding house and Betty is waiting for Johnny at the station house.

"The expense account, forget it, forget all of it. I only hope that someday, somehow I can repay Randy Singer, over his dead body though, because all he cared about was getting his hands on Caine. And, for some silly reason he seemed to think that I'd been helping him. What a guy."

NOTES:

- THIS PROGRAM MENTIONS DIRECT DIALING, WHICH WAS STARTING TO BE IMPLEMENTED IN THE EARLY 1960'S.

• THE ANNOUNCER IS JOHN WALD

| | | |
|---|---|---|
| Producer: | Jack Johnstone | Writers: Jack Johnstone |
| Cast: | Virginia Gregg, James McCallion, G. Stanley Jones, Herb Vigran, Jack Moyles, Junius Matthews, Lillian Buyeff, Paul Dubov | |

◆ ❖ ◆

| | |
|---|---|
| SHOW: | THE TOO MUCH MONEY MATTER |
| SHOW DATE: | 9/11/1960 |
| COMPANY: | FLOYDS OF ENGLAND |
| AGENT: | GEORGE REED |
| EXP. ACCT: | $0.00 |

SYNOPSIS: George Reed calls and tells Johnny that he has just received a frantic call from Alvin Peabody Cartwright. Alvin is an important client, and he wants Johnny on the West Coast immediately. Johnny tells George that the last time Alvin called someone was trying to kill him and the time before that was to give Johnny a Christmas present. Alvin is in Santa Barbara at the home of Rockland Rockwell, another extremely wealthy client of Floyds'. If this case involves Mr. Rockwell, it will be plenty serious. Johnny will be in touch.

Johnny flies to Los Angeles and rents a car. Johnny drives to Santa Barbara, California and gets directions to the Rockwell home, which is on ten acres and is well tended. The house is like a castle built of native stone. Alvin Cartwright meets Johnny at the door and tells Johnny that he wants Rocky to sell him the house and that the situation is serious. Alvin tells Johnny that he has had reason to think his life was in danger in the past, but poor old Rocky. Rocky is very brave and keeping up with his parties, pretending that nothing is wrong. All Rocky does is entertain, what with all his money. Right now Rocky and his friends are out on a foxhunt. Alvin is worried because he is going to be murdered.

Alvin tells Johnny that Rocky will be murdered unless Johnny can do something about it, but first Alvin takes Johnny on a tour of the house. The house was fabulous with marble, paneling and other expensive appointments. After the tour, Alvin tells Johnny that he might be able to buy the house for two or three million dollars. Alvin spots the party returning and Rocky is leading them. Alvin goes to get Rocky who turns out to be an obese, florid type of man who wheezes when he breathes. Johnny wonders how he (or the horse for that matter) survived the foxhunt. Rocky tells Johnny that many years ago he pulled a fast one on Lord Jacob Hunter Ashley. Ashley never even knew that Rocky had done it. Rocky had put him out of business, ruined him. Now Ashley's son Marvin, an actor, has found out what Rocky had done. A few months ago Marvin had written to say he was coming to take revenge for the poverty of the family. Rocky got a call a few days ago that Ashley was in the States. Rock told Ashley that he was a changed man, and would give him anything he wanted, but Ashley told him that he was going to kill Rocky. Rocky is sorry, but Johnny wonders if it is because he is in danger. Unless Johnny finds him, Ashley will murder Rocky.

Alvin tells Rocky that he is ashamed of him and tells Rocky that he made all of his money honestly; he inherited it! But it is Johnny's duty to protect Rocky. When Johnny tells him he is going to call in the police, Rocky tells Johnny that Ashley might even be in the house now, as he does not know all of his guests. Rocky only knows that Ashley is between thirty-five and forty and Johnny must find him. Johnny does not like this case because of Rockwell. At dinner Rocky is a good host, and Johnny does not spot anyone suspicious. After dinner Rocky tells Johnny that Ashley must be there, and Johnny must stay with him. They go down to the billiards room to play pool. None of the players call themselves Ashley. One of the players, Mr. Gibson mentions a "massa" shot, and he seems to recognize Johnny's name. Gibson tells Johnny that he runs a brokerage business in San Francisco. Johnny talks to Mr. Sam Edwards, who looks familiar, and excuses himself to get a drink. Gibson invites Johnny to have lunch with him the next time he is in San Francisco. They can go to the Cliff House. Johnny tries to sink the eight ball and manages to rip the cover of the table. Johnny tells them that the play is over for Gibson, but that is not his name. Johnny tells the group that Gibson had talked about making a "massa" shot, and only the British call it that. Americans call it a "masse" shot. Only and actor could make that slip. Johnny tells him that his real slip was calling the restaurant "Cliff House," not "Cliffhouse." Ashley pulls a gun to shoot Rocky and Johnny slugs him with a pool cue. "Hmm. Not as rusty as I thought!"

"You know something? Dear old Alvin Peabody Cartwright furnished the high-powered legal talent that got Ashley off with nothing more than deportation. And needless to say, Cartwright is really through with Rockwell, as it would be. Expense account, aw forget it. Alvin P. handed me a check big enough for three expense accounts.

NOTES:
- THIS IS AN **AFRS** PROGRAM WITH THE COMMERCIALS CUT OUT
- A MASSE SHOT IS ONE WHERE THE CUE BALL IS STRUCK IN SUCH A FASHION AS TO MOVE IN A CIRCULAR PATH, AROUND A BLOCKING BALL.
- SAM EDWARDS PLAYS A CHARACTER WITH HIS OWN NAME—TYPICAL JACK JOHNSTONE
- THE ANNOUNCER IS HUGH DOUGLAS

**Producer:**    Jack Johnstone      **Writers:**    Jack Johnstone
**Cast:**      G. Stanley Jones. Howard McNear, Chet Stratton, Marvin Miller, Sam Edwards

◆    ❖    ◆

**SHOW:**      THE REAL SMOKEY MATTER
**SHOW DATE:**    9/18/1960
**COMPANY:**    PHILADELPHIA MUTUAL LIFE & CASUALTY INSURANCE
**AGENT:**      HARRY BRANSON

EXP. ACCT:        $621.00

SYNOPSIS: Harry Branson calls Johnny and reminds him how he had convinced Harry to sell a policy to Smokey Sullivan. Harry is not sure if something has happened.

Johnny goes to Philadelphia, Pennsylvania where Harry tells Johnny that he did not say that anything was wrong, after all, Smokey is a criminal. Johnny reminds Harry about all the cases Smokey has helped him with. Harry shows Johnny a newspaper with the headline "Toy Factory Burned, work of Smokey Sullivan." The article relates how Smokey's body was found in the ashes, and was identified by a ring. Harry has tried to find Smokey but he has not been able to find him. Harry tells Johnny that he must find the real Smokey.

Johnny goes to the police and meets with Capt. Fletcher who takes Johnny to the morgue where Johnny sees Smokey's ring. Capt. Fletcher tells Johnny that by naming a suspect he has put the others off guard and tells Johnny to find Smokey. Johnny searches for Smokey and calls Marty Ross, a newspaper reporter and plants a story. Johnny rents a car and calls the police with the license number. Johnny calls Marty and then goes out and almost runs down a policeman, and Marty sees it and reports it. Johnny is put in jail and Capt. Fletcher comes to see him, but Johnny will not tell him why he did what he did.

Three days later Johnny goes before the judge who tells Johnny that his car was a deadly weapon and of the reporter who saw the accident. Johnny is told that Smokey Sullivan came to help and went to the scene of the fire and recognized the work of a crony called "The Twin" who wore the same type of ring that Smokey had. The judge tells Johnny that the newspaper article had worried him. Smokey enters the courtroom, and the judge tells Johnny that the next time he has a case, do not scare the police.

NOTES:
* THE ANNOUNCER IS JOHN WALD
* BOB BAILEY CONGRATULATES STATION KNX ON THEIR 40TH ANNIVERSARY.
* STORY INFORMATION OBTAINED FROM THE KNX COLLECTION IN THE THOUSAND OAKS LIBRARY

Producer:    Jack Johnstone        Writers    Jack Johnstone
Cast:        Harry Bartell, Stacy Harris, Vic Perrin, Lou Merrill, Tom Hanley, Bill James

◆    ❖    ◆

SHOW:        THE FIVE DOWN MATTER
SHOW DATE:   9/25/1960
COMPANY:     EVERYONE
AGENT:
EXP. ACCT:   $0.00

**SYNOPSIS:** Betty Lewis calls Johnny and comments about the concert that afternoon. "Let's make a day of it and have lunch, take a walk in the park, go to the concert, go somewhere and get married and have dinner together and find something to do this evening," offer Betty. "Sure, why not—whoa. Somewhere along the line I heard something about marriage. You know how I feel, but this job of mine," complains Johnny. "Dollar you dope" remarks Betty. The phone rings again but is it not Betty, it is Pat McCracken and he has an assignment and is coming right over. The phone rings again and it is George Reed, and he has an emergency regarding Alvin Peabody Cartwright. Johnny tells George that he is sorry, but he has a personal matter to attend to. "More important than murder?" asks George.

Three calls in five minutes all requesting my services. Johnny starts to call Betty when Harry Branson calls, and he needs Johnny for a case. Johnny tells him he will call him back. The phone rings again and Earle Poorman is on the line. Earle wants Johnny to come down, and Johnny tells him he will call back. The phone rings again and Buster Favor is on the line. Buster tells Johnny that since he is going to Los Angeles, he will drive over and meet him. The phone rings again and Alvin Peabody Cartwright is on the phone. Alvin tells Johnny that it is vital that he see him at his summer place in Beverly Hills. This time it is more serious, and Alvin cannot talk to Johnny about it on the phone. There is nothing more important Alvin implores.

Johnny muses that all of them require Johnny to be on the west coast. Johnny calls back all of the callers, but there is no answer. Johnny cabs to the airport and gets a call at the gate. Louis Du Marsac is calling. He must see Johnny. Johnny runs onto the plane. In New York, Johnny runs into Randy Singer who needs him to handle a case on the west coast. Randy tells Johnny that he will beat him there on a jet flight, but Johnny thinks that they are all full. Johnny wires everyone on a stopover in Chicago. In Los Angeles, California Johnny runs into Smokey Sullivan, who has a car for him. Smokey tells Johnny that it is awful about Alvin; you will never believe it.

Johnny and Smokey drive to the Cartwright house. Johnny knocks on Alvin's door and Alvin answers and tells him that he did not think Johnny would make it, what with all the bodies in the library. Bodies! Johnny goes to the library with his gun drawn. Inside the floor is strewn with the bodies of six people. Huh? Wait a minute. Among the bodies are Pat and George, and Johnny asks if he should put them out of their misery. Everyone gets up and congratulates Johnny. Alvin takes Johnny's gun from him, and it goes off! Pat McCracken tells Johnny that this gathering marks the end of 5 years of Johnny's series of investigations for a pretty good line up of insurance companies. So Happy Anniversary! It is also five solid years of the broadcasts of these cases on CBS. You have performed a service throughout this country to the insurance companies, no question about it. Your broadcasting has helped to expose a lot of crookedness, fraud, that sort of thing. Has saved the insurance companies a lot of money. And that means it has saved the people, their clients, the people who listen to your program every week. It saved them a lot of money too. Incidentally these CBS shows of yours have provided a lot of entertainment, a lot of pleasure to millions. In other words, Johnny, a lot of people think mighty well of you, and with very good reason. Pat has made a list of the people most involved in his cases, and Alvin demanded the right to give this party to show you how much we love and appreciate you. Johnny is flabbergasted, and almost breaks up, especially when Betty walks in, promising not to make Johnny marry him, not yet anyway. Alvin tells Johnny that he can have anything he wants, and Johnny only asks to hold on to the friendship of people like them.

"Oh, mighty wonderful people, all them, some others too, I mean behind the scenes in the job of bringing you these radio reports week after week. The associate directors on the show: Kenny Hodge, Bob Shue. The announcer Johnny Wald. A mighty wonderful technical crew: Bob Chadwick, Bill James, Tom Hanley, and I mean Jack Johnstone our producer and director who, he is the guy who makes it . . . what was that Jack? Ok. Give them a lot of credit, huh. Because believe me, they deserve it."

NOTES:
- THE ONLY COMMERCIAL BREAK IS A SMALL SEGMENT FOR EXLAX
- THIS IS A FIFTH ANNIVERSARY SHOW; FIVE YEARS OF THE BOB BAILEY RUN.
- THE ANNOUNCER IS JOHN WALD

Producer:   Jack Johnstone          Writers:   Jack Johnstone
Cast:       Virginia Gregg, Larry Dobkin, G. Stanley Jones,
            Harry Bartell, Vic Perrin, John Dehner, Howard McNear,
            Marvin Miller, Forrest Lewis, Herb Vigran

◆   ❖   ◆

SHOW:          THE STOPE OF DEATH MATTER
SHOW DATE:     10/2/1960
COMPANY:       TRI-WESTERN LIFE INSURANCE COMPANY
AGENT:         HAL BARKER
EXP. ACCT:     $248.75

SYNOPSIS: Hal Barker calls Johnny from Reno, Nevada. Hal wants Johnny to come out. A client, Walter Bisbee, has died in a mining accident in Virginia City, but Hal does not think it was an accident. Hal is convinced that Walter Bisbee was murdered, and he knows who did it and why. Come on out and get the details.

Johnny flies to Los Angeles and then to Reno, Nevada. Hal meets Johnny and drives him to Virginia City, Nevada, the largest of the old mining towns of the Comstock Lode. Hal tells Johnny that due to modern mining methods, Bisbee and his partners are pretty well-off. Bill Hargrave was his partner and they have a partnership policy for $35,000, double indemnity. The accident happened in the old Catterwall #2 mine. Walter was exploring a stope in the mine while Bill had gone to Carson City for supplies. When he returned, Bill said he discovered that the stope ceiling had collapsed. Hal had talked to a state geologist who knew the mine, and he told him that there was no way that the mine should have collapsed, unless someone helped it. That is the kind of bad luck Bisbee and Hargrave have been having lately, and the insurance would have come in handy. And, the geologist found signs of a charge of nitro. The police are not holding Hargrave because without Bisbee's body, there is no proof that he is dead. Hargrave has witnesses that he was in Carson City. When they arrive at the mine, Hargrave is waving at something. Hal and Johnny go to the mine where Hargrave tells them that he had gone down there and found Bisbee. But he was murdered!

Johnny recounts how Hargrave had been the prime suspect, and how he had rigged a hoist over an airshaft and lowered himself into the mine to find Bisbee's body. Hargrave is upset that his partner had been killed over a new find. Johnny agrees to go down with the sheriff to recover the body. Hargrave tells them that Bisbee would have wanted to be buried in the mine, and all the gold in the world cannot change that. Hargrave recounts how they worked together to recover gold from a number of mines. Without his partner, Hargrave says he is finished and does not want to see another mine. Hargrave tells the sheriff to leave Bisbee there and bury him in the mine. Johnny enters the mine with the sheriff. Johnny notes that the marks on Bisbee's face indicate he was knocked down and kicked to death with a hob nail boot. They note the right footmark of the man who kicked him. The sheriff notes that Bisbee is too big to get through the airshaft, so he will have to stay down there. Johnny notes that there are marks from a new pair of boots and Johnny wonders if Bisbee was killed and then the mine was blasted. Johnny thinks a timer might have been used to set off the explosion while Bill was in town. The sheriff is convinced that Bill did not kill Walter, but Johnny is not convinced. Johnny drives to Bill's shack with Hal, and Johnny wonders if they had had a falling out, what with separate quarters. Johnny tells Hal to bring the sheriff back to Bill's place.

Johnny has an idea and tells Hal to have the sheriff take a good look at the footprint in the mine. Bill is not home, so Johnny opens the door with a pocketknife and looks for a pair of shoes and something else. On the wall is an old lever action 30/30 rifle commonly found in the west. Johnny takes the gun down and puts it on the bed just as Bill comes back. Johnny tells him that he is looking at the habits of a murdered man, and his partner. Johnny asks what kind of timer Bill used. Too bad the stope did not fill up completely. You found a way in and you told us that Walter had been killed. Johnny tells Bill of the lone the footprint and the new boots marks. The one footprint is where you stood on your right foot and kicked him with your left. And now I find a rifle with a shiny spot on the right hand side of the stock caused by a left-handed man. Bill grabs the rifle and tells Johnny that he killed Walter. Johnny tells him that he had unloaded the gun, and when Bill checks the gun Johnny slugs him. "Phew, I guess I really should have thought to take the shells out of that thing."

"So maybe there are dozens of left handed men are around Virginia City, and who know maybe there were some right-handed men who kick with their left foot. Bill just didn't happen to think of that when he confessed to killing him."

NOTES:

- THE FIRST COMMERCIAL BREAK IS AN ELECTION CAMPAIGN CONTRIBUTION PUBLIC SERVICE MESSAGE
- THIS PROGRAM IS PROBABLY ONE OF THE MOST COMMONLY MISSPELLED TITLES. IT IS USUALLY THE "STROKE OF DEATH" RATHER THAN THE "STOPE OF DEATH." A STOPE IS DEFINED AS A STEP-LIKE EXCAVATION CAUSED BY THE REMOVAL OF ORE. INCIDENTALLY, THE TERM STOPE IS ALSO USED IN "THE DEEP DOWN MATTER."
- THE ANNOUNCER IS JOHN WALD

Producer:    Jack Johnstone          Writers:    Jack Johnstone
Cast:        Hershel Bernardi, Russell Thorson, Forrest Lewis

◆  ❖  ◆

SHOW:        THE RECOMPENSE MATTER
SHOW DATE:   10/9/1960
COMPANY:     TRI-SATE LIFE & CASUALTY COMPANY
AGENT:       DON BOOMHAUER
EXP. ACCT:   $0.00

SYNOPSIS: Don Boomhauer calls Johnny from Sarasota. Don tells Johnny that Earle Poorman has moved to California bag and baggage, so Don is still running the office. Don does not have a real problem, but a client, Bill Trasker the fishing guide, is dying. The insurance is negligible, only $2,500. Bill is in a coma and keeps asking for Johnny when he wakes up. He keeps trying to give a clue to a murder. Johnny is on his way.

Johnny flies to Sarasota, Florida where Don meets him at the airport and drives towards Sarasota. According to Doc Crutcher, nothing short of a miracle will cure Bill. The insurance will be enough to bury Bill and pay his bills. Bill was asking for Johnny and was very vague and only mentioned Gerald or Gerry. Doc Crutcher is waiting for Johnny at Bill's shack. At the shack Johnny learns that Doc has given Bill the last of seven doses of a new miracle drug. Inside Bill is awake and glad to see Johnny. Bill tells Johnny that it is too late now. Bill tells Johnny to tell the police that he did it, and he mentions Gerald Thornley and then tells Johnny that he did it again. Bill passes out, but Doc tells Johnny that Bill seems to be stronger. Doc calls for an ambulance and Don agrees, so they can investigate the confession of murder and try Bill for it.

Johnny puts Bill in Don's car and drives him to the hospital. Later Don tells Johnny that something is wrong in wanting to cure Bill so that he can be investigated for murder. Don wants Johnny to investigate what Bill said, and

Johnny tells him he will try. Later Doc calls and tells them to keep their fingers crossed. Then Lt. Barney Phillips calls and Johnny asks if he knows Gerald Thornley, and that they will investigate what Bill had told them. Lt. Phillips tells Johnny that Bill was the nicest man you could ever meet. He was always doing things for others since he got there seven years ago, even though he did not have much. Johnny tells Don that he wants no part of this, but Don convinces him to continue. Johnny borrows a car and drives to Bill's shack to search for Bill's past. All of Bill's clothes have New York labels. Johnny drives to the airport in Tampa and wires Ricky Keener, a friend on the New York Times and then flies to New York City. Rick picks up Johnny at the airport and tells him that he had written a story on Thornley. He was a crooked promoter who disappeared seven years ago. The police are convinced that he was murdered. Rick tells Johnny to nail the old guy for murder.

Rick tells Johnny that Thornley made millions and took money from poor people and left them hungry. Every deal was legal at the time, but he caused a lot of real estate laws to be rewritten. The feature that Rick wrote was about how he had left enough money to pay back all the people he had stolen from. Johnny tells Rick he may get a Pulitzer Prize yet. Johnny calls Randy Singer and then goes to his office and gets a set of fingerprints for Thornley. Johnny has a hunch as he goes back to Tampa. Johnny goes to the hospital where Bill is improving. Johnny takes Bill's fingerprints, and then Bill tells Johnny his story. At police headquarters, a technician compares the prints, and they are identical; Bill Trasker is Gerald Thornley. Johnny tells the chief that the dirty real estate tactics did not bother Bill until he came down with kidney problems. Then Thornley realized that he would die one of the most hated men in the world. Giving back the money was not enough, so he arranged his own disappearance to make it look like murder so he could get away and do good for people. Johnny tells Lt. Phillips that Bill had said "no murder," and that he "did not do it." Now we know what he did. Johnny tells Lt. Phillips that Thornley is legally dead, so it is Bill Trasker who is in the hospital.

"After sticking around for a few days to make sure that old Bill's recovery would be complete, well I changed my mind about giving Rick Keener the material for a feature, let him wonder about it. Expense account total, including the trip back to Hartford, $200 and uh, no Don, forget it, just forget it."

NOTES:
- THE FIRST COMMERCIAL BREAK IS AN **AFRS** SPOT WITH A MINI-BIOGRAPHY OF CYRUS W. FIELD, WHO LAID THE FIRST ATLANTIC CABLE.
- THE SECOND COMMERCIAL BREAK IS AN **AFRS** SPOT ABOUT THE 14TH AMENDMENT.
- THE ANNOUNCER IS JOHN WALD

| | | |
|---|---|---|
| **Producer:** | Jack Johnstone | **Writers:** Jack Johnstone |
| **Cast:** | Russell Thorson, Bart Robinson, Parley Baer, Barney Phillips, Dick Crenna, Herb Vigran | |

◆ ❖ ◆

| | |
|---|---|
| SHOW: | THE TWINS OF TAHOE MATTER |
| SHOW DATE: | 10/16/1960 |
| COMPANY: | INTERNATIONAL LIFE & CASUALTY INSURANCE COMPANY |
| AGENT: | MICHAEL J. KENDRY |
| EXP. ACCT: | $416.00 |

SYNOPSIS: Michael J. Kendry calls Johnny from Lake Tahoe. He is at the Seven Pines Lodge in Al Tahoe. Johnny comments on the great fishing in the lake, and Kendry tells Johnny that just what he might be doing, fishing for the body of Marvin W. Smedly. Huh?

Johnny flies to San Francisco and rents a car to drive to Lake Tahoe, Nevada along Route 50, which goes through a series of old mining towns. Johnny comments on the beauty of Lake Tahoe and it's clear blue waters dotted with boats and bathers. Johnny also comments on the bawdy gambling places on the Nevada side of the lake. At the Seven Pines Lodge, Johnny meets Kendry. Johnny gets a room next to Kendry and goes to talk to him in his cabin. Johnny is told that Smedly was a wealthy client. Johnny had passed a small stone house on the way in, and that is where Smedly lived with a housekeeper, Mrs. Turner, and twin nephews. Mrs. Turner woke up this morning to the sound of a shot. She went to see if the twins had heard it but they were not there. She remembered that Tracy had said he would be out gambling all night, and Alfred was at a house party at the upper end of the lake. She did not want to awaken old Mr. Smedly, so she decided it was a backfire and went to bed. In the morning she found the library a mess, and the safe opened. She told the police that Smedly used to get up at night and count his money in there. He did not trust the banks and kept all his money in the safe. The police were called and they found a set of footprints going down to the lake and signs of a body being dragged to the lake. Kendry is sure that it was one of the twins, as they had been mooching off Smedly for years. Both of the boys are in jail, but they have airtight alibis.

Johnny examines the walkway down to the lake and talks to Sgt. Bill Corter. The footprints were made from new shoes, but both of the boys dressed alike to cover up for each other. They were always mischief-makers and always swore that it was the other when they got into trouble. The police never knew which one to arrest and the boys always threatened to sue for false arrest. The uncle would always end up paying a fine to get the boys out of jail. Sgt. Corter tells Johnny that they have found the shoes, in the boy's shared closet. Johnny talks to May Turner, the housekeeper who is very upset. She tells Johnny that she knew something like this would happen. Everyone knew he kept all his money in the safe. Johnny tells Sgt. Corter that anyone could be a suspect. Mrs. Turner tells Johnny that she had warned Smedly about the boys; now one of them has gone and killed him. Johnny goes to the jail to talk to the twins, and they impress Johnny as high-spirited kids who are bored. They tell Johnny that it was good that their uncle died, as he had a lung condition and would not live too much longer. The boys tell Johnny that their uncle had toiled as a prospector, and did not want them to work, and told them that he was leaving them his insurance. One of them asks Johnny if he has proof that their uncle was killed. Al tells Johnny to look at the old prospectors who came back for handouts for suspects. Johnny goes to a local casino, and the manager tells Johnny that one of the twins was there all night at the craps table. He watches them so they do not pull tricks on the dealers, but he does not know which one was there. Johnny goes to the house where the party was held, and a girl tells Johnny that the party broke up around nine this morning, and one of the twins was there all night.

Both of the twins have alibis that are hard to break, but one of them must have killed their uncle. But something one of them said gives Johnny a hunch. Johnny calls Smedly's lawyer, Mr. Kenneth McMannis. Johnny visits him and asks one question about the will that gives Johnny a fresh start. Johnny calls Sgt. Corter and he tells Johnny that they have found the body about one hundred fifty feet out and hung up on a rock in twenty feet of water. There is a bullet hole in his head, but they will never find the gun. Johnny tells him that he is going to play a little bluff. Back at the house Mrs. Turner is told that Smedly is in the morgue. Johnny tells her that he has spoken with the lawyer, and that all the insurance goes to the twins. Johnny tells her that the rest of the estate goes to her, for her service. That was her motive. Johnny tells her that the gun and the body were found in the lake, and asks Mrs. Turner to give him a set of her fingerprints. She tells Johnny that half of her life she took care of him and he gave her nothing. She hated the boys but no one could have put it on them. He gave them all his money, so there was nothing left for her. "What's left for you now, Mrs. Turner?"

"Oh, sure. From here on in it's up to the courts, and no doubt the whole estate will go to the twins. You know something? I hate this kind of a case. It leaves a bad taste in my mouth."

## NOTES:

- THE FIRST COMMERCIAL BREAK IS A PUBLIC SERVICE ANNOUNCEMENT TO REDUCE CRIME AND DELINQUENCY BY TAKING THE FAMILY TO RELIGIOUS SERVICES.
- THE SECOND COMMERCIAL BREAK IS ABOUT THE CBS NETWORK WHERE STARS SHINE DURING THE DAYTIME, AND HAVE BEEN NAMED BY THEIR CELESTIAL FOREBEARS. THOSE NAMED ARE ARTHUR GODFREY, ART LINKLETTER, BING CROSBY, ROSE MARY CLOONEY, GARY MOORE AND DURWARD KIRBY. YOU WON'T FIND THEM IN YOUR BOOK OF THE PLANETS AND STARS. BUT NO COMPENDIUM OF SHOW BUSINESS LUMINARIES WOULD BE COMPLETE WITHOUT THEM. MONDAY THROUGH FRIDAY, YOU RADIO SET IS YOUR PERSONAL TELESCOPE ON THIS STAR-STUDDED DISPLAY, ON YOUR CBS RADIO STATION.
- THE FINAL COMMERCIAL FOR EXLAX.
- THE ANNOUNCER IS JOHN WALD

**Producer:** Jack Johnstone     **Writers:** Jack Johnstone

Cast:          **Virginia Gregg, Jean Tatum, Paul Dubov, Forrest Lewis, Sam Edwards, Herb Ellis, Tom Hanley, Bill James**

◆    ❖    ◆

SHOW:          THE UNWORTHY KIN MATTER
SHOW DATE:     10/23/1960
COMPANY:       TRI WESTERN LIFE INSURANCE
AGENT:         FRANK HARMON
EXP. ACCT:     $500.00

SYNOPSIS: Frank Harmon calls Johnny ands asks where he has been. Jack Price in Corpus Christi has been trying to get hold of Johnny. Jack has a big problem, and now it looks like Johnny has to prevent a murder.

Johnny is ready for a rest after the last case, but a job is a job. Johnny cabs to Frank's office where Frank is waiting for Jean Unworthy to arrive. Johnny is told that five years ago Eric Bean killed a prominent businessman in Ypsilanti, Michigan. Johnny remembers that it was a senseless murder because the victim did not give Bean a few dollars. Johnny was in on the case and was there during the trial when Bean promised he would get out and kill everyone involved in sending him to jail. Frank tells Johnny that Bean has escaped and over the past five days Bean has killed four of the people he promised to kill. The police have no idea where he is, or who he will hit next. Another victim is Albert Unworthy, who lives in Corpus Christi, and is insured for half a million dollars.

Frank tells Johnny that the whole case has been dumped in Frank's lap. Jean is demanding that Johnny be made a bodyguard to her father. Johnny realizes that by putting two people together, Bean can finish of his threats. Besides Johnny has to go to New York in the morning. Johnny does not want to be a bodyguard and turns the job down, until a beautiful Jean Unworthy enters the room. Boing! Johnny is totally taken by Jean, and can only say "wow!" Johnny tells Jean that he must be in New York tomorrow, but that is no problem because she has an appointment in New York tomorrow too. They can leave tonight and stay at the Pierre and have a wonderful time. Johnny flies to New York City and promises himself to behave, and gets a room at the Gotham Hotel. Dinner was over fifty bucks and the clubs were $130. The next day Johnny sees a newspaper and calls Frank Harmon to complain about the story of Johnny going to Corpus Christi. Frank tells Johnny that it was his idea to flush out Eric Bean. Johnny flies to Corpus Christi, Texas and would almost be ready to marry Jean if she asked. Doug Johnstone meets Johnny in the airport, and the story is all over the papers. Doug knows Jean's father and wants Johnny to put Jean in a cab so they can talk. Jean agrees and takes a cab home. In his office, Doug tells Johnny that Mr. Unworthy is loaded, in spite of Jean's efforts to spend it. There are rumblings that her father is getting ready to cut her off. The phone rings and Jean is on the phone and tells Johnny that Eric is in the house. There are two shots and Jean cries, "You killed him!"

Johnny rushes to the house and finds Mr. Unworthy dead, with three bullet holes in his temple. Jean tells Johnny that it was terrible and she is very upset. She tells Johnny that Mr. Unworthy had been so nice to her from the day he adopted her. She was alone when the man came in. He was short and heavyset with thick curly hair. The description is that of Eric Bean. She tells Johnny that she has never seen Bean before. He came in and knocked her down and shot her father. Doug calls the police and the family doctor. After getting a statement, the doctor who gives Jean a sedative. Before going out Jean tells Johnny that now he is in danger. Johnny and Doug go back to his office. Johnny uses the phone to call the police in Ypsilanti and talks to Sgt. Brauer. Sgt. Brauer tells Johnny that Bean has set a pattern of killing people in the area. Johnny tells Doug about how her father had gotten upset about her spending, and the too perfect description of Bean. Johnny realizes that he heard two shots on the phone, but there were three in the body. Johnny borrows a car and goes to Jean's house. Johnny tells Jean that he has found the murderer and wants to know what she did with the gun. She tells Johnny that it is in a fishpond under the library window." Not a chance for me?" she asks. "Not a chance," replies Johnny.

"And I learned about women from her. Following Eric Bean's pattern the police in Michigan were able to pick him up in less than two weeks, before he could kill again."

NOTES:
- THE FIRST COMMERCIAL BREAK IS FOR PEPSI
- THE SECOND COMMERCIAL BREAK IS FOR EXLAX
- THE ANNOUNCER IS JOHN WALD

Producer: Jack Johnstone    Writers:  Jack Johnstone
Cast:       Virginia Gregg, Dick Crenna, Frank Gerstle, Russell Thorson, Stacy Harris, James McCallion, Bill James, Gus Bayz

SHOW:        THE WHAT GOES MATTER
SHOW DATE:   10/30/1960
COMPANY:     TRI-STATE LIFE & CASUALTY INSURANCE COMPANY
AGENT:       EARLE POORMAN
EXP. ACCT:   $368.50

SYNOPSIS: Earle Poorman calls Johnny and one of Earle's important clients is in trouble, but he does not know who, what, when, where or why. Earle wants Johnny to come on down. "Ok, baby, you're paying for it."

Johnny flies to Los Angeles, California on a jet in a little over five hours. At the terminal, Johnny bumps into a man in the walkway. He apologizes and recognizes Johnny and wants to talk. He falls against Johnny again and tells Johnny that he will talk later and walks away. Earle meets Johnny who tells Earle that he was jostled, and checks to make sure he still has his wallet. Earle tells

Johnny that he loves it here, and lives on Bundy Drive. Earle tells Johnny that he got a phone call from a client who has a policy for a third of a million. Earle gives Johnny a cigarette and tells him that the man had to send for Johnny or they would lose him. Johnny tells Earle that this case makes no sense, then again there was the man in the airport. Earle asks Johnny "What goes?"

Johnny describes Earle and Mike's new house in Westwood, and the good company of the Poormans. Johnny wonders if Earle made up the whole thing. Maybe the man who bumped Johnny was the man, but why did he shy away when he saw Earl. Mike suggests that maybe the man was out to get a client and wanted to get rid of Johnny. The phone rings and the call is for Johnny. The caller asks if he really is Johnny Dollar and he admits being the man who bumped into Johnny at the airport, and who had called Earle. The caller mentions a connection with something, and when he bumped into Johnny, haven't you looked in your (click). Johnny tells Earle that the caller was the man from the airport, and the phone sounded like the wires were cut. Johnny goes to get his cigarettes from his topcoat, but Earle gives him one of his. Johnny wonders if the phone line was cut. Johnny and Earle decide to go to the office and look through the files. Johnny grabs his coat and they leave. The files are searched and the list of large policies comes to a dozen names that have to be called. Johnny muses that he should have realized he had the clue and had stopped bumming cigarettes.

Johnny calls the Branfords and Earle tells Johnny that they are in Florida. The last name is Bernard Sealegger. "Barney the Bum," "Barney the Butcher," alias "Sealegs Brown" and a bunch of other names exclaims Earl. Earle tells Johnny that Barney is wanted by the police for narcotics running. If he is the man, let him get bumped off! The policy is only six-months old, and Earle decides that they must find him. Johnny calls Lt. Jim Spaulding of the Los Angeles police. Lt. Spaulding tells Johnny that Barney had tried to call him as well, because he is helping the police. Earle reaches for a cigarette in Johnny's coat and finds a card with an address on Bundy Drive, not too far from where Earle lives. So Barney had slipped the card into his pocket when he bumped into Johnny at the airport. Johnny takes Earle's car and drives to the house and knocks at the door. Johnny notices a utility service box and when he goes to look at it a gun gets put into his back. The man takes Johnny's gun and hits Johnny when he gets smart with him. He takes Johnny to a window to see what Johnny will get after the stoolie is dead. In the window is a small air conditioner pumping air into the room with a gas bottle attached. The room is being filled with gas while Barney sleeps. Johnny struggles with the man and the gun goes off. The man starts to shoot Johnny with his own gun when Lt. Spaulding arrives.

"Yeah, Barney was still alive, but barely, which is more than you can say for his would be assassin. One of the lieutenant's bullets had caught him square in the head. So that is that."

## NOTES:

• COMMERCIAL BREAK #1 IS FOR SYLVANIA BLUE DOT FLASH BULBS TO BE

USED AT HALLOWEEN.

- COMMERCIAL #2 IS FOR US SAVINGS BONDS AND THE VARIOUS SAVINGS PLANS.
- BUNDY HAPPENS TO BE THE MAIDEN NAME OF JACK JOHNSTONE'S WIFE.
- THE ANNOUNCER IS JOHN WALD

Producer: Jack Johnstone     Writers: Jack Johnstone
Cast:     Virginia Gregg, Vic Perrin, Forrest Lewis, Frank Gerstle, Chet Stratton

◆ ❖ ◆

SHOW:        THE SUPER SALESMAN MATTER
SHOW DATE:   11/6/1960
COMPANY:     UNIVERSAL ADJUSTMENT BUREAU
AGENT:       PAT MCCRACKEN
EXP. ACCT:   $189.95

SYNOPSIS: Pat McCracken calls Johnny, who answers "Hello Master." Pat can only tell Johnny that the Rochemonte necklace is missing. The necklace is insured for $321,000, and Johnny is on his way!

Johnny cabs to Pat's office where Pat tells Johnny that the necklace was part of a collection of crown jewels. Mrs. Rochemonte, who is a wealthy widow living in Hartford, Connecticut bought the necklace. She puts the necklace in a bank vault whenever she travels, otherwise she keeps the necklace in a safe in her home, to which she is the only one with the combination, and no one has broken into it. A couple days ago she gave the necklace to a jeweler, Clayton Parker, to have it cleaned. Parker called on her in the middle of the night, barged in and gave her the necklace and told her it was paste. She then gave it to Wilson Brothers who told her that Parker was right. Pat tells Johnny about a similar case in 1956 in Chicago and one in Philadelphia in 1959, and the jeweler who discovered the switch meets the description of Parker. His shop has not been searched for legal reasons. Pat tells Johnny that Parker's shop does not have a burglar alarm or one the safe, and there is a dark ally in the rear. Pat is not asking Johnny to do anything illegal mind you. But, if someone unknown to us were to find the necklace in the shop muses Pat. "What did you say your name was?" asks Johnny. "I didn't. And yours?" asks Pat. "What's it to you." responds Johnny. "Ok?" "Ok." Johnny gives $100 to a friend named "Fingers," and that night Johnny gets into Parker's shop where he finds nothing when Fingers opens the safe. Fingers leaves and as Johnny exits the window he is slugged.

Johnny wakes up and leaves before the police arrive and cabs home. The next day Johnny is ready to call Pat and drop the case, but decides to think about the case. There are only two people who could have substituted the fake jewels, Mrs. Rochemonte or Parker. Johnny decides to go to Parker's home to search there. Johnny gets a wild idea and gets some business cards printed and buys a tank style vacuum cleaner and an old suitcase. Johnny drives to the Parker house and knocks at the door, posing as a door-to-door salesman. Mrs. Gloria Parker answers and Johnny tells her he is responding to a coupon she sent in, and gives her his card, "James Dakin, Sales Engineer." Gloria comments on Johnny's job selling and Johnny tells Gloria that she is much more attractive than other women he meets at the door. She tells Johnny that she did not send in a coupon, and Johnny tells her he is only there for the free demonstration. Johnny tells her that he will clean the whole house for her, as things have been tough this week. Gloria relents and lets Johnny in. Johnny unpacks and starts cleaning the house, regretting he did not read the instructions first. Johnny leaves the study for last. Gloria leaves to go fix some drinks and Johnny runs for the desk. In the third drawer of the desk Johnny finds the Rochemonte necklace. The phone on the desk rings and Johnny closes the drawer. Gloria comes back into the desk with a gun instead of the drinks.

Gloria tells Johnny that he should have been smarter. Her husband had just called, and he had recognized Johnny. Clayton did not call the police because he did not want them poking around. Johnny tells her that he has proof that her husband had stolen the necklace, but she sees that the desk is still locked, and tells Johnny he does not. Clayton comes in and Johnny tells him that he was welcomed into the house by Gloria. Johnny tells him to call in the police, and he tells Johnny that he does not want them involved. Clayton admits to exchanging the jewels and opens the desk, but the jewels are gone. Johnny is searched but he does not have the necklace. Clayton searches the house and makes Johnny strip to his shorts. The police come in with Pat McCracken and Clayton is shot. Pat tells Johnny the he was worried because Johnny did not call in, and he had seen Parker rush from his office, so it was obvious. "Do you want to see the necklace, somewhere inside this vacuum I didn't sell?"

"Parker is dead. His wife yammered all over the place in hopes of getting off easy. Optimist. So, that's that."

**NOTES:**

- THE FIRST COMMERCIAL BREAK IS FOR THE DANGERS OF FOREST FIRES CAUSED BY CARELESS FIRES
- THE SECOND COMMERCIAL BREAK IS FOR THE ACCURACY OF CBS NEWS
- CAST INFORMATION FROM THE KNX COLLECTION AT THE THOUSAND OAKS LIBRARY
- THE ANNOUNCER IS JOHN WALD

**Producer:** Jack Johnstone    **Writers:** Jack Johnstone
**Cast:**    Lawrence Dobkin, Russell Thorson, Virginia Gregg

**SHOW:**    THE BAD ONE MATTER
**SHOW DATE:**    11/13/1960
**COMPANY:**    MONO GUARANTEE INSURANCE COMPANY

**AGENT:**          **CULPEPPER WALKER**

**EXP. ACCT:**      **$231.20**

**SYNOPSIS:** Pat McCracken calls, and asks Johnny how old he is. "Just exactly thirty eh, why?" asks Johnny. Pat tells Johnny that he is young enough to remember how he felt when he was a young man. Pat wonders if Johnny ever got into any real trouble, and Johnny tells him that he was no mama's boy. If Johnny had a police record he would be just right for this case. Pat wants Johnny to go out and see Culpepper Walker in Little Rock. He is having problems with a kid, just a kid. And be sure to take along a pair of brass knuckles, a length of chain and maybe a switchblade knife. A real bad kid.

Johnny flies to Little Rock, Arkansas and arrives at 8:50 PM. Johnny comments on the changes in Little Rock since it was founded in 1772 and expansion in the surrounding countryside. Johnny meets with Walker the next morning and he tells Johnny all about Pete McGuire, who lives in an area called Milltown. Pete is eighteen or nineteen and works in a cotton mill. He is the only one who knows who killed Mr. Ambrose Briarly who was insured for $50,000. Briarly was driving with the payroll for a cotton mill. He had some car trouble, and it was dark before he got back on the road. His car was run off the road and someone took the $17,000 payroll. The skid marks on the road show just how it happened. The McGuire boy was caught running away from the scene by the police chief. The chief talked to McGuire and got nothing. The partners of the cotton mill are the ones who insisted that Johnny be brought out to investigate. Johnny rents a car and drives to Milltown. The police chief tells Johnny that he was there just after it happened. The bank had told him about Briarly's car trouble and he decided to make sure that the money got to the mill ok. When he got to the car, he saw another car driving away, and Pete trying to get his motorcycle started. The chief grabbed Pete, who told him he should have chased the other car. The chief tells Johnny that you could still see the tracks on the rainy road where the other car had shoved Briarly's car off the road. He could not read the tracks of the car, but he could read the marks from Pete's motorcycle. The Doc came along and Mr. Briarly said over and over that "you saw it, you tell 'em who did it," before he died. Pete is a no-good kid, and had been a troublemaker all his life. He is nothing but trouble. He is a cop hater, just like his old man who I had to kill one night in a robbery. The kid needs to go to the pen. The public defender, Percy Van Ashworthy got the judge to release Pete, but the chief will get him if he runs out. The chief tells Johnny that he will not retire with that kid running loose, him with no more money than when he started by walking a beat.

Johnny visits Percy Van Ashworthy "Ted" Tetwiler who tells Johnny that Pete has had the odds against him since he was born. He was a stupid little runt and the other kids bullied him and left him to get caught for their mischief. The chief never let up on him either, so he hates the cops. Ted got him released hoping he would open up to him. Ted sees Pete coming in and Johnny asks Ted to help him. Johnny asks Ted to tell Pete that Johnny is a troublemaker he is trying to get out of town. Pete comes in and Johnny puts on an act for Pete, who wants to talk.

Pete tells Ted that the police are following him and he knows that they are trying to trick him. Ted asks Pete to tell him what he knows, but Pete keeps quiet. Pete leaves and Johnny follows him. Johnny asks if Pete wants to learn how to shake a tail from an expert, and Johnny asks Pete if he can help Johnny learn the ropes around town. Pete agrees to meet Johnny on seven-mile road at a railroad crossing. Johnny is to walk down the gully to a tool shack by the railroad. Johnny is tailed by the police and meets Pete an hour later. Pete tells Johnny that he knows who he is, and Johnny tells him that the insurance company paid him to come, not the law. Pete admires Johnny and figures he can help him. Pete tells Johnny that the chief runs the town. Pete only thinks he knows who killed Briarly. The only car he saw was a police car coming from the direction of the mill. Pete tells Johnny that the chief is trying to trick him so he will run away and the chief can kill him. Johnny remembers how the chief had Ted release him and how the chief had to retire with no money and how the payroll would help out. Sure! Johnny smells kerosene and then the locked door starts burning. Johnny pulls the pins from the inside hinges, and the chief is outside. He tells Johnny that he saw the shack on fire, but Johnny tells him he set it on fire to cover up the killing of Briarly. The chief shoots at Pete and Johnny slugs him. Johnny gets the chief to agree to sign a confession.

"Yeah, pretty smart using that poor used kid as a means to keep any suspicion away from himself. But, believe me, not smart enough."

**NOTES:**
- CAST CREDIT FROM RADIOGOLDINDEX.
- THE ANNOUNCER IS JOHN WALD

Producer:   Jack Johnstone          Writers:   Jack Johnstone
Cast:        Lawrence Dobkin, James McCallion, Forrest Lewis, Russell
             Thorson, Sam Edwards

◆   ❖   ◆

SHOW:          THE DOUBLE DEAL MATTER
SHOW DATE:     11/20/1960
COMPANY:       PHILADELPHIA MUTUAL LIABILITY & CASUALTY COMPANY
AGENT:         HARRY BRANSON
EXP. ACCT:     $2,044.45
SYNOPSIS: [Opening is missing.] Johnny travels to Philadelphia, Pennsylvania and the Eastern Trust offices on Walnut Street. Ted Plainer tells Johnny that the case is about Michael Jonathan O'Banyon, known as "Mickey the Hood." He was an old rumrunner and gunrunner and who know what else back in the twenties. After being released on parole Mickey opened a small drug import company, and Bruce Terwilliger the previous agent sold him half a million coverage on his business and a quarter million on his life. The beneficiary is Mary "Toodles" Baker, a cheap stripper. Ted wants to take him off the books but the company

will not cancel the policies without proof. Johnny tells Ted that it is a police matter, but Ted tells Johnny that they cannot find anything on him. Ted is sure that something is going on, but Johnny does not want to try to frame Mickey. Call me when he does something illegal. Ted gets a phone call and the caller wants to talk to Johnny. On the phone is Harry Branson from Philadelphia Mutual Liability & Casualty Company. Something terrible has happened, and he must see John right away. The canary diamonds have been stolen again. Johnny tells Ted that Harry will pay him a lot of money for his case. Wouldn't it be nice if I could tie these two cases together? Bit fat chance.

Johnny goes to see Harry who tells him that the canary diamonds have been stolen. When Johnny brought the diamonds back from Paris they got so much publicity that a client, Mrs. Arthur Pierpont Galloway just had to buy them. She bought them and insured them with Harry for $515,000. She got a call from a magazine that wanted to take pictures of the diamonds there in her home. She thought the maid and chauffeur would be enough protection, but when the man came he tricked her into being alone with him and he walked off with the diamonds. The description is somewhat confused and the police think that they might know who the man was. Lt. Bernard Barry is in charge of the case, and Johnny wants to go see the police first. Harry is flustered that Johnny is acting so cool, but Johnny is just thinking of his commission. Johnny goes to see his friend Lt. Barry who tells him that the description is of a man who was wearing enough makeup for a whole chorus line. The chauffeur noticed that the man was trying to cover up a scar on his face by his left eye. Johnny thinks it might be "Mickey the Hood," and the police agree and have been tailing him, but they have found nothing, and he has an alibi. Johnny remembers that with his importing business he must ship things out, but Barry tells him that all his shipments are being searched. Johnny remembers that the diamonds were previously smuggled out in cans of fruit. The diamonds are so unique that he would have to get them out of the country. Johnny has no idea how he can trip up Mickey. Johnny goes to the O'Banyon Drug Imports store and only Mickey is there. Johnny poses as "Mr. Russell," a storeowner from the south looking for exotic drugs and medicines. A woman walks in that Mickey recognizes as Mrs. Peterson. He has the nerve pills for her, and they are free. She hopes that she can swallow the huge pills, and Mickey tells her to chew them and only take one a day. She thanks him and promises to sent a postcard from Hong Kong. Johnny asks if Mickey is always so nice to his customers. Mickey recognizes his voice from the radio, Johnny Dollar! Mickey should have realized it when Johnny mentioned a non-existent ad in the phone book. Mickey tells Johnny that he had nothing to do with diamonds and no one can prove it. So leave me alone, or else.

Johnny starts to add things up in the store and remembers Mickey's oriental contacts, having met Mrs. Peterson in a travel office, and the large bottle of pills he had made up. Would he be there to collect the remaining pills when she got to Hong Kong? Mickey tells Johnny he is smart enough to steal the diamonds, but he did not do it. Johnny realizes he should have followed Mrs. Peterson. Johnny calls all the travel companies in Philadelphia until he finds the one that arranged Mrs. Peterson's trip, and they tell Johnny that she is in the Belleview Stratford hotel. Johnny goes to the hotel and tells Mrs. Peterson that he needs the pills she got from the store. She gets upset and Johnny tells her to take one of her pills as he gets his credentials out. Johnny empties the bottle and Mrs. Peterson bites into a pill and then spits out a diamond into his hand. What a beautiful stunt! Johnny asks Mrs. Peterson how she would like a couple thousand dollars of extra spending money on the trip? All she has to do is go to the police and explain where she got the pills.

"Proof? It was all Lt. Berry needed. The Canary diamonds are home again, and that will save Philly Mutual from having to pay off a big claim. And Eastern Trust and Insurance has plenty of reasons to drop O'Banyon as a client. After all, he ought to be out of circulation for a long, long time."

NOTES:
- THE FIRST COMMERCIAL BREAK IS FOR VACUUM CLEANED COMMANDER CIGARETTES.
- THE SECOND COMMERCIAL BREAK IS FOR SYLVANIA BLUE DOT FLASHBULBS TO BE USED AT THANKSGIVING.
- THE THIRD COMMERCIAL BREAK IS FOR EXLAX.
- THE ANNOUNCER IS JOHN WALD

Producer: Jack Johnstone     Writers: Jack Johnstone
Cast: Virginia Gregg, Chet Stratton, Harry Bartell, Barney Phillips, Paul Frees

◆ ❖ ◆

SHOW: THE EMPTY THREAT MATTER
SHOW DATE: 11/27/1960
COMPANY: FLOYDS OF ENGLAND
AGENT: GEORGE REED
EXP. ACCT: $2,561.00

SYNOPSIS: George Reed calls, and Johnny asks how dear old Floyds of England is these days. George tells Johnny that that if he read the Wall Street Journal he would see that the leading insurance companies are doing quite well and Floyds is among the leaders. Johnny suggests that George has gotten a big fat raise and wants to take Johnny out for dinner tonight. George tells Johnny that he will get more than a free dinner out of this one. George has an unusual problem. George knows that Johnny does not like acting as bodyguard, but this case is different. Come on over to my office.

Johnny cabs to George's office where George tells Johnny that Charles Stockerly is a retired attorney. He has no regular address. He was highly successful, married and adopted two kids and lived the good life. His wife died two years ago, and he has a worthless hateful son to bother him. Stockerly has a lot of insurance, which is why he called George about the threats on his life. The threats are real, which is why he has been running away. Right now he is in Tahiti, in the town of Papeete. Johnny does not want this job, but will take it on, because all his life he has dreamed of seeing Tahiti. Johnny flies to New York and then to Fiji and then to Viti Levu. Then Johnny flies to Suva, a tropical paradise with attractive peoples. Then another flight to Papeete, Tahiti. It is an ideal place to get away from things, and Johnny can really relax there. Johnny finds Mr. Stockerly in a shack near the hotel, or rather what was left of him.

In the beachfront shack Johnny meets Dr. Dentley. Mr. Stockerly looks as though he had been beaten. The doctor tells Johnny that Stockerly was collecting flowers on a nearby mountain and had been followed. Stockerly thinks that he was shoved by someone, and fell sixty feet through the brush. Stockerly would have left the island if he were not sedated, and lives in a constant state of fear. Johnny decides to spend the night in the cabin to guard Stockerly. Johnny tells the doctor about his job, and he arranges to have some food brought to Johnny. That night every sound wakes Johnny up. At five-thirty Stockerly wakes up and tells Johnny that they must leave. On the flight Stockerly tells Johnny that the death of his wife really upset him and he would have lost his mind, had I not been for his daughter Joyce. His son Andrew had been given too much and has never done a day's work in his life. He also does not like his sister. Joyce supports herself and is happily married. Stockerly tells Johnny that the threats must have come from Harry Linker, a man he had sent to prison. Linker called him and threatened him before a trip to Europe, and in Paris he called again and Stockerly was almost run down by an American car. In London Stockerly was almost murdered. In Jakarta more threats and a poisonous reptile was found in his trunk, and scorpions in a briefcase in Stockholm. Stockerly had run and run, but Linker keeps following him. Johnny tries to explain it as coincidence and promises to stay awake and protect him. Sure, it was coincidence when they were almost hit by a baggage truck in San Francisco. In Hartford, Johnny puts Stockerly in his apartment. Stockerly has pulled down the shades, and when Johnny raises one of them, a bullet breaks the window. Another bullet enters the room, and Johnny thinks Stockerly might have a point.

Johnny digs a slug out of the wall and calls Dr. Bill Peters and tells him to come to the apartment, with a gun. Bill arrives, quiets Stockerly's nerves and agrees to stick around. Bill is sure that Stockerly will kill himself if he goes much farther. Johnny goes to police headquarters and they tell Johnny that Linker has changed and is running a hardware store. Johnny goes to the store and Linker convinces Johnny that he is sincere. Johnny calls on Stockerly's daughter, and she is upset about the situation and wants to bring her father there. Johnny gets a call and Bill Peters tells Johnny that he got a phone call and Stockerly took it. He got white as a sheet and started yelling, "No! You will never get me!" and lunged for the window. Bill gave him a shot and he is ok now. Suicide! What's the matter with me! Johnny goes to George Reed's office and looks at the policy, where Joyce is the sole beneficiary, and Andrew is specifically omitted irrevocably. And there is a suicide clause. So maybe Andrew could not get any of the money, but if Stockerly killed himself, neither would Joyce! And Andrew would love that. Maybe the attempts are a long campaign to drive Stockerly out of his mind. Johnny drives to Andrew's home and notices all the travel stickers on his luggage. He tells Johnny that no one can prove he tried to kill his foster father. Johnny is about to take the law into his own hands when Andrew pulls a gun. When Johnny tells him that he wants the gun so he can compare it with the slugs he pulled from his wall, Andrew says, "That was your apartment? But you drove him over there in a car. You left him there, and I thought." Johnny tells Andrew that he left Stockerly alone just long enough to park his car. Johnny takes the gun from Andrew and slugs him.

"All I hope is that they lock that bird up for the rest of his life. And that somehow Joyce and her husband can bring the poor old man back to normal."

NOTES:

- BOB BAILEY PREVIEWS THE NEXT WEEK'S SHOW WITH "NEXT WEEK A STORY OF REAL INTRIGUE, PLUS A COUPLE OF THE MOST INTRIGUING CHARACTERS I EVER MET."
- JOHN WALD ENDS WITH THE NORMAL "BE SURE TO JOIN US NEXT WEEK, SAME TIME AND STATION FOR ANOTHER EXCITING STORY OF YOURS TRULY JOHNNY DOLLAR." TOO BAD NEITHER OF THEM WOULD BE ON THE NEXT BROADCAST, AS THE SHOW WAS MOVED TO NEW YORK WITH A NEW CAST AND CREW AFTER THIS PROGRAM.

Producer:   Jack Johnstone     Writers:   Jack Johnstone
Cast:        Virginia Gregg, G. Stanley Jones, Ben Wright, Ralph Moody, Harry Bartell, Carleton G. Young

# Index

## VOLUME ONE: PAGES 1–414
## VOLUME TWO: PAGES 415–995
## VOLUME THREE: PAGES 996–1203

## B

### BACKGROUND

## C

### CASE LOCATIONS

## CAST MEMBERS

### CATALOGED STORIES

CBS Station Anniversary

### CBS STATIONS REFERENCED

### CBS STATIONS WELCOMED

### COMMERCIAL REFERENCES

## H

### HOME ADDRESS

### HOTELS USED

## M

### MARITAL STATUS

### MUSIC SUPERVISION

## P

### PHONE NUMBER

### POISONS USED

## R

### RECURRING CHARACTERS

CPSIA information can be obtained at www.ICGtesting.com
Printed in the USA
BVOW012044060313

314863BV00011B/611/P

9 781593 930905